fundamentals of

Human Resource Management

RAYMOND A. NOE
The Ohio State University

JOHN R. HOLLENBECK
Michigan State University

BARRY GERHART
University of Wisconsin–Madison

PATRICK M. WRIGHT
Cornell University

 Irwin

Boston   Burr Ridge, IL   Dubuque, IA   Madison, WI   New York   San Francisco   St. Louis
Bangkok   Bogotá   Caracas   Kuala Lumpur   Lisbon   London   Madrid   Mexico City
Milan   Montreal   New Delhi   Santiago   Seoul   Singapore   Sydney   Taipei   Toronto

Irwin

FUNDAMENTALS OF HUMAN RESOURCE MANAGEMENT

Published by McGraw-Hill/Irwin, a business unit of The McGraw-Hill Companies, Inc., 1221
Avenue of the Americas, New York, NY, 10020. Copyright © 2004, by The McGraw-Hill
Companies, Inc. All rights reserved. No part of this publication may be reproduced or distributed
in any form or by any means, or stored in a database or retrieval system, without the prior written
consent of The McGraw-Hill Companies, Inc., including, but not limited to, in any network or
other electronic storage or transmission, or broadcast for distance learning.
Some ancillaries, including electronic and print components, may not be available to customers
outside the United States.

The book is printed on acid-free paper.

domestic   3 4 5 6 7 8 9 0 QWV/QWV 0 9 8 7 6 5 4 3
international   2 3 4 5 6 7 8 9 0 QWV/QWV 0 9 8 7 6 5 4 3

ISBN 0-07-282567-7

Publisher: *John E. Biernat*
Executive editor: *John Weimeister*
Senior developmental editor: *Sarah Reed*
Senior marketing manager: *Ellen Cleary*
Producer, Media technology: *Mark Molsky*
Senior project manager: *Pat Frederickson*
Production supervisor: *Gina Hangos*
Designer: *Adam Rooke*
Photo research coordinator: *Jeremy Cheshareck*
Photo researcher: *Jennifer Blankenship*
Supplement producer: *Vicki Laird*
Senior digital content specialist: *Brian Nacik*
Cover image and design: *SIS/Dave Cutler*
Typeface: *10.5/12 Goudy*
Compositor: *ElectraGraphics, Inc.*
Printer: *Quebecor World Versailles Inc.*

Library of Congress Cataloging-in-Publication Data

Fundamentals of human resource management / Raymond A. Noe . . . [et al.].—1st ed.
    p. cm.
   Includes indexes.
    ISBN 0-07-282567-7 (alk. paper) — ISBN 0-07-121494-1 (International ed. : alk. paper)
    1. Personnel management.   I. Noe, Raymond A.
HF5549 .F86 2004
658.3—dc21

                        2002043219

INTERNATIONAL EDITION ISBN 0-07-121494-1
Copyright © 2004. Exclusive rights by The McGraw-Hill Companies, Inc. for manufacture and
export. This book cannot be re-exported from the country to which it is sold by McGraw-Hill.
The International Edition is not available in North America.

www.mhhe.com

About the Authors

Raymond A. Noe is the Robert and Anne Hoyt Professor of Management at The Ohio State University. He was previously a professor in the Department of Management at Michigan State University and the Industrial Relations Center of the Carlson School of Management, University of Minnesota. He received his BS in psychology from The Ohio State University and his MA and PhD in psychology from Michigan State University. Professor Noe conducts research and teaches undergraduate as well as MBA and PhD students in human resource management, managerial skills, quantitative methods, human resource information systems, training, employee development, and organizational behavior. He has published articles in the *Academy of Management Journal*, *Academy of Management Review*, *Journal of Applied Psychology*, *Journal of Vocational Behavior*, and *Personnel Psychology*. Professor Noe is currently on the editorial boards of several journals including *Personnel Psychology*, *Journal of Business and Psychology*, *Journal of Training Research*, and *Journal of Organizational Behavior*. Professor Noe has received awards for his teaching and research excellence, including the Herbert G. Heneman Distinguished Teaching Award in 1991 and the Ernest J. McCormick Award for Distinguished Early Career Contribution from the Society for Industrial and Organizational Psychology in 1993. He is also a fellow of the Society for Industrial and Organizational Psychology.

John R. Hollenbeck is Professor of Management at the Eli Broad Graduate School of Business Administration at Michigan State University. He received his PhD in management and organizational behavior from New York University in 1984. Professor Hollenbeck is the editor of *Personnel Psychology* and has served on the editorial boards of *Academy of Management Journal*, *Organizational Behavior and Human Decision Processes*, the *Journal of Management*, and the *Journal of Applied Psychology*. Professor Hollenbeck has been recognized for both his research and teaching. He was the first recipient of the Ernest J. McCormick Award for Distinguished Early Career Contributions to the field of Industrial and Organizational Psychology in 1992 and was the 1987 Teacher–Scholar Award winner at Michigan State University. Dr. Hollenbeck's research focuses on self-regulation theories of work motivation, employee separation and acquisition processes, and team decision making and performance.

Barry Gerhart is the John and Barbara Keller Distinguished Chair in Business at University of Wisconsin–Madison. He was previously the Frances Hampton Currey Professor and Area Coordinator, Organization Studies in the Owen School of Management at Vanderbilt University and Associate Professor and Chairman of the Department of Human Resource Studies, School of Industrial and Labor Relations at Cornell University. He received his BS in psychology from Bowling Green State University in 1979 and his PhD in industrial relations from the University of Wisconsin–Madison in 1985. His research is in the areas of compensation/rewards, human resource strategy staffing, and employee attitudes. Professor Gerhart has worked with a variety of organizations, including TRW, Corning, and Hewitt Associates. His work has appeared in the *Academy of Management Journal, Industrial Relations, Industrial and Labor Relations Review, Journal of Applied Psychology, Personnel Psychology,* and *Handbook of Industrial and Organizational Psychology,* and he has served on the editorial boards of the *Academy of Management Journal, Industrial and Labor Relations Review, Administrative Science Quarterly, International Journal of Human Resource Management,* and the *Journal of Applied Psychology.* He was a corecipient of the 1991 Scholarly Achievement Award, Human Resources Division, Academy of Management.

Patrick M. Wright is Professor of Human Resource Studies and Research Director of the Center for Advanced Human Resource Studies in the School of Industrial and Labor Relations at Cornell University. He was formerly Associate Professor of Management and Coordinator of the Master of Science in Human Resource Management program in the College of Business Administration and Graduate School of Business at Texas A & M University. He holds a BA in psychology from Wheaton College and an MBA and a PhD in organizational behavior/human resource management from Michigan State University. He teaches, conducts research, and consults in the areas of personnel selection, employee motivation, and strategic human resource management. His research articles have appeared in journals such as the *Academy of Management Journal, Journal of Applied Psychology, Organizational Behavior and Human Decision Processes, Journal of Management,* and *Human Resource Management Review.* He has served on the editorial boards of *Journal of Applied Psychology* and *Journal of Management* and also serves as an ad hoc reviewer for *Organizational Behavior and Human Decision Processes, Academy of Management Journal,* and *Academy of Management Review.* In addition, he has consulted for a number of organizations, including Whirlpool Corporation, Amoco Oil Company, and the North Carolina state government.

fundamentals of human RESOURCE Management

fundamentals of human RESOURCE Management

NOE

HOLLENBECK

GERHART

WRIGHT

FOCUSED.

ENGAGING.

APPLIED.

The first edition of *Fundamentals of Human Resource Management* has been developed to give students a brief introduction to HRM that is rich with examples and engaging in its application.

Please take a moment to page through some of the highlights of this new edition.

FEATURES

This successful author team has developed a new text that is geared toward students and classes that want to learn more about how human resource management is used in the everyday work environment.

WHAT DO I NEED TO KNOW?

These objectives open each chapter. They bring attention to the key topics in the chapter and are referenced in the margins of the chapter content so students can easily see where each topic is being discussed.

Learning objectives are referenced in the margins where that discussion begins. These refer to the What do I Need to Know objectives that open each chapter.

Chapter 8

Managing Employees' Performance

What Do I Need to Know? After reading this chapter, you should be able to:

1. Identify the activities involved in performance management.
2. Discuss the purposes of performance management systems.
3. Define five criteria for measuring the effectiveness of a performance management system.
4. Compare the major methods for measuring performance.
5. Describe major sources of performance information in terms of their advantages and disadvantages.
6. Define types of rating errors and explain how to minimize them.
7. Explain how to provide performance feedback effectively.
8. Summarize ways to produce improvement in unsatisfactory performance.
9. Discuss legal and ethical issues that affect performance management.

Introduction

When Synergy, a Philadelphia-based software company, was a start-up, its seven employees would regularly meet to discuss performance issues. Sitting around a table,

Organization Analysis

organization analysis
A process for determining the appropriateness of training by evaluating the characteristics of the organization.

Usually, the needs assessment begins with the [...] for determining the appropriateness of trainin[...] the organization. The organization analysis loo[...] ganization's strategy, resources available for tr[...] training activities.

Training needs will vary depending on whe[...] the training will be meaningful and helpfu[...]

After deciding on the goals and content[...] cide how the training will be conducted. [...] wide variety of methods is available. Train[...] of presentation methods, hands-on metho[...]

presentation methods
Training methods in which trainees receive information provided by instructors or via computers or other media.

With **presentation methods,** trainees r[...] or via computers or other media. Trainees [...] ture, or the material may be presented o[...] workbooks. Presentations are appropriate [...] or result in a significant improvement, relative[...]ing proposals with specific goals, timetables, [...]ccess.

hands-on method[s]
Actively involve th[e] trainee in trying ou[t] skills being taught

group-building methods

[...]nt, needs assessment turns to the remaining [...]erson analysis is a process for determining in[...]ing. It involves answering several questions:

[...]om a lack of knowledge, skill, or ability? (If so, [...]solutions are more relevant.)

[...]ng?

[...]e manager identify whether training is appro[...]ning. In certain situations, such as the intro[...]e, all employees may need training. However, [...] response to a performance problem, training

person analysis
A process for determining individuals' needs and readiness for training.

KEY TERMS

Key terms and definitions appear in the text margins, so terms are highlighted where they are discussed for each review and students can get to know the language of HRM.

BEST PRACTICES

Success in Global Fast Food Depends on Good Selection for Overseas Assignments

Team Spirit Makes Winners of Whole Foods Employees

BEST PRACTICES

The "Best Practices" boxes give specific company examples of what is working well in HRM. Illustrating real world examples of policies that have been put in place and have been successful helps students understand how to apply what they're learning in the text. Examples include: "Incentives for Tough Times," and "Deloitte Develops a Global Workforce."

E-HRM

The "E-HRM" boxes appear throughout the book and emphasize the increasing use of technology in human resource management today and how it is changing the way things are getting done. Examples include: "Will Unions Play a Role in High-Tech Industries" and "Getting Oriented Online."

HR HOW TO

Off to a Safe Start

Starting a new business usually entails long hours for the owners and managers. It's no wonder, when you think of all the issues involved—raising money, finding a place to work, crafting the details of a business plan, hiring all the employees. And regardless of whether the business will manufacture goods or consist entirely of office workers, the government expects that the owners will address health and safety issues from the very start.

OSHA regulations have a (sometimes justifiable) reputation for being complex and difficult to follow. Fortunately, the agency has prepared materials designed to help businesses, including start-ups, succeed. A good place to begin is to call the local OSHA office or visit the agency's website (www.osha.gov) and download the OSHA Fact Sheet titled "OSHA Help for New Businesses." This fact sheet

provides a basic summary of employers' duties and information about where to get more detailed help.

When planning the setup of operations, new-business owners can begin to identify potential hazards. Can any of these be avoided? Avoiding hazards may be as simple as arranging rooms so that electrical cords do not cause accidents. Under the OSH Act, these basic concerns are a legal requirement. Employers also must display OSHA's Safe and Healthful Workplaces poster in a location where it is conspicuous to employees and job candidates. The poster provides information about employees' rights and responsibilities under the OSH Act.

New-business owners also must obtain copies of OSHA's Log of Work-Related Injuries and Illnesses. Recording any work-related injuries and illnesses on the log is another

duty under the OSH Act. (Some businesses, such as employers in many services industries, are exempt, however.)

Employers can get guidance and training at OSHA area offices. They may request free and confidential on-site consultations to help them identify and correct hazards. Several OSHA training centers conduct courses related to worker safety and health. At the OSHA website, employers can also download interactive training materials on general and specific topics related to occupational safety and health.

By getting off to a safe start, employers help to create an environment in which employees recognize safety and health as important values of the organization.

SOURCE: Occupational Safety and Health Administration, "OSHA Help for New Businesses," OSHA Fact Sheet (2002); OSHA website, www.osha.gov, February 19, 2002.

HR HOW TO

The "HR How To" boxes discuss steps to creating HRM programs and include examples of how companies have tackled challenges. This feature helps students to understand the common functions of human resource professionals. Examples include: "Minimizing the Pain of Layoffs," "Keeping up with Change," and "Using Incentives to Motivate Salespeople."

E-HRM

Getting Oriented Online

If you take a job with ChemConnect, don't expect to be greeted on your first day with a dry lecture from human resource personnel. Rather, the San Francisco–based online seller of chemicals and plastics offers an orientation via its intranet. The online orientation, titled "Tour de Chem," is a takeoff on the Tour de France bicycle race. Trainees use a computer mouse to manipulate the image of a bicycle to travel online through various scenarios. Clicking on the front wheel to move forward and on the rear wheel to move backward, trainees take a tour through company jargon, a menu of employee services and benefits, and background about ChemConnect's leaders. For each stage of the tour, one of those executives rides along— shown as a stick figure with a photo of the executive's head patched on top. The whole tour takes about 90 minutes.

says ChemConnect's vice president of operations, Peter Navin. Navin, who is responsible for HRM, says, "If you look into a screen and see no creativity, you certainly get a sense of what you're joining."

No doubt, Jane Paradiso would applaud the Tour de Chem. Paradiso, leader of the recruiting solutions practice at the Watson Wyatt Worldwide consulting firm, says online orientations should be more than a video about the company plus a signup sheet for benefits. According to Paradiso, an online orientation should take advantage of the Internet's potential for communication. The orientation program should assign the new employee an e-mail address and a password to the intranet, let the employee schedule lunch with his or her boss, set up a connection between the new employee and his or her mentor, and describe the

the organization gives out a password for the system.

That's what Pinnacle Decision Systems does. The consulting and software development company, located in Middletown, Connecticut, sends new hires to a website it calls "HQ." There, the newly hired individuals can read policies and procedures, view the company's organization chart, or order business cards and company T-shirts. Thanks to these online services, employees are already acquainted with the company on their first day. During their first day at work, they meet with department heads to deepen their knowledge of the organization. Pinnacle believes that in-depth employee orientation and development require more than a virtual touch, however. Says Joanne Keller, Pinnacle's HR director, "We wouldn't want to lose the personal touch, where you pick

FEATURES

Summary

1. Identify the elements of the selection process.
   Selection typically begins with a review of candidates' employment applications and résumés. The organization administers tests to candidates who meet basic requirements, and qualified candidates undergo one or more interviews. Organizations check references and conduct background checks to verify the accuracy of information provided by candidates. A candidate is selected to fill each vacant position. Candidates who accept offers are placed in the positions for which they were selected.

2. Define ways to measure the success of a selection method.
   One criterion is reliability, which indicates the method is free from random error, so that measurements are consistent. A selection method should also be valid, meaning that performance on the measure (such as a test score) is related to what the measure is designed to assess (such as job performance). Criterion-related validity shows a correlation between test scores and job performance scores. Content validity shows consistency between the test items or problems and the kinds of situations or problems that occur on the job. Construct validity establishes that the test actually measures a specified construct, such as intelligence or leadership ability, which is presumed to be associated with success on the job. A selection method also should be generalizable, so that it applies to more than one specific situation. Each selection method should have utility, meaning it provides economic value greater than its cost. Finally, selection methods should meet the legal requirements for employment decisions.

3. Summarize the government's requirements for employee selection.
   The selection process must be conducted in a way that avoids discrimination and provides access to persons with disabilities. This means selection methods must be valid for job performance, and scores may not be ad-

Nearly all organizations gather information through employment applications and résumés. These methods are inexpensive, and an application form standardizes basic information received from all applicants. The information is not necessarily reliable, because each applicant provides the information. These methods are most valid when evaluated in terms of the criteria in a job description. References and background checks help to verify the accuracy of the information. Employment tests and work samples are more objective. To be legal, any test must measure abilities that actually are associated with successful job performance. Employment tests range from general to specific. General-purpose tests are relatively inexpensive and simple to administer. Tests should be selected to be related to successful job performance and avoid charges of discrimination. Interviews are widely used to obtain information about a candidate's interpersonal and communication skills [and to] gather more detailed information about a [candidate's] background. Structured interviews are more [valid than] unstructured ones. Situational interviews [have] greater validity than general questions. Int[erviews are] costly and may introduce bias into the selecti[on process]. Organizations can minimize the drawbac[ks with] preparation and training.

5. Describe major types of employment tests.
   Physical ability tests measure strength, end[urance,] chomotor abilities, and other physical abi[lities. They] can be accurate but can discriminate and are [not always] job related. Cognitive ability tests, or intelli[gence tests,] tend to be valid, especially for complex job[s or jobs] requiring adaptability. They are a relative[ly cheap] way to predict job performance but have [been chal-]lenged as discriminatory. Job performance t[ests can] be valid but are not always generalizable. U[sing a wide] variety of job performance tests can be exp[ensive. Per-]sonality tests measure personality traits suc[h as extro-]version and adjustment. Research supports [the valid-]ity for appropriate job situations, esp[ecially...]

CHAPTER SUMMARIES recap the "What Do I Need to Know?" objectives from the beginning of each chapter with brief summary discussions.

BusinessWeek Case

BusinessWeek It's Not Easy Making Pixie Dust

We are in the Utilidor—a series of tunnels below Disney World's Magic Kingdom theme park in Orlando. The tunnel complex is generally off-limits to outsiders, but not to 41 visiting managers whose companies have anted up $2,295 a head so they can learn about Walt Disney Company's approach to people management.

This underground city is a beehive of activity. Employees rush through the gray concrete tunnels, scrambling to put on costumes and assume their roles upstairs. Golf carts speed by with supplies. Makeup artists prepare an array of Cinderella and Snow White wigs.

Before coming to this $3\frac{1}{2}$-day seminar, I was skeptical. The program sounded like little more than a dream junket: three nights at the resort's most elegant hotel, plus four-day passes to Disney's theme parks. Besides, I thought, what could any manager possibly learn at Disney World? By the end of the first day's activities, however, my note pad was brimming with ideas and lessons dished out by Disney staff.

My colleagues, most of them human-resource managers, take the program seriously. Most are facing a slew of challenges in need of Disney-style magic. A delivery manager at Anheuser-Busch Companies is trying to make his drivers more responsive to retailers. Personnel managers at a fast-growing bagel chain in Florida worry about maintaining standards as they beef up the chain's ranks. And an employee trainer at South Africa's state-owned transportation conglomerate is looking for ways to streamline the company's hiring process.

Disney's reputation for cleanliness, attention to detail, and helpful employees is what has drawn them here. "Everyone knows how wonderful Disney is, so you figure they must be doing something right," says Kathleen Scapini, who works for Multi-Media in West Hartford, Connecticut. That "something right" is what Disney refers to as the "pixie-dust" formula, with four key ingredients—employee selection, training, support, and benefits. Our seminar, "Disney's Approach to People Management," promises to reveal how the company motivates employees.

Instructors, called facilitators, tell us that we cannot count on Tinkerbell. "The solutions are not complicated," assures Jeff Soluri, a Disney instructor. "It's attention to detail and hard-nosed business practices that produce the magic."

If there is pixie dust, it starts with the hiring process.

One of the first activities is a field trip to Disney's "casting center," a Venetian-style castle where job candidates view a video before being interviewed. The short film informs job seekers about the company's strict appearance guidelines (one ring per hand and no tattoos, please) and the rigors of the work. By being blunt and detailed, Disney says, it's able to weed out incompatible candidates at the first crack.

The critical part of the process, though, is employee training. New hires, who average less than $10 an hour, are treated to a visual company history. They are told that they are not just employees but pivotal "cast members" in a "show." From street sweepers to monorail pilots, each cast member must go out of his way to make the resort seem *unreal.* No matter how tired workers are or how deeply guests may try their patience, they must never lose composure. To do so, the company tells its cast, is to risk alienating a guest, spoiling the illusion, and damaging Disney's standing in entertainment and American culture.

Between excursions, participants share what they have learned—and what they might use. Disney staffers with wireless microphones dart Oprah-like through a conference room seeking comments. They get plenty. John Lealos, the Anheuser-Busch manager, says he wants to incorporate more of an appreciative, team feel into his unit's corporate culture. "If we can get that kind of atmosphere at our company, the productivity will go up," he says. Hugo Strydom, the training manager at South Africa's Transit Ltd., intends to use a Disney-style orientation to weed out weak candidates in a major hiring blitz.

SOURCE: Antonio Fins, "It's Not Easy Making Pixie Dust," *BusinessWeek,* September 19, 1997.

Questions
1. This case reveals much about what Disney looks for in a job applicant as well as what it does (realistic job previews) to get unsuitable job candidates to remove themselves from the process. What characteristics would you expect Disney to be selecting for?
2. Based on the information given, what selection methods might be appropriate for further screening job applicants?
3. Why is selection an important part of a maintaining a competitive advantage at Disney? Would it be equally important at a bank? Why or why not?

BUSINESSWEEK CASES look at events at real companies as reported by the nation's number one business weekly and encourage students to critically evaluate each situation and apply the chapter concepts.

VIDEO CASE

Developing a Diverse Workforce

Most jobs start with an interview, whether it's conducted in person, by phone, or even online. Interpersonal dynamics can affect those interviews, so a human resource manager who is looking to develop a diverse workforce to meet company needs must be able to ask the right questions of a candidate and listen to the answers in

located. So, it makes sense to recruit, develop, and retain employees who can relate to this broadening customer base and meet their needs in specific ways.

Managers at all companies, whether product or service oriented, can reap the rewards of diversity for their organizations if they practice

employee—employer relationship but also boosts overall productivity of the company. Managers must be aware of the possibility of a glass ceiling in their organization, an invisible barrier that separates female employees or those of different cultural or ethnic backgrounds from top levels of the organization. One way to guard against

---

VIDEO CASES at the end of each Part include questions to challenge students to view HRM issues and problems from different perspectives. Teaching notes to the video cases are included in the Instructor's Manual.

REVIEW AND DISCUSSION QUESTIONS at the end of each chapter help students nail down the concepts presented in the chapter and understand potential applications of the chapter material.

FINAL CASES in each chapter take another look at companies and how their practices illustrate or apply concepts from the chapter. They provide external examples to bring into a lecture, along with questions for assignments or classroom discussion.

---

ences and job-related behaviors. The interviewers also should be prepared to provide information about the job and the organization.

scores poorly with one method may be selected if he or she scores very high on another measure.

Review and Discussion Questions

1. What activities are involved in the selection process? Think of the last time you were hired for a job. Which of those activities were used in selecting you? Should the organization that hired you have used other methods as well?
2. Why should the selection process be adapted to fit the organization's job descriptions?
3. Choose two of the selection methods identified in this chapter. Describe how you can compare them in terms of reliability, validity, ability to generalize, utility, and compliance with the law.
4. Why does predictive validation provide better information than concurrent validation? Why is this type of validation more difficult?
5. How do U.S. laws affect organizations' use of each of the employment tests? Interviews?
6. Suppose your organization needs to hire several computer programmers, and you are reviewing résumés you obtained from an online service. What kinds of information will you want to gather from the "work experience" portion of these résumés? What kinds of information will you want to gather from the "education" portion of these résumés? What methods would you use for verifying or exploring this information? Why would you use those methods?
7. For each of the following jobs, select the two kinds of

a. City bus driver.
b. Insurance salesperson.
c. Member of a team that sells complex high-tech equipment to manufacturers.
d. Member of a team that makes a component of the equipment in (c).
8. Suppose you are a human resource professional at a large retail chain. You want to improve the company's hiring process by creating standard designs for interviews, so that every time someone is interviewed for a particular job category, that person answers the same questions. You also want to make sure the questions asked are relevant to the job and maintain equal employment opportunity. Think of three questions to include in interviews for each of the following jobs. For each question, state why you think it should be included.
   a. Cashier at one of the company's stores.
   b. Buyer of the stores' teen clothing line.
   c. Accounts payable clerk at company headquarters.
9. How can organizations improve the quality of their interviewing so that interviews provide valid information?
10. Some organizations set up a selection process that is long and complex. In some people's opinion, this kind of selection process not only is more valid but also has symbolic value. What can the use of a long, complex selection process symbolize to job seekers? How do the organization's ability

---

same time that companies were cutting retirement benefits for employees, for example, some were also creating special supplemental plans for their highest-paid executives that guaranteed lush retirements.

The crunched pay and benefits create more inequality. Employers are using variable pay to lavish financial resources on their most prized employees, creating a kind of corporate star system.

No doubt, dismantling the old entitlement culture is bound to create a whole new set of questions. "How do you communicate to a workforce that it isn't created equally?" asks Jay Schuster of Los Angeles–based compensation consultants Schuster-Zingheim & Associates. "How do you treat a workforce in which everyone has a different deal?"

SOURCE: M. Conlin, "A Little Less in the Envelope This Week," *BusinessWeek*, February 18, 2002, pp. 64+.

1. The case says many organizations shifted to greater use of variable pay during the 1990s, a time of rapid economic growth. What forms of variable pay are mentioned? What were some advantages of switching to variable pay during a growth period?
2. Variable pay helped IBM compete in the labor market during the 1990s. Since then, economic conditions have changed. How does variable pay affect IBM's competitiveness now?
3. At the end of this case, consultant Jay Schuster asks, "How do you communicate to a workforce that it isn't created equally?" and "How do you treat a workforce in which everyone has a different deal?" Considering that the way an organization implements its pay plan will affect that plan's success, how would you answer Schuster's questions?

Case: Paying for Good Employee Relations

Organizations understand that their ability to reach financial goals depends largely on how well they manage relationships with customers and employees. Therefore, many organizations link incentive pay to customer satisfaction and employee satisfaction. Eastman Kodak, for example, [...] inion results as one [...] upon which bonuses [...] s, which is employee [...] stem in which execu- [...] he results of employee [...] managers for good em- [...] appeal, this practice

plan that directly rewards employee satisfaction produce only the intended positive consequences? Or might this practice also produce unintended and less desirable consequences?

Eastman Kodak and United are two examples of companies that have decided some direct incentive makes sense, even if the incentive is small compared with the rewards for satisfying other measures such as financial performance. Other companies have shied away from these incentives out of concern for unintended consequences. In this way, we can see that the organizations' pay strategies are related to their business goals.

Which of those activities were used in selecting you? Should the organization that hired you have used other methods as well?

2. Why should the selection process be adapted to fit the organization's job descriptions?
3. Choose two of the selection methods identified in this chapter. Describe how you can compare them in terms of reliability, validity, ability to generalize, utility, and compliance with the law.
4. Why does predictive validation provide better information than concurrent validation? Why is this type of validation more difficult?
5. How do U.S. laws affect organizations' use of each of the employment tests? Interviews?
6. Suppose your organization needs to hire several computer programmers, and you are reviewing résumés you obtained from an online service. What kinds of information will you want to gather from the "work experience" portion of these résumés? What kinds of information will you want to gather from the "education" portion of these résumés? What methods would you use for verifying or exploring this information? Why would you use those methods?
7. For each of the following jobs, select the two kinds of tests you think would be most important to include in the selection process. Explain why you chose those tests.

c. Member of a team that sells complex high-tech equipment to manufacturers.
d. Member of a team that makes a component of the equipment in (c).
8. Suppose you are a human resource professional at a large retail chain. You want to improve the company's hiring process by creating standard designs for interviews, so that every time someone is interviewed for a particular job category, that person answers the same questions. You also want to make sure the questions asked are relevant to the job and maintain equal employment opportunity. Think of three questions to include in interviews for each of the following jobs. For each question, state why you think it should be included.
   a. Cashier at one of the company's stores.
   b. Buyer of the stores' teen clothing line.
   c. Accounts payable clerk at company headquarters.
9. How can organizations improve the quality of their interviewing so that interviews provide valid information?
10. Some organizations set up a selection process that is long and complex. In some people's opinion, this kind of selection process not only is more valid but also has symbolic value. What can the use of a long, complex selection process symbolize to job seekers? How do you think this would affect the organization's ability to attract the best employees?

What's Your HR IQ?

The Student CD-ROM offers two more ways to check what you've learned so far. Use the Self-Assessment exercise to test your knowledge of employee selection. Go online with the Web Exercise to see how well your knowledge works in cyberspace.

WHAT'S YOUR HR IQ? sections at the end of each chapter reference the assessment activities included on the Student CD with the desired outcomes of the Web exercises, which are hands-on activities to reinforce the specific chapter content.

supplements for students and instructors

INSTRUCTOR'S MANUAL
The Instructor's Manual includes chapter summaries, learning objectives, an extended chapter outline, key terms, description of text boxes, discussion questions, summary of end-of-chapter cases, video notes, additional activities, and references to Annual Editions articles.

TEST BANK
The test bank includes multiple choice, true/false, and essay questions for each chapter. Rationales and page references are also provided for the answers.

INSTRUCTOR PRESENTATION CD-ROM
This multimedia CD-ROM allows instructors to create dynamic classroom presentations by incorporating PowerPoint, videos and the Instructor's Manual and Test Bank.

BROWNSTONE'S DIPLOMA FOR WINDOWS
This test generator allows instructors to add and edit questions, create new versions of the test, and more.

VIDEOS
Five new videos on HRM issues accompany this edition. The accompanying video cases are included in the text at the end of each Part. Teaching notes are included in the Instructor's Manual.

POWERPOINT
This presentation program features 10–20 slides for each chapter, which are also found on the Instructor CD-ROM and on the Instructor Center of the Online Learning Center.

ONLINE LEARNING CENTER
(www.mhhe.com/fundamentals)
This text-specific website follows the text chapter by chapter. OLC content is ancillary and supplementary

germane to the textbook; as students read the book, they can go online to take self-grading quizzes, review material, or work through interactive exercises. OLCs can be delivered multiple ways—professors and students can access them directly through the textbook website, through PageOut, or within a course management system (i.e., WebCT, Blackboard, TopClass, or eCollege).

STUDENT CD-ROM
This NEW CD-ROM contains the Self-Assessment and Internet Activities that are referenced in the text. It also includes chapter review questions, flashcards to review key terms, and a link to **Human Resources Online**. Students will stay current and expand their knowledge in the field of human resources by completing approximately 20 online exercises in such areas as training and employee development, selection and recruitment, compensation and benefits, labor relations, employee separation and retention, as well as training and employee development. In each exercise, students will review one or more online resources, such as articles covering a recent HRM trend. They will then answer some challenging questions. For the busy instructor, **Human Resources Online** includes password-protected teaching notes that provide insights and answers to each question.

POWERWEB
Harness the assets of the Web to keep your course current with PowerWeb! This online resource provides high-quality, peer-reviewed content including up-to-date articles from leading periodicals and journals, current news, weekly updates with assessment, interactive exercises, Web research guide, study tips, and much more! Visit **www.dushkin.com/powerweb** or access through the OLC at www.mhhe.com/fundamentals.

Acknowledgments

The first edition of *Fundamentals of Human Resource Management* would not have been possible without the staff of McGraw-Hill/Irwin and Elm Street Publishing Services. John Weimeister, our editor, helped us in developing the vision for the book and gave us the resources we needed to develop a top-of-the-line HRM teaching package. Sarah Reed's organizational skills kept the author team on deadline and made the book more visually appealing than the authors could have ever produced on their own. Karen Hill of Elm Street worked diligently to help make sure that the book was interesting, practical, and readable, yet remained true to findings of human resource management research. We also thank Ellen Cleary for her marketing efforts for this new book.

Our supplements' authors deserve thanks for helping us create a first rate teaching package. Amit Shah of Frostburg State University wrote the *Instructor's Manual* and created the PowerPoint presentation. He also developed the quiz questions for the CD and website for use as student review questions. Fred Heidrich of Black Hills State University developed the new Test Bank. We would also like to thank Interactive Learning LLC for the important creation of HR Online.

We would also like to thank the professors who gave of their time to review this first edition text. Their helpful comments and suggestions have greatly helped us to shape this new book:

Cheryl Adkins
Longwood University

Wendy Becker
University of Albany

Jon Bryan
Bridgewater State College

Craig Cowles
Bridgewater State College

Vicki Mullenex
Davis & Elkins College

Mary Ellen Rosetti
Hudson Valley Community College

James Tan
University of Wisconsin–Stout

Steve Thomas
Southwest Missouri State University

Melissa Waite
SUNY Brockport

Barbara Warschawski
Schenectady County Community College

Steven Wolff
Marist College

Raymond A. Noe
John R. Hollenbeck
Barry Gerhart
Patrick M. Wright

Brief Contents

1 Managing Human Resources 1

■ PART 1
The Human Resource Environment 29

2 Trends in Human Resource Management 30

3 Providing Equal Employment Opportunity and a Safe Workplace 66

4 Analyzing Work and Designing Jobs 101

VIDEO CASE Southwest Airlines Competes by Putting People First 130

■ PART 2
Acquiring and Preparing Human Resources 133

5 Planning for and Recruiting Human Resources 134

6 Selecting Employees and Placing Them in Jobs 170

7 Training Employees 199

VIDEO CASE Developing a Diverse Workforce 234

■ PART 3
Assessing Performance and Developing Employees 237

8 Managing Employees' Performance 238

9 Developing Employees for Future Success 273

10 Separating and Retaining Employees 308

VIDEO CASE Creative Staffing Solutions Pairs Workers with Employers 340

■ PART 4
Compensating Human Resources 343

11 Establishing a Pay Structure 344

12 Recognizing Employee Contributions with Pay 373

13 Providing Employee Benefits 402

VIDEO CASE Compensating Workers through Pay and Benefits 437

■ PART 5
Meeting Other HR Goals 439

14 Collective Bargaining and Labor Relations 440

15 Managing Human Resources Globally 477

16 Creating and Maintaining High-Performance Organizations 513

VIDEO CASE Workplace Ergonomics Is Good Business 540

Glossary 542

Photo Credits 553

Name and Company Index 555

Subject Index 561

Contents

1 Managing Human Resources 1

Introduction 1

Human Resources and Company Performance 3

Responsibilities of Human Resource Departments 5

Analyzing and Designing Jobs 6
Recruiting and Hiring Employees 6

BEST PRACTICES
Success in Global Fast Food Depends on Good Selection for Overseas Assignments 7

Training and Developing Employees 8
Managing Performance 9
Planning and Administering Pay and Benefits 10
Maintaining Positive Employee Relations 11
Establishing and Administering Personnel Policies 11
Ensuring Compliance with Labor Laws 11
Supporting the Organization's Strategy 13

Skills of HRM Professionals 13

HR HOW TO
Winning the War for Talent 14

Human Relations Skills 14
Decision-Making Skills 15
Leadership Skills 16
Technical Skills 16

HR Responsibilities of Supervisors 16

Ethics in Human Resource Management 17

Employee Rights 18
Standards for Ethical Behavior 19

Careers in Human Resource Management 20

Organization of This Book 21

Summary 23

Review and Discussion Questions 24

What's Your HR IQ? 25

BusinessWeek **BusinessWeek Case**
The Human Factor 25

Case: The Container Store: Human Resource Management Excellence Takes Different Forms 26

Notes 27

■ **PART 1**
The Human Resource Environment 29

2 Trends in Human Resource Management 30

Introduction 30

Change in the Labor Force 32

An Aging Workforce 32
A Diverse Workforce 32
Skill Deficiencies of the Workforce 36

High-Performance Work Systems 36

HR HOW TO
Keeping Up with Change 37

Knowledge Workers 37
Employee Empowerment 40
Teamwork 40

BEST PRACTICES
Team Spirit Makes Winners of Whole Foods Employees 41

Focus on Strategy 42

High Quality Standards 43
Mergers and Acquisitions 44
Downsizing 44
Expanding into Global Markets 46
Reengineering 48
Outsourcing 49

Technological Change in HRM 49

A Changing Economy 50
Human Resources in E-Business 51
E-HRM Applications in Other Organizations 52

E-HRM
Help Yourself to HRM 54

Change in the Employment Relationship 55

A New Psychological Contract 55
Flexibility 56

Summary 58

Review and Discussion Questions 60

What's Your HR IQ? 60

BusinessWeek *BusinessWeek* **Case**
Click Here for HR 61

Case: HRM Flies through Turbulence at Delta
Air Lines 62

Notes 63

3 Providing Equal Employment
Opportunity and a Safe Workplace 66

Introduction 66

**Regulation of Human Resource
Management 68**

Equal Employment Opportunity 68

Constitutional Amendments 69
Legislation 69

BEST PRACTICES
Blind Feeding the Blind 76

Executive Orders 77

**The Government's Role in Providing for Equal
Employment Opportunity 77**

Equal Employment Opportunity Commission
(EEOC) 77
Office of Federal Contract Compliance
Procedures (OFCCP) 81

**Businesses' Role in Providing for Equal
Employment Opportunity 82**

Avoiding Discrimination 82
Providing Reasonable Accommodation 85
Preventing Sexual Harassment 86
Valuing Diversity 87

**Occupational Safety and Health Act
(OSH Act) 88**

General and Specific Duties 88

HR HOW TO
Off to a Safe Start 90

Enforcement of the OSH Act 91
Employee Rights and Responsibilities 92
Impact of the OSH Act 93

**Employer-Sponsored Safety and Health
Programs 94**

Identifying and Communicating Job
Hazards 94
Reinforcing Safe Practices 95
Promoting Safety Internationally 95

Summary 95

Review and Discussion Questions 96

What's Your HR IQ? 97

BusinessWeek *BusinessWeek* **Case**
Racism in the Workplace 97

Case: Home Depot's Bumpy Road
to Equality 98

Notes 99

4 Analyzing Work and Designing
Jobs 101

Introduction 101

Work Flow in Organizations 102

Work Flow Analysis 102
Work Flow in Organizations 104

BEST PRACTICES
Team-Based Jobs Put the Focus on Patient Care 105

Job Analysis 105

HR HOW TO
Writing a Job Description 106

Job Descriptions 106
Job Specifications 108
Sources of Job Information 110
Position Analysis Questionnaire 111
Task Analysis Inventory 112
Fleishman Job Analysis System 112
Importance of Job Analysis 113
Trends in Job Analysis 115

Job Design 116

Designing Efficient Jobs 116
Designing Jobs That Motivate 117
Designing Ergonomic Jobs 122

Designing Jobs That Meet Mental Capabilities and Limitations 124

Summary 125

Review and Discussion Questions 126

What's Your HR IQ? 127

BusinessWeek *BusinessWeek* **Case**
The New Factory Worker 127

Case: From Big Blue to Efficient Blue 128

Notes 129

VIDEO CASE
Southwest Airlines Competes by Putting People First 130

■ PART 2
Acquiring and Preparing Human Resources 133

5 Planning for and Recruiting Human Resources 134

Introduction 134

The Process of Human Resource Planning 135

Forecasting 136

Goal Setting and Strategic Planning 139

BEST PRACTICES
Just Enough People at ZF Micro Devices 140

HR HOW TO
Minimizing the Pain of Layoffs 143

Implementing and Evaluating the HR Plan 147

Applying HR Planning to Affirmative Action 148

Recruiting Human Resources 148

Personnel Policies 149

Internal versus External Recruiting 150

Lead-the-Market Pay Strategies 150

Employment-at-Will Policies 152

Image Advertising 152

Recruitment Sources 153

Internal Sources 153

External Sources 155

E-HRM
Web Opens the Door to a Global Labor Market 159

Evaluating the Quality of a Source 160

Recruiter Traits and Behaviors 161

Characteristics of the Recruiter 161

Behavior of the Recruiter 163

Enhancing the Recruiter's Impact 163

Summary 164

Review and Discussion Questions 165

What's Your HR IQ? 165

BusinessWeek *BusinessWeek* **Case**
Forget the Huddled Masses: Send Nerds 165

Case: Southwest Airlines Focuses on Takeoffs, Not Layoffs 166

Notes 167

6 Selecting Employees and Placing Them in Jobs 170

Introduction 170

Selection Process 171

Reliability 172

Validity 173

Ability to Generalize 175

Practical Value 175

Legal Standards for Selection 176

Job Applications and Résumés 178

Application Forms 178

Résumés 180

References 180

Background Checks 181

Employment Tests and Work Samples 182

Physical Ability Tests 182

Cognitive Ability Tests 182

Job Performance Tests and Work Samples 184

Personality Inventories 184

Honesty Tests and Drug Tests 185

BEST PRACTICES
Impairment Tests: Ready or Not, Here They Come 186

Medical Examinations 187

Interviews 187

Interviewing Techniques 187

Advantages and Disadvantages of Interviewing 189

Preparing to Interview 189

HR HOW TO
Interviewing Effectively 190

Selection Decisions 191

How Organizations Select Employees 191

Communicating the Decision 192

Summary 193

Review and Discussion Questions 194

What's Your HR IQ? 194

[BusinessWeek] *BusinessWeek* Case
It's Not Easy Making Pixie Dust 195

Case: Never Having to Say "You Never Know" 195

Notes 196

7 Training Employees 199

Introduction 199

Training Linked to Organizational Needs 200

Needs Assessment 201

Organization Analysis 202
Person Analysis 203
Task Analysis 203

Readiness for Training 205

Employee Readiness Characteristics 205
Work Environment 205

Planning the Training Program 206

Objectives of the Program 207
In-House or Contracted Out? 207

HR HOW TO
Administering a Training Program 209

Choice of Training Methods 210

Training Methods 210

Classroom Instruction 210
Audiovisual Training 212
Computer-Based Training 212

BEST PRACTICES
Humanizing e-Learning 214

On-the-Job Training 214
Simulations 216
Business Games and Case Studies 216
Behavior Modeling 217
Experiential Programs 217
Team Training 218
Action Learning 218

Implementing the Training Program: Principles of Learning 219

Measuring Results of Training 221

Evaluation Methods 222
Applying the Evaluation 223

Applications of Training 224

Orientation of New Employees 224

Diversity Training 225

E-HRM
Getting Oriented Online 226

Summary 227

Review and Discussion Questions 229

What's Your HR IQ? 229

[BusinessWeek] *BusinessWeek* Case
Look Who's Building Online Classrooms 230

Case: Training Helps the Rubber Hit the Road at Tires Plus 231

Notes 232

VIDEO CASE
Developing a Diverse Workforce 234

■ **PART 3**
Assessing Performance and Developing Employees 237

8 Managing Employees' Performance 238

Introduction 238

The Process of Performance Management 239

BEST PRACTICES
Managing Performance to Build Unity across Cultures and Jobs 241

Purposes of Performance Management 242

Criteria for Effective Performance Management 242

Methods for Measuring Performance 244

Making Comparisons 244
Rating Individuals 247
Measuring Results 253
Total Quality Management 254

Sources of Performance Information 255

Managers 255

E-HRM
Otis Elevator's Appraisals Move Up, Down, and Sideways 256

Peers 257
Subordinates 257
Self 257

Customers 258

Errors in Performance Measurement 258

Types of Rating Errors 258
Ways to Reduce Errors 260
Political Behavior in Performance Appraisals 260

Giving Performance Feedback 260

Scheduling Performance Feedback 261
Preparing for a Feedback Session 261

HR HOW TO
Delivering Performance Feedback 262

Conducting the Feedback Session 263

Finding Solutions to Performance Problems 263

Legal and Ethical Issues in Performance Management 264

Legal Requirements for Performance Management 265
Electronic Monitoring and Employee Privacy 266

Summary 266

Review and Discussion Questions 268

What's Your HR IQ? 269

BusinessWeek **BusinessWeek Case**
Focusing on the Softer Side of Managing 269

Case: The Trials and Tribulations of Performance Management at Ford 270
Notes 271

9 Developing Employees for Future Success 273

Introduction 273

Training, Development, and Career Management 274

Development and Training 274
Development for Careers 275

Approaches to Employee Development 276

Formal Education 277

E-HRM
E-Learning Helps Build Management Talent at IBM 278

Assessment 279
Job Experiences 285
Interpersonal Relationships 289

HR HOW TO
Setting Up a Mentoring Program 290

Systems for Career Management 291

Self-Assessment 292
Reality Check 293
Goal Setting 294
Action Planning 294

Development-Related Challenges 296

The Glass Ceiling 296

BEST PRACTICES
Procter & Gamble Selling Women on Careers 297

Succession Planning 298
Dysfunctional Managers 299

Summary 301

Review and Discussion Questions 302

What's Your HR IQ? 303

BusinessWeek **BusinessWeek Case**
Basic Training for CEOs 303

Case: Developing Employees Reduces Risk for First USA Bank 304

Notes 305

10 Separating and Retaining Employees 308

Introduction 308

Managing Voluntary and Involuntary Turnover 309

Employee Separation 310

Principles of Justice 310
Legal Requirements 312
Progressive Discipline 315
Alternative Dispute Resolution 318
Employee Assistance Programs 319
Outplacement Counseling 320

Job Withdrawal 320

Job Dissatisfaction 321
Behavior Change 323
Physical Job Withdrawal 324
Psychological Withdrawal 324

Job Satisfaction 321

Personal Dispositions 325
Tasks and Roles 326

BEST PRACTICES
Attracting Workers with Technology 327

Supervisors and Coworkers 328
Pay and Benefits 330

Monitoring Job Satisfaction 330

HR HOW TO
Measuring Employee Satisfaction 331

Summary 333
Review and Discussion Questions 334
What's Your HR IQ? 334

[BusinessWeek] *BusinessWeek* **Case**
Low-Wage Lessons 334

Case: Feeling Insecure about Airline
Security 336

Notes 336

VIDEO CASE

Creative Staffing Solutions Pairs Workers
with Employers 340

■ PART 4
Compensating Human
Resources 343

11 Establishing a Pay Structure 344

Introduction 344

Decisions about Pay 345

Legal Requirements for Pay 346

Equal Employment Opportunity 346
Minimum Wage 347
Overtime Pay 348
Child Labor 349
Prevailing Wages 349

Economic Influences on Pay 350

Product Markets 350
Labor Markets 350
Pay Level: Deciding What to Pay 351
Gathering Information about Market Pay 352

HR HOW TO
Gathering Wage Data at the BLS Website 353

Employee Judgments about Pay Fairness 354

Judging Fairness 354
Communicating Fairness 355

BEST PRACTICES
No More Secrets at Two Financial Companies 355

Job Structure: Relative Value of Jobs 356

Pay Structure: Putting It All Together 358

Pay Rates 358

Pay Grades 359
Pay Ranges 360
Pay Differentials 361
Alternatives to Job-Based Pay 362

Pay Structure and Actual Pay 363

Current Issues Involving Pay Structure 364

Pay during Military Duty 365
Pay for Executives 365

Summary 367

Review and Discussion Questions 369

What's Your HR IQ? 369

[BusinessWeek] *BusinessWeek* **Case**
Revenge of the "Managers" 369

Case: Corning Hopes Pay Structure Can Make It
Nimble 370

Notes 371

12 Recognizing Employee Contributions
with Pay 373

Introduction 373

Incentive Pay 374

Pay for Individual Performance 376

Piecework Rates 376
Standard Hour Plans 378
Merit Pay 378
Performance Bonuses 379

HR HOW TO
Using Incentives to Motivate Salespeople 381

Sales Commissions 381

Pay for Group Performance 382

Gainsharing 382
Group Bonuses and Team Awards 385

Pay for Organizational Performance 385

Profit Sharing 386

BEST PRACTICES
Incentives for Tough Times 387

Stock Ownership 388

Balanced Scorecard 391

Processes That Make Incentives Work 392

Participation in Decisions 393
Communication 393

Incentive Pay for Executives 393

Performance Measures for Executives 394

Ethical Issues 395

Summary 396

Review and Discussion Questions 397

What's Your HR IQ? 398

BusinessWeek *BusinessWeek* **Case**

A Little Less in the Envelope This Week 398

Case: Paying for Good Employee Relations 399

Notes 400

13 Providing Employee Benefits 402

Introduction 402

The Role of Employee Benefits 403

Benefits Required by Law 404

Social Security 405
Unemployment Insurance 406
Workers' Compensation 407
Unpaid Family and Medical Leave 407

Optional Benefits Programs 408

Paid Leave 408
Group Insurance 410

BEST PRACTICES
Giving Employees the Health Care Benefits They
Want 412

Retirement Plans 415
"Family-Friendly" Benefits 420
Other Benefits 422

Selecting Employee Benefits 422

Organization's Objectives 423
Employees' Expectations and Values 424
Benefits' Costs 425

HR HOW TO
Controlling the Cost of Benefits 426

**Legal Requirements for Employee
Benefits 427**

Tax Treatment of Benefits 427
Antidiscrimination Laws 428

E-HRM
Tapping into Benefits Online 429

Accounting Requirements 430

Communicating Benefits to Employees 430

Summary 431

Review and Discussion Questions 432

What's Your HR IQ? 433

BusinessWeek *BusinessWeek* **Case**
Dr. Goodnight's Company Town 433

Case: Is Retirement a Luxury? 434

Notes 435

VIDEO CASE
Compensating Workers through Pay
and Benefits 437

■ **PART 5**
Meeting Other HR Goals 439

14 Collective Bargaining and Labor
Relations 440

Introduction 440

Role of Unions and Labor Relations 441

National and International Unions 442
Local Unions 444
Trends in Union Membership 444

E-HRM
Will Unions Play a Role in High-Tech Industries? 446

Unions in Government 448
Impact of Unions on Company Performance 448

Goals of Each Group 449

Goals of Management 449
Goals of Labor Unions 450
Goals of Society 451

**Laws and Regulations Affecting Labor
Relations 451**

National Labor Relations Act (NLRA) 451

HR HOW TO
Avoiding Unfair Labor Practices 453

Laws Amending the NLRA 453
National Labor Relations Board (NLRB) 454

Union Organizing 456

The Process of Organizing 456
Management Strategies 457
Union Strategies 459
Decertifying a Union 460

Collective Bargaining 460

Bargaining over New Contracts 462
When Bargaining Breaks Down 463

Contract Administration 465

Labor-Management Cooperation 467

BEST PRACTICES
Brass Factory Polishes Employees' Understanding—
And Morale, Too 468

Summary 470

Review and Discussion Questions 471

What's Your HR IQ? 471

BusinessWeek *BusinessWeek* **Case**
A World of Sweatshops 472

Case: Verizon Strikes Out against Unions 473

Notes 474

15 Managing Human Resources
Globally 477

Introduction 477
HRM in a Global Environment 478
Employees in an International Workforce 479
Employers in the Global Marketplace 479
**Factors Affecting HRM in International
Markets 481**
Culture 481
Education and Skill Levels 484
Economic System 484
Political-Legal System 486
**Human Resource Planning in a Global
Economy 486**
**Selecting Employees in a Global Labor
Market 487**
**Training and Developing a Global
Workforce 489**
Training Programs for an International
Workforce 489
Cross-Cultural Preparation 491
Global Employee Development 491
BEST PRACTICES
Deloitte Develops a Global Workforce 492

**Performance Management across National
Boundaries 492**
**Compensating an International
Workforce 493**
Pay Structure 493
Incentive Pay 495
Employee Benefits 495
International Labor Relations 496
Managing Expatriates 497

Selecting Expatriate Managers 497
Preparing Expatriates 500
Compensating Expatriates 501
HR HOW TO
Communicating across Language Barriers 502

Helping Expatriates Return Home 504

Summary 506

Review and Discussion Questions 507

What's Your HR IQ? 508

BusinessWeek *BusinessWeek* **Case**
The High Cost of France's Aversion
to Layoffs 508

Case: Human Resource Management in a World
with Terrorism 509

Notes 510

16 Creating and Maintaining High-
Performance Organizations 513

Introduction 513
High-Performance Work Systems 514
Elements of a High-Performance Work
System 515
Outcomes of a High-Performance Work
System 516
**Conditions That Contribute to High
Performance 517**
Teamwork and Empowerment 518
Knowledge Sharing 518
Job Satisfaction 520
Ethics 521
HRM's Contribution to High Performance 522
Job Design 522
BEST PRACTICES
HR Policies Deliver High Performance for FedEx 523

Recruitment and Selection 524
Training and Development 524
Performance Management 525
Compensation 526
HRM Technology 527
HR HOW TO
Using Information Systems in a Learning
Organization 527
E-HRM
Oracle Spells Human Resource Management
"B2E" 530

Effectiveness of Human Resource Management 531

Human Resource Management Audits 532
Analyzing the Effect of HRM Programs 534

Summary 534

Review and Discussion Questions 535

What's Your HR IQ? 536

BusinessWeek *BusinessWeek* **Case**
From Devastation to High Performance 536

Case: A Giant Falls 537

Notes 538

VIDEO CASE

Workplace Ergonomics Is Good Business 540

Glossary 542

Photo Credits 553

Name and Company Index 555

Subject Index 561

Managing Human Resources

1. Define human resource management and explain how HRM contributes to an organization's performance.

2. Identify the responsibilities of human resource departments.

3. Summarize the types of skills needed for human resource management.

4. Explain the role of supervisors in human resource management.

5. Discuss ethical issues in human resource management.

6. Describe typical careers in human resource management.

Introduction

Can a company operate without people? Moffatt/Rosenthal, a Portland, Oregon, ad agency, came dangerously close to finding out. Toward the end of the 1990s, when the search for talented employees was a challenge for almost any company, all but one of the agency's 13 employees left. Some were lured to the exciting world of Internet commerce; others were laid off when clients shifted work to other agencies, as often happens in the advertising business. Employees move on to new opportunities all the time, but agency founders Al Moffatt and Rob Rosenthal were stunned by the impact on their firm. Almost too late, they realized they needed to focus on their staff, not just on their clients.

Moffatt and Rosenthal committed themselves to finding and keeping good people. To make room in the budget for a top-notch business development executive, the

human resource management (HRM)
The policies, practices, and systems that influence employees' behavior, attitudes, and performance.

partners cut their own salaries. They studied the company's history and concluded that employees who initially had been stimulated by the challenge of building a new company had grown bored once the company had established itself with a few big accounts. The partners now found new employees and set out to make them want to stay. They began to encourage greater employee creativity, taking on pro bono (charitable) assignments and giving employees free rein in creating promotional pieces for the agency. They selected a challenging mission for Moffatt/Rosenthal—focusing on brand promotion, a prestigious advertising specialty—to stimulate excitement and long-term commitment among the new set of employees. Two years later, Moffatt/Rosenthal had earned its biggest profits ever and was planning a big party to celebrate its 10th anniversary.[1]

The changes that revitalized Moffatt/Rosenthal centered around **human resource management (HRM),** the policies, practices, and systems that influence employees' behavior, attitudes, and performance. Many companies refer to HRM as involving "people practices." Figure 1.1 emphasizes that there are several important HRM practices: analyzing work and designing jobs, attracting potential employees (recruiting), choosing employees (selection), teaching employees how to perform their jobs and preparing them for the future (training and development), evaluating their performance (performance management), rewarding employees (compensation), creating a positive work environment (employee relations), and supporting the organization's strategy (HR planning and change management). An organization performs best when all of these practices are managed well. At companies with effective HRM, employees and customers tend to be more satisfied, and the companies tend to be more innovative, have greater productivity, and develop a more favorable reputation in the community.[2]

In this chapter, we introduce the scope of human resource management. We begin by discussing why human resource management is an essential element of an organization's succcess. We then turn to the elements of managing human resources: the roles and skills needed for effective human resource management. Next, the chapter describes how all managers, not just human resource professionals, participate in the activities related to human resource management. The following section of the chap-

FIGURE 1.1

Human Resource Management Practices

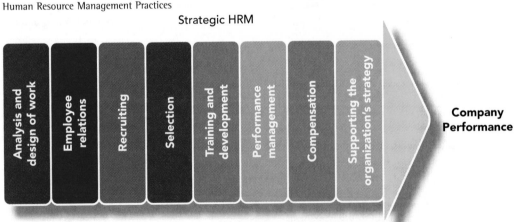

Strategic HRM

Analysis and design of work | Employee relations | Recruiting | Selection | Training and development | Performance management | Compensation | Supporting the organization's strategy → **Company Performance**

ter addresses some of the ethical issues that arise with regard to human resource management. We then provide an overview of careers in human resource management. The chapter concludes by highlighting the HRM practices covered in the remainder of this book.

Human Resources and Company Performance

Managers and economists traditionally have seen human resource management as a necessary expense, rather than as a source of value to their organizations. Economic value is usually associated with *capital*—equipment, technology, and facilities. However, research has demonstrated that HRM practices can be valuable.[3] Decisions such as whom to hire, what to pay, what training to offer, and how to evaluate employee performance directly affect employees' motivation and ability to provide goods and services that customers value. Companies that attempt to increase their competitiveness by investing in new technology and promoting quality throughout the organization also invest in state-of-the-art staffing, training, and compensation practices.[4]

The concept of "human resource management" implies that employees are *resources* of the employer. As a type of resource, **human capital** means the organization's employees, described in terms of their training, experience, judgment, intelligence, relationships, and insight—the employee characteristics that can add economic value to the organization. In other words, whether it manufactures automobiles or forecasts the weather, for an organization to succeed at what it does, it needs employees with certain qualities, such as particular kinds of training and experience. This view means employees in today's organizations are not interchangeable, easily replaced parts of a system but the source of the company's success or failure. By influencing *who* works for the organization and *how* those people work, human resource management therefore contributes to such basic measures of an organization's success as quality, profitability, and customer satisfaction. Figure 1.2 shows this relationship.

Athleta Corporation, a catalog and Internet retailer of sports apparel, based in Petaluma, California, demonstrates the importance of human capital to the company's

human capital
An organization's employees, described in terms of their training, experience, judgment, intelligence, relationships, and insight.

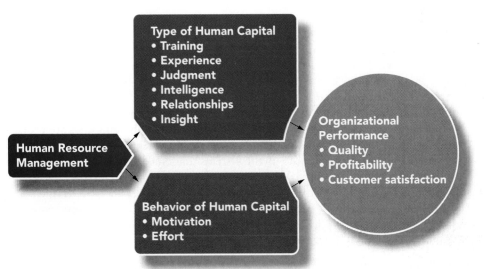

FIGURE 1.2

Impact of Human Resource Management

At Southwest Airlines, the company's focus is on keeping employees loyal, motivated, trained, and compensated. In turn, there is a low turnover rate and a high rate of customer satisfaction.

bottom line. Athleta's workforce is so committed to the company that turnover is less than 1 percent (1 out of 100 employees leave the company in an average year), productivity (output per worker) is increasing, and the company's growth is skyrocketing—it grew by five times in 2000 alone. One way the company has built a committed workforce is by cultivating a positive work environment. Most of Athleta's 60 employees set their own work schedules and are permitted to take personal time during the day. Employees take the initiative to learn one another's jobs, so they can fill in for one another during the day. Those who take time off for personal reasons willingly work odd hours. The company encourages employees to take breaks for physical activity, and employees can even bring along their dogs, which join employees outside for a run or to play catch. Employees use the open space preserve behind Athleta's facility to run, or they work out with the gym equipment set up in the company's storage area.[5]

Human resource management is critical to the success of organizations because human capital has certain qualities that make it valuable. In terms of business strategy, an organization can succeed if it has a *sustainable competitive advantage* (is better than competitors at something, and can hold that advantage over a sustained period of time). Therefore, we can conclude that organizations need the kind of resources that will give them such an advantage. Human resources have these necessary qualities:

- Human resources are *valuable*. High-quality employees provide a needed service as they perform many critical functions.
- Human resources are *rare* in the sense that a person with high levels of the needed skills and knowledge is not common. An organization may spend months looking for a talented and experienced manager or technician.
- Human resources *cannot be imitated*. To imitate human resources at a high-performing competitor, you would have to figure out which employees are providing the advantage and how. Then you would have to recruit people who can do precisely the same thing and set up the systems that enable those people to imitate your competitor.
- Human resources have *no good substitutes*. When people are well trained and highly motivated, they learn, develop their abilities, and care about customers. It is difficult to imagine another resource that can match committed and talented employees.

These qualities imply that human resources have enormous potential. An organization realizes this potential through the ways it practices human resource management.

Effective management of human resources can form the foundation of a **high-performance work system**—an organization in which technology, organizational structure, people, and processes all work together to give an organization an advantage in the competitive environment. As technology changes the ways organizations manufacture, transport, communicate, and keep track of information, human resource management must ensure that the organization has the right kinds of people to meet the new challenges. Maintaining a high-performance work system may include development of training programs, recruitment of people with new skill sets, and establishment of rewards for such behaviors as teamwork, flexibility, and learning. In the next chapter, we will see some of the changes that human resource managers are planning for, and Chapter 16 examines high-performance work systems in greater detail.

high-performance work system
An organization in which technology, organizational structure, people, and processes all work together to give an organization an advantage in the competitive environment.

Responsibilities of Human Resource Departments

LO2

In all but the smallest organizations, a human resource department is responsible for the functions of human resource management. On average, an organization has one HR staff person for every 100 employees served by the department. Table 1.1 details the responsibilities of human resource departments. These responsibilities include the practices introduced in Figure 1.1 plus two areas of responsibility that support those practices: (1) establishing and administering personnel policies and (2) ensuring compliance with labor laws.

FUNCTION	RESPONSIBILITIES
Analysis and design of work	Work analysis; job design; job descriptions
Recruitment and selection	Recruiting; job postings; interviewing; testing; coordinating use of temporary labor
Training and development	Orientation; skills training; career development programs
Performance management	Performance measures; preparation and administration of performance appraisals; discipline
Compensation and benefits	Wage and salary administration; incentive pay; insurance; vacation leave administration; retirement plans; profit sharing; stock plans
Employee relations	Attitude surveys; labor relations; employee handbooks; company publications; labor law compliance; relocation and outplacement services
Personnel policies	Policy creation; policy communication; record keeping; HR information systems
Compliance with laws	Policies to ensure lawful behavior; reporting; posting information; safety inspections; accessibility accommodations
Support for strategy	Human resource planning and forecasting; change management

TABLE 1.1

Responsibilities of HR Departments

SOURCE: Based on SHRM-BNA Survey No. 66, "Policy and Practice Forum: Human Resource Activities, Budgets, and Staffs, 2000–2001," *Bulletin to Management,* Bureau of National Affairs Policy and Practice Series (Washington, DC: Bureau of National Affairs, June 28, 2001).

Although the human resource department has responsibility for these areas, many of the tasks may be performed by supervisors or others inside or outside the organization. No two human resource departments have precisely the same roles because of differences in organization sizes and characteristics of the workforce, the industry, and management's values. In some companies, the HR department handles all the activities listed in Table 1.1. In others, it may share the roles and duties with managers of other departments such as finance, operations, or information technology. In some companies, the HR department actively advises top management. In others, the department responds to top-level management decisions and implements staffing, training, and compensation activities in light of company strategy and policies.

Let's take an overview of the HR functions and some of the options available for carrying them out. Human resource management involves both the selection of which options to use and the activities of using those options. Later chapters of the book will explore each function in greater detail.

Analyzing and Designing Jobs

job analysis
The process of getting detailed information about jobs.

To produce their given product or service (or set of products or services) companies require that a number of tasks be performed. The tasks are grouped together in various combinations to form jobs. Ideally, the tasks should be grouped in ways that help the organization to operate efficiently and to obtain people with the right qualifications to do the jobs well. This function involves the activities of job analysis and job design. **Job analysis** is the process of getting detailed information about jobs. **Job design** is the process of defining the way work will be performed and the tasks that a given job requires.

job design
The process of defining the way work will be performed and the tasks that a given job requires.

In general, jobs can vary from having a narrow range of simple tasks to having a broad array of complex tasks requiring multiple skills. At one extreme is a worker on an assembly line at a poultry-processing facility; at the other extreme is a doctor in an emergency room. In the past, many companies have emphasized the use of narrowly defined jobs to increase efficiency. With many simple jobs, a company can easily find workers who can quickly be trained to perform the jobs at relatively low pay. However, greater concern for innovation and quality have shifted the trend to more use of broadly defined jobs. Also, as we will see in Chapters 2 and 4, some organizations assign work even more broadly, to teams instead of individuals.

recruitment
The process through which the organization seeks applicants for potential employment.

Recruiting and Hiring Employees

selection
The process by which the organization attempts to identify applicants with the necessary knowledge, skills, abilities, and other characteristics that will help the organization achieve its goals.

Based on job analysis and design, an organization can determine the kinds of employees it needs. With this knowledge, it carries out the function of recruiting and hiring employees. **Recruitment** is the process through which the organization seeks applicants for potential employment. **Selection** refers to the process by which the organization attempts to identify applicants with the necessary knowledge, skills, abilities, and other characteristics that will help the organization achieve its goals. An organization makes selection decisions in order to add employees to its workforce, as well as to transfer existing employees to new positions. Selecting employees for overseas assignments can be especially challenging, as described in the nearby "Best Practices" box.

Approaches to recruiting and selection involve a variety of alternatives. The organization may actively recruit from many external sources, such as Internet job postings, newspaper want-ads, and college recruiting events. Other organizations may rely

Success in Global Fast Food Depends on Good Selection for Overseas Assignments

As companies expand globally, they are spending more time and energy assessing employees' cultural fit for overseas assignments. By one estimate, the cost of a failed overseas assignment ranges from $200,000 to $500,000. These costs result from lost productivity, relocation, recruitment, and severance pay. The most common reason for a failed overseas assignment is choosing people who have the technical skills needed to perform the job but lack the necessary personality characteristics and family support. In other words, overseas assignments typically fail because the employee or family becomes homesick, or the employee cannot interact well with people in a different culture.

Tricon Restaurants International has planned extensively to avoid these pitfalls. Dallas-based Tricon is the franchiser for over 10,000 overseas Kentucky Fried Chicken, Pizza Hut, and Taco Bell restaurants. The company has 100 expatriates, including 20 Americans working overseas. Rather than choosing candidates who are merely excited about an overseas assignment and who have the technical skills to perform the job, Tricon is taking a closer look at whether the candidates also have the necessary personality characteristics. In particular, Tricon looks for the ability to adapt to different situations and the family support needed to succeed in overseas assignments.

To identify employees for overseas assignments, Tricon interviews candidates about the position, the country's culture, and its marketplace. If there is any doubt whether the candidate can make the adjustment, the company hires a consulting firm to further assess whether the candidate has the personality needed to succeed in an overseas assignment. Some of the personality characteristics needed include empathy, adaptability, and the ability to interact with others (sociability). If candidates pass the interview, their peers and manager complete a feedback survey about their strengths and weaknesses to provide an evaluation of their skills.

If the evaluation is positive, the company sends the candidates and their families overseas for a week. During the visit, local managers evaluate each candidate while the family evaluates the community. The family spends time touring local schools, exploring potential housing locations, and meeting with other expatriates in the country, who tell them about the local culture and environment. If the local managers find the candidate acceptable, the candidate, with input from his or her family, can accept or reject the position.

SOURCE: Based on C. Patton, "Match Game," *Human Resource Executive*, 2001, pp. 36–41.

heavily on promotions from within and applicants referred by current employees. The choice of recruiting methods is influenced by the types of positions to be be filled, as well as by characteristics of the employer. A well-known employer in a large city may receive so many applications for entry-level jobs that it need not recruit very actively. Other positions are harder to fill. For ATX Forms, a developer of tax software, the big challenge is the company's location in cold, out-of-the way Caribou, Maine—not the destination of choice for the majority of college graduates. ATX decided to focus its recruiting on people who already have ties to the area. The company publicized its generous pay for programmers, as well as a $5,000 bonus for signing on. ATX

TABLE 1.2

Top 10 Qualities Employers Seek in Job Candidates

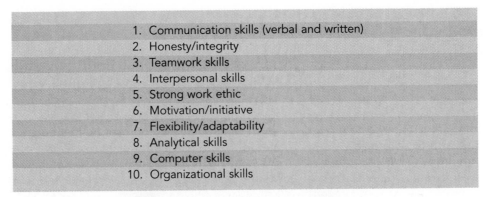

1. Communication skills (verbal and written)
2. Honesty/integrity
3. Teamwork skills
4. Interpersonal skills
5. Strong work ethic
6. Motivation/initiative
7. Flexibility/adaptability
8. Analytical skills
9. Computer skills
10. Organizational skills

SOURCE: National Association of Colleges and Employers, "Job Outlook 2002," online version, www.jobweb.com.

employees and their neighbors began encouraging their adult children to return to Caribou; other adults who had planned to move away changed their minds in favor of taking positions with ATX.[6]

At some organizations the selection process may focus on specific skills, such as experience with a particular programming language or type of equipment. At other organizations, selection may focus on general abilities, such as the ability to work as part of a team or find creative solutions. The focus an organization favors will affect many choices, from the way the organization measures ability, to the questions it asks in interviews, to the places it recruits. Table 1.2 lists the top 10 qualities that employers say they are looking for in job candidates, based on a survey by the National Association of Colleges and Employers.

Training and Developing Employees

training
A planned effort to enable employees to learn job-related knowledge, skills, and behavior.

development
The acquisition of knowledge, skills, and behaviors that improve an employee's ability to meet changes in job requirements and in customer demands.

Although organizations base hiring decisions on candidates' existing qualifications, most organizations provide ways for their employees to broaden or deepen their knowledge, skills, and abilities. To do this, organizations provide for employee training and development. **Training** is a planned effort to enable employees to learn job-related knowledge, skills, and behavior. For example, many organizations offer safety training to teach employees safe work habits. **Development** involves acquiring knowledge, skills, and behavior that improve employees' ability to meet the challenges of a variety of new or existing jobs, including the client and customer demands of those jobs. Development programs often focus on preparing employees for management responsibility. Likewise, if a company plans to set up teams to manufacture products, it might offer a development program to help employees learn the ins and outs of effective teamwork. Figure 1.3 illustrates examples of training and development designed to increase the value of an organization's human capital.

Decisions related to training and development include whether the organization will emphasize enabling employees to perform their current jobs, preparing them for future jobs, or both. An organization may offer programs to a few employees in whom the organization wants to invest, or it may have a philosophy of investing in the training of all its workers. Some organizations, especially large ones, may have extensive formal training programs, including classroom sessions and training programs on CD-ROM. Other organizations may prefer a simpler, more flexible approach of encourag-

FIGURE 1.3

How Training and Development Can Increase the Value of Human Capital

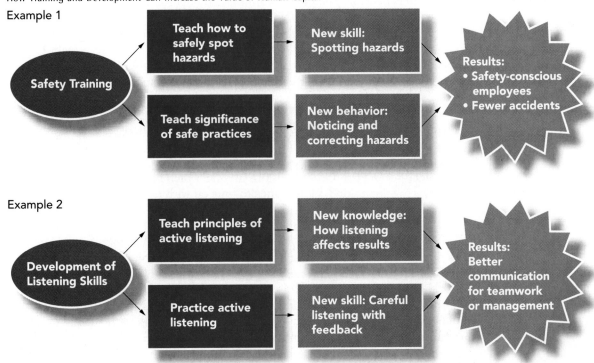

ing employees to participate in outside training and development programs as needs are identified.

Managing Performance

Managing human resources includes keeping track of how well employees are performing relative to objectives such as job descriptions and goals for a particular position. The process of ensuring that employees' activities and outputs match the organization's goals is called **performance management.** The activities of performance management include specifying the tasks and outcomes of a job that contribute to the organization's success. Then various measures are used to compare the employee's performance over some time period with the desired performance. Often, rewards—the topic of the next section—are developed to encourage good performance.

The human resource department may be responsible for developing or obtaining questionnaires and other devices for measuring performance. The performance measures may emphasize observable behaviors (for example, answering the phone by the second ring), outcomes (number of customer complaints and compliments), or both. When the person evaluating performance is not familiar with the details of the job, outcomes tend to be easier to evaluate than specific behaviors.[7] The evaluation may focus on the short term or long term and on individual employees or groups. Typically, the person who completes the evaluation is the employee's supervisor. Often employees also evaluate their own performance, and in some organizations, peers and subordinates participate, too.

performance management
The process of ensuring that employees' activities and outputs match the organization's goals.

Planning and Administering Pay and Benefits

The pay and benefits that employees earn play an important role in motivating them. This is especially true when rewards such as bonuses are linked to the individual's or group's achievements. Decisions about pay and benefits also can support other aspects of an organization's strategy. For example, a company that wants to provide an exceptional level of service or be exceptionally innovative might pay significantly more than competitors in order to attract and keep the best employees. At other companies, a low-cost strategy requires knowledge of industry norms, so that the company does not spend more than it must.

Planning pay and benefits involves many decisions, often complex and based on knowledge of a multitude of legal requirements. An important decision is how much to offer in salary or wages, as opposed to bonuses, commissions, and other performance-related pay. Other decisions involve which benefits to offer, from retirement plans to various kinds of insurance to time off with pay. All such decisions have implications for the organization's bottom line, as well as for employee motivation.

Pay and benefits have the greatest impact when they are based on what employees really want and need. Sherman Assembly Systems, located in San Antonio, Texas, hires many unskilled workers, including a large number who moved off the welfare rolls to take jobs at Sherman. These employees need benefits that help them enter the world of earning a regular paycheck. Sherman arranges to have its bank send representatives to the worksite to help employees apply for checking accounts with low minimum balances. In addition, the company gives workers without a high school diploma an opportunity to take Internet-based courses so they can earn their GED.[8] The work situation at Cronin and Company, a small advertising agency in Glastonbury, Connecticut, is far different. With Cronin's offices located midway between Boston and New York, the challenge is to keep talent from leaving for the many attractions of those major cities. Cronin's benefits therefore include making the workplace attractive, with an environment that makes people want to linger. The company has built a posh employee lounge featuring leather chairs, piped-in jazz, and a cappucino machine. The lounge is meant to be an opportunity to stimulate creative interaction, as well as a way to keep employees happy.[9]

Administering pay and benefits is another big responsibility. Organizations need systems for keeping track of each employee's earnings and benefits. Employees need information about their health plan, retirement plan, and other benefits. Keeping track of this involves extensive record keeping and reporting to management, employees, the government, and others.

In December 2001, Jason Giambi smiles during a press conference in which the New York Yankees announced they had signed Giambi to a seven-year, $120 million contract. The employer (the Yankees) is paying so much because it believes Giambi will contribute more to the organization than anyone else could.

Maintaining Positive Employee Relations

Organizations often depend on human resource professionals to help them identify and perform many of the tasks related to maintaining positive relations with employees. This function often includes providing for communications to employees. Many organizations prepare and distribute employee handbooks that detail company policies, and large organizations often have company publications, such as a monthly newsletter or a website on the organization's intranet (an Internet service limited to use within the organization). Preparing these communications may be a regular task for employees in the human resource department.

The human resource department also can expect to handle certain kinds of communications from individual employees. Employees turn to this department for answers to questions about benefits and company policy. If employees feel they have been discriminated against, see safety hazards, or have other problems and are dissatisfied with their supervisor's response, they may turn to the HR department for help. Members of the department should be prepared with a way to address such problems.

In organizations where employees belong to a union, employee relations entails additional responsibilities. The organization periodically conducts collective bargaining to negotiate an employment contract with union members. The HR department also maintains communication with union representatives to ensure that problems are resolved as they arise.

Establishing and Administering Personnel Policies

All the human resource activities described so far require fair and consistent decisions, and most require substantial record keeping. Organizations depend on their HR department to help establish policies related to hiring, discipline, promotions, benefits, and the other activities of human resource management. For example, if the company has a policy in place that an intoxicated worker will be immediately terminated, the company can handle such a situation more fairly and objectively than if it addressed such incidents on a case-by-case basis. The company can communicate the policy to every employee, so that everyone knows its importance. And if anyone violates the rule, the supervisor can quickly intervene—confident that the employee knew the consequences and that any other employee would be treated the same way. Such policies not only promote fair decision making, they also promote other objectives, such as workplace safety and customer service.

All aspects of human resource management require careful and discreet record keeping. From the preparation of employee handbooks, to processing job applications, performance appraisals, benefits enrollment, and government-mandated reports, handling records about employees requires accuracy as well as sensitivity to employee privacy. Whether the organization keeps records in file cabinets or on a sophisticated computer information system, it must have methods for ensuring accuracy and for balancing privacy concerns with easy access for those who need information and are authorized to see it.

Ensuring Compliance with Labor Laws

As we will discuss in later chapters, especially Chapter 3, the government has many laws and regulations concerning the treatment of employees. These laws govern such matters as equal employment opportunity, employee safety and health, employee pay and benefits, employee privacy, and job security. Requirements include filing reports and displaying posters, as well as avoiding unlawful behavior. Most managers depend on human resource professionals to help them keep track of these requirements.

Ensuring compliance with laws requires that human resource personnel keep watch over a rapidly changing legal landscape. For example, the increased use of and access to electronic databases by employees and employers suggest that in the near future legislation will be needed to protect employee privacy rights. Currently, no federal laws outline how to use employee databases in order to protect employees' privacy while also meeting employers' and society's concern for security.

The requirement that employers give people with disabilities access to the workplace is a topic of continuing debate and court action. The Americans with Disabilities Act (ADA), discussed in Chapter 3, covers access of disabled persons to the physical work environment and attempts to eliminate discrimination against these persons in hiring and other HRM practices. However, no law helps eliminate disabled persons' disadvantages in access to technology such as the Internet, cell phones, and other electronic devices. Disabled people's computer usage and Internet access are only about half the level of persons without disabilities. Future laws may require that persons with disabilities receive access to such technology.[10] Accessibility might include adding screen readers to websites, providing voice recognition technology to computer users, or changing computer design to make computers easier for employees with limited mobility to use.

Another area of continued debate likely will be laws designed to prohibit discrimination by employers and health insurers against employees based on their genetic makeup. Advances in medicine and genetics allow scientists to predict from DNA samples a person's likelihood of contracting certain diseases. To reduce health care costs, companies may want to use this information to screen out job candidates or reassign current employees who have a genetic predisposition to a disease that is triggered by exposure to certain working conditions. Congress has debated laws that restrict genetic testing to monitoring the adverse effects of exposure to hazardous workplace substances (such as chemicals) and that prohibit employers from requiring employees or job candidates to provide predictive genetic information.

Also in the realm of fair employment practices, we are likely to see more challenges to sex and race discrimination focusing on lack of access to training and development opportunities needed for an employee to be considered for top management. Although women and minorities are advancing into top management positions, "glass ceilings" still exist between top management and female and minority employees. A recent survey showed that 97 percent of top U.S. managers are white, and at least 95 percent are male.[11]

Another subject of lawsuits that will continue to have a major influence on HRM practices is job security. As companies are forced to close facilities and lay off employees because of economic or competitive conditions, cases dealing with the illegal discharge of employees have increased. The issue of what constitutes "employment at will"—that is, the principle that an employer may terminate employment at any time without notice—will be debated. As the age of the overall workforce increases, as described in the next chapter, the number of cases dealing with age discrimination in layoffs, promotions, and benefits will likely rise. Employers will need to review work rules, recruitment practices, and performance evaluation systems, revising them if necessary to ensure that they do not falsely communicate employment agreements the company does not intend to honor (such as lifetime employment) or discriminate on the basis of age.

Supporting the Organization's Strategy

At one time, human resource management was primarily an administrative function. The HR department focused on filling out forms and processing paperwork. However, as more organizations have come to appreciate the significance of highly skilled human resources, many HR departments have taken on a more active role in supporting the organization's strategy.

An important element of this responsibility is **human resource planning,** identifying the numbers and types of employees the organization will require in order to meet its objectives. Using these estimates, the human resource department helps the organization forecast its needs for hiring, training, and reassigning employees. Planning also may show that the organization will need *fewer* employees to meet anticipated needs. In that situation, human resource planning includes how to handle or avoid layoffs. The "HR How To" box draws on several companies' experience to describe some ways of planning for human resource needs.

Often, an organization's strategy requires some type of change—for example, adding, moving, or closing facilities; applying new technology; or entering markets in other regions or countries. Common reactions to change include fear, anger, and confusion. The organization may turn to its human resource department for help in managing the change process. Skilled human resource professionals can apply knowledge of human behavior, along with performance management tools, to help the organization manage change constructively.

human resource planning
Identifying the numbers and types of employees the organization will require in order to meet its objectives.

Skills of HRM Professionals

LO3

With such varied responsibilities, the human resource department needs to bring together a large pool of skills. These skills fall into the four basic categories shown in Figure 1.4: human relations skills, decision-making skills, leadership skills, and technical skills.

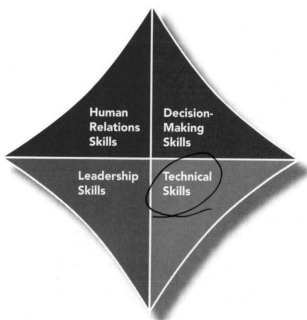

FIGURE 1.4

Skills of HRM Professionals

Winning the War for Talent

Throughout the 1990s, a booming economy and rapidly changing technology transformed the task of recruiting employees into a war for talent. Even with an economic slowdown at the beginning of the 21st century, the war for talent continues in many fields. How can HR practices help a company win that war? Here are strategies that have worked for several companies:

Avoid Layoffs. When money is tight, avoiding layoffs requires creativity. Sun Microsystems has tried closing plants only over the summer. Cisco Systems didn't quite cut ties with employees, even when it concluded it needed layoffs. Cisco is paying some of them one-third of their previous salaries and continuing to provide full benefits, including health insurance, use of a laptop, and access to the company gym. The company also promised that after a year, Cisco would pay an additional two months' salary to help pay for a job search inside Cisco.

Lure Them Back. Other companies that have cut back have tried to stay connected to former employees, so they will want to return when times improve. Charles Schwab is promising a $7,500 rehiring bonus to any of the 2,100 employees laid off who return within 18 months. Many companies are considering rehiring retired employees on a part-time basis or as consultants, and rather than offering all-or-none retirement programs, they are allowing employees to gradually phase out of work. For example, Monsanto Corporation has developed its own in-house temporary employment agency, the Retiree Resource Corporation (RRC), to utilize retirees' talents.

Teach Managers to Keep Employees. Macy's West has developed a comprehensive retention strategy that includes three elements: (1) advising managers on how to run meetings and conduct performance evaluations in a way that will motivate associates; (2) flexible work schedules; and (3) development opportunities to prepare associates to be managers. Executives at Macy's are also held accountable for retention of the employees who report to them.

Create a Positive Work Environment. SAS Institute makes employees want to stay by giving them an opportunity to do interesting work in a comfortable environment that gives them time for their personal lives. SAS Institute is a privately held worldwide company that develops and markets statistical software (80

Human Relations Skills

The ability to understand and work well with other people is important to virtually any career, but human relations skills have taken on new significance for human resource management today. As organizations' managers increasingly appreciate the significance of human resources, many are calling for HRM to become the "source of people expertise" in the organization.[12] HR managers therefore need knowledge of how people can and do play a role in giving the organization an advantage against the competition, as well as of the policies, programs, and practices that can help the organization's people do so. Some of the human relations skills that are particularly important for today's HR professionals are communicating, negotiating, and team development.

percent of the Fortune 500 are customers). SAS Institute operates on the basis of trust. The company's policy for sick leave is that employees can take as many days as they need (assuming they don't abuse the policy). SAS Institute is most famous for its generous, family-friendly benefits and pleasant physical environment. Every employee has a nice private office with computer equipment. Company policy is for employees to work 35 hours a week: a nine-to-five day with an hour for lunch or exercise. The company closes at 5 P.M. The company has an on-site medical facility, on-site day care, and a fitness center. Every Wednesday afternoon, plain and peanut M&Ms are distributed to snack areas on every floor in every building. Not surprisingly, in spite of competition from many nearby high-tech firms, SAS Institute has low turnover. The company's work environment encourages employees to stay even if they have opportunities at other companies.

Think Globally. Companies are relying on the global labor market to find employees with specific talent. In India, computer programmers and call center employees work part-time on contracts for numerous companies around the world. Companies such as Conseco, an insurance firm, are finding that by contracting business to Indian firms, they can find a greater supply of better-educated persons than in the United States. The Indian employees are excited about the type of customer service work offered and are loyal and eager to learn, taking the initiative to improve business processes and please their customers. In the United States it is difficult to find and retain the same type of employees, and pay and benefits tend to be much higher. Similarly, many companies are setting up facilities in countries where human resources are plentiful. In Ireland more than 100 international companies have set up telemarketing operations, and the country is attracting employees from all over Europe.

SOURCE: K. Clark, "You're Laid Off! Kind of. Firms Look beyond Pink Slips," *U.S. News and World Report*, July 2, 2001, pp. 50–53; L. Phillon and J. Brugger, "Encore! Retirees Give Top Performance as Temporaries," *HR Magazine*, October 1994, pp. 74–77; N. Breuer, "Shelf Life," *Workforce*, August 2000, pp. 29–34; C. A. O'Reilly III and J. Pfeffer, *Hidden Value* (Boston: Harvard Business School Press, 2000); Conseco website (June 2001), www.conseco.com; Society for Human Resource Management, "Globalization and the Human Resources Profession: Workplace Visions," no. 5 (2000).

Decision-Making Skills

Human resource managers must make a wide variety of decisions that affect whether employees are qualified and motivated and whether the organization is operating efficiently and complying with the law. Especially at organizations that give HRM departments a role in supporting strategy, HR decision makers also must be able to apply decision-making skills to strategic issues. This requires knowledge of the organization's line of business and the ability to present options in terms of costs and benefits to the organization, stated in terms of dollars.[13] Decisions also must take into account social and ethical implications of the alternatives.

The Hewlett-Packard/Compaq merger is a high-profile example of organizations going through significant change. Companies turn to human resource departments for help with change management as "people issues" and standardizing practices become increasingly prevalent in the new economy.

Leadership Skills

Through their knowledge, communication skills, and other abilities, HR managers need to play a leadership role with regard to the organization's human resources. In today's environment, leadership often requires helping the organization manage change. Fulfilling this leadership role includes diagnosing problems, implementing organizational changes, and evaluating results, especially in terms of employees' skills and attitudes. Changes typically produce conflict, resistance, and confusion among the people who must implement the new plans or programs. HR professionals must oversee the change in a way that ensures success. HRM provides tools for overcoming resistance to change, teaching employees to operate under new conditions, and even encouraging innovation. A survey of Fortune 500 companies found that in 87 percent of the companies, organization development and change were managed by the HR department.[14]

Technical Skills

In any field, including management, "technical skills" are the specialized skills of that field. In human resource management, professionals need knowledge of state-of-the-art practices in such areas as staffing, development, rewards, organizational design, and communication. New selection techniques, performance appraisal methods, training programs, and incentive plans are constantly being developed. These developments often include the use of new software and computer systems. New laws are passed every year, and technical skills require knowledge of how to comply.

Professionals must be able to evaluate the worth of the techniques that are available for carrying out HRM activities. Some of the new methods and tools will provide value to the organization, whereas others may be no more than the HRM equivalent of snake oil. HRM professionals must be able to critically evaluate new techniques in light of HRM principles and business value to determine which are beneficial.

LO4

HR Responsibilities of Supervisors

Although many organizations have human resource departments, HR activities are by no means limited to the specialists who staff those departments. In large organizations, HR departments advise and support the activities of the other departments. In small organizations, there may be an HR specialist, but many HR activities are carried out by line supervisors. Either way, non-HR managers need to be familiar with the basics of HRM and their role with regard to managing human resources.

FIGURE 1.5

Supervisors' Involvement in HRM: Common Areas of Involvement

At a start-up company, the first supervisors are the company's founders. Not all founders recognize their HR responsibilities, but those who do have a powerful advantage. When Rene Larrave and two partners founded the consulting firm they called Tactica, Larrave felt certain that the only way the firm could grow profitably was with a clear vision of the numbers and kinds of employees who could enable that growth. Larrave and his partners drew up career paths for all the employees they planned to hire, including the requirements for the jobs to which they would be promoted during the company's first few years. To help their future employees find their way along those career paths, they published the details in their company's Employee Atlas. The partners also set up a plan for reviewing performance by collecting feedback from peers as well as supervisors. Using this plan, implemented by its HR department, Tactica in several years grew to a $40 million firm, staffed by almost 200 highly committed, hardworking employees—most of them holding the positions that Larrave and his partners had planned for them.[15]

As we will see in later chapters, supervisors typically have responsibilities related to all the HR functions. Figure 1.5 shows some HR responsibilities that supervisors are likely to be involved in. Organizations depend on supervisors to help them determine what kinds of work need to be done (job analysis and design) and in what quantities (HR planning). Supervisors typically interview job candidates and participate in the decisions about which candidates to hire. Many organizations expect supervisors to train employees in some or all aspects of the employees' jobs. Supervisors conduct performance appraisals and may recommend pay increases. And, of course, supervisors play a key role in employee relations, because they are most often the voice of management for their employees, representing the company on a day-to-day basis. Throughout all these activities, supervisors can participate in HRM by taking into consideration the ways that decisions and policies will affect their employees. Understanding the principles of communication, motivation, and other elements of human behavior can help supervisors inspire the best from the organization's human resources.

Ethics in Human Resource Management

LO5

Whenever people's actions affect one another, ethical issues arise, and business decisions are no exception. **Ethics** refers to the fundamental principles of right and wrong; ethical behavior is behavior that is consistent with those principles. Business decisions, including HRM decisions, should be ethical, but the evidence suggests that is

ethics
The fundamental principles of right and wrong.

U.S. companies are becoming more aware of the need to act responsibly and ethically. The obvious example is the impact of the Enron debacle on employees' retirement funds.

not always what happens. Recent surveys indicate that the general public and managers do not have positive perceptions of the ethical conduct of U.S. businesses. For example, in a survey conducted by the *Wall Street Journal*, 4 out of 10 executives reported they had been asked to behave unethically.[16]

As a result of unfavorable perceptions of U.S. business practices and an increased concern for better serving customers, U.S. companies are becoming more aware of the need for all company representatives to act responsibly.[17] They have an interest in the way their employees behave because customer, government agency, and vendor perceptions of the company affect the relationships necessary to sell goods and services.

Employee Rights

In the context of ethical human resource management, HR managers must view employees as having basic rights. Such a view reflects ethical principles embodied in the U.S. Constitution and Bill of Rights. A widely adopted understanding of human rights, based on the work of the philosopher Immanuel Kant, as well as the tradition of the Enlightenment, assumes that in a moral universe, every person has certain basic rights:

- *Right of free consent*—People have the right to be treated only as they knowingly and willingly consent to be treated. An example that applies to employees would be that employees should know the nature of the job they are being hired to do; the employer should not deceive them.
- *Right of privacy*—People have the right to do as they want in their private lives, and they have the right to control what they reveal about private activities. One way an employer respects this right is by keeping employees' medical records confidential.
- *Right of freedom of conscience*—People have the right to refuse to do what violates

their moral beliefs, as long as these beliefs reflect commonly accepted norms. A supervisor who demands that an employee do something that is unsafe or environmentally damaging may be violating this right if it conflicts with the employee's values. (Such behavior could be illegal as well as unethical.)

- *Right of freedom of speech*—People have the right to criticize an organization's ethics, if they do so in good conscience and their criticism does not violate the rights of individuals in the organization. Many organizations address this right by offering hot lines or policies and procedures designed to handle complaints from employees.
- *Right to due process*—If people believe their rights are being violated, they have the right to a fair and impartial hearing. As we will see in Chapter 3, Congress has addressed this right in some circumstances by establishing agencies to hear complaints when employees believe their employer has not provided a fair hearing. For example, the Equal Employment Opportunity Commission may prosecute complaints of discrimination if it believes the employer did not fairly handle the problem.

One way to think about ethics in business is that the morally correct action is the one that minimizes encroachments on and avoids violations of these rights.

As the examples above suggest, organizations often face situations in which the rights of employees are affected. In particular, the right of privacy has received much attention in recent years. Computerized record keeping and computer networks have greatly increased the ways people can gain (authorized or unauthorized) access to records about individuals. Human resource records can be particularly sensitive. HRM responsibilities therefore include the ever-growing challenge of maintaining confidentiality.

Standards for Ethical Behavior

Ethical, successful companies act according to four principles.[18] First, in their relationships with customers, vendors, and clients, ethical and successful companies emphasize mutual benefits. Second, employees assume responsibility for the actions of the company. Third, such companies have a sense of purpose or vision that employees value and use in their day-to-day work. Finally, they emphasize fairness; that is, another person's interests count as much as their own.

The Raytheon Company gives each employee a checklist including several questions intended to help employees determine whether an action they are contemplating is ethical:[19]

- Is the action legal?
- Is it right?
- Who will be affected?
- Does it fit with Raytheon's values?
- How will I feel afterward?
- How will it look in the newspaper?
- Will it reflect poorly on the company?

Raytheon reinforces its ethics codes with formal training programs, a toll-free "ethics line," and full-time ethics offices and officers in all its major business units. Case studies are used in mandatory one-hour ethics classes for all employees to make them aware of the ethical problems that may occur at work.

FIGURE 1.6

Standards for Identifying
Ethical Practices

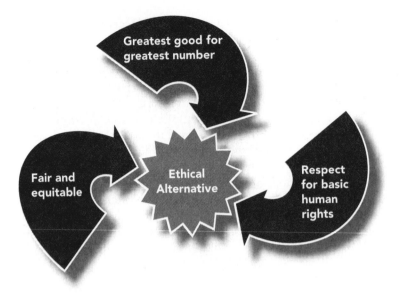

For human resource practices to be considered ethical, they must satisfy the three basic standards summarized in Figure 1.6.[20] First, HRM practices must result in the greatest good for the largest number of people. Second, employment practices must respect basic human rights of privacy, due process, consent, and free speech. Third, managers must treat employees and customers equitably and fairly. These standards are most vexing when none of the alternatives in a situation meet all three of them. For instance, most employers hesitate to get involved in the personal affairs of employees, and this attitude is in keeping with employees' right to privacy. But when personal matters include domestic violence, employees' safety may be in jeopardy, both at home and in the workplace. For Barbara Marlowe of the Boston law firm Mintz Levin Cohn Ferris Glovsky and Popeo, the choice is clear: Helping employees protect themselves does good for employees and also helps employees do better on the job, she says. Mintz Levin set up a group called Employers Against Domestic Violence. Companies that join the group take measures such as posting the phone number of a victim help line, allowing employees to keep flexible hours (to shake off stalkers), and removing victims' names from dial-by-name directories (so harassers can't easily call and disturb them at work).[21]

To explore how ethical principles apply to a variety of decisions, throughout the book we will highlight ethical dilemmas in human resource management practices.

Careers in Human Resource Management

LO6

There are many different types of jobs in the HRM profession. Figure 1.7 shows selected HRM positions and their salaries. The salaries vary depending on education and experience, as well as the type of industry in which the person works. As you can see from Figure 1.7, some positions involve work in specialized areas of HRM such as recruiting, training, or labor and industrial relations. Usually, HR generalists make between $50,000 and $70,000, depending on their experience and education level. Generalists usually perform the full range of HRM activities, including recruiting, training, compensation, and employee relations.

The vast majority of HRM professionals have a college degree, and many also have

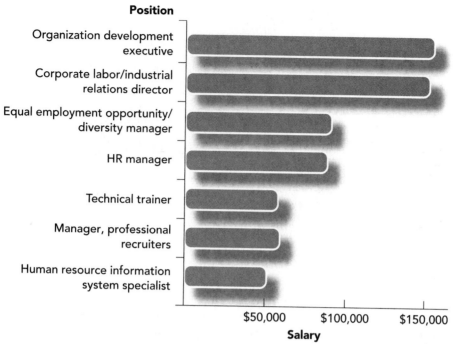

Position

FIGURE 1.7

Median Salaries for HRM Positions

SOURCE: Based on Society for Human Resource Management—Mercer Survey 2001 as reported in the Bureau of National Affairs website, www.bna.com, August 28, 2001.

completed postgraduate work. The typical field of study is business (especially human resources or industrial relations), but some HRM professionals have degrees in the social sciences (economics or psychology), the humanities, and law programs. Those who have completed graduate work have master's degrees in HR management, business management, or a similar field. A well-rounded educational background will likely serve a person well in an HRM position. As one HR professional noted, "One of the biggest misconceptions is that [HRM] is all warm and fuzzy communications with the workers. Or that it is creative and involved in making a more congenial atmosphere for people at work. Actually it is both of those some of the time, but most of the time it is a big mountain of paperwork which calls on a myriad of skills besides the 'people' type. It is law, accounting, philosophy, and logic as well as psychology, spirituality, tolerance, and humility."[22]

Some HRM professionals have a professional certification in HRM, but many more are members of professional associations. The primary professional organization for HRM is the Society for Human Resource Management (SHRM). SHRM is the world's largest human resource management association, with more than 160,000 professional and student members throughout the world. SHRM provides education and information services, conferences and seminars, government and media representation, and online services and publications (such as *HR Magazine*). You can visit SHRM's website to see their services at www.shrm.org.

Organization of This Book

This chapter has provided an overview of human resource management, to give you a sense of its scope. In this book, the topics are organized according to the broad areas

SHRM provides education, information services (such as this conference), seminars, government and media representation, and online services and publications.

of human resource management shown in Table 1.3. The numbers in the table refer to the part and chapter numbers.

Part I discusses several aspects of the human resource environment. To be effective, human resource management must begin with an awareness of the trends shaping this field, including changes in the workforce, technology, and society. Such trends are the topic of Chapter 2. On a more detailed level, human resource management must also ensure that the organization's actions comply with legal requirements, the topic of Chapter 3. And within the organization itself, human resource management looks at the types of work required and designs jobs that meet a variety of objectives, balancing safety, efficiency, mental demands, and motivation. Chapter 4 covers the topics of analyzing work and designing jobs.

Part II explores the responsibilities involved in acquiring and preparing human resources. Chapter 5 explains how to plan for human resource needs and recruit candidates to meet those needs. Chapter 6 discusses the selection of employees and their

TABLE 1.3

Topics Covered in This Book

I.   The Human Resource Environment
   2. Trends in Human Resource Management
   3. Providing Equal Employment Opportunity and a Safe Workplace
   4. Analyzing Work and Designing Jobs

II. Acquiring and Preparing Human Resources
   5. Planning for and Recruiting Human Resources
   6. Selecting Employees and Placing Them in Jobs
   7. Training Employees

III. Assessing Performance and Developing Employees
   8. Managing Employees' Performance
   9. Developing Employees for Future Success
   10. Separating and Retaining Employees

IV. Compensating Human Resources
   11. Establishing a Pay Structure
   12. Recognizing Employee Contributions with Pay
   13. Providing Employee Benefits

V.   Meeting Other HR Goals
   14. Collective Bargaining and Labor Relations
   15. Managing Human Resources Globally
   16. Creating and Maintaining High-Performance Organizations

placement into jobs or teams. Chapter 7 addresses various ways organizations train their employees to perform their jobs.

In Part III, the discussion turns to the assessment and development of human resources. Chapter 8 describes the various activities involved in managing performance, including regular performance appraisals. Chapter 9 describes practices related to employee development—preparing employees for future jobs and helping to establish career paths that take into account employees' work interests, goals, values, and other career issues. Despite these activities, organizations at times determine they no longer need certain positions or no longer wish to retain certain employees. To address these situations, Chapter 10 discusses appropriate ways to handle employee separation. It also discusses the flip side: how organizations can keep valuable employees from wanting to leave.

An important element of employee satisfaction is the employee's belief that he or she is being fairly compensated for the work performed. Part IV addresses several topics related to compensation. Chapter 11 explores decisions related to the organization's overall pay structure. Chapter 12 discusses ways organizations can use pay to recognize individual and group contributions to the organization's performance. Chapter 13 considers benefits—forms of compensation other than pay (for example, insurance and paid vacation time).

The last part of the book addresses a number of special topics that human resource managers face today. Chapter 14 discusses responsibilities of human resource management in organizations where employees have or are seeking union representation. Chapter 15 explores issues that arise when the organization has human resources working in more than one nation. And Chapter 16, the last chapter, returns to the topic of high-performance organizations, taking a closer look at how human resource management can contribute to creating and maintaining such an organization.

Each chapter includes principles and examples showing how the human resource management practice covered in that chapter helps a company maintain high performance. "Best Practices" boxes highlight success stories related to these topics. "HR How To" boxes provide a more detailed look at how to carry out a practice in each of these areas. Many chapters also include an "e-HRM" box identifying the ways that human resource professionals are applying information technology and the Internet to help their organizations excel in the fast-changing modern world.

Summary

1. Define human resource management and explain how HRM contributes to an organization's performance.
Human resource management consists of an organization's "people practices"—the policies, practices, and systems that influence employees' behavior, attitudes, and performance. HRM influences who works for the organization and how those people work. These human resources, if well managed, have the potential to be a source of sustainable competitive advantage, contributing to basic objectives such as quality, profits, and customer satisfaction.

2. Identify the responsibilities of human resource departments.

By carrying out HR activities or supporting line management, HR departments have responsibility for a variety of functions related to acquiring and managing employees. The HRM process begins with analyzing and designing jobs, then recruiting and selecting employees to fill those jobs. Training and development equip employees to carry out their present jobs and follow a career path in the organization. Performance management ensures that employees' activities and outputs match the organization's goals. Human resource departments also plan and administer the organization's pay and benefits. They carry out activities in support of employee relations, such as communications programs and collective bargaining. Conducting all these activities involves the establishment and administration of personnel policies. Management also depends on human resource professionals for help in ensuring compliance with labor laws, as well as for support for the organization's strategy—for example, human resource planning and change management.

3. Summarize the types of skills needed for human resource management.
Human resource management requires substantial human relations skills, including skill in communicating, negotiating, and team development. Human resource professionals also need decision-making skills based on knowledge of the HR field as well as the organization's line of business. Leadership skills are necessary, especially for managing conflict and change. Technical skills of human resource professionals include knowledge of current techniques, applicable laws, and computer systems.

4. Explain the role of supervisors in human resource management.
Although many organizations have human resource departments, non-HR managers must be familiar with the basics of HRM and their own role with regard to managing human resources. Supervisors typically have responsibilities related to all the HR functions. Supervisors help analyze work, interview job candidates, participate in selection decisions, provide training, conduct performance appraisals, and recommend pay

increases. On a day-to-day basis, supervisors represent the company to their employees, so they also play an important role in employee relations.

5. Discuss ethical issues in human resource management.
Like all managers and employees, HR professionals should make decisions consistent with sound ethical principles. Their decisions should result in the greatest good for the largest number of people; respect basic rights of privacy, due process, consent, and free speech; and treat employees and customers equitably and fairly. Some areas in which ethical issues arise include concerns about employee privacy, protection of employee safety, and fairness in employment practices (for example, avoiding discrimination).

6. Describe typical careers in human resource management.
Careers in human resource management may involve specialized work in fields such as recruiting, training, or labor relations. HR professionals may also be generalists, performing the full range of HR activities described in this chapter. People in these positions usually have a college degree in business or the social sciences. Human resource management means enhancing communication with employees and concern for their well-being, but also involves a great deal of paperwork, and a variety of non-people skills as well as knowledge of business and laws.

Review and Discussion Questions

1. How can human resource management contribute to a company's success?
2. Imagine that a small manufacturing company decides to invest in a materials resource planning (MRP) system. This is a computerized information system that improves efficiency by automating such work as planning needs for resources, ordering materials, and scheduling work on the shop floor. The company hopes that with the new MRP system, it can grow by quickly and efficiently processing small orders for a variety of products. Which of the human resource functions are likely to be affected by this change? How can human resource management help the organization carry out this change successfully?
3. What skills are important for success in human resource management? Which of these skills are already strengths of yours? Which would you like to develop?
4. Traditionally, human resource management practices were developed and administered by the company's human resource department. Line managers are now

playing a major role in developing and implementing HRM practices. Why do you think non-HR managers are becoming more involved?
5. If you were to start a business, which aspects of human resource management would you want to entrust to specialists? Why?
6. Why do all managers and supervisors need knowledge and skills related to human resource management?
7. Federal law requires that employers not discriminate on the basis of a person's race, sex, national origin, or age over 40. Is this also an ethical requirement? A competitive requirement? Explain.
8. When a restaurant employee slipped on spilled soup and fell, requiring the evening off to recover, the owner realized that workplace safety was an issue to which she had not devoted much time. A friend warned the owner that if she started creating a lot of safety rules and procedures, she would lose her focus on customers and might jeopardize the future of the restaurant. The safety problem is beginning to feel like an ethical

dilemma. Suggest some ways the restaurant owner might address this dilemma. What aspects of human resource management are involved?

9. Does a career in human resource management, based on this chapter's description, appeal to you? Why or why not?

What's Your HR IQ?

The Student CD-ROM offers two more ways to check what you've learned so far. Use the Self-Assessment exercise to see whether you have what it takes for a career in HR. Go online with the Web Exercise to learn about the Society for Human Resource Management and its publication *HR Magazine*.

BusinessWeek Case

BusinessWeek **The Human Factor** ✳

Julie Jones jumped at the chance to take a sabbatical when Accenture Ltd. offered one in June. Although she had been a consultant in the firm's Chicago office for just two and a half years, the 25-year-old expert in accounts payable software had long wanted to work for Ameri-Corps, the national volunteer group. So in July, Jones, who's single, headed out to Los Angeles for a year to join an AmeriCorps group that helps nonprofits with technology problems. Accenture—formerly the consulting subsidiary of Andersen Worldwide and now an independent consulting firm—will pay 20 percent of her salary, plus benefits, and let her keep her work phone number, laptop, and e-mail. "This gives me the security of knowing I'll have a job when I come back," says Jones.

Accenture hopes the program will offer it some security, too. The economic slowdown has pinched the company's business, forcing it to rein in costs. But after years of scrambling to find scarce talent, Accenture is reluctant to lay off workers it hopes to need when the economy turns north again. Accenture did cut 600 support staff jobs in June 2001. But to retain skilled employees, it cooked up the idea of partially paid sabbaticals, such as the one Jones is taking. About 1,000 employees took up the offer, which allows them to do whatever they want for 6 to 12 months, says Larry Solomon, Accenture's managing partner in charge of internal operations. "This is a way to cut costs that gives us the ability to hang onto people we spent so much time recruiting and training," he says.

Plenty of other employers are feeling the same way. The slumping economy has put pressure on companies to slash expenses and boost sagging profits. But the United States has just sailed through five years of labor shortfalls on a scale not seen in more than three decades. What's more, the unemployment rate, while rising, remains at historically low levels. Many employers are wary about dumping too many workers just to find themselves scrambling later to refill the positions.

Even companies that have handed out pink slips often did so with caution rather than abandon. When Charles Schwab Corporation first saw business deteriorate last fall, it put projects on hold and cut back on such expenses as travel and entertainment to avoid layoffs, says human resources vice president Ruth K. Ross. In December, as it became clear that more was needed, top executives all took pay cuts: 50 percent for the company's two co-CEOs, 20 percent for executive vice presidents, 10 percent for senior vice presidents, and 5 percent for vice presidents.

Schwab took further steps this year before finally cutting staff. It encouraged employees to take unused vacation and to take unpaid leaves of up to 20 days. Management designated three Fridays in February and March as voluntary days off without pay for employees who didn't have clients to deal with. Only in March, after the outlook darkened yet again, did Schwab announce 2,000 layoffs out of a workforce of 25,000. Even then, the severance package includes a $7,500 "hire-back" bonus that any employee will get if they're rehired within 18 months. "We felt the markets will turn at some point, and the cost of hiring people back with the bonus is small compared to what it would be to pay for recruiting and retraining new employees," says Ross.

Employers also are trying to protect their core workers by axing temps and contract employees. Throughout the 1990s, many companies built up buffer workforces—workers performing jobs under contract, rather than as employees—to get work done during a period of high demand. The buffer workforces were intended to allow companies to more easily adjust staffing levels. Since 1990 the number of temporary employees tripled, to a peak of 3.6 million in the fall of 2000. But since then their ranks have fallen by half a million as companies have tried to adjust to slower sales by reducing their use of contract and temporary workers.

Slashing work hours is another way to reduce payroll

without lopping off heads. The workweek has edged steadily downward as the economy slowed, to 34.3 hours for most of 2001. Manufacturers, hit the hardest by the economic slump, have dialed back the most. Factory overtime has fallen by about 15 percent from last year, to four hours a week in June 2001. The factory workweek has plunged by a similar amount, to 40.7 hours. "Businesses have aggressively cut hours worked, which is the first thing you do if you want to hang onto staff," says Mark M. Zandi, chief economist at Economy.com Inc. in West Chester, Pennsylvania.

The result of all these trends has been a relatively modest upturn in unemployment. The jobless rate has jumped up to 4.5 percent since hitting a 30-year low of 3.9 percent last fall. But that's still below the 5 percent or even 6 percent that most experts had considered full employment for some two decades. It's also much lower than the spike that occurred during the last recession, in 1991. Back then, unemployment soared from a low of 5 percent to a peak of 7.8 percent. The rate probably will continue to inch higher through the year as companies face up to the fact that the sales volumes they had geared up for in 2000 aren't going to materialize. But if the consensus among economists is right, labor, especially the more skilled kind, will remain scarce for the foreseeable future. "Even if we get unemployment up over 5 percent, it won't free up more nurses or computer programmers," says David Wyss, chief economist at Standard & Poor's. "There aren't enough of them to go around."

Even high-tech workers are likely to remain in demand. Employers will have about 900,000 job openings in 2001 for programmers, software engineers, tech-support personnel, and similar workers, according to an April survey by the Information Technology Association of America (ITAA), an industry group based in Arlington, Virginia. That's down sharply from 1.6 million openings in 2000. But the survey found that even this year, companies believe that they will be unable to fill nearly half of those

jobs, or 420,000 positions. "Demand for workers remains strong," the report concluded.

Part of the reason is that most of these posts aren't at high-tech companies, which have borne the brunt of the sharp falloff in demand for computers and telecom equipment. Roughly 90 percent of the country's 10.4 million tech workers are employed by non-high-tech companies, the ITAA found in its survey. Employers say they will have a total of about 640,000 openings this year.

Still, even battered tech companies would like to hire 260,000 skilled workers this year—and expect to be able to find just half of those they need, according to the survey. "We're still hiring for some critical areas, like electrical engineers," says Matt McKinney, a spokesman for Texas Instruments Inc., which announced 2,500 layoffs in April. "Every year, the universities graduate fewer students in these areas, so the available talent pool is shrinking. Yet demand still goes up."

Absent a full-blown recession, skilled workers are likely to remain in short supply. The same may not hold true at the bottom of the labor market, which is unlikely to see solid wage growth without a return to the extraordinary growth levels of 2000. That leaves the United States facing renewed social cleavages as those on the top continue to gain while the rest struggle to keep up.

SOURCE: A. Bernstein, "The Human Factor," *BusinessWeek*, August 27, 2001.

Questions

1. Why have some organizations looked for alternatives to laying off employees? How does this fit with the idea of employees being "human capital"?
2. What ethical issues are involved in decisions about whether to lay off employees?
3. While many employees have been laid off recently, there is still a shortage of skilled workers in certain fields. What HRM practices may be useful for attracting these workers?

Case: The Container Store: Human Resource Management Excellence Takes Different Forms

The management of human resources is critical to an organization's success. But the way that an organization manages human resources takes many different forms. Consider, for example, the approach of The Container Store. The Container Store has a small human resource function and expects managers to actively participate in HR activities such as recruiting.

The Container Store is a retailer of boxes, bags, racks, and shelves that organize everything from shoes to spices. The interior of each store has an open layout, which is divided into sections marked with brightly colored banners

with descriptions such as Closet, Kitchen, Office, and Laundry. Wherever you look in the store, someone in a blue apron is ready to help solve storage problems from the tiniest of issues to the most intimidating of organizational challenges.

The Dallas-based company, which has 2,000 employees in 22 states, has become respected for its commitment to employees. The Container Store has gained many rewards for its HRM leadership. It has been ranked as the best U.S. organization to work for by *Fortune* and has received other awards for its outstanding people management strategies, including the *Workforce* magazine Optimas Award in 2001.

The company attributes its success to a 15 to 20 percent turnover rate in an industry where 100 percent turnover is common. Credit for the low turnover and employees' high level of service goes directly to The Container Store culture. The company issues a few uncomplicated guidelines, such as always being flexible, based on a set of humanistic philosophies that emphasize treating others as you want to be treated. A strong emphasis on customer service allows employees to take ownership of the company and make decisions they believe will benefit customers. The company treats employees with respect, and in turn employees enthusiastically serve customers. Employees' ability to create a customized product solution for each customer's organizational needs increases the stores' sales.

The Container Store does not have a large HRM department. In fact, until recently, managers viewed HRM as working against the company's culture. According to Elizabeth Barrett, vice president of operations, the company has always trusted supervisors to attract, motivate, and retain employees. Managers are responsible for many traditional HRM tasks because they are closest to employees. The Container Store believes that people have to fit into the company's culture to succeed.

The company has a focused people strategy: hire for fit, train comprehensively, and pay and support for long tenure. Forty-one percent of new employees are people recommended by current employees. Many new employees are the company's customers. They are typically college educated and want their quality of life at work to reflect their lifestyle, beliefs, and values. The company invests more than 235 hours of training in first-year employees, far above the industry average of 7 hours per year. After their first year, employees receive an average of 160 hours of training each year. In contrast to other retailers, the company spends considerable time measuring the direct impact of training on store sales. Most retailers focus primarily on merchandise. The Container Store's managers believe that loyal employees will pay off handsomely with increased sales and customer service, so the company pays employees two to three times the industry average. It also shares financial information with everyone and offers benefits to both full- and part-time employees.

The company now has a semiformal HRM structure with recruiting, training, payroll, and benefits departments. HR managers are also given responsibility for other areas of the company, such as store operations, and are required to take store-level positions so they can better understand the company's purpose—to serve customers. Most HRM employees start out as salespeople so they will understand more about serving customer needs. Despite the new HRM structure, managers continue to take the lead in recruiting and evaluating potential employees, as well as in the extensive employee training. The company has seen its human resource strategy pay off. The Container Store is continuing to expand in the United States and beyond, and retail sales have increased at an average rate of 20 to 25 percent a year.

SOURCE: Based on R. Laglow, "The Container Store Does Great HRM—Even without an HR Department," *Human Resource Executive,* August 2001, p. 23; J. Labbs, "Thinking outside the Box at The Container Store," *Workforce,* March 2001, pp. 34–38; The Container Store website, www.containerstore.com.

Questions

1. Consider the areas of human resource management listed in Table 1.3. For each area, summarize how The Container Store handles these activities.
2. For each of the functions identified in Question 1, what is the role of the HR department? What is the role of the company's line managers?
3. What advantages might there be to assigning more of these tasks to the HR department or to line managers? Would you expect these advantages to be different in a larger or smaller organization?

Notes

1. Susan Greco, "As the Talent Turns," *Inc.*, June 2001, pp. 88–89.
2. A. S. Tsui and L. R. Gomez-Mejia, "Evaluating Human Resource Effectiveness," in *Human Resource Management: Evolving Rules and Responsibilities,* ed. L. Dyer (Washington, DC: BNA Books, 1988), pp. 1187–227; M. A. Hitt, B. W. Keats, and S. M. DeMarie, "Navigating in the New Competitive Landscape: Building Strategic Flexibility and Competitive Advantage in the 21st Century," *Academy of Management Executive* 12, no. 4 (1998), pp. 22–42; J. T. Delaney and M. A. Huselid, "The Impact of Human Resource Management Practices on Perceptions of Organizational Performance," *Academy of Management Journal* 39 (1996), pp. 949–69.
3. W. F. Cascio, *Costing Human Resources: The Financial Impact of Behavior in Organizations,* 3rd ed. (Boston: PWS-Kent, 1991).
4. S. A. Snell and J. W. Dean, "Integrated Manufacturing and Human Resource Management: A Human Capital Perspective," *Academy of Management Journal* 35 (1992), pp. 467–504; M. A. Youndt, S. Snell, J. W. Dean Jr., and D. P. Lepak, "Human Resource Management, Manufacturing Strategy, and Firm Performance," *Academy of Management Journal* 39 (1996), pp. 836–66.

5. Athleta Corporation website, www.athleta.com, September 22, 2001; K. Dobbs, "Knowing How to Keep Your Best and Brightest," *Workforce*, April 2001, pp. 56–60.

6. Rifka Rosenwein, "Hot Tips: Using Mom as the Ultimate Recruiting Tool," *Inc.*, June 2001, p. 76.

7. S. Snell, "Control Theory in Strategic Human Resource Management: The Mediating Effect of Administrative Information," *Academy of Management Journal* 35 (1992), pp. 292–327.

8. Leigh Buchanan, "City Lights," *Inc.*, May 2001, pp. 66–71.

9. Jill Hecht Maxwell, "New to the HR Brew," *Inc.*, April 2001, p. 100.

10. J. Britt, "Disability Advocates Aim at Technology Barriers," *HR News* 20, no. 9 (2001), pp. 1, 9.

11. S. Nelton, "Nurturing Diversity," *Nation's Business*, June 1995, pp. 25–27.

12. G. McMahan and R. Woodman, "The Current Practice of Organization Development within the Firm: A Survey of Large Industrial Corporations," *Group and Organization Studies* 17 (1992), pp. 117–34.

13. G. Jones and P. Wright, "An Economic Approach to Conceptualizing the Utility of Human Resource Management Practices," *Research in Personnel/Human Resources* 10 (1992), pp. 271–99.

14. R. Schuler and J. Walker, "Human Resources Strategy: Focusing on Issues and Actions," *Organizational Dynamics*, Summer 1990, pp. 5–19.

15. Kate O'Sullivan, "Why You're Hiring All Wrong," *Inc.*, February 2002, p. 86.

16. R. Ricklees, "Ethics in America," *The Wall Street Journal*, October 31–November 3, 1983, p. 33.

17. C. Lee, "Ethics Training: Facing the Tough Questions," *Training*, March 31, 1986, pp. 33, 38–41.

18. M. Pastin, *The Hard Problems of Management: Gaining the Ethics Edge* (San Francisco: Jossey-Bass, 1986).

19. D. Fandray, "The Ethical Company," *Workforce*, December 2000, pp. 75–77.

20. G. F. Cavanaugh, D. Moberg, and M. Velasquez, "The Ethics of Organizational Politics," *Academy of Management Review* 6 (1981), pp. 363–74.

21. Mike Hofman, "The Shadow of Domestic Violence," *Inc.*, March 2001, p. 85.

22. J. Wiscombe, "Your Wonderful, Terrible HR Life," *Workforce*, June 2001, pp. 32–38.

Part 1

The Human Resource Environment

Chapter 2
Trends in Human Resource Management

Chapter 3
Providing Equal Employment Opportunity and a Safe Workplace

Chapter 4
Analyzing Work and Designing Jobs

Trends in Human Resource Management

What Do I Need to Know?
After reading this chapter, you should be able to:

1. Describe trends in the labor force composition and how they affect human resource management.

2. Summarize areas in which human resource management can support the goal of creating a high-performance work system.

3. Define employee empowerment and explain its role in the modern organization.

4. Identify ways HR professionals can support organizational strategies for quality, growth, efficiency, and international operations.

5. Summarize the role of human resource management in an Internet economy.

6. Discuss how technological developments are affecting human resource management.

7. Explain how the nature of the employment relationship is changing.

8. Discuss how the need for flexibility affects human resource management.

Introduction

The early years of the 21st century have shaken the complacency of U.S. workers and forced them to take a fresh look at the ways they are working. A decade of turbulent economic growth gave way to decline, or at least stagnation. Terrorist attacks on U.S. soil forced a new sense of life's uncertainties. And a revolution in information technology has redefined such fundamental notions as what it means to be "in touch" or "at work." More and more voices at the workplace, in the community, and in the media tell of people who are mulling over why they work the way they do—and whether they want to keep working that way.

Jessica Hsu is a case in point. At age 25, Hsu was experiencing an economic slowdown for the first time, and she questioned her past role as an ad writer for a dot-com business. Says Hsu, " I was writing ads to convince people to buy things they really did not need." She decided to switch to more meaningful work and signed up with the Peace Corps. She was far from the only one. According to the Peace Corps, enrollment has surged since the stocks of Internet companies plunged in 2001. Some of these volunteers had lost their jobs, but others just said they were sick of the intense pace of work and wanted to do something more significant.[1]

Difficult times have given business owner Richard Schachtman more appreciation for his employees. Schachtman, who runs the six-store Now! Audio Video chain in North Carolina, struggled to avoid laying off workers. For 27 years, he had never made any cuts in his payroll. But after the September 11, 2001, attacks intensified the economic slowdown, his business simply could not support all his employees. He laid off three employees and reduced or eliminated annual bonuses for the rest. At the end of the year, he spent hours trying to write a heartfelt thank-you to the remaining 132 employees. Says Schachtman, "We're a family company, and these people deserved thousands [of dollars in bonuses], but were getting just hundreds." The employees responded to the situation with an understanding that Schachtman calls "almost noble."[2]

Other employees are holding onto their jobs—and barely holding onto their nonwork lives. In fact, their jobs seem to be creeping out of the workplace and into their homes and cars. People are using the latest technology to make phone calls and check e-mail wherever they can carry a cell phone or pager. *Multitasking* has become a new buzzword as people become increasingly creative with their travel time. One New York official even admitted to a *Wall Street Journal* columnist that he has figured out how to change his pants while driving (he insists he has a safe driving record). On a more serious note, many workers have turned their cars into traveling conference centers. Greg Xikes and coworkers at a company that provides networking services have carried on conference calls from Xikes's car, with all of them dialing into the same number from their cell phones. Not everyone likes multitasking, though. A sales manager in Rhode Island works from his car, even though he hates it, because he believes it is a necessary part of keeping up with the competition. Kimberly Cooper, a data analyst in Florida, simply decided not to participate in this aspect of modern life. She leaves her car at home and rides a bike to work. Cooper says

Multitasking has become a way of life for many employees who need to make the most of every minute. This is a new, but prevalent, trend that is affecting human resource management and the employees it supports.

distracted multitaskers lose an amazing amount of the fruits of their busyness: "You should see the 'road kill'—a dropped wallet, a case with over $135 in CDs."[3]

These are the kinds of people and situations that shape the nature of human resource management today. This chapter describes major trends that are affecting human resource management. It begins with an examination of the modern labor force, including trends that are determining who will participate in the workforce of the future. Next, we explore ways HRM can support a number of trends in organizational strategy, from efforts to maintain high-performance work systems to changes in the organization's size and structure. Often, growth includes the use of human resources on a global scale, as more and more organizations hire immigrants or open operations overseas. The chapter then turns to major changes in technology, especially the role of the Internet. As we will explain, the Internet is changing organizations themselves, as well as providing new ways to carry out human resource management. Finally, we explore the changing nature of the employment relationship, in which careers and jobs are becoming more flexible.

Change in the Labor Force

LO1

internal labor force
An organization's workers (its employees and the people who have contracts to work at the organization).

external labor market
Individuals who are actively seeking employment.

The *labor force* is a general way to refer to all the people willing and able to work. For an organization, the **internal labor force** consists of the organization's workers—its employees and the people who have contracts to work at the organization. This internal labor force is drawn from the organization's **external labor market,** that is, individuals who are actively seeking employment. The number and kinds of people in the external labor market determine the kinds of human resources available to an organization (and their cost). Human resource professionals need to be aware of trends in the composition of the external labor market, because these trends affect the organization's options for creating a well-skilled, motivated internal labor force.

An Aging Workforce

In the United States, the Bureau of Labor Statistics (BLS), an agency of the Department of Labor, tracks changes in the composition of the U.S. labor force and forecasts employment trends. The BLS has projected that from 1996 to 2006, the total U.S. labor force will grow from 134 million to 149 million workers.[4] This 11 percent increase represents somewhat slower growth than during the preceding decade. As that growth occurs, the composition of the labor force will change because of shifts in the U.S. population.

Some of the expected change involves the distribution of workers by age. During the 1996–2006 period, the youth labor force (workers between the ages of 16 and 24) is expected to grow faster than the overall labor force for the first time in 25 years. However, the fastest-growing age segment will be workers aged 45 to 64, as the baby boom generation (born from 1946 to 1964) continues to age. Therefore, in spite of the growing numbers of young workers, the overall work force will be aging. Figure 2.1 shows the change in age distribution, as forecast by the Bureau of Labor Statistics, between 1990 and 2010. The BLS forecasts that by 2015, the number of workers at least 40 years old will exceed the number under 40 for the first time ever.[5] Human resource professionals will therefore spend much of their time on concerns related to retirement planning, retraining older workers, and motivating workers whose careers

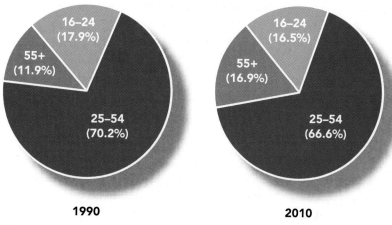

FIGURE 2.1

Age Distribution of U.S. Labor Force, 1990 and 2010

SOURCE: H. N. Fullerton Jr. and M. Toossi, "Labor Force Projections to 2010: Steady Growth and Changing Composition," *Monthly Labor Review* 124, no. 11 (November 2001), downloaded at www.bls.gov.

have plateaued. Organizations will struggle with ways to control the rising costs of health care and other benefits. At the same time, organizations will have to find ways to attract, retain, and prepare the youth labor force.

In doing so, organizations will be reminded that values tend to change from one generation to the next, as well as when people reach different life stages.[6] For example, members of Generation Y (born between 1976 and 1995) begin their career with the assumption they will frequently change jobs. They are likely to place a high value on money as well as on helping others. Most employees, however, value several aspects of work, regardless of their age. Employees view work as a means to self-fulfillment—that is, a means to more fully use their skills and abilities, meet their interests, and live a desirable lifestyle.[7] One report indicates that if employees receive opportunities to fully use and develop their skills, have greater job responsibilities, believe the promotion system is fair, and have a trustworthy manager who represents the employee's best interests, they are more committed to their companies.[8] Fostering these values requires organizations to develop HRM practices that provide more opportunity for individual contribution and entrepreneurship (in this context, taking responsibility for starting up something new).[9] Because many employees place more value on the quality of nonwork activities and family life than on pay and production, employees will demand more flexible work policies that allow them to choose work hours and the places where they work.

Employers will likely find that many talented older workers want to continue contributing through their work, though not necessarily in a traditional nine-to-five job. For organizations to attract and keep talented older workers, many will have to rethink the ways they design jobs. Phyllis Ostrowsky, in her mid-fifties, enjoyed her position as a store manager for 13 years, and she went out of her way to provide good customer service. But her job responsibilities and hours expanded to the point they became excessive. She eventually was working 12-hour days and was too busy to give customers the personal touch she liked to deliver. Ostrowsky therefore left her store job for a position as an office manager with another company.[10]

A Diverse Workforce

Another kind of change affecting the U.S. labor force is that it is growing more diverse in racial and ethnic terms. As Figure 2.2 shows, the 2006 workforce will be 72 percent white (and non-Hispanic), 11 percent black, 12 percent Hispanic, and 5 percent Asian and other minorities. The fastest-growing of these categories are "Asian and other" and Hispanics because these groups are experiencing immigration and birthrates above the national average. Along with the greater racial and ethnic diversity, more women are in the paid labor force than in the past. Since 1994, women have been 46 percent of the U.S. labor force. Three-quarters of them work full-time.[11]

The greater diversity of the U.S. labor force challenges employers to create HRM practices that ensure they fully utilize the talents, skills, and values of all employees. The growth in the labor market of female and minority populations will exceed the growth of white non-Hispanic persons. As a result, organizations cannot afford to ignore or discount the potential contributions of women and minorities. Employers will have to ensure that employees and HRM systems are free of bias and value the perspectives and experience that women and minorities can contribute to organizational goals such as product quality and customer service. As we will discuss further in the next chapter, managing cultural diversity involves many different activities. These include creating an organizational culture that values diversity, ensuring that HRM systems are bias-free, encouraging career development for women and minorities, promoting knowledge and acceptance of cultural differences, ensuring involvement in education both within and outside the organization, and dealing with employees' resistance to diversity.[12] Figure 2.3 summarizes ways in which HRM can support the management of diversity for organizational success.

Many U.S. companies have already committed themselves to ensuring that they recognize the diversity of their internal labor force and use it to gain a competitive advantage. According to a recent survey of HR professionals, the most common approaches include recruiting efforts with the goal of increasing diversity and training programs related to diversity.[13] The majority of respondents believed that these efforts were beneficial; 91 percent said they helped the company maintain a competitive advantage.

Texaco developed a state-of-the-art diversity program after the company had to

FIGURE 2.2

Projected Racial/Ethnic Makeup of the U.S. Workforce, 2006

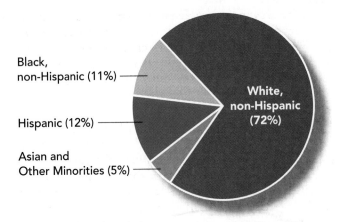

Black, non-Hispanic (11%)

Hispanic (12%)

Asian and Other Minorities (5%)

White, non-Hispanic (72%)

SOURCE: Bureau of Labor Statistics, "BLS Releases New 1996–2006 Employment Projections," www.bls.gov/new.release/ecopro.nws.htm.

FIGURE 2.3

HRM Practices That Support Diversity Management

Communication:
Communicate with employees from a variety of backgrounds.

Development:
Provide career development for employees with different backgrounds and abilities.

Performance Appraisal:
Provide feedback based on objective outcomes.

Employee Relations:
Create a work environment that is comfortable for all and fosters creativity.

SOURCE: Based on M. Loden and J. B. Rosener, *Workforce America!* (Homewood, IL: Business One Irwin, 1991).

pay more than $175 million to settle a racial discrimination lawsuit.[14] The lawsuit publicly accused company executives of using racial slurs. Before the lawsuit, Texaco's diversity program consisted of a workshop presented to top executives on practical tips for managing a diverse workforce. Today all Texaco employees are required to attend a two-day diversity "learning experience" that emphasizes awareness of what it feels like to be excluded, develops employee sensitivity to others, and improves communication skills needed for interacting with diverse peers. However, managing diversity at Texaco goes far beyond attending workshops; it is part of a culture change. As you will see in Chapter 7, Texaco's diversity effort includes programs designed to stop discrimination in hiring, retention, and promotion.

The practices required for successfully managing diversity do more than meet employee needs; they reduce turnover costs and ensure that customers receive the best service possible. For instance, Molina Healthcare operates clinics whose clients are mostly African American, Hispanic, and Southeast Asian. The company tries to hire staffers who live in the clinics' neighborhoods and speak their patients' languages. This commitment to diversity helps improve communications and the quality of health care provided by the company.[15]

Throughout this book, we will show how diversity affects HRM practices. For example, from a staffing perspective, it is important to ensure that tests used to select employees are not unfairly biased against minority groups. From the perspective of work design, employees need flexible schedules that allow them to meet nonwork needs. In terms of training, it is clear that employees must be made aware of the damage that stereotypes can do. With regard to compensation, organizations are providing benefits such as elder care and day care as a way to accommodate the needs of a diverse workforce. As we will see later in the chapter, successfully managing diversity is also critical for companies that compete in international markets.

Skill Deficiencies of the Workforce

The increasing use of computers to do routine tasks has shifted the kinds of skills needed for employees in the U.S. economy. Such qualities as physical strength and mastery of a particular piece of machinery are no longer important for many jobs. More employers are looking for mathematical, verbal, and interpersonal skills, such as the ability to solve math problems or reach decisions as part of a team. Often, when organizations are looking for technical skills, they are looking for skills related to computers and using the Internet. Today's employees must be able to handle a variety of responsibilities, interact with customers, and think creatively.

To find such employees, most organizations are looking for educational achievements. A college degree is a basic requirement for many jobs today. Competition for qualified college graduates in many fields is intense. At the other extreme, workers with less education often have to settle for low-paying jobs. Some companies are unable to find qualified employees and instead rely on training to correct skill deficiencies.[16] Other companies team up with universities, community colleges, and high schools to design and teach courses ranging from basic reading to design blueprint reading.

Not all the skills employers want require a college education. Employers surveyed by the National Association of Manufacturers report a deficiency in employees with such basic skills as getting to work on time and working hard. The school district in Kent, Washington, surveyed local businesses and learned that its graduates were not well prepared to handle such challenges as working well with others. According to Tony Proscio, a researcher who prepared a report on the subject for a Philadelphia think tank, there have always been many people lacking these soft skills, but a lower-than-usual employment rate has forced employers to consider hiring these unqualified workers: "In the late 1990s, employers weren't able to pass them over anymore, because there simply wasn't anyone [else] left." Proscio expects that when the recent economic slowdown reverses, the problem will again become severe.[17] The gap between skills needed and skills available has decreased U.S. companies' ability to compete because they sometimes lack the skills to upgrade technology, reorganize work, and empower employees.

LO2

high-performance work systems
Organizations that have the best possible fit between their social system (people and how they interact) and technical system (equipment and processes).

High-Performance Work Systems

Human resource management is playing an important role in helping organizations gain and keep an advantage over competitors by becoming **high-performance work systems.** These are organizations that have the best possible fit between their social system (people and how they interact) and technical system (equipment and processes).[18] As the nature of the workforce and the technology available to organizations have changed, so have the requirements for creating a high-performance work system. Customers are demanding high quality and customized products, employees are seeking flexible work arrangements, and employers are looking for ways to tap people's creativity and interpersonal skills. Such demands require that organizations make full use of their people's knowledge and skill, and skilled human resource management can help organizations do this.

Among the trends that are occurring in today's high-performance work systems are reliance on knowledge workers; the empowerment of employees to make decisions; and the use of teamwork. The following sections describe those three trends, and Chapter 16 will explore the ways HRM can support the creation and maintenance of

Keeping Up with Change

Many of the changes in today's business environment have a direct impact on human resource management. Changes in the population, in technology, in employees' expectations, and other aspects of the business environment place heavy demands on modern HR professionals—and anyone else involved in management. The career advantage goes to those who keep an eye on what's happening in the business environment. Here are some ways to keep up with change:

Know Your Specialty. Join and participate in trade and professional groups. In human resource management, the largest group is the Society for Human Resource Management. Attendance at meetings and visits to the SHRM home page will help you stay abreast of the latest ideas in the field.

Know Your Business. To support your organization's strategy, you have to know the company's line of work. Read industry and general business publications, with an eye on news about what's happening in your company's industry. You can customize Web portals and news websites to deliver headlines related to your industry.

Follow Trends. Government agencies publish news releases and data related to their area of responsibility. Pay regular visits to relevant agency websites, such as those for the Bureau of Labor Statistics (www.bls.gov), the Equal Employment Opportunity Commission (www.eeoc.gov), and the Occupational Safety and Health Administration (www.osha.gov) to find the latest information.

Listen at Work. When employees and management are talking about their work and the organization's performance, listen for the HR implications. Does the organization have the right amounts and kinds of knowledge, skills, and motivation to carry out its goals? Can some of the new ideas in your field help your organization?

Keep Your Résumé Up-to-Date. If new job or career opportunities become available with your current employer (or another organization), you will be ready to take advantage of them.

Take Time Out to Relax. Change creates long work hours and stress. Work can become all-consuming. If you are stressed out, you are not a valuable employee or a happy person to be around. Make sure you take time for leisure activities you enjoy. Dance, read, exercise—have fun!

a high-performance work system. HR professionals who keep up with change are well positioned to help create high-performance work systems. The nearby "HR How To" box suggests ways HR professionals can make a commitment to adapt to change in order to keep up with a fast-changing work environment.

Knowledge Workers

The growth in e-commerce, plus the shift from a manufacturing to a service and information economy, has changed the nature of employees that are most in demand. Figure 2.4 shows the number of job openings forecast by the Bureau of Labor Statistics for a variety of job classes. The numbers include new positions created by existing and start-up organizations, as well as openings that result from employees leaving jobs for retirement, disability, or other reasons.

FIGURE 2.4

Types of Job Openings Forecast by the Bureau of Labor Statistics

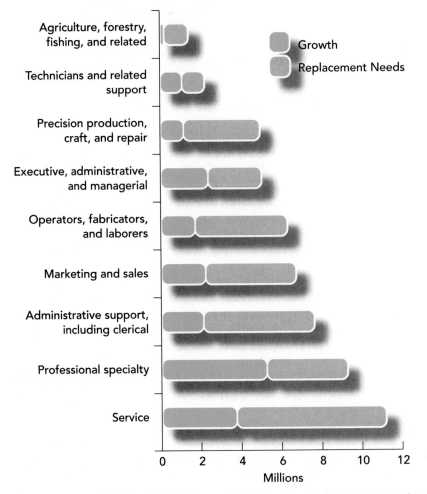

SOURCE: "Tomorrow's Jobs" in the *2000–01 Occupational Outlook Handbook*, chart 11. From website http://stats.bls.gov/oco/oco2003.htm.

In terms of numbers, the greatest job growth will be in service occupations. The number of service jobs has important implications for human resource management. Research shows that if employees have a favorable view of HRM practices—say, their career opportunities, training, pay, and feedback on performance—they are more likely to provide good service to customers. Therefore, quality HRM for service employees can translate into customer satisfaction. The second-largest category of new jobs is professional specialties. Most of the new jobs in this category will be for teachers, librarians, and counselors; computer, mathematical, and operations research positions; and health assessment and treatment occupations.

According to the Bureau of Labor Statistics, the fastest growth rate for jobs over the next few years will include computer-related positions such as computer engineers, computer support specialists, system analysts, and computer database administrators.[19] The largest number of job openings will be in occupations requiring a bachelor's degree and on-the-job training. Most of the opportunities for unskilled workers will be in retailing.

What most of these high-growth jobs have in common is specialized knowledge.

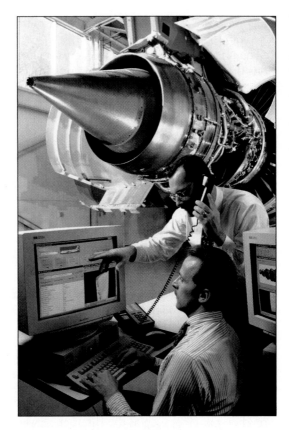

Knowledge workers are employees whose value to their employers stems primarily from what they know. Engineers such as the ones pictured here have in-depth knowledge of their field and are hard to replace because of their special knowledge.

To meet their human capital needs, companies are increasingly trying to attract, develop, and retain knowledge workers. **Knowledge workers** are employees whose main contribution to the organization is specialized knowledge, such as knowledge of customers, a process, or a profession. Knowledge workers are especially needed for jobs in health services, business services, social services, engineering, and management.

Knowledge workers are in a position of power, because they own the knowledge that the company needs in order to produce its products and services, and they must share their knowledge and collaborate with others in order for their employer to succeed. An employer cannot simply order these employees to perform tasks. Managers depend on the employees' willingness to share information. Furthermore, skilled knowledge workers have many job opportunities, even in a slow economy. If they choose, they can leave a company and take their knowledge to another employer. Replacing them may be difficult and time-consuming.

As more organizations become knowledge-based, they must promote and capture learning at the level of employees, teams, and the overall organization. Buckman Laboratories, for example, is known for its knowledge management practices.[20] Buckman Laboratories develops and markets specialty chemicals. Buckman's CEO, Robert Buckman, has developed an organizational culture, technology, and work processes that encourage the sharing of knowledge. Employees have laptop computers so they can share information anywhere and anytime via the Internet. The company set up rewards for innovation and for creating and exchanging knowledge. The rewards are based on performance measures related to the percentage of sales of new products. Buckman also changed the focus of the company's information systems department,

knowledge workers
Employees whose main contribution to the organization is specialized knowledge, such as knowledge of customers, a process, or a profession.

renaming it the "knowledge transfer department" to better match the service it is supposed to provide.

The reliance on knowledge workers also affects organizations' decisions about the kinds of people they are recruiting and selecting.[21] They are shifting away from focusing on specific skills, such as how to operate a particular kind of machinery, and toward a greater emphasis on general cognitive skills (thinking and problem solving) and interpersonal skills. Employers are more interested in evidence that job candidates will excel at working in teams or interacting with customers. These skills also support an employee's ability to gather and share knowledge, helping the organization to innovate and meet customer needs. To the extent that technical skills are important, employers often are most interested in the ability to use information technology, including the Internet and statistical software.

Employee Empowerment

To completely benefit from employees' knowledge, organizations need a management style that focuses on developing and empowering employees. **Employee empowerment** means giving employees responsibility and authority to make decisions regarding all aspects of product development or customer service.[22] Employees are then held accountable for products and services. In return, they share the resulting losses and rewards.

HRM practices such as performance management, training, work design, and compensation are important for ensuring the success of employee empowerment. Jobs must be designed to give employees the necessary latitude for making a variety of decisions. Employees must be properly trained to exert their wider authority and use information resources such as the Internet, as well as tools for communicating information. Employees also need feedback to help them evaluate their success. Pay and other rewards should reflect employees' authority and be related to successful handling of their responsibility. In addition, for empowerment to succeed, managers must be trained to link employees to resources within and outside the organization, such as customers, coworkers in other departments, and websites with needed information. Managers must also encourage employees to interact with staff throughout the organization, must ensure that employees receive the information they need, and must reward cooperation.

As with the need for knowledge workers, use of employee empowerment shifts the recruiting focus away from technical skills and toward general cognitive and interpersonal skills. Employees who have responsibility for a final product or service must be able to listen to customers, adapt to changing needs, and creatively solve a variety of problems.

Teamwork

Modern technology places the information that employees need for improving quality and providing customer service right at the point of sale or production. As a result, the employees engaging in selling and producing must also be able to make decisions about how to do their work. Organizations need to set up work in a way that gives employees the authority and ability to make those decisions. One of the most popular ways to increase employee responsibility and control is to assign work to teams. **Teamwork** is the assignment of work to groups of employees with various skills who interact to assemble a product or provide a service. Work teams often assume

---

LO3

employee empowerment
Giving employees responsibility and authority to make decisions regarding all aspects of product development or customer service.

teamwork
The assignment of work to groups of employees with various skills who interact to assemble a product or provide a service.

Team Spirit Makes Winners of Whole Foods Employees

Every year, *Fortune* magazine evaluates nominations for the "100 Best Companies to Work For," based on the companies' work life and culture, including such elements as employee attitudes, company benefits, and training opportunities. One company that has consistently made the list is Whole Foods Market, a chain of natural-foods stores headquartered in Austin, Texas.

For employees at Whole Foods, the emphasis is on teams. Work is assigned to teams, rather than to individual jobs. Each store is operated by about 10 teams, each handling a product area such as produce, prepared foods, or groceries. Teams are responsible for decisions about hiring, ordering, and pricing. Every team has a set of goals and a team leader. The team leaders, in turn, are members of a leadership team. The leader of that team for each store is part of a regional team. The company's regional team leaders are a company leadership team.

To support decision making by these teams, the company shares information. Any employee can see data on store and team sales, profit margins, and salaries. Teams also use the information to help them compete with the other

teams, stores, and regions. The company provides rewards (bonuses, recognition, and promotions) to those that deliver the best profits, service, productivity, and quality. The performance-related rewards and open information sharing can help team members focus on goals. Whole Foods' chief executive, John Mackey, says leaders often come to him with questions like, "How come you are paying this regional president this much, and I'm making this much?" Continues Mackey, "I have to say, 'Because that person is more valuable. If you accomplish what this person has accomplished, I'll pay you that, too.' "

Complementing the notion of teamwork is a sense of equality. In contrast to many American corporations, where the top executives earn far more than the rank and file, Whole Foods limits its top pay to eight times the company's average wage.

Some employees would say that "team" does not begin to describe the relationships among Whole Foods employees. Becky Ellis, specialty team leader at a Whole Foods store in Austin, says what she likes most about the company is its people. She says, "They seem to be more

like your family, not just your coworkers." Whole Foods sponsors an emergency fund designed to let employees help one another out in emergencies by donating benefit hours.

Besides the good feelings of being part of a work community, Whole Foods gives employees the good feelings of participating in their outside community. Whole Foods has a community service program that pays employees to do volunteer work. Employees can earn their regular hourly wage for doing up to 40 hours of service work in their community each year.

Of course, there are practical benefits to working at Whole Foods. The company rewards employees with career opportunities, by filling most positions through promotions from within. Aly Winningham, a Whole Foods employee who has held several positions over seven years, says the company's willingness to give her the work experience "makes me feel that the company believes in me and wants to see me grow."

SOURCE: C. Royal, "Finding Fame in *Fortune*," *Austin Business Journal*, August 11, 2000, downloaded at http://austin.bcentral.com; C. Fishman, "Whole Foods Is All Teams," *Fast Company*, April 1996, downloaded at www.fastcompany.com.

many activities traditionally reserved for managers, such as selecting new team members, scheduling work, and coordinating work with customers and other units of the organization. Work teams also contribute to total quality by performing inspection and quality-control activities while the product or service is being completed.

In some organizations, technology is enabling teamwork even when workers are at different locations or work at different times. These organizations use *virtual teams*—teams that rely on communications technology such as videoconferences, e-mail, and cell phones to keep in touch and coordinate activities.

Teamwork can motivate employees by making work more interesting and significant. The nearby "Best Practices" box tells how teamwork contributes to a positive work environment at Whole Foods Market. At organizations that rely on teamwork, labor costs may be lower as well. Spurred by such advantages, a number of companies are reorganizing assembly operations—abandoning the assembly line in favor of operations that combine mass production with jobs in which employees perform multiple tasks, use many skills, control the pace of work, and assemble the entire final product.[23] One example of this type of teamwork is Compaq Computer's assembly cells. In manufacturing sites in Scotland and Texas, four-person teams build the computers. One person assembles parts, another builds components, and two people assemble the finished computer unit. The new teams have helped raise labor productivity (the amount produced per worker) 51 percent.

LO4

Focus on Strategy

As we saw in Chapter 1, traditional management thinking treated human resource management primarily as an administrative function, but managers today are beginning to see a more central role for HRM. They are beginning to look at HRM as a means to support a company's *strategy*—its plan for meeting broad goals such as profitability, quality, and market share.[24] This strategic role for HRM has evolved gradually. At many organizations, managers still treat HR professionals primarily as experts in designing and delivering HR systems. But at a growing number of organizations, HR professionals are strategic partners with other managers.[25] This means they use their knowledge of the business and of human resources to help the organization develop strategies and to align HRM policies and practices with those strategies. To do this, human resource managers must focus on the future as well as the present, and on company goals as well as human resource activities.

Continental Airlines used HRM as a strategic partner to plan and implement a dramatic turnaround a few years ago. The airline, which had been struggling with low customer satisfaction and financial problems, brought in Gordon Bethune as CEO to develop a new strategy. The strategy Bethune launched had four elements: Fly to Win (achieve profit margins in the top one-fourth of the industry), Fund the Future (reduce the company's heavy load of debt), Make Reliability a Reality (improve the quality of the company's services to make them best in the industry), and Working Together (make the company an organization that employees are glad to work for). Bethune charged Ken Carrig, Continental's vice president of human resources, with leading HRM in the development of systems and plans to execute that strategy. For example, a new pay system helped to give the company a cost advantage but also rewarded employees for doing well. Base pay was low compared with that of other airlines, but employees were eligible for bonuses and profit sharing. If in any month, Continental ranked in the top three airlines for on-time arrivals, every employee would receive a

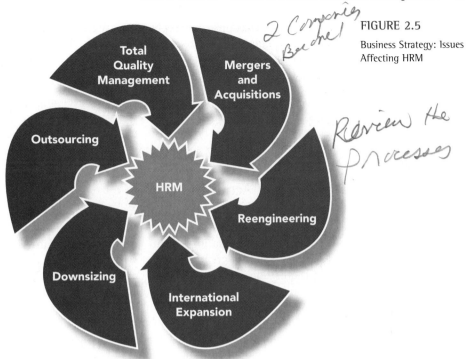

2 Companies Become 1

Review the Processes

FIGURE 2.5

Business Strategy: Issues Affecting HRM

check for $65. Employees quickly began contributing ideas to improve on-time performance, and as customers began returning to the new and improved Continental, the employees began to receive profit-sharing payments as well.[26]

The specific ways in which human resource professionals support the organization's strategy vary according to their level of involvement and the nature of the strategy. Strategic issues include emphasis on quality and decisions about growth and efficiency. Human resource management can support strategies that involve such changes as mergers, acquisitions, downsizing, or international expansion. Decisions to use reengineering and outsourcing can make an organization more efficient and also give rise to many human resource challenges. Figure 2.5 summarizes these strategic issues facing human resource management.

High Quality Standards

To compete in today's economy, companies need to provide high-quality products and services. If companies do not adhere to quality standards, they will have difficulty selling their product or service to vendors, suppliers, or customers. Therefore, many organizations have adopted some form of **total quality management (TQM)**—a companywide effort to continuously improve the ways people, machines, and systems accomplish work.[27] TQM has several core values:[28]

- Methods and processes are designed to meet the needs of internal and external customers (that is, whomever the process is intended to serve).
- Every employee in the organization receives training in quality.
- Quality is designed into a product or service so that errors are prevented from occurring, rather than being detected and corrected in an error-prone product or service.

total quality management (TQM)
A companywide effort to continuously improve the ways people, machines, and systems accomplish work.

- The organization promotes cooperation with vendors, suppliers, and customers to improve quality and hold down costs.
- Managers measure progress with feedback based on data.

Based on these values, the TQM approach provides guidelines for all the organization's activities, including human resource management. To promote quality, organizations need an environment that supports innovation, creativity, and risk taking to meet customer demands. Problem solving should bring together managers, employees, and customers. Employees should communicate with managers about customer needs.

Mergers and Acquisitions

Increasingly, organizations are joining forces through *mergers* (two companies becoming one) and *acquisitions* (one company buying another). Some mergers and acquisitions result in consolidation within an industry, meaning that two firms in one industry join to hold a greater share of the industry. For example, British Petroleum's recent acquisition of Amoco Oil represents a consolidation, or reduction of the number of companies in the oil industry. Other mergers and acquisitions cross industry lines. In a merger to form Citigroup, Citicorp combined its banking business with Traveller's Group's insurance business. Furthermore, these deals more frequently take the form of global megamergers, or mergers of big companies based in different countries (as in the case of BP-Amoco).

These deals do not always meet expectations, however. According to a report by the Conference Board, one of the major reasons for their failure may be "people issues." Recognizing this, some companies now heavily weigh the other organization's culture before they embark on a merger or acquisition. For example, before acquiring ValueRx, executives at Express Scripts interviewed senior executives and middle managers at ValueRx in order to get a sense of its values and practices.[29] Even so, in a recent survey, fewer than one-third of the HRM executives said they had a major influence in how mergers are planned. Not surprisingly, 80 percent of them said people issues have a significant impact after the deals go through.[30]

HRM should have a significant role in carrying out a merger or acquisition. Differences between the businesses involved in the deal make conflict inevitable. Training efforts should therefore include development of skills in conflict resolution. Also, HR professionals have to sort out differences in the two companies' practices with regard to compensation, performance appraisal, and other HR systems. Settling on a consistent structure to meet the combined organization's goals may help to bring employees together. Cisco Systems heads off conflict following its acquisitions by preparing employees at the firm to be acquired. Cisco tries to make sure that employees of the acquired firm understand that major change will follow the acquisition, so that they will not be surprised afterward. Cisco also addresses career paths. It provides significant roles for the acquired company's top talent in order to keep them on board with challenging opportunities. With such HR-related efforts, Cisco outperforms most firms in retaining talented employees after an acquisition.[31]

Downsizing

It would have been hard to ignore the massive "war for talent" that went on during the late 1990s, particularly with the dot-com craze, as Internet-based companies seemingly became rich overnight. During this time, organizations sought to become

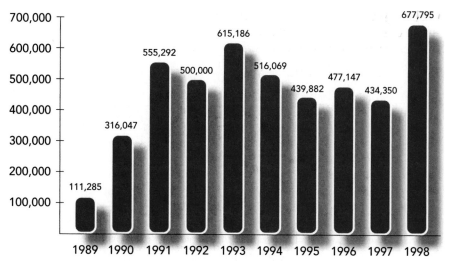

FIGURE 2.6

Number of Employees Laid Off During the 1990s

SOURCE: Challenger, Gray, and Christmas, 1998.

"employers of choice," to establish "employment brands," and to develop "employee value propositions." All these slogans were meant as ways to ensure that the organizations would be able to attract and retain talented employees. However, what was less noticeable was that in spite of the hiring craze, massive layoffs also were occurring. In fact, as shown in Figure 2.6, 1998, the height of the war for talent, also saw the largest number of layoffs in the decade.[32]

This pattern seems to represent a "churning" of employees. In other words, organizations apparently were laying off employees with outdated skills or cutting whole businesses that were in declining markets while simultaneously building businesses and employee bases in newer, higher-growth markets. For example, IBM cut 69,256 people yet increased its workforce by 16,000 in 1996. Although downsizing always poses problems for human resource management, the impact can be especially confusing in an organization that "churns" employees. How can such an organization develop a reputation as an employer of choice and motivate employees to care about the organization? The way organizations answer such questions will play a significant part in determining the quality of employees on the payroll.

Whether or not the organization is churning employees, downsizing presents a number of challenges and opportunities for HRM. In terms of challenges, the HRM function must "surgically" reduce the workforce by cutting only the workers who are less valuable in their performance. Achieving this is difficult because the best workers are most able (and often willing) to find alternative employment and may leave voluntarily before the organization lays off anyone. In 1992 General Motors and the United Auto Workers agreed to an early-retirement program for individuals between the ages of 51 and 65 who had been employed for 10 or more years. For those who agreed to retire, even if they obtained employment elsewhere, the program provided full pension benefits and as much as $13,000 toward the purchase of a GM car.[33] Such early-retirement programs are humane, but they essentially reduce the workforce with a "grenade" approach—not distinguishing good from poor performers but rather eliminating an entire group of employees. In fact, research indicates that when companies downsize by offering early-retirement programs, they usually end up rehiring to replace essential talent within a year. Often the company does not achieve its cost-cutting goals because it spends 50 to 150 percent of the departing employee's salary in hiring and retraining new workers.[34]

Another HRM challenge is to boost the morale of employees who remain after the reduction; this is discussed in greater detail in Chapter 5. Survivors may feel guilt over keeping their jobs when their friends were laid off. Or they may envy their friends who retired with attractive severance and pension benefits. Their reduced satisfaction and lower commitment to the organization may interfere with their performance of their work. To address these problems, HR professionals should maintain open communication with remaining employees to build their trust and commitment, rather than withholding information.[35] All employees should be informed why the downsizing is necessary, what costs are to be cut, how long the downsizing will last, and what strategies the organization intends to pursue. Finally, HRM can provide downsized employees with outplacement services to help them find new jobs. Such services are ways an organization can show that it cares about its employees, even though it cannot afford to keep all of them on the payroll.

Expanding into Global Markets

Companies are finding that to survive they must compete in international markets as well as fend off foreign competitors' attempts to gain ground in the United States. To meet these challenges, U.S. businesses must develop global markets, keep up with competition from overseas, hire from an international labor pool, and prepare employees for global assignments.

Study of companies that are successful and widely admired suggests that these companies not only operate on a multinational scale, but also have workforces and corporate cultures that reflect their global markets.[36] These companies, which include General Electric, Coca-Cola, Microsoft, Walt Disney, and Intel, focus on customer satisfaction and innovation. In addition, they operate on the belief that people are the company's most important asset. Placing this value on employees requires the companies to emphasize human resource practices, including rewards for superior performance, measures of employee satisfaction, careful selection of employees, promotion from within, and investment in employee development.

The Global Workforce

For today's and tomorrow's employers, talent comes from a global workforce. Organizations with international operations hire at least some of their employees in the foreign countries where they operate. And even small businesses that stick close to home often find that qualified candidates include some immigrants to the United States.

Technology is lowering barriers to overseas operations. Mark Braxton, chief technology officer for GM Onstar-Europe, believes that new technologies will open up opportunities for underdeveloped villages and communities in Africa, Asia, Europe, the United States, Central America, and South America by making it practical for employers to locate telephone service centers in places companies once would not have considered.[37] Already, economically deprived communities in Ireland, Brazil, and Mexico are being equipped with satellite links that give them access to universities, local government offices, and businesses. Hiring in such areas gives employers access to people with potential to be eager to work yet who will accept lower wages than elsewhere in the world. Challenges, however, may include employees' lack of famil-

Starbucks Coffee chairman Howard Schultz, left, poses with Yuji Tsunoda, president of Starbucks Japan, during the opening of the Seattle-based coffee-chain giant's 208th shop in Japan. Starbucks, which opens three stores a day worldwide, is a prime example of how companies can successfully compete in international markets.

iarity with technology and corporate practices, as well as political and economic instability in the areas.

Despite the risks, many organizations that have hired globally are realizing high returns. For example, ABB Asea Brown Boveri (Europe's largest engineering company and a competitor to General Electric) was one of the first Western companies to seize a business opportunity when Asia was experiencing economic difficulties in the late 1990s.[38] With over 219,000 employees worldwide, ABB was considered a global company well before then. But when economic crisis lowered the cost of operating in Asia, the company laid off employees in Europe and North America, shifting production to low-cost countries in Asia. The changes required massive HR efforts for the layoffs and hiring, as well as training for the new Asian workers. For example, ABB sent employees to its electric motor facility in Shanghai, China, to train plant managers in ABB quality standards.

For an organization to operate in other countries, its HR practices must take into consideration differences in culture and business practices. Consider how Starbucks Coffee handled its expansion into Beijing, China.[39] Demand for qualified managers in Beijing exceeds the local supply. Employers therefore have to take steps to attract and retain managers. Starbucks researched the motivation and needs of potential managers. The company learned that in traditional Chinese-owned companies, rules and regulations allowed little creativity and self-direction. Also, in many joint U.S.-China ventures, local managers were not trusted. Starbucks distinguished itself as an employer by emphasizing its casual culture and opportunities for career development. The company also spends considerable time training employees. It sends new managers to Tacoma, Washington, where they learn the corporate culture as well as the secrets of brewing flavorful coffee. Another company that trains foreign workers in the United States is Boeing. The aircraft maker brings workers from Poland and India to the United States. They return home with needed knowledge in aircraft design and manufacturing.[40]

Even hiring at home may involve selection of employees from other countries. The 1990s and beginning of the 21st century, like the beginning of the last century, have been years of significant immigration. Immigrants will likely account for an additional million persons in the U.S. workforce each year through 2006.[41] Figure 2.7 shows the distribution of immigration by continent of origin. The impact of immigration will be especially large in some regions of the United States. In 2000 about one-fourth of immigrants settled in California; another 32 percent headed for New York, Florida, and Texas.[42] In the states on the Pacific Coast, 7 out of 10 entrants to the labor force are immigrants.[43] About 70 percent of immigrant workers will be Hispanics and Asians. Employers in tight labor markets—such as those seeking experts in computer science,

FIGURE 2.7

Where Immigrants to the United States Came from in 2000

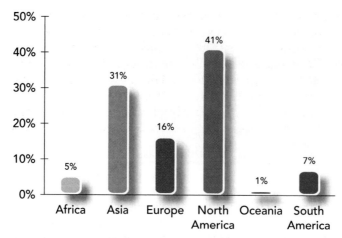

SOURCE: Office of Policy and Planning, Immigration and Naturalization Service, "Legal Immigration, Fiscal Year 2000," *Annual Report,* January 2002, downloaded at www.ins.gov.

engineering, and information systems—are especially likely to recruit international students.[44]

International Assignments

expatriates
Employees who take assignments in other countries.

Besides hiring an international workforce, organizations must be prepared to send employees to other countries. This requires HR expertise in selecting employees for international assignments and preparing them for those assignments. Employees who take assignments in other countries are called **expatriates.**

U.S. companies must better prepare employees to work in other countries. The failure rate for U.S. expatriates is greater than that for European and Japanese expatriates.[45] To improve in this area, U.S. companies must carefully select employees to work abroad based on their ability to understand and respect the cultural and business norms of the host country. Qualified candidates also need language skills and technical ability. In the "Best Practices" box in Chapter 1, we saw how Tricon Restaurants is overcoming the common mistake of hiring for international assignments based on technical skills alone. In Chapter 15, we discuss practices for training employees to understand other cultures.

Reengineering

reengineering
A complete review of the organization's critical work processes to make them more efficient and able to deliver higher quality.

Rapidly changing customer needs and technology have caused many organizations to rethink the way they get work done. For example, when an organization adopts new technology, its existing processes may no longer result in acceptable quality levels, meet customer expectations for speed, or keep costs to profitable levels. Therefore, many organizations have undertaken **reengineering**—a complete review of the organization's critical work processes to make them more efficient and able to deliver higher quality.

Ideally, reengineering involves reviewing all the processes performed by all the organization's major functions, including production, sales, accounting, and human resources. Therefore, reengineering affects human resource management in two ways. First, the way the HR department itself accomplishes its goals may change dramatically. Second, the fundamental change throughout the organization requires the HR department to help design and implement change so that all employees will be committed to the success of the reengineered organization. Employees may need training for their reengineered jobs. The organization may need to redesign the structure of its pay and benefits to make them more appropriate for its new way of operating. It also may need to recruit employees with a new set of skills. Often, reengineering results in employees being laid off or reassigned to new jobs, as the organization's needs change. HR professionals should help with this transition, as described above in the case of downsizing.

Outsourcing

Many organizations are increasingly outsourcing business activities. **Outsourcing** refers to the practice of having another company (a vendor, third-party provider, or consultant) provide services. For instance, a manufacturing company might outsource its accounting and transportation functions to businesses that specialize in these activities. Outsourcing gives the company access to in-depth expertise and is often more economical as well.

outsourcing
The practice of having another company (a vendor, third-party provider, or consultant) provide services.

Not only do HR departments help with a transition to outsourcing, but many HR functions are being outsourced. A survey by the Society for Human Resource Management found that almost three-quarters of companies outsource at least one HR function.[46] HR functions that are commonly outsourced include payroll administration, training, and recruitment and selection of employees. For example, Bank of America signed a 10-year contract with Exult Inc. to manage much of the bank's HR function.[47] Among the functions that Bank of America is outsourcing are payroll, accounts payable, and benefits administration. Other services Exult is handling include delivery of HR services and a call center to provide employees with information about human resources and benefits. Bank of America retained the HR functions of recruiting and compensation, as well as legal counsel. This arrangement frees HR managers at Bank of America to work on strategy and vision, focusing them on HRM responsibilities that add value to the business.

Technological Change in HRM

Advances in computer-related technology have had a major impact on the use of information for managing human resources. Large quantities of employee data (including training records, skills, compensation rates, and benefits usage and cost) can easily be stored on personal computers and manipulated with user-friendly spreadsheets or statistical software. Often these features are combined in a **human resource information system (HRIS),** a computer system used to acquire, store, manipulate, analyze, retrieve, and distribute information related to an organization's human resources.[48] An HRIS can support strategic decision making, help the organization avoid lawsuits, provide data for evaluating programs or policies, and support day-to-day HR decisions. Table 2.1 describes some of the new technologies that may be included in an organization's HRIS.

human resource information system (HRIS)
A computer system used to acquire, store, manipulate, analyze, retrieve, and distribute information related to an organization's human resources.

The support of an HRIS can help HR professionals navigate the challenges of today's complex business environment. For example, rapidly changing technology can cause employees' skills to become obsolete. Organizations must therefore carefully monitor their employees' skills and the organization's needed skills. Often the

TABLE 2.1

New Technologies
Influencing HRM

TECHNOLOGY	WHAT IT DOES	EXAMPLE
Internet portal	Combines data from several sources into a single site; lets user customize data without programming skills.	A company's manager can track labor costs by work group.
Shared service centers	Consolidate different HR functions into a single location; eliminate redundancy and reduce administrative costs; process all HR transactions at one time.	AlliedSignal combined more than 75 functions, including finance and HR, into a shared service center.
Application service provider (ASP)	Lets companies rent space on a remote computer system and use the system's software to manage its HR activities, including security and upgrades.	KPMG Consulting uses an ASP to host the company's computerized learning program.
Business intelligence	Provides insight into business trends and patterns and helps businesses improve decisions.	Managers use the system to analyze labor costs and productivity among different employee groups.

employees and needs are distributed among several locations, perhaps among several countries, requiring a global HRIS. Northern Telecom (a Canadian telecommunications company that has facilities in 90 countries, including the United Kingdom, China, and the United States) needed access to information about employees located worldwide. The company has created a central database built on a common set of core elements. Anyone with authorization can view employee records from around the globe. Data on the number of employees, salaries, and recruiting efforts are continually updated as changes are made around the world. The system is customized to specific country needs, but several common data fields and elements are used globally. Northern Telecom's system has enabled managers around the world to obtain up-to-date employee data to meet customer needs and address internal staffing issues.[49]

LO5

A Changing Economy

The way business is conducted has changed rapidly during the past few years and will continue to do so. Many companies are connecting to the Internet to gain an advantage over (or keep up with) competitors. Over half of all Americans went online in September 2001, and 2 million more people are trying the Internet each month.[50] Greater use of the Internet has prompted the spread of **electronic business (e-business)**—any process that a business conducts electronically, especially business involving use of the Internet. E-business includes several forms of buying and selling goods and business services:

electronic business (e-business)
Any process that a business conducts electronically, especially business involving use of the Internet.

- Business-to-consumer transactions, such as purchasing books and tickets and conducting services, including banking, online.
- Business-to-business transactions, including sales among manufacturers, retailers, wholesalers, and construction firms.

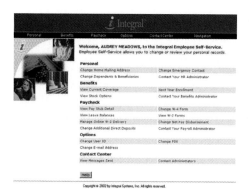

Integral, a designer of human resource intranet systems, creates company intranets that can deliver such HR services as benefits enrollment and paycheck information online.

- Consumer-to-consumer transactions—in particular, individuals buying and selling through auctions.

E-business relies on the Internet to enable buyers to obtain product information on-line, directly order products and services, receive after-sale technical support, and view the status of orders and deliveries. Internet sites may also allow the customer and seller to communicate with each other through e-mail, chat, and voice connections. Companies may set up customer service centers offering e-mail and live telephone connections to provide help, advice, or product information not found on their websites.

Consumers have been slower than expected in taking their business to the Internet. To win the hearts of consumers, e-commerce has to be better, cheaper, and faster than traditional retailers, entertainment providers, and information sources.[51] One thing the Internet can do better than any other medium is search through information. The Internet-based companies ("dot-coms") that take advantage of this feature lower the costs of making sales and therefore improve profits.[52] Some e-businesses, such as those in the online travel business dealing with purchasing airline tickets, reserving hotel rooms, and renting cars online, have been successful. The profitable dot-coms provide services that are information-intensive, rely on old-economy roots, and require little or no physical transportation of products. For example, eBay takes a cut of each sale on its auction site but is not directly involved in transporting items from sellers to buyers. Monster.com charges companies to post job openings and see résumés but does not set up interviews between job candidates and employees. Travel websites such as Travelocity earn a commission if the customer purchases a ticket, rents a car, or books a hotel room. Other old-economy businesses with strong brand recognition, such as FTD, the floral delivery service, have successfully used the Internet to complement telephone and flower store business. FTD can rely on local retailers to receive and ship orders using their own delivery vehicles. The Internet has given customers a new way to place orders.

Human Resources in E-Business

LO6

E-business creates many HRM challenges.[53] The fast pace of change in information technology requires that e-business companies quickly identify and hire talented employees. At the same time, competition for such employees is stiff. Many dot-coms are relatively new and may lack management expertise in keeping and motivating employees. As companies start, struggle, and sometimes fail, they require HR expertise to help work through the stresses of downsizing or restructuring without making legal missteps. For example, within the first six months of Jessica Keim's tenure as HR manager for Multex.com, the company grew from 350 to 500 employees by acquiring two companies.

Dot-coms are vulnerable to potential legal problems related to human resources. Many of these companies have started with young, inexperienced managers who created a fraternity-party culture, which was intended to foster innovation and creativity but risked cultivating sexual harassment. It's also not unusual to find incomplete personnel folders or poor documentation about when and why employees were terminated. This occurs because successful dot-coms have to focus so intently on bringing a product or service to market and making sales to survive that they do not find time to develop HRM policies, procedures, or standards. Also, the work environment tends to be casual, dress codes may be loose, and work schedules are flexible.

In this context, HRM needs to maintain a balance between accommodating the unique needs of an unstructured and creative workforce and enforcing necessary policies and procedures. Managers and employees often don't know how to nurture or mentor people, so counseling is needed. One HR professional summarized the experience as being like "a counselor at a day care camp."

Despite these challenges, dot-coms offer a dynamic, exciting HRM work environment. Their small size allows HR professionals to speak directly to the chief executive. HRM professionals also have the opportunity to build the HR function from scratch, something that is virtually impossible in a large, more established company. Because of the important role that HRM practices such as recruiting, selection, and compensation play in a growing company, HRM is asked to get involved with strategic decision making. In the words of Beth Skrzyniarz, vice president of HRM for Net-Folio, an Internet-based investment adviser firm, "You're invited to sit at the table a lot more . . . you are heard a lot more than you would be in a big corporation." Because of the numerous HRM needs of small dot-coms, HRM sees its decisions implemented, quickly sees the impact on the business, and receives personal recognition for successful actions.

E-HRM Applications in Other Organizations

The development of e-business has included ways to move HRM activities onto the Internet. Electronic HRM applications let employees enroll in and participate in training programs online. Employees can go online to select from items in a benefits package and enroll in the benefits they choose. They can look up answers to HR-related questions and read company news. This processing and transmission of digitized HR information is called **electronic human resource management (e-HRM).**

electronic human resource management (e-HRM)
The processing and transmission of digitized HR information, especially using computer networking and the Internet.

E-HRM has the potential to change all traditional HRM functions. Table 2.2 shows some major implications of e-HRM. For example, employees in different geographic areas can work together. Use of the Internet lets companies search for talent without geographic limitations. Recruiting can include online job postings, applications, and candidate screening from the company's website or the websites of companies that specialize in online recruiting, such as Monster.com or HotJobs. Employees from different geographic locations can all receive the same training over the company's computer network.

Privacy is an important issue in e-HRM. A great deal of HR information is confidential and not suitable for posting on a website for everyone to see. Therefore, e-HRM typically is set up on an *intranet*, which is a network that uses Internet tools but limits access to authorized users in the organization.

HRM PRACTICES	IMPLICATIONS OF E-HRM
Analysis and design of work	Employees in geographically dispersed locations can work together in virtual teams using video, e-mail, and the Internet.
Recruiting	Post job openings online; candidates can apply for jobs online.
Training	Online learning can bring training to employees anywhere, anytime.
Selection	Online simulations, including tests, videos, and e-mail, can measure job candidates' ability to deal with real-life business challenges.
Compensation and benefits	Employees can review salary and bonus information and seek information about and enroll in benefit plans.

TABLE 2.2

Implications of e-HRM for HRM Practices

Sharing of Human Resource Information

Information technology is changing the way HR departments handle record keeping and information sharing. Today, HR employees use modern technology to automate much of their work in managing employee records and giving employees access to information and enrollment forms for training, benefits, and other programs. As a result, HR employees play a smaller role in maintaining records, and employees now get information through **self-service.** This means employees have online access to information about HR issues such as training, benefits, compensation, and contracts; go online to enroll themselves in programs and services; and provide feedback through online surveys. The "e-HRM" box tells how self-service has improved HRM at General Motors and Channell Commercial Corporation.

Another example is MCI Worldcom, which offers an extensive system of self-service. Employees look up information in online employee directories, handbooks, and databases of employee records. Using the Internet, employees at MCI Worldcom can purchase stock and reallocate the investments in their retirement accounts. They use the system to fill out electronic forms and view electronic pay stubs. They can also view streaming video of managers providing briefings or discussing strategy, see examples of best practices, and sign up for training courses, provided via desktop computers.[54]

self-service
System in which employees have online access to information about HR issues and go online to enroll themselves in programs and provide feedback through surveys.

Linking Employees and Teams Electronically

Business today operates on a global scale. Many organizations therefore need employees throughout the world, and employees need to collaborate with coworkers in different places. HR professionals must identify potential recruits, provide training, and assess skills in many parts of the world. Organizations can save travel costs and time by applying e-HRM to a variety of HR practices. For example, members of a team could make hiring decisions during an online videoconference or chat session, and training technologies range from downloadable text files to streaming video.

Electronic links pose a challenge that is especially significant for human resource management: they lack the personal touch of face-to-face communication. When e-HRM includes sensitive matters, such as discrimination complaints, the lack of a personal touch can prevent an organization from seeing important problems or meeting important needs. In Detroit, two former employees filed a sexual harassment lawsuit against a software company that had arranged for an outside company to provide

Help Yourself to HRM

At General Motors, employees who want information know that it's as close as the nearest computer. General Motors provides a Web portal called My Socrates, with links to the kinds of information employees are looking for. They can use online forms to sign up for insurance and other benefits. They can authorize direct deposits and submit address changes. Links from the My Socrates page take employees to pages of information about health care and other benefits. New employees get information about the corporation and their department.

In 1998, the first information that GM put on this intranet was for the company's employee savings plan. Employees can look up bank statements detailing their transactions over any time frame they specify. Initially, a small share of employees went online for the information, but today almost half do their banking with the intranet. With employees helping themselves to transaction information, GM was able to cut the number of people required to administer the plan from 150 to just 4. Although the cost savings are substantial, Dick O'Brien, GM's executive director of employee benefits and personnel services, says the main reason for switching to self-service "was to support the employees, to get the information they need to get the work done."

O'Brien says the intranet also frees HR professionals at GM for more interesting work. Now HRM's role is to support corporate strategy. Says O'Brien, "[The intranet] will provide us with the ability to focus on more strategic work, such as management development, cultural and organizational change, development of a learning organization, and skill building among GM employees."

Some organizations are taking their intranets to a higher level: "smart" self-service, in which a knowledge base links different kinds of information to provide answers to HR-related questions. Channell Commercial Corporation originally set up its system just to dispense benefits enrollment forms, but now it supports management decisions with a software tool called HR AnswerSource. Users enter questions, and the system searches the company's knowledge base to assemble an answer. For example, when one of Channell's manufacturing facilities was preparing to switch to a four-day workweek, the plant manager entered the question "Can we change working hours?" The system provided the manager with the company's policy regarding work hours, plus state and federal guidelines, summaries of relevant laws, model documents, and news reports concerning alternative work schedules.

Channell's e-HRM system also provides managers with regular reports on HR topics. For example, it tells managers about which training modules employees are using. In addition, the system provides information related to harassment complaints, disciplinary actions, and performance appraisals. Top managers can use data from the system to help them plan development opportunities for the company's managers, individually and as a team.

At Channell, as at GM, the benefits of e-HRM go beyond cost savings. Channell's expenses for HR staffing have fallen by one-fifth, and e-HRM has freed HR professionals to provide better service. Employees and managers both express much greater satisfaction with the HR department since it began offering smart self-service.

SOURCE: B. Calandra, "Window to Their World," *Human Resource Executive*, September 2001, pp. 87–88; B. Shutan, "Self-Service Gets Smart," *Human Resource Executive*, March 6, 2002, pp. 49–50, 52–53.

its HR services online. In their complaint, the former employees said the software company's human resource provider had failed to respond appropriately when they reported the harassment. As a result, the former employer might be held responsible for the e-HRM provider's inaction.[55] The lesson for organizations interested in e-HRM is to plan how they will hear and respond to employees' concerns when most communications take place online.

Change in the Employment Relationship

LO7

Economic downturns will continue to occur, resulting in layoffs in all industries. For example, recently Xerox laid off 12,000 employees, and Cisco Systems 3,000 employees. Excessive optimism about the Internet fueled heavy investment in e-business, and when investors pulled back, dot-coms began going out of business. The trend reached a peak in the early part of 2001, when dozens of Internet companies closed every month. Such layoffs and bankruptcies have played a major role in changing the basic relationship between employers and employees.

A New Psychological Contract

We can think of that relationship in terms of a **psychological contract,** a description of what an employee expects to contribute in an employment relationship and what the employer will provide the employee in exchange for those contributions.[56] Unlike a written sales contract, the psychological contract is not formally put into words. Instead, it describes unspoken expectations that are widely held by employers and employees. In the traditional version of this psychological contract, organizations expected their employees to contribute time, effort, skills, abilities, and loyalty. In return, the organizations would provide job security and opportunities for promotion.

However, this arrangement is being replaced with a new type of psychological contract.[57] To stay competitive, modern organizations must frequently change the quality, innovation, creativeness, and timeliness of employee contributions and the skills needed to make those contributions. This need has led to organizational restructuring, mergers and acquisitions, layoffs, and longer hours for many employees. Companies demand excellent customer service and high productivity levels. They expect employees to take more responsibility for their own careers, from seeking training to balancing work and family. These expectations result in less job security for employees, who can count on working for several companies over the course of a career. Today, the average length of time a person holds a job is seven years (compared with eight years in 2000 and nine years in 1999).[58]

In exchange for top performance and working longer hours without job security, employees want companies to provide flexible work schedules, comfortable working conditions, more control over how they accomplish work, training and development opportunities, and financial incentives based on how the organization performs. (Figure 2.8 provides a humorous look at an employee who seems to have benefited from this modern psychological contract by obtaining a family-friendly work arrangement.) Employees realize that companies cannot provide employment security, so they want *employability*. This means they want their company to provide training and job experiences to help ensure that they can find other employment opportunities.

MTW, an information technology company, is exceptional in that it puts its psychological contracts into writing. Whenever a new employee joins the company,

psychological contract
A description of what an employee expects to contribute in an employment relationship and what the employer will provide the employee in exchange for those contributions.

FIGURE 2.8

A Family-Friendly Work
Arrangement

SPEED BUMP   **Dave Coverly**

that person writes an "expectations agreement" stating his or her most important goals. Every six months or so, the employee and the team leader of the employee's project team review the expectations agreement and modify it if the employee's expectations have changed. For example, Dan Carier's expectations agreement said he would stay knowledgeable about a type of software and that the company would let him continue work on his project, even if he had to move out of state (his wife had a job that might require relocation). Says Carier of the agreement, "I felt I was in control of my destiny." MTW's treatment of employees has translated into business success. Employee turnover is just 6.7 percent a year, in contrast to an industry average of 30 percent, and in a tough job market, most of the company's new hires come from referrals by existing employees. Revenues have grown at a rate of 50 percent a year, and an impressive 14 percent of that revenue is profits.[59]

LO1

**alternative work
arrangements**
Methods of staffing
other than the
traditional hiring of
full-time employees
(for example, use of
independent
contractors, on-call
workers, temporary
workers, and
contract company
workers).

Flexibility

The new psychological contract largely results from the HRM challenge of building a committed, productive workforce in turbulent economic conditions that offer opportunity for financial success but can also quickly turn sour, making every employee expendable. From the organization's perspective, the key to survival in a fast-changing environment is flexibility. Organizations want to be able to change as fast as customer needs and economic conditions change. Flexibility in human resource management includes flexible staffing levels and flexible work schedules.

Flexible Staffing Levels

A flexible workforce is one the organization can quickly reshape and resize to meet its changing needs. To be able to do this without massive hiring and firing campaigns, organizations are using more alternative work arrangements. **Alternative work arrangements** are methods of staffing other than the traditional hiring of full-time employees. There are a variety of methods, with the following being most common:

The Bureau of Labor Statistics estimates that there are approximately 12.2 million nontraditional workers. Many of these workers (independent contractors, contract workers, etc.) have this work arrangement by choice.

- *Independent contractors* are self-employed individuals with multiple clients.
- *On-call workers* are persons who work for an organization only when they are needed.
- *Temporary workers* are employed by a temporary agency; client organizations pay the agency for the services of these workers.
- *Contract company workers* are employed directly by a company for a specific time specified in a written contract.

The Bureau of Labor Statistics estimates that there are 12.2 million "nontraditional workers," including 8.2 million independent contractors, 2 million on-call workers, 1.2 million temporary workers, and approximately 800,000 contract company workers. Altogether, these work arrangements cover about 10 percent of U.S. employees.[60]

More workers in alternative employment relationships are choosing these arrangements, but preferences vary. Most independent contractors and contract workers have this type of arrangement by choice. In contrast, temporary agency workers and on-call workers are likely to prefer traditional full-time employment. There is some debate about whether nontraditional employment relationships are good or bad. Some labor analysts argue that alternative work arrangements are substandard jobs featuring low pay, fear of unemployment, poor health insurance and retirement benefits, and dissatisfying work. Others claim that these jobs provide flexibility for companies and employees alike. With alternative work arrangements, organizations can more easily modify the number of their employees. Continually adjusting staffing levels is especially cost-effective for an organization that has fluctuating demand for its products and services. And when an organization downsizes by laying off temporary and part-time employees, the damage to morale among permanent full-time workers is likely to be less severe. From employees' perspective, alternative work arrangements provide some flexibility for balancing work and nonwork activities. Of course, the flexibility often means these employees are the first to go when an organization downsizes. In the last three quarters of 2001, 3 out of 10 jobs cut were at temporary-help agencies, even though these jobs account for just 2.2 percent of total payrolls.[61]

Flexible Work Schedules

The globalization of the world economy and the development of e-commerce have made the notion of a 40-hour work week obsolete. As a result, companies need to be staffed 24 hours a day, seven days a week. Employees in manufacturing environments and service call centers are being asked to work 12-hour days or to work afternoon or midnight shifts. Similarly, professional employees face long hours and work demands that spill over into their personal lives. E-mail, pagers, and cell phones bombard employees with information and work demands. In the car, on vacation, on planes, and even in the bathroom, employees can be interrupted by work demands. More demanding work results in greater employee stress, less satisfied employees, loss of productivity, and higher turnover—all of which are costly for companies.

Many organizations are taking steps to provide more flexible work schedules, to protect employees' free time, and to more productively use employees' work time. Workers consider flexible schedules a valuable way to ease the pressures and conflicts of trying to balance work and nonwork activities. Employers are using flexible schedules to recruit and retain employees and to increase satisfaction and productivity. For example, International Paper plants must run paper-producing machinery 24 hours a day, seven days a week. The challenge for the company was to devise a schedule that keeps the machines running while allowing employees to balance work and rest. At International Paper's plant in DePere, Wisconsin, employees are asked to rotate between daytime work hours to nighttime shifts and back again. Typically, such rotating shifts force employees to continually adjust to different sleep patterns and disrupt social activities. At the DePere plant, shifts have been extended from 8 hours to 12. The typical rotation follows a pattern of four days on, two off, three on, three off, three on, and four off. Employees work only 190 days a year and can balance the demands of work and family life. Another example is Hewlett-Packard, which redesigned work schedules in response to the loss of talented computer service employees who were forced to answer calls late at night and on weekends. HP allowed employees to volunteer to work either during the week or on weekends. As a result, turnover rates decreased and customer response times improved.[62]

To protect employees' nonwork time, some companies, such as the consulting firm Ernst & Young, allow employees to wait until they return to work to answer weekend or vacation voice mail and e-mail messages.[63] At SCJohnson in Racine, Wisconsin, employees often had to take work home on the weekends because they were so tied up in meetings from Monday through Friday that they had to finish duties on their own time.[64] SCJohnson now bans all meetings for two Fridays each month. The policy helps employees rest on at least two weekends and work at home on those Fridays because they won't be afraid of missing a meeting.

Flexible work schedules and flexible job assignments also provide organizations with a way to adjust to slow periods without laying off valued workers. Lincoln Electric Company responded to slow demand by moving salaried employees to clerical jobs at hourly wages that vary according to the assignment. Lincoln's production workers also are trained to handle varied jobs, according to the size and types of orders the company receives from its customers. In the recession of the early 1980s, which hit the company hard, engineers and factory workers from Lincoln went on the road to try peddling Lincoln's welding and cutting parts to potential customers. Of course, employees prefer the higher-paying jobs, not the demands of lean times. Still, they are glad for Lincoln's commitment to keep them on the payroll—and on the receiving end of benefits like pensions and insurance.[65]

Summary

1. Describe trends in the labor force composition and how they affect human resource management.

An organization's internal labor force comes from its external labor market—individuals who are actively seeking employment. In the United States, this labor market is aging and becoming more racially and ethnically diverse. The share of women in the U.S. workforce has grown to nearly half of the total. To compete for talent, organizations must be flexible enough to meet the needs of older workers, possibly redesigning jobs. Organizations must recruit from a diverse population, establish bias-free HR systems, and help employees understand and appreciate cultural differences. Organizations also need employees with skills in decision making, customer service, and teamwork, as well as technical skills. The competition for such talent is intense. Organizations facing a skills shortage often hire employees who lack certain skills, then train them for their jobs.

2. Summarize areas in which human resource management can support the goal of creating a high-performance work system.
HRM can help organizations find and keep the best possible fit between their social system and technical system. Organizations need employees with broad skills and strong motivation. Recruiting and selection decisions are especially important for organizations that rely on knowledge workers. Job design and appropriate systems for assessment and rewards have a central role in supporting employee empowerment and teamwork.

3. Define employee empowerment and explain its role in the modern organization.
Employee empowerment means giving employees responsibility and authority to make decisions regarding all aspects of product development or customer service. The organization holds employees accountable for products and services, and in exchange, the employees share in the rewards (or losses) that result. Selection decisions should provide the organization people who have the necessary decision-making and interpersonal skills. HRM must design jobs to give employees latitude for decision making and train employees to handle their broad responsibilities. Feedback and rewards must be appropriate for the work of empowered employees. HRM can also play a role in giving employees access to the information they need.

4. Identify ways HR professionals can support organizational strategies for quality, growth, efficiency, and international operations.
HR professionals should be familiar with the organization's strategy and may even play a role in developing the strategy. Specific HR practices vary according to the type of strategy. Job design is essential for empowering employees to practice total quality management. In organizations planning major changes such as a merger or acquisition, downsizing, or reengineering,

HRM must provide leadership for managing the change in a way that includes skillful employee relations and meaningful rewards. HR professionals can bring "people issues" to the attention of the managers leading these changes. They can provide training in conflict resolution skills, as well as knowledge of the other organization involved in a merger or acquisition. HR professionals also must resolve differences between the companies' HR systems, such as benefits packages and performance appraisals. For a downsizing, the HR department can help to develop voluntary programs to reduce the workforce or can help identify the least valuable employees to lay off. Employee relations can help maintain the morale of employees who remain after a downsizing. Organizations with international operations hire employees in foreign countries where they operate, so they need knowledge of differences in culture and business practices. Even small businesses serving domestic markets discover that qualified candidates include immigrants, as they account for a significant and growing share of the U.S. labor market, so HRM requires knowledge of different cultures. Organizations also must be able to select and prepare employees for overseas assignments. In reengineering, the HR department can lead in communicating with employees and providing training. It will also have to prepare new approaches for recruiting and appraising employees that are better suited to the reengineered jobs. Outsourcing presents similar issues related to job design and employee selection.

5. Summarize the role of human resource management in an Internet economy.
Information systems have become a tool for more HR professionals, and often these systems are provided through the Internet. In addition, e-business plays a role in a growing number of organizations. At organizations that provide some or all of their services online, HRM must compete for talent in a labor market with heavy demand for expertise. Also, dot-coms often lack depth of management experience and may rely heavily on HR professionals to provide guidance in personnel matters.

6. Discuss how technological developments are affecting human resource management.
The widespread use of the Internet includes HRM applications. Organizations search for talent globally using online job postings and screening candidates online. Organizations' websites feature information directed toward potential employees. Employees may receive training online. At many companies, online information sharing enables employee self-service for many HR needs, from application forms to training

modules to information about the details of company policies and benefits. Online communications also may link employees and teams, enabling organizations to structure work that involves collaboration among employees at different times and places. In such situations, HR professionals must ensure that communications remain effective enough to detect and correct problems when they arise.

7. Explain how the nature of the employment relationship is changing.

The employment relationship takes the form of a "psychological contract" that describes what employees and employers expect from the employment relationship. It includes unspoken expectations that are widely held. In the traditional version, organizations expected their employees to contribute time, effort, skills, abilities, and loyalty in exchange for job security and opportunities for promotion. Today, modern organizations' needs are constantly changing, so organizations are requiring top performance and longer work hours but cannot provide job security. Instead, employees are looking for flexible work schedules, comfortable working conditions, greater autonomy, opportunities for training and development, and performance-related financial incentives. For HRM, the changes require planning for flexible staffing levels.

8. Discuss how the need for flexibility affects human resource management.

Organizations seek flexibility in staffing levels through alternatives to the traditional employment relationship. They may use outsourcing as well as temporary and contract workers. The use of such workers can affect job design, as well as the motivation of the organization's permanent employees. Organizations also may seek flexible work schedules, including shortened workweeks. They may offer flexible schedules as a way for employees to adjust work hours to meet personal and family needs. Organizations also may move employees to different jobs to meet changes in demand.

Review and Discussion Questions

1. How does each of the following labor force trends affect HRM?
   a. Aging of the labor force.
   b. Diversity of the labor force.
   c. Skill deficiencies of the labor force.
2. At many organizations, goals include improving people's performance by relying on knowledge workers, empowering employees, and assigning work to teams. How can HRM support these efforts?
3. Merging, downsizing, and reengineering all can radically change the structure of an organization. Choose one of these changes, and describe HRM's role in making the change succeed. If possible, apply your discussion to an actual merger, downsizing, or reengineering effort that has recently occurred.
4. When an organization decides to operate facilities in other countries, how can HRM practices support this change?
5. Why do organizations outsource HRM functions? How does outsourcing affect the role of human resource professionals? Would you be more attracted to the role of HR professional in an organization that outsources many HR activities or in the outside firm that has the contract to provide the HR services? Why?
6. Suppose you have been hired to manage human resources for a small dot-com start-up. The 12-person company has spent the last year preparing to launch on the Internet, and the company's two founders realize that they will need to prepare for the growth they expect when they go online next month. What challenges will you need to prepare the company to meet? How will you begin?
7. What e-HRM resources might you use to meet the challenges in Question 4?
8. What HRM functions could an organization provide through self-service? What are some advantages and disadvantages of using self-service for these functions?
9. How is the employment relationship typical of modern organizations different from the relationship of a generation ago?

What's Your HR IQ?

The Student CD-ROM offers two more ways to check what you've learned so far. Use the Self-Assessment exercise to test your knowledge of trends in human resource management. Go online with the Web Exercise to see how well your knowledge works in cyberspace.

BusinessWeek Case

BusinessWeek Click Here for HR

Cardstore.com Inc., an Emeryville, California, online retailer with about 35 employees, is in a hiring frenzy. So you might expect to find the company's human resource manager, Rhonda Mae Botello, buried in forms for payroll, health coverage, taxes, and the like. She's busy all right, but not with paperwork. When a new worker comes on board, Botello simply logs on to the Web, surfs over to eBenefits.com, and enters the new name and start date. The system spits out an I.D. code and password. Then the new hire logs on to the site, fills out forms online, and selects benefits by completing a series of dialog boxes. Botello approves the choices and ships the package to the insurance company and other providers. "This frees HR up to focus on the things that matter," she says. "Like more hiring."

EBenefits is one of a handful of application service providers (ASPs) designed to manage human resources. ASPs deliver software applications over the Web to companies that lack the time, money, or inclination to do it themselves. Analysts predict that entrepreneurs will soon use ASPs to run nearly every aspect of their companies. ASP sales reached nearly $400 million in 1998 and are expected to hit $10 billion by 2003, says Rebecca Scholl, an analyst at Dataquest in Mountain View, California.

At present, an ASP with a solid track record is the one that promises to manage one of any company's most onerous and paper-clogged chores, human resources, offering sophisticated HR software systems for a relative pittance in monthly charges.

What's the catch? For one thing, new technology is never foolproof, and few ASPs have the track record of traditional HR systems. Meanwhile, the products primarily handle paperwork, and do not address the "human" aspect of human resources. "This is not a magic formula," says John Donovan, a managing partner at Deloitte Consulting in Minneapolis. ASPs also lack flexibility. Botello of Cardstore.com wishes she could create custom blanks in the electronic forms to record employees' favorite foods and beverages. (Both are free at Cardstore.com.) A bigger problem: eBenefits still requires paper because it isn't linked up electronically to all of its providers. Still, for $30 a month flat, Botello is not complaining.

If you want a more integrated—and expensive—system, check out Employease Inc. Employease doesn't just provide software; it links up small companies with their various providers. To terminate an employee, an employer needs to notify the payroll service, insurance company, and 401(k) administrator—providing the same information over and over. With Employease, you simply click

Yours for the ASPing: A Sampling of Major Online Human Resources Service Providers

COMPANY	WHAT THEY OFFER
eBenefits.com	Benefits management; employee record keeping; time-off tracking; legal compliance.
ADP (www.adp.com)	Maintains employee records; tracks attendance; monitors compliance with federal regulations.
Employease.com	Maintains payroll and benefit data; self-service access for employees; employee performance tracking.
Interpath Communications (www.interpath.com)	Internet hosting for SAP's HR applications; e-commerce ASPs for no additional cost.
Employeeservice.com	Benefits management; payroll; employee self-service; report generation; new-hire automation; in-person HR consulting.
Corio (www.corio.com)	Hosts PeopleSoft HR software; one of the most comprehensive and customizable HR systems.

DATA: BW Frontier.

"terminate," and the message goes out to all of them. Employease requires a one-time $2,500 fee for implementation, and a monthly fee, ranging from $2 to $6 per employee, depending on whether employees have access to the system.

For many companies, it's worth the cost. Insight Management, an Atlanta info-tech incubation company, has 30 employees, 75 percent of whom work in remote locations. "Wherever they are, they can go online and see what kind of insurance they are enrolled in or change their 401(k) contribution," says Colleen Verner, the company's HR coordinator.

What about security? How safe are your data? Employease uses a system similar to E*Trade Group Inc. or Yahoo! Inc.—with password protection, firewalls, secure socket-layer encryption, even armed guards. A similar system exists at eBenefits. But with all the high-tech safeguards, common sense says that nothing is completely secure. "You just have to take a leap of faith," admits Botello.

Some entrepreneurs have another reservation. Numerous "high-touch" aspects of HR—mediating disputes, providing career-path strategy—are unsuited to the Web, says Gus Stieber, director of business development at VMC Behavioral Health Care Services, an employee assistance program in Gurnee, Illinois. "There's still no substitute for face-to-face," Stieber says.

ASP boosters would argue that Stieber has it backwards, that using the Web reduces administrative chores, freeing up time to focus on workers' needs. But if you want an ASP with a human touch, look at San Francisco's EmployeeService.com. It provides the same services as Employease—and also sends people out to assist with HR problems, which can include everything from setting up the human resources system to answering employee questions. The handholding drives up the cost to $80 to $130 per employee per month. Customized systems cost even more.

The main reason to consider paying the premium: integration with other ASPs, including customer service, sales, and e-commerce software—which eventually paves the way for businesses to move more of their operations to the Web without having to go through multiple ASPs. Integrated systems are probably the wave of the future, says Scholl at Dataquest. But for now, most users would settle for anything that helps take the "paper" out of paperwork.

SOURCE: A. S. Wellner, "Click Here for HR," *BusinessWeek*, April 24, 2000.

Questions

1. Compare the descriptions of software in this case with the HR functions described in Chapter 1. Which functions are available through application service providers? Which additional functions can you envision ASPs adding? Are there HR functions that could not appropriately be outsourced to an ASP? Explain.
2. Does the use of ASPs, as described in this case, fit well with the trend toward employee empowerment? Why or why not?
3. Visit the websites of one or two ASPs listed in the table. How have their services changed since the *BusinessWeek* article was written? Can you identify any trends that would explain these changes?

Case: HRM Flies through Turbulence at Delta Air Lines

In 1994 executives at Delta Air Lines faced a crucial decision about the company's direction. Delta had established a reputation in the industry for having highly committed employees who delivered the highest-quality customer service. In fact, Delta employees were so committed to the airline that in the 1980s they had pitched in and bought Delta a new plane. But the company had been losing money—at a rate of $10 for every share of stock—for two straight years. There were several reasons. The company had spent $491 million to acquire Pan Am in 1991, and then war in the Persian Gulf had driven up fuel costs. Delta's cost per available seat mile (the cost to fly one passenger one mile) was 9.26 cents, among the highest in the industry. A recession in the early 1990s lowered the demand for air travel, and a growing share of those who did fly chose discount carriers. The company had to act, and whatever it did, the changes were sure to affect Delta's human resources.

Chairman and chief executive officer Ron Allen launched a cost-cutting strategy, which he named Leadership 7.5. To reduce the cost per available seat mile to 7.5 cents, Delta would have to cut labor costs, the largest single controllable cost for any airline. The company began downsizing, cutting 11,458 people from its 69,555-employee workforce over three years through buyouts, early retirement, extended leaves, and layoffs. The company laid off many experienced customer service representatives, replacing them with lower-paid, inexperienced, part-time workers. Delta outsourced the cleaning of planes and baggage handling, again laying off long-term Delta employees. The numbers of maintenance workers and flight attendants were reduced substantially. Outsourcing saved a lot of money. For example, Delta had often hired college graduates to clean its planes; these employees were willing to start at $7.80 an hour to get their foot in the company's door. The outside contractors received lower wages, fewer benefits, and no travel privileges.

These cuts improved the company's financial performance, but by other measures, Delta was worse off. Customer complaints about dirty airplanes rose from 219 in 1993 to 358 in 1994 and 634 in 1995. On-time performance became so bad that passengers joked that Delta stands for "Doesn't Ever Leave The Airport." In passenger ratings of airline performance, Delta slipped from fourth to seventh in baggage handling among the top 10 carriers. Employee morale hit an all-time low, and unions were beginning to make headway toward organizing some of Delta's employee groups.

CEO Allen was convinced the changes were necessary. In 1996 he was quoted as saying, "This has tested our people. There have been some morale problems. But so be it. You go back to the question of survival, and it makes the decision very easy." Shortly after that, employees began donning buttons bearing a cynical "so be it" slogan.

Delta's board of directors began to question whether the company had given enough attention to its human resources. The directors saw union organizers stirring workers' discontent, employee morale destroyed, Delta's reputation for customer service in shambles, and senior managers exiting the company in droves. Less than a year after his notorious comments, Allen was fired, despite Delta's financial turnaround. His firing came "not because the company was going broke, but because its spirit was broken."

Delta is still trying to compose a happy ending to this story. With the family atmosphere gone and the bond between management and rank-and-file employees broken, employees sought other ways to gain voice and security. In the fall of 2001, two union organizing drives were under way, involving Delta's flight attendants and mechanics. Although less than one-third of eligible flight attendants voted in favor of the union (which is seeking a new election), the union activity has driven up labor costs. The pilots earlier that year signed a lucrative five-year contract giving them the highest pay in the industry. To head off the mechanics' organizing drive, Delta gave the mechanics raises to put them at the industry top. Not surprisingly, the flight attendants are seeking industry-leading pay for themselves.

Delta's replacement for Allen, Leo Mullin, has declared customer service and employee relations to be top priorities. Under Mullin's leadership, Delta employees have heard speeches emphasizing leadership and received such incentives as pay raises, discounts on computers, and more generous benefits. Mullin says his focus on restoring customer service improves morale. As employees see the company succeed, they "feel good about Delta." Delta has conducted employee surveys that show morale improving substantially. Explains Mullin, "I think the most important ingredient [in this change] was just to create a winning company. People feel good if they believe they're part of a company that's committed to excellent customer ser-vice." Customers see a difference, too. In a recent Airline Quality Rating, an annual survey of airline performance, Delta for the first time was rated best in overall quality and customer service.

An economic slowdown and fear of terrorism devastated the demand for air travel in 2001, testing Delta's new focus on employees. In September 2001, Delta determined that reduced demand would require cutting flight capacity and reducing the workforce by up to 13,000 jobs. To minimize the pain, the company offered voluntary programs, including early retirement, a package of benefits to those who accepted voluntary layoffs, and leaves of absence ranging from one to five years. Over 9,500 employees opted for these arrangements.

An antagonistic relationship between workers and managers is just one of the perils that can await organizations that fail to adequately address human resource issues. However, Mullin sees evidence that such a relationship can be changed when the goals are right.

SOURCE: M. Brannigann and E. De Lisser, "Cost Cutting at Delta Raises the Stock Price but Lowers the Service," *The Wall Street Journal*, June 20, 1996, pp. A1, A8; M. Brannigan and J. White, "So Be It: Why Delta Air Lines Decided It Was Time for CEO to Take Off," *The Wall Street Journal*, May 30, 1997, p. A1; M. Brannigan, "Delta Lifts Mechanics' Pay to Top of Industry Amid Push by Union," *The Wall Street Journal*, Interactive Edition, August 16, 2001; M. Adams, "Delta May See Second Big Union," *USA Today*, August 27, 2001, p. 1B; M. Sanchanta, "Delta Pilots Ratify Contract," *Financial Times*, October 26, 2001, http://news.ft.com; A. Higgins, "Delta Family Has Grown Dysfunctional," *Cincinnati Enquirer*, April 15, 2001, http://enquirer.com; "How Did They Do That?" *Leaders*, January 2001, p. 161; M. Brannigan, "Delta Wins Round in Fight over Union for Flight Attendants," *The Wall Street Journal*, Interactive Edition, February 4, 2002; "Delta Workers Sign Up for Voluntary Separation," *The Wall Street Journal*, October 26, 2001, p. A4; "Delta Tops Poll," *Travel Agent*, April 9, 2001, downloaded from FindArticles.com.

Questions

1. How might human resource management support a strategy like Leadership 7.5?
2. When an organization is losing money, as Delta has been, can human resource management enable a more positive outcome than Delta experienced with Leadership 7.5? Explain.
3. How has human resource management changed under CEO Mullin? What additional changes or actions can you recommend?

Notes

1. Vincent J. Schodolski, "Peace Corps Applications Rise after Dot-Com Fall," *Chicago Tribune*, August 25, 2001, sec. 1, pp. 1, 13.
2. Kortney Stringer, "Time Out," *The Wall Street Journal*, Interactive Edition, March 27, 2002.
3. Sue Shellenbarger, "Americans Spend So Much Time in Cars, Living Takes a Back Seat," *The Wall Street Journal*, Interactive Edition, February 13, 2002.
4. H. N. Fullerton, "Labor Force 2006: Slowing Down and Changing Composition," *Monthly Labor Review*,

November 1997, pp. 23–28. Also see the Bureau of Labor Statistics employment projections on the Web at www.bls.gov.

5. S. Shellenbarger, "Companies Must Try Harder to Attract Older Employees," *The Wall Street Journal*, Interactive Edition, May 23, 2001.

6. C. M. Solomon, "Managing the Baby Busters," *Personnel Journal*, March 1992, pp. 52–59; J. Wallace, "After X Comes Y," *HR Magazine*, April 2001, p. 192.

7. B. Wooldridge and J. Wester, "The Turbulent Environment of Public Personnel Administration: Responding to the Challenge of the Changing Workplace of the Twenty-First Century," *Public Personnel Management* 20 (1991), pp. 207–24; J. Laabs, "The New Loyalty: Grasp It. Earn It. Keep It," *Workforce*, November 1998, pp. 34–39.

8. "Employee Dissatisfaction on Rise in Last 10 Years, New Report Says," *Employee Relations Weekly* (Washington, DC: Bureau of National Affairs, 1986).

9. D. T. Hall and J. Richter, "Career Gridlock: Baby Boomers Hit the Wall," *The Executive* 4 (1990), pp. 7–22.

10. S. Shellenbarger, "Companies Must Try Harder to Attract Older Employees," *The Wall Street Journal*, Interactive Edition, May 23, 2001.

11. Women's Bureau, U.S. Department of Labor, "Facts on Working Women," Labor Department Web site, www.dol.gov, March 2000.

12. T. H. Cox and S. Blake, "Managing Cultural Diversity: Implications for Organizational Competitiveness," *The Executive* 5 (1991), pp. 45–56.

13. "Impact of Diversity Initiatives on the Bottom Line Survey," *SHRM/Fortune*, June 2001.

14. H. Rosin, "Cultural Revolution at Texaco," *The New Republic*, February 2, 1998, pp. 15–18; K. Labich, "No More Crude at Texaco," *Fortune*, September 6, 1999, pp. 205–12.

15. T. Singer, "Comeback Markets," *Inc.*, May 2001, pp. 53–57+.

16. "Industry Report 2000," *Training*, October 2000, p. 48.

17. N. Learner, "Frontline Makeover," *Christian Science Monitor*, March 11, 2002, downloaded at www.csmonitor.com.

18. J. A. Neal and C. L. Tromley, "From Incremental Change to Retrofit: Creating High-Performance Work Systems," *Academy of Management Executive* 9 (1995), pp. 42–54.

19. U.S. Bureau of Labor Statistics Employment Projections, "The Ten Fastest-Growing Occupations, 1998–2008," Table 3b, http://stats.bls.gov.

20. "CIO Panel: Knowledge-Sharing Roundtable," *Information Week Online, News in Review*, April 26, 1999, www.informationweek.com; Buckman Laboratories website, www.buckman.com.

21. A. Carnevale and D. Desrochers, "Training in the Dilbert Economy," *Training & Development*, December 1999, pp. 32–36.

22. Conseco website, June 2001, www.conseco.com.

23. M. Williams, "Some Plants Tear Out Long Assembly Lines, Switch to Craft Work," *The Wall Street Journal*, October 24, 1994, pp. A1, A4.

24. D. Ulrich, *Human Resource Champions* (Boston: Harvard Business School Press, 1998).

25. A. Halcrow, "Survey Shows HRM in Transition," *Workforce*, June 1998, pp. 73–80; J. Laabs, "Why HR Can Win Today," *Workforce*, May 1998, pp. 62–74; C. Cole, "Kodak Snapshots," *Workforce*, June 2000, pp. 65–72; Towers Perrin, *Priorities for Competitive Advantage: An IBM Study Conducted by Towers Perrin*, 1992.

26. K. Carrig, "Reshaping Human Resources for the Next Century: Lessons from a High-Flying Airline," *Human Resource Management* 36, no. 2 (1997), pp. 277–89.

27. J. R. Jablonski, *Implementing Total Quality Management: An Overview* (San Diego: Pfeiffer, 1991).

28. R. Hodgetts, F. Luthans, and S. Lee, "New Paradigm Organizations: From Total Quality to Learning to World-Class," *Organizational Dynamics*, Winter 1994, pp. 5–19.

29. G. Fairclough, "Business Bulletin," *The Wall Street Journal*, March 5, 1998, p. A1.

30. P. Sebastian, "Business Bulletin," *The Wall Street Journal*, October 2, 1997, p. A1.

31. C. O'Reilly and J. Pfeffer, *Hidden Value: How Great Companies Achieve Extraordinary Results with Ordinary People* (Cambridge, MA: Harvard Business School Press, 2000).

32. J. Laabs, "Has Downsizing Missed Its Mark?" *Workforce*, April 1999, pp. 31–38.

33. N. Templin, "UAW to Unveil Pact on Slashing GM's Payroll," *The Wall Street Journal*, December 15, 1992, p. A3.

34. J. Lopez, "Managing: Early-Retirement Offers Lead to Renewed Hiring," *The Wall Street Journal*, January 26, 1993, p. B1.

35. A. Church, "Organizational Downsizing: What Is the Role of the Practitioner?" *Industrial-Organizational Psychologist* 33, no. 1 (1995), pp. 63–74.

36. J. Kahn, "The World's Most Admired Companies," *Fortune*, October 26, 1998, pp. 206–26; A. Fisher, "The World's Most Admired Companies," *Fortune*, October 27, 1997, p. 232.

37. M. Braxton, "HR's Role in a New Global Economy," *HRTX iLinx*, May/June 2001, pp. 1, 14.

38. C. Fleming and L. Lopez, "No Boundaries," *The Wall Street Journal,* September 9, 1998, p. R16.

39. J. L. Young, "Starbucks Expansion into China Is Slated," *The Wall Street Journal,* October 5, 1998, p. B13C.

40. G. P. Zachary, "Stalled U.S. Workers' Objections Grow as More of Their Jobs Shift Overseas," *The Wall Street Journal,* October 9, 1995, pp. A2, A9.

41. M. Cohen, *Labor Shortages as America Approaches the Twenty-First Century* (Ann Arbor, Mich.: University of Michigan Press, 1995); "Human Resources and Their Skills," in *The Changing Nature of Work,* ed. A. Howard (San Francisco: Jossey-Bass, 1995), pp. 211–22; H. Fullerton, "Another Look at the Labor Force," *Monthly Labor Review,* November 1993, pp. 31–40.

42. Office of Policy and Planning, Immigration and Naturalization Service, "Legal Immigration, Fiscal Year 2000," *Annual Report,* January 2002, downloaded at www.ins.gov.

43. "The People Problem," *Inc.,* State of Small Business 2001 issue, May 29, 2001, pp. 84–85.

44. National Association of Colleges and Employers, "Job Outlook 2002," www.jobweb.com.

45. R. L. Tung, "Expatriate Assignments: Enhancing Success and Minimizing Failure," *Academy of Management Executive* 12, no. 4 (1988), pp. 93–106.

46. "More HR Being Outsourced," *HR Daily News,* March 1, 2002, HRnext.com.

47. E. Zimmerman, "B of A and Big-Time Outsourcing," *Workforce,* April 2001, pp. 50–54.

48. M. J. Kavanaugh, H. G. Guetal, and S. I. Tannenbaum, *Human Resource Information Systems: Development and Application* (Boston: PWS-Kent, 1990).

49. S. Greengard, "When HRMS Goes Global: Managing the Data Highway," *Personnel Journal,* June 1995, pp. 91–106.

50. CyberAtlas, "U.S. Internet Population Continues to Grow," *Internet Advertising Report,* February 6, 2002, www.internetnews.com.

51. R. D. Blackwell and K. Stephan, *Customers Rule! Why the E-Commerce Honeymoon Is Over and Where Winning Businesses Go from Here* (Crown Publishing, 2001).

52. J. Angwin, "Latest Dot-Com Fad Is a Bit Old-Fashioned: It's Called 'Profitability,' " *The Wall Street Journal,* August 14, 2001, pp. A1, A6.

53. This section is based on L. Grensing-Pophal, "Are You Suited for a Dot-Com?" *HR Magazine,* November 2000, pp. 75–80.

54. S. Greengard, "Technology Finally Advances HR," *Workforce,* January 2000, pp. 38–41.

55. C. Tejada, "For Many, Taking Work Home Is Often a Job without Reward," *The Wall Street Journal,* Interactive Edition, March 5, 2002.

56. D. M. Rousseau, "Psychological and Implied Contracts in Organizations," *Employee Rights and Responsibilities Journal* 2 (1989), pp. 121–29.

57. D. Rousseau, "Changing the Deal While Keeping the People," *Academy of Management Executive* 11 (1996), pp. 50–61; M. A. Cavanaugh and R. Noe, "Antecedents and Consequences of the New Psychological Contract," *Journal of Organizational Behavior* 20 (1999), pp. 323–40.

58. Tejada, "For Many, Taking Work Home Is Often a Job without Reward."

59. E. O. Welles, "Great Expectations," *Inc.,* March 2001, pp. 68–70, 72–73.

60. M. DiNatale, "Characteristics of and Preferences for Alternative Work Arrangements, 1999," *Monthly Labor Review,* March 2001, pp. 28–49.

61. J. C. Cooper and K. Madigan, "Labor's New Flexibility Cuts Two Ways," *BusinessWeek,* December 24, 2001, downloaded from http://library.northernlight.com.

62. C. Johnson, "Don't Forget Your Shift Workers," *HR Magazine,* February 1999, pp. 80–84.

63. J. Cook, "Keeping Work at Work," *Human Resource Executive,* July 2001, pp. 68–71.

64. Ibid.

65. C. Ansberry, "Old Industries Adopt Flex Staffing to Adapt to Rapid Pace of Change," *The Wall Street Journal,* Interactive Edition, March 22, 2002.

3

Providing Equal Employment Opportunity and a Safe Workplace

What Do I Need to Know? After reading this chapter, you should be able to:

1. Explain how the three branches of government regulate human resource management.

2. Summarize the major federal laws requiring equal employment opportunity.

3. Identify the federal agencies that enforce equal employment opportunity, and describe the role of each.

4. Describe ways employers can avoid illegal discrimination and provide reasonable accommodation.

5. Define sexual harassment and tell how employers can eliminate or minimize it.

6. Explain employers' duties under the Occupational Safety and Health Act.

7. Describe the role of the Occupational Safety and Health Administration.

8. Discuss ways employers promote worker safety and health.

Introduction

Following the September 2001 terrorist attacks in New York City and Washington, DC, President George W. Bush declared that the U.S. response would not include

Cari M. Dominguez, the EEOC administrator. The EEOC is part of the executive branch. One of Dominguez's first actions was to call a meeting to hear testimony about backlash discrimination against Arab-Americans (and people wrongly thought to be of Arab descent) following the terrorist attacks of 2001.

prejudice against any ethnic group, and he expressed respect for Islam and for law-abiding Arab-Americans. Responding to that theme two months later, the first meeting of the federal Equal Employment Opportunity Commission under Cari M. Dominguez examined treatment of Arab-Americans in the workplace. After hearing testimony, Dominguez asserted, "The important things have *not* changed since September 11. The EEOC remains focused on its enduring mission: to ensure that working men and women have the freedom to compete without the barriers of unlawful discrimination and the indignities of illegal harassment."[1]

As we saw in Chapter 1, human resource management takes place in the context of the company's goals and society's expectations for how a company should operate. In the United States, the federal government has set some limits on how an organization can practice human resource management. Among these limits are requirements intended to prevent discrimination in hiring and employment practices and to protect the health and safety of workers while they are on the job. Questions about a company's compliance with these requirements can result in lawsuits and negative publicity that often cause serious problems for a company's success and survival. Conversely, a company that skillfully navigates the maze of regulations can gain an advantage over its competitors.

This chapter provides an overview of the ways government bodies regulate equal employment opportunity and workplace safety and health. It introduces you to major laws affecting employers in these areas, as well as the agencies charged with enforcing those laws. The chapter also discusses ways organizations can develop practices that ensure they are in compliance with the laws.

One point to make at the outset is that managers often want a list of do's and don'ts that will keep them out of legal trouble. Some managers rely on strict rules such as "Don't ever ask a female applicant if she is married," rather than learning the reasons behind those rules. Clearly, certain practices are illegal or at least inadvisable, and this chapter will provide guidance on avoiding such practices. However, managers who merely focus on how to avoid breaking the law are not thinking about how to be ethical or how to acquire and use human resources in the best way to carry out the company's mission. This chapter introduces ways to think more creatively and constructively about fair employment and workplace safety.

Regulation of Human Resource Management

LO1

All three branches of the U.S. government—legislative, executive, and judicial—play an important role in creating a legal environment for human resource management. The legislative branch, which consists of the two houses of Congress, has enacted a number of laws governing human resource activities. Senators and U.S. Representatives generally develop these laws in response to perceived societal needs. For example, during the civil rights movement of the early 1960s, Congress enacted Title VII of the Civil Rights Act to ensure that various minority groups received equal opportunities in many areas of life.

The executive branch, including the many regulatory agencies that the president oversees, is responsible for enforcing the laws passed by Congress. Agencies do this through a variety of actions, from drawing up regulations detailing how to abide by the laws to filing suit against alleged violators. Some federal agencies involved in regulating human resource management include the Equal Employment Opportunity Commission and the Occupational Safety and Health Administration. In addition, the president may issue executive orders, which are directives issued solely by the president, without requiring congressional approval. Some executive orders regulate the activities of organizations that have contracts with the federal government. For example, President Lyndon Johnson signed Executive Order 11246, which requires all federal contractors and subcontractors to engage in affirmative-action programs designed to hire and promote women and minorities. (We will explore the topic of affirmative action later in this chapter.)

The judicial branch, the federal court system, influences employment law by interpreting the law and holding trials concerning violations of the law. The U.S. Supreme Court, at the head of the judicial branch, is the court of final appeal. Decisions made by the Supreme Court are binding; they can be overturned only through laws passed by Congress. The Civil Rights Act of 1991 was partly designed to overturn Supreme Court decisions.

equal employment opportunity (EEO)
The condition in which all individuals have an equal chance for employment, regardless of their race, color, religion, sex, age, disability, or national origin.

Equal Employment Opportunity

Among the most significant efforts to regulate human resource management are those aimed at achieving **equal employment opportunity (EEO)**—the condition in which all individuals have an equal chance for employment, regardless of their race, color, religion, sex, age, disability, or national origin. The federal government's efforts to create equal employment opportunity include constitutional amendments, legislation, and executive orders, as well as court decisions that interpret the laws. Table 3.1 summarizes major EEO laws discussed in this chapter. These are U.S. laws; equal employment laws in other countries may differ.

Constitutional Amendments

Two amendments to the U.S. Constitution—the Thirteenth and Fourteenth—have implications for human resource management. The Thirteenth Amendment abolished slavery in the United States. Though you might be hard-pressed to cite an example of race-based slavery in the United States today, the Thirteenth Amendment has been applied in cases where discrimination involved the "badges" (symbols) and "incidents" of slavery.

The Fourteenth Amendment forbids the states from taking life, liberty, or property without due process of law and prevents the states from denying equal protection of the laws. Recently it has been applied to the protection of whites in charges of reverse discrimination. In a case that marked the early stages of a move away from race-based quotas, Alan Bakke alleged that as a white man he had been discriminated against in the selection of entrants to the University of California at Davis medical school.[2] The university had set aside 16 of the available 100 places for "disadvantaged" applicants who were members of racial minority groups. Under this quota system, Bakke was able to compete for only 84 positions, whereas a minority applicant was able to compete for all 100. The federal court ruled in favor of Bakke, noting that this quota system had violated white individuals' right to equal protection under the law.

An important point regarding the Fourteenth Amendment is that it applies only to the decisions or actions of the government or of private groups whose activities are deemed government actions. Thus, a person could file a claim under the Fourteenth Amendment if he or she had been fired from a state university (a government organization) but not if the person had been fired by a private employer.

Legislation

The periods following the Civil War and during the civil rights movement of the 1960s were times when many voices in society pressed for equal rights for all without regard to a person's race or sex. In response, Congress passed laws designed to provide for equal opportunity. In later years, Congress has passed additional laws that have extended EEO protection more broadly.

Civil Rights Acts of 1866 and 1871

During Reconstruction, Congress passed two Civil Rights Acts to further the Thirteenth Amendment's goal of abolishing slavery. The Civil Rights Act of 1866 granted all persons the same property rights as white citizens, as well as the right to enter into and enforce contracts. Courts have interpreted the latter right as including employment contracts. The Civil Rights Act of 1871 granted all citizens the right to sue in federal court if they feel they have been deprived of some civil right. Although these laws might seem outdated, they are still used because they allow the plaintiff to recover both compensatory and punitive damages (that is, payment to compensate them for their loss plus additional damages to punish the offender).

TABLE 3.1

Summary of Major EEO Laws and Regulations

ACT	REQUIREMENTS	COVERS	ENFORCEMENT AGENCY
Thirteenth Amendment	Abolished slavery	All individuals	Court system
Fourteenth Amendment	Provides equal protection for all citizens and requires due process in state action	State actions (e.g., decisions of government organizations)	Court system
Civil Rights Acts (CRAs) of 1866 and 1871 (as amended)	Grant all citizens the right to make, perform, modify, and terminate contracts and enjoy all benefits, terms, and conditions of the contractual relationship	All individuals	Court system
Equal Pay Act of 1963	Requires that men and women performing equal jobs receive equal pay	Employers engaged in interstate commerce	EEOC
Title VII of CRA	Forbids discrimination based on race, color, religion, sex, or national origin	Employers with 15 or more employees working 20 or more weeks per year; labor unions; and employment agencies	EEOC
Age Discrimination in Employment Act of 1967	Prohibits discrimination in employment against individuals 40 years of age and older	Employers with 15 or more employees working 20 or more weeks per year; labor unions; employment agencies; federal government	EEOC
Rehabilitation Act of 1973	Requires affirmative action in the employment of individuals with disabilities	Government agencies; federal contractors and subcontractors with contracts greater than $2,500	OFCCP
Pregnancy Discrimination Act of 1978	Treats discrimination based on pregnancy-related conditions as illegal sex discrimination	All employees covered by Title VII	EEOC
Americans with Disabilities Act of 1990	Prohibits discrimination against individuals with disabilities	Employers with more than 15 employees	EEOC
Executive Order 11246	Requires affirmative action in hiring women and minorities	Federal contractors and subcontractors with contracts greater than $10,000	OFCCP
Civil Rights Act of 1991	Prohibits discrimination (same as Title VII)	Same as Title VII, plus applies Section 1981 to employment discrimination cases	EEOC
Uniformed Services Employment and Reemployment Rights Act of 1994	Requires rehiring of employees who are absent for military service, with training and accommodations as needed	Veterans and members of reserve components	Veterans' Employment and Training Service

Equal Pay Act of 1963

Under the Equal Pay Act of 1963, if men and women in an organization are doing equal work, the employer must pay them equally. The act defines *equal* in terms of skill, effort, responsibility, and working conditions. However, the act allows for reasons why men and women performing the same job might be paid differently. If the pay differences result from differences in seniority, merit, quantity or quality of production, or any factor other than sex (such as participating in a training program or working the night shift), then the differences are legal.

A former employee of Outback Steakhouse was recently awarded $2.2 million by a federal district court when she demonstrated that she had not received equal pay. Dena Zechella worked for Outback's construction department, and as the company grew, Zechella assumed more and more responsibility until she was handling the acquisition and development of about 100 new restaurant sites a year. About a year and a half after Zechella's hiring, Outback hired a male employee to perform the same job functions. After Zechella trained the man, he took over most of Zechella's duties. Zechella complained, and the company transferred her to a clerical job. Zechella later learned that the man had been hired at almost twice her salary. After she complained again, the company fired her. The court awarded Zechella back wages plus $50,000 in compensatory damages for her emotional pain and suffering and $2.1 million in punitive damages.[3]

✳Title VII of the Civil Rights Act of 1964 ✳

The major law regulating equal employment opportunity in the United States is Title VII of the Civil Rights Act of 1964. Title VII directly resulted from the civil rights movement of the early 1960s, led by such individuals as Dr. Martin Luther King Jr. To ensure that employment opportunities would be based on character or ability rather than on race, Congress wrote and passed Title VII, and President Lyndon Johnson signed it into law in 1964. The law is enforced by the **Equal Employment Opportunity Commission (EEOC),** an agency of the Department of Justice.

Title VII prohibits employers from discriminating against individuals because of their race, color, religion, sex, or national origin. An employer may not use these characteristics as the basis for not hiring someone, for firing someone, or for discriminating against them in the terms of their pay, conditions of employment, or privileges of employment. In addition, an employer may not use these characteristics to limit, segregate, or classify employees or job applicants in any way that would deprive any individual of employment opportunities or otherwise adversely affect his or her status as an employee. The act applies to organizations that employ 15 or more persons working 20 or more weeks a year and that are involved in interstate commerce, as well as state and local governments, employment agencies, and labor organizations.

Title VII also states that employers may not retaliate against employees for either "opposing" a perceived illegal employment practice or "participating in a proceeding" related to an alleged illegal employment practice. *Opposition* refers to expressing to someone through proper channels that you believe an illegal employment act has taken place or is taking place. *Participation in a proceeding* refers to testifying in an investigation, hearing, or court proceeding regarding an illegal employment act. The purpose of this provision is to protect employees from employers' threats and other forms of intimidation aimed at discouraging employees from bringing to light acts they believe to be illegal. Companies that violate this prohibition may be liable for punitive damages, as in the earlier mentioned case involving Outback Steakhouse.

Equal Employment Opportunity Commission (EEOC)
Agency of the Department of Justice charged with enforcing Title VII of the Civil Rights Act of 1964 and other antidiscrimination laws.

Age Discrimination in Employment Act (ADEA)

One category of employees not covered by Title VII is older workers. Older workers sometimes are concerned that they will be the targets of discrimination, especially when a company is downsizing. Older workers tend to be paid more, so a company that wants to cut labor costs may save by laying off its oldest workers. To counter such discrimination, Congress in 1967 passed the Age Discrimination in Employment Act (ADEA), which prohibits discrimination against workers who are over the age of 40. Similar to Title VII, the ADEA outlaws hiring, firing, setting compensation rates, or other employment decisions based on a person's age being over 40.

Recently, many firms have offered early-retirement incentives as an alternative or supplement to involuntary layoffs. Because this approach to workforce reduction focuses on older employees, who would be eligible for early retirement, it may be in violation of the ADEA. Early-retirement incentives require that participating employees sign an agreement waiving their rights to sue under the ADEA. Courts have tended to uphold the use of early-retirement incentives and waivers as long as the individuals were not coerced into signing the agreements, the agreements were presented in a way the employees could understand, and the employees had enough time to make a decision.[4]

Still, age discrimination complaints make up a large percentage of the complaints filed with the Equal Employment Opportunity Commission, and whenever the economy is slow, the number of complaints grows. For example, as shown in Figure 3.1, the number of age discrimination cases increased during the early 1990s, when many firms were downsizing. Another increase in age discrimination claims accompanied the economic recession in 2001.[5] These cases can be costly; most are settled out of court, but the settlements run from $50,000 to $400,000 per employee.[6] In cases that go to court, punitive damages can bring the total cost much higher. Several years ago, Fred Maiorino was awarded millions in a lawsuit against Schering-Plough. The company fired Maiorino after he had worked with Schering-Plough for 35 years and twice failed to accept an early-retirement offer made to all sales representatives. After hearing testimony that Maiorino's boss had plastered his file with negative paperwork aimed at firing him, rather than trying to help him improve his performance, the ju-

FIGURE 3.1

Age Discrimination Complaints, 1991–2000

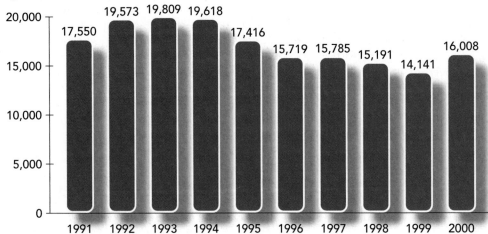

SOURCE: Equal Employment Opportunity Commission.

rors unanimously decided Maiorino had been discriminated against because of his age. They awarded him $435,000 in compensatory damages and $8 million in punitive damages.[7]

In today's environment, in which firms are seeking talented individuals to achieve the company's goals, older employees can be a tremendous pool of potential resources. Bonne Bell, maker of cosmetics popular with teenage girls, even set up an assembly line staffed entirely with older workers. The company's president, Jess Bell, thought older workers might appreciate working apart from younger workers' conversations and music. The line's supervisor, Juliana Carlton, age 65, notes, "I raised my kids. It's my turn to be with people my own age group. We can talk to each other. We don't have to compete [with young employees]." The department has grown from 16 workers to 50, with an average age of 70. Bonne Bell has a dedicated workforce (almost no turnover) that has met shipment goals and saved the company almost $1 million.[8]

Vocational Rehabilitation Act of 1973

In 1973, Congress passed the Vocational Rehabilitation Act to enhance employment opportunity for individuals with disabilities. This act covers executive agencies and contractors and subcontractors that receive more than $2,500 annually from the federal government. These organizations must engage in affirmative action for individuals with disabilities. **Affirmative action** is an organization's active effort to find opportunities to hire or promote people in a particular group. Thus, Congress intended this act to encourage employers to recruit qualified individuals with disabilities and to make reasonable accommodations to all those people to become active members of the labor market. The Department of Labor's Employment Standards Administration enforces this act.

affirmative action
An organization's active effort to find opportunities to hire or promote people in a particular group.

Vietnam Era Veteran's Readjustment Act of 1974

Similar to the Rehabilitation Act, the Vietnam Era Veteran's Readjustment Act of 1974 requires federal contractors and subcontractors to take affirmative action toward employing veterans of the Vietnam War (those serving between August 5, 1964, and May 7, 1975). The Office of Federal Contract Compliance Procedures, discussed later in this chapter, has authority to enforce this act.

Pregnancy Discrimination Act of 1978

An amendment to Title VII of the Civil Rights Act of 1964, the Pregnancy Discrimination Act of 1978 defines discrimination on the basis of pregnancy, childbirth, or related medical conditions to be a form of illegal sex discrimination. According to the EEOC, this means that employers must treat "women affected by pregnancy or related conditions . . . in the same manner as other applicants or employees with similar abilities or limitations."[9] For example, an employer may not refuse to hire a woman because she is pregnant. Decisions about work absences or accommodations must be based on the same policies as the organization uses for other disabilities. Benefits, including health insurance, should cover pregnancy and related medical conditions in the same way that it covers other medical conditions.

Americans with Disabilities Act (ADA) of 1990

One of the farthest-reaching acts concerning the management of human resources is the Americans with Disabilities Act. This 1990 law protects individuals with disabilities from being discriminated against in the workplace. It prohibits discrimination based on disability in all employment practices such as job application procedures, hiring, firing, promotions, compensation, and training. Other employment activities covered by the ADA are employment advertising, recruitment, tenure, layoff, leave, and fringe benefits.

disability
Under the Americans with Disabilities Act, a physical or mental impairment that substantially limits one or more major life activities, a record of having such an impairment, or being regarded as having such an impairment.

The ADA defines **disability** as a physical or mental impairment that substantially limits one or more major life activities, a record of having such an impairment, or being regarded as having such an impairment. The first part of the definition refers to individuals who have serious disabilities—such as epilepsy, blindness, deafness, or paralysis—that affect their ability to perform major life activities such as walking, seeing, performing manual tasks, learning, caring for oneself, and working. The second part refers to individuals who have a history of disability, such as someone who has had cancer but is currently in remission, someone with a history of mental illness, and someone with a history of heart disease. The third part of the definition, "being regarded as having a disability," refers to people's subjective reactions, as in the case of someone who is severely disfigured; an employer might hesitate to hire such a person on the grounds that people will react negatively to such an employee.[10]

Because the ADA is still relatively new, court rulings continue to define who is protected. At present, the ADA is understood to cover specific physiological disabilities such as cosmetic disfigurement and anatomical loss affecting the body's systems. In addition, it covers mental and psychological disorders such as mental retardation, organic brain syndrome, emotional or mental illness, and learning disabilities. Conditions *not* covered include obesity, substance abuse, eye and hair color, and left-handedness.[11] Figure 3.2 shows the types of disabilities associated with complaints filed under the ADA.

In contrast to other EEO laws, the ADA goes beyond prohibiting discrimination to require that employees take steps to accommodate individuals covered under the act. If a disabled person is selected to perform a job, the employer (perhaps in consultation with the disabled employee) determines what accommodations are necessary for the employee to perform the job. Examples include using ramps and lifts to

FIGURE 3.2

Disabilities Associated with Complaints Filed under ADA

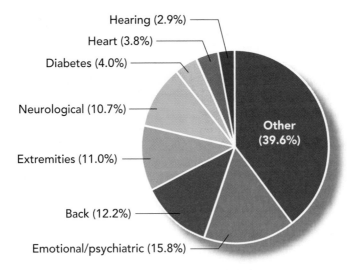

Total complaints: 17,007

SOURCE: Equal Employment Opportunity Commission, data for 1999.

EMPLOYER SIZE	DAMAGE LIMIT
14 to 100 employees	$ 50,000
101 to 200 employees	100,000
201 to 500 employees	200,000
More than 500 employees	300,000

TABLE 3.2

Maximum Punitive Damages Allowed under the Civil Rights Act of 1991

make facilities accessible, redesigning job procedures, and providing technology such as TDD lines for hearing-impaired employees. Some employers have feared that accommodations under the ADA would be expensive. However, a study by Sears Roebuck & Co. found that 69 percent of all accommodations cost nothing, 29 percent cost less than $1,000, and only 3 percent cost more than $1,000.[12] Some companies have even found that accommodating disabled individuals gives them an advantage in the marketplace, as in the example in the nearby "Best Practices" box.

Civil Rights Act of 1991

In 1991 Congress broadened the relief available to victims of discrimination by passing a Civil Rights Act (CRA 1991). CRA 1991 amends Title VII of the Civil Rights Act of 1964, as well as the Civil Rights Act of 1866, the Americans with Disabilities Act, and the Age Discrimination in Employment Act of 1967. One major change in EEO law under CRA 1991 has been the addition of compensatory and punitive damages in cases of discrimination under Title VII and the Americans with Disabilities Act. Before CRA 1991, Title VII limited damage claims to *equitable relief,* which courts have defined to include back pay, lost benefits, front pay in some cases, and attorney's fees and costs. CRA 1991 allows judges to award compensatory and punitive damages when the plaintiff proves the discrimination was intentional or reckless. Compensatory damages include such things as future monetary loss, emotional pain, suffering, and loss of enjoyment of life. Punitive damages are a punishment; by requiring violators to pay the plaintiff an amount beyond the actual losses suffered, the courts try to discourage employers from discriminating.

Recognizing that one or a few discrimination cases could put an organization out of business, and so harm many innocent employees, Congress has limited the amount of punitive damages. As shown in Table 3.2, the amount of damages depends on the size of the organization charged with discrimination. The limits range from $50,000 per violation at a small company (14 to 100 employees) to $300,000 at a company with more than 500 employees. A company has to pay punitive damages only if it discriminated intentionally or with malice or reckless indifference to the employee's federally protected rights.

Uniformed Services Employment and Reemployment Rights Act of 1994

When members of the armed services were called up following the terrorist attacks of September 2001, a 1994 employment law—the Uniformed Services Employment and Reemployment Rights Act (USERRA)—assumed new significance. Under this law, employers must reemploy workers who left jobs to fulfill military duties for up to five years. When service members return from active duty, the employer must reemploy

Blind Feeding the Blind

Many teachers use an exercise where students must walk around blindfolded for a few hours to help them appreciate the situation of those who are truly blind. Until recently, however, nobody actually made a business out of this.

At the Blind Cow restaurant in Zurich, Switzerland, nothing looks good to eat. The reason is not that the food is bad, but that patrons dine in total darkness. The Rev. Jorge Spielman, a 37-year-old blind pastor, came up with the idea while tending bar at a public exhibit in Zurich. The exhibit required sighted people to grope their way through various dark rooms to experience what it is like to be blind. Spielman and four blind colleagues decided to create a restaurant that would help sighted people appreciate the situation of the blind and that would also provide jobs for the blind and visually impaired.

A blind waitress leads diners to their tables, asking one guest to place both hands on her shoulders, and each of the other guests to do likewise to the guest in front of him or her. The waitress explains the rules: no flashlights, no iridescent watches, and no wandering. Waitresses and waiters should be called by shouting, and guests who need to use the rest rooms must be led by a waitress. The staff all wear bells to allow them to avoid colliding with one another while carrying hot plates of food.

The restaurant has been an unarguable success. Although the Rev. Spielman worried that the novelty would wear off after a few months, a year after its opening the restaurant was still booked solid for the following three months. In addition, the breakage of dishes and glasses is no different from that at other restaurants, because guests are extremely careful. In fact, the business has been such a success that the owners are considering expanding into big U.S. cities like New York and Los Angeles.

Such expansion could succeed because the atmosphere provides for a variety of novel experiences. For instance, a group of three couples dined there, and when the women went to the rest room, the men changed places. When they returned, the men planted kisses on their "new" dates; not all the women noticed that the lips kissing them were unfamiliar ones. In addition, the restaurant was the site for a "blind date." The woman arrived early and sipped a drink until the man was led to her table. Unfortunately, according to the staff, they departed separately.

Finally, the Rev. Spielman has some ideas to keep the restaurant fresh. He plans to make Monday night "date night," bringing in guest speakers to discuss sex and relationships. He explains, "People can ask all kinds of questions in the dark."

SOURCE: J. Costello, "Swiss Eatery Operated by the Blind Keeps Diners Completely in the Dark," *The Wall Street Journal,* November 28, 2001, p. 1.

them in the job they would have held if they had not left to serve in the military, including the same seniority, status, and pay. Disabled veterans also have up to two years to recover from injuries received during their service or training, and employers must make reasonable accommodations for a remaining disability.

Service members also have duties under USERRA. Before leaving for duty, they are to give their employers notice, if possible. After their service, the law sets time limits for applying to be reemployed. Depending on the length of service, these limits range from approximately 2 to 90 days. Veterans with complaints under USERRA can obtain assistance from the Veterans' Employment and Training Service of the Department of Labor.

Executive Orders

Two executive orders that directly affect human resource management are Executive Order 11246, issued by Lyndon Johnson, and Executive Order 11478, issued by Richard Nixon. Executive Order 11246 prohibits federal contractors and subcontractors from discriminating based on race, color, religion, sex, or national origin. In addition, employers whose contracts meet minimum size requirements must engage in affirmative action to ensure against discrimination. Those receiving more than $10,000 from the federal government must take affirmative action, and those with contracts exceeding $50,000 must develop a written affirmative-action plan for each of their establishments. This plan must be in place within 120 days of the beginning of the contract. This executive order is enforced by the Office of Federal Contract Compliance Procedures.

Executive Order 11478 requires the federal government to base all its employment policies on merit and fitness. It specifies that race, color, sex, religion, and national origin may not be considered. Along with the government, the act covers all contractors and subcontractors doing at least $10,000 worth of business with the federal government. The U.S. Office of Personnel Management is in charge of ensuring that the government is in compliance, and the relevant government agencies are responsible for ensuring the compliance of contractors and subcontractors.

The Government's Role in Providing for Equal Employment Opportunity   LO3

At a minimum, equal employment opportunity requires that employers comply with EEO laws. To enforce those laws, the executive branch of the federal government uses the Equal Employment Opportunity Commission and the Office of Federal Contract Compliance Procedures.

Equal Employment Opportunity Commission (EEOC)

The Equal Employment Opportunity Commission (EEOC) is responsible for enforcing most of the EEO laws, including Title VII, the Equal Pay Act, and the Americans with Disabilities Act. To do this, the EEOC investigates and resolves complaints about discrimination, gathers information, and issues guidelines.

When individuals believe they have been discriminated against, they may file a complaint with the EEOC or a similar state agency. They must file the complaint within 180 days of the incident. Figure 3.3 illustrates the number of charges filed with the EEOC for different types of discrimination in 2001. Many individuals file more than one type of charge (for instance, both race discrimination and retaliation), so the total number of complaints filed with the EEOC is less than the total of the amounts in each category.

After the EEOC receives a charge of discrimination, it has 60 days to investigate the complaint. If the EEOC either does not believe the complaint to be valid or fails

FIGURE 3.3

Types of Charges Filed with the EEOC

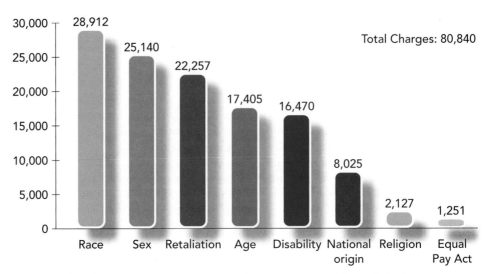

SOURCE: Equal Employment Opportunity Commission website, www.eeoc.gov, February 22, 2002.

to complete the investigation within 60 days, the individual has the right to sue in federal court. If the EEOC determines that discrimination has taken place, its representatives will attempt to work with the individual and the employer to try to achieve a reconciliation without a lawsuit. Sometimes the EEOC enters into a consent decree with the discriminating organization. This decree is an agreement between the agency and the organization that the organization will cease certain discriminatory practices and possibly institute additional affirmative-action practices to rectify its history of discrimination. A settlement with the EEOC can be costly, including such remedies as back pay, reinstatement of the employee, and promotions.

If the attempt at a settlement fails, the EEOC has two options. It may issue a "right to sue" letter to the alleged victim. This letter certifies that the agency has investigated the victim's allegations and found them to be valid. The EEOC's other option, which it uses less often, is to aid the alleged victim in bringing suit in federal court.

EEO-1 report
The EEOC's Employer Information Report, which details the number of women and minorities employed in nine different job categories.

Uniform Guidelines on Employee Selection Procedures
Guidelines issued by the EEOC and other agencies to identify how an organization should develop and administer its system for selecting employees so as not to violate antidiscrimination laws.

The EEOC also monitors organizations' hiring practices. Each year organizations that are government contractors or subcontractors or have 100 or more employees must file an Employer Information Report (EEO-1) with the EEOC. The **EEO-1 report,** shown in Figure 3.4, details the number of women and minorities employed in nine different job categories. The EEOC computer analyzes those reports to identify patterns of discrimination, which the agency can then attack through class-action lawsuits. Employers must display EEOC posters detailing employment rights. These posters must be in prominent and accessible locations—for example, in a company's cafeteria or near its time clock. Also, employers should retain copies of documents related to employment decisions—recruitment letters, announcements of jobs, completed job applications, selections for training, and so on. Employers must keep these records for at least six months or until a complaint is resolved, whichever is later.

Besides resolving complaints and suing alleged violators, the EEOC issues guidelines designed to help employers determine when their decisions violate the laws enforced by the EEOC. These guidelines are not laws themselves. However, the courts give great consideration to them when hearing employment discrimination cases. For example, the *Uniform Guidelines on Employee Selection Procedures* is a set of guidelines issued by the EEOC and other government agencies. The guidelines iden-

FIGURE 3.4

EEOC Form 100: Employer Information Report

Standard Form 100
(Rev. 3/97)

O.M.B. No. 3046-0007
EXPIRES 10/31/99
100-214

Joint Reporting
Committee

- **Equal Employment Opportunity Commission**
- **Office of Federal Contract Compliance Programs (Labor)**

EQUAL EMPLOYMENT OPPORTUNITY

EMPLOYER INFORMATION REPORT EEO—1

SAMPLE

Section A—TYPE OF REPORT
Refer to instructions for number and types of reports to be filed.

1. Indicate by marking in the appropriate box the type of reporting unit for which this copy of the form is submitted (MARK ONLY ONE BOX).

   (1) ☐ Single-establishment Employer Report

   Multi-establishment Employer:
   (2) ☐ Consolidated Report (Required)
   (3) ☐ Headquarters Unit Report (Required)
   (4) ☐ Individual Establishment Report (submit one for each establishment with 50 or more employees)
   (5) ☐ Special Report

2. Total number of reports being filed by this Company (Answer on Consolidated Report only) _____

Section B—COMPANY IDENTIFICATION *(To be answered by all employers)*

OFFICE USE ONLY

1. Parent Company

   a. Name of parent company (owns or controls establishment in item 2) omit if same as label

   a.

   Address (Number and street)

   b.

City or town	State	ZIP code

   c.

2. Establishment for which this report is filed. (Omit if same as label)

   a. Name of establishment

   d.

Address (Number and street)	City or Town	County	State	ZIP code

   e.

   b. Employer Identification No. (IRS 9-DIGIT TAX NUMBER)

   f.

   c. Was an EEO–1 report filed for this establishment last year? ☐ Yes ☐ No

Section C—EMPLOYERS WHO ARE REQUIRED TO FILE *(To be answered by all employers)*

☐ Yes ☐ No 1. Does the entire company have at least 100 employees in the payroll period for which you are reporting?

☐ Yes ☐ No 2. Is your company affiliated through common ownership and /or centralized management with other entities in an enterprise with a total employment of 100 or more?

☐ Yes ☐ No 3. Does the company or any of its establishments (a) have 50 or more employees AND (b) is not exempt as provided by 41 CFR 60-1.5, AND either (1) is a prime government contractor or first-tier subcontractor and has a contract, subcontract, or purchase order amounting to $50,000 or more, or (2) serves as a depository of Government funds in any amount or is a financial institution which is an issuing and paying agent for U.S. Savings Bonds and Savings Notes?
If the response to question C-3 is yes, please enter your Dun and Bradstreet identification number (it you have one): ☐☐☐☐☐☐☐☐☐

NOTE: If the answer is yes to questions 1, 2, or 3, complete the entire form, otherwise skip to Section G.

FIGURE 3.4

EEOC Form 100: Employer Information Report (continued)

Section D—EMPLOYMENT DATA

Employment at this establishment—Report all permanent full-time and part-time employees including apprentices and on-the-job trainees unless specifically excluded as set forth in the instructions. Enter the appropriate figures on all lines and in all columns. Blank spaces will be considered as zeros.

JOB CATEGORIES		OVERALL TOTALS (SUM OF COL. B THRU K)	MALE					FEMALE				
			WHITE (NOT OF HISPANIC ORIGIN)	BLACK (NOT OF HISPANIC ORIGIN)	HISPANIC	ASIAN OR PACIFIC ISLANDER	AMERICAN INDIAN OR ALASKAN NATIVE	WHITE (NOT OF HISPANIC ORIGIN)	BLACK (NOT OF HISPANIC ORIGIN)	HISPANIC	ASIAN OR PACIFIC ISLANDER	AMERICAN INDIAN OR ALASKAN NATIVE
		A	B	C	D	E	F	G	H	I	J	K
Officials and Managers	1											
Professionals	2											
Technicians	3											
Sales Workers	4											
Office and Clerical	5											
Craft Workers (Skilled)	6											
Operatives (Semi-Skilled)	7											
Laborers (Unskilled)	8											
Service Workers	9											
TOTAL	10											
Total employment reported in previous EEO–1 report	11											

NOTE: Omit questions 1 and 2 on the Consolidated Report.

1. Date(s) of payroll period used: 2. Does this establishment employ apprentices?   1 ☐ Yes   2 ☐ No

Section E—ESTABLISHMENT INFORMATION *(Omit on the Consolidated Report)*

1. What is the major activity of this establishment? (Be specific, i.e., manufacturing steel castings, retail grocer, wholesale plumbing supplies, title insurance, etc. Include the specific type of product or type of service provided, as well as the principal business or industrial activity.)

OFFICE USE ONLY

g.

Section F—REMARKS

Use this item to give any identification data appearing on last report which differs from that given above, explain major changes in composition of reporting units and other pertinent information.

Section G—CERTIFICATION *(See Instructions G)*

Check one
1 ☐ All reports are accurate and were prepared in accordance with the instructions (check on consolidated only).
2 ☐ This report is accurate and was prepared in accordance with the instructions.

Name of Certifying Official	Title	Signature	Date
Name of person to contact regarding this report (Type or print)	Address (Number and Street)		
Title	City and State	ZIP Code	Telephone Number (including Area Code)	Extension

All reports and information obtained from individual reports will be kept confidential as required by Section 709(e) of Title VII.
WILLFULLY FALSE STATEMENTS ON THIS REPORT ARE PUNISHABLE BY LAW, U.S. CODE, TITLE 18, SECTION 1001.

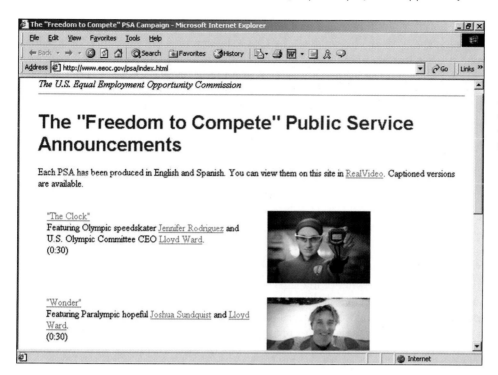

The EEOC's recent "Freedom to Compete" Olympics-related ad campaign illustrates their enforcement of equal opportunity and how individuals can succeed in business no matter their gender, physical abilities, or race.

tify ways an organization should develop and administer its system for selecting employees so as not to violate Title VII. The courts often refer to the *Uniform Guidelines* to determine whether a company has engaged in discriminatory conduct. Similarly, in the *Federal Register,* the EEOC has published guidelines providing details about what the agency will consider illegal and legal in the treatment of disabled individuals under the Americans with Disabilities Act.

Office of Federal Contract Compliance Procedures (OFCCP)

The **Office of Federal Contract Compliance Procedures (OFCCP)** is the agency responsible for enforcing the executive orders that cover companies doing business with the federal government. As we stated earlier in the chapter, businesses with contracts for more than $50,000 may not discriminate in employment based on race, color, religion, national origin, or sex, and they must have a written affirmative-action plan on file. This plan must include three basic components:

1. *Utilization analysis*—A comparison of the race, sex, and ethnic composition of the employer's workforce with that of the available labor supply. The percentages in the employer's workforce should not be greatly lower than the percentages in the labor supply.
2. *Goals and timetables*—The percentages of women and minorities the organization seeks to employ in each job group, and the dates by which the percentages are to be attained. These are meant to be more flexible than quotas, requiring only that the employer have goals and be seeking to achieve the goals.
3. *Action steps*—A plan for how the organization will meet its goals. Besides working toward its goals for hiring women and minorities, the company must take affirmative steps toward hiring Vietnam veterans and individuals with disabilities.

Office of Federal Contract Compliance Procedures (OFCCP)
The agency responsible for enforcing the executive orders that cover companies doing business with the federal government.

Each year, the OFCCP audits government contractors to ensure they are actively pursuing the goals in their plans. The OFCCP examines the plan and conducts on-site visits to examine how individual employees perceive the company's affirmative-action policies. If the agency finds that a contractor or subcontractor is not complying with the requirements, it has several options. It may notify the EEOC (if there is evidence of a violation of Title VII), advise the Department of Justice to begin criminal proceedings, request that the Secretary of Labor cancel or suspend any current contracts with the company, and forbid the firm from bidding on future contracts. For a company that depends on the federal government for a sizable share of its business, that last penalty is severe.

LO4

Businesses' Role in Providing for Equal Employment Opportunity

Rare is the business owner or manager who wants to wait for the government to identify that the business has failed to provide for equal employment opportunity. Instead, out of motives ranging from concern for fairness to the desire to avoid costly lawsuits and settlements, most companies recognize the importance of complying with these laws. Often, management depends on the expertise of human resource professionals to help in identifying how to comply. These professionals can help organizations take steps to avoid discrimination and provide reasonable accommodation.

Avoiding Discrimination

How would you know if you had been discriminated against? Decisions about human resources are so complex that discrimination is often difficult to identify and prove. However, legal scholars and court rulings have arrived at some ways to show evidence of discrimination.

Disparate Treatment

disparate treatment
Differing treatment of individuals, where the differences are based on the individuals' race, color, religion, sex, national origin, age, or disability status.

One sign of discrimination is **disparate treatment**—differing treatment of individuals, where the differences are based on the individuals' race, color, religion, sex, national origin, age, or disability status. For example, disparate treatment would include hiring or promoting one person over an equally qualified person because of the individual's race. Another instance of disparate treatment is the Outback Steakhouse example we saw earlier in which a man was paid twice as much as a woman to perform the same job. Or suppose a company fails to hire women with school-age children (claiming the women will be frequently absent) but hires men with school-age children. In that situation, the women are victims of disparate treatment, because they are being treated differently based on their sex. To sustain a claim of discrimination based on disparate treatment, the women would have to prove that the employer intended to discriminate.

To avoid disparate treatment, companies can evaluate the questions and investigations they use in making employment decisions. These should be applied equally. For example, if the company investigates conviction records of job applicants, it should investigate them for all applicants, not just for applicants from certain racial groups. Companies may want to avoid some types of questions altogether. For example, questions about marital status can cause problems, because interviewers may unfairly make different assumptions about men and women. (Common stereotypes about women have been that a married woman is less flexible or more likely to get pregnant than a single woman, in contrast to the assumption that a married man is more stable and committed to his work.)

Sometimes a company can develop a more appropriate approach by focusing on the job requirement behind or implied by a question it would rather not ask. At the Teachers' College of Columbia University in New York, interviewers avoid questions about candidates' child care arrangements. Instead, says Diane Dobry, director of communications for the college, the interviewers discuss the work schedule. Dobry explains, "We say there are evening hours and weekend hours, but we don't ask [candidates] how they'll manage it. It's up to them."[13]

Is disparate treatment ever legal? The courts have held that in some situations, a factor such as sex or race may be a **bona fide occupational qualification (BFOQ),** that is, a necessary (not merely preferred) qualification for performing a job. A typical example is a job that includes handing out towels in a locker room. Requiring that employees who perform this job in the women's locker room be female is a BFOQ. However, it is very difficult to think of many jobs where criteria such as sex and race are BFOQs. In a widely publicized case from the 1990s, Johnson Controls, a manufacturer of car batteries, instituted a "fetal protection" policy that excluded women of childbearing age from jobs that would expose them to lead, which can cause birth defects. Johnson Controls argued that the policy was intended to provide a safe workplace and that sex was a BFOQ for jobs that involved exposure to lead. However, the Supreme Court disagreed, ruling that BFOQs are limited to policies directly related to a worker's ability to do the job.[14]

bona fide occupational qualification (BFOQ)
A necessary (not merely preferred) qualification for performing a job.

Disparate Impact

Another way to measure discrimination is by identifying **disparate impact**—a condition in which employment practices are seemingly neutral yet disproportionately exclude a protected group from employment opportunities. In other words, the company's employment practices lack obvious discriminatory content, but they affect one group differently than others. A commonly used test of disparate impact is the **four-fifths rule,** which finds evidence of discrimination if the hiring rate for a minority group is less than four-fifths the hiring rate for the majority group. Keep in mind that this rule of thumb compares *rates* of hiring, not numbers of employees hired. Figure 3.5 illustrates how to apply the four-fifths rule.

An important distinction between disparate treatment and disparate impact is the role of the employer's intent. Proving disparate treatment in court requires showing that the employer intended the disparate treatment, but a plaintiff need not show intent in the case of disparate impact. It is enough to show that the result of the treatment was unequal. For example, the requirements for some jobs, such as firefighters or pilots, have sometimes included a minimum height. Although the intent may be to identify people who can perform the jobs, an unintended result may be disparate impact on groups that are shorter than average. Women, for example, tend to be shorter than men, and people of Asian ancestry tend to be shorter than people of European ancestry.

One way employers can avoid disparate impact is to be sure that employment decisions are really based on relevant, valid measurements. If a job requires a certain amount of strength and stamina, the employer would want measures of strength and stamina, not simply individuals' height and weight. The latter numbers are easier to

disparate impact
A condition in which employment practices are seemingly neutral yet disproportionately exclude a protected group from employment opportunities.

four-fifths rule
Rule of thumb that finds evidence of discrimination if an organization's hiring rate for a minority group is less than four-fifths the hiring rate for the majority group.

FIGURE 3.5

Applying the Four-Fifths Rule

Example: A new hotel has to hire employees to fill 100 positions. Out of 300 total applicants, 200 are black, and the remaining 100 are white. The hotel hires 40 of the black applicants and 60 of the white applicants.

Step 1: Find the Rates

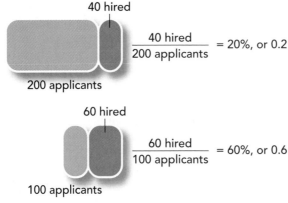

40 hired

$$\frac{40 \text{ hired}}{200 \text{ applicants}} = 20\%, \text{ or } 0.2$$

200 applicants

60 hired

$$\frac{60 \text{ hired}}{100 \text{ applicants}} = 60\%, \text{ or } 0.6$$

100 applicants

Step 2: Compare the Rates

$$\frac{0.2}{0.6} = 0.33 \qquad \frac{4}{5} = 0.8$$

$$0.33 < 0.8$$

The four-fifths requirement is not satisfied, and thus discrimination is proved.

obtain but more likely to result in charges of discrimination. Assessing validity of a measure can be a highly technical exercise requiring the use of statistics. The essence of such an assessment is to show that test scores or other measurements are significantly related to job performance.

EEO Policy

Employers can also avoid discrimination and defend against claims of discrimination by establishing and enforcing an EEO policy. The policy should define and prohibit unlawful behaviors, as well as provide procedures for making and investigating complaints. The policy also should require that employees at all levels engage in fair conduct and respectful language. Derogatory language can support a court claim of discrimination.

Affirmative Action and Reverse Discrimination

In the search for ways to avoid discrimination, some organizations have used affirmative-action programs, usually to increase the representation of minorities. In its original form, affirmative action was meant as taking extra effort to attract and retain minority employees. These efforts have included extensively recruiting minority candidates on college campuses, advertising in minority-oriented publications, and providing educational and training opportunities to minorities. However, over the years, many organizations have resorted to quotas, or numerical goals for the proportion of certain minority groups, to ensure that their workforce mirrors the proportions of the labor market. Sometimes these organizations act voluntarily; in other cases, the quotas are imposed by the courts or the EEOC.

Regina Genwright talks to a voice-activated copier at the American Foundation for the Blind. The copier has a Braille keyboard and wheelchair-accessible height. Equipment like this can help employers make reasonable accommodation for their disabled employees.

Whatever the reasons for these hiring programs, by increasing the proportion of minority or female candidates hired or promoted, they necessarily reduce the proportion of white or male candidates hired or promoted. In many cases, white and/or male individuals have fought against affirmative action and quotas, alleging what is called *reverse discrimination*. In other words, the organizations are allegedly discriminating against white males by preferring women and minorities. Affirmative action remains a controversial issue in the United States. Surveys have found that Americans are least likely to favor affirmative action when programs use quotas.[15]

Providing Reasonable Accommodation

Especially in situations involving religion and individuals with disabilities, equal employment opportunity may require that an employer make **reasonable accommodation.** In employment law, this term refers to an employer's obligation to do something to enable an otherwise qualified person to perform a job. Wal-Mart recently settled a number of lawsuits related to the Americans with Disabilities Act in which the company agreed to provide various accommodations, from letting an employee who worked as a People Greeter occasionally sit down to developing computer-based learning modules in American Sign Language for hearing-impaired employees.[16]

In the context of religion, this principle recognizes that for some individuals, religious observations and practices may present a conflict with work duties, dress codes, or company practices. For example, some religions require head coverings, or individuals might need time off to observe the sabbath or other holy days, when the company might have them scheduled to work. When the employee has a legitimate religious belief requiring accommodation, the employee should demonstrate this need to the employer. Assuming that it would not present an undue hardship, employers are required to accommodate such religious practices. They may have to adjust schedules so that employees do not have to work on days when their religion forbids it, or they may have to alter dress or grooming requirements.

For employees with disabilities, reasonable accommodations also vary according to the individuals' needs. As shown in Figure 3.6, employers may restructure jobs, make facilities in the workplace more accessible, modify equipment, or reassign an employee to a job that the person can perform. In some situations, a disabled individual may provide his or her own accommodation, which the employer allows, as in the case of a blind worker who brings a guide dog to work.

If accommodating a disability would require significant expense or difficulty, however, the employer may be exempt from the reasonable accommodation requirement (although the employer may have to defend this position in court). An accommodation

reasonable accommodation
An employer's obligation to do something to enable an otherwise qualified person to perform a job.

FIGURE 3.6

Examples of Reasonable Accommodations under the ADA

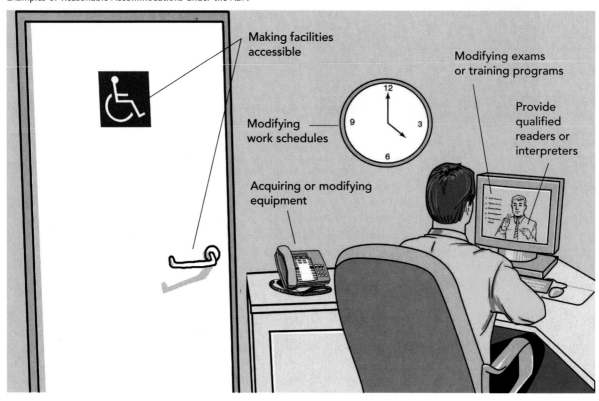

Note: Reasonable accommodations do *not* include hiring an unqualified person, lowering quality standards, or compromising coworkers' safety.

SOURCE: Equal Employment Opportunity Commission, "The ADA: Questions and Answers," www.eeoc.gov, January 15, 1997.

is considered "reasonable" if it does not impose an undue hardship on the employer, such as an expense that is large in relation to a company's resources.

LO5

sexual harassment
Unwelcome sexual advances as defined by the EEOC.

Preventing Sexual Harassment

Based on Title VII's prohibition of sex discrimination, the EEOC defines sexual harassment of employees as unlawful employment discrimination. **Sexual harassment** refers to unwelcome sexual advances. The EEOC has defined the types of behavior and the situations under which this behavior constitutes sexual harassment:

> Unwelcome sexual advances, requests for sexual favors, and other verbal or physical contact of a sexual nature constitute sexual harassment when
>
> 1. Submission to such conduct is made either explicitly or implicitly a term of condition of an individual's employment,
> 2. Submission to or rejection of such conduct by an individual is used as the basis for employment decisions affecting such individual, or
> 3. Such conduct has the purpose or effect of unreasonably interfering with an individual's work performance or creating an intimidating, hostile, or offensive working environment.[17]

Under these guidelines, preventing sexual discrimination includes managing the workplace in a way that does not tolerate anybody's threatening or intimidating employees through sexual behavior.

In general, the most obvious examples of sexual harassment involve *quid pro quo harassment,* meaning that a person makes a benefit (or punishment) contingent on an employee's submitting to (or rejecting) sexual advances. For example, a manager who promises a raise to an employee who will participate in sexual activities is engaging in quid pro quo harassment. Likewise, it would be sexual harassment to threaten to reassign someone to a less desirable job if that person refuses sexual favors.

A more subtle, and possibly more pervasive, form of sexual harassment is to create or permit a "hostile working environment." This occurs when someone's behavior in the workplace creates an environment in which it is difficult for someone of a particular sex to work. Common complaints in sexual harassment lawsuits include claims that harassers ran their fingers through the plaintiffs' hair, made suggestive remarks, touched intimate body parts, posted pictures with sexual content in the workplace, and used sexually explicit language or told sex-related jokes. The reason that these behaviors are considered discrimination is that they treat individuals differently based on their sex.

Although a large majority of sexual harassment complaints received by the EEOC involve women being harassed by men, sexual harassment can affect anyone. Men have filed complaints that they were harassed by women, and in at least one case, a male employee won a lawsuit claiming sexual harassment by his male boss.[18]

To ensure a workplace free from sexual harassment, organizations can follow some important steps. First, the organization can develop a policy statement making it very clear that sexual harassment will not be tolerated in the workplace. Second, all employees, new and old, can be trained to identify inappropriate workplace behavior. In addition, the organization can develop a mechanism for reporting sexual harassment in a way that encourages people to speak out. Finally, management can prepare to act promptly to discipline those who engage in sexual harassment, as well as to protect the victims of sexual harassment.

Valuing Diversity

As we mentioned in Chapter 2, the United States is a diverse nation, and becoming more so. In addition, many U.S. companies have customers and operations in more than one country. Managers differ in how they approach the challenges related to this diversity. Some define a diverse workforce as a competitive advantage that brings them a wider pool of talent and greater insight into the needs and behaviors of their diverse customers. These organizations say they have a policy of *valuing diversity.*

The practice of valuing diversity has no single form; it is not written into law or business theory. Organizations that value diversity may practice some form of affirmative action, discussed earlier. They may have policies stating their value of understanding and respecting differences. Wal-Mart's website includes a statement that reinforces the company's folksy image along with its policy with regard to diversity: "All kinds of people work and shop at Wal-Mart—and we like it that way."[19] Organizations may try to hire, reward, and promote employees who demonstrate respect for others. They may sponsor training programs designed to teach employees about differences among groups. Whatever their form, these efforts are intended to make each individual feel respected. Also, these actions can support equal employment opportunity by cultivating an environment in which individuals feel welcome and able to do their best.

Occupational Safety and Health Act (OSH Act)
U.S. law authorizing the federal government to establish and enforce occupational safety and health standards for all places of employment engaging in interstate commerce.

Occupational Safety and Health Act (OSH Act)

Like equal employment opportunity, the protection of employee safety and health is regulated by the government. Through the 1960s, workplace safety was primarily an issue between workers and employers. By 1970, however, roughly 15,000 work-related fatalities occurred every year. That year, Congress enacted the **Occupational Safety and Health Act (OSH Act),** the most comprehensive U.S. law regarding worker safety. The OSH Act authorized the federal government to establish and enforce occupational safety and health standards for all places of employment engaging in interstate commerce.

The OSH Act divided enforcement responsibilities between the Department of Labor and the Department of Health. Under the Department of Labor, the **Occupational Safety and Health Administration (OSHA)** is responsible for inspecting employers, applying safety and health standards, and levying fines for violation. The Department of Health is responsible for conducting research to determine the criteria for specific operations or occupations and for training employers to comply with the act. Much of the research is conducted by the National Institute for Occupational Safety and Health (NIOSH).

Occupational Safety and Health Administration (OSHA)
Labor Department agency responsible for inspecting employers, applying safety and health standards, and levying fines for violation.

General and Specific Duties

The main provision of the OSH Act states that each employer has a general duty to furnish each employee a place of employment free from recognized hazards that cause or are likely to cause death or serious physical harm. This is called the act's *general-duty clause.* Employers also must keep records of work-related injuries and illnesses and post an annual summary of these records from February 1 to April 30 in the following year. Figure 3.7 shows a sample of OSHA's Form 300A, the annual summary that must be posted, even if no injuries or illnesses occurred.

The act also grants specific rights; for example, employees have the right to:

- Request an inspection.
- Have a representative present at an inspection.
- Have dangerous substances identified.
- Be promptly informed about exposure to hazards and be given access to accurate records regarding exposure.
- Have employer violations posted at the work site.

The nearby "HR How To" box summarizes key points from OSHA's guidance on how new companies can ensure that they follow *these requirements.*

The Department of Labor recognizes many specific types of hazards, and employers must comply with all the occupational safety and health standards published by NIOSH. NIOSH has, for instance, determined that a noise level of 85 decibels (comparable to the noise of heavy city traffic) is potentially dangerous. A person exposed to this much noise over a long enough period of time could experience hearing loss as a result. Researchers in San Francisco measured noise levels at five local restaurants and found that the levels reached 85 decibels and often reached 105 decibels. Such levels could be a health risk for waiters working in the restaurant for eight hours at a time. Employers could respond in a number of ways, from permitting ear plugs to educating workers to reconsidering restaurant design (large bars, open kitchens, and high ceilings are a number of features that intensify noise levels).[20]

FIGURE 3.7

OSHA Form 300A: Summary of Work-Related Injuries and Illnesses

OSHA's Form 300A

Summary of Work-Related Injuries and Illnesses

Year 20___ ___

U.S. Department of Labor
Occupational Safety and Health Administration

Form approved OMB no. 1218-0176

All establishments covered by Part 1904 must complete this Summary page, even if no work-related injuries or illnesses occurred during the year. Remember to review the Log to verify that the entries are complete and accurate before completing this summary.

Using the Log, count the individual entries you made for each category. Then write the totals below, making sure you've added the entries from every page of the Log. If you had no cases, write "0."

Employees, former employees, and their representatives have the right to review the OSHA Form 300 in its entirety. They also have limited access to the OSHA Form 301 or its equivalent. See 29 CFR Part 1904.35, in OSHA's recordkeeping rule, for further details on the access provisions for these forms.

Number of Cases

Total number of deaths	Total number of cases with days away from work	Total number of cases with job transfer or restriction	Total number of other recordable cases
______ (G)	______ (H)	______ (I)	______ (J)

Number of Days

Total number of days of job transfer or restriction	Total number of days away from work
______ (K)	______ (L)

Injury and Illness Types

Total number of . . .
(M)

(1) Injuries ______

(2) Skin disorders ______

(3) Respiratory conditions ______

(4) Poisonings ______

(5) All other illnesses ______

Post this Summary page from February 1 to April 30 of the year following the year covered by the form.

Public reporting burden for this collection of information is estimated to average 50 minutes per response, including time to review the instructions, search and gather the data needed, and complete and review the collection of information. Persons are not required to respond to the collection of information unless it displays a currently valid OMB control number. If you have any comments about these estimates or any other aspects of this data collection, contact: US Department of Labor, OSHA Office of Statistics, Room N-3644, 200 Constitution Avenue, NW, Washington, DC 20210. Do not send the completed forms to this office.

Establishment information

Your establishment name ______________________

Street ______________________

City ______________ State ____ ZIP ______

Industry description (*e.g., Manufacture of motor truck trailers*)

____

Standard Industrial Classification (SIC), if known (*e.g., SIC 3715*)

__ __ __ __

Employment information *(If you don't have these figures, see the Worksheet on the back of this page to estimate.)*

Annual average number of employees ______

Total hours worked by all employees last year ______

Sign here

Knowingly falsifying this document may result in a fine.

I certify that I have examined this document and that to the best of my knowledge the entries are true, accurate, and complete.

______________________ Company executive ______ Title

( ) ______________ Phone / / Date

Off to a Safe Start

Starting a new business usually entails long hours for the owners and managers. It's no wonder, when you think of all the issues involved—raising money, finding a place to work, crafting the details of a business plan, hiring all the employees. And regardless of whether the business will manufacture goods or consist entirely of office workers, the government expects that the owners will address health and safety issues from the very start.

OSHA regulations have a (sometimes justifiable) reputation for being complex and difficult to follow. Fortunately, the agency has prepared materials designed to help businesses, including start-ups, succeed. A good place to begin is to call the local OSHA office or visit the agency's website (www.osha.gov) and download the OSHA Fact Sheet titled "OSHA Help for New Businesses." This fact sheet provides a basic summary of employers' duties and information about where to get more detailed help.

When planning the setup of operations, new-business owners can begin to identify potential hazards. Can any of these be avoided? Avoiding hazards may be as simple as arranging rooms so that electrical cords do not cause accidents. Under the OSH Act, these basic concerns are a legal requirement. Employers also must display OSHA's Safe and Healthful Workplaces poster in a location where it is conspicuous to employees and job candidates. The poster provides information about employees' rights and responsibilities under the OSH Act.

New-business owners also must obtain copies of OSHA's Log of Work-Related Injuries and Illnesses. Recording any work-related injuries and illnesses on the log is another duty under the OSH Act. (Some businesses, such as employers in many services industries, are exempt, however.)

Employers can get guidance and training at OSHA area offices. They may request free and confidential on-site consultations to help them identify and correct hazards. Several OSHA training centers conduct courses related to worker safety and health. At the OSHA website, employers can also download interactive training materials on general and specific topics related to occupational safety and health.

By getting off to a safe start, employers help to create an environment in which employees recognize safety and health as important values of the organization.

SOURCE: Occupational Safety and Health Administration, "OSHA Help for New Businesses," OSHA Fact Sheet (2002); OSHA website, www.osha.gov, February 19, 2002.

Although NIOSH publishes numerous standards, it is clearly impossible for regulators to anticipate all possible hazards that could occur in the workplace. Thus, the general-duty clause requires employers to be constantly alert for potential sources of harm in the workplace (as defined by the standard of what a reasonably prudent person would do) and to correct them. For example, managers at Amoco's plant in Joliet, Illinois, realized that over the years some employees had created undocumented shortcuts and built them into their process for handling flammable materials. These changes appeared to be labor saving but created a problem: workers did not have uniform procedures for dealing with flammable products. This became an urgent issue because many of the experienced workers were reaching retirement age, and the plant

You Have a Right to a Safe
and Healthful Workplace.

IT'S THE LAW!

- You have the right to notify your employer or OSHA about workplace hazards. You may ask OSHA to keep your name confidential.
- You have the right to request an OSHA inspection if you believe that there are unsafe and unhealthful conditions in your workplace. You or your representative may participate in the inspection.
- You can file a complaint with OSHA within 30 days of discrimination by your employer for making safety and health complaints or for exercising your rights under the *OSH Act*.
- You have a right to see OSHA citations issued to your employer. Your employer must post the citations at or near the place of the alleged violation.
- Your employer must correct workplace hazards by the date indicated on the citation and must certify that these hazards have been reduced or eliminated.
- You have the right to copies of your medical records or records of your exposure to toxic and harmful substances or conditions.
- Your employer must post this notice in your workplace.

The *Occupational Safety and Health Act of 1970 (OSH Act)*, P.L. 91-596, assures safe and healthful working conditions for working men and women throughout the Nation. The Occupational Safety and Health Administration, in the U.S. Department of Labor, has the primary responsibility for administering the *OSH Act*. The rights listed here may vary depending on the particular circumstances. To file a complaint, report an emergency, or seek OSHA advice, assistance, or products, call 1-800-321-OSHA or your nearest OSHA office: • Atlanta (404) 562-2300 • Boston (617) 565-9860 • Chicago (312) 353-2220 • Dallas (214) 767-4731 • Denver (303) 844-1600 • Kansas City (816) 426-5861 • New York (212) 337-2378 • Philadelphia (215) 861-4900 • San Francisco (415) 975-4310 • Seattle (206) 553-5930. Teletypewriter (TTY) number is 1-877-889-5627. To file a complaint online or obtain more information on OSHA federal and state programs, visit OSHA's website at www.osha.gov. If your workplace is in a state operating under an OSHA-approved plan, your employer must post the required state equivalent of this poster.

1-800-321-OSHA
www.osha.gov

U.S. Department of Labor   •   Occupational Safety and Health Administration   •   OSHA 3165

OSHA is responsible for inspecting businesses, applying safety and health standards, and levying fines for violations. OSHA regulations prohibit notifying employers of inspections in advance.

was in danger of losing critical technical expertise. To solve this problem, the plant adopted a training program that met all the standards required by OSHA. It conducted a needs analysis that highlighted each task new employees had to learn, and it documented all these processes in written guidelines. The company gave new employees hands-on training in the new procedures, after which their supervisor certified them in writing. The plant installed a computer tracking system to monitor who was handling flammable materials, and the system immediately identified anyone who was not certified. The plant uses the same approach to safety training in other areas.[21]

Enforcement of the OSH Act

To enforce the OSH Act, the Occupational Safety and Health Administration conducts inspections. OSHA compliance officers typically arrive at a workplace unannounced; for obvious reasons, OSHA regulations prohibit notifying employers of inspections in advance. After presenting credentials, the compliance officer tells the employer the reasons for the inspection and describes, in a general way, the procedures necessary to conduct the investigation.

An OSHA inspection has four major components. First, the compliance officer reviews the company's records of deaths, injuries, and illnesses. OSHA requires this kind of record keeping at all firms with 11 or more full- or part-time employees. Next, the officer—typically accompanied by a representative of the employer (and perhaps by a representative of the employees)—conducts a "walkaround" tour of the employer's premises. On this tour, the officer notes any conditions that may violate specific published standards or the less specific general-duty clause. The third component of the inspection, employee interviews, may take place during the tour. At this time, anyone who is aware of a violation can bring it to the officer's attention. Finally, in a closing conference, the compliance officer discusses the findings with the employer, noting any violations.

Following an inspection, OSHA gives the employer a reasonable time frame within which to correct the violations identified. If a violation could cause serious injury or death, the officer may seek a restraining order from a U.S. District Court. The restraining order compels the employer to correct the problem immediately. In addition, if an OSHA violation results in citations, the employer must post each citation in a prominent place near the location of the violation.

Besides correcting violations identified during the inspection, employers may have to pay fines. These fines range from $20,000 for violations that result in death of an employee to $1,000 for less serious violations. Other penalties include criminal charges for falsifying records that are subject to OSHA inspection or for warning an employer of an OSHA inspection without permission from the Department of Labor.

Employee Rights and Responsibilities

Although the OSH Act makes employers responsible for protecting workers from safety and health hazards, employees have responsibilities as well. They have to follow OSHA's safety rules and regulations governing employee behavior. Employees also have a duty to report hazardous conditions.

right-to-know laws
State laws that require employers to provide employees with information about the health risks associated with exposure to substances considered hazardous.

Along with those responsibilities go certain rights. Employees may file a complaint and request an OSHA inspection of the workplace, and their employers may not retaliate against them for complaining. Employees also have a right to receive information about any hazardous chemicals they handle in the course of their jobs. OSHA's Hazard Communication Standard and many states' **right-to-know laws** require employers to provide employees with information about the health risks associated with exposure to substances considered hazardous. State right-to-know laws may be more stringent than federal standards, so organizations should obtain requirements from their state's health and safety agency, as well as from OSHA.

material safety data sheets (MSDSs)
Forms on which chemical manufacturers and importers identify the hazards of their chemicals.

Under OSHA's Hazard Communication Standard, organizations must have **material safety data sheets (MSDSs)** for chemicals that employees are exposed to. An MSDS is a form that details the hazards associated with a chemical; the chemical's producer or importer is responsible for identifying these hazards and detailing them on the form. Employers must also ensure that all containers of hazardous chemicals are labeled with information about the hazards, and they must train employees in safe handling of the chemicals. Office workers who encounter a chemical infrequently (such as a secretary who occasionally changes the toner in a copier) are not covered by these requirements. In the case of a copy machine, the Hazard Communication

Incidences per 100 Full-Time Workers

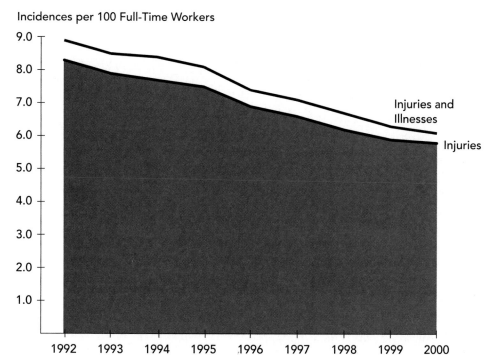

FIGURE 3.8

Rates of Occupational
Injuries and Illnesses

Note: Data do not include fatal work-related injuries and illnesses.
SOURCE: Occupational Safety and Health Administration, www.osha.gov, February 19, 2002.

Standard would apply to someone whose job involves spending a large part of the day servicing or operating such equipment.

Impact of the OSH Act

The OSH Act has unquestionably succeeded in raising the level of awareness of occupational safety. Yet legislation alone cannot solve all the problems of work site safety. Indeed, the rate of occupational illnesses more than doubled between 1985 and 1990, according to the Bureau of Labor Statistics, while the rate of injuries rose by about 8 percent. However, as depicted in Figure 3.8, both rates showed an overall downward trend during the 1990s.[22]

Many industrial accidents are a product of unsafe behaviors, not unsafe working conditions. Because the act does not directly regulate employee behavior, little behavior change can be expected unless employees are convinced of the standards' importance.[23] This principle has been recognized by labor leaders. For example, Lynn Williams, president of the United Steelworkers of America, has noted, "We can't count on government. We can't count on employers. We must rely on ourselves to bring about the safety and health of our workers."[24]

Because conforming to the law alone does not necessarily guarantee their employees will be safe, many employers go beyond the letter of the law. In the next section we examine various kinds of employer-initiated safety awareness programs that comply with OSHA requirements and, in some cases, exceed them.

LO8

Employer-Sponsored Safety and Health Programs

Many employers establish safety awareness programs to go beyond mere compliance with the OSH Act and attempt to instill an emphasis on safety. A safety awareness program has three primary components: identifying and communicating hazards, reinforcing safe practices, and promoting safety internationally.

Identifying and Communicating Job Hazards

job hazard analysis technique
Safety promotion technique that involves breaking down a job into basic elements, then rating each element for its potential for harm or injury.

Employees, supervisors, and other knowledgeable sources need to sit down and discuss potential problems related to safety. One method for doing this is the **job hazard analysis technique**.[25] With this technique, each job is broken down into basic elements, and each of these is rated for its potential for harm or injury. If there is agreement that some job element has high hazard potential, the group isolates the element and considers possible technological or behavior changes to reduce or eliminate the hazard.

technic of operations review (TOR)
Method of promoting safety by determining which specific element of a job led to a past accident.

Another means of isolating unsafe job elements is to study past accidents. The **technic of operations review (TOR)** is an analysis method for determining which specific element of a job led to a past accident.[26] The first step in a TOR analysis is to establish the facts surrounding the incident. To accomplish this, all members of the work group involved in the accident give their initial impressions of what happened. The group must then, through discussion, come to an agreement on the single, systematic failure that most likely contributed to the incident, as well as two or three major secondary factors that contributed to it.

An analysis of jobs at Burger King, for example, revealed that certain jobs required employees to walk across wet or slippery surfaces, which led to many falls. Specific corrective action was taken based on analysis of where people were falling and what conditions led to those falls. Now Burger King provides mats at critical locations and has generally upgraded its floor maintenance. The company also makes slip-resistant shoes available to employees in certain job categories.[27]

To communicate with employees about job hazards, managers should talk directly with their employees about safety. Memos also are important, because the written communication helps establish a "paper trail" that can later document a history of the employer's concern regarding the job hazard. Posters, especially if placed near the hazard, serve as a constant reminder, reinforcing other messages.

In communicating risk, managers should recognize that different groups of individuals may constitute different audiences. Research by the National Safety Council indicates that 40 percent of accidents happen to individuals in the 20-to-29 age group and that 48 percent of accidents happen to workers during their first year on the job.[28] The employer's primary concern with respect to younger workers is to inform them. Training should include specific information about safe procedures, first aid, and any protective equipment related to the job.

Experienced employees need retraining to jar them from complacency about the real dangers associated with their work.[29] This is especially the case if the hazard in question poses a greater threat to older employees. For example, accidents that involve falling off a ladder are a greater threat to older workers than to younger ones. Over 20 percent of such falls lead to a fatality for workers in the 55-to-65 age group, compared with 10 percent for all other workers.[30]

Reinforcing Safe Practices

To ensure safe behaviors, employers should not only define how to work safely but reinforce the desired behavior. One common technique for reinforcing safe practices is implementing a safety incentive program to reward workers for their support of and commitment to safety goals. Such programs start by focusing on monthly or quarterly goals or by encouraging suggestions for improving safety. Possible goals might include good housekeeping practices, adherence to safety rules, and proper use of protective equipment. Later, the program expands to include more wide-ranging, long-term goals. Typically, the employer distributes prizes in highly public forums, such as company or department meetings. Using merchandise for prizes, instead of cash, provides a lasting symbol of achievement. A good deal of evidence suggests that such incentive programs are effective in reducing the number and cost of injuries.[31]

Besides focusing on specific jobs, organizations can target particular types of injuries or disabilities, especially those for which employees may be at risk. For example, the National Society to Prevent Blindness estimates that 1,000 eye injuries occur every day in occupational settings.[32] Organizations can prevent such injuries through a combination of job analysis, written policies, safety training, protective eyewear, rewards and sanctions for safe and unsafe behavior, and management support for the safety effort. Similar practices for preventing other types of injuries are available in trade publications, through the National Safety Council, and on the website of the Occupational Safety and Health Administration (www.osha.gov).

Promoting Safety Internationally

Given the increasing focus on international management, organizations also need to consider how to ensure the safety of their employees regardless of the nation in which they operate. Cultural differences may make this more difficult than it seems. For example, a study examined the impact of one standardized corporationwide safety policy on employees in three different countries: the United States, France, and Argentina. The results of this study indicate that employees in the three countries interpreted the policy differently because of cultural differences. The individualistic, control-oriented culture of the United States stressed the role of top management in ensuring safety in a top-down fashion. However, this policy failed to work in Argentina, where the culture is more "collectivist" (emphasizing the group). Argentine employees tend to feel that safety is everyone's joint concern, so the safety programs needed to be defined from the bottom of the organization up.[33]

Summary

1. Explain how the three branches of government regulate human resource management.
   The legislative branch develops laws such as those governing equal employment opportunity and worker safety and health. The executive branch establishes agencies such as the Equal Employment Opportunity Commission and Occupational Safety and Health Administration to enforce the laws by publishing regulations, filing lawsuits, and other activities. The president may also issue executive orders, such as requirements for federal contractors. The judicial branch hears cases related to employment law and interprets the law.

2. Summarize the major federal laws requiring equal employment opportunity.
   The Civil Rights Acts of 1866 and 1871 granted all persons equal property rights, contract rights, and the right to sue in federal court if they have been deprived of civil rights. The Equal Pay Act of 1963 requires

equal pay for men and women who are doing work that is equal in terms of skill, effort, responsibility, and working conditions. Title VII of the Civil Rights Act of 1964 prohibits employment discrimination on the basis of race, color, religion, sex, or national origin. The Age Discrimination in Employment Act prohibits employment discrimination against persons older than 40. The Vocational Rehabilitation Act of 1973 requires that federal contractors engage in affirmative action in the employment of persons with disabilities. The Vietnam Era Veteran's Readjustment Act of 1974 requires affirmative action in employment of veterans who served during the Vietnam War. The Pregnancy Discrimination Act of 1978 treats discrimination based on pregnancy-related conditions as illegal sex discrimination. The Americans with Disabilities Act requires reasonable accommodations for qualified workers with disabilities. The Civil Rights Act of 1991 provides for compensatory and punitive damages in cases of discrimination. The Uniformed Services Employment and Reemployment Rights Act of 1994 requires that employers reemploy service members who left jobs to fulfill military duties.

3. Identify the federal agencies that enforce equal employment opportunity, and describe the role of each.
The Equal Employment Opportunity Commission is responsible for enforcing most of the EEO laws, including Title VII and the Americans with Disabilities Act. It investigates and resolves complaints, gathers information, and issues guidelines. The Office of Federal Contract Compliance Procedures is responsible for enforcing executive orders that call for affirmative action by companies that do business with the federal government. It monitors affirmative-action plans and takes action against companies that fail to comply.

4. Describe ways employers can avoid illegal discrimination and provide reasonable accommodation.
Employers can avoid discrimination by avoiding disparate treatment of job applicants and employees, as well as policies that result in disparate impact. Companies can develop and enforce an EEO policy coupled with policies and practices that demonstrate a high value placed on diversity. Affirmative action may correct past discrimination, but quota-based activities can result in charges of reverse discrimination. To provide reasonable accommodation, companies should recog-

nize needs based on individuals' religion or disabilities. Employees may need to make such accommodations as adjusting schedules or dress codes, making the workplace more accessible, or restructuring jobs.

5. Define sexual harassment and tell how employers can eliminate or minimize it.
Sexual harassment is unwelcome sexual advances and related behavior that makes submitting to the conduct a term of employment or the basis for employment decisions, or that interferes with an individual's work performance or creates a work environment that is intimidating, hostile, or offensive. Organizations can prevent sexual harassment by developing a policy that defines and forbids it, training employees to recognize and avoid this behavior, and providing a means for employees to complain and be protected.

6. Explain employers' duties under the Occupational Safety and Health Act.
Under the Occupational Safety and Health Act, employers have a general duty to provide employees a place of employment free from recognized safety and health hazards. They must inform employees about hazardous substances, maintain and post records of accidents and illnesses, and comply with NIOSH standards about specific occupational hazards.

7. Describe the role of the Occupational Safety and Health Administration.
The Occupational Safety and Health Administration publishes regulations and conducts inspections. If OSHA finds violations, it discusses them with the employer and monitors the employer's response in correcting the violation.

8. Discuss ways employers promote worker safety and health.
Besides complying with OSHA regulations, employers often establish safety awareness programs designed to instill an emphasis on safety. They may identify and communicate hazards through the job hazard analysis technique or the technic of operations review. They may adapt communications and training to the needs of different employees, such as differences in experience levels or cultural differences from one country to another. Employers may also establish incentive programs to reward safe behavior.

Review and Discussion Questions

1. What is the role of each branch of the federal government with regard to equal employment opportunity?

2. For each of the following situations, identify one or more constitutional amendments, laws, or executive orders that might apply.

a. A veteran of the Vietnam conflict experiences lower-back pain after sitting for extended periods of time. He has applied for promotion to a supervisory position that has traditionally involved spending most of the workday behind a desk.

b. One of two female workers on a road construction crew complains to her supervisor that she feels uncomfortable during breaks, because the other employees routinely tell off-color jokes.

c. A manager at an architectural firm receives a call from the local newspaper. The reporter wonders how the firm wishes to respond to calls from two of its employees alleging racial discrimination. About half of the firm's employees (including all of its partners and most of its architects) are white. One of the firm's clients is the federal government.

3. For each situation in the preceding question, what actions, if any, should the organization take?

4. The Americans with Disabilities Act requires that employers make reasonable accommodations for individuals with disabilities. How might this requirement affect law enforcement officers and fire fighters?

5. To identify instances of sexual harassment, the courts may use a "reasonable woman" standard of what constitutes offensive behavior. This standard is based on the idea that women and men have different ideas of what behavior is appropriate. What are the implications of this distinction? Do you think this distinction is helpful or harmful? Why?

6. Given that the "reasonable woman" standard referred to in Question 5 is based on women's ideas of what is appropriate, how might an organization with mostly male employees identify and avoid behavior that could be found to be sexual harassment?

7. What are an organization's basic duties under the Occupational Safety and Health Act?

8. OSHA penalties are aimed at employers, rather than employees. How does this affect employee safety?

9. How can organizations motivate employees to promote safety and health in the workplace?

10. For each of the following occupations, identify at least one possible hazard and at least one action employers could take to minimize the risk of an injury or illness related to that hazard.

a. Worker in a fast-food restaurant

b. Computer programmer

c. Truck driver

d. House painter

What's Your HR IQ?

The Student CD-ROM offers two more ways to check what you've learned so far. Use the Self-Assessment exercise to test your knowledge of equal employment opportunity. Go online with the Web Exercise to see how well your knowledge of safety issues works in cyberspace.

BusinessWeek Case

BusinessWeek Racism in the Workplace

When Wayne A. Elliott was transferred in 1996 from a factory job to a warehouse at Lockheed Martin Corporation's sprawling military aircraft production facilities in Marietta, Georgia, he says he found himself face to face with naked racism. Anti-black graffiti were scrawled on the restroom walls. His new white colleagues harassed him, Elliott recalls, as did his manager, who would yell at him, call him "boy," and tell him to "kiss my butt." He complained, but Elliott says the supervisor was no help. Instead he assigned Elliott, now 46, to collecting parts to be boxed, which involves walking about 10 miles a day. Meanwhile, the eight whites in his job category sat at computer terminals and told him to get a move on—even though Elliott outranked them on the union seniority list.

The atmosphere got even uglier when Elliott and a few other blacks formed a small group in 1997 called Workers Against Discrimination, which led to the filing of two class actions. One day, he and the other two black men among the 30 warehouse workers found "back-to-Africa tickets" on their desks. They reported this, but the Lockheed security officials who responded took the three victims away in their security cars as if they were the wrongdoers, he says, and interrogated them separately.

Then, one day in 1999, according to Elliott, a hangman's noose appeared near his desk. "You're going to end up with your head in here," Elliott recalls a white coworker threatening. Another noose appeared last November, Elliott says. The white coworker and the other whites "hassle me all the time now, unplugging my computer so I lose work, hiding my bike or chair; it's constant," says Elliott, who gets counseling from a psychologist for the stress and says he has trouble being attentive to his two children, ages 7 and 8, when he's at home.

Racial hatred is not confined to small southern cities

such as Marietta. In addition to high-profile suits at Lockheed, Boeing, and Texaco, dozens of other household names face complaints of racism in their workforce. Noose cases have been prosecuted in cosmopolitan San Francisco and in Detroit, with a black population among the largest in the nation.

It's true that minorities' share of the workforce grew over the decade, which could have led to a corresponding rise in clashes. Yet racial harassment charges have jumped by 100 percent since 1990, while minority employment grew by 36 percent. What's more, most charges involve multiple victims, so each year the cases add up to tens of thousands of workers—mostly blacks, but also Hispanics and Asians.

It's hard to reconcile such ugly episodes with an American culture that is more accepting of its increasing diversity than ever before. To some extent, the rise in harassment cases may actually reflect America's improved race relations. Because more minorities believe that society won't tolerate blatant bigotry any more, they file EEOC charges rather than keep quiet out of despair that their complaints won't be heard, says Susan Sturm, a Columbia University law professor who studies workplace discrimination. Many cases involve allegations of harassment that endured for years.

But many experts say they are seeing a disturbing increase in incidents of harassment. Minority workers endure the oldest racial slurs in the book. They're asked if they eat "monkey meat," denigrated as inferior to whites, or find "KKK" and other intimidating graffiti on the walls at work.

Worse yet are hangman's nooses, a potent symbol of mob lynchings in America's racist history. The EEOC has handled 25 noose cases in the past 18 months, "something that only came along every two or three years before," says Ida L. Castro, outgoing EEOC chairwoman. Management lawyers concur that racial harassment has jumped sharply. "I've seen more of these cases in the last few years than in the previous 10, and it's bad stuff," says Steve Poor, a partner at Seyfarth, Shaw, Fairweather & Geraldson, a law firm that helps companies defend harassment and discrimination suits.

Because racial harassment allegations can be embarrassing, they pose a difficult challenge for companies. Some quickly go on the offensive and take steps to change. Other employers hunker down for a fight, arguing that allegations are inaccurate or exaggerated. Northwest Airlines Corporation is fighting charges made by black construction workers who found a noose last July at the airline's new terminal at Detroit Metro Airport. Northwest also recently settled two noose-related suits, although it denied liability. Northwest spokeswoman Kathleen M. Peach says the noose incidents do not "rise to the level of harassment. You have to ask was it a joke at a construction site? Or was it in a cargo area where a lot of ropes are used? It's not as cut-and-dried as it seems."

In the end, racist behavior by employees lands at the door of corporate executives. Until more employers confront the rise of ugly racism head on, Americans will continue to see behavior they thought belonged to a more ignominious age and lawsuits in response to it.

SOURCE: *BusinessWeek* online, www.businessweek.com, October 23, 2001.

Questions

1. Do you think racism still exists in the workplace? Why or why not?
2. What can organizations do to ensure that racism does not pervade their workplaces?

Case: Home Depot's Bumpy Road to Equality

Home Depot is the largest U.S. home products firm, selling home repair products for the do-it-yourselfer. Founded 20 years ago, the company now boasts 100,000 employees and more than 500 warehouse stores throughout the United States. Home Depot's success is based on the dual strategies of building stores within a half-hour's drive of every U.S. customer and providing superior service. To achieve its goals for service quality, the company hires people who are knowledgeable about home repair and can teach customers how to do home repairs.

Along the way, however, Home Depot has run into some legal problems. During the company's growth, hiring followed a clear pattern: Of the merchandise employees (those directly involved in selling lumber, electrical supplies, hardware, and other merchandise), about 70 percent are men. In contrast, of the operations employees (cashiers, accountants, back-office staff, and others), about 70 percent are women. Because of this difference, several years ago a lawsuit was filed on behalf of 17,000 current and former employees, as well as up to 200,000 job applicants who were not hired. According to the lawsuit, Home Depot's pattern of hiring reinforced stereotypes about men and women.

Home Depot explained the disparity in hiring in terms of work experience. The company said most female job applicants had experience as cashiers, so the company placed them in cashier positions. In contrast, most male applicants expressed an interest in or aptitude for home repair work, such as carpentry or plumbing, so the company put them to work selling related products.

Along with sex discrimination, Home Depot has separately been charged with race discrimination. Five former

Home Depot employees sued the company, charging that it had discriminated against African-American workers at two stores in southeast Florida. The five plaintiffs alleged they were paid less than white workers at the stores, passed over for promotion, and received critical performance reviews based on their race. Home Depot spokesman Jerry Shields responds, "The company takes exception to the charges and believes they are without merit." However, the company has faced other racial discrimination suits as well, including one filed by the Michigan Department of Civil Rights.

In settling its sex discrimination lawsuit, Home Depot agreed to pay $65 million to women who had been steered to cashier's jobs and had been denied promotions. In addition, the company promised that every applicant would get a "fair shot." Home Depot's solution to achieving fairness has been to apply modern technology to its hiring practices. Home Depot has instituted its Job Preference Program, an automated hiring and promotion system, across its 900 stores at a cost of $10 million. It has set up kiosks where potential applicants can log on to a computer, complete an application, and take a set of pre-screening tests. The process weeds out unqualified applicants. For the managers who will interview candidates who pass the prescreening, the system prints out test scores along with structured interview questions and samples of good and bad answers. The system also supports decisions about promoting employees. Employees are asked to update their skills and career aspirations so they can be identified and considered for promotion opportunities at nearby stores.

The system has been an unarguable success. Managers love it because they are able to get high-quality applicants without having to sift through mounds of résumés. In addition, the system seems to have accomplished its main purpose. The number of female managers has increased 30 percent, and the number of minority managers by 28 percent since the introduction of the system. In fact, David

Borgen, co-counsel for the plaintiffs in the original lawsuit, states, "No one can say it can't be done anymore, because Home Depot is doing it bigger and better than anyone I know."

Home Depot has identified other ways to avoid discrimination. The company has broadened its written policy against discrimination by adding a new protected category, sexual orientation. In addition, company president and CEO Bob Nardelli announced in the fall of 2001 that Home Depot would take special steps to protect benefits for its more than 500 employees who serve in the Army reserves and were activated. "We will make up any difference between their Home Depot pay and their military pay if it's lower," said Nardelli. "When they come home [from duty], their jobs and their orange aprons are waiting for them."

SOURCE: "Home Depot Says Thanks to America's Military; Extends Associates/Reservists' Benefits, Announces Military Discount," company news release, October 9, 2001; S. Jaffe, "New Tricks in Home Depot's Toolbox?" *BusinessWeek Online*, June 5, 2001, www.businessweek.com; "HRC Lauds Home Depot for Adding Sexual Orientation to Its Non-Discrimination Policy," *Human Rights Campaign*, May 14, 2001, www.hrc.org; "Former Home Depot Employees File Racial Discrimination Lawsuit," *Diversity at Work*, June 2000, www.diversityatwork.com; "Michigan Officials File Discrimination Suit against Home Depot," *Diversity at Work*, February 2000, www.diversityatwork.com; M. Boot, "For Plaintiffs' Lawyers, There's No Place Like Home Depot," *The Wall Street Journal*, interactive edition, February 12, 1997.

Questions

1. If Home Depot was correct in that it was not discriminating, but simply filling positions consistent with those who applied for them (and very few women were applying for customer service positions), was the firm guilty of discrimination? Why or why not?
2. How does this case illustrate the application of new technology to solving issues that had seemed unrelated to technology? How else might technology be used to address issues related to diversity and equal employment opportunity?

Notes

1. Equal Employment Opportunity Commission, "EEOC Confers with Minority Groups on Combating September 11 Backlash Discrimination," news release, December 12, 2001.
2. *Bakke v. Regents of the University of California*, 17 F.E.P.C. 1000 (1978).
3. Equal Employment Opportunity Commission, "Jury Finds Outback Steakhouse Guilty of Sex Discrimination and Illegal Retaliation; Awards Victim $2.2 Million," news release, September 19, 2001.
4. "Labor Letter," *The Wall Street Journal*, August 25, 1987, p. 1.
5. T. Shawn Taylor, "Age Bias Complaints Rising in Hard Times," *Chicago Tribune*, February 27, 2002, sec. 6, p. 1.
6. J. Woo, "Ex-Workers Hit Back with Age-Bias Suits," *The Wall Street Journal*, December 8, 1992, p. B1.
7. W. Carley, "Salesman's Treatment Raises Bias Questions at Schering-Plough," *The Wall Street Journal*, May 31, 1995, p. A1.
8. C. Ansberry, "Bonne Bell Retires Stereotypes with Seniors-Only Department," *The Wall Street Journal*, February 5, 2001, p. 1.
9. Equal Employment Opportunity Commission, "Facts

about Pregnancy Discrimination," EEOC website, www.eeoc.gov, January 15, 1997.

10. "ADA: The Final Regulations (Title I): A Lawyer's Dream/An Employer's Nightmare," *Employment Law Update* 16, no. 9 (1991), p. 1.

11. "ADA Supervisor Training Program: A Must for Any Supervisor Conducting a Legal Job Interview," *Employment Law Update* 7, no. 6 (1992), pp. 1–6.

12. J. Reno and D. Thornburgh, "ADA—Not a Disabling Mandate," *The Wall Street Journal*, July 26, 1995, p. A12.

13. Jacqueline Fitzgerald, "Drawing the Line in Interviews," *Chicago Tribune*, February 20, 2002, sec. 8, p. 2.

14. *UAW v. Johnson Controls, Inc.* (1991).

15. D. Kravitz and J. Platania, "Attitudes and Beliefs about Affirmative Action: Effects of Target and of Respondent Sex and Ethnicity," *Journal of Applied Psychology* 78 (1993), pp. 928–38.

16. Equal Employment Opportunity Commission, "Wal-Mart Agrees to Air TV Ad and Pay $427,500 after Court Finds Retailer in Contempt of Court," news release, September 20, 2001; EEOC, "Wal-Mart Violates Disabilities Act Again; EEOC Files 16th ADA Suit against Retail Giant," news release, June 21, 2001; Wal-Mart Stores, "Wal-Mart Demonstrates Commitment to Americans with Disabilities Act," company statement, Wal-Mart website, February 13, 2002.

17. EEOC guideline based on the Civil Rights Act of 1964, Title VII.

18. B. Carton, "At Jenny Craig, Men Are Ones Who Claim Sex Discrimination," *The Wall Street Journal*, November 29, 1995, p. A1; "Male-on-Male Harassment Suit Won," *Houston Chronicle*, August 12, 1995, p. 21A.

19. Wal-Mart Stores, "Diversity as a Way of Life," Wal-Mart website, February 13, 2002.

20. National Safety Council, "Waiters' Work Is Risky Business," *Safety and Health Magazine*, NSC website, www.nsc.org, September 2000.

21. V. F. Estrada, "Are Your Factory Workers Know-It-Alls?" *Personnel Journal*, September 1995, pp. 128–34.

22. Occupational Safety and Health Administration, "Occupational Injury & Illness Incidence Rates per 100 Full-Time Workers, 1973–98," OSHA website, www.osha.gov, February 19, 2002; OSHA, "Statement of Labor Secretary Elaine L. Chao on Historic Lows in Workplace Injury and Illness," OSHA website, www.osha.gov, December 18, 2001.

23. J. Roughton, "Managing a Safety Program through Job Hazard Analysis," *Professional Safety* 37 (1992), pp. 28–31.

24. M. A. Verespec, "OSHA Reform Fails Again," *Industry Week*, November 2, 1992, p. 36.

25. Roughton, "Managing a Safety Program."

26. R. G. Hallock and D. A. Weaver, "Controlling Losses and Enhancing Management Systems with TOR Analysis," *Professional Safety* 35 (1990), pp. 24–26.

27. H. Herbstman, "Controlling Losses the Burger King Way," *Risk Management* 37 (1990), pp. 22–30.

28. J. F. Mangan, "Hazard Communications: Safety in Knowledge," *Best's Review* 92 (1991), pp. 84–88.

29. T. Markus, "How to Set Up a Safety Awareness Program," *Supervision* 51 (1990), pp. 14–16.

30. J. Agnew and A. J. Saruda, "Age and Fatal Work-Related Falls," *Human Factors* 35 (1994), pp. 731–36.

31. R. King, "Active Safety Programs, Education Can Help Prevent Back Injuries," *Occupational Health and Safety* 60 (1991), pp. 49–52.

32. T. W. Turriff, "NSPB Suggests 10-Step Program to Prevent Eye Injury," *Occupational Health and Safety* 60 (1991), pp. 62–66.

33. M. Janssens, J. M. Brett, and F. J. Smith, "Confirmatory Cross-Cultural Research: Testing the Viability of a Corporation-wide Safety Policy," *Academy of Management Journal* 38 (1995), pp. 364–82.

Chapter 4

Analyzing Work and Designing Jobs

What Do I Need to Know? After reading this chapter, you should be able to:

1. Summarize the elements of work flow analysis.

2. Describe how work flow is related to an organization's structure.

3. Define the elements of a job analysis, and discuss their significance for human resource management.

4. Tell how to obtain information for a job analysis.

5. Summarize recent trends in job analysis.

6. Describe methods for designing a job so that it can be done efficiently.

7. Identify approaches to designing a job to make it motivating.

8. Explain how organizations apply ergonomics to design safe jobs.

9. Discuss how organizations can plan for the mental demands of a job.

Introduction

Teach for America, a national organization that encourages college graduates to take teaching jobs in inner-city schools, received three times as many applications in 2001 as in the year before and predicted still more in 2002. Elissa Clapp, the organization's vice president of recruitment and selection, says that one reason is a teacher's ability to make a difference in the lives of others: "People are seeking to ensure that all parts of their lives—professional as well as personal—are fulfilling and meaningful." Kay McElroy, a high school teacher and mother, sees another attraction: a work schedule that matches her children's school schedule. Along with the academic schedule and the ability to make a difference in children's lives comes a job that combines great responsibility with an administrative trend toward greater oversight of school performance. Teachers must plan lessons that meet wide differences in skill levels and learning styles, and their success is regularly evaluated with a battery of standardized tests administered to their students. Typically, the result is a workload that extends beyond classroom hours and walls. For Carrie McGill, who teaches in Albuquerque, New Mexico, "There are so many rules and so many guidelines these days, I don't feel like I can just walk in and know it." The paperwork piled in the back of her 10-year-old Saab makes the car an extension of her workplace.[1]

Heavy responsibility, duties that range from planning to paperwork to inspiring children, and a work schedule that runs from September to June—all these are elements of the teacher's job. These elements give rise to the types of skills and personalities required for success, and they in turn help to narrow the field of people who will succeed at teaching. Consideration of such elements is at the heart of analyzing work, whether in a school district or a multinational corporation.

This chapter discusses the analysis and design of work and, in doing so, lays out some considerations that go into making informed decisions about how to create and link jobs. The chapter begins with a look at the big-picture issues related to analyzing work flow and organizational structure. The discussion then turns to the more specific issues of analyzing and designing jobs. Traditionally, job analysis has emphasized the study of existing jobs in order to make decisions such as employee selection, training, and compensation. In contrast, job design has emphasized making jobs more efficient or more motivating. However, as this chapter shows, the two activities are interrelated.

work flow design
The process of analyzing the tasks necessary for the production of a product or service.

position
The set of duties (job) performed by a particular person.

job
A set of related duties.

LO1

Work Flow in Organizations

Informed decisions about jobs take place in the context of the organization's overall work flow. Through the process of **work flow design,** managers analyze the tasks needed to produce a product or service. With this information, they assign these tasks to specific jobs and positions. (A **job** is a set of related duties. A **position** is the set of duties performed by one person. A school has many teaching *positions*; the person filling each of those positions is performing the *job* of teacher.) Basing these decisions on work flow design can lead to better results than the more traditional practice of looking at jobs individually.

Work Flow Analysis

Before designing its work flow, the organization's planners need to analyze what work needs to be done. Figure 4.1 shows the elements of a work flow analysis. For each type of work, such as producing a product line or providing a support service (accounting, legal support, and so on), the analysis identifies the output of the process, the activities involved, and three categories of inputs: raw inputs (materials and information), equipment, and human resources.

Outputs are the products of any work unit, whether a department, team, or individual. An output can be as readily identifiable as a completed purchase order, an employment test, or a hot, juicy hamburger. An output can also be a service, such as transportation, cleaning, or answering questions about employee benefits. Even at an organization that produces tangible goods, such as computers, many employees pro-

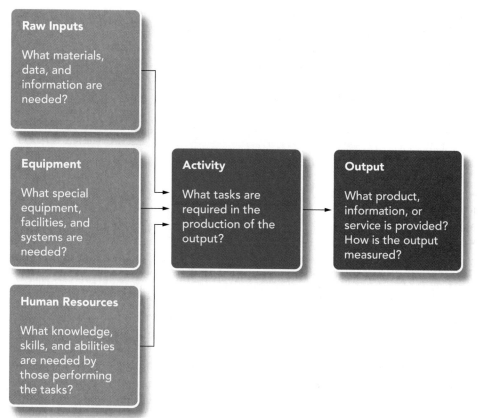

FIGURE 4.1

Developing a Work-Unit
Activity Analysis

duce other outputs, such as components of the computers, marketing plans, and building security. Work flow analysis identifies the outputs of particular work units. The analysis considers not only the amount of output but also quality standards. This attention to outputs has only recently gained attention among HRM professionals. However, it gives a clearer view of how to increase the effectiveness of each work unit.

For the outputs identified, work flow analysis then examines the work processes used to generate those outputs. Work processes are the activities that members of a work unit engage in to produce a given output. Every process consists of operating procedures that specify how things should be done at each stage of developing the output. These procedures include all the tasks that must be performed in producing the output. Usually, the analysis breaks down the tasks into those performed by each person in the work unit. This analysis helps with design of efficient work systems by clarifying which tasks are necessary. Typically, when a unit's work load increases, the unit adds people, and when the work load decreases, some members of the unit may busy themselves with unrelated tasks in an effort to appear busy. Without knowledge of work processes, it is more difficult to identify whether the work unit is properly staffed. For example, Microsoft, currently the most successful computer software company in the world, deliberately understaffs its product teams in "small bands of people with a mission." This approach ensures a lean organization and high levels of motivation.[2]

The final stage in work flow analysis is to identify the inputs used in the development of the work unit's product. As shown in Figure 4.1, these inputs can be broken down into the raw inputs (materials and knowledge), equipment, and human skills needed to perform the tasks. Makers of athletic shoes need nylon and leather, shoe-

Firefighters work as a team. They and their equipment are the "inputs" (they do the work), and the "output" is an extinguished fire and the rescue of people and pets. In any organization or team, workers need to be cross-trained in several skills to create an effective team. If these firefighters are trained to do any part of the job, the chief can deploy them rapidly as needed.

making machinery, and workers to operate the machinery, among other inputs. Nike and Reebok minimize the cost of inputs by subcontracting manufacturing to factories in countries where wages are low. In contrast, New Balance Athletic Shoes operates a factory in Norridgewock, Maine, where modern technology and worker training enable the company to afford U.S. workers. Teams of employees use automated equipment that operates over 20 sewing machines simultaneously. The employees are cross-trained in all tasks. The highly efficient factory produces shoes much faster than a typical Chinese shoe factory.[3]

LO2

Work Flow in Organizations

Besides looking at the work flow of each process, it is important to see how the work fits within the context of the organization's structure. Within an organization, units and individuals must cooperate to create outputs. Ideally, the organization's structure brings together the people who must collaborate in order to efficiently produce the desired outputs. The structure may do this in a way that is highly centralized (that is, with authority concentrated in a few people at the top of the organizaton) or decentralized (with authority spread among many people). The organization may group jobs according to functions (for example, welding, painting, packaging), or it may set up divisions to focus on products or customer groups.

Although there is an infinite number of ways to combine the elements of an organization's structure, we can make some general observations about structure and work design. If the structure is strongly based on function, workers tend to have low authority and to work alone at highly specialized jobs. Jobs that involve teamwork or broad responsibility tend to require a structure based on divisions other than functions. When the goal is to empower employees, companies therefore need to set up structures and jobs that enable broad responsibility, such as jobs that involve employees in serving a particular group of customers or producing a particular product, rather than performing a narrowly defined function. The "Best Practices" box illustrates a way of applying this principle to hospitals.

Work design often emphasizes the analysis and design of jobs, as described in the remainder of this chapter. Although all of these approaches can succeed, each focuses on one isolated job at a time. These approaches do not necessarily consider how that single job fits into the overall work flow or structure of the organization. To use these techniques effectively, human resources personnel should also understand their organization as a whole. Without this big-picture appreciation, they might redesign a job in a way that makes sense for the particular job but is out of line with the organization's work flow, structure, or strategy.

Team-Based Jobs Put the Focus on Patient Care

One way hospitals are improving patient care is to empower employees by organizing work around teams. In Bethesda, Maryland, Suburban Hospital has adopted a team-based approach in its intensive-care unit (ICU). Each team includes an ICU specialist, a pharmacist, a nutritionist, a social worker, a nurse, a respiratory specialist, and a chaplain. These employees go room to room each morning, visiting every patient, sometimes accompanied by a family member. The team meets with each patient's bedside nurse to discuss and debate the best action for this patient from all possible angles.

This focus on teamwork has a long tradition in other high-pressure work contexts such as aviation and the military, and it is increasingly being adopted in many businesses and industries. Indeed, enhanced communication technologies such as e-mail, teleconferencing, and videoconferencing have allowed the creation of "virtual teams" that work together despite team members' separation in space and time. The use of these technologies eliminates the need for travel and truly allows organizations to put together the best teams possible, free of traditional constraints.

At Suburban Hospital, this team-based approach is credited with reducing errors, shortening the time patients spend in the small (12-bed) ICU, and improving the communication among patients, their families, and the medical staff. It also has reduced the time patients spend on ventilators by 25 percent, which is critical because the use of ventilators increases the chances of pneumonia, which, in turn, greatly increases both costs and the chance of patients dying. Indeed, the cost savings from avoiding complications more than offsets the increased expense associated with forming teams, and this does not even calculate the reduced amount of human suffering.

As Dr. Joseph Fontan, an ICU specialist at Suburban, notes, "It's good to have people with different backgrounds and opinions looking at the same problem—it makes a huge difference because small problems that can turn into big ones are headed off early."

SOURCE: J. Appleby and R. Davis, "Teamwork Used to Be a Money Saver: Now It's a Lifesaver," *USA Today,* March 1, 2001, pp. B1–B2; L. Kohn, J. Corrigan, and M. Donaldson, *To Err Is Human: Building a Safer Health System* (Washington, DC: National Academy Press, 2001); C. M. Solomon, "Managing Virtual Teams," *Workforce,* June 2001, pp. 61–65.

Job Analysis

LO3

To achieve high-quality performance, organizations have to understand and match job requirements and people. This understanding requires **job analysis,** the process of getting detailed information about jobs. Analyzing jobs and understanding what is required to carry out a job provide essential knowledge for staffing, training, performance appraisal, and many other HR activities. For instance, a supervisor's evaluation of an employee's work should be based on performance relative to job requirements. In very small organizations, line managers may perform a job analysis, but usually the work is done by a human resource professional. A large company may have a compensation management department that includes job analysts (also called personnel analysts). Organizations may also contract with firms that provide this service.

job analysis
The process of getting detailed information about jobs.

Writing a Job Description

Preparing a job description begins with gathering information from sources who can identify the details of performing a task. These sources may include persons already performing the job, the supervisor or team leader, or if the job is new, the managers who are creating the new position. Asking the purpose of the new position can provide insight into what the company expects this person to accomplish. Besides people, sources of information may include the company's human resource files, such as past job advertisements and job descriptions, as well as general sources of information about similar jobs, such as O*NET (http://online.onetcenter.org).

There are several ways to gather information about the duties of a job:

- Employees can fill out a questionnaire that asks about what they do or complete a diary that details their activities over several days.

- A job analyst can visit the workplace and watch or videotape an employee performing the job. This method is most appropriate for jobs that are repetitive and involve physical activity.
- A job analyst can visit the workplace and ask an employee to show what the job entails. This method is most appropriate for clerical and technical jobs.
- A manager or supervisor can imagine what a well-done job would look like. What would the outputs be? Would customers feel the job holder had answered their questions fully and politely? Would a product be assembled correctly and in some quantity? Would coworkers have access to up-to-date information? The analyst can identify the activities necessary to create the outputs.
- A supervisor or job analyst can review company records related to performing the job—for example, work

orders or summaries of customer calls. These records can show the kinds of problems a person solves in the course of doing a job.

After gathering such information, the next thing to do is list all the activities, then evaluate whether all of them or which ones are essential duties. One way to do this is to rate all the duties on a scale of 1 to 5, where 1 is most important. A rating scale also could rank the tasks according to how much time the person spends on them. Perhaps the ratings will show that some tasks are desirable but not essential. The tasks listed as essential duties on the job description should be only the ones that the job analysis identifies as essential.

Gathering information from many sources helps to verify which tasks are essential. Perhaps the job holder is aware of some activities that others do not notice. Or on the other hand, perhaps the job holder performs activities that are not

Job Descriptions

job description
A list of the tasks, duties, and responsibilities (TDRs) that a particular job entails.

An essential part of job analysis is the creation of job descriptions. A **job description** is a list of the tasks, duties, and responsibilities (TDRs) that a job entails. TDRs are observable actions. For example, a clerical job requires the jobholder to type. If you were to observe someone in that position for a day, you would certainly see some typing. When a manager attempts to evaluate job performance, it is most important to have detailed information about the work performed in the job (that is, the TDRs). This information makes it possible to determine how well an individual is meeting each job requirement.

essential but are merely habits or holdovers from a time when they were essential. When different people analyzing a job come to different conclusions about which activities are essential, the person writing the job description should compare the listed activities with the company's goals and work flow to see which are essential. A group discussion also may help categorize tasks as essential, ideal, and unnecessary.

From these sources, the writer of the job description thus obtains the important elements of the description:

- *Title of the job*—The title should be descriptive and, if appropriate, indicate the job's level in the organization by using terms such as *junior, senior, assistant,* and *executive.*
- *Administrative information about the job*—Depending on the company's size and requirements, the job description may identify a division, department, supervisor's title, date of the analysis, name of the analyst, and other information for administering the company's human resource activities.
- *Summary of the job, focusing on its purpose and duties*—This summary should be brief and as specific as possible, including types of responsibilities, tools and equipment used, and level of authority (for example, the degree of authority and responsibility of the job holder—how much the person is supervised and how much the person supervises others or participates in teamwork).
- *Essential duties of the job*—These should be listed in order of importance to successful performance of the job and should include details such as physical requirements (for example, the amount of weight to be lifted), the persons with whom an employee in this job interacts, and the results to be accomplished.
- *Additional responsibilities*—The job description may have a section stating that the position requires additional responsibilities as requested by the supervisor.
- *Job specifications*—The specifications cover the knowledge, skills, abilities, and other characteristics required for a person to be qualified to perform the job successfully. These may appear at the end of the job description or as a separate document.

SOURCE: D. B. Bordeaux, "Writing Job Descriptions," *Motor Age,* November 2001, downloaded from Findarticles.com; "Job Descriptions and the ADA," HRNext, www.hrnext.com, downloaded March 7, 2002; "Simple Job Analysis," HRNext, www.hrnext.com, downloaded March 7, 2002; C. Joinson, "Refocusing Job Descriptions," *HR Magazine,* January 2001, downloaded from Findarticles.com.

A job description typically has the format shown in Figure 4.2. It includes the job title, a brief description of the TDRs, and a list of the essential duties with detailed specifications of the tasks involved in carrying out each duty. Although organizations may modify this format according to their particular needs, all job descriptions within an organization should follow the same format. This helps the organization make consistent decisions about such matters as pay and promotions. It also helps the organization show that it makes human resource decisions fairly.

Whenever the organization creates a new job, it needs to prepare a job description, using a process such as the one detailed in the "HR How To" box nearby. Job descriptions should then be reviewed periodically (say, once a year) and updated if necessary.

FIGURE 4.2

Sample Job Description

Sales Associate

Customer service and interaction with customers are key responsibilities of this position. A sales associate must work effectively with customers and other store associates and provide information about products and/or projects. This position also involves stocking merchandise, using tools and equipment, and maintenance duties (e.g., sweeping aisles, down-stocking shelves, etc.).

Major Tasks and Responsibilities
- Presenting a consistent, pleasant, and service-oriented image to customers
- Listening and asking appropriate questions to assist customers in completing projects
- Assisting and working with other store associates in order to complete job tasks
- Using computers, phones, and other equipment
- Cleaning and maintaining shelves, end caps, and aisles

SOURCE: "Retail Careers by Title," Home Depot website, www.homedepot.com, April 2, 2002.

Performance appraisals can provide a good opportunity for updating job descriptions, as the employee and supervisor compare what the employee has been doing against the details of the job description.

When organizations prepare many job descriptions, the process can become repetitive and time consuming. To address this challenge, a number of companies have developed software that provides forms into which the job analyst can insert details about the specific job. Typically, the job analyst would use a library of basic descriptions, selecting one that is for a similar type of job and then modifying it to fit the organization's needs.

Organizations should give each newly hired employee a copy of his or her job description. This helps the employee to understand what is expected, but it shouldn't be presented as limiting the employee's commitment to quality and customer satisfaction. Ideally, employees will want to go above and beyond the listed duties when the situation and their abilities call for that. Many job descriptions include the phrase *and other duties as requested* as a way to remind employees not to tell their supervisor, "But that's not part of my job."

Job Specifications

job specification
A list of the knowledge, skills, abilities, and other characteristics (KSAOs) that an individual must have to perform a particular job.

Whereas the job description focuses on the activities involved in carrying out a job, a **job specification** looks at the qualities of the person performing the job. It is a list of the knowledge, skills, abilities, and other characteristics (KSAOs) that an individual must have to perform the job. *Knowledge* refers to factual or procedural information that is necessary for successfully performing a task. For example, this course is providing you with knowledge in how to manage human resources. A *skill* is an individual's level of proficiency at performing a particular task—that is, the capability to perform it well. With knowledge and experience, you could acquire skill in the task of preparing job specifications. *Ability*, in contrast to skill, refers to a more general enduring capability that an individual possesses. A person might have the ability to cooperate with others or to write clearly and precisely. Finally, *other characteristics* might be personality traits such as someone's persistence or motivation to achieve. Some jobs also have legal requirements, such as licensing or certification. Figure 4.3 is a set of sample job specifications for the job description in Figure 4.2.

In developing job specifications, it is important to consider all of the elements of KSAOs. As with writing a job description, the information can come from a combination of people performing the job, people supervising or planning for the job, and trained job analysts. At Acxiom Corporation, job specifications are based on an analysis of employees' roles and competencies (what they must be able to do), stated in terms of behaviors. To reach these definitions, groups studied what the company's good performers were doing and looked for the underlying abilities. For example, according to Jeff Standridge, Acxiom's organizational development leader, they might ask a panel about a high-performing software developer, and panel members might identify the employee's knowledge of the Java and C++ programming languages. Then, Standridge says, the job analysts would probe for the abilities behind this knowledge: "When we asked, 'If Java becomes obsolete in five years, will this person

---

FIGURE 4.3

Sample Job Specifications

Sales Associate

Major Skills and Competencies
- Customer Focus: Ability to maintain a positive customer service orientation when dealing with customers on the phone and in person
- Stress Tolerance: Ability to work effectively under stressful work conditions (e.g., dealing with multiple customers who need help quickly)
- Teamwork: Ability to work well with others to achieve common goals
- Listening/Communicating: Ability to listen attentively to others, ask appropriate questions, and speak in a clear and understandable manner

Minimum Job Requirements
- 18 years or older
- Pass a drug test
- Be able to work a flexible schedule including weekends, evenings, and holidays
- Pass a sales associate test

SOURCE: "Retail Careers by Title," Home Depot website, www.homedepot.com, April 2, 2002.

When a job entails working night shifts, job specifications should reflect this requirement. Some people who work at night experience emotional and physical stress. The organization needs to help these employees handle the challenges of night work.

no longer be successful?' the panel responded, 'Oh no, he'll update his skills and be great in the new language.' . . . The employee's strength was not just in his specific skills but in his ability to learn."[4]

In contrast to tasks, duties, and responsibilities, KSAOs are characteristics of people and are not directly observable. They are observable only when individuals are carrying out the TDRs of the job. Thus, if someone applied for a clerical job, you could not simply look at the individual to determine whether he or she possessed typing skills. However, you could assess the level of typing skill by observing the person type a document and reviewing the document.

Accurate information about KSAOs is especially important for making decisions about who will fill a job. A manager attempting to fill a position needs information about the characteristics required, and about the characteristics of each applicant. Interviews and selection decisions should therefore focus on KSAOs. In the earlier example of computer programming at Acxiom, the company would look for someone who knows the computer languages currently used, but also has a track record of taking the initiative to learn new computer languages as they are developed.

Operations that need to run 24 hours a day have special job requirements. For example, shutting down certain equipment at night may be inefficient or may cause production problems, or some industries, such as security and health care, may have customers who demand services around the clock. Globalization often means that operations take place across many time zones, requiring management at all hours. When a job entails working night shifts, job specifications should reflect this requirement. For most people, working at night disrupts their normal functioning and may cause disorders such as fatigue, depression, and obesity. However, people show wide variability in how well they respond to working at night. Research has found that people who work well at night tend to prefer sleeping late in the morning and staying up late. They also tend to sleep easily at different times of day, like to take naps, and exercise regularly. When job specifications call for nighttime work, a person's ability to handle a nocturnal work life may be the most critical KSAO.[5]

Sources of Job Information

LO4

Information for analyzing an existing job often comes from incumbents, that is, people who currently hold that position in the organization. They are a logical source of information, because they are most acquainted with the details of the job. Incumbents should be able to provide very accurate information.

A drawback of relying solely on incumbents' information is that they may have an incentive to exaggerate what they do, to appear more valuable to the organization. Information from incumbents should therefore be supplemented with information from observers, such as supervisors. Supervisors should review the information provided by incumbents, looking for a match between what incumbents are doing and what they are supposed to do. Research suggests that incumbents may provide the most accurate estimates of the actual time spent performing job tasks, while supervisors may be more accurate in reporting information about the importance of job duties.[6]

The government also provides background information for analyzing jobs. In the 1930s, the U.S. Department of Labor created the *Dictionary of Occupational Titles* **(DOT)** as a vehicle for helping the new public employment system link the demand for skills and the supply of skills in the U.S. workforce. The government perceived a need to lower the high unemployment rate by helping to match workers and employers. The *DOT* described over 12,000 jobs, as well as some of the requirements of successful job holders. Employment agencies and private employers used the *DOT* to help them staff jobs efficiently. It was also a valuable resource for workers because it listed the skills and educational requirements they would need for certain occupations.

> **Dictionary of Occupational Titles**
> Created by the Department of Labor in the 1930s, the *DOT* listed over 12,000 jobs and requirements.

This system served the United States well for over 60 years, but it became clear to Labor Department officials that jobs in the new economy were so different that the *DOT* no longer served its purpose. Technological change, global competition, and greater emphasis on flexibility were making the system obsolete. The Labor Department therefore abandoned the *DOT* in 1998 and introduced a new system, called the Occupational Information Network (O*NET). Instead of relying on fixed job titles and narrow task descriptions, O*NET uses a common language that generalizes across jobs to describe the abilities, work styles, work activities, and work context required for 1,000 broadly defined occupations. Many employers and employment agencies began using O*NET even before it was fully developed. For example, in preparing to move its headquarters from Seattle, Boeing used O*NET to help find jobs for the workers it was laying off. The state of Texas has used the O*NET to identify emerging occupations within the state and identify areas where the state should encourage more training to prepare Texans for the workplace of the future. Educational organizations such as the Boys and Girls Club of America have used the O*NET to help design activities to improve the career prospects of children from disadvantaged backgrounds.[7]

Position Analysis Questionnaire

After gathering information, the job analyst uses the information to analyze the job. One of the broadest and best-researched instruments for analyzing jobs is the **Position Analysis Questionnaire (PAQ).** This is a standardized job analysis questionnaire containing 194 items that represent work behaviors, work conditions, and job characteristics that apply to a wide variety of jobs. The questionnaire organizes these items into six sections concerning different aspects of the job:

> **Position Analysis Questionnaire (PAQ)**
> A standardized job analysis questionnaire containing 194 questions about work behaviors, work conditions, and job characteristics that apply to a wide variety of jobs.

1. *Information input*—Where and how a worker gets information needed to perform the job.
2. *Mental processes*—The reasoning, decision making, planning, and information-processing activities involved in performing the job.
3. *Work output*—The physical activities, tools, and devices used by the worker to perform the job.

4. *Relationships with other persons*—The relationships with other people required in performing the job.
5. *Job context*—The physical and social contexts where the work is performed.
6. *Other characteristics*—The activities, conditions, and characteristics other than those previously described that are relevant to the job.

The person analyzing a job determines whether each item on the questionnaire applies to the job being analyzed. The analyst rates each item on six scales: extent of use, amount of time, importance to the job, possibility of occurrence, applicability, and special code (special rating scales used with a particular item). The PAQ headquarters uses a computer to score the questionnaire and generate a report that describes the scores on the job dimensions.

Using the PAQ provides an organization with information that helps in comparing jobs, even when they are dissimilar. The PAQ also has the advantage that it considers the whole work process, from inputs through outputs. However, the person who fills out the questionnaire must have college-level reading skills, and the PAQ is meant to be completed only by job analysts trained in this method.[8] Also, the descriptions in the PAQ reports are rather abstract, so the reports may not be useful for writing job descriptions or redesigning jobs.

Task Analysis Inventory

task analysis inventory
Job analysis method that involves listing the tasks performed in a particular job and rating each task according to a defined set of criteria.

Another type of job analysis method, the **task analysis inventory,** focuses on the tasks performed in a particular job. This method has several variations. In one, the task inventory–CODAP method, subject-matter experts such as job incumbents generate a list of the tasks performed in a job. Then they rate each task in terms of time spent on the task, frequency of task performance, relative importance, relative difficulty, and length of time required to learn the job. The CODAP computer program organizes the responses into dimensions of similar tasks.[9]

Task analysis inventories can be very detailed, including 100 or more tasks. This level of detail can be helpful for developing employment tests and criteria for performance appraisal. However, they do not directly identify KSAOs needed for success in a job.

Fleishman Job Analysis System

Fleishman Job Analysis System
Job analysis technique that asks subject-matter experts to evaluate a job in terms of the abilities required to perform the job.

To gather information about worker requirements, the **Fleishman Job Analysis System** asks subject-matter experts (typically job incumbents) to evaluate a job in terms of the abilities required to perform the job.[10] The survey is based on 52 categories of abilities, ranging from written comprehension to deductive reasoning, manual dexterity, stamina, and originality. As in the example in Figure 4.4, the survey items are arranged into a scale for each ability. Each begins with a description of the ability and a comparison to related abilities. Below this is a seven-point scale with phrases describing extemely high and low levels of the ability. The person completing the survey indicates which point on the scale represents the level of the ability required for performing the job being analyzed.

When the survey has been completed in all 52 categories, the results provide a picture of the ability requirements of a job. Such information is especially useful for employee selection, training, and career development.

Written Comprehension

This is the ability to understand written sentences and paragraphs.
How written comprehension is different from other abilities:

FIGURE 4.4

Example of an Ability
from the Fleishman Job
Analysis System

This ability		**Other Abilities**
Understand written English words, sentences, and paragraphs.	vs.	*Oral comprehension* (1): *Listen and understand spoken* English words and sentences.
	vs.	*Oral expression* (3): and *written expression* (4): *Speak or write* English words and sentences so others will understand.

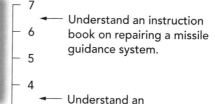

Requires understanding of complex or detailed information in **writing** containing unusual words and phrases and involving fine distinctions in meaning among words.

7
6 ← Understand an instruction book on repairing a missile guidance system.
5
4
3 ← Understand an apartment lease.
2
1 ← Read a road map.

Requires understanding short, simple **written** information containing common words and phrases.

SOURCE: E. A. Fleishman and M. D. Mumford, "Evaluating Classifications of Job Behavior: A Construct Validation of the Ability Requirements Scales," *Personnel Psychology* 44 (1991), pp. 523–76. The complete set of ability requirement scales, along with instructions for their use, may be found in E. A. Fleishman, *Fleishman Job Analysis Survey (F-JAS)* (Palo Alto, CA: Consulting Psychologists Press, 1992). Used with permission.

Importance of Job Analysis

Job analysis is so important to HR managers that it has been called the building block of everything that personnel does.[11] The fact is that almost every human resource management program requires some type of information that is gleaned from job analysis:[12]

- *Work redesign*—Often an organization seeks to redesign work to make it more efficient or to improve quality. The redesign requires detailed information about the existing job(s). In addition, preparing the redesign is similar to analyzing a job that does not yet exist.
- *Human resource planning*—As planners analyze human resource needs and how to meet those needs, they must have accurate information about the levels of skill

required in various jobs, so that they can tell what kinds of human resources will be needed.

- *Selection*—To identify the most qualified applicants for various positions, decision makers need to know what tasks the individuals must perform, as well as the necessary knowledge, skills, and abilities.
- *Training*—Almost every employee hired by an organization will require training. Any training program requires knowledge of the tasks performed in a job, so that the training is related to the necessary knowledge and skills.
- *Performance appraisal*—An accurate performance appraisal requires information about how well each employee is performing in order to reward employees who perform well and to improve their performance if it is below standard. Job analysis helps in identifying the behaviors and the results associated with effective performance.
- *Career planning*—Matching an individual's skills and aspirations with career opportunities requires that those in charge of career planning know the skill requirements of the various jobs. This allows them to guide individuals into jobs in which they will succeed and be satisfied.
- *Job evaluation*—The process of job evaluation involves assessing the relative dollar value of each job to the organization in order to set up fair pay structures. If employees do not believe pay structures are fair, they will become dissatisfied and may quit, or they will not see much benefit in striving for promotions. To put dollar values on jobs, it is necessary to get information about different jobs and compare them.

IHS Help Desk, which provides computer-related advice to companies, found out the importance of job descriptions by trying to operate without them. When the company started, management thought employees would be more flexible in assisting customers if they weren't limited by detailed descriptions of their jobs. However, when employees left the company, they expressed confusion during their exit interviews, according to Jean Rall, IHS's chief operating officer: "We started hearing employees say . . . , 'I got hired to do this and I do it well, but you haven't provided me with any vision about what I'm doing next.' Employees didn't see a professional identity or career path, and we couldn't manage employee expectations." Preparing job descriptions helped the company end such confusion and keep employees longer. Rall says job descriptions haven't limited employees, but have helped supervisors and employees with career development.[13]

Job analysis is also important from a legal standpoint. As we saw in Chapter 3, the government imposes requirements related to equal employment opportunity. Detailed, accurate, objective job specifications help decision makers comply with these regulations by keeping the focus on tasks and abilities. These documents also provide evidence of efforts made to engage in fair employment practices. For example, to enforce the Americans with Disabilities Act, the Equal Employment Opportunity Commission may look at job descriptions to identify the essential functions of a job and determine whether a disabled person could have performed those functions with reasonable accommodations. Likewise, lists of duties in different jobs could be compared to evaluate claims under the Equal Pay Act. However, job descriptions and job specifications are not a substitute for fair employment practices. In the words of John Fraser, deputy administrator for the Labor Department's Wage and Hour Division, "With respect to the laws that we administer, job descriptions per se aren't relevant . . . It's what people do, not what's on paper" that the agencies and courts are interested in.[14]

Besides helping human resource professionals, job analysis helps supervisors and other managers carry out their duties. Data from job analysis can help managers identify the types of work in their units, as well as provide information about the work flow process, so that managers can evaluate whether work is done in the most efficient way. Job analysis information also supports managers as they make hiring decisions, review performance, and recommend rewards.

Trends in Job Analysis   LO5

As we noted in the earlier discussion of work flow analysis, organizations are beginning to appreciate the need to analyze jobs in the context of the organization's structure and strategy. In addition, organizations are recognizing that today's workplace must be adaptable and is constantly subject to change. Thus, although we tend to think of "jobs" as something stable, they actually tend to change and evolve over time. Those who occupy or manage jobs often make minor adjustments to match personal preferences or changing conditions.[15] Indeed, although errors in job analysis can have many sources, most inaccuracy is likely to result from job descriptions being outdated. For this reason, job analysis must not only define jobs when they are created, but also detect changes in jobs as time passes.

In today's world of rapidly changing products and markets, some observers have even begun to suggest that the concept of a "job" is obsolete. Some researchers and businesspeople have observed a trend they call *dejobbing*—viewing organizations as a field of work needing to be done, rather than as a set or series of jobs held by individuals. For example, at Amazon.com, HR director Scott Pitasky notes, "Here, a person might be in the same 'job,' but three months later be doing completely different work."[16] This means Amazon.com puts more emphasis on broad worker specifications ("entrepreneurial and customer-focused") than on detailed job descriptions ("HTML programming"), which may not be descriptive one year down the road.

These changes in the nature of work and the expanded use of "project-based" organizational structures require the type of broader understanding that comes from an analysis of work flows. Because the work can change rapidly and it is impossible to rewrite job descriptions every week, job descriptions and specifications need to be flexible. At the same time, legal requirements (as discussed in Chapter 3) may discourage organizations from writing flexible job descriptions. So, organizations must balance the need for flexibility with the need for legal documentation. This presents one of the major challenges to be faced by HRM departments in the next decade. Many professionals are meeting this challenge with a greater emphasis on careful job design.

Amazon.com practices "dejobbing," or designing work by project rather than by jobs. What would appeal to you about working for a company organized like this?

Job Design

Although job analysis, as just described, is important for an understanding of existing jobs, organizations also must plan for new jobs and periodically consider whether they should revise existing jobs. When an organization is expanding, supervisors and human resource professionals must help plan for new or growing work units. When an organization is trying to improve quality or efficiency, a review of work units and processes may require a fresh look at how jobs are designed.

These situations call for **job design,** the process of defining how work will be performed and what tasks will be required in a given job, or *job redesign*, a similar process that involves changing an existing job design. To design jobs effectively, a person must thoroughly understand the job itself (through job analysis) and its place in the larger work unit's work flow process (through work flow analysis). Having a detailed knowledge of the tasks performed in the work unit and in the job, a manager then has many alternative ways to design a job. As shown in Figure 4.5, the available approaches emphasize different aspects of the job: the mechanics of doing a job efficiently, the job's impact on motivation, the use of safe work practices, and the mental demands of the job.

job design
The process of defining how work will be performed and what tasks will be required in a given job.

Designing Efficient Jobs

LO6

If workers perform tasks as efficiently as possible, not only does the organization benefit from lower costs and greater output per worker, but workers should be less fatigued. This point of view has for years formed the basis of classical **industrial engineering,** which looks for the simplest way to structure work in order to maximize efficiency. Typically, applying industrial engineering to a job reduces the complexity of the work, making it so simple that almost anyone can be trained quickly and easily to perform the job. Such jobs tend to be highly specialized and repetitive.

In practice, the scientific method traditionally seeks the "one best way" to perform a job by performing time-and-motion studies to identify the most efficient movements for workers to make. Once the engineers have identified the most efficient sequence

industrial engineering
The study of jobs to find the simplest way to structure work in order to maximize efficiency.

FIGURE 4.5

Approaches to Job Design

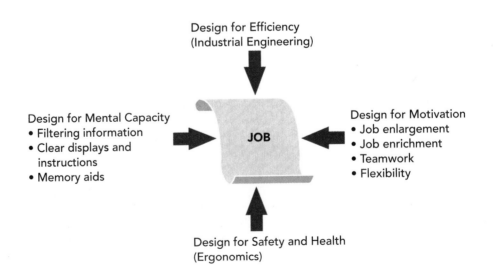

of motions, the organization should select workers based on their ability to do the job, then train them in the details of the "one best way" to perform that job. The company also should offer pay structured to motivate workers to do their best. (Chapters 11 and 12 discuss pay and pay structures.)

Despite the logical benefits of industrial engineering, a focus on efficiency alone can create jobs that are so simple and repetitive that workers get bored. Workers performing these jobs may feel their work is meaningless. Hence, most organizations combine industrial engineering with other approaches to job design.

Designing Jobs That Motivate   LO7

Especially when organizations must compete for employees, depend on skilled knowledge workers, or need a workforce that cares about customer satisfaction, a pure focus on efficiency will not achieve human resource objectives. These organizations need jobs that employees find interesting and satisfying, and job design should take into account factors that make jobs motivating to employees.

The quest for meaningful work draws people to such career paths as teaching and service in the Peace Corps. When the recent economic slowdown, especially the end of the boom in e-commerce, ended widespread dreams of getting rich by working for a dot-com, many workers began to change their dreams. The new dream of some has been the opportunity to work with young people in a learning context where the teacher has some control over the work. For example, when Patrick Bernhardt was laid off from his job as a marketing executive in an e-commerce start-up, he seized the chance to switch fields. Bernhardt became a computer science teacher at John Muir Middle School and enrolled in night classes in order to qualify for a teaching license. When he switched to this job, Bernhardt took a 50 percent pay cut, but he doesn't mind: "This is the hardest thing I've ever done, but the sense of satisfaction makes it worth it."[17]

A model that shows how to make jobs more motivating is the Job Characteristics Model, developed by Richard Hackman and Greg Oldham. This model describes jobs in terms of five characteristics:[18]

1. *Skill variety*—The extent to which a job requires a variety of skills to carry out the tasks involved.
2. *Task identity*—The degree to which a job requires completing a "whole" piece of work from beginning to end (for example, building an entire component or resolving a customer's complaint).
3. *Task significance*—The extent to which the job has an important impact on the lives of other people.
4. *Autonomy*—The degree to which the job allows an individual to make decisions about the way the work will be carried out.
5. *Feedback*—The extent to which a person receives clear information about performance effectiveness from the work itself.

As shown in Figure 4.6, the more of each of these characteristics a job has, the more motivating the job will be, according to the Job Characteristics Model. The model predicts that a person with such a job will be more satisfied and will produce more and better work. This approach to designing jobs includes such techniques as job enlargement, job enrichment, self-managing work teams, flexible work schedules, and telework.

FIGURE 4.6

Characteristics of a Motivating Job

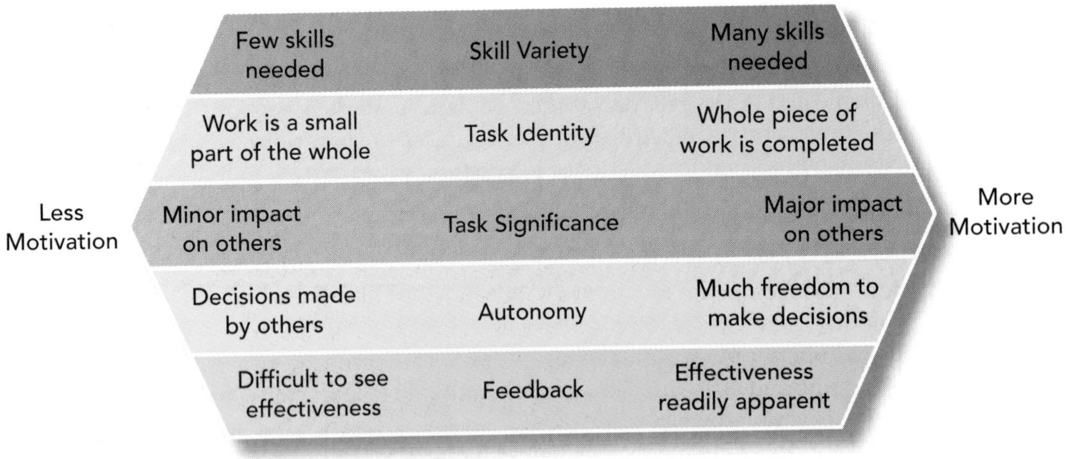

Less Motivation		More Motivation
Few skills needed	Skill Variety	Many skills needed
Work is a small part of the whole	Task Identity	Whole piece of work is completed
Minor impact on others	Task Significance	Major impact on others
Decisions made by others	Autonomy	Much freedom to make decisions
Difficult to see effectiveness	Feedback	Effectiveness readily apparent

Job Enlargement

job enlargement
Broadening the types of tasks performed in a job.

In a job design, **job enlargement** refers to broadening the types of tasks performed. The objective of job enlargement is to make jobs less repetitive and more interesting. Methods of job enlargement include job extension and job rotation.

Job extension is enlarging jobs by combining several relatively simple jobs to form a job with a wider range of tasks. An example might be combining the jobs of receptionist, typist, and file clerk into jobs containing all three kinds of work. This approach to job enlargement is relatively simple, but if all the tasks are dull, workers will not necessarily be more motivated by the redesigned job.

job extension
Enlarging jobs by combining several relatively simple jobs to form a job with a wider range of tasks.

Job rotation does not actually redesign the jobs themselves, but moves employees among several different jobs. This approach to job enlargement is common among production teams. During the course of a week, a team member may carry out each of the jobs handled by the team. Team members might assemble components one day and pack products into cases another day. As with job extension, the enlarged jobs may still consist of repetitious activities, but with greater variation among those activities.

job rotation
Enlarging jobs by moving employees among several different jobs.

Job Enrichment

job enrichment
Empowering workers by adding more decision-making authority to jobs.

The idea of **job enrichment,** or empowering workers by adding more decision-making authority to their jobs, comes from the work of Frederick Herzberg. According to Herzberg's two-factor theory, individuals are motivated more by the intrinsic aspects of work (for example, the meaningfulness of a job) than by extrinsic rewards such as pay. Herzberg identified five factors he associated with motivating jobs: achievement, recognition, growth, responsibility, and performance of the entire job. Thus, ways to enrich a manufacturing job might include giving employees authority to stop production when quality standards are not being met and having each employee perform several tasks to complete a particular stage of the process, rather than dividing up the tasks among the employees. For a salesperson in a store, job enrichment might involve the authority to resolve customer problems, including the authority to decide whether to issue refunds or replace merchandise.

Employees who have enriched jobs and/or work in self-managed teams can be motivated when they feel they have decision-making authority.

Self-Managing Work Teams

Instead of merely enriching individual jobs, some organizations empower employees by designing work to be done by self-managing work teams. As described in Chapter 2, these teams have authority for an entire work process or segment. Team members typically have authority to schedule work, hire team members, resolve problems related to the team's performance, and perform other duties traditionally handled by management. Teamwork can give a job such motivating characteristics as autonomy, skill variety, and task identity.

Because team members' responsibilities are great, their jobs usually are defined broadly and include sharing of work assignments. Team members may, at one time or another, perform every duty of the team. The challenge for the organization is to provide enough training so that the team members can learn the necessary skills. Another approach, when teams are responsible for particular work processes or customers, is to assign the team responsibility for the process or customer, then let the team decide which members will carry out which tasks.

Teamwork can certainly make jobs more interesting, but teamwork's effectiveness is not guaranteed. Self-managing teams are most likely to accomplish their goals if they involve 6 to 18 employees who share the same technology (tools or ideas), location, and work hours. Such teams can be especially beneficial when a group's skills are relatively easy to learn (so that employees can readily learn one another's jobs) and demand for particular activities shifts from day to day (requiring flexibility). In addition, the job specifications should help the organization identify employees who will be willing and able to cooperate for the team's success. Such employees likely will have good problem-solving skills and be able to communicate well.

A study of work teams at a large financial services company found that the right job design was associated with effective teamwork.[19] In particular, when teams are self-managed and team members are highly involved in decision making, teams are more productive, employees more satisfied, and managers more pleased with performance. Teams also tend to do better when each team member performs a variety of tasks and when team members view their effort as significant.

Flexible Work Schedules

One way in which an organization can give employees some say in how their work is structured is to offer flexible work schedules. Depending on the requirements of the organization and the individual jobs, organizations may be able to be flexible in terms of when employees work. As introduced in Chapter 2, types of flexibility include flextime and job sharing. Figure 4.7 illustrates alternatives to the traditional 40-hour workweek.

Flextime is a scheduling policy in which full-time employees may choose starting and ending times within guidelines specified by the organization. The flextime policy may require that employees be at work between certain hours, say, 10:00 AM and 3:00 PM. Employees work additional hours before or after this period in order to work the full day. One employee might arrive early in the morning in order to leave at 3:00 PM to pick up children after school. Another employee might be a night owl who prefers to arrive at 10:00 AM and work until 6:00, 7:00, or even later in the evening. A flextime policy also may enable workers to adjust a particular day's hours in order to make time for doctor's appointments, children's activities, hobbies, or volunteer work. A

flextime
A scheduling policy in which full-time employees may choose starting and ending times within guidelines specified by the organization.

FIGURE 4.7

Alternatives to the 8-to-5 Work Job

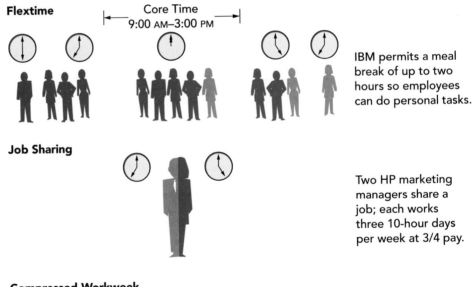

Flextime

Core Time
9:00 AM–3:00 PM

IBM permits a meal break of up to two hours so employees can do personal tasks.

Job Sharing

Two HP marketing managers share a job; each works three 10-hour days per week at 3/4 pay.

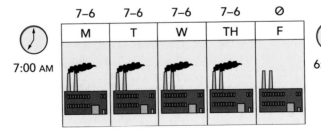

Compressed Workweek

	7–6	7–6	7–6	7–6	Ø
	M	T	W	TH	F

7:00 AM   6:00 PM

All employees of Red Dot Corporation have the option of working 10 hours per day, Monday through Thursday.

work schedule that allows time for community and family interests can be extremely motivating for some employees.

Job sharing is a work option in which two part-time employees carry out the tasks associated with a single job. Such arrangements can enable an organization to attract or retain valued employees who want more time to attend school or to care for family members. The job requirements in such an arrangement include the ability to work cooperatively and coordinate the details of one's job with another person.

Although not strictly a form of flexibility on the level of individual employees, another scheduling alternative is the *compressed workweek*. A compressed workweek is a schedule in which full-time workers complete their weekly hours in fewer than five days. For example, instead of working eight hours a day for five days, the employees could complete 40 hours of work in four 10-hour days. This alternative is most common, but some companies use other alternatives, such as scheduling 80 hours over nine days (with a three-day weekend every other week) or reducing the workweek from 40 to 38 or 36 hours. Employees may appreciate the extra days available for leisure, family, or volunteer activities. An organization might even use this schedule to offer a kind of flexibility—for example, letting workers vote whether they want a compressed workweek during the summer months. This type of schedule has a couple of drawbacks, however. One is that employees may become exhausted on the longer workdays. Another is that if the arrangement involves working more than 40 hours during a week, the Fair Labor Standards Act requires the payment of overtime wages to nonsupervisory employees.

job sharing
A work option in which two part-time employees carry out the tasks associated with a single job.

Telework

Flexibility can extend to work locations as well as work schedules. Before the Industrial Revolution, most people worked either close to or inside their own homes. Mass production technologies changed all this, separating work life from home life, as people began to travel to centrally located factories and offices. Today, however, skyrocketing prices for office space, combined with drastically reduced prices for portable communication and computing devices, seem ready to reverse this trend. The broad term for doing one's work away from a centrally located office is *telework* or telecommuting. Studies reveal that the cost savings from telework programs can top $8,000 per employee annually.

An example of a company that has benefited from telework is IBM, which initiated a program in which the company gave each teleworker an IBM ThinkPad notebook computer, printer, and extra home phone line. Marketing employees also were supplied with cell phones, pagers, faxes, and personal copiers. These workers, when

Saving commuting time and avoiding distractions, employees working at home or in a nontraditional workplace may be more productive. Would you like to work at home, or would you find it difficult to separate your home and work roles?

not sharing office space at IBM headquarters, could use their equipment to work at home or at a customer's site. IBM found that teleworkers' productivity was higher than that of traditional workers, primarily because of the savings in commuting time and avoidance of distractions from coworkers. In addition, teleworkers were able to choose their most efficient times to work (sometimes very early in the morning or late at night) and were better able to fit work around personal obligations such as caring for a sick child. However, some teleworkers reported difficulty in maintaining the same level of teamwork and in separating home and work roles.[20]

Given the possible benefits, it is not surprising that telework is a growing trend. Definitions (and, therefore, statistics) differ, but the evidence suggests the trend is significant. According to the Institute for the Study of Distributed Work, the number of corporate employees who work outside the office at least two days a week has risen from 6.3 million in 1995 to 10.4 million in 2002. The institute predicts that 13.7 million, or over 9 percent of the workforce, will be teleworkers in 2005. The researcher IDC found that telecommuting began to decline in early 2001, but after the September 11 terrorist attacks that year, telecommuting rose significantly, perhaps as a way for workers to avoid the risks of working in skyscrapers. Another force behind telework is technology. Satellite communications and the Internet make it easier to work almost anywhere. Bob Long, a global field-sales support manager for Dow Chemical, spends only 10 percent of his time at headquarters in Michigan, and the rest is divided between his New Jersey home office and trips to his customers.[21]

Designing Ergonomic Jobs

LO8

The way people use their bodies when they work—whether toting heavy furniture onto a moving van or sitting quietly before a computer screen—affects their physical well-being and may affect how well and how long they can work. The study of the interface between individuals' physiology and the characteristics of the physical work environment is called **ergonomics.** The goal of ergonomics is to minimize physical strain on the worker by structuring the physical work environment around the way the human body works. Ergonomics therefore focuses on outcomes such as reducing physical fatigue, aches and pains, and health complaints.

ergonomics
The study of the interface between individuals' physiology and the characteristics of the physical work environment.

Ergonomic job design has been applied in redesigning equipment used in jobs that are physically demanding. Such redesign is often aimed at reducing the physical demands of certain jobs so that anyone can perform them. In addition, many interventions focus on redesigning machines and technology—for instance, adjusting the height of a computer keyboard to minimize occupational illnesses, such as carpal tunnel syndrome. The design of chairs and desks to fit posture requirements is very important in many office jobs. One study found that having employees participate in an ergonomic redesign effort significantly reduced the number and severity of cumulative trauma disorders (injuries that result from performing the same movement over and over), lost production time, and restricted-duty days.[22]

Often, redesigning work to make it more worker-friendly also leads to increased efficiencies. For example, at International Truck and Engine Corporation, one of the most difficult aspects of truck production was pinning the axles to the truck frame. Traditionally, the frame was lowered onto the axle and a crew of six people, armed with oversized hammers and crowbars, forced the frame onto the axle. Because the workers could not see the bolts they had to tighten under the frame, the bolts were often fastened improperly, and many workers injured themselves in the process. After

Ergonomically designed work equipment can minimize the strain on employees and lead to increased efficiencies.

a brainstorming session, the workers and engineers concluded that it would be better to flip the frame upside down and attach the axles from above. The result was a job that could be done twice as fast by half as many workers, who were much less likely to make mistakes or get injured.[23]

Similarly, at 3M's plant in Tonawanda, New York, the company spent $60,000 on new ramps and forklifts specifically to help its aging workers lift crates filled with the company's product. The crates weighed over 125 pounds and were the source of numerous employee complaints. The result of this change in work processes was that productivity went up (expressed in terms of time to load trucks) and workers' compensation claims in the factory went to zero in the next year—down from an average of 20 over the last five years. These positive outcomes far outstripped the cost of the changes, again illustrating how a change aimed at improving the work from an ergonomic point of view often leads to cost savings as well.[24]

In 2001 the Occupational Safety and Health Administration issued regulations related to ergonomics. The OSHA regulations identify five specific high-risk work practices that employers need to avoid:[25]

1. Using a keyboard for four hours straight without a break.
2. Lifting more than 75 pounds.
3. Kneeling or squatting for more than two hours a day.
4. Working with the back, neck, or wrists bent more than two hours a day.
5. Using large vibrating equipment such as chainsaws or jackhammers more than 30 minutes a day.

Although these regulations have been challenged and may change, they do identify characteristics of jobs that may pose problems for employees. When jobs have these characteristics, employers should be vigilant about opportunities to improve work design, for the benefit of both workers and the organization.

LO9

Designing Jobs That Meet Mental Capabilities and Limitations

Just as the human body has capabilities and limitations, addressed by ergonomics, the mind, too, has capabilities and limitations. Besides hiring people with certain mental skills, organizations can design jobs so that they can be accurately and safely performed given the way the brain processes information. Generally, this means reducing the information-processing requirements of a job. In these simpler jobs, workers may be less likely to make mistakes or have accidents. Of course, the simpler jobs also may be less motivating.

There are several ways to simplify a job's mental demands. One is to limit the amount of information and memorization that the job requires. Organizations can also provide adequate lighting, easy-to-understand gauges and displays, simple-to-operate equipment, and clear instructions. Often, employees try to simplify some of the mental demands of their own jobs by creating checklists, charts, or other aids. Finally, every job requires some degree of thinking, remembering, and paying attention, so for every job, organizations need to evaluate whether their employees can handle the job's mental demands.

Applying the perceptual approach to the job of cashier, electronic cash registers have simplified some aspects of this job. In the past, a cashier read the total price displayed by a cash register, received payment, then calculated any change due the customer. Today, most stores have cash registers that compute the change due and display that amount. The cash register display makes the job easier. However, some cashiers may have been proud of their ability to figure change due, and for these people, the introduction of electronic cash registers may have reduced their job satisfaction. In this way, simplifying the mental demands of a job can also make it less interesting.

Because of this drawback to simplifying jobs, it can be most beneficial to simplify jobs where employees will most appreciate having the mental demands reduced (as in a job that is extremely challenging) or where the costs of errors are severe (as in the job of a surgeon or air-traffic controller). A relatively recent source of complexity in many jobs is the need to process a daily flood of e-mail messages. As shown in Figure

FIGURE 4.8

Number of E-Mail Messages Sent from North American Businesses

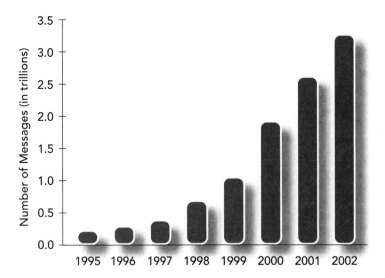

SOURCE: E. Weinstein, "Rising Flood of Office E-Mail Messages Threatens to Drown the Unorganized," *The Wall Street Journal*, Interactive Edition, February 7, 2002.

4.8, business sources alone are sending well over 2 trillion messages every day. Although the total from all sources is difficult to count, it is clear that e-mail has taken over a significant share of an 8-hour workday. Various studies estimate that office workers spend nearly an hour a day handling e-mail, and top managers may spend four times that much handling their messages. After the 2001 anthrax scare triggered concerns about the handling of postal mail, the growth rate of e-mail usage began to exceed even the rapid increases of the preceding few years.

Organizations take various steps to manage this challenge. Many have established policies—for example, limiting personal use of company e-mail and restricting the number of Internet discussion groups to which employees may subscribe. Some companies delete e-mail messages once a month. Another alternative is to install software that filters spam (electronic "junk mail"). Programs such as SpamKiller, Spam Buster, and Brightmail look for and block messages that match spam databases or have characteristics of spam. Of course, generators of spam continuously look for ways to evade these filters, so individual employees must develop ways of managing e-mail, just as they have simplified other aspects of their jobs in the past.[26]

Summary

1. **Summarize the elements of work flow analysis.**
   The analysis identifies the amount and quality of a work unit's outputs, which may be products, parts of products, or services. Next, the analyst determines the work processes required to produce these outputs, breaking down tasks into those performed by each person in the work unit. Finally, the work flow analysis identifies the inputs used to carry out the processes and produce the outputs.

2. **Describe how work flow is related to an organization's structure.**
   Within an organization, units and individuals must cooperate to create outputs, and the organization's structure brings people together for this purpose. The structure may be centralized or decentralized, and people may be grouped according to function or into divisions focusing on particular products or customer groups. A functional structure is most appropriate for people who perform highly specialized jobs and hold relatively little authority. Employee empowerment and teamwork succeed best in a divisional structure. Because of these links between structure and types of jobs, considering such issues improves the success of job design.

3. **Define the elements of a job analysis, and discuss their significance for human resource management.**
   Job analysis is the process of getting detailed information about jobs. It includes preparation of job descriptions and job specifications. A job description lists the tasks, duties, and responsibilities of a job. Job specifications look at the qualities needed in a person performing the job. They list the knowledge, skills, abilities, and other characteristics that are required for successful performance of a job. Job analysis provides a foundation for carrying out many HRM responsibilities, including work redesign, human resource planning, employee selection and training, performance appraisal, career planning, and job evaluation to determine pay scales.

4. **Tell how to obtain information for a job analysis.**
   Information for analyzing an existing job often comes from incumbents and their supervisors. The Labor Department publishes general background information about jobs in the *Dictionary of Occupational Titles* and Occupational Information Network (O*NET). Job analysts, employees, and managers may complete a Position Analysis Questionnaire or task analysis inventory, or fill out a survey for the Fleishman Job Analysis System.

5. **Summarize recent trends in job analysis.**
   Some organizations are "dejobbing," or viewing organizations in terms of a field of work needing to be done, rather than as a set or series of jobs. These organizations look for employees who can take on different responsibilities as the field of work changes. Organizations are also adopting project-based structures and teamwork, which also require flexibility and the ability to handle broad responsibilities.

6. **Describe methods for designing a job so that it can be done efficiently.**
   The basic technique for designing efficient jobs is industrial engineering, which looks for the simplest way

to structure work in order to maximize efficiency. Through methods such as time-and-motion studies, the industrial engineer creates jobs that are relatively simple and typically repetitive. These jobs may bore workers because they are so simple.

7. Identify approaches to designing a job to make it motivating.

According to the Job Characteristics Model, jobs are more motivating if they have greater skill variety, task identity, task significance, autonomy, and feedback about performance effectiveness. Ways to create such jobs include job enlargement (through job extension or job rotation) and job enrichment. In addition, self-managing work teams offer greater skill variety and task identity. Flexible work schedules and telework offer greater autonomy.

8. Explain how organizations apply ergonomics to design safe jobs.

The goal of ergonomics is to minimize physical strain on the worker by structuring the physical work environment around the way the human body works. Er-

gonomic design may involve modifying equipment to reduce the physical demands of performing certain jobs or redesigning the jobs themselves to reduce strain. Ergonomic design may target work practices associated with injuries, including using a keyboard for hours at a time, lifting heavy weights, extensive kneeling or squatting, using large vibrating equipment, and working with back, neck, or wrists bent for several hours a day.

9. Discuss how organizations can plan for the mental demands of a job.

Employers may seek to reduce mental as well as physical strain. The job design may limit the amount of information and memorization involved. Adequate lighting, easy-to-read gauges and displays, simple-to-operate equipment, and clear instructions also can minimize mental strain. Computer software can simplify jobs—for example, by performing calculations or filtering out spam from important e-mail. Finally, organizations can select employees with the necessary abilities to handle a job's mental demands.

Review and Discussion Questions

1. Assume you are the manager of a fast-food restaurant. What are the outputs of your work unit? What are the activities required to produce those outputs? What are the inputs?

2. Based on question 1, consider the cashier's job in the restaurant. What are the outputs, activities, and inputs for that job?

3. Consider the "job" of college student. Perform a job analysis on this job. What tasks are required in the job? What knowledge, skills, and abilities are necessary to perform those tasks? Prepare a job description based on your analysis.

4. Discuss how the following trends are changing the skill requirements for managerial jobs in the United States:
   a. Increasing use of computers and the Internet.
   b. Increasing international competition.
   c. Increasing work-family conflicts.

5. How can a job analysis of each job in the work unit help a supervisor to do his or her job?

6. Consider the job of a customer service representative who fields telephone calls from customers of a retailer that sells online and through catalogs. What measures can an employer take to design this job to make it efficient? What might be some drawbacks or challenges of designing this job for efficiency?

7. How might the job in question 6 be designed to make it more motivating? How well would these considerations apply to the cashier's job in question 1?

8. What ergonomic considerations might apply to each of the following jobs? For each job, what kinds of costs would result from addressing ergonomics? What costs might result from failing to address ergonomics?
   a. A computer programmer.
   b. A UPS delivery person.
   c. A child care worker.

9. The chapter said that modern electronics have eliminated the need for a store's cashiers to calculate change due on a purchase. How does this development modify the job description for a cashier? If you were a store manager, how would it affect the skills and qualities of job candidates you would want to hire? Does this change in mental processing requirements affect what you would expect from a cashier? How?

10. Consider a job you hold now or have held recently. Would you want this job to be redesigned to place more emphasis on efficiency, motivation, ergonomics, or mental processing? What changes would you want, and why? (Or why do you not want the job to be redesigned?)

What's Your HR IQ?

The Student CD-ROM offers two more ways to check what you've learned so far. Use the Self-Assessment exercise to learn more about the Department of Labor's Occu- pational Information Network (O*NET). Go online with the Web Exercise to learn more about ergonomics in the workplace.

BusinessWeek Case

BusinessWeek The New Factory Worker

Fred Price gropes his way downstairs in the dark, grabs a Danish, and races off to work at 4 AM. Today is a special day for the 29-year-old North Carolina factory hand. He will schedule orders as usual for the tiny tool-and-die shop where he doubles as a supervisor when he's not bending metal himself. But at midday, test results are coming in from the state Labor Department. These aptitude exams for all 43 workers at Northeast Tool & Manufacturing Company, outside Charlotte, measure everything from math and mechanical skills to leadership and adaptability. And they come with a prescription. It appears that Price will have less time for bird hunting and the kids' go-cart. Like tens of thousands of factory workers across America, Fred Price is going back to school.

Growing up, Price liked to work with his hands more than his head. He would help his father fix the family's old Ford pickup, and once they rigged up a hydraulic log split- ter. In high school, he excelled in shop class but not in English and math. These days, with even factory work de- fined by blips on a computer screen, more schooling is the only road ahead. Northeast Tool will use the employee tests to select training for each worker. Some will enroll at a nearby community college. Others will take remote courses through computers set up at the plant. A few will attend afternoon classes with professors brought right into the mill. Price wants to pursue a two-year degree in met- allurgy, even if it requires long hours on weekends. "Someday I hope to manage the plant," he says.

Until recently, Americans divided ranks in high school between shop kids such as Price, who went on to industrial or service work, and college-bound students headed for white-collar or professional jobs. They parted ways at graduation and moved into distinct categories of manual and knowledge workers.

Today, thinned-out ranks of managers have equipped factory workers with industrial robots and taught them to use computer controls to operate masssive steel casters and stamp presses. Managers are funneling information through the computers, bringing employees into the data loop. Workers learn to watch inventories, to know suppli- ers and customers, cost and prices. Knowledge that long separated brain workers from hand workers is now avail- able via computer on the factory floor. At Northeast Tool, Rusty Arant, Fred Price's manager, points to a computer he rigged up to a milling machine and says, "I crammed it with memory because I want these guys to be managing the business from the shop floor."

"There's a real rise in companies' willingness to invest in their workforces," says Pamela J. Tate, president of the Council for Adult & Experiential Learning, a Chicago consulting group. This investment carries a blunt message for manufacturing workers: Hone your skills or risk being left behind. U.S. workers are being pushed to raise their technical savvy, develop leadership skills, and take a role in managing that's a far cry from the traditional top-down structure.

Indeed, the old formula of company loyalty, a strong back, and showing up on time no longer guarantees job se- curity or even a decent paycheck. Industrial workers will thrive only if they use their wits and keep adding to their skills. It's a rich irony: Millions of Americans who headed for the factory because they didn't like school, among other reasons, now face a career-long dose of it.

Workers must meet the challenge so their employers can compete. In 1985, when the then 18-year-old Fred Price started at Northeast Tool, the job shop sold custom- made metal pieces primarily to local Carolina customers. Today, as markets become global, Northeast must boost quality enough to land contracts from the likes of BMW and Siemens. These companies want metal fashioned to precise tolerances. Many demand that suppliers be certified to tough European standards, a goal Northeast is pursuing.

This requires more training than Price, a high school graduate, had gained through work experience. For him, the payoff is a shot at advancement and improving his $15-an-hour pay. From manager Arant's perspective, there is no choice. Arant plans to use his higher-skilled work- force to bid for more lucrative business and expand. If he didn't, Northeast could fall behind, as Arant thinks some rivals may do.

Until recently, workers such as Price probably would have been out of luck. Northeast, with annual revenues of less than $5 million, simply wouldn't have been able to af- ford its ambitious training program. Many companies, large and small, avoided investing too much in workers, only to lose them later. Now, though, more companies feel they can't afford not to train.

The education message rings so loudly that some job seekers actually target high-performance employers just to get the schooling. In fact, such companies are replacing the military as a blue-collar training ground and an inexpensive way to get some college education, or its equivalent. Many companies are willing to sink money into training if they feel confident the employee has the profile of a lifelong learner. "We look for people who want change, who don't see it as troublesome, but as an opportunity," says David P. Jones, an official of Aon Consulting, a Chicago firm that helps manufacturers with testing and hiring.

SOURCE: Adapted from S. Baker, "The New Factory Worker," *BusinessWeek,* September 30, 1996.

Questions

1. What changes does this article describe in Fred Price's job? What benefits was his employer seeking from job redesign?
2. How does the redesign of factory jobs, as described in this article, affect the tasks, duties, and responsibilities required for these jobs? How does the redesign change the needed knowledge, skills, abilities, and other characteristics of an individual performing the job?
3. What challenges to human resource management result from these changes? Suggest some ways organizations might meet these challenges.

Case: From Big Blue to Efficient Blue

IBM was long known as "Big Blue" because of its size, in terms of both the number of employees and the amount of revenue and costs associated with its operations. However, as the old saying goes, "The bigger they are, the harder they fall." In 1993 IBM racked up over $8 billion in losses when it was blindsided by a switch in consumer preferences from mainframe computers to smaller, networked personal computers.

Then-incoming CEO, Lou Gerstner, needed to engineer one of the greatest turnarounds in modern business; he started with a new vision of what the company would become, as well as a strategy for getting where the company needed to be. The strategy had both an external aspect, focused on changing from an old-fashioned manufacturing company to a modern service provider, and an internal aspect of restructuring operations to reduce costs and promote efficiencies.

Nowhere was this internal strategy change felt more strongly than in the human resource division. In 1993, the HRM function of IBM was large, decentralized, and regionally based, with branch offices all over the world employing over 3,500 people. By the year 2000, there was only one single, centralized unit located in Raleigh, North Carolina. This unit employed fewer than 1,000 people.

The key to the successful downsizing effort was its emphasis on matching size changes with changes in structure and the substitution of technology for labor. Instead of interacting face-to-face with the local human resources office, all communication would be technologically mediated and directed to the central Raleigh facility via telephone, e-mail, or fax. Moreover, user-friendly software was developed to help employees answer their questions without any other human involvement.

The sprawling, geographically dispersed units were replaced with an efficient three-tier system. The first tier was composed of broadly trained human resource generalists who received telephone calls from any of IBM's 700,000 HRM "customers" (employees) and tried to respond to any queries that could not be handled via the automated system. The second tier, a smaller number of highly trained specialists (such as in 401(k) plans, OSHA requirements, or selection standards), took any calls that exceeded the knowledge level of the generalists. Finally, the third tier consisted of an even smaller number of top executives charged with keeping the HRM practices in line with the overall corporate strategy being developed by Gerstner.

Amazingly, despite the radical downsizing of this unit, employee satisfaction with service actually increased to over 90 percent of employees saying they were satisfied. Gerstner singled out the reengineering of the HR division as a success story that should serve as a benchmark for the rest of the company's divisions. Moreover, the restructuring and redesign of these IBM jobs have formed a "blue"-print for many other HRM departments in other organizations.

SOURCE: S. N. Mehta, "What Lucent Can Learn from IBM," *Fortune,* June 25, 2001, p. 40; G. Flynn, "Out of the Red, into the Blue," *Workforce,* March 2000, pp. 50–52; P. Gilster, "Making Online Self-Service Work," *Workforce,* January 2001, pp. 54–61; J. Hutchins, "The U.S. Postal Service Delivers an Innovative HR Strategy," *Workforce,* October 2000, pp. 116–18.

Questions

1. Based on this chapter, how did IBM's change affect the organization's overall structure? How might these changes affect IBM's basic work flow?
2. How would the changes in organizational structure affect the kinds of job design suitable for IBM, especially in its HR division?
3. How would the changes influence the kinds of employee skills that IBM needs for its HR division?

Notes

1. C. Tejada, "Home Office: Millions Don't Leave Work at Work," *The Wall Street Journal,* Interactive Edition, March 5, 2002; C. Richards, " 'Pink-Collar' Pressure," *Chicago Tribune,* March 6, 2002, sec. 8, pp. 1, 7.
2. M. Fefer, "Bill Gates' Next Challenge," *Fortune,* December 14, 1992, pp. 30–41.
3. D. Shook, "Why Nike Is Dragging Its Feet," *BusinessWeek Online,* March 19, 2001; A. Bernstein, "Backlash: Behind the Anxiety over Globalization," *BusinessWeek,* April 20, 2000, pp. 38–43; A. Bernstein, "Low Skilled Jobs: Do They Have to Move?" *BusinessWeek,* February 26, 2001.
4. C. Joinson, "Refocusing Job Descriptions," *HR Magazine,* January 2001, downloaded from Findarticles.com.
5. G. Koretz, "Perils of the Graveyard Shift: Poor Health and Low Productivity," *BusinessWeek,* March 10, 1997, p. 22; C. R. Maiwald, J. L. Pierce, and J. W. Newstrom, "Workin' 8 P.M. to 8 A.M. and Lovin' Every Minute of It," *Workforce,* July 1997, pp. 30–36.
6. A. O'Reilly, "Skill Requirements: Supervisor-Subordinate Conflict," *Personnel Psychology* 26 (1973), pp. 75–80; J. Hazel, J. Madden, and R. Christal, "Agreement between Worker-Supervisor Descriptions of the Worker's Job," *Journal of Industrial Psychology* 2 (1964), pp. 71–79.
7. N. G. Peterson, M. D. Mumford, W. C. Borman, P. R. Jeanneret, and E. A. Fleishman, *An Occupational Information System for the 21st Century: The Development of O*NET* (Washington, DC: American Psychological Association, 1999); N. G. Peterson, M. D. Mumford, W. C. Borman, P. R. Jeanneret, E. A. Fleishman, K. Y. Levin, M. A. Campion, M. S. Mayfield, F. P. Morgenson, K. Pearlman, M. K. Gowing, A. R. Lancaster, M. B. Silver, and D. M. Dye, "Understanding Work Using the Occupational Information Network (O*NET): Implications for Practice and Research," *Personnel Psychology* 54 (2001), pp. 451–92; S. Holmes, "Lots of Green Left in the Emerald City," *BusinessWeek Online,* March 28, 2000; D. Dyer, "O*NET in Action," O*NET website, http://online.onetcenter.org.
8. *PAQ Newsletter,* August 1989.
9. E. Primhoff, *How to Prepare and Conduct Job Element Examinations* (Washington, DC: U.S. Government Printing Office, 1975).
10. E. Fleishman and M. Reilly, *Handbook of Human Abilities* (Palo Alto, CA: Consulting Psychologists Press, 1992); E. Fleishman and M. Mumford, "Ability Requirements Scales," in *The Job Analysis Handbook for Business, Industry, and Government,* pp. 917–35.
11. W. Cascio, *Applied Psychology in Personnel Management,* 4th ed. (Englewood Cliffs, NJ: Prentice Hall, 1991).
12. P. Wright and K. Wexley, "How to Choose the Kind of Job Analysis You Really Need," *Personnel,* May 1985, pp. 51–55.
13. C. Joinson, "Refocusing Job Descriptions."
14. Ibid.
15. M. K. Lindell, C. S. Clause, C. J. Brandt, and R. S. Landis, "Relationship between Organizational Context and Job Analysis Ratings," *Journal of Applied Psychology* 83 (1998), pp. 769–76.
16. S. Caudron, "Jobs Disappear when Work Becomes More Important," *Workforce,* January 2000, pp. 30–32.
17. P. Gogoi, "Going to the Head of the Class," *BusinessWeek,* December 10, 2001, pp. 53–54.
18. R. Hackman and G. Oldham, *Work Redesign* (Boston: Addison-Wesley, 1980).
19. M. A. Campion, G. J. Medsker, and A. C. Higgs, "Relations between Work Group Characteristics and Effectiveness: Implications for Designing Effective Work Groups," *Personnel Psychology* 46 (1993), pp. 823–50.
20. M. Werner, "Working at Home—the Right Way to Be a Star in Your Bunny Slippers," *Fortune,* March 3, 1997, pp. 165–66; P. Coy, "Home Sweet Office," *BusinessWeek,* April 6, 1998, p. 30; E. J. Hill, B. C. Miller, S. P. Weiner, and J. Colihan, "Influences of the Virtual Office on Aspects of Work and Work/Life Balance," *Personnel Psychology* 51 (1998), pp. 667–83.
21. S. Shellenbarger, "Workers Get Creative Finding Places to Sit and 'Telework,' " *The Wall Street Journal,* Interactive Edition, January 23, 2002.
22. D. May and C. Schwoerer, "Employee Health by Design: Using Employee Involvement Teams in Ergonomic Job Redesign," *Personnel Psychology* 47 (1994), pp. 861–86.
23. S. F. Brown, "International's Better Way to Build Trucks," *Fortune,* February 19, 2001, pp. 210k–210v.
24. C. Haddad, "OSHA's New Regs Will Ease the Pain—for Everybody," *BusinessWeek,* December 4, 2000, pp. 90–94.
25. G. Flynn, "Now Is the Time to Prepare for OSHA's Sweeping New Ergonomics Standard," *Workforce,* March 2001, pp. 76–77.
26. E. Weinstein, "Rising Flood of Office E-Mail Messages Threatens to Drown the Unorganized," *The Wall Street Journal,* Interactive Edition, January 10, 2002; Associated Press, "With Mountain of Junk Mail Set to Grow, Companies Promote Tools to Reduce 'Spam,' " *The Wall Street Journal,* Interactive Edition, December 17, 2001.

Southwest Airlines Competes by Putting People First

Whenever Southwest Airlines founder Herb Kelleher did a song and dance routine for his employees, they laughed —then they got up to sing and dance with him. Kelleher is well known for his energy, enthusiasm, and drive, not only throughout the airline industry but also throughout American industry as a whole. Thirty years ago, he founded the Dallas-based airline with a few planes scheduled for short hauls within the state of Texas. In the late 1970s, Southwest expanded to inter-state—but still short-haul—flights, and it now serves nearly 60 cities in 30 states, usually operating out of smaller, less-congested airports. Consumers love the low-cost, quick-turnaround flights staffed by cheerful, energetic employees. Southwest employees love the atmosphere in which they work. "We do have a good time here, and we work hard," notes Laura Rollheiser, supervisor of ramp agents. And everyone loves Kelleher, who decided to step down as chief executive when he turned 70 years old in the spring of 2001. In three decades, Kelleher created a successful organization based on strategic management so that when he transferred power to Southwest's vice president and general counsel James F. Parker, the company was ready. "It's an exceedingly orderly transition," said Kelleher.

Southwest Airlines is an organization that has built its business and corporate culture on the principles of total quality management. Customer focus, employee involvement and empowerment, and continuous improvement are not just buzzwords to Southwest employees or to its executives. Employ-

ees are included in business strategy planning, they are selected for their team skills, and they are cross-trained in a variety of areas. Then they are given the freedom to make decisions that will help customers and improve efficiency—any way they can. Once, when five students who commuted weekly to an out-of-state medical school informed Southwest that the most convenient flight still got them to class 15 minutes late, Southwest employees moved the departure time of the flight up by a quarter of an hour. Customers are involved, too. Frequent fliers may be asked to assist HR managers in interviewing and selecting prospective flight attendants, and focus groups are used to help measure passenger response to new services and generate new ideas for improvement. The approximately 1,000 customers who write the company each week receive a personal response within four weeks. It's not surprising that Southwest has been a frequent winner of the U.S. Department of Transportation's Triple Crown Award for best on-time performance, best baggage handling, and fewest customer complaints. All of these successes are no accident—they are based on superior strategy.

THE AIRLINE INDUSTRY

No one could have predicted the tragic events that occurred on September 11, 2001, when two hijacked American Airlines flights and two hijacked United Airlines flights crashed with hundreds of people on board— two into the World Trade Center in New York, one into the Pentagon in Washington, DC, and one in western

Pennsylvania. It would take many months to sort through the devastating losses, both in terms of human lives and financial repercussions. The airline industry itself was already suffering in an uncertain economy, and when airspace was completely shut down for two days after the terrorist attacks, some of the smaller airlines such as Midway folded. Other airlines slashed jobs, routes, and schedules in an effort to stay aloft. A month after the tragedy, Southwest was still hanging tough, flying a full schedule (despite many empty seats because the public wasn't flying) and keeping all of its workers on payroll. By year's end, it was expected to be the only major carrier to show a profit—perhaps small comfort amid so much loss and turmoil.

SOUTHWEST'S CORPORATE STRATEGY

From the beginning, Herb Kelleher developed a strategy based on regional markets; Southwest could fly shorter routes with a single type of reliable aircraft—the Boeing 737. While other airlines busily built hubs, Southwest simply flew point-to-point, operating out of smaller airports. Instead of serving expensive meals, Southwest offered snacks and nuts. The airline encouraged its employees to interact with customers in a friendly, casual manner. Its much-touted 15-minute turnaround time was the envy of the industry. And the single aircraft choice increased flexibility for changes in flight crew and schedules. Ultimately, Southwest achieved the goal of every airline—the lowest cost per seat in the industry. Still, Southwest was able to charge less per ticket than most other airlines.

All the while, Herb Kelleher was preparing the company for change—part of his overall corporate strategy. When James Parker took over as CEO, Kelleher noted that although Parker had previously maintained a low profile, he had been part of upper-level decision making for a "long, long time." Colleen Barrett, who began her career as Kelleher's legal secretary, moved into the position of president and chief operating officer. Employees at other levels were—and continue to be—groomed to take on more responsibility. As one business writer notes, "These people have been in a leadership lab where they've had an opportunity to study and learn firsthand from [Kelleher] for many years. They have seen the airline through good and bad times. The company wouldn't be what it is today without them collectively."

ORGANIZATIONAL CULTURE AND HRM PRACTICES

The organizational culture at Southwest promotes safety, customer satisfaction, and consistency. Employees feel that they are part of a team and that they can view their contributions to the success of Southwest with unity and pride. "We're all in it together," notes Chris Wahlenheimer, a station manager. Employees at all levels of the company are linked to the overall business strategy.

The positive employee relations enjoyed by Southwest are unusual in an industry where antagonistic labor-management relations are common. How does the company build cooperation with a workforce that is more than 80 percent unionized? First led by Kelleher and now by his successors,

the corporation has developed a culture that treats employees the same way it treats its passengers—by paying attention, being responsive, and involving them in decisions. Southwest places high value on employees' enjoying their jobs but places equal value on their performance. Employees are encouraged—and trained—to be flexible. And they are given lots of feedback about how they are doing. When they do well, they are publicly recognized. When Southwest won the Triple Crown Award for the fifth year in a row, the company dedicated an airplane to all the employees, and engraved their names on the outside of overhead bins. Business practices as described above help position Southwest Airlines as a company that can easily recruit, and more importantly keep, talented employees.

A LOOK TOWARD THE FUTURE

As other airlines struggle to survive, Southwest looks for ways to thrive. Shortly after the September 11 tragedies, the company sought ways to convince the public to fly regularly again. It kept workers going. And it went ahead with previous plans to open new routes. "They're doing what they do best, which is to shine in the hours of trouble," noted Mo Garfinkle, president of an aviation consulting firm. "This, to me, is not a gamble. This is a very shrewd strategic move." Still, chief financial officer Gary Kelly cautioned that the company would not be making any outrageous moves. "The fact of the matter is we can be patient and we should be patient," noted Kelly. "We're in the mode where we are thinking very tactically."

Ultimately, no one doubts that Southwest will spread its wings again.

SOURCES: Melanie Trottman and Susan Carey, "Southwest, Alaska Saw Profits in Quarter," *The Wall Street Journal*, October 19, 2001, p. A2; Melanie Trottman, "Up in the Air," *The Wall Street Journal*, pp. A1, A10; Melanie Trottman, "Southwest Airlines' Formula for Success to Be Tested in a More Cautious Market," *The Wall Street Journal*, September 24, 2001, p. A8; Kevin and Jackie Freiberg, "Southwest Can Find Another Pilot," *The Wall Street Journal*, March 26, 2001, p. A22; Ann Zimmerman, Elliot Spagat, and Scott McCartney, "Southwest Airlines' Kelleher, Who Kept Costs Low and Morale High, Cuts Duties," *The Wall Street Journal*, March 20, 2001, p. A3, A10.

Questions

1. What are some of the major challenges that Southwest has faced in recent years? In what ways has the company dealt with these challenges?
2. Name at least two values that the organizational culture of Southwest promotes. In what ways do these two values affect the way the company is managed?
3. Would you want to work for Southwest? Cite at least three reasons why or why not.
4. Do you think that Southwest's success is more a result of business practices, human resource practices, or the interaction between the two? Can HR practices help a company be successful without good business practices?
5. One of the challenges of the new economy is finding and keeping new employees. Describe what you believe are the most important features of Southwest Airlines that help the company gain a competitive advantage through finding and keeping new employees. Visit Southwest Airlines website at www.iflyswa.com to find out more about the company.

Part 2

Acquiring and Preparing Human Resources

Chapter 5

Planning for and Recruiting Human Resources

Chapter 6

Selecting Employees and Placing Them in Jobs

Chapter 7

Training Employees

Chapter 5

Planning for and Recruiting Human Resources

What Do I Need to Know? After reading this chapter, you should be able to:

1. Discuss how to plan for human resources needed to carry out the organization's strategy.

2. Determine the labor demand for workers in various job categories.

3. Summarize the advantages and disadvantages of ways to eliminate a labor surplus and avoid a labor shortage.

4. Describe recruitment policies organizations use to make job vacancies more attractive.

5. List and compare sources of job applicants.

6. Describe the recruiter's role in the recruitment process, including limits and opportunities.

Introduction

Business news often contains stories of layoffs, as organizations react to falling demand by cutting their workforce. Others go out of their way to find alternatives. Stacey Scott, founder and chief executive of Elgia, a provider of Web conferencing services, had trouble getting enough financing, so she kept her start-up afloat by moving away from high-cost Silicon Valley. At Elgia's new location in Roswell, Georgia, rents and salaries are far cheaper. Moving didn't require layoffs. Elgia's sales representative stayed in California and continued working there until she found another job. Since then, Scott has hired three employees in Georgia.[1]

With a bigger workforce, an established company needs more creativity to avoid layoffs. At Parker Hannifin's Daedal division in Irwin, Pennsylvania, general manager Ken Sweet went to great lengths to keep workers on the payroll during the economic slowdown of 2001. He reassigned many employees to help sell the division's automation equipment. Assembly workers built demonstration models, other production workers ran batches of parts the company had formerly bought from suppliers, and some even spent a few hours a week phoning prospective customers. As Sweet waited for sales to rebound, he had workers vote on a choice of layoffs or unpaid time off. Most factory workers chose time off, so Sweet announced they would have three or four days off each month. Fewer of the office workers preferred that alternative, so Sweet said they would have two unpaid days off a month, and their salary increases would be delayed several months.[2]

As these two examples show, trends and events that affect the economy also create opportunities and problems in obtaining human resources. When customer demand rises (or falls), organizations may need more (or fewer) employees. When the labor market changes—say, when more people go to college or when a sizable share of the population retires—the supply of qualified workers may grow, shrink, or change in nature. Organizations recently have had difficulty filling information technology jobs because the demand for people with these skills outstrips the supply. To prepare for and respond to these challenges, organizations engage in *human resource planning*—defined in Chapter 1 as identifying the numbers and types of employees the organization will require to meet its objectives.

This chapter describes how organizations carry out human resource planning. In the first part of the chapter, we lay out the steps that go into developing and implementing a human resource plan. Throughout each section, we focus especially on recent trends and practices, including downsizing, employing temporary workers, and outsourcing. The remainder of the chapter explores the process of recruiting. We describe the process by which organizations look for people to fill job vacancies and the usual sources of job candidates. Finally, we discuss the role of recruiters.

The Process of Human Resource Planning   LO1

Organizations should carry out human resource planning so as to meet business objectives and gain an advantage over competitors. To do this, organizations need a clear idea of the strengths and weaknesses of their existing internal labor force. They also must know what they want to be doing in the future—what size they want the organization to be, what products and services it should be producing, and so on. This knowledge helps them define the number and kinds of employees they will need. Human resource planning compares the present state of the organization with its goals for the future, then identifies what changes it must make in its human resources to meet those goals. The changes may include downsizing, training existing employees in new skills, or hiring new employees.

These activities give a general view of HR planning. They take place in the human resource planning process shown in Figure 5.1. The process consists of three stages: forecasting, goal setting and strategic planning, and program implementation and evaluation.

FIGURE 5.1

Overview of the Human Resource Planning Process

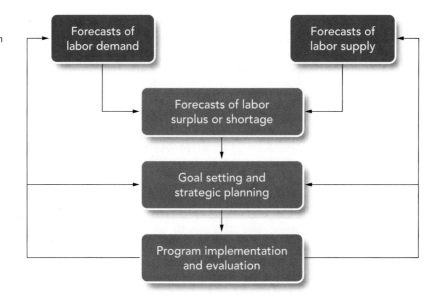

Forecasting

forecasting
The attempts to determine the supply of and demand for various types of human resources to predict areas within the organization where there will be labor shortages or surpluses.

The first step in human resource planning is **forecasting,** as shown in the top portion of Figure 5.1. In personnel forecasting, the HR professional tries to determine the supply of and demand for various types of human resources. The primary goal is to predict which areas of the organization will experience labor shortages or surpluses.

Forecasting supply and demand can use statistical methods or judgment. Statistical methods capture historic trends in a company's demand for labor. Under the right conditions, these methods predict demand and supply more precisely than a human forecaster can using subjective judgment. But many important events in the labor market have no precedent. When such events occur, statistical methods are of little use. To prepare for these situations, the organization must rely on the subjective judgments of experts. Pooling their "best guesses" is an important source of ideas about the future.

LO2

Forecasting the Demand for Labor

trend analysis
Constructing and applying statistical models that predict labor demand for the next year, given relatively objective statistics from the previous year.

leading indicators
Objective measures that accurately predict future labor demand.

Usually, an organization forecasts demand for specific job categories or skill areas. After identifying the relevant job categories or skills, the planner investigates the likely demand for each. The planner must forecast whether the need for people with the necessary skills and experience will increase or decrease. There are several ways of making such forecasts.

At the most sophisticated level, an organization might use **trend analysis,** constructing and applying statistical models that predict labor demand for the next year, given relatively objective statistics from the previous year. These statistics are called **leading indicators**—objective measures that accurately predict future labor demand. They might include measures of the economy (such as sales or inventory levels), actions of competitors, changes in technology, and trends in the composition of the workforce. For example, a manufacturer of automobile parts that sells its product primarily to the Big Three automakers would use statistics on the Big Three automakers, using the numbers from recent time periods to predict the demand for the company's product in a later time period.

Statistical planning models are useful when there is a long, stable history that can be used to reliably detect relationships among variables. However, these models almost always have to be complemented with subjective judgments of experts. There are simply too many "once-in-a-lifetime" changes to consider, and statistical models cannot capture them.

Determining Labor Supply

Once a company has forecast the demand for labor, it needs an indication of the firm's labor supply. Determining the internal labor supply calls for a detailed analysis of how many people are currently in various job categories or have specific skills within the organization. The planner then modifies this analysis to reflect changes expected in the near future as a result of retirements, promotions, transfers, voluntary turnover, and terminations.

One type of statistical procedure that can be used for this purpose is the analysis of a **transitional matrix.** This is a chart that lists job categories held in one period and shows the proportion of employees in each of those job categories in a future period. It answers two questions: "Where did people who were in each job category go?" and "Where did people now in each job category come from?" Table 5.1 is an example of a transitional matrix.

This example lists job categories for an auto parts manufacturer. The jobs listed at the left were held in 1998; the numbers at the right show what happened to the people in 2001. The numbers represent proportions. For example, .95 means 95 percent of the people represented by a row in the matrix. The column headings under 2001 refer to the row numbers. The first row is sales managers, so the numbers under column (1) represent people who became sales managers. Reading across the first row, we see that 95 of the people who were sales managers in 1998 are still sales managers in 2001. The other 5 percent correspond to position (8), "Not in organization," meaning the 5 percent of employees who are not still sales managers have left the organization. In the second row are sales representatives. Of those who were sales reps in 1998, 5 percent were promoted to sales manager, 60 percent are still sales reps, and 35 percent have left the organization. In row (3), half (50 percent) of sales apprentices are still in that job, but 20 percent are now sales reps, and 30 percent have left the organization. This pattern of jobs shows a career path from sales apprentice to sales representative to sales manager. Of course, not everyone is promoted, and some of the people leave instead.

transitional matrix
A chart that lists job categories held in one period and shows the proportion of employees in each of those job categories in a future period.

1998	2001							
	(1)	(2)	(3)	(4)	(5)	(6)	(7)	(8)
(1) Sales manager	.95							.05
(2) Sales representative	.05	.60						.35
(3) Sales apprentice		.20	.50					.30
(4) Assistant plant manager				.90	.05			.05
(5) Production manager				.10	.75			.15
(6) Production assembler					.10	.80		.10
(7) Clerical							.70	.30
(8) Not in organization	.00	.20	.50	.00	.10	.20	.30	

TABLE 5.1

Transitional Matrix: Example for an Auto Parts Manufacturer

Reading down the columns provides another kind of information: the sources of employees holding the positions in 2001. In the first column, we see that most sales managers (95 percent) held that same job three years earlier. The other 5 percent were promoted from sales representative positions. Skipping over to column (3), half the sales apprentices on the payroll in 2001 held the same job three years before, and the other half were hired from outside the organization. This suggests that the organization fills sales manager positions primarily through promotions, so planning for this job would focus on preparing sales representatives. In contrast, planning to meet the organization's needs for sales apprentices would emphasize recruitment and selection of new employees.

Matrices such as this one are extremely useful for charting historical trends in the company's supply of labor. More important, if conditions remain somewhat constant, they can also be used to plan for the future. For example, if we believe that that we are going to have a surplus of labor in the production assembler job category in the next three years, we can plan to avoid layoffs. Still, historical data may not always reliably indicate future trends. Planners need to combine statistical forecasts of labor supply with expert judgments. For example, managers in the organization may see that a new training program will likely increase the number of employees qualified for new openings. Forecasts of labor supply also should take into account the organization's pool of skills. Many organizations include inventories of employees' skills in an HR database. When the organization forecasts that it will need new skills in the future, planners can consult the database to see how many existing employees have those skills.

Besides looking at the labor supply within the organization, the planner should examine trends in the external labor market. The planner should keep abreast of labor market forecasts, including the size of the labor market, the unemployment rate, and the kinds of people who will be in the labor market. For example, we saw in Chapter 2 that the U.S. labor market is aging and that immigration is an important source of new workers. Important sources of data on the external labor market include the *Occupational Outlook Quarterly* and the *Monthly Labor Review*, published by the Labor Department's Bureau of Labor Statistics. Details and news releases are available at the website of the Bureau of Labor Statistics (**www.bls.gov**).

Determining Labor Surplus or Shortage

Based on the forecasts for labor demand and supply, the planner can compare the figures to determine whether there will be a shortage or surplus of labor for each job category. Determining expected shortages and surpluses allows the organization to plan how to address these challenges.

Japan's Matsushita Corporation has benefited from accurate forecasting. Much of Matsushita's revenues come from exporting, so a leading indicator for its labor demand is the value of the Japanese yen against other currencies. When the yen is high, sales in other countries tend to be low, because Matsushita's prices are relatively high. When the yen's value falls, Matsushita's prices in other currencies fall, so sales in other countries rise. Logically, when sales of Japanese products rise or fall, the demand for Japanese labor changes in the same direction. In 1988 Matsushita's planners accurately forecasted a large increase in the price of the yen, which could cause falling demand and an oversupply of Japanese labor. Rather than expanding in Japan, Matsushita opened "export centers," which designed and produced televisions and air conditioners in Malaysia, China, and the United States. When the yen's price rose as expected, Matsushita's export centers were very successful.[3] Meanwhile, Japanese companies that had failed to accurately predict labor demand had to lay off workers—an act almost unprecedented in Japan until that time.[4]

Goal Setting and Strategic Planning

LO4

The second step in human resource planning is goal setting and strategic planning, as shown in the middle of Figure 5.1. The purpose of setting specific numerical goals is to focus attention on the problem and provide a basis for measuring the organization's success in addressing labor shortages and surpluses. The goals should come directly from the analysis of labor supply and demand. They should include a specific figure indicating what should happen with the job category or skill area and a specific timetable for when the results should be achieved.

For each goal, the organization must choose one or more human resource strategies. A variety of strategies is available for handling expected shortages and surpluses of labor. The top of Table 5.2 shows major options for reducing an expected labor surplus, and the bottom of the table lists options for avoiding an expected labor shortage.

This planning stage is critical. The options differ widely in their expense, speed, and effectiveness. Options for reducing a labor surplus cause differing amounts of human suffering. The options for avoiding a labor shortage differ in terms of how easily the organization can undo the change if it no longer faces a labor shortage. For example, an organization probably would not want to handle every expected labor surplus by hiring new employees. The process is relatively slow and involves expenses to

OPTIONS FOR REDUCING A SURPLUS		
OPTION	SPEED OF RESULTS	AMOUNT OF SUFFERING CAUSED
Downsizing	Fast	High
Pay reductions	Fast	High
Demotions	Fast	High
Transfers	Fast	Moderate
Work sharing	Fast	Moderate
Hiring freeze	Slow	Low
Natural attrition	Slow	Low
Early retirement	Slow	Low
Retraining	Slow	Low

OPTIONS FOR AVOIDING A SHORTAGE		
OPTION	SPEED OF RESULTS	ABILITY TO CHANGE LATER
Overtime	Fast	High
Temporary employees	Fast	High
Outsourcing	Fast	High
Retrained transfers	Slow	High
Turnover reductions	Slow	Moderate
New external hires	Slow	Low
Technological innovation	Slow	Low

TABLE 5.2

HR Strategies for Addressing a Labor Shortage or Surplus

Just Enough People at ZF Micro Devices

Sure, ZF Micro Devices is growing fast. Even in the softening economy of 2001, the company was forecasting that its sales would triple from the previous year. ZF offers customers an entire processing unit's worth of computer power on a single microchip—a technology in heavy demand as companies continue to automate functions. Even so, ZF's founder, David L. Feldman, insists that the company hire new people only when it absolutely must.

Instead of reflexively hiring for growth, ZF Micro Devices treats each decision to add to the payroll as a major step. Feldman requires his own signature of approval for any new job posting. He encourages employees to contract for work, rather than hire employees. The company works closely with its contractors. With one group of engineers, ZF even counseled them on how to submit bills so that they would be paid faster.

Just as companies invest in the capabilities of their employees, ZF invests in the long-term success of the firms that meet its outsourcing needs.

A necessary consequence of a conservative hiring policy at a fast-growing organization is that employees are under tremendous pressure. Feldman describes the pace of work as "absolutely hectic." For example, just two employees are assigned to handling calls for technical support. When they became swamped, the company tried pulling engineers away from their work to help handle calls. Then the company tried minimizing the need for more labor through better use of technology. ZF set up a database that could deliver answers to common questions via e-mail.

But why not hire faster? The answer lies in the experience of David Feldman. He previously ran a company called Ampro Computers, which barely survived a plunge in sales

brought on by Operation Desert Storm in 1990, followed by a dip in the U.S. economy. Ampro negotiated a payment plan with creditors, but to stay afloat Feldman and his cofounder realized they would have to cut back from 65 workers to 36. Laying off employees, knowing they all had families to support, was a painful task that still troubles Feldman a decade later. That memory fuels Feldman's determination never to repeat the situation.

For Feldman, human resource planning is a matter of hiring only when the company has exhausted the alternatives. He says to his managers, "If you hire someone and it's one too many, you're the one who's going to have to tell that person. . . . You're not just bringing a body in here—it's a life."

SOURCE: Mike Hofman, "Sins of the Founder," *Inc.*, August 2001, pp. 66–68, 70 (interview with David Feldman).

---

find and train new employees. Also, if the shortage becomes a surplus, the organization will have to consider laying off some of the employees. Layoffs involve another set of expenses, such as severance pay, and they are costly in terms of human suffering. The "Best Practices" box above describes how ZF Micro Devices has addressed these issues.

Another consideration in choosing an HR strategy is whether the employees needed will contribute directly to the organization's success. Organizations are most likely to benefit from hiring and retaining employees who provide a **core competency**—that is, a set of knowledges and skills that make the organization superior to competitors and create value for customers. At a store, for example, core competen-

core competency
A set of knowledges and skills that make the organization superior to competitors and create value for customers.

cies include choosing merchandise that shoppers want and providing shoppers with excellent service. For other work that is not a core competency—say, cleaning the store and providing security—the organization may benefit from using HR strategies other than hiring full-time employees.

Organizations try to anticipate labor surpluses far enough ahead that they can freeze hiring and let natural attrition (people leaving on their own) reduce the labor force. Unfortunately for many workers, in the past decade, the typical way organizations have responded to a surplus of labor has been downsizing, which delivers fast results. Beyond the obvious economic impact, downsizing has a psychological impact that spills over and affects families, increasing the rates of divorce, child abuse, and drug and alcohol addiction.[5] To handle a labor shortage, organizations typically hire temporary employees or use outsourcing. Because downsizing, using temporary employees, and outsourcing are most common, we will look at each of these in greater detail in the following sections.

Downsizing

As we discussed in Chapter 2, **downsizing** is the planned elimination of large numbers of personnel with the goal of enhancing the organization's competitiveness. Many organizations adopted this option in the late 1980s and early 1990s, especially in the United States. Over 85 percent of the Fortune 1000 firms downsized between 1987 and 2001, resulting in more than 8 million permanent layoffs—an unprecedented figure in U.S. economic history. The jobs eliminated were not temporary losses due to downturns in the business cycle, but permanent losses resulting from changes in the competitive pressures faced by businesses today. In fact, 8 out of every 10 companies that underwent downsizing were earning a profit at the same time.[6]

> **downsizing**
> The planned elimination of large numbers of personnel with the goal of enhancing the organization's competitiveness.

The primary reason organizations engage in downsizing is to promote future competitiveness. According to surveys, they do this by meeting four objectives:

1. *Reducing costs*—Labor is a large part of a company's total costs, so downsizing is an attractive place to start cutting costs.
2. *Replacing labor with technology*—Closing outdated factories, automating, or introducing other technological changes reduces the need for labor. Often, the labor savings outweighs the cost of the new technology.
3. *Mergers and acquisitions*—When organizations combine, they often need less bureaucratic overhead, so they lay off managers and some professional staff members. In the mid-1990s, talk of health care reform caused many pharmaceutical companies to hold back on price increases. To maintain their profits, they merged so they could produce and sell the same products with fewer staff members.
4. *Moving to more economical locations*—Some organizations move from one area of the United States to another, especially from the Northeast, Midwest, and California to the South and the mountain regions of the West. Universal Studios moved many of its operations out of Los Angeles to Orlando, Florida, where the costs of producing television shows are a fraction of the costs in Los Angeles.[7] Other moves have shifted jobs to other countries. Fruit of the Loom announced that the relatively high cost of U.S. labor was the reason it moved production to Mexico, cutting 2,900 U.S. jobs.[8]

Although the jury is still out on whether these downsizing efforts have enhanced performance, some indications are that the results have *not* lived up to expectations. According to a recent study of 52 Fortune 100 firms, most firms that announced a

A Japanese worker passes by a laid-off white-collar worker in Tokyo's Hibiya park. The park is a common place for white-collar victims of downsizing to spend their days. Layoffs can be costly because of severance pay, and have severe repercussions in terms of human suffering.

downsizing campaign showed worse, rather than better, financial performance in the years that followed.[9]

Why do so many downsizing efforts fail to meet expectations? There seem to be several reasons. First, although the initial cost savings give a temporary boost to profits, the long-term effects of an improperly managed downsizing effort can be negative. Downsizing leads to a loss of talent, and it often disrupts the social networks through which people are creative and flexible.[10] When Roche Holding acquired Syntex Corporation, half the Syntex jobs were eliminated. Most of the employees left voluntarily, taking advantage of a lucrative severance package that included two to three years of full compensation. Many felt that this downsizing strategy encouraged turnover among the best, most marketable scientists and managers.[11]

Also, many companies wind up rehiring. Downsizing campaigns often eliminate people who turn out to be irreplaceable. In one survey, 80 percent of the firms that had downsized wound up replacing some of the very people they had laid off. One senior manager of a *Fortune* 100 firm described a situation in which a bookkeeper making $9 an hour was let go. Later, the company realized she knew many things about the company that no one else knew, so she was hired back as a consultant—for $42 an hour.[12] Hiring back formerly laid-off workers has become so routine that many organizations track their laid-off employees, using software formerly used for tracking job applicants. If the organization ever faces a labor shortage, it can quickly contact these former workers and restore them to the payroll.[13]

Finally, downsizing efforts often fail because employees who survive the purge become self-absorbed and afraid to take risks. Motivation drops because any hope of future promotions—or any future—with the company dies. Many employees start looking for other employment opportunities. The negative publicity associated with a downsizing campaign can also hurt the company's image in the labor market, so it is harder to recruit employees later. The key to avoiding this kind of damage is to ensure that the need for the layoff is well explained and that procedures for carrying out the layoff are fair.[14] Although this advice may sound like common sense, organizations are often reluctant to provide complete information, especially when a layoff results from top-level mismanagement.[15]

Many problems with downsizing can be reduced with better planning. The "HR How To" box offers guidelines for carrying out downsizing. Still, downsizing hardly guarantees an increase in an organization's competitiveness. Organizations should more carefully consider using all the other avenues for eliminating a labor surplus (shown in Table 5.2). Many of these take effect slowly, so organizations must improve their forecasting or be stuck with downsizing as their only viable option.

Minimizing the Pain of Layoffs

Although layoffs are always painful, handling the task well can maintain employees' dignity and improve the organization's long-term health. When layoffs increased in 2001, *Inc.* magazine asked Helen Drinan, chief executive officer of the Society for Human Resource Management, to offer advice on minimizing the pain of layoffs. Here's what she recommended:

- *Communicate fully.* As soon as you know about layoffs, tell employees the news, in detail. First tell the people who will be laid off. Then tell the whole group what you are doing and why. If there's information you *don't* know, disclose that, too.
- *Empower managers to make choices.* The company's executives shouldn't decide precisely which people to

lay off. People who are closer to the situation should be involved in such decisions.

- *Ask laid-off employees to leave immediately, but be humane about it.* It's probably unwise to let employees hang around for days, using the company's phones and computers. Still, you don't have to send over a security guard to usher the employees out of the building. Ways to be humane include offering to stay late and help pack personal belongings, providing an outplacement service, and offering to be a reference in the laid-off employee's job hunt.
- *Budget for layoffs.* Plan to give laid-off employees at least two weeks' severance pay, plus more based on years of employment. If possible, include

outplacement services in the layoff budget.

- *Plan ahead.* Even when times are good, managers know that downsizing is often part of an organization's strategy. Drinan recommends the mental exercise of asking what you would do if the organization had to reduce its staff by 10 percent.

Why go to all this trouble for a change that is essentially about cutting costs? Quite simply, because even after layoffs, an organization still needs dedicated, talented people. In Drinan's words, "You want to treat [laid-off] people well, because this becomes an object lesson for everyone in your organization about how you treat employees."

SOURCE: Mike Hofman, "Five Rules for Making Layoffs Less Painful," *Inc.,* April 2001, pp. 97–98.

Early-Retirement Programs

Another popular way to reduce a labor surplus is with an early-retirement program. As we discussed in Chapter 2, the average age of the U.S. workforce is increasing. But even though many baby boomers are approaching traditional retirement age, early indications are that this group has no intention of retiring soon.[16] Several forces fuel the drawing out of older workers' careers. First, the improved health of older people in general, combined with the decreased physical labor required by many jobs, has made working longer a viable option. Also, many workers fear Social Security will be cut and have skimpy employer-sponsored pensions that may not cover their expenses. Finally, age discrimination laws and the outlawing of mandatory retirement ages have limited organizations' ability to induce older workers to retire. Under the pressures associated with an aging labor force, many employers try to encourage older workers to leave voluntarily by offering a variety of early-retirement incentives. The more lucrative of these programs succeed by some measures. Research suggests that these programs encourage lower-performing older workers to retire.[17] Sometimes they work so well that too many workers retire.

Many organizations are moving from early-retirement programs to phased-retirement programs. In a *phased-retirement program*, the organization can continue to enjoy the experience of older workers while reducing the number of hours that these employees work, as well as the cost of those employees. This option also can give older employees the psychological benefit of easing into retirement, rather than being thrust entirely into a new way of life.[18]

Employing Temporary Workers

While downsizing has been a popular way to reduce a labor surplus, the most widespread methods for eliminating a labor shortage are hiring temporary workers and outsourcing work. As we saw in Chapter 2, the federal government estimated that organizations are using over a million temporary workers. Temporary employment is popular with employers because it gives them flexibility they need to operate efficiently when demand for their products changes rapidly.

In addition to flexibility, temporary employment offers lower costs. Using temporary workers frees the employer from many administrative tasks and financial burdens associated with being the "employer of record." The cost of employee benefits, including health care, pension, life insurance, workers' compensation, and unemployment insurance, accounted for 40 percent of payroll expenses for permanent employees. To lower some of these costs, McDonnell Douglas raised the percentage of temporary workers from 4.3 percent of its labor force to 15 percent.

Agencies that provide temporary employees also may handle some of the tasks associated with hiring. Small companies that cannot afford their own testing programs often get employees who have been tested by a temporary agency. Aligned Fiber Composites, a small manufacturer in Chatfield, Minnesota, has adopted this solution. The company's temporary agency recruits and tests workers. Aligned Fiber signs up the workers for 90 days, and if it is satisfied with their performance, it hires them as permanent employees. The company has hired 17 percent of its permanent employees in this way.[19]

Many temporary agencies train employees before sending them to employers. This reduces employers' training costs and eases the transition for the temporary worker and employer. When United Parcel Service (UPS) signed on with a temporary agency to supply data-entry personnel, the agency designed a computer screen that simulates those used at UPS. A temporary worker assigned to UPS must be able to enter data at a minimum speed on the simulated screens.[20]

Key Resources, an agency in Greensboro, North Carolina, gives employers access to a segment of the workforce they otherwise might not be able to use: immigrants. The company has found reliable, hardworking employees in the local Hispanic and Vietnamese immigrant communities. Because many of these workers are unable to speak English, the agency also hires translators. For simple jobs, the agency can provide a translator for a day or two at no charge. For more complex jobs, the agency charges the client for a translator who stays on for the entire project and also performs other duties.[21]

Finally, temporary workers may offer benefits not available from permanent employees. Because the temporary worker has little experience at the employer's organi-

Companies such as McDonnell Douglas employ a significant percentage of temporary workers, lowering costs, bringing new perspectives into the organization, and helping after a downsizing. Sometimes using temporary workers is a way of finding good permanent hires. Using temporary workers can be a good strategy in times of frequent downsizing.

zation, this person brings an objective point of view to the organization's problems and procedures. Also, a temporary worker may have a great deal of experience in other organizations. A temporary worker at Lord, Abbett and Company, an investment firm in New York, suggested an efficient software program for managing investment portfolios. The worker had been trained with that program at a different firm.

To benefit from using temporary workers, organizations must overcome the disadvantages associated with this type of labor force. One drawback is that tension often exists between temporary and permanent employees. According to surveys, one-third of full-time employees perceive temporary workers as a threat to their own job security. Such an attitude can interfere with cooperation and, in some cases, lead to outright sabotage if the situation is not well managed.

One way organizations should manage this situation is to complete any downsizing efforts before bringing in temporary workers. Surviving a downsizing is almost like experiencing a death in the family. In this context, a decent time interval needs to occur before new temporary workers are introduced. Without the delay, the surviving employees will associate the downsizing effort (which was a threat) with the new temporary employees (who could be perceived as outsiders brought in to replace old friends). If an upswing in demand follows a downsizing effort, the organization should probably begin meeting its expanded demand for labor by granting overtime to core employees. If the demand persists, the organization will be more certain that the upswing will last and future layoffs will be unnecessary. The extended stretches of overtime will eventually tax the full-time employees, so they will accept using temporary workers to help lessen their load.

Organizations that use temporary workers must avoid treating them as second-class citizens. One way to do this is to ensure that the temporary agency provides temporaries with benefits that are comparable with those enjoyed by the organization's permanent workers. For example, one temporary agency, MacTemps, gives its workers long-term health coverage, full disability insurance, and complete dental coverage. This not only reduces the benefit gap between the temporary and permanent workers but also helps attract the best temporary workers in the first place.

Outsourcing

outsourcing
Contracting with another organization to perform a broad set of services.

Instead of using a temporary employee to fill a single job, an organization might want a broader set of services. Contracting with another organization to perform a broad set of services is called **outsourcing.** American Airlines used its own employees as ticket agents at major airports but outsourced that function at smaller "second-tier" airports. American entered into a contract with Johnson Controls to provide 500 ticket agents for American's operations at 28 airports. The main reason was cost control. American paid its veteran ticket agents $19 an hour plus benefits, the market rate for the airline industry. Johnson Controls, in contrast, paid the local market wage, just $8 an hour.

A major reason outsourcing can save money is that the outside company specializes in the services and can benefit from economies of scale (the economic principle that producing something in large volume tends to cost less for each additional unit than producing in small volume). Several years ago, Ford Motor Company had a unit that processed applications for financing from people who wanted to buy Ford cars and trucks. Now Ford hands this work over to MCN Corporation, which can do the same job with fewer people than Ford had used. MCN's computers and staff are dedicated to processing data for Ford (and over 25 other companies). Their efficiency comes from a narrow focus on data entry and analysis, free from the need to produce automobiles. Outsourcing is logical when an organization lacks certain kinds of expertise and doesn't want to invest in developing that expertise.

Outsourcing in manufacturing often involves designing products in the United States and shipping manufacturing responsibilities overseas, where production costs can be 10 to 60 percent less. Apple introduced a laptop computer produced by Sony, and Motorola set up equipment production centers in Hong Kong. In the service industry, data-entry jobs often are outsourced. Metropolitan Life Insurance has its medical claims analyzed in Ireland, where operating costs are about 35 percent less than in the United States. The labor forces of countries like China, India, Jamaica, and those of Eastern Europe are creating an abundant supply of labor for unskilled and low-skilled work.

Technological advances in computer networks and transmission have speeded up the outsourcing process and have helped it spread beyond manufacturing areas and low-skilled jobs. For companies that perform design engineering, India is a fertile ground for outsourcing this type of work. Indian computer scientists earn, on average, one-fourth the salaries paid in the United States.[22]

Although outsourcing manufacturing may make good sense in the short term, it may hurt U.S. firms' competitiveness. Outsourcing reduces manufacturing costs, but companies eventually will have more and more difficulty designing products that apply innovations in technology. According to this argument, unrestrained outsourcing starts a downward spiral of more and more outsourcing until the organization no longer produces anything of value. Companies that manufacture goods develop their own design teams and compete directly and with a substantial competitive advantage.

Overtime and Expanded Hours

Organizations facing a labor shortage may be reluctant to hire employees, even temporary workers, or to commit to an outsourcing arrangement. Especially if the organization expects the shortage to be temporary, it may prefer an arrangement that is simpler and less costly. Under some conditions, these organizations may try to garner more hours from the existing labor force. Many employers opted for this strategy during the 1990s. As a result, 6 percent of the automobiles assembled in North America in 1997 resulted from overtime production—equivalent to the output of an additional four auto plants running on straight time (no overtime).[23]

A major downside of overtime is that the employer must pay nonmanagement employees one-and-a-half times their normal wages for work done overtime. Even so, employers see overtime pay as preferable to the costs of hiring and training new employees. The preference is especially strong if the organization doubts that the current higher level of demand for its products will last long.

For a short time at least, many workers appreciate the added compensation for working overtime. Over extended periods, however, employees feel stress and frustration from working long hours. Overtime therefore is best suited for short-term labor shortages.

Implementing and Evaluating the HR Plan

For whatever HR strategies are selected, the final stage of human resource planning involves implementing the strategies and evaluating the outcomes. This stage is represented by the bottom part of Figure 5.1. When implementing the HR strategy, the organization must hold some individual accountable for achieving the goals. That person also must have the authority and resources needed to accomplish those goals. It is also important that this person issue regular progress reports, so the organization can be sure that all activities occur on schedule and that the early results are as expected.

In evaluating the results, the most obvious step is checking whether the organization has succeeded in avoiding labor shortages or surpluses. Along with measuring these numbers, the evaluation should identify which parts of the planning process contributed to success or failure.

A good example of evaluation is Bell Atlantic's attempt at downsizing during the 1990s. In 1994 the company was convinced it would need fewer workers. Layoffs were out of the question, because employees were represented by the Communication Workers of America, which staunchly opposed layoffs. Bell Atlantic therefore developed a high-priced *buyout plan*, a voluntary program that offered a package of benefits in exchange for leaving the company before the workers' contract expired in 1998.

By June 1998, almost one-third of Bell Atlantic's unionized workforce (14,000 people) stood ready to accept the buyout offer. But by then the company saw that forecasts for product demand had been far too low. Bell Atlantic had forecasted lower demand for copper wiring, but orders surged to accommodate new phone lines for faxes and modems. Bell Atlantic's reduced workforce could not keep up. The company stretched the hours of the remaining employees, but the strategy did not work in many metropolitan areas. As a result, while many experienced employees were walking away with lucrative buyouts, Bell Atlantic had to replace them with inexperienced new hires amid a labor shortage in the overall U.S. economy. To avert disaster, the company had to offer a 25 percent hike in its already generous pension plan to any employee who would stay. The overall effect: an extravagant bonus system that rewarded employees for either staying or leaving.[24]

Applying HR Planning to Affirmative Action

As we discussed in Chapter 3, many organizations have a human resource strategy that includes affirmative action to manage diversity or meet government requirements. Meeting affirmative-action goals requires that employers carry out an additional level of human resource planning aimed at those goals. In other words, besides looking at its overall workforce and needs, the organization looks at the representation of subgroups in its labor force—for example, the proportion of women and minorities.

Affirmative-action plans forecast and monitor the proportion of employees who are members of various protected groups (typically, women and racial or ethnic minorities). The planning looks at the representation of these employees in the organization's job categories and career tracks. The planner can compare the proportion of employees who are in each group with the proportion each group represents in the labor market. For example, the organization might note that in a labor market that is 25 percent Hispanic, 60 percent of its customer service personnel are Hispanic. This type of comparison is called a **workforce utilization review.** The organization can use this process to determine whether there is any subgroup whose proportion in the relevant labor market differs substantially from the proportion in the job category.

If the workforce utilization review indicates that some group—for example, African Americans—makes up 35 percent of the relevant labor market for a job category but that this same group constitutes only 5 percent of the employees actually in the job category at the organization, this is evidence of underutilization. That situation could result from problems in selection or from problems in internal movement (promotions or other movement along a career path). One way to diagnose the situation would be to use transitional matrices, such as the matrix shown in Table 5.1 earlier in this chapter.

The steps in a workforce utilization review are identical to the steps in the HR planning process shown in Figure 5.1. The organization must assess current utilization patterns, then forecast how these are likely to change in the near future. If these analyses suggest the organization is underutilizing certain groups and if forecasts suggest this pattern is likely to continue, the organization may need to set goals and timetables for changing. The planning process may identify new strategies for recruitment or selection. The organization carries out these HR strategies and evaluates their success.

workforce utilization review
A comparison of the proportion of employees in protected groups with the proportion that each group represents in the relevant labor market.

LO4

Recruiting Human Resources

As the first part of this chapter shows, it is difficult to always predict exactly how many (if any) new employees the organization will have to hire in a given year in a given job category. The role of human resource recruitment is to build a supply of potential new hires that the organization can draw on if the need arises. In human resource management, **recruiting** consists of any practice or activity carried on by the organization with the primary purpose of identifying and attracting potential employees.[25] It thus creates a buffer between planning and the actual selection of new employees (the topic of the next chapter).

Because of differences in companies' strategies, they may assign different degrees of importance to recruiting.[26] In general, however, all companies have to make decisions in three areas of recruiting: personnel policies, recruitment sources, and the characteristics and behavior of the recruiter. As shown in Figure 5.2, these aspects of recruiting have different effects on whom the organization ultimately hires. Personnel policies influence the characteristics of the positions to be filled. Recruitment sources

recruiting
Any activity carried on by the organization with the primary purpose of identifying and attracting potential employees.

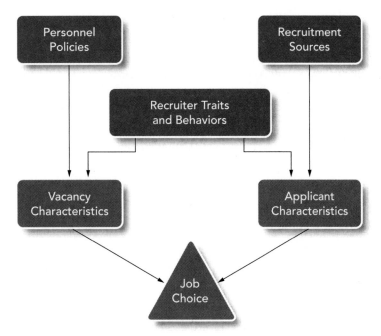

FIGURE 5.2

Three Aspects of
Recruiting

influence the kinds of job applicants an organization reaches. And the nature and behavior of the recruiter affect the characteristics of both the vacancies and the applicants. Ultimately, an applicant's decision to accept a job offer—and the organization's decision to make the offer—depend on the match between vacancy characteristics and applicant characteristics.

Kelsey August has experienced the impact of this principle as she has struggled to find entry-level employees, including packers, shippers, and production workers, for her direct-marketing company, Lone Star Direct. Unskilled workers were just as happy to work for McDonald's and Wendy's, which were paying wages of $10 to $12 per hour in Austin, Texas, where Lone Star is located. After such desperate efforts as hiring away the cashiers in stores where she shopped, August tried running a newspaper ad for part-time jobs. To August's surprise, a flood of applications poured in, mostly from women with children. Lone Star revised its personnel policies to suit this new group of employees, with benefits emphasizing flexible work hours and perks that appeal to young mothers. Many of these employees are high school dropouts, so Lone Star brings in instructors to help them prepare for their high school equivalency diplomas. The company also started paying a $200 bonus to employees who refer candidates—which enabled the company to cut its budget for job advertising.[27]

The remainder of this chapter explores these three aspects of recruiting: personnel policies, recruitment sources, and recruiter traits and behaviors.

Personnel Policies

An organization's *personnel policies* are its decisions about how it will carry out human resource management, including how it will fill job vacancies. These policies influence the nature of the positions that are vacant. According to the research on recruitment, it is clear that characteristics of the vacancy are more important than recruiters or recruiting sources for predicting job choice.[28] Several personnel policies are especially relevant to recruitment:

- Recruiting existing employees to fill vacancies or hiring from outside the organization.
- Meeting or exceeding the market rate of pay.
- Emphasizing job security or the right to terminate employees.
- Images of the organization conveyed in its advertising.

Let's explore the impact of each of these policy areas.

Internal versus External Recruiting

Opportunities for advancement make a job more attractive to applicants and employees. Organizations with policies to "promote from within" try to fill upper-level vacancies by recruiting candidates internally—that is, finding candidates who already work for the organization. In a 2001 survey of students pursuing a master's degree in business administration (MBA), a policy of promotion from within was the students' top consideration when they were evaluating jobs at a company.[29]

As personnel policies, decisions about internal versus external recruiting affect the nature of jobs. As we will discuss later in the chapter, they also influence recruitment sources and the nature of applicants. For now, we will focus on the impact of these decisions as personnel policies. Promote-from-within policies signal to job applicants that the company provides opportunities for advancement, both for the present vacancy and for later vacancies created when people are promoted to fill higher-level vacancies.

McDonald's restaurants provide a good example of the virtues of promoting from within. McDonald's has a program with the goal of enabling low-income managers to buy franchises. Phil Hagans was once a cook at a McDonald's restaurant, who worked his way up, and thanks to his hard work and the McDonald's program for low-income employees, now owns two franchises. Hagans's restaurants not only turn a profit but also perform a valuable social function by providing needed employment and work experience for many inner-city youths in the Houston area. In Hagans's view, programs such as this make McDonald's "the best company for African American entrepreneurs" such as himself.[30]

Lead-the-Market Pay Strategies

Pay is an important job characteristic for almost all applicants. Organizations have a recruiting advantage if their policy is to take a "lead-the-market" approach to pay—that is, pay more than the current market wages for a job. Higher pay can also make up for a job's less desirable features. For example, many organizations pay employees more for working midnight shifts than daytime shifts. (This practice is called paying a *shift differential*; we will take a closer look at these and other decisions about pay in Chapters 11 and 12.)

Increasingly, organizations that compete for applicants based on pay do so using forms of pay other than wages or salary. For example, a 1997 survey found that close to 4 out of 10 employers used signing bonuses rather than higher wages to attract new hires. Almost 2 out of 10 were using lucrative stock option plans (the right to buy company stock at a set price at a specified time).[31] Many employers prefer bonuses and stock options because, unlike wages and salary, they tend not to grow over time (as

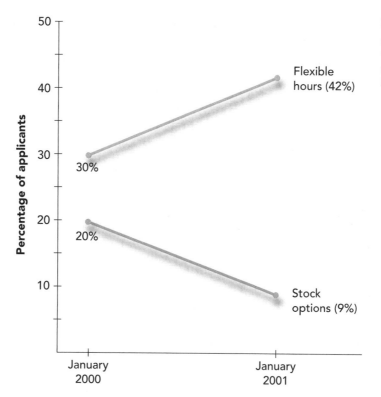

with a 5 percent raise every year) and can be administered more flexibly. However, after the recent downturn in the economy and the accompanying dip in stock prices, job applicants are showing less interest in stock options. As Figure 5.3 shows, the share of students who listed stock options as their most important incentive fell by more than half between January 2000 and January 2001. At the same time, the share of students who most valued flexible hours increased substantially.[32]

These changing attitudes intensified following the Enron bankruptcy at the end of 2001. Some low-level and mid-level Enron employees held stock options whose value made them millionaires on paper. But as Enron's stock price began to slide in the second half of 2001, the company prevented the employees from cashing in their options while it was a good deal for employees. Instead, the employees watched helplessly as the stock price fell so low that their options became worthless. Enron employees also had another type of stock-related benefit—401(k) retirement savings plans that consisted largely of Enron stock. Those plans, too, lost much of their value. Suspicions about top management's role in the disaster grew following reports that Enron's executives had sold many of their own shares of stock for $1 billion just before the company announced its bankruptcy.[33]

In reaction to the Enron experience, many employees have become suspicious of the value of benefits tied to their company's stock. To attract top talent, employers are placing more emphasis on salary and more traditional benefits. Employees who do participate in benefits like 401(k) plans are insisting that the funds permit them to diversify their investments.

Employment-at-Will Policies

Within the laws of the state where they are operating, employers have latitude to set policies about their rights in an employment relationship. A widespread policy follows the principle of **employment at will,** which holds that if there is no specific employment contract saying otherwise, the employer or employee may end an employment relationship at any time, regardless of cause. An alternative to employment at will is to establish extensive **due-process policies,** which formally lay out the steps an employee may take to appeal an employer's decision to terminate that employee. When employees have sued on the grounds that employers discharged them wrongfully, court decisions of the last few decades have eroded employers' rights to terminate employees with impunity.[34] To protect organizations from being sued on the grounds of wrongful discharge, their lawyers have sometimes recommended that they make sure all their recruitment documents say the employment is "at will." Organizations have been advised to avoid any mention of due process in company handbooks, personnel manuals, and recruiting brochures.[35]

In decisions about employment-at-will policies, organizations should consider not only the legal advantages of employment at will but also the effect of such policies on recruitment. For many applicants, job security is important. If the organization's recruiting materials emphasize due process, rights of appeal, and mechanisms for filing grievances, the message is that the company is concerned about protecting employees, and job security is high. Materials that emphasize employment at will send a message that job security is minimal. Job applicants are more attracted to organizations with due-process policies than to organizations with employment-at-will policies.[36]

Image Advertising

Besides advertising specific job openings, as discussed in the next section, organizations may advertise themselves as a good place to work in general.[37] Advertising designed to create a generally favorable impression of the organization is called *image advertising*. Image advertising is particularly important for organizations in highly competitive labor markets that perceive themselves as having a bad image.[38]

Many people are attracted to the challenge and responsibility associated with a job. Dow Chemical in the early 1990s ran an advertising campaign that presented the company as offering such jobs. Its $60 million television campaign hammered home the message "Dow lets you do great things," clearly aimed at affecting the general public's view of the work at Dow.[39] The U.S. Army's "Be all that you can be" campaign pursued

---

employment at will
Employment principle that if there is no specific employment contract saying otherwise, the employer or employee may end an employment relationship at any time, regardless of cause.

due-process policies
Policies that formally lay out the steps an employee may take to appeal the employer's decision to terminate that employee.

Image advertising, such as in this campaign to recruit nurses, promotes a whole profession or organization as opposed to a specific job opening. This ad is designed to create a positive impression of the profession, which is now facing a shortage of workers.

a similar objective. These ads focused on the challenge associated with army jobs. They also attempted to offset certain negative attributes of the work, such as the fact that, in some of its jobs at certain times, other people are systematically trying to kill you.

Although the programs described here try to promote the employer in the labor market in general, other image advertising programs target specific groups within the overall labor market. For example, many large corporations with agricultural ties, such as DuPont and Cargill, struggle to attract minority applicants. Hispanics, Asians, and African Americans each constitute only 3 to 4 percent of all agricultural and food scientists. Lisa Barrios, a Mexican American who grew up in Chicago, notes, "I assumed everything was just farming . . . if you didn't have a rural background, then you wouldn't be able to do it." After working at a special minority internship program at Monsanto's Hybritech unit in Indiana, however, Barrios changed her major from chemical engineering to agricultural engineering.[40]

Whether the goal is to influence the perception of the public in general or specific segments of the labor market, job seekers form beliefs about the nature of the organizations well before they have any direct interviewing experience with these companies. Thus, organizations must assess their reputation in the labor market and correct any shortcomings they detect in people's actual image of them.[41]

Recruitment Sources

LO5

Another critical element of an organization's recruitment strategy is its decisions about where to look for applicants. The total labor market is enormous and spread over the entire globe. As a practical matter, an organization will draw from a small fraction of that total market. The methods the organization chooses for communicating its labor needs and the audiences it targets will determine the size and nature of the labor market the organization taps to fill its vacant positions.[42] A person who responds to a job advertisement on the Internet is likely to be different from a person responding to a sign hanging outside a factory. Figure 5.4 summarizes major sources from which organizations draw recruits. Each source has advantages and disadvantages.

job posting
The process of communicating information about a job vacancy on company bulletin boards, in employee publications, on corporate intranets, and anywhere else the organization communicates with employees.

Internal Sources

As we discussed with regard to personnel policies, an organization may emphasize internal or external sources of job applicants. Internal sources are employees who currently hold other positions in the organization. Organizations recruit existing employees through **job posting,** or communicating information about the vacancy

Retailers tend to promote from within their organizations, a policy that is attractive to many workers.

FIGURE 5.4

Recruitment Sources

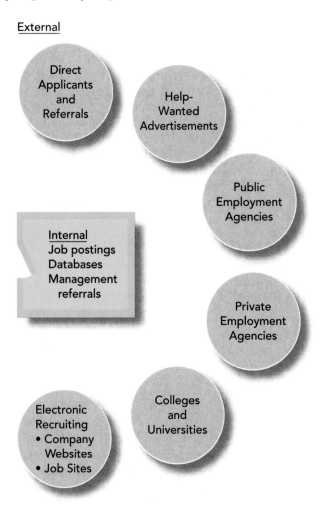

on company bulletin boards, in employee publications, on corporate intranets, and anywhere else the organization communicates with employees. Managers also may identify candidates to recommend for vacancies. Policies that emphasize promotions and even lateral moves to achieve broader career experience can give applicants a favorable impression of the organization's jobs. The use of internal sources also affects what kinds of people the organization recruits.

For the employer, relying on internal sources offers several advantages.[43] First, it generates applicants who are well known to the organization. In addition, these applicants are relatively knowledgeable about the organization's vacancies, which minimizes the possibility they will have unrealistic expectations about the job. Finally, filling vacancies through internal recruiting is generally cheaper and faster than looking outside the organization.

Inova Health Systems, a Virginia-based consortium of hospitals, enjoyed these benefits of internal recruiting when it centralized its human resource functions to cut the cost of recruitment. Before that, Inova's many hospitals separately managed their own recruitment and selection efforts. Often facilities were competing with one another for the same applicants. No individual facility had exorbitant costs, but their combined spending on recruitment advertising was $500,000, and the huge pool of applicants required more than 3,000 interviews.

To consolidate these activities, Inova created a database containing records of all personnel, as well as an internal computer network to promote communication among the hospitals. The information in the database showed how many openings in one area could be filled through transfers and promotions from areas experiencing a labor surplus. Inova posted the vacancies on its network, and decisions about which applicants to interview gave priority to Inova employees. This policy improved current employees' job satisfaction by increasing their chances of promotion and enhancing the fit between individuals and jobs (employees could transfer readily to jobs that fit their skills). Inova also had less need for external recruitment and the related costs of generating and processing so many applications.[44]

External Sources

Despite the advantages of internal recruitment, organizations often have good reasons to recruit externally.[45] For entry-level positions and perhaps for specialized upper-level positions, the organization has no internal recruits from which to draw. Also, bringing in outsiders may expose the organization to new ideas or new ways of doing business. An organization that uses only internal recruitment can wind up with a workforce whose members all think alike and therefore may be poorly suited to innovation.[46] So organizations often recruit through direct applicants and referrals, advertisements, employment agencies, schools, and websites.

Direct Applicants and Referrals

Even without a formal effort to reach job applicants, an organization may hear from candidates through direct applicants and referrals. **Direct applicants** are people who apply for a vacancy without prompting from the organization. **Referrals** are people who apply because someone in the organization prompted them to do so. These two sources of recruits share some characteristics that make them excellent pools from which to draw.

One advantage is that many direct applicants are to some extent already "sold" on the organization. Most have done some research and concluded there is enough fit between themselves and the vacant position to warrant submitting an application, a process called *self-selection,* which, when it works, eases the pressure on the organization's recruiting and selection systems. A form of aided self-selection occurs with referrals. Many job seekers look to friends, relatives, and acquaintances to help find employment. Using these social networks not only helps the job seeker, but also simplifies recruitment for employers.[47] Current employees (who are familiar with the vacancy as well as the person they are referring) decide that there is a fit between the person and the vacancy, so they convince the person to apply for the job.

An additional benefit of using such sources is that it costs much less than formal recruiting efforts. Considering these combined benefits, referrals and direct applications are among the best sources of new hires. Some employers offer current employees financial incentives for referring applicants who are hired and perform acceptably on the job (for example, if they stay 180 days).[48] Other companies play off their good reputations in the labor market to generate direct applications. For

direct applicants
People who apply for a vacancy without prompting from the organization.

referrals
People who apply for a vacancy because someone in the organization prompted them to do so.

example, minorities constitute about one-fourth of the managerial and professional employees at Avon Products, and this relatively high representation of minorities enhances Avon's ability to recruit other minority applicants. As Al Smith, Avon's director of managing diversity, notes, "I get a lot of résumés from people of all cultures and ethnicities because Avon has a good reputation." This takes the place of expensive and sometimes unreliable outreach programs.[49]

The major downside of referrals is that they limit the likelihood of exposing the organization to fresh viewpoints. People tend to refer others who are like themselves. Furthermore, sometimes referrals contribute to hiring practices that are or that appear unfair, an example being **nepotism,** or the hiring of relatives. Employees may resent the hiring and rapid promotion of "the boss's son" or "the boss's daughter," or even the boss's friend.

nepotism
The practice of hiring relatives.

Advertisements in Newspapers and Magazines

Open almost any newspaper or magazine and you can find advertisements of job openings. These ads typically generate a less desirable group of applicants than direct applications or referrals, and do so at greater expense. However, few employers can fill all their vacancies purely through direct applications and referrals, so they usually need to advertise. Also, an employer can take many steps to increase the effectiveness of recruitment through advertising.

The person designing a job advertisement needs to answer two questions:

1. What do we need to say?
2. To whom do we need to say it?

With respect to the first question, an ad should give readers enough information to evaluate the job and its requirements, so they can make a well-informed judgment about their qualifications. Providing enough information may require long advertisements, which cost more. The employer should evaluate the additional costs against the costs of providing too little information: Vague ads generate a huge number of applicants, including many who are not reasonably qualified or would not accept the job if they learned more about it. Reviewing all these applications to eliminate unsuitable applicants is expensive.

Specifying whom to reach with the message helps the advertiser decide where to place the ad. The most common medium for advertising jobs is the classified section of local newspapers. These ads are relatively inexpensive yet reach many people in a specific geographic area who are currently looking for work (or at least interested enough to be reading the classifieds). On the downside, this medium offers little ability to target skill levels. Typically, many of the people reading classified ads are either over- or underqualified for the position. Also, people who are not looking for work rarely read the classifieds. These people may include candidates the organization could lure from their current employers. For reaching a specific part of the labor market, including certain skill levels and more people who are employed, the organization may get better results from advertising in professional or industry journals. Some employers also advertise on television—particularly cable television.[50]

Public Employment Agencies

The Social Security Act of 1935 requires that everyone receiving unemployment compensation be registered with a local state employment office. These state employment offices work with the U.S. Employment Service (USES) to try to ensure that unemployed individuals eventually get off state aid and back on employer payrolls. To accomplish this, agencies collect information from the unemployed people about their skills and experience.

Employers can register their job vacancies with their local state employment office, and the agency will try to find someone suitable, using its computerized inventory of local unemployed individuals. The agency refers candidates to the employer at no charge. The organization can interview or test them to see if they are suitable for its vacancies. Besides offering access to job candidates at low cost, public employment agencies can be a useful resource for meeting certain diversity objectives. Laws often mandate that the agencies maintain specialized "desks" for minorities, disabled individuals, and Vietnam War veterans. Employers that feel they currently are underutilizing any of these subgroups of the labor force may find the agencies to be an excellent source.

The government also provides funding to a variety of nonprofit employment agencies. Many of these support "welfare to work" efforts, teaching skills such as punctuality and conflict resolution, then lining up candidates for job interviews. The welfare reform passed by Congress in 1996 (the Personal Responsibility and Work Opportunity Act) dramatically increased the pressure on welfare recipients to find jobs, either through public employment agencies or other means. Under this law, most people have a five-year limit on benefits and must find jobs within two years. The law also gives employers incentives—tax credits of up to $8,500—for each welfare recipient they hire. An agency that specializes in helping welfare recipients find work is the Independence Center, a mental health rehabilitation center in St. Louis. The Independence Center filled unskilled clerical jobs for Kirkwood Insurance Agency, offering a guarantee that all the workers would be on the job as required. Kirkwood's president, Rick Kalina, says the Independence Center eliminated the company's "constant" job turnover.[51]

Private Employment Agencies

In contrast to public employment agencies, which primarily serve the blue-collar labor market, private employment agencies provide much the same service for the white-collar labor market. Workers interested in finding a job can sign up with a private employment agency whether or not they are currently unemployed. Another difference between the two types of agencies is that private agencies charge the employers for providing referrals. Therefore, using a private employment agency is more expensive than using a public agency, but the private agency is a more suitable source for certain kinds of applicants.

For managers or professionals, an employer may use the services of a type of private agency called an *executive search firm (ESF)*. People often call these agencies "headhunters" because, unlike other employment agencies, they find new jobs for people almost exclusively already employed. For example, when BMW was preparing to open a new plant in the United States, it used an executive search firm to help "liberate" Allen Kinzer and Edwin Buker from Honda. These two executives were vice presidents for Honda's U.S. operations, and by hiring them, BMW hoped to re-create Honda's success.[52]

For job candidates, dealing with executive search firms can be sensitive. Typically, executives do not want to advertise their availability, because it could trigger a negative reaction from their current employer. ESFs serve a buffer, providing confidentiality between the employer and the recruit. That benefit may give an employer access to candidates it cannot recruit in other, more direct ways.

Employing an executive search firm may be expensive because of direct and indirect costs. According to a 1997 survey, ESFs often charge one-third to one-half the salary of the executive who is eventually placed with the client.[53] Also, convincing a person to consider changing jobs requires that the employer offer something more attractive. A company in a growing industry may have to offer as much as 50 percent more than the executive's current pay.[54]

Colleges and Universities

Most colleges and universities have placement services that seek to help their graduates obtain employment. On-campus interviewing is the most important source of recruits for entry-level professional and managerial vacancies.[55] Organizations tend to focus especially on colleges that have strong reputations in areas for which they have critical needs—say, chemical engineering or public accounting.[56] The recruiting strategy at 3M includes concentrating on 25 to 30 selected universities. The company has a commitment to those selected universities and returns to them each year with new job openings. HR professionals make sure that the same person works with the same university year in and year out, to achieve "continuity of contact."[57]

Many employers have found that successfully competing for the best students requires more than just signing up prospective graduates for interview slots. One of the best ways to establish a stronger presence on a campus is with a college internship program. Dun & Bradstreet funds a summer intern program for minority MBA students. D&B often hires these interns for full-time positions when they graduate.[58] Internship programs give an organization early access to potential applicants and let the organization assess their capabilities directly.

Another way of increasing the employer's presence on campus is to participate in university job fairs. In general, a job fair is an event where many employers gather for a short time to meet large numbers of potential job applicants. Although job fairs can be held anywhere (such as at a hotel or convention center), campuses are ideal locations because of the many well-educated, yet unemployed, individuals who are there. Job fairs are an inexpensive means of generating an on-campus presence. They can even provide one-on-one dialogue with potential recruits—dialogue that would be impossible through less interactive media, such as newspaper ads.

FIGURE 5.5

Sources of Recruits

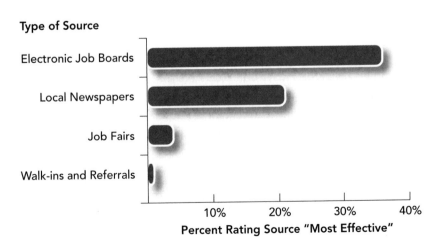

Type of Source

Web Opens the Door to a Global Labor Market

The Internet's audience is a global one, so by definition, e-cruiting reaches an international labor market. An organization that posts a job on the World Wide Web might just hear from people as far away as Dublin or Sri Lanka. Some organizations regard this as an opportunity and develop recruitment strategies that target job seekers in other countries.

An obvious challenge in global recruiting is language differences. Aside from translation concerns, even websites targeting job seekers in English-speaking parts of the world such as Australia and Hong Kong need to adapt their English for local usages. Symbols or graphics as well as words have different meanings in different cultures, too. A thumb's-up gesture meant to signal a positive thought would be obscene in Sicily.

Countries also differ in terms of their recruitment laws and customs. Job candidates in Holland and France expect that employers will ask about such characteristics as age, gender, and marital status—questions that would violate federal law if asked in the United States. In Germany, companies must give employees six months' notice before firing them, so recruiting methods should recognize the existence of German employees who know they will need a new job in a few months. Countries also vary in the degree to which they protect applicants' privacy. The European Union prohibits countries with "inadequate" privacy protection (including the United States) from transferring data outside the EU unless the data provider gives them permission.

Online recruiters also need to consider the values and expectations of job seekers. In contrast to Americans, Europeans tend to be more reluctant to share information about themselves on the Internet—especially if they don't know who wants the information and how it will be used. These workers also are more likely to hunt for a job using an intermediary, such as an executive search firm.

How can recruiters plan for all these differences? A good place to start is to talk to recruiters and employees in the countries from which the organization hopes to draw job candidates. People who work for global advertising agencies and some HR consulting and Web consulting firms are also knowledgeable about communicating globally.

SOURCE: Anne Freedman, "The Web World-Wide," *Human Resource Executive*, March 6, 2002, pp. 44–48.

Electronic Recruiting

The Internet has opened up new vistas for organizations trying to recruit talent. There are many ways to employ the Internet for recruiting. Increasingly, organizations are refining their use of this medium. As shown in Figure 5.5, over one-third of HR executives responding to a 2001 survey indicated that electronic job boards were the most effective source of recruits for their organization.[59] As the "e-HRM" box above describes, online recruiting also expands the labor market from which the organization can draw.

One of the easiest ways to get into "e-cruiting" is simply to use the organization's own website to solicit applications. Less than a quarter of the websites of the world's largest firms were using this approach in 1998. But by 2000, 88 percent were doing this—not surprisingly, since this practice is effective and extremely efficient for large organizations.[60]

Providing a way to submit applications at the company website is not so successful for smaller and less well-known organizations, because fewer people are likely to visit the website. These organizations may get better results by going to the websites that are set up to attract job seekers, such as Monster.com, HotJobs, and CareerBuilder, which attract a vast array of applicants. At these sites, job seekers submit standardized résumés. Employers can search the site's database for résumés that include specified key terms, and they can also submit information about their job opportunities, so that job seekers can search that information by key term. With both employers and job seekers submitting information to and conducting searches on them, these sites offer an efficient way to find matches between job seekers and job vacancies. However, a drawback is that the big job websites can provide too many leads of inferior quality because they are so huge and serve all job seekers and employers, not a select segment. In the words of an HR executive, "The last thing you need is to get a thousand résumés, 990 of which don't meet your needs."[61]

Because of this limitation of the large websites, smaller, more tailored websites called "niche boards" focus on certain industries, occupations, or geographic areas. Telecommcareers.net, for example, is a site devoted to, as the name implies, the telecommunications industry. CIO.com, a companion site to *CIO Magazine*, specializes in openings for chief information officers. The San Francisco Bay Area features craiglist.com, a job board for applicants who live in that area and have no intention of relocating. The best evidence in favor of these niche boards is that the major websites are scrambling to create more focused subsections of their own.[62]

Evaluating the Quality of a Source

yield ratio
A ratio that expresses the percentage of applicants who successfully move from one stage of the recruitment and selection process to the next.

In general, there are few rules that say what recruitment source is best for a given job vacancy. Therefore, it is wise for employers to monitor the quality of all their recruitment sources. One way to do this is to develop and compare **yield ratios** for each source.[63] A yield ratio expresses the percentage of applicants who successfully move from one stage of the recruitment and selection process to the next. For example, the organization could find the number of candidates interviewed as a percentage of the total number of résumés generated by a given source (that is, number of interviews divided by number of résumés). A high yield ratio (large percentage) means that the source is an effective way to find candidates to interview. By comparing the yield ratios of different recruitment sources, HR professionals can determine which source is the best or most efficient for the type of vacancy.

Another measure of recruitment success is the *cost per hire*. To compute this amount, find the cost of using a particular recruitment source for a particular type of vacancy. Then divide that cost by the number of people hired to fill that type of vacancy. A low cost per hire means that the recruitment source is efficient; it delivers qualified candidates at minimal cost.

To see how HR professionals use these measures, look at the examples in Table 5.3. This table shows the results for a hypothetical organization that used five kinds of recruitment sources to fill a number of vacancies. For each recruitment source, the table shows four yield ratios and the cost per hire. To fill these jobs, the best two sources of recruits were local universities and employee referral programs. Newspaper ads generated the largest number of recruits (500 résumés). However, only 50 were judged acceptable, of which only half accepted employment offers, for a cumulative yield ratio of 25/500, or 5 percent. Recruiting at renowned universities generated highly qualified applicants, but relatively few of them ultimately accepted positions with the or-

TABLE 5.3

Results of a Hypothetical Recruiting Effort

	RECRUITING SOURCE				
	LOCAL UNIVERSITY	RENOWNED UNIVERSITY	EMPLOYEE REFERRALS	NEWSPAPER AD	EXECUTIVE SEARCH FIRMS
Résumés generated	200	400	50	500	20
Interview offers accepted	175	100	45	400	20
Yield ratio	87%	25%	90%	80%	100%
Applicants judged acceptable	100	95	40	50	19
Yield ratio	57%	95%	89%	12%	95%
Accept employment offers	90	10	35	25	15
Yield ratio	90%	11%	88%	50%	79%
Cumulative yield ratio	90/200 45%	10/400 3%	35/50 70%	25/500 5%	15/20 75%
Cost	$30,000	$50,000	$15,000	$20,000	$90,000
Cost per hire	$333	$5,000	$428	$800	$6,000

ganization. Executive search firms produced the highest cumulative yield ratio. These generated only 20 applicants, but all of them accepted interview offers, most were judged acceptable, and 79 percent of these acceptable candidates took jobs with the organization. However, notice the cost per hire. The executive search firms charged $90,000 for finding these 15 employees, resulting in the largest cost per hire. In contrast, local universities provided modest yield ratios at the lowest cost per hire. Employee referrals provided excellent yield ratios at a slightly higher cost.

Recruiter Traits and Behaviors   LO6

As we showed in Figure 5.2, the third influence on recruitment outcomes is the recruiter, including this person's characteristics and the way he or she behaves. The recruiter affects the nature of both the job vacancy and the applicants generated. However, the recruiter often becomes involved late in the recruitment process. In many cases, by the time a recruiter meets some applicants, they have already made up their minds about what they desire in a job, what the vacant job has to offer, and their likelihood of receiving a job offer.[64]

Many applicants approach the recruiter with some skepticism. Knowing it is the recruiter's job to sell them on a vacancy, some applicants discount what the recruiter says, in light of what they have heard from other sources, such as friends, magazine articles, and professors. For these and other reasons, recruiters' characteristics and behaviors seem to have limited impact on applicants' job choices.

Characteristics of the Recruiter

Most organizations must choose whether their recruiters are specialists in human resources or are experts at particular jobs (that is, those who currently hold the same

FIGURE 5.6

Recruits Who Were Offended by Recruiters

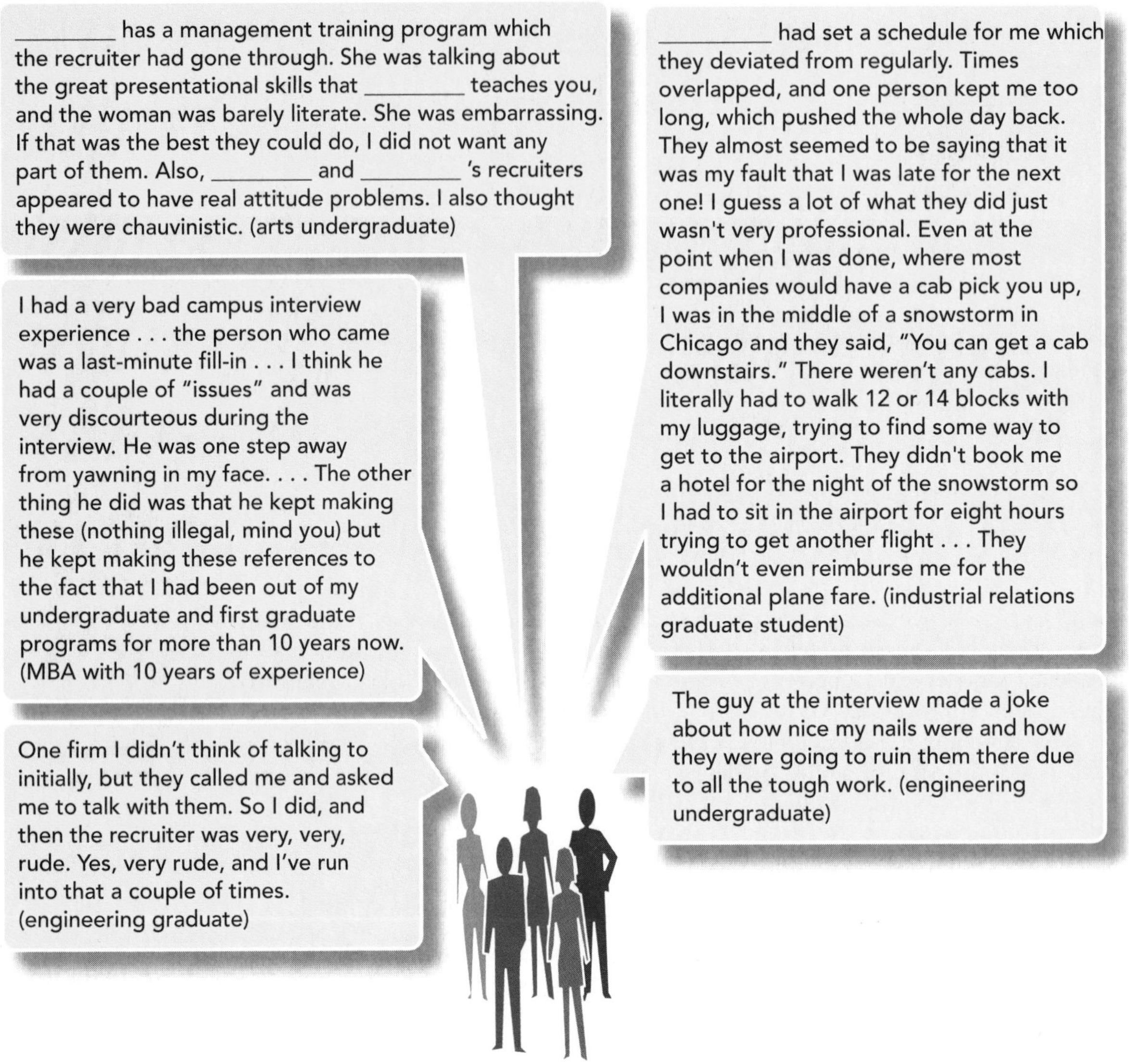

_____ has a management training program which the recruiter had gone through. She was talking about the great presentational skills that _____ teaches you, and the woman was barely literate. She was embarrassing. If that was the best they could do, I did not want any part of them. Also, _____ and _____ 's recruiters appeared to have real attitude problems. I also thought they were chauvinistic. (arts undergraduate)

I had a very bad campus interview experience . . . the person who came was a last-minute fill-in . . . I think he had a couple of "issues" and was very discourteous during the interview. He was one step away from yawning in my face. . . . The other thing he did was that he kept making these (nothing illegal, mind you) but he kept making these references to the fact that I had been out of my undergraduate and first graduate programs for more than 10 years now. (MBA with 10 years of experience)

One firm I didn't think of talking to initially, but they called me and asked me to talk with them. So I did, and then the recruiter was very, very, rude. Yes, very rude, and I've run into that a couple of times. (engineering graduate)

_____ had set a schedule for me which they deviated from regularly. Times overlapped, and one person kept me too long, which pushed the whole day back. They almost seemed to be saying that it was my fault that I was late for the next one! I guess a lot of what they did just wasn't very professional. Even at the point when I was done, where most companies would have a cab pick you up, I was in the middle of a snowstorm in Chicago and they said, "You can get a cab downstairs." There weren't any cabs. I literally had to walk 12 or 14 blocks with my luggage, trying to find some way to get to the airport. They didn't book me a hotel for the night of the snowstorm so I had to sit in the airport for eight hours trying to get another flight . . . They wouldn't even reimburse me for the additional plane fare. (industrial relations graduate student)

The guy at the interview made a joke about how nice my nails were and how they were going to ruin them there due to all the tough work. (engineering undergraduate)

kinds of jobs or supervise people who hold the jobs). According to some studies, applicants perceive HR specialists as less credible and are less attracted to jobs when recruiters are HR specialists.[65] The evidence does not completely discount a positive role for personnel specialists in recruiting. It does indicate, however, that these specialists need to take extra steps to ensure that applicants perceive them as knowledgeable and credible.

In general, applicants respond positively to recruiters whom they perceive as warm and informative. "Warm" means the recruiter seems to care about the applicant and to be enthusiastic about the applicant's potential to contribute to the organization. "Informative" means the recruiter provides the kind of information the applicant is seeking. The evidence of impact of other characteristics of recruiters—including their age, sex, and race—is complex and inconsistent.[66]

Behavior of the Recruiter

Recruiters affect results not only by providing plenty of information, but by providing the right kind of information. Perhaps the most-researched aspect of recruiting is the level of realism in the recruiter's message. Because the recruiter's job is to attract candidates, recruiters may feel pressure to exaggerate the positive qualities of the vacancy and to downplay its negative qualities. Applicants are highly sensitive to negative information. The highest-quality applicants may be less willing to pursue jobs when this type of information comes out.[67] But if the recruiter goes too far in a positive direction, the candidate can be misled and lured into taking a job that has been misrepresented. Then unmet expectations can contribute to a high turnover rate. When recruiters describe jobs unrealistically, people who take those jobs may come to believe that the employer is deceitful.[68]

Many studies have looked at how well **realistic job previews**—background information about jobs' positive and negative qualities—can get around this problem and help organizations minimize turnover among new employees. On the whole, the research suggests that realistic job previews have a weak and inconsistent effect on turnover.[69] Although recruiters can go overboard in selling applicants on the desirability of a job vacancy, there is little support for the belief that informing people about the negative characteristics of a job will "inoculate" them so that the negative features don't cause them to quit.[70]

Finally, for affecting whether people choose to take a job, but even more so, whether they stick with a job, the recruiter seems less important than an organization's personnel policies that directly affect the job's features (pay, security, advancement opportunities, and so on).

realistic job preview
Background information about a job's positive and negative qualities.

Enhancing the Recruiter's Impact

Nevertheless, although recruiters are probably not the most important influence on people's job choices, this does not mean recruiters cannot have an impact. Most recruiters receive little training.[71] If we were to determine what does matter to job candidates, perhaps recruiters could be trained in those areas.

Researchers have tried to find the conditions in which recruiters do make a difference. Such research suggests that an organization can take several steps to increase the positive impact that recruiters have on job candidates:

- Recruiters should provide timely feedback. Applicants dislike delays in feedback. They may draw negative conclusions about the organization (for starters, that the organization doesn't care about their application).
- Recruiters should avoid offensive behavior. They should avoid behaving in ways that might convey the wrong impression about the organization.[72] Figure 5.6 quotes applicants who felt they had extremely bad experiences with recruiters. Their statements provide examples of behaviors to avoid.
- The organization can recruit with teams rather than individual recruiters. Applicants view job experts as more credible than HR specialists, and a team can include both kinds of recruiters. HR specialists on the team provide knowledge about company policies and procedures.

Through such positive behavior, recruiters can give organizations a better chance of competing for talented human resources. In the next chapter, we will describe how an organization selects the candidates that best meet its needs.

Summary

1. Discuss how to plan for human resources needed to carry out the organization's strategy.
   The first step in human resource planning is personnel forecasting. Through trend analysis and good judgment, the planner tries to determine the supply of and demand for various human resources. Based on whether a surplus or a shortage is expected, the planner sets goals and creates a strategy for achieving those goals. The organization then implements its HR strategy and evaluates the results.

2. Determine the labor demand for workers in various job categories.
   The planner can look at leading indicators, assuming trends will continue in the future. Multiple regression can convert several leading indicators into a single prediction of labor needs. Analysis of a transitional matrix can help the planner identify which job categories can be filled internally and where high turnover is likely.

3. Summarize the advantages and disadvantages of ways to eliminate a labor surplus and avoid a labor shortage.
   To reduce a surplus, downsizing, pay reductions, and demotions deliver fast results but at a high cost in human suffering that may hurt surviving employees' motivation and future recruiting. Also, the organization may lose some of its best employees. Transferring employees and requiring them to share work are also fast methods and the consequences in human suffering are less severe. A hiring freeze or natural attrition is slow to take effect but avoids the pain of layoffs. Early-retirement packages may unfortunately induce the best employees to leave and may be slow to implement; however, they, too, are less painful than layoffs. Retraining can improve the organization's overall pool of human resources and maintain high morale, but it is relatively slow and costly.
   To avoid a labor shortage, requiring overtime is the easiest and fastest strategy, which can easily be changed if conditions change. However, overtime may exhaust workers and can hurt morale. Using temporary employees and outsourcing do not build an in-house pool of talent, but by these means staffing levels can be quickly and easily modified. Transferring and retraining employees require investment of time and money, but can enhance the quality of the organization's human resources; however, this may backfire if a labor surplus develops. Hiring new employees is slow and expensive but strengthens the organization if labor needs are expected to expand for the long term. Using technology as a substitute for labor can be slow to implement and costly, but it may improve the organization's long-term performance. New technology and hiring are difficult to reverse if conditions change.

4. Describe recruitment policies organizations use to make job vacancies more attractive.
   Internal recruiting (promotions from within) generally makes job vacancies more attractive because candidates see opportunities for growth and advancement. Lead-the-market pay strategies make jobs economically desirable. Due-process policies signal that employers are concerned about employee rights. Image advertising can give candidates the impression that the organization is a good place to work.

5. List and compare sources of job applicants.
   Internal sources, promoted through job postings, generate applicants who are familiar to the organization and motivate other employees by demonstrating opportunities for advancement. However, internal sources are usually insufficient for all of an organization's labor needs. Direct applicants and referrals tend to be inexpensive and to generate applicants who have self-selected; this source risks charges of unfairness, especially in cases of nepotism. Newspaper and magazine advertising reaches a wide audience and may generate many applications, although many are likely to be unsuitable. Public employment agencies are inexpensive and typically have screened applicants. Private employment agencies charge fees but may provide many services. Another inexpensive channel is schools and colleges, which may give the employer access to top-notch entrants to the labor market. Electronic recruiting gives organizations access to a global labor market, tends to be inexpensive, and allows convenient searching of databases.

6. Describe the recruiter's role in the recruitment process, including limits and opportunities.
   Through their behavior and other characteristics, recruiters influence the nature of the job vacancy and the kinds of applicants generated. Applicants tend to perceive job experts as more credible than recruiters who are HR specialists. They tend to react more favorably to recruiters who are warm and informative. Recruiters should not mislead candidates. Realistic job previews

are helpful, but have a weak and inconsistent effect on job turnover compared to personnel policies and actual job conditions. Recruiters can improve their impact by providing timely feedback, avoiding behavior that contributes to a negative impression of the organization, and teaming up with job experts.

Review and Discussion Questions

1. Suppose an organization expects a labor shortage to develop in key job areas over the next few years. Recommend general responses the organization could make in each of the following areas:
   a. Recruitment.
   b. Training.
   c. Compensation (pay and employee benefits).
2. Review the sample transitional matrix shown in Table 5.1. What jobs experience the greatest turnover (employees leaving the organization)? How might an organization with this combination of jobs reduce the turnover?
3. In the same transitional matrix, which jobs seem to rely the most on internal recruitment? Which seem to rely most on external recruitment? Why?
4. Why do organizations combine statistical and judgmental forecasts of labor demand, rather than relying on statistics or judgment alone? Give an example of a situation in which each type of forecast would be inaccurate.
5. Some organizations have detailed affirmative-action plans, complete with goals and timetables, for women and minorities, yet have no formal human resource plan for the organization as a whole. Why might this be the case? What does this practice suggest about the role of human resource management in these organizations?

6. Give an example of a personnel policy that would help attract a larger pool of job candidates. Give an example of a personnel policy that would likely reduce the pool of candidates. Would you expect these policies to influence the quality as well as the number of applicants? Why or why not?
7. Discuss the relative merits of internal versus external recruitment. Give an example of a situation in which each of these approaches might be particularly effective.
8. List the jobs you have held. How were you recruited for each of these? From the organization's perspective, what were some pros and cons of recruiting you through these methods?
9. Recruiting people for jobs that require international assignments is increasingly important for many organizations. Where might an organization go to recruit people interested in such assignments?
10. A large share of HR professionals have rated e-cruiting as their best source of new talent. What qualities of electronic recruiting do you think contribute to this opinion?
11. How can organizations improve the effectiveness of their recruiters?

What's Your HR IQ?

The Student CD-ROM offers two more ways to check what you've learned so far. Use the Self-Assessment exercise to test your knowledge of HR planning and recruiting.

Go online with the Web Exercise to see how well your knowledge works in cyberspace.

BusinessWeek Case

BusinessWeek **Forget the Huddled Masses: Send Nerds**

As a headhunter, George Van Derven has an unlikely connection: Russia's former state airline, Aeroflot. Not that Van Derven trades in pilots, flight mechanics, or surly Russian flight attendants. But in a former career, he sold a computerized reservation system to Aeroflot and came to know the talented programmers stashed in the back offices. When Aeroflot broke up into regional carriers in

1992, Van Derven promptly tapped its brain pool. Now, as president of Alternative Technology Resources Inc. in Sacramento, Van Derven is mining a rich lode of programming talent and busily dispatching it to understaffed computer departments throughout the Western world.

Other recruiters should be so lucky. High-tech headhunters for Andersen Consulting [now Accenture] tramp through technical schools in Budapest and job fairs in Manila. At a training session for programmers in Holland, Microsoft Corporation hired bouncers to keep head-hunters at bay. And a recruiter for IBM's Global Services Division, who is trying to hire 15,000 software hands, in-troduces himself as James R. Bunch, "as in bunch of jobs."

The Information Revolution is racing ahead of its vital raw material: brainpower. As demand explodes for com-puterized applications, companies are finding themselves strapped for programmers. In the United States alone, which accounts for two-thirds of the world's market in software products and services, some 190,000 high-tech jobs stand open, most of them for programmers, according to the Information Technology Association.

Relief is nowhere in sight. Experts predict the gap be-tween computer science students and expected demand won't ease for a decade, if then. Too many bright young people, especially in Europe and the United States, con-sider programming geek work and choose other careers. In the United States, the number of computer science grad-uates has plummeted in the past decade or so.

How did the shortage get so bad? For years, tech compa-nies had little reason to fret. In the early 90s, the industry snapped up hundreds of thousands of workers who were dropped into the job market when large corporations down-sized—a source now running dry. At the same time, the work of writing software has not sped up despite the com-puter revolution and the terabytes of information hurtling around the globe. Today, even the best of programmers painstakingly turns out some 10 lines of code a day—while even a cellular telephone requires some 300,000 lines of code. To whip up today's software programs takes armies of programmers laboriously writing away.

No surprise, then, that companies are trying any re-cruiting tactic, including the World Wide Web. Since the Net is where most programmers spend idle hours, growing numbers of recruiters are using it to chase them down. That's where Michael L. McNeal casts his global net. McNeal, human resources chief at Cisco Systems, needs to hire 1,000 people each quarter, many of them program-mers. Like other recruiters, he buys ads on popular web-sites like the Dilbert page, which funnels traffic to Cisco's website. There the company lists some 500 current job openings. Applicants in foreign countries can hit hot but-tons to translate the page into Cantonese, Mandarin, Russian. And, by filling out a short questionnaire, they can create a résumé and zap it to Cisco.

Cisco's Web page draws 500,000 job searches per month. This gives Cisco gobs of data about the job mar-ket, including which companies have interested employ-ees. Armed with the best prospects, McNeal then turns to Cisco employees for help, asking them to call recruits, who speak the same language.

Like the others, Microsoft recruits on the Web and snaps up start-ups for talent—some 20 companies in 1996 alone. But to get its software up and running throughout the world, Microsoft relies on service companies, which are grossly understaffed. Microsoft calculates that its ser-vice partners are short 41,000 professionals trained to in-stall Microsoft products. This is forcing the company to educate new recruits. With an effort known as Skills 2000, Microsoft has been pushing into 350 schools and colleges around the world. It hammers out curricula that will pro-duce more programmers, such as adding computer training in business schools. A big part of the effort is in Europe, a major market that has 18 million unemployed workers. Microsoft's solution is to invite jobless Europeans in 11 countries into free training programs. In the past year, 3,000 Europeans have gone through the program, with 98 percent of them landing jobs.

As recruiters travel, they focus on regional specialties. The Russians are whizzes at math. India's university at Puna has a strong Japanese language program. South African programmers learned to cope during the years of the antiapartheid boycott with a motley collection of jury-rigged mainframes, making them especially adept at up-grading old computer systems.

SOURCE: "Forget the Huddled Masses: Send Nerds," *BusinessWeek*, July 21, 1997.

Questions

1. This chapter described several options for avoiding a labor shortage. Which of those options have the com-panies in this case used? Which options do you think can be most successful?
2. How has e-cruiting helped employers find program-mers?
3. If you were responsible for recruiting programmers for a bank, how would you help your company succeed in this highly competitive labor market? How (if at all) would your approach differ if you were recruiting for a firm that provides programmers to companies that want to outsource this work?

Case: Southwest Airlines Focuses on Takeoffs, Not Layoffs

In the summer of 2001, the airline industry was facing se-vere problems caused by slumping business travel and va-cationer demand. Northwest Airlines slashed its schedules and service. Midway Airlines declared bankruptcy, blam-ing its decision on "calamitous" decline in air traffic. Then the situation got worse.

The September 2001 terrorist attacks on New York and Washington, DC, devastated the whole nation, but few segments of the economy felt the impact as dramatically as the already struggling airline industry. Even after the airlines had reduced scheduled flights by more than 20 percent, most planes were taking off with fewer than half their seats filled. The value of airline stock fell by one-third. To make ends meet, most airlines needed to cut costs drastically. Over 100,000 employees were laid off at American Airlines, United Airlines, US Airways, Continental Airlines, and America West.

One airline stood out as the exception to this trend: Southwest Airlines. Despite the regular ups and downs of the airline industry, Southwest has never, in its 30 years of operation, laid off employees. Remarkably, Southwest was able to maintain this record even during the difficult fall of 2001.

Southwest has a no-layoff policy that is one of its core values. Insiders stress that this human resource policy is one of the main reasons why the workforce at Southwest is so fiercely loyal, productive, and flexible. The high productivity of these workers helps keep labor costs low, and the savings are passed on to travelers in the form of lower prices—sometimes half the fares offered by competitors. Job security also promotes a willingness of Southwest employees to innovate on the job without fearing that they will be punished for any mistakes. Southwest also finds that satisfied employees help create satisfied customers and can even help in recruiting new employees when the economy is growing.

To keep its no-layoff record in 2001, Southwest executives assembled into an emergency command and control center in Dallas. There they brainstormed methods to cut costs without laying off employees. The executives decided to delay the company's plans to purchase new planes and to scrap plans to renovate the company's headquarters. Southwest has no debt and over a billion dollars in cash, so it drew from its "rainy-day" fund to get through the tough times. The process was difficult and painful, but as CEO Jim Parker noted, "We are willing to suffer some damage, even to our stock price, to protect the jobs of our people."

Southwest Airlines' steadfast refusal to lay off workers, despite external pressure, was simply an extension of a long-term culture at Southwest. It was in keeping with Southwest's culture to follow a policy of using methods other than layoffs as a means of managing the labor surplus.

SOURCE: M. Arndt, "Suddenly, Carriers Can't Get off the Ground," *BusinessWeek,* September 3, 2001, pp. 36–37; M. Arndt, "What Kind of Rescue?" *BusinessWeek,* October 1, 2001, pp. 36–37; W. Zeller, "Southwest: After Kelleher, More Blue Skies," *BusinessWeek,* April 2, 2001, p. 45; M. Conlin, "Where Layoffs Are a Last Resort," *BusinessWeek,* October 8, 2001, p. 42.

Questions

1. If other organizations want to pattern themselves after Southwest Airlines, what steps can they take to avoid layoffs when business is slow?
2. How would you predict that Southwest's treatment of employees influences its selection of recruitment sources? What sources would you expect Southwest to rely on?
3. Suppose the demand for air travel skyrockets in the near future. How will Southwest's past practices affect its ability to manage the accompanying labor shortage?

Notes

1. Stacy Forster, "New Ventures Meet the Challenges of a Struggling Start-up Climate," *The Wall Street Journal Online,* March 27, 2002, http://online.wsj.com.
2. Timothy Aeppel, "A Factory Manager Improvises to Save Jobs Amid a Downturn," *The Wall Street Journal,* Interactive Edition, December 27, 2001, http://interactive.wsj.com.
3. B. Schlender, "Matsushita Shows How to Go Global," *Fortune,* July 11, 1994, pp. 159–66.
4. P. Smith, "Salariless Man," *The Economist,* September 16, 1995, p. 79.
5. M. Conlin, "Savaged by the Slowdown," *BusinessWeek,* September 17, 2001, pp. 74–77.
6. W. F. Cascio, "Whither Industrial and Organizational Psychology in a Changing World of Work?" *American Psychologist* 50 (1995), pp. 928–39.
7. K. Kabich, "The Geography of an Emerging America," *Fortune,* June 27, 1994, pp. 88–94.
8. D. Greising, "It's the Best of Times—or Is It?" *BusinessWeek,* January 12, 1998, pp. 35–38.
9. K. P. DeMeuse, P. A. Vanderheiden, and T. J. Bergmann, "Announced Layoffs: Their Effect on Corporate Financial Performance," *Human Resource Management* 33 (1994), pp. 509–30.
10. P. P. Shaw, "Network Destruction: The Structural Implications of Downsizing," *Academy of Management Journal* 43 (2000), pp. 101–12.
11. R. T. King, "Is Job Cutting by Drug Makers Bad Medicine?" *The Wall Street Journal,* August 23, 1995, pp. B1–B3.
12. W. F. Cascio, "Downsizing: What Do We Know? What Have We Learned?" *Academy of Management Executive* 7 (1993), pp. 95–104.
13. J. Schu, "Internet Helps Keep Goodwill of Downsized Employees," *Workforce,* July 2001, p. 15.
14. D. Skatlicki, J. H. Ellard, and B. R. C. Kellin, "Third

Party Perceptions of a Layoff: Procedural, Derogation, and Retributive Aspects of Justice," *Journal of Applied Psychology* 83 (1998), pp. 119–27.

15. R. Folger and D. P. Skarlicki, "When Tough Times Make Tough Bosses: Managerial Distancing as a Function of Layoff Blame," *Academy of Management Journal* 41 (1998), pp. 79–87.

16. R. Stodghill, "The Coming Job Bottleneck," *BusinessWeek*, March 24, 1997, pp. 184–85.

17. S. Kim and D. Feldman, "Healthy, Wealthy, or Wise: Predicting Actual Acceptances of Early Retirement Incentives at Three Points in Time," *Personnel Psychology* 51 (1998), pp. 623–42.

18. D. Fandray, "Gray Matters," *Workforce*, July 2000, pp. 27–32.

19. S. Caudron, "Contingent Work Force Spurs HR Planning," *Personnel Journal*, July 1994, pp. 52–59.

20. G. Flynn, "Contingent Staffing Requires Serious Strategy," *Personnel Journal*, April 1995, pp. 50–58.

21. Rifka Rosenwein, "Help (Still) Wanted," *Inc.*, April 2001, pp. 51–52, 54–55.

22. K. Bradsher, "American Workers Watch as Jobs Go Overseas," *International Herald Tribune*, August 29, 1995, pp. C1–C2.

23. G. Koretz, "Overtime versus New Factories," *BusinessWeek*, May 4, 1998, p. 34.

24. A. Bernstein, "Bell Atlantic North Faces a Monstrous Labor Crunch," *BusinessWeek*, June 8, 1998, p. 38.

25. A. E. Barber, *Recruiting Employees* (Thousand Oaks, CA: Sage, 1998).

26. J. D. Olian and S. L. Rynes, "Organizational Staffing: Integrating Practice with Strategy," *Industrial Relations* 23 (1984), pp. 170–83.

27. Rosenwein, "Help (Still) Wanted."

28. G. T. Milkovich and J. M. Newman, *Compensation* (Homewood, IL.: Richard D. Irwin, 1990).

29. S. J. Marks, "After School," *Human Resources Executive*, June 15, 2001, pp. 49–51.

30. J. Kaufman, "A McDonald's Owner Becomes a Role Model for Black Teenagers," *The Wall Street Journal*, August 23, 1995, p. A1.

31. K. Clark, "Reasons to Worry about Rising Wages," *Fortune*, July 7, 1997, pp. 31–32.

32. Jobtrack.com, "Changing Views on Valued Benefits," June 30, 2001, p. 1.

33. W. Zellner, "The Fall of Enron," *BusinessWeek*, December 17, 2001, pp. 30–36.

34. M. Leonard, "Challenges to the Termination-at-Will Doctrine," *Personnel Administrator* 28 (1983), pp. 49–56.

35. C. Schowerer and B. Rosen, "Effects of Employment-at-Will Policies and Compensation Policies on Corporate Image and Job Pursuit Intentions," *Journal of Applied Psychology* 74 (1989), pp. 653–56.

36. Ibid.

37. M. Magnus, "Recruitment Ads at Work," *Personnel Journal* 64 (1985), pp. 42–63.

38. S. L. Rynes and A. E. Barber, "Applicant Attraction Strategies: An Organizational Perspective," *Academy of Management Review* 15 (1990), pp. 286–310; J. A. Breaugh, *Recruitment: Science and Practice* (Boston: PWS-Kent, 1992), p. 34.

39. J. Bussey, "Dow Chemical Tries to Shed Tough Image and Court the Public," *The Wall Street Journal*, November 20, 1987, p. 1.

40. R. Thompson, "More Diversity in Agriculture: A Hard Row," *The Wall Street Journal*, September 19, 1995, p. B1.

41. D. M. Cable, L. Aiman-Smith, P. Mulvey, and J. R. Edwards, "The Sources and Accuracy of Job Applicants' Beliefs about Organizational Culture," *Academy of Management Journal* 43 (2000), pp. 1076–85.

42. M. A. Conrad and S. D. Ashworth, "Recruiting Source Effectiveness: A Meta-Analysis and Re-examination of Two Rival Hypotheses," paper presented at the annual meeting of the Society of Industrial/Organizational Psychology, Chicago, 1986.

43. Breaugh, *Recruitment*.

44. P. A. Savill, "HR at Inova Reengineers Recruitment Process," *Personnel Journal*, June 1995, pp. 109–14.

45. Breaugh, *Recruitment*, pp. 113–114.

46. R. S. Schuler and S. E. Jackson, "Linking Competitive Strategies with Human Resource Management Practices," *Academy of Management Executive* 1 (1987), pp. 207–19.

47. C. R. Wanberg, R. Kanfer, and J. T. Banas, "Predictors and Outcomes of Networking Intensity among Job Seekers," *Journal of Applied Psychology* 85 (2000), pp. 491–503.

48. A. Halcrow, "Employers Are Your Best Recruiters," *Personnel Journal* 67 (1988), pp. 42–49.

49. G. Flynn, "Do You Have the Right Approach to Diversity?" *Personnel Journal*, October 1995, pp. 68–75.

50. Breaugh, *Recruitment*, p. 87.

51. Rosenwein, "Help (Still) Wanted."

52. J. Mitchell, "BMW Names 2 Honda Executives to Oversee New U.S. Assembly Plant," *The Wall Street Journal*, November 29, 1992, p. B4.

53. J. Reingold, "Casting for a Different Set of Characters," *BusinessWeek*, December 8, 1997, pp. 38–39.

54. J. Greenwald, "Invasion of the Body Snatchers," *Time*, April 23, 1984, p. 41.

55. P. Smith, "Sources Used by Employers When Hiring College Grads," *Personnel Journal*, February 1995, p. 25.

56. J. W. Boudreau and S. L. Rynes, "Role of Recruitment in Staffing Utility Analysis," *Journal of Applied Psychology* 70 (1985), pp. 354–66.

57. D. Anfuso, "3M's Staffing Strategy Promotes Produc-

tivity and Pride," *Personnel Journal*, February 1995, pp. 28–34.

58. L. Winter, "Employers Go to School on Minority Recruiting," *The Wall Street Journal*, December 15, 1992, p. B1.

59. J. Smith, "Is Online Recruiting Getting Easier?" *Workforce*, September 2, 2001, p. 1.

60. C. Timberlake, "Corporate Websites Increasingly Offer Chances to Apply for Open Jobs Online," *The Wall Street Journal*, October 30, 2001, p. 1.

61. S. Bills, "A Wider Net for Hiring," *CNN/Money Online*, July 26, 2000, p. 1.

62. A. Salkever, "A Better Way to Float Your Résumé," *BusinessWeek Online*, October 9, 2000, pp. 1–2.

63. R. Hawk, *The Recruitment Function* (New York: American Management Association, 1967).

64. C. K. Stevens, "Effects of Preinterview Beliefs on Applicants' Reactions to Campus Interviews," *Academy of Management Journal* 40 (1997), pp. 947–66.

65. M. S. Taylor and T. J. Bergman, "Organizational Recruitment Activities and Applicants' Reactions at Different Stages of the Recruitment Process," *Personnel Psychology* 40 (1984), pp. 261–85; C. D. Fisher, D. R. Ilgen, and W. D. Hoyer, "Source Credibility, Information Favorability, and Job Offer Acceptance," *Academy of Management Journal* 22 (1979), pp. 94–103.

66. L. M. Graves and G. N. Powell, "The Effect of Sex Similarity on Recruiters' Evaluation of Actual Applicants: A Test of the Similarity-Attraction Paradigm," *Personnel Psychology* 48 (1995), pp. 85–98.

67. R. D. Tretz and T. A. Judge, "Realistic Job Previews: A Test of the Adverse Self-Selection Hypothesis," *Journal of Applied Psychology* 83 (1998), pp. 330–37.

68. P. Hom, R. W. Griffeth, L. E. Palich, and J. S. Bracker, "An Exploratory Investigation into Theoretical Mechanisms Underlying Realistic Job Previews," *Personnel Psychology* 51 (1998), pp. 421–51.

69. G. M. McEvoy and W. F. Cascio, "Strategies for Reducing Employee Turnover: A Meta-Analysis," *Journal of Applied Psychology* 70 (1985), pp. 342–53; S. L. Premack and J. P. Wanous, "A Meta-Analysis of Realistic Job Preview Experiments," *Journal of Applied Psychology* 70 (1985), pp. 706–19.

70. P. G. Irving and J. P. Meyer, "Reexamination of the Met-Expectations Hypothesis: A Longitudinal Analysis," *Journal of Applied Psychology* 79 (1995), pp. 937–49.

71. R. W. Walters, "It's Time We Become Pros," *Journal of College Placement* 12 (1985), pp. 30–33.

72. S. L. Rynes, R. D. Bretz, and B. Gerhart, "The Importance of Recruitment in Job Choice: A Different Way of Looking," *Personnel Psychology* 44 (1991), pp. 487–522.

Chapter 6

Selecting Employees and Placing Them in Jobs

What Do I Need to Know? After reading this chapter, you should be able to:

1. Identify the elements of the selection process.

2. Define ways to measure the success of a selection method.

3. Summarize the government's requirements for employee selection.

4. Compare the common methods used for selecting human resources.

5. Describe major types of employment tests.

6. Discuss how to conduct effective interviews.

7. Explain how employers carry out the process of making a selection decision.

Introduction

Unlike a lot of entrepreneurs, Jeff Soderberg specifically avoids hiring workaholics. He knows better, because he once was one himself. Soderberg cofounded a software business, and as he devoted every waking hour to the company, he sacrificed his marriage along with his leisure time, only to be fired one day. Later, when Soderberg started Software Technology Group (STG), he decided he needed a new style that would keep him in business for the long run. STG provides information technology experts on a contract basis, helping clients with their software projects. Client companies want to get their software running as fast as possible, and STG insists that clients hire enough staff, rather than forcing programmers to work around the clock. According to Soderberg, "We have to make sure that our consultants don't burn out. We have to think long-term. . . . We can't afford to think only about the finish line of the current software project." With regard to hiring, that means Soderberg asks prospective employees about their hobbies. Applicants who call themselves workaholics don't get a job offer. Soderberg explains, "To put a workaholic on the staff would be like trying to mix oil and water. You have to create a team that shares the same values, and having a healthy lifestyle is one of our values."[1]

As Jeff Soderberg knows, hiring decisions are about finding the people who will be a good fit with the job and the organization. Any organization that appreciates the competitive edge provided by good people must take the utmost care in choosing its members. The organization's decisions about selecting personnel are central to its ability to survive, adapt, and grow. Selection decisions become especially critical when organizations face tight labor markets or must compete for talent with other organizations in the same industry. If a competitor keeps getting the best applicants, the remaining companies must make do with who is left.

This chapter will familiarize you with ways to minimize errors in employee selection and placement. The chapter starts by describing the selection process and how to evaluate possible methods for carrying out that process. It then takes an in-depth look at the most widely used methods: applications and résumés, employment tests, and interviews. The chapter ends by describing the process by which organizations arrive at a final selection decision.

Selection Process

LO1

Through **personnel selection,** organizations make decisions about who will or will not be allowed to join the organization. Selection begins with the candidates identified through recruitment and attempts to reduce their number to the individuals best qualified to perform the available jobs. At the end of the process, the selected individuals are placed in jobs with the organization.

The process of selecting employees varies considerably from organization to organization and from job to job. At most organizations, however, selection includes the steps illustrated in Figure 6.1. First, a human resource professional reviews the applications received to see which meet the basic requirements of the job. For candidates who meet the basic requirements, the organization administers tests and reviews work samples to rate the candidates' abilities. Those with the best abilities are invited to the organization for one or more interviews. Often, supervisors and team members are involved in this stage of the process. By this point, the decision makers are beginning to form opinions about which candidates are most desirable. For the top few

personnel selection The process through which organizations make decisions about who will or will not be allowed to join the organization.

FIGURE 6.1

Steps in the Selection Process

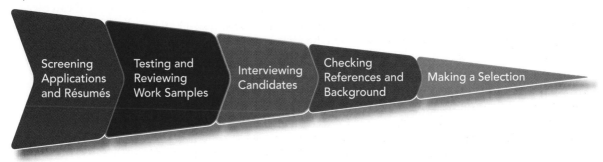

Screening Applications and Résumés

Testing and Reviewing Work Samples

Interviewing Candidates

Checking References and Background

Making a Selection

FIGURE 6.2

Criteria for Evaluating
Selection Methods

candidates, the organization should check references and conduct background checks to verify that the organization's information is correct. Then supervisors, teams, and other decision makers select a person to receive a job offer. In some cases, the candidate may negotiate with the organization regarding salary, benefits, and the like. If the candidate accepts the job, the organization places him or her in that job.

How does an organization decide which of these elements to use, and in what order? Some organizations simply repeat a selection process that is familiar. If members of the organization underwent job interviews, they conduct job interviews, asking familiar questions. However, what organizations *should* do is to create a selection process in support of its job descriptions. In Chapter 3, we explained that a job description identifies the knowledge, skills, abilities, and other characteristics required for successfully performing a job. The selection process should be set up in such a way that it lets the organization identify people who have the necessary KSAOs. For example, when Diversified Communications Group, a Massachusetts recruiting firm, hires for sales positions, it looks for people who have the same psychological traits as its best current sales reps. The company also wants skill in handling phone calls to prospective customers. Therefore, the selection process for these positions includes a personality test and two half-day sessions of placing phone calls to actual prospects of Diversified. Candidates who survive those steps also spend time in an interview with Tony Natella, the company's chief executive.[2]

LO2

This kind of strategic approach to selection requires ways to measure the effectiveness of selection tools. From science, we have basic standards for this. The best selection methods will provide information that is reliable and valid and can be generalized to apply to the organization's group of candidates. In addition, selection should measure characteristics that have practical benefits for the organization. Finally, selection criteria must meet the legal requirements in effect where the organization operates. Figure 6.2 summarizes these criteria.

reliability
The extent to which
a measurement is
from random error.

Reliability

The **reliability** of a type of measurement indicates how free that measurement is from random error.[3] A reliable measurement therefore generates consistent results. Assuming that a person's intelligence is fairly stable over time, a reliable test of intelligence should generate consistent results if the same person takes the test several times. Organizations that construct intelligence tests therefore should be able to provide (and explain) information about the reliability of their tests.

Usually, this information involves statistics such as *correlation coefficients*. These statistics measure the degree to which two sets of numbers are related. A higher correlation coefficient signifies a stronger relationship. At one extreme, a correlation coefficient of 1.0 means a perfect positive relationship—as one set of numbers goes up, so does the other. If you took the same vision test three days in a row, those scores would probably have nearly a perfect correlation. At the other extreme, a correlation of –1.0 means a perfect negative correlation—when one set of numbers goes up, the other goes down. In the middle, a correlation of 0 means there is no correlation at all. For example, the correlation between weather and intelligence would be at or near 0. A reliable test would be one for which scores by the same person (or people with similar attributes) have a correlation close to 1.0.

Validity

For a selection measure, **validity** describes the extent to which performance on the measure (such as a test score) is related to what the measure is designed to assess (such as job performance). Although we can reliably measure such characteristics as weight and height, these measurements do not provide much information about how a person will perform most kinds of jobs. Thus, for most jobs height and weight provide little validity as selection criteria. One way to determine whether a measure is valid is to compare many people's scores on that measure with their job performance. For example, suppose people who score above 60 words per minute on a keyboarding test consistently get high marks for their performance in data-entry jobs. This observation suggests the keyboarding test is valid for predicting success in that job.

As with reliability, information about the validity of selection methods often uses correlation coefficients. A strong positive (or negative) correlation between a measure and job performance means the measure should be a valid basis for selecting (or rejecting) a candidate. This information is important, not only because it helps organizations identify the best employees, but also because organizations can demonstrate fair employment practices by showing that their selection process is valid. The federal government's *Uniform Guidelines on Employee Selection Procedures* accept three ways of measuring validity: criterion-related, content, and construct validity.

Criterion-Related Validity

The first category, **criterion-related validity,** is a measure of validity based on showing a substantial correlation between test scores and job performance scores. In the example in Figure 6.3, a company compares two measures—an intelligence test and college grade point average—with performance as sales representative. In the left graph, which shows the relationship between the intelligence test scores and job performance, the points for the 20 sales reps fall near the 45-degree line. The correlation coefficient is near .90 (for a perfect 1.0, all the points would be on the 45-degree line). In the graph at the right, the points are scattered more widely. The correlation between college GPA and sales reps' performance is much lower. In this hypothetical example, the intelligence test is more valid than GPA for predicting success at this job.

Two kinds of research are possible for arriving at criterion-related validity:

validity
The extent to which performance on a measure (such as a test score) is related to what the measure is designed to assess (such as job performance).

criterion-related validity
A measure of validity based on showing a substantial correlation between test scores and job performance scores.

FIGURE 6.3

Criterion-Related Measurements of a Student's Aptitude

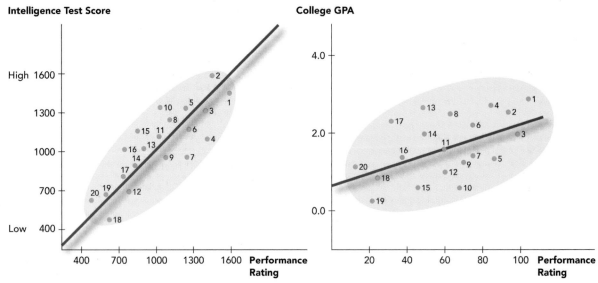

1. **Predictive validation**—This research uses the test scores of all applicants and looks for a relationship between the scores and future performance. The researcher administers the tests, waits a set period of time, and then measures the performance of the applicants who were hired.
2. **Concurrent validation**—This type of research administers a test to people who currently hold a job, then compares their scores to existing measures of job performance. If the people who score highest on the test also do better on the job, the test is assumed to be valid.

Predictive validation is more time consuming and difficult, but it is the best measure of validity. Job applicants tend to be more motivated to do well on the tests, and their performance on the tests is not influenced by their firsthand experience with the job. Also, the group studied is more likely to include people who perform poorly on the test—a necessary ingredient to accurately validate a test.[4]

Content and Construct Validity

Another way to show validity is to establish **content validity**—that is, consistency between the test items or problems and the kinds of situations or problems that occur on the job.[5] A test that is "content valid" exposes the job applicant to situations that are likely to occur on the job. It tests whether the applicant has the knowledge, skills, or ability to handle such situations.

For example, a general contracting firm that constructs tract housing needed to hire a construction superintendent.[6] This job involved organizing, supervising, and inspecting the work of many subcontractors. The tests developed for this position attempted to mirror the job. One test was a scrambled subcontractor test. The applicant had to take a random list of subcontractors (roofing, plumbing, electrical, and so on) and put them in the order that each firm should appear on the construction site. A second test measured recognition of construction errors. In this test, the applicant

predictive validation
Research that uses the test scores of all applicants and looks for a relationship between the scores and future performance of the applicants who were hired.

concurrent validation
Research that consists of administering a test to people who currently hold a job, then comparing their scores to existing measures of job performance.

content validity
Consistency between the test items or problems and the kinds of situations or problems that occur on the job.

went into a shed that was specially constructed to have 25 common and expensive errors, including faulty wiring and upside-down windows. The applicant was supposed to record all the problems he or she could detect. The content of these tests so closely parallels the content of the job that it was safe to use test performance as the basis for predicting job performance.

The usual basis for deciding that a test has content validity is through expert judgment. Experts can rate the test items according to whether they mirror essential functions of the job. Because establishing validity is based on the experts' subjective judgments, content validity is most suitable for measuring behavior that is concrete and observable.

For tests that measure abstract qualities such as intelligence or leadership ability, establishment of validity may have to rely on **construct validity.** This involves establishing that tests really do measure intelligence, leadership ability, or other such "constructs," as well as showing that mastery of this construct is associated with successful performance of the job. For example, if you could show that a test measures something called "mechanical ability," and that people with superior mechanical ability perform well as assemblers, then the test has construct validity for the assembler job. Tests that measure a construct usually measure a combination of behaviors thought to be associated with the construct.

construct validity
Consistency between a high score on a test and high level of a construct such as intelligence or leadership ability, as well as between mastery of this construct and successful performance of the job.

Ability to Generalize

Along with validity in general, we need to know whether a selection method is valid in the context in which the organization wants to use it. A **generalizable** method applies not only to the conditions in which the method was originally developed—job, organization, people, time period, and so on. It also applies to other organizations, jobs, applicants, and so on. In other words, is a selection method that was valid in one context also valid in other contexts?

Researchers have studied whether tests of intelligence and thinking skills (called *cognitive ability*) can be generalized. The research has supported the idea that these tests are generalizable across many jobs. However, as jobs become more complex, the validity of many of these tests increases. In other words, they are most valid for complex jobs.[7]

generalizable
Valid in other contexts beyond the context in which the selection method was developed.

Practical Value

Not only should selection methods such as tests and interview responses accurately predict how well individuals will perform, they should produce information that actually benefits the organization. Being valid, reliable, and generalizable adds value to a method. Another consideration is the cost of using the selection method. Selection procedures such as testing and interviewing cost money. They should cost significantly less than the benefits of hiring the new employees. Methods that provide economic value greater than the cost of using them are said to have **utility.**

The choice of a selection method may differ according to the job being filled. If the job involves providing a product or service of high value to the organization, it is worthwhile to spend more to find a top performer. At a company where salespeople are responsible for closing million-dollar deals, the company will be willing to invest more in selection decisions. At a fast-food restaurant, such an investment will not be worthwhile; the employer will prefer faster, simpler ways to select workers who ring up orders, prepare food, and keep the facility clean.

utility
The extent to which something provides economic value greater than its cost.

Two issues facing Advanced Financial Solutions are the company's high-tech workforce and its location in Oklahoma City, far from the glamour of New York City or California's Silicon Valley. Because scarce information technology professionals can easily find jobs elsewhere, there is high utility in methods of identifying people who will be happy to live and work in Oklahoma City. Therefore, AFS pays to have candidates visit for a week during the selection process. Many companies would pay only for short visits by a few top candidates. But after AFS has conducted phone interviews and checked references, it invites qualified applicants to visit the company and meet employees at all levels. Candidates and their spouses from as far away as Brazil and Singapore have time to look at housing and schools, as well as get a sense of the city's climate and lifestyle. Although the week-long interviewing process costs about $7,500 for each employee hired, AFS believes it has practical value. Turnover is just 1 percent a year, so the savings from not replacing employees more than compensates for the high selection costs.[8]

LO3

Legal Standards for Selection

As we discussed in Chapter 3, the U.S. government imposes legal limits on selection decisions. The government requires that the selection process be conducted in a way that avoids discrimination and provides access to employees with disabilities. The laws described in Chapter 3 have many applications to the selection process:

- The Civil Rights Act of 1991 places requirements on the choice of selection methods. An employer that uses a neutral-appearing selection method that damages a protected group is obligated to show that there is a business necessity for using that method. For example, if an organization uses a test that eliminates many candidates from minority groups, the organization must show that the test is valid for predicting performance of that job.
- The Civil Rights Act of 1991 also prohibits preferential treatment in favor of minority groups. In the case of an organization using a test that tends to reject members of minority groups, the organization may not simply adjust minority applicants' scores upward. Such practices, besides being illegal, can interfere with motivation. According to research, when employees perceive selection decisions to be based partially on membership in some group (minority group or women), this perception undermines the confidence of members of the supposedly protected group. Their job performance suffers as well.[9]
- Equal employment opportunity laws affect the kinds of information an organization may gather on application forms and in interviews. As summarized in Table 6.1, the organization may not ask questions that gather information about a person's protected status, even indirectly. For example, requesting the dates a person attended high school and college could indirectly gather information about an applicant's age.
- The Americans with Disabilities Act (ADA) of 1991 requires employers to make "reasonable accommodation" to disabled individuals and restricts many kinds of questions during the selection process.[10] Under the ADA, preemployment questions may not investigate disabilities, but must focus on job performance. An interviewer may ask, "Can you meet the attendance requirements for this job?" but may not ask, "How many days did you miss work last year because you were sick?" Also, the employer may not, in making hiring decisions, use employment physical exams or other tests that could reveal a psychological or physical disability.

PERMISSIBLE QUESTIONS	IMPERMISSIBLE QUESTIONS
What is your full name? Have you ever worked under a different name?	What was your maiden name? What's the nationality of your name?
Are you at least 18 years old?	How old are you?
Do you understand the job requirements? Are you able to perform this job, with or without reasonable accommodation?	What is your height? your weight? Do you have any disabilities? Have you been seriously ill? Please provide a photograph of yourself.
What languages do you speak? [Statement that employment is subject to verification of applicant's identity and employment eligibility under immigration laws]	What is your ancestry? Are you a citizen of the United States? Where were you born? How did you learn to speak that language?
What schools have you attended? What degrees have you earned? What was your major?	Is that school affiliated with [religious group]? When did you attend high school? [to learn applicant's age]
[No questions about religion]	What is your religion? What religious holidays do you observe?
Please provide the names of any relatives currently employed by this employer.	What is your marital status? Would you like to be addressed as Mrs., Ms., or Miss? Do you have any children?
Have you ever been convicted of a crime?	Have you ever been arrested?
Please give the name and address of a person we may contact in case of an emergency.	Please give the name and address of a relative we may contact in case of an emergency.
What organizations or groups do you belong to (excluding those that indicate members' race, religion, color, national origin, or ancestry)?	What organizations or groups do you belong to?

TABLE 6.1

Permissible and Impermissible Questions for Applications and Interviews

Note: This table provides examples and is not intended as a complete listing of permissible and impermissible questions. The examples are based on federal requirements; state laws vary and may affect these examples.

SOURCE: Examples based on "Legal and Illegal Preemployment Inquiries," Inc.com, Human Resources Advice pages, www.inc.com, downloaded March 7, 2002; S. Kahn, B. B. Brown, M. Lanzarone, *Legal Guide to Human Resources* (Boston, MA: Warren, Gorham & Lamont, 1995).

Along with equal employment opportunity, organizations must be concerned about candidates' privacy rights. The information gathered during the selection process may include information that employees consider confidential. For some jobs, background checks look at candidates' credit history. The Fair Credit Reporting Act requires that employers obtain a candidate's consent before using a third party to check the candidate's credit history or references. If the employer then decides to take an adverse action (such as not hiring) based on the report, the employer must give the applicant a copy of the report and summary of the applicant's rights *before* taking the action.

Another legal requirement is that employers hiring people to work in the United States must ensure that anyone they hire is eligible for employment in this country. Under the Immigration Reform and Control Act of 1986, employers must verify and maintain records on the legal rights of applicants to work in the United States. They do this by having applicants fill out the Immigration and Naturalization Service's Form I-9 and present documents showing their identity and eligibility to work. Employers must complete their portion of each Form I-9, check the applicant's documents, and retain the Form I-9 for at least three years. At the same time, assuming a person is eligible to work under this law, the law prohibits the employer from discriminating against the person on the basis of national origin or citizenship status.

An important principle of selection is to combine several sources of information about candidates, rather than relying solely on interviews or a single type of testing. The sources should be chosen carefully to relate to the characteristics identified in the job description. When organizations do this, they are increasing the validity of the decision criteria. They are more likely to make hiring decisions that are fair and unbiased. They also are more likely to choose the best candidates.

Job Applications and Résumés

LO4

Nearly all employers gather background information on applicants at the beginning of the selection process. The usual ways of gathering background information are by asking applicants to fill out application forms and provide résumés. Organizations also verify the information by checking references and conducting background checks.

Asking job candidates to provide background information is inexpensive. The organization can get reasonably accurate information by combining applications and résumés with background checks and well-designed interviews.[11]

Application Forms

Asking each applicant to fill out an employment application is a low-cost way to gather basic data from many applicants. It also ensures that the organization has certain standard categories of information, such as mailing address and employment history, from each. Figure 6.4 is an example of an application form.

Employers can buy general-purpose application forms from an office supply store, or they can create their own forms to meet unique needs. Either way, employment applications include areas for applicants to provide several types of information:

- *Contact information*—The employee's name, address, phone number, and e-mail address.
- *Work experience*—Companies the applicant worked for, job titles, and dates of employment.
- *Educational background*—High school, college, and universities attended and degree(s) awarded.
- *Applicant's signature*—Signature following a statement that the applicant has provided true and complete information.

The application form may include other areas for the applicant to provide additional information, such as specific work experiences, technical skills, or memberships in professional or trade groups. Also, including the date on an application is useful for keeping up-to-date records of job applicants. The application form should not request

FIGURE 6.4

Sample Job Application Form

APPLICATION FOR EMPLOYMENT
An Equal Opportunity Employer

FIRST NAME	MIDDLE NAME	LAST NAME		SOCIAL SECURITY NUMBER
LOCAL	STREET ADDRESS	CITY AND STATE	ZIP CODE	TELEPHONE
PERMANENT	STREET ADDRESS	CITY AND STATE	ZIP CODE	TELEPHONE

ELECTRONIC MAIL ADDRESS

PLEASE ANSWER ALL ITEMS. IF NOT APPLICABLE, WRITE N/A.

ARE YOU A U.S. CITIZEN OR AUTHORIZED TO BE LEGALLY EMPLOYED ON AN ONGOING BASIS IN THE U.S. BASED ON YOUR VISA OR IMMIGRATION STATUS? ☐ YES ☐ NO

ARE YOU OVER 18 YEARS OF AGE? YES ☐ NO ☐

DO YOU CURRENTLY HAVE A NONIMMIGRANT U.S. VISA? ☐ YES ☐ NO   IF YES, PLEASE SPECIFY:

DO YOU HAVE ANY RELATIVES EMPLOYED HERE? ☐ NO ☐ YES
IF YES, GIVE NAME, RELATIONSHIP AND LOCATION WHERE THEY WORK

DO YOU HAVE ANY RELATIVES EMPLOYED BY THE COMPETITION? ☐ NO ☐ YES   WHAT COMPANY?

ARE YOU ABLE TO TRAVEL AS REQUIRED FOR THE POSITION SOUGHT? ☐ YES ☐ NO

ARE YOU WILLING TO RELOCATE? ☐ YES ☐ NO

ARE THERE GEOGRAPHICAL AREAS WHICH YOU WOULD PREFER OR REFUSE? ☐ NO ☐ YES   IF YES, PLEASE SPECIFY:

HAVE YOU EVER BEEN CONVICTED OR PLED GUILTY TO ANY FELONY OR MISDEMEANOR OTHER THAN FOR A MINOR TRAFFIC VIOLATION? ☐ NO ☐ YES
IF YES, STATE THE DATE(S) AND LOCATION(S):

WHEN   WHERE   NATURE OF OFFENSE(S)

WORK PREFERENCE

SPECIFIC POSITION FOR WHICH YOU ARE APPLYING

NUMBER OF YEARS OF RELATED EXPERIENCE

LIST COMPUTER SOFTWARE PACKAGES OR PROGRAMMING LANGUAGE SKILLS

STARTING SALARY EXPECTED | DATE AVAILABLE TO START WORK | HOW DID YOU HAPPEN TO APPLY FOR A POSITION HERE?

HAVE YOU EVER WORKED AT, OR APPLIED FOR WORK HERE BEFORE? ☐ NO ☐ YES
IF YES, WHEN?   WHERE?

LIST EMPLOYMENT REFERENCES HERE, IF NOT INCLUDED ON ATTACHED RESUME

TURN OVER

COMPLETE THIS SECTION IF INFORMATION IS NOT INCLUDED ON ATTACHED RESUME

EDUCATION CIRCLE THE HIGHEST GRADE COMPLETED: ELEMENTARY 6 7 8   HIGH SCHOOL 1 2 3 4   COLLEGE 1 2 3 4 5 6 7 8

	NAME(S)	LOCATION(S)	GRADUATED	MAJOR FIELDS OF STUDY AND PRINCIPAL PROFESSOR (OR ADVISOR)	GRADE AVERAGE	DEGREE(S) RECEIVED	CLASS RANK ___ OUT OF ___
HIGH SCHOOL							
COLLEGE	NAME(S)	LOCATION(S)	☐ YES ☐ NO		DEGREE(S) RECEIVED		OVERALL AND MAJOR GPA'S

ACADEMIC HONORS OR OTHER SPECIAL RECOGNITION

FOREIGN LANGUAGES READ   FOREIGN LANGUAGES SPOKEN

HAVE YOU TAKEN THE GMAT, GRE, SAT OR OTHER ACADEMIC ENTRANCE TEST(S) WITHIN THE LAST TEN YEARS? ☐ YES ☐ NO
IF YES, LIST TEST(S), DATE(S) AND HIGHEST SCORE(S).

	DATE TAKEN		SCORE(S)
SAT		VERBAL: ___	MATHEMATICAL: ___
ACT		ENGLISH: ___ VERBAL: ___ MATHEMATICS: ___	READING: ___ SCIENCE: ___
GRE (GENERAL TEST)		VERBAL: ___ QUANTITATIVE: ___	ANALYTICAL: ___
GMAT		VERBAL: ___ MATH: ___	AWA: ___
OTHER			

EMPLOYMENT AND MILITARY RECORD LIST MOST RECENT FIRST. I AGREE TO FURNISH VERIFICATION IF REQUESTED. ATTACH RESUME. RESPOND BELOW IF INFORMATION IS NOT INCLUDED ON RESUME.

NAME AND ADDRESS OF EMPLOYER	POSITION HELD	PRIMARY RESPONSIBILITIES AND ACCOUNTABILITIES	SALARY START	SALARY FINISH	DATES FROM	DATES TO	REASON FOR LEAVING

ENCIRCLE THOSE EMPLOYERS YOU DO NOT WANT US TO CONTACT
TURN OVER

information that could violate equal employment opportunity standards. For example, questions about an applicant's race, marital status, or number of children would be inappropriate.

By reviewing application forms, HR personnel can identify which candidates meet minimum requirements for education and experience. They may be able to rank applicants—for example, giving applicants with 10 years' experience a higher ranking than applicants with 2 years' experience. In this way, the applications enable the organization to narrow the pool of candidates to a number it can afford to test and interview.

Résumés

The usual way that applicants introduce themselves to a potential employer is to submit a résumé. An obvious drawback of this information source is that applicants control the content of the information, as well as the way it is presented. This type of information is therefore biased in favor of the applicant and (although this is unethical) may not even be accurate. However, this inexpensive way to gather information does provide employers with a starting point. Organizations typically use résumés as a basis for deciding which candidates to investigate further.

As with employment applications, an HR staff member reviews the résumés to identify candidates meeting such basic requirements as educational background, related work performed, and types of equipment the person has used. Because résumés are created by the job applicants (or the applicants have at least approved résumés created by someone they hire), they also may provide some insight into how candidates communicate and present themselves. Employers tend to decide against applicants whose résumés are unclear, sloppy, or full of mistakes. On the positive side, résumés may enable applicants to highlight accomplishments that might not show up in the format of an employment application. Review of résumés is most valid when the content of the résumés is evaluated in terms of the elements of a job description.

References

Application forms often ask that applicants provide the names of several references. Applicants provide the names and phone numbers of former employers or others who can vouch for their abilities and past job performance. In some situations, the applicant may provide letters of reference written by those people. It is then up to organization to have someone contact the references to gather information or verify the accuracy of the information provided by the applicant.

As you might expect, references are not an unbiased source of information. Most applicants are careful to choose references who will say something positive. In addition, former employers and others may be afraid that if they express negative opinions, they will be sued. Their fear is understandable. In the many thousands of lawsuits that have been filed over such matters, damage awards can run over $500,000.[12] Intuit Corporation, producer of Quicken software, gets around this problem by requiring as many as 12 letters of reference. Typically, the first two or three people listed provide glowing references, but people further down the list provide a fuller picture of the candidate.[13]

Usually the organization checks references after it has determined that the applicant is a finalist for the job. Contacting references for all applicants would be time-consuming, and it does pose some burden on the people contacted. Part of that burden is the risk of giving information that is seen as too negative or too positive. If the person who is a reference gives negative information, there is a chance the candidate will claim *defamation*, meaning the person damaged the applicant's reputation by making statements that cannot be proved truthful.[14] At the other extreme, if the person gives a glowing statement about a candidate, and the new employer later learns of misdeeds such as sexual misconduct or workplace violence, the new employer might sue the former employer for misrepresentation.[15]

Because such situations occasionally arise, often with much publicity, people who give references tend to give as little information as possible. Most organizations have policies that the human resource department will handle all requests for references and that they will only verify employment dates and sometimes the employee's final salary. In organizations without such a policy, HR professionals should be careful—and train managers to be careful—to stick to observable, job-related behaviors and to avoid broad opinions that may be misinterpreted. In spite of these drawbacks of references, the risks of not learning about significant problems in a candidate's past outweigh the possibility of getting only a little information. Potential employers should check references.

Background Checks

A background check is a way to verify that applicants are as they represent themselves to be. APCOA, a Cleveland-based company that operates parking facilities in 42 states, uses a variety of resources for background checks: driving records, credit history, criminal record, and verification of education and employment history. The company varies the background check according to the type of position to be filled. According to Bobbi Navarro, a human resource professional at APCOA, the effort is worthwhile: "The hiring process can set you apart from the competition, and nowadays, you have to know who the people are who work for you."[16]

Avert Inc. provides HR services, including background checks on prospective employees. In its experience, nearly one-fourth of candidates misrepresented something in their employment or educational background, more than one in eight had employers who said they would not rehire them if given the chance, and about 1 out of

Background checks have become more important and popular recently, especially for security jobs or others requiring a high level of trustworthiness and attention to detail. The employer needs to know that people are what they represent themselves to be and that their past doesn't show evidence they shouldn't be trusted. What are some of the risks associated with hiring the wrong person?

16 had records of criminal behavior within recent years. Numbers like these make a lot of employers think background checks are a wise investment. Caution has become even more the watchword following the terrorist attacks of September 2001. Avert, for example, experienced a major jump in requests for background checks in the months following the attacks.[17]

Verifying credentials and conducting background checks is more complicated when candidates are not U.S. citizens. Their education may include degrees from schools outside the United States. In such cases, the organization has to determine how the institution and the degree awarded compare with schools and degrees in the United States. Some companies, including Mobil Corporation, get around this issue by conducting their own screening tests for basic skills in reading and math. Other companies, such as the Knowledge Company in Fairfax, Virginia, use work sample tests. For example, an applicant for an engineering job would have to submit designs for a certain product, and experts evaluate the drawings. Criminal background checks also are difficult. Except for serious crimes, U.S. records contain little about crimes committed outside the United States. These and other hurdles can discourage U.S. employers from hiring foreign nationals. Organizations that overcome the hurdles therefore can gain an advantage in hiring the best of this talent.[18]

LO5

Employment Tests and Work Samples

When the organization has identified candidates whose applications or résumés indicate they meet basic requirements, the organization continues the selection process with this narrower pool of candidates. Often, the next step is to gather objective data through one or more employment tests. These tests fall into two broad categories:

aptitude tests
Tests that assess how well a person can learn or acquire skills and abilities.

1. **Aptitude tests** assess how well a person can learn or acquire skills and abilities. In the realm of employment testing, the best-known aptitude test is the General Aptitude Test Battery (GATB), used by the U.S. Employment Service.
2. **Achievement tests** measure a person's existing knowledge and skills. For example, government agencies conduct civil service examinations to see whether applicants are qualified to perform certain jobs.

achievement tests
Tests that measure a person's existing knowledge and skills.

Employment tests may assess general abilities, such as physical strength, or specific skills, such as keyboarding speed. Some organizations also use personality tests to find applicants who have personality traits associated with successful job performance, as well as integrity tests to weed out dishonest candidates. In addition, drug testing and medical examinations try to ensure that candidates meet physical job requirements and will not be impaired on the job. Before using any test, organizations should investigate the test's validity and reliability. Besides asking the testing service to provide this information, it is wise to consult more impartial sources of information, such as the ones identified in Table 6.2.

Physical Ability Tests

Physical strength and endurance play less of a role in the modern workplace than in the past, thanks to the use of automation and modern technology. Even so, many jobs still require certain physical abilities or psychomotor abilities (those connecting brain and body, as in the case of eye-hand coordination). When these abilities are essential to job performance or avoidance of injury, the organization may use physical ability tests. These evaluate one or more of the following areas of physical ability: muscular

Mental Measurements Yearbook	Descriptions and reviews of tests that are commercially available	**TABLE 6.2** Sources of Information about Employment Tests
Principles for the Validation and Use of Personnel Selection Procedures Society for Industrial and (Organizational Psychology)	Guide to help organizations evaluate tests	
Standards for Educational and Psychological Tests (American Psychological Association)	Description of standards for testing programs	
Tests: A Comprehensive Reference for Assessments in Psychology, Education, and Business	Descriptions of thousands of tests	
Test Critiques	Reviews of tests, written by professionals in the field	

tension, muscular power, muscular endurance, cardiovascular endurance, flexibility, balance, and coordination.[19]

Although these tests can accurately predict success at certain kinds of jobs, they also tend to exclude women and people with disabilities. As a result, use of physical ability tests can make the organization vulnerable to charges of discrimination. It is therefore important to be certain that the abilities tested for really are essential to job performance or that the absence of these abilities really does create a safety hazard.

Cognitive Ability Tests

Although fewer jobs require muscle power today, brainpower is essential for most jobs. Organizations therefore benefit from people who have strong mental abilities. **Cognitive ability tests**—sometimes called "intelligence tests"—are designed to measure such mental abilities as verbal skills (skill in using written and spoken language), quantitative skills (skill in working with numbers), and reasoning ability (skill in thinking through the answer to a problem). Many jobs require all of these cognitive skills, so employers often get valid information from general tests. Many reliable tests are commercially available. The tests are especially valid for complex jobs and for those requiring adaptability in changing circumstances.[20]

cognitive ability tests
Tests designed to measure such mental abilities as verbal skills, quantitative skills, and reasoning ability.

The evidence of validity, coupled with the relatively low cost of these tests, makes them appealing, except for one problem: concern about legal issues. These concerns arise from a historical pattern in which use of the tests has had an adverse impact on African Americans. Some organizations responded with *race norming*, establishing different norms for hiring members of different racial groups. Race norming poses its own problems, not the least of which is the negative reputation it bestows on the minority employees selected using a lower standard. In addition, the Civil Rights Act of 1991 forbids the use of race or sex norming. Organizations that want to base selection decisions on cognitive ability therefore must make difficult decisions about how to measure this ability while avoiding legal problems. One possibility is a concept called *banding*. This concept treats a range of scores as being similar, as when an instructor gives the grade of A to any student whose average test score is at least 90. All applicants within a range of scores, or band, are treated as having the same score. Then within the set of "tied" scores, employers give preference to underrepresented groups. This is a controversial practice, and some have questioned its legality.[21]

Pilots require high cognitive ability. Cognitive ability tests may be used to select individuals for such positions. What other positions might require some measure of an individual's ability to handle their complexities?

Job Performance Tests and Work Samples

Many kinds of jobs require candidates that excel at performing specialized tasks, such as operating a certain machine, handling phone calls from customers, or designing advertising materials. To evaluate candidates for such jobs, the organization may administer tests of the necessary skills. Sometimes the candidates take tests that involve a sample of work, or they may show existing samples of their work. Examples of job performance tests include tests of keyboarding speed and *in-basket tests*. An in-basket test measures the ability to juggle a variety of demands, as in a manager's job. The candidate is presented with simulated memos and phone messages describing the kinds of problems that confront a person in the job. The candidate has to decide how to respond to these messages, and in what order. Examples of jobs for which candidates provide work samples include graphic designers and writers.

assessment center
A wide variety of specific selection programs that use multiple selection methods to rate applicants or job incumbents on their management potential.

Tests for selecting managers may take the form of an **assessment center**—a wide variety of specific selection programs that use multiple selection methods to rate applicants or job incumbents on their management potential. An assessment center typically includes in-basket tests, tests of more general abilities, and personality tests. Combining several assessment methods increases the validity of this approach.

Job performance tests have the advantage of being job specific—that is, tailored to the kind of work done in a specific job. These tests therefore have a high level of validity, especially when combined with cognitive ability tests and a highly structured interview.[22] This advantage can become a disadvantage, however, if the organization wants to generalize the results of a test for one job to candidates for other jobs. Also, developing different tests for different jobs can become expensive. One way to save money is to prepare computerized tests that can be delivered online to various locations.

Personality Inventories

In some situations, employers may also want to know about candidates' personalities. For example, one way that psychologists think about personality is in terms of the "Big Five" traits: extroversion, adjustment, agreeableness, conscientiousness, and inquisitiveness (explained in Table 6.3). There is evidence that people who score high on conscientiousness tend to excel at work, especially when they also have high cognitive ability.[23] For people-related jobs like sales and management, extroversion and agreeableness also seem to be associated with success.[24]

The usual way to identify a candidate's personality traits is to administer one of the personality tests that are commercially available. The employer pays for the use of the test, and the organization that owns the test then scores the responses and provides a report about the test taker's personality. An organization that provides such tests should be able to discuss the test's validity and reliability. Assuming the tests are valid

1. Extroversion	Sociable, gregarious, assertive, talkative, expressive
2. Adjustment	Emotionally stable, nondepressed, secure, content
3. Agreeableness	Courteous, trusting, good-natured, tolerant, cooperative, forgiving
4. Conscientiousness	Dependable, organized, persevering, thorough, achievement-oriented
5. Inquisitiveness	Curious, imaginative, artistically sensitive, broadminded, playful

TABLE 6.3

Five Major Personality Dimensions Measured by Personality Inventories

for the organization's jobs, they have advantages. Administering commercially available personality tests is simple,[25] and these tests have generally not violated equal opportunity employment requirements.[26]

Some people think they can identify personality traits by analyzing a person's handwriting. Research has not found a relationship between the results of handwriting analysis and job performance. However, handwriting analysis is a popular selection method in Europe. According to one estimate, 8 out of 10 companies in Western Europe use it in their selection process. U.S. organizations rarely use handwriting analysis, but in today's global business climate, HR professionals may want to know that it is common in other parts of the world.[27]

Honesty Tests and Drug Tests

No matter what employees' personalities may be like, organizations want employees to be honest and to behave safely. Some organizations are satisfied to assess these qualities based on judgments from reference checks and interviews. Others investigate these characteristics more directly through the use of honesty tests and drug tests.

The most famous kind of honesty test is the polygraph, the so-called lie detector test. However, in 1988 the passage of the Polygraph Act banned the use of polygraphs for screening job candidates. As a result, testing services have developed paper-and-pencil honesty (or integrity) tests. Generally these tests ask applicants directly about their attitudes toward theft and their own experiences with theft. Table 6.4 shows a sample of the items on such a test. Most of the research into the validity of these tests has been conducted by the testing companies, but evidence suggests they do have some ability to predict such behavior as theft of the employer's property.[28]

As concerns about substance abuse have grown during recent decades, so has the use of drug testing. As a measure of a person's exposure to drugs, chemical testing has high reliability and validity. However, these tests are controversial for several reasons.

TABLE 6.4

Sample Items from a Typical Honesty Test

1. It's OK to take something from a company that is making too much profit.
2. Stealing is just a way of getting your fair share.
3. When a store overcharges its customers, it's OK to change price tags on merchandise.
4. If you could get into a movie without paying and not get caught, would you do it?
5. Is it OK to go around the law if you don't actually break it?

SOURCE: "T or F? Honesty Tests," p. 104. Reprinted with permission, *Inc.* magazine, February 1992. © Copyright 1992 by Goldhirsh Group, Inc., 38 Commercial Wharf, Boston, MA 02110.

Impairment Tests: Ready or Not, Here They Come

Making workplaces safe for organizations' workers and customers is a critical responsibility. For years, this has been the primary defense of those who have advocated mandatory drug-testing programs conducted by employers. From the mid-1980s to the mid-1990s, the percentage of employers using urine drug tests increased steadily, peaking at 81 percent in 1996. Since then, the percentage of employers relying on drug testing has steadily fallen, moving below 70 percent in 2001. Concerns about privacy and the competition for scarce workers have made these tests less desirable.

Another critique of testing for exposure to drugs is that these tests do not directly assess whether employees' off-work behavior actually affects their on-the-job performance. Research conducted by the National Academy of Sciences has debunked several of the fundamental assumptions behind the use of such testing— including the assumption that testing reduces on-the-job accidents and injuries. An academy spokesperson notes that drug testing is "a pathetic excuse for a safety program, because it misses 95 percent of the problem—most people who have accidents on the job are not drug users but instead [the accidents are] caused by alcohol or fatigue."

A growing number of organizations are therefore replacing drug testing with *impairment testing*, also known as *fitness-for-duty testing*. These testing programs measure whether a worker is alert and mentally able to perform critical tasks at the time of the test. The test does not investigate the cause of any impairment—whether the employee scores poorly because of illegal drugs, alcohol, prescription drugs, over-the-counter medicines, or simple fatigue.

A typical impairment test looks like a video game. The employee looks into a dark viewport and tries to follow a randomly moving point of light with his or her eyes. The equipment analyzes the person's performance and compares it with a baseline to see if the person is fit for duty at that moment. Results are available in as little as two minutes. Because this test measures involuntary physical responses, employees cannot cheat (as some have done on urine or blood tests).

So far, the high cost of the technology has limited the use of impairment testing. The price of the tests has been falling, however. Moreover, in many high-stakes industries (such as building aircraft, spacecraft, or surgical equipment), if a technology can prevent even one or two errors, it more than pays for itself over time. To get a feel for how you would do on an impairment test, try one at www.pmifit.com. Are you fit to be reading this textbook right now?

SOURCE: E. Beck, "Is the Time Right for Impairment Testing?" *Workforce*, February 2001, pp. 69–71; J. Farley, "Better than Caffeine," *USA Today*, March 9, 2001, p. C1; J. Hamilton, "A Video Game That Tells if Employees Are Fit for Work," *BusinessWeek*, June 3, 1991, pp. 34–35.

Some people are concerned that they invade individuals' privacy. Others object from a legal perspective. When all applicants or employees are subject to testing, whether or not they have shown evidence of drug use, the tests might be an unreasonable search and seizure or a violation of due process. Taking urine and blood samples involves invasive procedures, and accusing someone of drug use is a serious matter. To address these issues, some organizations are taking a different approach to drug testing. As described in the "Best Practices" box, they use tests that focus on whether a person's ability to work is impaired.

Employers considering the use of drug tests should ensure that their drug-testing programs conform to some general rules. First, the tests should be administered systematically to all applicants for the same job. If some applicants for a machinist's job are tested, then all applicants for that job should take the same test. Second, testing seems most defensible for jobs that involve safety hazards when not performed properly. For example, it is easier to justify drug testing for a roofer's job than for the job of answering the telephone at the roofing company. In addition, the applicant should receive a report of the test results and should know how to appeal those results (and perhaps be retested). The organization also should respect applicants' privacy. As far as possible, the tests should be conducted in an environment that is not intrusive, and the results should be strictly confidential. Finally, when the organization tests current employees, the testing program should be part of a wider organizational program that provides rehabilitation counseling.[29]

Medical Examinations

Especially for physically demanding jobs, organizations may wish to conduct medical examinations to see that the applicant can meet the job's requirements. Employers may also wish to establish an employee's physical condition at the beginning of employment, so that there is a basis for measuring whether the employee has suffered a work-related disability later on. At the same time, as described in Chapter 3, organizations may not discriminate against individuals with disabilities who could perform a job with reasonable accommodations. Likewise, they may not use a measure of size or strength that discriminates against women, unless those requirements are valid in predicting the ability to perform a job. Furthermore, to protect candidates' privacy, medical exams must be related to job requirements and may not be given until the candidate has received a job offer. Therefore, organizations must be careful in how they use medical examinations. Many organizations make selection decisions first, then conduct the exams to confirm that the employee can handle the job, with any reasonable accommodations required. Limiting the use of medical exams in this way also holds down the cost of what tends to be an expensive process.

Interviews

LO6

Supervisors and team members most often get involved in the selection process at the stage of employment interviews. These interviews bring together job applicants and representatives of the employer to obtain information and evaluate the applicant's qualifications. While the applicant is providing information, he or she is also forming opinions about what it is like to work for the organization. Most organizations use interviewing as part of the selection process. In fact, this method is used more than any other.

Interviewing Techniques

An interview may be nondirective or structured. In a **nondirective interview,** the interviewer has great discretion in choosing questions to ask each candidate. For example, the interviewer might ask, "What is your greatest accomplishment in your current position?" The candidate's reply might suggest to the interviewer what other questions to ask. Often, these interviews include open-ended questions about the candidate's strengths, weaknesses, career goals, and work experience. Because

nondirective interview
A selection interview in which the interviewer has great discretion in choosing questions to ask each candidate.

structured interview
A selection interview that consists of a predetermined set of questions for the interviewer to ask.

situational interviews
A structured interview in which the interviewer describes a situation likely to arise on the job, then asks the candidate what he or she would do in that situation.

behavior description interview (BDI)
A structured interview in which the interviewer asks the candidate to describe how he or she handled a type of situation in the past.

nondirective interviews give the interviewer wide latitude, their reliability is not great. Also, interviewers do not necessarily ask valid questions. Inexperienced or poorly informed interviewers may ask questions that are irrelevant or even illegal.

To manage the risks of a nondirective interview, many organizations substitute the use of a **structured interview,** which establishes a set of questions for the interviewer to ask. Ideally, these questions are related to the requirements set out in the job description. They should cover the candidate's knowledge required to perform this type of job, his or her experience in handling job-related situations, and other job-related personal requirements such as willingness to travel, work overtime, or learn new skills. The interviewer asks questions from the list and is supposed to avoid asking questions that are not on the list. Some interviewers object to being limited in this way, but a list of well-written questions can provide more valid and reliable results.

Some of the best results of interviewing come from the use of **situational interviews.** In this type of structured interview, the interviewer describes a situation likely to arise on the job, then asks the candidate what he or she would do in that situation. Situational interviews have been shown to have high validity in predicting job performance.[30] A variation is the **behavior description interview (BDI),** in which the interviewer asks the candidate to describe how he or she handled a type of situation in the past. Questions about the candidates' actual experiences tend to have the highest validity.[31]

When Andrew Kindler was a hiring manager, he used open-ended BDI-style questions to good effect. When interviewing candidates for management positions, he would ask them to describe the most difficult ethical dilemma they had to solve at work. Kindler's objective was to learn about each candidate's ethics and problem-solving style. In one instance, a candidate for a position as the corporation's general counsel (an important legal position) said he had never encountered an ethical dilemma. Kindler quickly eliminated that candidate from consideration, on the grounds that "a lawyer who has never encountered an ethical dilemma doesn't have ethics."[32]

The common setup for either a nondirected or structured interview is for an individual (an HR professional or the supervisor for the vacant position) to interview each candidate face to face. However, variations on this approach are possible. In a **panel interview,** several members of the organization meet to interview each candi-

When interviewing candidates, it's valid to ask about willingness to travel if that is part of the job. Interviewers might ask questions about previous business travel experiences and/or how interviewees handled situations requiring flexibility and self-motivation (qualities that would be an asset in someone who is traveling alone and solving business problems on the road).

date. A panel interview gives the candidate a chance to meet more people and see how people interact in that organization. It provides the organization with the judgments of more than one person, to reduce the effect of personal biases in selection decisions. Panel interviews can be especially appropriate in organizations that use teamwork. At the other extreme, some organizations conduct interviews without any interviewers; they use a computerized interviewing process. The candidate sits at a computer and enters replies to the questions presented by the computer. Such a format eliminates a lot of personal bias—along with the opportunity to see how people interact. Therefore, computer interviews are useful for gathering objective data, rather than assessing people skills.

panel interview
Selection interview in which several members of the organization meet to interview each candidate.

Advantages and Disadvantages of Interviewing

The wide use of interviewing is not surprising. People naturally want to see prospective employees firsthand. As we noted in Chapter 1, the top qualities that employers seek in new hires include communication skills and interpersonal skills. Talking face to face can provide evidence of these skills. Interviews can give insights into candidates' personalities and interpersonal styles. They are more valid, however, when they focus on job knowledge and skill.

Despite these benefits, interviewing is not necessarily the most accurate basis for making a selection decision. Research has shown that interviews can be unreliable, low in validity,[33] and biased against a number of different groups.[34] Interviews are also costly. They require that at least one person devote time to interviewing each candidate, and the applicants typically have to be brought to one geographic location. Interviews are also subjective, so they place the organization at greater risk of discrimination complaints by applicants who were not hired, especially if those individuals were asked questions not entirely related to the job. The Supreme Court has held that subjective selection methods like interviews must be validated, using methods that provide criterion-related or content validation.[35]

Organizations can avoid some of these pitfalls.[36] Human resource staff should keep the interviews narrow, structured, and standardized. The interview should focus on accomplishing a few goals, so that at the end of the interview, the organization has ratings on several observable measures, such as ability to express ideas. The interview should not try to measure abilities and skills—for example, intelligence—that tests can measure better. As noted earlier, situational interviews are especially effective for doing this. Organizations can prevent problems related to subjectivity by training interviewers and using more than one person to conduct interviews. Training typically includes focusing on the recording of observable facts, rather than on making subjective judgments, as well as developing interviewers' awareness of their biases.[37] Levi Strauss handles subjectivity by giving women and minority interviewers a significant role, to ensure that many perspectives are included in selection decisions.[38] Finally, to address costs of interviewing, many organizations videotape interviews and send the tapes (rather than the applicants) from department to department. The nearby "HR How To" box provides more specific guidelines for successful interviewing.

Preparing to Interview

Organizations can reap the greatest benefits from interviewing if they prepare carefully. A well-planned interview should be standardized, comfortable for the participants, and focused on the job and the organization. The interviewer should have a quiet place in which to conduct interviews without interruption. This person should

Interviewing Effectively

Interviewing is one HR function that almost all managers become involved with at some point. Most managers and team leaders want a role in interviewing candidates for the positions that report to them. Therefore, HR professionals need to teach as well as learn effective interviewing skills. Here are some ways to conduct interviews that identify the best candidates:

- *Decide what you're looking for.* Review the job description for the vacant position, and identify the qualifications, motivations, behaviors, and values of a successful employee in that position.
- *Plan the interview.* Write questions that relate to the qualifications, motivations, behaviors, and values you are looking for. Make sure the questions are legally permissible (if you aren't sure, get legal advice). Also, prepare the information you will be giving the candidates: description of job duties and background about the organization.

- *Put the applicant at ease.* Often, people who interview for a job are nervous, or at least cautious. Spend the first few minutes of the interview making the applicant comfortable. Chat about casual matters—the weather, the traffic, the fishing trophy on your wall—and wait for the candidate to relax. You can't learn much about someone who is tense.
- *Work from a list.* If you prepared well, you have a list of job-related questions to cover with each candidate. These should include behavior-based questions that meet the objectives you defined during the planning phase. Let candidates know that everyone is answering the same questions. If you cover all the questions on your list with each candidate, you will have a more valid basis for comparison.
- *Avoid vague or clichéd questions.* One advantage of working from a list is that you can avoid falling back on the vague questions that

people associate with interviews—like "What is your greatest weakness?" Such questions become so notorious that candidates rehearse answers they think interviewers are looking for, rather than revealing much about themselves. According to one recent account, the most popular response to the "weakness" question is currently, "I put so much pressure on myself to be perfect that I sometimes work until 3 AM, so it's hard for me to balance work and family." An answer like that sounds so fake that the interviewer might as well have skipped the question.

SOURCE: G. P. Smith, "Improve Your Interviewing Techniques," *BLR Online HR Newsletter* (Business & Legal Reports), www.blr.com, downloaded March 20, 2002; G. Gabriel, "Pick the Super Performers," *Job Resources*, National Association for Female Executives website, http://nafe.com, downloaded March 19, 2002; P. Kitchen, "Be Strong on the 'Weakness' Question," *Hartford Courant*, April 1, 2002, online edition, www.ctnow.com.

be trained in how to ask objective questions, what subject matter to avoid, and how to detect and handle his or her own personal biases or other distractions in order to fairly evaluate candidates.

The interviewer should have enough documents to conduct a complete interview. These should include a list of the questions to be asked in a structured interview, with plenty of space for recording the responses. When the questions are prepared, it is also helpful to determine how the answers will be scored. For example, if questions ask how interviewees would handle certain situations, consider what responses are best in terms of meeting job requirements. If the job requires someone who motivates others, then a response that shows motivating behavior would receive a higher score. The interviewer also should have a copy of the interviewee's employment application and résumé, to review before the interview and refer to during the interview. If possible, the interviewer should also have printed information about the organization and the job. Near the beginning of the interview, it is a good idea to go over the job specifications, organizational policies, and so on, so that the interviewee has a clearer understanding of the organization's needs.

The interviewer should schedule enough time to review the job requirements, discuss the interview questions, and give the interviewee a chance to ask questions. To close, the interviewer should thank the candidate for coming and provide information about what to expect—for example, that the organization will contact a few finalists within the next two weeks or that a decision will be made by the end of the week.

Selection Decisions   LO7

After reviewing applications, scoring tests, conducting interviews, and checking references, the organization needs to make decisions about which candidates to place in which jobs. In practice, most organizations find more than one qualified candidate to fill an open position. The selection decision typically combines ranking based on objective criteria along with subjective judgments about which candidate will make the greatest contribution.

How Organizations Select Employees

The selection decision should not be a simple matter of whom the supervisor likes best or which candidate will take the lowest offer. Rather, the people making the selection should look for the best fit between candidate and position. In general, the person's performance will result from a combination of ability and motivation. Often, the selection is a choice among a few people who possess the basic qualifications. The decision makers therefore have to decide which of those people have the best combination of ability and motivation to fit in the position and in the organization as a whole. Figure 6.5 illustrates an extreme example of such a candidate.

FIGURE 6.5

Fit for the Job

ZITS

Copyright © Zits Partnership. Reprinted with special permission of King Features Syndicate.

multiple-hurdle model
Process of arriving at a selection decision by eliminating some candidates at each stage of the selection process.

compensatory model
Process of arriving at a selection decision in which a very high score on one type of assessment can make up for a low score on another.

The usual process for arriving at a selection decision is to gradually narrow the pool of candidates for each job. This approach, called the **multiple-hurdle model,** is based on a process such as the one shown earlier in Figure 6.1. Each stage of the process is a hurdle, and candidates who overcome a hurdle continue to the next stage of the process. For example, the organization reviews applications and/or résumés of all candidates, conducts some tests on those who meet minimum requirements, conducts initial interviews with those who had the highest test scores, follows up with additional interviews or testing, and then selects a candidate from the few who survived this process. Another, more expensive alternative is to take most applicants through all steps of the process and then to review all the scores to find the most desirable candidates. With this alternative, decision makers may use a **compensatory model,** in which a very high score on one type of assessment can make up for a low score on another.

Whether the organization uses a multiple-hurdle model or conducts the same assessments on all candidates, the decision maker(s) needs criteria for choosing among qualified candidates. An obvious strategy is to select the candidates who score highest on tests and interviews. However, employee performance depends on motivation as well as ability. It is possible that a candidate who scores very high on an ability test might be "overqualified"—that is, the employee might be bored by the job the organization needs to fill, and a less-able employee might actually be a better fit. Similarly, a highly motivated person might learn some kinds of jobs very quickly, potentially outperforming someone who has the necessary skills. Furthermore, some organizations have policies of developing employees for career paths in the organization. Such organizations might place less emphasis on the skills needed for a particular job and more emphasis on hiring candidates who share the organization's values, show that they have the people skills to work with others in the organization, and are able to learn the skills needed for advancement.

Finally, organizations have choices about who will make the decision. Usually a supervisor makes the final decision, often alone. This person may couple knowledge of the job with a judgment about who will fit in best with others in the department. The decision could also be made by a human resource professional using standardized, objective criteria. Especially in organizations that use teamwork, selection decisions may be made by a work team or other panel of decision makers.

Communicating the Decision

The human resource department is often responsible for notifying applicants about the results of the selection process. When a candidate has been selected, the organization should communicate the offer to the candidate. The offer should include the job responsibilities, work schedule, rate of pay, starting date, and other relevant details. If placement in a job requires that the applicant pass a physical examination, the offer should state that contingency. The person communicating the offer should also indicate a date by which the candidate should reply with an acceptance or rejection of the offer. For some jobs, such as management and professional positions, the candidate and organization may negotiate pay, benefits, and work arrangements before they arrive at a final employment agreement.

The person who communicates this decision should keep accurate records of who was contacted, when, and for which position, as well as of the candidate's reply. The HR department and the supervisor also should be in close communication about the job offer. When an applicant accepts a job offer, the HR department must notify the supervisor, so that he or she can be prepared for the new employee's arrival.

Summary

1. Identify the elements of the selection process.
   Selection typically begins with a review of candidates' employment applications and résumés. The organization administers tests to candidates who meet basic requirements, and qualified candidates undergo one or more interviews. Organizations check references and conduct background checks to verify the accuracy of information provided by candidates. A candidate is selected to fill each vacant position. Candidates who accept offers are placed in the positions for which they were selected.

2. Define ways to measure the success of a selection method.
   One criterion is reliability, which indicates the method is free from random error, so that measurements are consistent. A selection method should also be valid, meaning that performance on the measure (such as a test score) is related to what the measure is designed to assess (such as job performance). Criterion-related validity shows a correlation between test scores and job performance scores. Content validity shows consistency between the test items or problems and the kinds of situations or problems that occur on the job. Construct validity establishes that the test actually measures a specified construct, such as intelligence or leadership ability, which is presumed to be associated with success on the job. A selection method also should be generalizable, so that it applies to more than one specific situation. Each selection method should have utility, meaning it provides economic value greater than its cost. Finally, selection methods should meet the legal requirements for employment decisions.

3. Summarize the government's requirements for employee selection.
   The selection process must be conducted in a way that avoids discrimination and provides access to persons with disabilities. This means selection methods must be valid for job performance, and scores may not be adjusted to discriminate against or give preference to any group. Questions may not gather information about a person's membership in a protected class, such as race, sex, or religion, nor may the employer investigate a person's disability status. Employers must respect candidates' privacy rights and ensure that they keep personal information confidential. They must obtain consent before conducting background checks and notify candidates about adverse decisions made as a result of background checks.

4. Compare the common methods used for selecting human resources.

Nearly all organizations gather information through employment applications and résumés. These methods are inexpensive, and an application form standardizes basic information received from all applicants. The information is not necessarily reliable, because each applicant provides the information. These methods are most valid when evaluated in terms of the criteria in a job description. References and background checks help to verify the accuracy of the information. Employment tests and work samples are more objective. To be legal, any test must measure abilities that actually are associated with successful job performance. Employment tests range from general to specific. General-purpose tests are relatively inexpensive and simple to administer. Tests should be selected to be related to successful job performance and avoid charges of discrimination. Interviews are widely used to obtain information about a candidate's interpersonal and communication skills and to gather more detailed information about a candidate's background. Structured interviews are more valid than unstructured ones. Situational interviews provide greater validity than general questions. Interviews are costly and may introduce bias into the selection process. Organizations can minimize the drawbacks through preparation and training.

5. Describe major types of employment tests.
   Physical ability tests measure strength, endurance, psychomotor abilities, and other physical abilities. They can be accurate but can discriminate and are not always job related. Cognitive ability tests, or intelligence tests, tend to be valid, especially for complex jobs and those requiring adaptability. They are a relatively low-cost way to predict job performance but have been challenged as discriminatory. Job performance tests tend to be valid but are not always generalizable. Using a wide variety of job performance tests can be expensive. Personality tests measure personality traits such as extroversion and adjustment. Research supports their validity for appropriate job situations, especially for individuals who score high on conscientiousness, extroversion, and agreeableness. These tests are relatively simple to administer and generally meet legal requirements. Organizations may use paper-and-pencil honesty tests, which can predict certain behaviors, including employee theft. Organizations may not use polygraphs to screen job candidates. Organizations may also administer drug tests (if all candidates are tested and drug use can be an on-the-job safety hazard). A more job-related approach is to use impairment testing. Passing a medical examination may be a condition of employment, but to avoid discrimination against persons with

disabilities, organizations usually administer a medical exam only after making a job offer.

6. Discuss how to conduct effective interviews.
   Interviews should be narrow, structured, and standardized. Interviewers should identify job requirements and create a list of questions related to the requirements. Interviewers should be trained to recognize their own personal biases and conduct objective interviews. Panel interviews can reduce problems related to interviewer bias. Interviewers should put candidates at ease in a comfortable place that is free of distractions. Questions should ask for descriptions of relevant experiences and job-related behaviors. The interviewers also should be prepared to provide information about the job and the organization.

7. Explain how employers carry out the process of making a selection decision.
   The organization should focus on the objective of finding the person who will be the best fit with the job and organization. This includes an assessment of ability and motivation. Decision makers may use a multiple-hurdle model in which each stage of the selection process eliminates some of the candidates from consideration at the following stages. At the final stage, only a few candidates remain, and the selection decision determines which of these few is the best fit. An alternative is a compensatory model, in which all candidates are evaluated with all methods. A candidate who scores poorly with one method may be selected if he or she scores very high on another measure.

Review and Discussion Questions

1. What activities are involved in the selection process? Think of the last time you were hired for a job. Which of those activities were used in selecting you? Should the organization that hired you have used other methods as well?
2. Why should the selection process be adapted to fit the organization's job descriptions?
3. Choose two of the selection methods identified in this chapter. Describe how you can compare them in terms of reliability, validity, ability to generalize, utility, and compliance with the law.
4. Why does predictive validation provide better information than concurrent validation? Why is this type of validation more difficult?
5. How do U.S. laws affect organizations' use of each of the employment tests? Interviews?
6. Suppose your organization needs to hire several computer programmers, and you are reviewing résumés you obtained from an online service. What kinds of information will you want to gather from the "work experience" portion of these résumés? What kinds of information will you want to gather from the "education" portion of these résumés? What methods would you use for verifying or exploring this information? Why would you use those methods?
7. For each of the following jobs, select the two kinds of tests you think would be most important to include in the selection process. Explain why you chose those tests.

a. City bus driver.
b. Insurance salesperson.
c. Member of a team that sells complex high-tech equipment to manufacturers.
d. Member of a team that makes a component of the equipment in (c).

8. Suppose you are a human resource professional at a large retail chain. You want to improve the company's hiring process by creating standard designs for interviews, so that every time someone is interviewed for a particular job category, that person answers the same questions. You also want to make sure the questions asked are relevant to the job and maintain equal employment opportunity. Think of three questions to include in interviews for each of the following jobs. For each question, state why you think it should be included.

a. Cashier at one of the company's stores.
b. Buyer of the stores' teen clothing line.
c. Accounts payable clerk at company headquarters.

9. How can organizations improve the quality of their interviewing so that interviews provide valid information?
10. Some organizations set up a selection process that is long and complex. In some people's opinion, this kind of selection process not only is more valid but also has symbolic value. What can the use of a long, complex selection process symbolize to job seekers? How do you think this would affect the organization's ability to attract the best employees?

What's Your HR IQ?

The Student CD-ROM offers two more ways to check what you've learned so far. Use the Self-Assessment exercise to test your knowledge of employee selection. Go online with the Web Exercise to see how well your knowledge works in cyberspace.

BusinessWeek Case

BusinessWeek It's Not Easy Making Pixie Dust

We are in the Utilidor—a series of tunnels below Disney World's Magic Kingdom theme park in Orlando. The tunnel complex is generally off-limits to outsiders, but not to 41 visiting managers whose companies have anted up $2,295 a head so they can learn about Walt Disney Company's approach to people management.

This underground city is a beehive of activity. Employees rush through the gray concrete tunnels, scrambling to put on costumes and assume their roles upstairs. Golf carts speed by with supplies. Makeup artists prepare an array of Cinderella and Snow White wigs.

Before coming to this $3^1/_2$-day seminar, I was skeptical. The program sounded like little more than a dream junket: three nights at the resort's most elegant hotel, plus four-day passes to Disney's theme parks. Besides, I thought, what could any manager possibly learn at Disney World? By the end of the first day's activities, however, my note pad was brimming with ideas and lessons dished out by Disney staff.

My colleagues, most of them human-resource managers, take the program seriously. Most are facing a slew of challenges in need of Disney-style magic. A delivery manager at Anheuser-Busch Companies is trying to make his drivers more responsive to retailers. Personnel managers at a fast-growing bagel chain in Florida worry about maintaining standards as they beef up the chain's ranks. And an employee trainer at South Africa's state-owned transportation conglomerate is looking for ways to streamline the company's hiring process.

Disney's reputation for cleanliness, attention to detail, and helpful employees is what has drawn them here. "Everyone knows how wonderful Disney is, so you figure they must be doing something right," says Kathleen Scapini, who works for Multi-Media in West Hartford, Connecticut. That "something right" is what Disney refers to as the "pixie-dust" formula, with four key ingredients—employee selection, training, support, and benefits. Our seminar, "Disney's Approach to People Management," promises to reveal how the company motivates employees.

Instructors, called facilitators, tell us that we cannot count on Tinkerbell. "The solutions are not complicated," assures Jeff Soluri, a Disney instructor. "It's attention to detail and hard-nosed business practices that produce the magic."

If there is pixie dust, it starts with the hiring process.

One of the first activities is a field trip to Disney's "casting center," a Venetian-style castle where job candidates view a video before being interviewed. The short film informs job seekers about the company's strict appearance guidelines (one ring per hand and no tattoos, please) and the rigors of the work. By being blunt and detailed, Disney says, it's able to weed out incompatible candidates at the first crack.

The critical part of the process, though, is employee training. New hires, who average less than $10 an hour, are treated to a visual company history. They are told that they are not just employees but pivotal "cast members" in a "show." From street sweepers to monorail pilots, each cast member must go out of his way to make the resort seem *unreal*. No matter how tired workers are or how deeply guests may try their patience, they must never lose composure. To do so, the company tells its cast, is to risk alienating a guest, spoiling the illusion, and damaging Disney's standing in entertainment and American culture.

Between excursions, participants share what they have learned—and what they might use. Disney staffers with wireless microphones dart Oprah-like through a conference room seeking comments. They get plenty. John Lealos, the Anheuser-Busch manager, says he wants to incorporate more of an appreciative, team feel into his unit's corporate culture. "If we can get that kind of atmosphere at our company, the productivity will go up," he says. Hugo Strydom, the training manager at South Africa's Transit Ltd., intends to use a Disney-style orientation to weed out weak candidates in a major hiring blitz.

SOURCE: Antonio Fins, "It's Not Easy Making Pixie Dust," *BusinessWeek*, September 19, 1997.

Questions

1. This case reveals much about what Disney looks for in a job applicant as well as what it does (realistic job previews) to get unsuitable job candidates to remove themselves from the process. What characteristics would you expect Disney to be selecting for?
2. Based on the information given, what selection methods might be appropriate for further screening job applicants?
3. Why is selection an important part of a maintaining a competitive advantage at Disney? Would it be equally important at a bank? Why or why not?

Case: Never Having to Say "You Never Know"

Seymour Schlager had an impressive résumé. He had medical and law degrees, as well as a doctorate in microbiology. He had experience as a director of established AIDS research at Abbott Laboratories, and he had been an entrepreneur who started a small pharmaceutical company. He seemed like a perfect fit for the job of medical director when that position was open at Becton Dickinson. The company, which makes medical devices, hired him on the spot.

However, one fact about Schlager did not come out during the application process: He had been convicted of attempted murder in 1991 and had spent several years in prison as a result of this crime. Any reader of this book could type Schlager's name into almost any Internet search engine and uncover at least one of the 24 news articles written about his case—some of which were front-page material in the *Chicago Tribune*. But apparently no one at Becton Dickinson had felt this was necessary.

Although this situation is extreme, many job applicants do engage in stretching, shading, or spinning the information on their résumés. Some even include outright lies. For organizations hiring complete strangers, it pays to "be afraid—be very afraid." However, many organizations fail to conduct routine background checks on their hires.

Organizations that provide the service of background checking can point to some startling statistics. Kroll Associates, one of the leading investigative agencies for top-level executives, notes that of the 70 background checks it performed in 2000, almost 4 out of 10 turned up problems such as fraud, bankruptcy, and SEC violations that were serious enough to nix the employment offers being considered.

One reason that organizations haven't been careful about checking candidates' backgrounds is the labor shortage of the last decade. When there is intense competition for qualified employees, too many employers are in a rush to hire. For example, when Pinpoint Networks was searching for a new chief executive officer, it hired a firm called Christian and Timbers to conduct the search. By the time Christian and Timbers had narrowed the field to six can-

didates, Pinpoint's young founders were infatuated with the résumé of one applicant. They closed the search and took over the remainder of the selection process. They hired their desired candidate, Anthony J. Blake, and 13 weeks later, they discovered Blake was not who he claimed to be. It was too late. Without a seasoned chief executive, Pinpoint blew the opportunity to attract venture capital when this kind of start-up funding was widely available. When the technology sector of the economy tanked later the same year, Pinpoint had to lay off one-third of its workforce.

Experiences such as these are prompting other employers to slow down the hiring process. They are taking more time to get a much better idea of exactly whom they are asking to join their organization. Along with background checks, some organizations are using extensive psychological testing to ensure that a person is who he or she claims to be and also fits the culture of the organization. You never know what these kinds of investigations will uncover—unless, of course, you fail to perform them.

SOURCE: G. David, "You Just Hired Him: Should You Have Known Better?" *Fortune*, October 29, 2001, pp. 205–6; D. Foust, "When the CEO Is Too Good to Be True," *BusinessWeek*, July 16, 2001, pp. 62–63; C. Daniels, "Does This Man Need a Shrink?" *Fortune*, February 5, 2001.

Questions

1. If you were hiring the medical director of a hospital, what would you want to know about candidates' backgrounds?
2. How would you recommend gathering and checking the information you identified in question 1?
3. Why do you think some organizations fail to conduct background checks on candidates for executive positions?

Notes

1. E. Watters, "*Inc.* 500 Balancing Act: 'Come Here, Work, and Get Out of Here. You Don't Live Here. You Live Someplace Else,' " *Inc.*, October 30, 2001, pp. 56–58, 60–61.
2. S. Greco, "Sales: What Works Now," *Inc.*, February 2002, pp. 52–59.
3. J. C. Nunnally, *Psychometric Theory* (New York: McGraw-Hill, 1978).
4. N. Schmitt, R. Z. Gooding, R. A. Noe, and M. Kirsch, "Meta-Analysis of Validity Studies Published between 1964 and 1982 and the Investigation of Study Characteristics," *Personnel Psychology* 37 (1984), pp. 407–22.
5. C. H. Lawshe, "Inferences from Personnel Tests and Their Validity," *Journal of Applied Psychology* 70 (1985), pp. 237–38.
6. D. D. Robinson, "Content-Oriented Personnel Selection in a Small Business Setting," *Personnel Psychology* 34 (1981), pp. 77–87.
7. F. L. Schmidt and J. E. Hunter, "The Future of Criterion-Related Validity," *Personnel Psychology* 33 (1980), pp. 41–60; F. L. Schmidt, J. E. Hunter, and K. Pearlman, "Task Differences as Moderators of Aptitude Test Validity: A Red Herring," *Journal of Applied Psychology* 66 (1982), pp. 166–85; R. L. Gutenberg, R. D. Arvey, H. G. Osburn, and R. P. Jeanneret, "Moderating Effects of Decision-Making/Information Processing Dimensions on Test Validities," *Journal of Applied Psychology* 68 (1983), pp. 600–8.
8. J. S. MacNeil, "Hey, Look Us Over," *Inc., Inc.* 500 issue, October 30, 2001, p. 146.
9. M. E. Heilman, W. S. Battle, C. E. Keller, and R. A.

Lee, "Type of Affirmative Action Policy: A Determinant of Reactions to Sex-Based Preferential Selection," *Journal of Applied Psychology* 83 (1998), pp. 190–205.

10. B. S. Murphy, "EEOC Gives Guidance on Legal and Illegal Inquiries under ADA," *Personnel Journal*, August 1994, p. 26.

11. T. W. Dougherty, D. B. Turban, and J. C. Callender, "Confirming First Impressions in the Employment Interview: A Field Study of Interviewer Behavior," *Journal of Applied Psychology* 79 (1994), pp. 659–65.

12. J. B. Copeland, "Revenge of the Fired," *Newsweek*, February 16, 1987, pp. 46–47.

13. S. Greengard, "Are You Well Armed to Screen Applicants?" *Personnel Journal*, December 1995, pp. 84–95.

14. A. Ryan and M. Lasek, "Negligent Hiring and Defamation: Areas of Liability Related to Pre-employment Inquiries," *Personnel Psychology* 44 (1991), pp. 293–319.

15. A. Long, "Addressing the Cloud over Employee References: A Survey of Recently Enacted State Legislation," *William and Mary Law Review* 39 (October 1997), pp. 177–228.

16. Greengard, "Are You Well Armed to Screen Applicants?"

17. R. Theim, "Psychometric Testing," *Chicago Tribune*, March 6, 2002, sec. 6, pp. 1, 4.

18. C. J. Bachler, "Global Inpats—Don't Let Them Surprise You," *Personnel Journal*, June 1996, pp. 54–65; R. Horn, "Give Me Your Huddled . . . High-Tech Ph.D.s: Are High Skilled Foreigners Displacing U.S. Workers?" *BusinessWeek*, November 6, 1995, pp. 161–62; S. Greengard, "Gain the Edge in the Knowledge Race," *Personnel Journal*, August 1996, pp. 52–56.

19. L. C. Buffardi, E. A. Fleishman, R. A. Morath, and P. M. McCarthy, "Relationships between Ability Requirements and Human Errors in Job Tasks," *Journal of Applied Psychology* 85 (2000), pp. 551–64; J. Hogan, "Structure of Physical Performance in Occupational Tasks," *Journal of Applied Psychology* 76 (1991), pp. 495–507.

20. M. J. Ree, J. A. Earles, and M. S. Teachout, "Predicting Job Performance: Not Much More than *g*," *Journal of Applied Psychology* 79 (1994), pp. 518–24; L. S. Gottfredson, "The *g* Factor in Employment," *Journal of Vocational Behavior* 29 (1986), pp. 293–96; J. E. Hunter and R. H. Hunter, "Validity and Utility of Alternative Predictors of Job Performance," *Psychological Bulletin* 96 (1984), pp. 72–98; Gutenberg et al., "Moderating Effects of Decision-Making/Information Processing Dimensions on Test Validities"; F. L. Schmidt, J. G. Berner, and J. E. Hunter, "Racial Differences in Validity of Employment Tests: Reality or

Illusion," *Journal of Applied Psychology* 58 (1974), pp. 5–6; J. A. LePine, J. A. Colquitt, and A. Erez, "Adaptability to Changing Task Contexts: Effects of General Cognitive Ability, Conscientiousness, and Openness to Experience," *Personnel Psychology* 53 (2000), pp. 563–93.

21. D. A. Kravitz and S. L. Klineberg, "Reactions to Versions of Affirmative Action among Whites, Blacks, and Hispanics," *Journal of Applied Psychology* (2000), pp. 597–611.

22. F. L. Schmidt and J. E. Hunter, "The Validity and Utility of Selection Methods in Personnel Psychology: Practical and Theoretical Implications of 85 Years of Research Findings," *Psychological Bulletin* 124 (1998), pp. 262–74.

23. W. S. Dunn, M. K. Mount, M. R. Barrick, and D. S. Ones, "Relative Importance of Personality and General Mental Ability on Managers' Judgments of Applicant Qualifications," *Journal of Applied Psychology* 79 (1995), pp. 500–9; P. M. Wright, K. M. Kacmar, G. C. McMahan, and K. Deleeuw, "P = *f*(M × A): Cognitive Ability as a Moderator of the Relationship between Personality and Job Performance," *Journal of Management* 21 (1995), pp. 1129–39.

24. M. Mount, M. R. Barrick, and J. P. Strauss, "Validity of Observer Ratings of the Big Five Personality Factors," *Journal of Applied Psychology* 79 (1994), pp. 272–80.

25. Ryan and Lasek, "Negligent Hiring and Defamation."

26. L. Joel, *Every Employee's Guide to the Law* (New York: Pantheon, 1993).

27. R. Gatewood and H. Feild, *Human Resource Selection* (Fort Worth, TX: Dryden, 1998); A. Rafaeli and R. Klimoski, "Predicting Sales Success through Handwriting Analysis: An Evaluation of the Effects of Training and Handwriting Sample Content," *Journal of Applied Psychology* 68 (1983), pp. 212–17.

28. D. S. One, C. Viswesvaran, and F. L. Schmidt, "Comprehensive Meta-Analysis of Integrity Test Validities: Findings and Implications for Personnel Selection and Theories of Job Performance," *Journal of Applied Psychology* 78 (1993), pp. 679–703; H. J. Bernardin and D. K. Cooke, "Validity of an Honesty Test in Predicting Theft among Convenience Store Employees," *Academy of Management Journal* 36 (1993), pp. 1079–1106.

29. K. R. Murphy, G. C. Thornton, and D. H. Reynolds, "College Students' Attitudes toward Drug Test Programs," *Personnel Psychology* 43 (1990), pp. 615–31.

30. M. A. McDaniel, F. P. Morgeson, E. G. Finnegan, M. A. Campion, and E. P. Braverman, "Use of Situational Judgment Tests to Predict Job Performance: A Clarification of the Literature," *Journal of Applied Psychology* 86 (2001), pp. 730–40; J. Clavenger, G. M. Perreira, D. Weichmann, N. Schmitt, and V. S. Har-

vey, "Incremental Validity of Situational Judgment Tests," *Journal of Applied Psychology* 86 (2001), pp. 410–17.

31. M. A. Campion, J. E. Campion, and J. P. Hudson, "Structured Interviewing: A Note of Incremental Validity and Alternative Question Types," *Journal of Applied Psychology* 79 (1994), pp. 998–1002; E. D. Pulakos and N. Schmitt, "Experience-Based and Situational Interview Questions: Studies of Validity," *Personnel Psychology* 48 (1995), pp. 289–308.

32. J. Cleaver, "What Kind of Question Is That?" *Chicago Tribune*, April 24, 2002, sec. 6, pp. 1, 4.

33. Hunter and Hunter, "Validity and Utility of Alternative Predictors of Job Performance."

34. R. Pingitore, B. L. Dugoni, R. S. Tindale, and B. Spring, "Bias against Overweight Job Applicants in a Simulated Interview," *Journal of Applied Psychology* 79 (1994), pp. 184–90.

35. *Watson v. Fort Worth Bank and Trust*, 108 Supreme Court 2791 (1988).

36. M. A. McDaniel, D. L. Whetzel, F. L. Schmidt, and S. D. Maurer, "The Validity of Employment Interviews: A Comprehensive Review and Meta-Analysis," *Journal of Applied Psychology* 79 (1994), pp. 599–616; A. I. Huffcutt and W. A. Arthur, "Hunter and Hunter (1984) Revisited: Interview Validity for Entry-Level Jobs," *Journal of Applied Psychology* 79 (1994), pp. 184–90.

37. Y. Ganzach, A. N. Kluger, and N. Klayman, "Making Decisions from an Interview: Expert Measurement and Mechanical Combination," *Personnel Psychology* 53 (2000), pp. 1–21; G. Stasser and W. Titus, "Effects of Information Load and Percentage of Shared Information on the Dissemination of Unshared Information during Group Discussion," *Journal of Personality and Social Psychology* 53 (1987), pp. 81–93.

38. A. Cuneo, "Diverse by Design," *BusinessWeek*, June 6, 1992, p. 72.

Chapter **7**

Training Employees

What Do I Need to Know? After reading this chapter, you should be able to:

1. Discuss how to link training programs to organizational needs.

2. Explain how to assess the need for training.

3. Explain how to assess employees' readiness for training.

4. Describe how to plan an effective training program.

5. Compare widely used training methods.

6. Summarize how to implement a successful training program.

7. Evaluate the success of a training program.

8. Describe training methods for employee orientation and diversity management.

Introduction

The problem facing Espresso Connection was that sales were flat. The chain of drive-through coffee stands, based in Everett, Washington, used a variety of advertising media, but the customers attracted by the ads simply weren't coming back. Espresso Connection's owner, Christian Kar, identified the source of this problem as poor customer service. He decided he needed to teach employees how to impress customers.

Espresso Connection hired several part-time trainers and set up a practice facility. Newly hired employees no longer rely on their coworkers to teach them what to do. Instead, they spend a week in the practice facility, learning to use the equipment, followed by another week of on-the-job training at a store. The first week prepares employees to work fast, a goal that quickly affects Espresso Connection's bottom line. Says Kar, "Our locations are really, really small. Unless our staff really focuses on getting customers through there more efficiently, we quickly would hit a brick wall in terms of revenues." Moving fast also cuts the waiting time for Espresso Connection's customers. The other major goal of the training is to teach employees specific skills related to customer service—for example, keeping the window open while serving customers. A few years after Espresso Connection started the training, the company saw its sales nearly double.[1]

training
An organization's planned efforts to help employees acquire job-related knowledge, skills, abilities, and behaviors, with the goal of applying these on the job.

Training consists of an organization's planned efforts to help employees acquire job-related knowledge, skills, abilities, and behaviors, with the goal of applying these on the job. A training program may range from formal classes to one-on-one mentoring, and it may take place on the job or at remote locations. No matter what its form, training can benefit the organization when it is linked to organizational needs and when it motivates employees.

This chapter describes how to plan and carry out an effective training program. We begin by discussing how to develop effective training in the context of the organization's strategy. Next, we discuss how organizations assess employees' training needs. We then review training methods and the process of evaluating a training program. The chapter concludes by discussing some special applications of training: orientation of new employees and the management of diversity.

LO1

Training Linked to Organizational Needs

The nature of the modern business environment makes training more important today than it ever has been. Rapid change, especially in the area of technology, requires that employees continually learn new skills, from the use of robots to collaboration on the Internet. The new psychological contract, described in Chapter 2, has created the expectation that employees invest in their own career development. Employees with this expectation will value employment at an organization that provides learning opportunities. Growing reliance on teamwork creates a demand for the ability to solve problems in teams, an ability that often requires formal training. Finally, the diversity of the U.S. population, coupled with the globalization of business, requires that employees be able to work well with people who are different from them. Successful organizations often take the lead in developing this ability.

With training so essential in modern organizations, it is important to provide training that is effective. An effective training program actually teaches what it is designed to teach, and it teaches skills and behaviors that will help the organization achieve its goals. Training programs may prepare employees for future positions in the organization, enable the organization to respond to change, reduce turnover, enhance worker safety, improve customer service and product design, and meet many other

instructional design
A process of systematically developing training to meet specified needs.

goals. To achieve those goals, HR professionals approach training through **instructional design**—a process of systematically developing training to meet specified needs.

A complete instructional design process includes the steps shown in Figure 7.1. It begins with an assessment of the needs for training—what the organization requires that its people learn. Next, the organization ensures that employees are ready for training in terms of their attitudes, motivation, basic skills, and work environment. The third step is to plan the training program, including the program's objectives, instructors, and methods. The organization then implements the program. Finally, evaluating the results of the training provides feedback for planning future training programs.

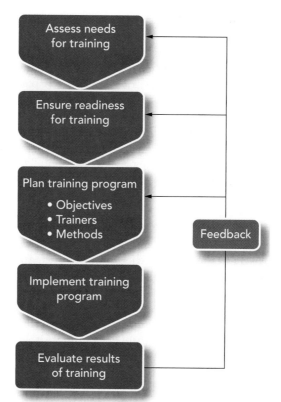

FIGURE 7.1

Stages of Instructional Design

Needs Assessment

Instructional design logically should begin with a **needs assessment,** the process of evaluating the organization, individual employees, and employees' tasks to determine what kinds of training, if any, are necessary. As this definition indicates, the needs assessment answers questions in the three broad areas shown in Figure 7.2:[2]

1. *Organization*—What is the context in which training will occur?
2. *Person*—Who needs training?
3. *Task*—What subjects should the training cover?

LO2

needs assessment
The process of evaluating the organization, individual employees, and employees' tasks to determine what kinds of training, if any, are necessary.

FIGURE 7.2

Needs Assessment

The answers to these questions provide the basis for planning an effective training program.

A variety of conditions may prompt an organization to conduct a needs assessment. Management may observe that some employees lack basic skills or are performing poorly. Decisions to produce new products, apply new technology, or design new jobs should prompt a needs assessment, because these changes tend to require new skills. The decision to conduct a needs assessment also may be prompted by outside forces, such as customer requests or legal requirements.

The outcome of the needs assessment is a set of decisions about how to address the issues that prompted the needs assessment. These decisions do not necessarily include a training program, because some issues should be resolved through methods other than training. For example, suppose a company uses delivery trucks to transport anesthetic gases to medical facilities. A driver of one of these trucks mistakenly hooked up the supply line of a mild anesthetic from the truck to the hospital's oxygen system, contaminating the hospital's oxygen supply. This performance problem prompts a needs assessment. Whether or not the hospital decides to provide more training will depend partly on the reasons the driver erred. The driver may have hooked up the supply lines incorrectly because of a lack of knowledge about the appropriate line hookup, anger over a request for a pay raise being denied, or mislabeled valves for connecting the supply lines. Out of these three possibilities, only the lack of knowledge can be corrected through training. Other outcomes of a needs assessment might include plans for better rewards to improve motivation, better hiring decisions, and better safety precautions.

The remainder of this chapter discusses needs assessments and then what the organization should do when they indicate a need for training. The possibilities include offering existing training programs to more employees; buying or developing new training programs; and improving existing training programs. Before we consider the available training options, let's examine the elements of the needs assessment in more detail.

Organization Analysis

organization analysis
A process for determining the appropriateness of training by evaluating the characteristics of the organization.

Usually, the needs assessment begins with the **organization analysis.** This is a process for determining the appropriateness of training by evaluating the characteristics of the organization. The organization analysis looks at training needs in light of the organization's strategy, resources available for training, and management's support for training activities.

Training needs will vary depending on whether the organization's strategy is based on growing or shrinking its personnel, whether it is seeking to serve a broad customer base or focusing on the specific needs of a narrow market segment, and various other strategic scenarios. A company that is cutting costs with a downsizing strategy may need to train employees in job search skills. The employees who will remain following a downsizing may need cross-training so that they can handle a wider variety of responsibilities. An organization that concentrates on serving a niche market may need to continually update its workforce on a specialized skills set. Transocean Offshore, a contractor that drills offshore oil wells for oil companies such as BP Amoco, focuses exclusively on deep-water drilling. Contracts for these jobs last four or five years, longer than contracts for other types of well drilling. Deep-water drilling also requires modern technology and new ships, such as the high-tech *Discoverer Enterprise,* which boasts numerous workstations, computer systems, and automated drilling systems. In contrast to most drilling companies, which merely provide safety training, Transocean must provide training for specialized job skills, as well as training for general rig safety.[3]

Even if training fits the organization's strategy, it can be viable only if the organization is willing to invest in this type of activity. Managers increase the success of training when they support it through such actions as helping trainees see how they can use their newly learned knowledge, skills, and behaviors on the job.[4] Conversely, the managers will be most likely to support training if the people planning it can show that it will solve a significant problem or result in a significant improvement, relative to its cost. Managers appreciate training proposals with specific goals, timetables, budgets, and methods for measuring success.

Person Analysis

Following the organizational assessment, needs assessment turns to the remaining areas of analysis: person and task. The **person analysis** is a process for determining individuals' needs and readiness for training. It involves answering several questions:

- Do performance deficiencies result from a lack of knowledge, skill, or ability? (If so, training is appropriate; if not, other solutions are more relevant.)
- Who needs training?
- Are these employees ready for training?

person analysis
A process of determining individuals' needs and readiness for training.

The answers to these questions help the manager identify whether training is appropriate and which employees need training. In certain situations, such as the introduction of a new technology or service, all employees may need training. However, when needs assessment is conducted in response to a performance problem, training is not always the best solution.

The person analysis is therefore critical when training is considered in response to a performance problem. In assessing the need for training, the manager should identify all the variables that can influence performance. The primary variables are the person's ability and skills, his or her attitudes and motivation, the organization's input (including clear directions, necessary resources, and freedom from interference and distractions), performance feedback (including praise and performance standards), and positive consequences to motivate good performance. Of these variables, only ability and skills can be affected by training. Therefore, before planning a training program, it is important to be sure that any performance problem results from a deficiency in knowledge and skills. Otherwise, training dollars will be wasted, because the training is unlikely to have much effect on performance.

The person analysis also should determine whether employees are ready to undergo training. In other words, the employees to receive training not only should require additional knowledge and skill, but must be willing and able to learn. (After this discussion of the needs assessment, we will explore the topic of employee readiness in greater detail.)

Task Analysis

The third area of needs assessment is **task analysis,** the process of identifying the tasks, knowledge, skills, and behaviors that training should emphasize. Usually, task analysis is conducted along with person analysis. Understanding shortcomings in performance usually requires knowledge about the tasks and work environment as well as the employee.

task analysis
The process of identifying and analyzing tasks to be trained for.

FIGURE 7.3

Sample Task Statement
Questionnaire

Name _____ Date _____
Position _____

Instructions: Please rate each of the task statements according to three factors: the **importance** of the task for effective performance, how **frequently** the task is performed, and the degree of **difficulty** required to become effective in the task.

Use the following scales in making your ratings.

Importance
4 = Task is critical for effective performance.
3 = Task is important but not critical for effective performance.
2 = Task is of some importance for effective performance.
1 = Task is of no importance for effective performance.
0 = Task is not performed.

Frequency
4 = Task is performed once a day.
3 = Task is performed once a week.
2 = Task is performed once every few months.
1 = Task is performed once or twice a year.
0 = Task is not performed.

Difficulty
4 = Effective performance of the task requires extensive prior experience and/or training (12–18 months or longer).
3 = Effective performance of the task requires minimal prior experience and training (6–12 months).
2 = Effective performance of the task requires a brief period of prior training and experience (1–6 months).
1 = Effective performance of the task does not require specific prior training and/or experience.
0 = Task is not performed.

Task (circle the number from the scales above)	*Importance*	*Frequency*	*Difficulty*
1. Ensuring maintenance on equipment, tools, and safety controls	0 1 2 3 4	0 1 2 3 4	0 1 2 3 4
2. Monitoring employee performance	0 1 2 3 4	0 1 2 3 4	0 1 2 3 4
3. Scheduling employees	0 1 2 3 4	0 1 2 3 4	0 1 2 3 4
4. Using statistical software on the computer	0 1 2 3 4	0 1 2 3 4	0 1 2 3 4
5. Monitoring changes made in processes using statistical methods	0 1 2 3 4	0 1 2 3 4	0 1 2 3 4

To carry out the task analysis, the HR professional looks at the conditions in which tasks are performed. These conditions include the equipment and environment of the job, time constraints (for example, deadlines), safety considerations, and performance standards. These observations form the basis for a description of work activities, or the tasks required by the person's job. For a selected job, the analyst interviews employees and their supervisors to prepare a list of tasks performed in that job. Then the analyst validates the list by showing it to employees, supervisors, and other subject-matter experts and asking them to complete a questionnaire about the importance, frequency, and difficulty of the tasks. Figure 7.3 is an example of a task statement questionnaire. In this example, the questionnaire begins by defining categories that specify a task's importance, frequency, and difficulty. Then, for a production supervisor's job, the questionnaire lists five tasks. For each task, the subject-matter expert uses the scales to rate the task's importance, frequency, and difficulty.

The information from these questionnaires is the basis for determining which tasks will be the focus of the training. The person or committee conducting the needs assessment must decide what levels of importance, frequency, and difficulty signal a need for training. Logically, training is most needed for tasks that are important, frequent, and at least moderately difficult. For each of these tasks, the analysts must identify the knowledge, skills, and abilities required to perform the task. This information usually comes from interviews with subject-matter experts, such as employees who currently hold the job.

Readiness for Training

LO3

Effective training requires not only a program that addresses real needs, but also a condition of employee readiness. **Readiness for training** is a combination of employee characteristics and positive work environment that permit training. The necessary employee characteristics include ability to learn the subject matter, favorable attitudes toward the training, and motivation to learn. A positive work environment is one that encourages learning and avoids interfering with the training program.

readiness for training
A combination of employee characteristics and positive work environment that permit training.

Employee Readiness Characteristics

Employees learn more from training programs when they are highly motivated to learn—that is, when they really want to learn the content of the training program.[5] Employees tend to feel this way if they believe they are able to learn, see potential benefits from the training program, are aware of their need to learn, see a fit between the training and their career goals, and have the basic skills needed for participating in the program. Managers can influence a ready attitude in a variety of ways. For example, they can provide feedback that encourages employees, establish rewards for learning, and communicate with employees about the organization's career paths and future needs.

Work Environment

Readiness for training also depends on two broad characteristics of the work environment: situational constraints and social support.[6] *Situational constraints* are the limits on training's effectiveness that arise from the situation or the conditions within the organization. Constraints can include a lack of money for training, lack of time for training or practicing, and failure to provide proper tools and materials for learning or applying the lessons of training. Conversely, trainees are likely to apply what they learn if the organization gives them opportunities to use their new skills and if it rewards them for doing so.[7]

Social support refers to the ways the organization's people encourage training, including giving trainees praise and encouraging words, sharing information about participating in training programs, and expressing positive attitudes toward the organization's training programs. Managers play an especially important role in providing social support. Besides offering positive feedback, they can emphasize the importance of training, show how training programs relate to employees' jobs, and provide opportunities for employees to apply what they learn. Table 7.1 summarizes some ways in which managers can support training. At the minimum, they should allow trainees to participate in training programs. At the other extreme, managers who not only encourage training but conduct the training sessions themselves are most likely to back up training by reinforcing new skills, providing feedback on progress, and giving trainees opportunities to practice.

Support can come from employees' peers as well as from supervisors and managers. The organization can formally provide peer support by establishing groups of employees who meet regularly to discuss their progress. Such a group might hold face-to-face meetings or communicate by e-mail or over the organization's intranet, sharing ideas as well as encouragement. For example, group members can share how they coped with challenges related to what they have learned and how they obtained resources they needed for applying their training. Another way to encourage peer

TABLE 7.1

What Managers
Should Do to
Support Training

Understand the content of the training.

Know how training relates to what you need employees to do.

In performance appraisals, evaluate employees on how they apply training to their jobs.

Support employees' use of training when they return to work.

Ensure that employees have the equipment and technology needed to use training.

Prior to training, discuss with employees how they plan to use training.

Recognize newly trained employees who use training content.

Give employees release time from their work to attend training.

Explain to employees why they have been asked to attend training.

Give employees feedback related to skills or behavior they are trying to develop.

SOURCE: Based on A. Rossett, "That Was a Great Class, but . . . " *Training and Development*, July 1997, p. 21.

support is for the human resource department or others in the organization to publish a newsletter with articles relevant to training. The newsletter might include interviews with employees who successfully applied new skills. Finally, the organization can assign experienced employees as mentors to trainees, providing advice and support related to the training.

LO4

Planning the Training Program

When the needs assessment indicates a need for training and employees are ready to learn, the person responsible for training should plan a training program that directly relates to the needs identified. Planning begins with establishing objectives for the training program. Based on those objectives, the planner decides who will provide the training, what topics the training will cover, what training methods to use, and how to evaluate the training.

Companies such as Tires Plus provide intensive training and educational programs for their employees. This company supports training by making resources available. Management has a favorable attitude toward training, which motivates employees to stay with the company and work toward advancement.

Objectives of the Program

Formally establishing objectives for the training program has several benefits. First, a training program based on clear objectives will be more focused and more likely to succeed. In addition, when trainers know the objectives, they can communicate them to the employees participating in the program. Employees learn best when they know what the training is supposed to accomplish. Finally, down the road, establishing objectives provides a basis for measuring whether the program succeeded, as we will discuss later in this chapter.

Effective training objectives have three components:

1. A statement of what the employee is expected to do (performance or outcome).
2. A statement of the quality or level of performance that is acceptable.
3. A statement of the conditions under which the trainee is expected to apply what he or she learned (for instance, physical conditions, mental stresses, or equipment failure).[8]

If possible, the objectives should include measurable performance standards. Suppose a training objective for a store's customer service training program is: "After training, the employee will be able to express concern to all irate customers with a brief (fewer than 10 words) apology, only after the customer has stopped talking, and no matter how upset the customer is." Here, measures include the length and timing of the apology.

Finally, training objectives should identify any resources required to carry out the desired performance or outcome. This helps the organization ensure that employees will be able to apply what they have learned.

A related issue at the outset is who will participate in the training program. Some training programs are developed for all employees of the organization or all members of a team. Other training programs identify individuals who lack desirable skills or have potential to be promoted, then provide training in the areas of need that are identified for the particular employees. When deciding whom to include in training, the organization has to avoid illegal discrimination. The organization should not— intentionally or unintentionally—exclude members of protected groups, such as women, minorities, and older employees. During the training, all participants should receive equal treatment, such as equal opportunities for practice. In addition, the training program should provide reasonable accommodation for trainees with disabilities. The kinds of accommodations that are appropriate will vary according to the type of training and type of disability. One employee might need an interpreter, whereas another might need to have classroom instruction provided in a location accessible to wheelchairs.

In-House or Contracted Out?

An organization can provide an effective training program, even if it lacks expertise in training. Many companies and consultants provide training services to organizations. Community colleges often work with employers to train employees in a variety of skills. PepsiCo needs highly skilled maintenance workers to take care of the sophisticated machinery at the Gatorade factory in Tolleson, Arizona. So PepsiCo and a neighboring manufacturer arranged for Maricopa Community College to provide courses in topics such as math and electricity. The college provides the instructor, and PepsiCo company provides the equipment to practice on.[9]

Businesses can outsource training services to organizations such as The American Society for Training and Development (an association of professional trainers). How can outsourcing training help businesses?

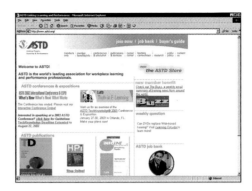

To select a training service, an organization can mail several vendors a *request for proposal (RFP)*, which is a document outlining the type of service needed, the type and number of references needed, the number of employees to be trained, the date by which the training is to be completed, and the date by which proposals should be received. A complete RFP also indicates funding for the project and the process by which the organization will determine its level of satisfaction. Putting together a request for proposal is time-consuming but worthwhile because it helps the organization clarify its objectives, compare vendors, and measure results.

Vendors that believe they are able to provide the services outlined in the RFP submit proposals that provide the types of information requested. The organization reviews the proposals to eliminate any vendors that do not meet requirements and to compare the vendors that do qualify. They check references and select a candidate, based on the proposal and the vendor's answers to questions such as those listed in Table 7.2.

The cost of purchasing training from a contractor can vary substantially. In general, it is much costlier to purchase specialized training that is tailored to the organization's unique requirements than to participate in a seminar or training course that teaches general skills or knowledge. According to estimates by consultants, preparing a training program can take 10 to 20 hours for each hour of instruction. Highly technical content that requires the developer to meet often with experts in the subject can take 50 percent longer.[10]

Even in organizations that send employees to outside training programs, someone in the organization may be responsible for coordinating the overall training program. Called *training administration*, this is typically the responsibility of a human resources

TABLE 7.2

Questions to Ask Vendors and Consultants

How much and what type of experience does your company have in designing and delivering training?
What are the qualifications and experiences of your staff?
Can you provide demonstrations or examples of training programs you have developed?
Would you provide references of clients for whom you worked?
What evidence do you have that your programs work?

SOURCE: Based on R. Zemke and J. Armstrong, "Evaluating Multimedia Developers," *Training*, November 1996, pp. 33–38. Adapted with permission. Lakewood Publications, Minneapolis, MN.

Administering a Training Program

For a training program to succeed, someone must be responsible for the nuts and bolts of the effort, from making sure there is an appropriate space to handling the paperwork. Usually, an organization's human resource department is responsible for this training administration. Carrying out that responsibility includes the following activities:

- *Communicate with employees.* The company newsletter, intranet, and postings on bulletin boards are possible ways to tell employees about the organization's overall training program and specific courses that are available. Messages should include the objectives as well as the topic of the training.
- *Enroll employees in courses and programs.* This may entail sending forms to schools, registering employees for in-house training sessions, or making sure employees have access to the Web if course enrollment is available online.
- *Prepare and process pretests to be administered or materials to be read before*

class begins. The training administrator may be also asked to prepare materials for handouts during the course. Training materials may include books, handouts, videotapes, and CD-ROMs.

- *Arrange the training facility.* The administrator may have to reserve a room, order refreshments, and make sure space is clean and ready for the training session. The administrator ensures that trainees and trainer are not distracted by an uncomfortable room or missing items. Visual aids should be easy to see. The setup should be appropriate for the course objectives. If the course objectives call for group interaction, the chairs should be arranged to encourage this.
- *Test equipment that will be used during the instruction.* In case of equipment failure, the administrator should be prepared with backup materials, such as replacement bulbs, a laptop computer, or photocopies of slides.
- *Provide support during instruction.* The administrator

should be nearby (physically or by phone), in case needs arise during a training session. Trainees should have full information about the schedule, including starting and finishing times and break times.

- *Distribute materials for evaluating the course*—for example, surveys or tests.
- *Provide for communication between the trainer and trainees.* For example, if the trainer will handle follow-up questions via e-mail, the administrator should ensure that trainees have the person's e-mail address.
- *Maintain records of course completion.* Usually, this information goes in employees' personnel files. The administrator should also keep records of the course evaluations. If the training is provided in-house, the records would include course materials such as handouts and videotapes.

SOURCE: Based on material in B. J. Smith and B. L. Delahaye, *How to Be an Effective Trainer*, 2nd ed. (New York: Wiley, 1987); M. Van Wart, N. J. Cayer, and S. Cook, *Handbook of Training and Development for the Public Sector* (San Francisco: Jossey-Bass, 1993).

professional. Training administration includes activities before, during, and after training sessions. The "HR How To" box describes what is involved in training administration.

Choice of Training Methods

Whether the organization prepares its own training programs or buys training from other organizations, it is important to verify that the content of the training relates directly to the training objectives. Such relevance to the organization's needs and objectives ensures that training money is well spent. Tying training content closely to objectives also improves trainees' learning, because it increases the likelihood that the training will be meaningful and helpful.

After deciding on the goals and content of the training program, planners must decide how the training will be conducted. As we will describe in the next section, a wide variety of methods is available. Training methods fall into the broad categories of presentation methods, hands-on methods, and group-building methods.[11]

presentation methods
Training methods in which trainees receive information provided by instructors or via computers or other media.

With **presentation methods,** trainees receive information provided by instructors or via computers or other media. Trainees may assemble in a classroom to hear a lecture, or the material may be presented on videotapes, CD-ROMs, websites, or in workbooks. Presentations are appropriate for conveying facts or comparing alternative processes. Computer-based training methods tend to be less expensive than bringing trainees together in a classroom.

hands-on methods
Training methods which actively involve the trainee in trying out skills being taught.

In contrast to presentation methods, **hands-on methods** actively involve the trainee in learning by trying out the behaviors being taught. Someone may help the trainee learn skills while on the job. Hands-on methods away from the job include simulations, games, role-plays, and interactive learning on computers. Hands-on training is appropriate for teaching specific skills and helping trainees understand how skills and behaviors apply to their jobs. These methods also help trainees learn to handle interpersonal issues, such as handling problems with customers.

group-building methods
Training methods in which trainees share ideas and experiences, build group identity, understand interpersonal relationships, and learn the strengths and weaknesses of themselves and their coworkers.

Group-building methods help trainees share ideas and experiences, build group or team identity, understand how interpersonal relationships work, and get to know their own strengths and weaknesses and those of their coworkers. The various techniques available involve examining feelings, perceptions, and beliefs about the trainees' group. Participants discuss how to apply what they learn in the training program to the group's performance at work. Group-building methods are appropriate for establishing teams or work groups, or for improving their performance.

Training programs may use these methods alone or in combination. The methods used should be suitable for the course content and the learning abilities of the participants. The following section explores the options in greater detail.

LO5

Training Methods

A wide variety of methods is available for conducting training. Figure 7.4 shows the percentages of companies using various training methods: classroom instruction, training videos, role-plays, case studies, several forms of computer-based training, learning games, and experiential programs. Of these methods, the most widely used are classroom training, videotapes, role-plays, and CD-ROMs.

Classroom Instruction

At school, we tend to associate learning with classroom instruction, and that type of training is most widely used in the workplace, too. Classroom instruction typically involves a trainer lecturing a group. Trainers often supplement lectures with slides,

FIGURE 7.4

Overview of Use of Instructional Methods

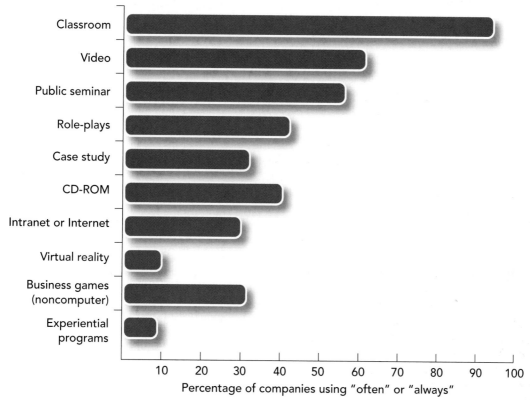

SOURCE: Based on "Industry Report 2001," *Training*, October 2001, p. 56.

discussions, case studies, question-and-answer sessions, and role playing. Actively involving trainees enhances learning.

When the course objectives call for presenting information on a specific topic to many trainees, classroom instruction is one of the least expensive and least time-consuming ways to accomplish that goal. Learning will be more effective if trainers enhance lectures with job-related examples and opportunities for hands-on learning.

Modern technology has expanded the notion of the classroom to classes of trainees scattered in various locations. With *distance learning*, trainees at different locations attend programs over phone and computer lines. Through audio- and videoconferencing, they can hear and see lectures and participate in discussions. Computers can enable participants to share documents as well. Satellite networks allow companies to link up with industry-specific and educational courses for which employees receive college credit and job certification. IBM, Digital Equipment, and Eastman Kodak are among the many companies that subscribe to the National Technological University, which broadcasts courses throughout the United States. Technical employees take these courses to obtain advanced degrees in engineering.[12] Distance learning provides many of the benefits of classroom training without the cost and time of travel to a shared classroom. The major disadvantage of distance learning is that interaction between the trainer and audience may be limited. To overcome this hurdle, distance learning usually provides a communications link between trainees and trainer. Also, on-site instructors or facilitators should be available to answer questions and moderate question-and-answer sessions.

Audiovisual Training

Presentation methods need not require that trainees attend a class. Trainees can also work independently, using course material prepared on audiotapes and videotapes or in workbooks. Audiovisual techniques such as overhead transparencies, slides, and videos can also supplement classroom instruction.

Training with videotapes has been used for improving communications skills, interviewing skills, and customer service skills. Videotapes can also be effective for demonstrating how to follow procedures, such as welding methods. Morse-Brothers provides training to the drivers of its ready-mix trucks with a series of videos. A mentor-driver selects a weekly video, schedules viewing sessions, keeps attendance records, and guides a wrap-up discussion. The short (10 minutes or less) videos cover topics such as safe driving, avoidance of excessive idling, and observing product tests at job sites. The mentor-drivers are trained in leading the discussion that follows the video, including how to call attention to key learning points and relate the topics to issues the drivers encounter on the job.[13]

Users of audiovisual training often have some control over the presentation. They can review material and may be able to slow down or speed up the lesson. Videotapes and video clips on CD-ROM can show situations and equipment that cannot be easily demonstrated in a classroom. Another advantage of audiovisual presentations is that they give trainees a consistent presentation, not affected by an individual trainer's goals and skills. The problems associated with these methods may include their trying to present too much material, poorly written dialogue, overuse of features such as humor or music, and drama that distracts from the key points. A well-written and carefully produced video can overcome these problems.

Computer-Based Training

Although almost all organizations use classroom training, new technologies are gaining in popularity as technology improves and becomes cheaper. With computer-based training, participants receive course materials and instruction distributed over the Internet or on CD-ROM. Often, these materials are interactive, so participants can answer questions and try out techniques, with course materials adjusted according to participants' responses. Online training programs may allow trainees to submit questions via e-mail and to participate in online discussions. Multimedia capabilities enable computers to provide sounds, images, and video presentations, along with text.

Computer-based training is generally less expensive than putting an instructor in a classroom of trainees. The low cost to deliver information gives the company flexibility in scheduling training, so that it can fit around work requirements. Training can be delivered in smaller doses, so material is easier to remember.[14] Finally, it is easier to customize computer-based training for individual learners.

Federal Express uses a form of computer-based training called *interactive video*. With this format, a monitor presents a training program stored on videodisk or CD-

ROM. Trainees use the keyboard or touch the monitor to interact with the program. Federal Express's 25-disk curriculum includes courses on customer etiquette, defensive driving, and delivery procedures.[15] Employees decide what aspects of the training program they want to view. They can skip ahead when they feel competent or review topics when they believe they need to do so. The program gives trainees immediate feedback on their learning progress.

Electronic Performance Support Systems

Computers can support trainees in applying training content to their jobs. *Electronic performance support systems (EPSSs)* are computer applications that provide access to skills training, information, and expert advice when a problem occurs on the job.[16] An EPSS gives trainees an electronic information source that they can refer to as they try applying new skills on the job. For example, Atlanta-based poultry processor Cagle's uses an EPSS for employees who maintain the chicken-processing machines.[17] The makers of machines that measure and cut chickens are continually improving this equipment, so that companies have no practical way to train technicians in the equipment's details. Instead, companies train technicians in the basic procedures for maintaining the machinery. When a problem occurs, the technicians combine the basic training with the EPSS to obtain enough information to fix the problem. On the EPSS, the technicians can look up detailed instructions for repairs, check parts availability, and find replacement parts in inventory.

E-Learning

Receiving training via the Internet or the organization's intranet is called **e-learning** or online learning. E-learning may bring together Web-based training, distance learning, virtual classrooms, and the use of CD-ROMs. Course content is presented with a combination of text, video, graphics, and sound. E-learning has three important characteristics. First, it involves electronic networks that enable the delivery, sharing, and updating of information and instruction. Second, e-learning is delivered to the trainee via computers with Internet access. Finally, it goes beyond traditional training objectives to offer tools and information that will help trainees improve performance. The system also may handle course enrollment, testing and evaluation of participants, and monitoring of progress.

e-learning
Receiving training via the Internet or the organization's intranet.

With e-learning, trainees have a great deal of control. They determine what they learn, how fast they progress through the program, how much time they practice, and when they learn. E-learners also may choose to collaborate or interact with other trainees and experts. They may use the training system's links to other learning resources such as reference materials, company websites, and other training programs.

Like other forms of computer-based learning, e-learning can reduce training costs and time. Trainees often appreciate the multimedia capabilities, which appeal to several senses, and the opportunity to actively participate in learning and apply it to situations on the job. The best e-learning combines the advantages of the Internet with the principles of a good learning environment. It takes advantage of the Web's dynamic nature and ability to use many positive learning features, including hyperlinks to other training sites and content, control by the trainee, and ability for trainees to collaborate. As described in the nearby "Best Practices" box, some of the most successful uses of e-learning combine online resources with face-to-face meetings.

Humanizing e-Learning

Despite all the hoopla about e-learning, posting some training modules on the organization's website will barely make an impression on the organization's employees. However computer savvy they may be, most people still appreciate a personal touch. Among the organizations that are benefiting most from e-learning are those combining it with traditional face-to-face methods such as classroom instruction.

Cablevision, for example, uses online training to prepare employees for more satisfactory classroom instruction. Before Cablevision's call center employees head for a classroom, they complete online courses, working at their own pace and completing an online assessment when they have finished. This gives them the background they need for participating in Cablevision's classroom instruction, and it shrinks classroom time from three days to one.

· Similarly, StorageTek's employees must complete online training before they go to class. Each employee works independently and must successfully complete learning assessments before taking the class. This setup makes the classroom time more rewarding, because classroom instruction can assume that everyone shares certain basic knowledge. In the words of StorageTek's manager of e-learning, Julie Bisiar, the online learning means trainees are "not just coming for three weeks to headquarters to take endless classes, some of which they already know, and some of which have nothing to do with them."

At Unisys, individual online learning precedes training in a *virtual classroom*. For the company's Coaching in the Workplace class, trainees complete computer-based training ahead of time, then participate in online discussions. A facilitator or faculty member leads those discussions.

Another company using virtual classrooms is Centra Software. These online sessions offer greater flexibility as well as lower costs. With Centra's system able to host classes of up to 250 students, discussions may require dividing the class into smaller groups. Centra's training system permits everyone to stay online while dividing into groups of any size from 1 person to 125. Participants can voice-chat or use "whiteboard" software that lets them look at one another's written work. Instructors can move from one online group to another, answering questions and looking at work. After the discussion, the subgroups can reunite and look at the work on one another's whiteboards. Still, even with all these bells and whistles, Centra cannot provide hands-on practice in a virtual classroom. When training requires the handling of equipment, the company sends trainees to one of its training locations around the globe, where students can meet in person with instructors and mentors.

SOURCE: G. Yohe, "The Best of Both?" *Human Resource Executive*, March 6, 2002, pp. 35, 38–39.

on-the-job training (OJT)
Training methods in which a person with job experience and skill guides trainees in practicing job skills at the workplace.

On-the-Job Training

Although people often associate training with classrooms, much learning occurs while employees are performing their jobs. **On-the-job training (OJT)** refers to training methods in which a person with job experience and skill guides trainees in practicing job skills at the workplace. This type of training takes various forms, including apprenticeships and internships.

APPRENTICESHIP	INTERNSHIP
Bricklayer	Accountant
Carpenter	Doctor
Electrician	Journalist
Plumber	Lawyer
Printer	Nurse
Welder	

TABLE 7.3

Typical Jobs for Apprentices and Interns

An **apprenticeship** is a work-study training method that teaches job skills through a combination of on-the-job training and classroom training.[18] The OJT component of an apprenticeship involves the apprentice assisting a certified tradesperson (a journeyman) at the work site. Typically, the classroom training is provided by local trade schools, high schools, and community colleges. Under state and federal guidelines, apprenticeship programs must require at least 144 hours of classroom instruction plus 2,000 hours (one year) of one-the-job experience.[19] Some apprenticeship programs are sponsored by individual companies, others by employee unions. As shown in the left column of Table 7.3, most apprenticeship programs are in the skilled trades, such as plumbing, carpentry, and electrical work. Apprenticeship programs are more widely used in Western European countries (including Germany and Denmark) than in the United States.[20] For trainees, a major advantage of apprenticeship is the ability to earn an income while learning a trade. In addition, training through an apprenticeship is usually effective because it involves hands-on learning and extensive practice.

apprenticeship
A work-study training method that teaches job skills through a combination of on-the-job training and classroom training.

An **internship** is on-the-job learning sponsored by an educational institution as a component of an academic program. The sponsoring school works with local employers to place students in positions where they can gain experience related to their area of study. For example, in Cedar Rapids, Iowa, Kirkwood Community College participates in an organization called Workplace Learning Connection, which finds students internships at hundreds of local companies.[21] High school students who pass a screening by the Workplace Learning Connection participate in semester-long internships. Many interns hope the internship will not only teach them about a workplace, but also lead to a job offer. Brian Whitlatch interned at the Iowa 80 Truck Stop, where he helped mechanics work on trucks. He worked without pay as an intern, but he received course credit and, three weeks before graduation, a job offer. Many internships prepare students for professions such as those listed in the right column of Table 7.3.

internship
On-the-job learning sponsored by an educational institution as a component of an academic program.

To be effective, OJT programs should include several characteristics:

- The organization should issue a policy statement describing the purpose of OJT and emphasizing the organization's support for it.
- The organization should specify who is accountable for conducting OJT. This accountability should be included in the relevant job descriptions.
- The organization should review OJT practices at companies in similar industries.
- Managers and peers should be trained in OJT principles.
- Employees who conduct OJT should have access to lesson plans, checklists, procedure manuals, training manuals, learning contracts, and progress report forms.
- Before conducting OJT with an employee, the organization should assess the employees' level of basic skills.[22]

The OJT program at Borden's North American Pasta Division has many of these characteristics.[23] Borden's carefully selects, trains, and rewards the managers and peers who act as trainers. The train-the-trainer course involves classroom training as well as time on the manufacturing floor to learn how to operate machinery such as pasta machines and correctly teach other employees how to use the equipment. Trainees in the OJT program complete a checklist in which they verify that the trainer helped them learn the skills needed and used effective teaching techniques.

Simulations

simulation
A training method that represents a real-life situation, with trainees making decisions resulting in outcomes that mirror what would happen on the job.

A **simulation** is a training method that represents a real-life situation, with trainees making decisions resulting in outcomes that mirror what would happen on the job. Simulations enable trainees to see the impact of their decisions in an artificial, risk-free environment. They are used to teaching production and process skills as well as management and interpersonal skills. At Motorola's Programmable Automation Literacy Lab, employees who may never have worked with computers or robots learn to operate them.[24] After completing a two-hour introduction to factory automation, trainees use a simulator to become familiar with the equipment by designing a product (a personalized memo holder). Success in simple exercises with the simulator increases trainees' confidence about working in an automated manufacturing environment.

Simulators must have elements identical to those found in the work environment. The simulator needs to respond exactly as equipment would under the conditions and response given by the trainee. For this reason, simulators are expensive to develop and need constant updating as new information about the work environment becomes available. Still, they are an excellent training method when the risks of a mistake on the job are great. Trainees do not have to be afraid of the impact of wrong decisions when using the simulator, as they would be with on-the-job training.

virtual reality
A computer-based technology that provides an interactive, three-dimensional learning experience.

A recent development in simulations is the use of virtual reality technology. **Virtual reality** is a computer-based technology that provides an interactive, three-dimensional learning experience. Using specialized equipment or viewing the virtual model on a computer screen, trainees move through the simulated environment and interact with its components.[25] Devices relay information from the environment to the trainees' senses. For example, audio interfaces, gloves that provide a sense of touch, treadmills, or motion platforms create a realistic but artificial environment. Devices also communicate information about the trainee's movements to a computer. Virtual reality is a feature of the simulated environment of the advanced manufacturing courses in Motorola's Pager Robotic Assembly facility. Employees wear a head-mount display that lets them view a virtual world of lab space, robots, tools, and the assembly operation. The trainees hear the sounds of using the real equipment. The equipment responds as if trainees were actually using it in the factory.[26]

Business Games and Case Studies

Training programs use business games and case studies to develop employees' management skills. A case study is a detailed description of a situation that trainees study and discuss. Cases are designed to develop higher-order thinking skills, such as the ability to analyze and evaluate information. They also can be a safe way to encourage trainees to take appropriate risks, by giving them practice in weighing and acting on uncertain outcomes. There are many sources of case studies, including Harvard Business School, the Darden Business School at the University of Virginia, and McGraw-Hill publishing company.

With business games, trainees gather information, analyze it, and make decisions that influence the outcome of the game. For instance, Market Share, part of a marketing management course, requires participants to use strategic thinking (such as analyzing competitors) to increase their share of the market.[27] Games stimulate learning because they actively involve participants and mimic the competitive nature of business. A realistic game may be more meaningful to trainees than presentation techniques such as classroom instruction.

Training with case studies and games requires that participants come together to discuss the cases or the progress of the game. This requires face-to-face or electronic meetings. Also, participants must be willing to be actively involved in analyzing the situation and defending their decisions.

Behavior Modeling

Research suggests that one of the most effective ways to teach interpersonal skills is through behavior modeling.[28] This involves training sessions in which participants observe other people demonstrating the desired behavior, then have opportunities to practice the behavior themselves. For example, a training program could involve four-hour sessions, each focusing on one interpersonal skill, such as communicating or coaching. At the beginning of each session, participants hear the reasons for using the key behaviors, then they watch a videotape of a model performing the key behaviors. They practice through role-playing and receive feedback about their performance. In addition, they evaluate the performance of the model in the videotape and discuss how they can apply the behavior on the job.

Experiential Programs

To develop teamwork and leadership skills, some organizations enroll their employees in a form of training called **experiential programs.** This type of program uses challenging, structured outdoor activities, which may include difficult sports such as dogsledding or mountain climbing. Other activities may be structured tasks like climbing walls, completing rope courses, climbing ladders, or making "trust falls" (in which each trainee stands on a table and falls backward into the arms of other group members).

experiential programs
A teamwork and leadership training program based on the use of challenging, structured outdoor activities.

For example, a manager of a Chili's restaurant was required to scale a wall that was three stories high. About two-thirds of the way from the top, the manager became very tired. Still, she succeeded in reaching the top by using the advice and encouragement shouted by team members on the ground. When asked what she had learned from the experience, the manager said the exercise made her realize that reaching personal success depends on other people. At her restaurant, everyone has to work together to make the customers happy.[29]

Do experiential programs work? The impact of these programs has not been rigorously tested, but participants report they gained a greater understanding of themselves and the ways they interact with their coworkers. One key to the success of such programs may be that the organization insist that entire work groups participate together. This encourages people to see, discuss, and correct the kinds of behavior that keep the group from performing well. Organizations should make sure that the exercises are related to the types of skills employees need to develop. Experiential programs should end with a discussion of what happened during the exercise, what participants learned, and how they can apply what they learned to their work.[30]

Before requiring employees to participate in experiential programs, the organization should consider the possible drawbacks. Because these programs are usually physically demanding and often require participants to touch each other, companies face certain risks. Some employees may be injured or may feel that they were sexually harassed or that their privacy was invaded. Also, the Americans with Disabilities Act (discussed in Chapter 3) raises questions about requiring employees with disabilities to participate in physically demanding training experiences.

Team Training

A possible alternative to experiential programs is team training, which coordinates the performance of individuals who work together to achieve a common goal. An organization may benefit from providing such training to groups when group members must share information and group performance depends on the performance of the individual group members. Examples include the military, nuclear power plants, and commercial airlines. In those work settings, much work is performed by crews, groups, or teams. Success depends on individuals' coordinating their activities to make decisions, perhaps in dangerous situations.

cross-training
Team training in which team members understand and practice each other's skills so that they are prepared to step in and take another member's place.

Ways to conduct team training include cross-training and coordination training.[31] In **cross-training,** team members understand and practice each other's skills so that they are prepared to step in and take another member's place. In a factory, for example, production workers could be cross-trained to handle all phases of assembly. This enables the company to move them to the positions where they are most needed to complete an order on time.

coordination training
Team training that teaches the team how to share information and make decisions to obtain the best team performance.

Coordination training trains the team in how to share information and decisions to obtain the best team performance. This type of training is especially important for commercial aviation and surgical teams. Both of these kinds of teams must monitor different aspects of equipment and the environment at the same time sharing information to make the most effective decisions regarding patient care or aircraft safety and performance.

action learning
Training in which teams get an actual problem, work on solving it and commit to an action plan, and are accountable for carrying it out.

For both kinds of team training, the training program usually brings together several training methods. To teach communication skills, training could begin with a lecture about communicating, followed by an opportunity for team members to role-play scenarios related to communication on the team. Boeing combined a number of methods in a team training program designed to improve the effectiveness of the 250 teams designing the Boeing 777.[32] Teams include members from a variety of specialties, from design engineers to marketing professionals. These team members had to understand how the process or product they were designing would fit with the rest of the finished jet. Boeing's training started with an extensive orientation emphasizing how team members were supposed to work together. Then the teams received their work assignments. Trainers helped the teams work through problems as needed, with assistance in communication skills, conflict resolution, and leadership.

Action Learning

Another form of group building, widely used in Europe, is **action learning.** In this type of training, teams or work groups get an actual problem, work on solving it and

One of the most important features of organizations today is teamwork. Experiential programs include team-building exercises like rope courses and wall climbing to help build trust and cooperation among employees.

commit to an action plan, and are accountable for carrying out the plan.[33] Typically, 6 to 30 employees participate in action learning; sometimes the participants include customers and vendors. For instance, a group might include a customer that buys the product involved in the problem to be solved. Another arrangement is to bring together employees from various functions affected by the problem. Whirlpool used action learning to solve a problem related to importing compressors from Brazil. The company had to pay duties (import taxes) on the compressors. It was overpaying and was trying to recover the overpayment. Members of the group responsible for obtaining the parts formed a team to implement Whirlpool's strategies for cost reduction and inventory control. Through action learning, they developed a process for recovering the overpayment, saving the company hundreds of thousands of dollars a year.

The effectiveness of action learning has not been formally evaluated. This type of training seems to result in a great deal of learning, however, and employees are able to apply what they learn because action learning involves actual problems the organization is facing. The group approach also helps teams identify behaviors that interfere with problem solving.

Implementing the Training Program: Principles of Learning

LO6

Learning permanently changes behavior. For employees to acquire knowledge and skills in the training program and apply what they have learned in their jobs, the training program must be implemented in a way that applies what we know about how people learn. Researchers have identified a number of ways employees learn best.[34] Table 7.4 summarizes ways that training can best encourage learning. In general, effective training communicates learning objectives clearly, presents information in distinctive and memorable ways, and helps trainees link the subject matter to their jobs.

TABLE 7.4

Ways That Training Helps Employees Learn

TRAINING ACTIVITY	WAYS TO PROVIDE TRAINING ACTIVITY
Communicate the learning objective.	Demonstrate the performance to be expected. Give examples of questions to be answered.
Use distinctive, attention-getting messages.	Emphasize key points. Use pictures, not just words.
Limit the content of training.	Group lengthy material into chunks. Provide a visual image of the course material. Provide opportunities to repeat and practice material.
Guide trainees as they learn.	Use words as reminders about sequence of activities. Use words and pictures to relate concepts to one another and to their context.
Elaborate on the subject.	Present the material in different contexts and settings. Relate new ideas to previously learned concepts. Practice in a variety of contexts and settings.
Provide memory cues.	Suggest memory aids. Use familiar sounds or rhymes as memory cues.
Transfer course content to the workplace.	Design the learning environment so that it has elements in common with the workplace. Require learners to develop action plans that apply training content to their jobs. Use words that link the course to the workplace.
Provide feedback about performance.	Tell trainees how accurately and quickly they are performing their new skill. Show how trainees have met the objectives of the training.

SOURCE: Adapted from R. M. Gagne, "Learning Processes and Instruction," *Training Research Journal* 1 (1995/96), pp. 17–28.

Employees are most likely to learn when training is linked to their current job experiences and tasks.[35] There are a number of ways trainers can make this link. Training sessions should present material using familiar concepts, terms, and examples. As far as possible, the training context—such as the physical setting or the images presented on a computer—should mirror the work environment. Along with physical elements, the context should include emotional elements. In the earlier example of training store personnel to handle upset customers, the physical context is more relevant if it includes trainees acting out scenarios of personnel dealing with unhappy customers. The role-play interaction between trainees adds emotional realism and further enhances learning.

To fully understand and remember the content of the training, employees need a chance to demonstrate and practice what they have learned. Trainers should provide ways to actively involve the trainees, have them practice repeatedly, and have them complete tasks within a time that is appropriate in light of the learning objectives. Practice requires physically carrying out the desired behaviors, not just describing them. Practice sessions could include role-playing interactions, filling out relevant forms, or operating machinery or equipment to be used on the job. The more the trainee practices these activities, the more comfortable he or she will be in applying the skills on the job. People tend to benefit most from practice that occurs over several sessions, rather than one long practice session.[36] For complex tasks, it may be most effective to practice a few skills or behaviors at a time, then combine them in later practice sessions.

Trainees need to understand whether or not they are succeeding. Therefore, training sessions should offer feedback. Effective feedback focuses on specific behaviors and is delivered as soon as possible after the trainees practice or demonstrate what they have learned.[37] One way to do this is to videotape trainees, then show the video while indicating specific behaviors that do or do not match the desired outcomes of the training. Feedback should include praise when trainees show they have learned material, as well as guidance on how to improve.

Well-designed training helps people remember the content. Training programs need to break information into chunks that people can remember. Research suggests that people can attend to no more than four to five items at a time. If a concept or procedure involves more than five items, the training program should deliver information in shorter sessions or chunks.[38] Other ways to make information more memorable include presenting it with visual images and practicing some tasks enough that they become automatic.

Written materials should have an appropriate reading level. A simple way to assess **readability**—the difficulty level of written materials—is to look at the words being used and at the length of sentences. In general, it is easiest to read short sentences and simple, standard words. If training materials are too difficult to understand, several adjustments can help. The basic approach is to rewrite the material looking for ways to simplify it.

readability
The difficulty level of written materials.

- Substitute simple, concrete words for unfamiliar or abstract words.
- Divide long sentences into two or more short sentences.
- Divide long paragraphs into two or more short paragraphs.
- Add checklists (like this one) and illustrations to clarify the text.

Another approach is to substitute videotapes, hands-on learning, or other nonwritten methods for some of the written material. A longer-term solution is to use tests to identify employees who need training to improve their reading levels and to provide that training first.

Measuring Results of Training

LO7

After a training program ends, or at intervals during an ongoing training program, organizations should ensure that the training is meeting objectives. The stage to prepare for evaluating a training program is when the program is being developed. Along with designing course objectives and content, the planner should identify how to measure achievement of objectives. Depending on the objectives, the evaluation can use one or more of the measures shown in Figure 7.5—trainee satisfaction with the program, knowledge or abilities gained, use of new skills and behavior on the job (transfer of training), and improvements in individual and organizational performance. The usual way to measure whether participants have acquired information is to administer tests on paper or electronically. Trainers or supervisors can observe whether participants demonstrate the desired skills and behaviors. Surveys measure changes in attitude. Changes in company performance have a variety of measures, many of which organizations keep track of for preparing performance appraisals, annual reports, and other routine documents in order to demonstrate the final measure of success shown in Figure 7.5—return on investment.

FIGURE 7.5

Measures of Training
Success

Evaluation Methods

transfer of training
On-the-job use of
knowledge, skills,
and behaviors
learned in training.

Evaluation of training should look for **transfer of training,** or on-the-job use of
knowledge, skills, and behaviors learned in training. Transfer of training requires that
employees actually learn the content of the training program and that the necessary
conditions are in place for employees to apply what they learned. Thus, the assessment can look at whether employees have an opportunity to perform the skills related
to the training. The organization can measure this by asking employees three questions about specific training-related tasks:

1. Do you perform the task?
2. How many times do you perform the task?
3. To what extent do you perform difficult and challenging learned tasks?

Frequent performance of difficult training-related tasks would signal great opportunity
to perform. If there is low opportunity to perform, the organization should conduct
further needs assessment and reevaluate readiness to learn. Perhaps the organization
does not fully support the training activities in general or the employee's supervisor
does not provide opportunities to apply new skills. Lack of transfer can also mean that
employees have not learned the course material. The organization might offer a re-
fresher course to give trainees more practice. Another reason for poor transfer of
training is that the content of the training may not be important for the employee's
job.

Assessment of training also should evaluate training *outcomes,* that is, what (if anything) has changed as a result of the training. The relevant training outcomes are the
ones related to the organization's goals for the training and its overall performance.
Possible outcomes include the following:

- Information such as facts, techniques, and procedures that trainees can recall after
  the training.
- Skills that trainees can demonstrate in tests or on the job.
- Trainee and supervisor satisfaction with the training program.
- Changes in attitude related to the content of the training (for example, concern
  for safety or tolerance of diversity).
- Improvements in individual, group, or company performance (for example, greater
  customer satisfaction, more sales, fewer defects).

Training is a significant part of many organizations' budgets. Therefore, economic measures are an important way to evaluate the success of a training program. Businesses that invest in training want to achieve a high *return on investment*—the monetary benefits of the investment compared to the amount invested, expressed as a percentage. For example, IBM's e-learning program for new managers, Basic Blue, costs $8,708 per manager.[39] The company has measured an improvement in each new manager's performance worth $415,000. That gives IBM a benefit of $415,000 − $8,708 = $406,292 for each manager. This is an extremely large return on investment: $406,292/$8,708 = 46.65, or 4,665 percent! In other words, for every $1 IBM invests in Basic Blue, it receives almost $47.

For any of these methods, the most accurate but most costly way to evaluate the training program is to measure performance, knowledge, or attitudes among all employees before the training, then to train only part of the employees. After the training is complete, the performance, knowledge, or attitudes are again measured, and the trained group is compared to the untrained group. A simpler but less accurate way to assess the training is to conduct the pretest and posttest on all trainees, comparing their performance, knowledge, or attitudes before and after the training. This form of measurement does not rule out the possibility that change resulted from something other than training (for example, a change in the compensation system). The simplest approach is to use only a posttest. Of course, this type of measurement does not enable accurate comparisons, but it may be sufficient, depending on the cost and purpose of the training.

Applying the Evaluation

The purpose of evaluating training is to help with future decisions about the organization's training programs. Using the evaluation, the organization may identify a need to modify the training and gain information about the kinds of changes needed. The organization may decide to expand on successful areas of training and cut back on training that has not delivered significant benefits.

At Walgreens, evaluation of training for pharmacy technicians convinced the company that formal training was economically beneficial. The drugstore chain developed a training course as an alternative to on-the-job training from pharmacists. Some of the newly hired technicians participated in the test of the program, taking part in 20 hours of classroom training and 20 hours of supervision on the job. Other technicians relied on the old method of being informally trained by the pharmacists who had hired them. After the training had ended, pharmacists who supervised the technicians completed surveys about the technicians' performance. The surveys indicated that formally trained technicians were more efficient and wasted less of the

Walgreens measured the success of training their pharmacy technicians. The formally trained technicians did show higher sales. Do you think Walgreens should invest in an even higher rate of training?

pharmacists' time. Also, sales in pharmacies with formally trained technicians exceeded sales in pharmacies with technicians trained on the job by an average of $9,500 each year.[40]

LO8

Applications of Training

Two categories of training that have become widespread among U.S. companies are orientation of new employees and training in how to manage workforce diversity.

Orientation of New Employees

orientation
Training designed to prepare employees to perform their jobs effectively, learn about their organization, and establish work relationships.

Many employees receive their first training during their first days on the job. This training is the organization's **orientation** program—its training designed to prepare employees to perform their job effectively, learn about the organization, and establish work relationships. Organizations provide for orientation because, no matter how realistic the information provided during employment interviews and site visits, people feel shock and surprise when they start a new job.[41] Also, employees need to become familiar with job tasks and learn the details of the organization's practices, policies, and procedures.

The objectives of orientation programs include making new employees familiar with the organization's rules, policies, and procedures. Table 7.5 summarizes the con-

TABLE 7.5

Content of a Typical Orientation Program

Company-level information
Company overview (e.g., values, history, mission)
Key policies and procedures
Compensation
Employee benefits and services
Safety and accident prevention
Employee and union relations
Physical facilities
Economic factors
Customer relations

Department-level information
Department functions and philosophy
Job duties and responsibilities
Policies, procedures, rules, and regulations
Performance expectations
Tour of department
Introduction to department employees

Miscellaneous
Community
Housing
Family adjustment

SOURCE: J. L. Schwarz and M. A. Weslowski, "Employee Orientation: What Employers Should Know," *Journal of Contemporary Business Issues*, Fall 1995, p. 48. Used with permission.

tent of a typical orientation program. Such a program provides information about the overall company and about the department in which the new employee will be working. The topics include social as well as technical aspects of the job. Miscellaneous information helps employees from out of town learn about the surrounding community.

Orientation of new engineers at Pillsbury addresses these issues. Before being assigned to a production facility, engineers work for one year at headquarters. To provide orientation, Pillsbury assigns a senior engineer to serve as a mentor, showing the new engineer the technical resources available within the company. The mentor also helps the new engineer become familiar with the community and handle issues related to relocation. The new employees attend seminars at which engineers from various product divisions explain the role of engineering. New employees also meet key managers.[42]

At The Container Store, orientation is about more than job skills.[43] The company also wants employees to care about what they are doing and to be committed to the organization. New employees at The Container Store participate in a one-week training program called Foundation Week. During the first day of Foundation Week, employees learn the company's philosophy, and they spend most of the day with the store manager. On the following days, they learn about the way merchandise is arranged in the stores, various selling techniques, roles of employees in different positions, and ways to provide customer service. Only after completing the entire week of training do employees receive the apron they wear while at work. The manager presents the apron during a ceremony intended to encourage the new hires. According to Barbara Anderson, The Container Store's director of community services and staff development, "The psychological effect of having to wait for that apron is incredible." Anderson says that since the company started its Foundation Week program, newly hired employees are more self-confident and productive, and they tend to stay with the company longer.

Orientation programs may combine various training methods such as printed and audiovisual materials, classroom instruction, on-the-job training, and e-learning. Decisions about how to conduct the orientation depend on the type of material to be covered and the number of new employees, among other factors. The "e-HRM" box describes how some organizations are applying e-learning to orientation programs.

Diversity Training

In response to Equal Employment Opportunity laws and market forces, many organizations today are concerned about managing diversity—creating an environment that allows all employees to contribute to organizational goals and experience personal growth. This kind of environment includes access to jobs as well as fair and positive treatment of all employees. Chapter 3 described how organizations manage diversity by complying with the law. Besides these efforts, many organizations provide training designed to teach employees attitudes and behaviors that support the management of diversity. Such training may have some or all of the following goals:

- Employees should understand how their values and stereotypes influence their behavior toward others of different gender and ethnic, racial, and religious backgrounds.
- Employees should gain an appreciation of cultural differences among themselves.
- Employees should avoid and correct behaviors that isolate and intimidate minority group members.

E-HRM

Getting Oriented Online

If you take a job with ChemConnect, don't expect to be greeted on your first day with a dry lecture from human resource personnel. Rather, the San Francisco–based online seller of chemicals and plastics offers an orientation via its intranet. The online orientation, titled "Tour de Chem," is a takeoff on the Tour de France bicycle race. Trainees use a computer mouse to manipulate the image of a bicycle to travel online through various scenarios. Clicking on the front wheel to move forward and on the rear wheel to move backward, trainees take a tour through company jargon, a menu of employee services and benefits, and background about ChemConnect's leaders. For each stage of the tour, one of those executives rides along—shown as a stick figure with a photo of the executive's head patched on top. The whole tour takes about 90 minutes.

The entertaining presentation keeps new hires engaged long after they might have nodded off in front of a benefits manual or lecture. The format also tells employees something about the company,

says ChemConnect's vice president of operations, Peter Navin. Navin, who is responsible for HRM, says, "If you look into a screen and see no creativity, you certainly get a sense of what you're joining."

No doubt, Jane Paradiso would applaud the Tour de Chem. Paradiso, leader of the recruiting solutions practice at the Watson Wyatt Worldwide consulting firm, says online orientations should be more than a video about the company plus a signup sheet for benefits. According to Paradiso, an online orientation should take advantage of the Internet's potential for communication. The orientation program should assign the new employee an e-mail address and a password to the intranet, let the employee schedule lunch with his or her boss, set up a connection between the new employee and his or her mentor, and describe the organization's ethics policy, among other features. In fact, such a system could begin building the organization's relationship with new employees even before their first day on the job, assuming

the organization gives out a password for the system.

That's what Pinnacle Decision Systems does. The consulting and software development company, located in Middletown, Connecticut, sends new hires to a website it calls "HQ." There, the newly hired individuals can read policies and procedures, view the company's organization chart, or order business cards and company T-shirts. Thanks to these online services, employees are already acquainted with the company on their first day. During their first day at work, they meet with department heads to deepen their knowledge of the organization. Pinnacle believes that in-depth employee orientation and development require more than a virtual touch, however. Says Joanne Keller, Pinnacle's HR director, "We wouldn't want to lose the personal touch, where you pick up the clues of how the company really works and what's expected of you."

SOURCE: Tom Starner, "Welcome E-Board," *Human Resource Executive*, March 6, 2002, pp. 40–43.

---

diversity training
Training designed to change employee attitudes about diversity and/or develop skills needed to work with a diverse workforce.

Training designed to change employee attitudes about diversity and/or develop skills needed to work with a diverse workforce is called **diversity training.** These programs generally emphasize either attitude awareness and change or behavior change.

Programs that focus on attitudes have objectives to increase participants' awareness of cultural and ethnic differences, as well as differences in personal characteristics and physical characteristics (such as disabilities). These programs are based on the assumption that people who become aware of differences and their stereotypes about those differences will be able to avoid letting stereotypes influence their interactions with people. Many of these programs use videotapes and experiential exercises to increase employees' awareness of the negative emotional and performance effects of stereotypes and resulting behaviors on members of minority groups. A risk of these programs is that they may actually reinforce stereotypes by focusing on differences rather than similarities among coworkers.[44] But it is generally held that greater awareness has a positive effect.

Programs that focus on behavior aim at changing the organizational policies and individual behaviors that inhibit employees' personal growth and productivity. Sometimes these programs identify incidents that discourage employees from working up to their potential. Employees work in groups to discuss specific promotion opportunities or management practices that they believe were handled unfairly. Another approach is to teach managers and employees basic rules of behavior in the workplace.[45] Trainees may be more positive about receiving this type of training than other kinds of diversity training. Finally, some organizations provide diversity training in the form of *cultural immersion*, sending employees directly into communities where they have to interact with persons from different cultures, races, and nationalities. Participants might talk with community members, work in community organizations, or learn about events that are significant to the community they visit. For example, AT&T sent several managers on a scavenger hunt in New York City's Harlem. In this eclectic community of Asian Americans, African Americans, Hispanic Americans, and Puerto Rican Americans, the managers had to look for a variety of items, including a bilingual community directory, a Jamaican meat patty, and soul food. The hunt required the team to interact with a variety of people.[46]

Although many organizations have used diversity training, few have provided programs lasting more than a day, and few have researched their long-term effectiveness.[47] The existing evidence regarding diversity training does, however, suggest that some characteristics make diversity training more effective.[48] Most important, the training should be tied to business objectives, such as understanding customers. The support and involvement of top management, and the involvement of managers at all levels, also are important. Diversity training should emphasize learning behaviors and skills, not blaming employees. Finally, the program should be well structured, connected to the organization's rewards for performance, and include a way to measure the success of the training.

Summary

1. Discuss how to link training programs to organizational needs.

   Organizations need to establish training programs that are effective. In other words, they teach what they are designed to teach, and they teach skills and behaviors that will help the organization achieve its goals. Organizations create such programs through instructional design. This process begins with a needs assessment. The organization then ensures readiness for training, including employee characteristics and organizational support. Next, the organization plans a training program, implements the program, and evaluates the results.

2. Explain how to assess the need for training.

   Needs assessment consists of an organization analysis, person analysis, and task analysis. The organization analysis determines the appropriateness of training by evaluating the characteristics of the organization, including its strategy, resources, and management support. The person analysis determines individuals' needs and readiness for training. The task analysis identifies the tasks, knowledge, skills, and behaviors that training should emphasize. It is based on examination of the conditions in which tasks are performed, including equipment and environment of the job, time constraints, safety considerations, and performance standards.

3. Explain how to assess employees' readiness for training.
Readiness for training is a combination of employee characteristics and positive work environment that permit training. The necessary employee characteristics include ability to learn the subject matter, favorable attitudes toward the training, and motivation to learn. A positive work environment avoids situational constraints such as lack of money and time. In a positive environment, both peers and management support training.

4. Describe how to plan an effective training program.
Planning begins with establishing objectives for the training program. These should define an expected performance or outcome, the desired level of performance, and the conditions under which the performance should occur. Based on the objectives, the planner decides who will provide the training, what topics the training will cover, what training methods to use, and how to evaluate the training. Even when organizations purchase outside training, someone in the organization, usually a member of the HR department, often is responsible for training administration. The training methods selected should be related to the objectives and content of the training program. Training methods may include presentation methods, hands-on methods, or group-building methods.

5. Compare widely used training methods.
Classroom instruction is most widely used and is one of the least expensive and least time-consuming ways to present information on a specific topic to many trainees. It also allows for group interaction and may include hands-on practice. Audiovisual and computer-based training need not require that trainees attend a class, so they can reduce time and money spent on training. Computer-based training may be interactive and may provide for group interaction. On-the-job training methods such as apprenticeships and internships give trainees first-hand experiences. A simulation represents a real-life situation, enabling trainees to see the effects of their decisions without dangerous or expensive consequences. Business games and case studies are other methods for practicing decision-making skills. Participants need to come together in one location or

collaborate online. Behavior modeling gives trainees a chance to observe desired behaviors, so this technique can be effective for teaching interpersonal skills. Experiential programs provide an opportunity for group members to interact in challenging circumstances but may exclude members with disabilities. Team training focuses a team on achievement of a common goal. Action learning offers relevance, because the training focuses on an actual work-related problem.

6. Summarize how to implement a successful training program.
Implementation should apply principles of learning. In general, effective training communicates learning objectives, presents information in distinctive and memorable ways, and helps trainees link the subject matter to their jobs. Employees are most likely to learn when training is linked to job experiences and tasks. Employees learn best when they demonstrate or practice what they have learned and when they receive feedback that helps them improve. Trainees remember information better when it is broken into small chunks, presented with visual images, and practiced many times. Written materials should be easily readable by trainees.

7. Evaluate the success of a training program.
Evaluation of training should look for transfer of training by measuring whether employees are performing the tasks taught in the training program. Assessment of training also should evaluate training outcomes, such as change in attitude, ability to perform a new skill, and recall of facts or behaviors taught in the training program. Training should result in improvement in the group's or organization's outcomes, such as customer satisfaction or sales. An economic measure of training success is return on investment.

8. Describe training methods for employee orientation and diversity management.
Employee orientation is training designed to prepare employees to perform their job effectively, learn about the organization, and establish work relationships. Organizations provide for orientation because, no matter how realistic the information provided during employment interviews and site visits, people feel shock and surprise when they start a new job, and they need to learn the details of how to perform the job. A typical orientation program includes information about the overall company and the department in which the new employee will be working, covering social as well as technical aspects of the job. Orientation programs may combine several training methods, from printed materials to on-the-job training to e-learning. Diversity training is designed to change employee attitudes

about diversity and/or develop skills needed to work with a diverse workforce. Evidence regarding these programs suggests that diversity training is most effec- tive if it is tied to business objectives, has management support, emphasizes behaviors and skills, and is well structured with a way to measure success.

Review and Discussion Questions

1. "Melinda!" bellowed Toran to the company's HR spe- cialist, "I've got a problem, and you've got to solve it. I can't get people in this plant to work together as a team. As if I don't have enough trouble with our com- petitors and our past-due accounts, now I have to put up with running a zoo. You're responsible for seeing that the staff gets along. I want a training proposal on my desk by Monday." Assume you are Melinda.
    a. Is training the solution to this problem? How can you determine the need for training?
    b. Summarize how you would conduct a needs assess- ment.
2. How should an organization assess readiness for learn- ing? In question 1, how do Toran's comments suggest readiness (or lack of readiness) for learning?
3. Assume you are the human resource manager of a small seafood company. The general manager has told you that customers have begun complaining about the quality of your company's fresh fish. Currently, train- ing consists of senior fish cleaners showing new em- ployees how to perform the job. Assuming your needs assessment indicates a need for training, how would you plan a training program? What steps should you take in planning the program?
4. Many organizations turn to e-learning as a less expen- sive alternative to classroom training. What are some other advantages of substituting e-learning for class- room training? What are some disadvantages?
5. Suppose the managers in your organization tend to avoid delegating projects to the people in their groups. As a result, they rarely meet their goals. A training needs analysis indicates that an appropriate solution is training in management skills. You have identified two outside training programs that are con- sistent with your goals. One program involves ex- periential programs, and the other is an interactive computer program. What are the strengths and weak- nesses of each technique? Which would you choose? Why?
6. Consider your current job or a job you recently held. What types of training did you receive for the job? What types of training would you like to receive? Why?
7. A manufacturing company employs several mainte- nance employees. When a problem occurs with the equipment, a maintenance employee receives a de- scription of the symptoms and is supposed to locate and fix the source of the problem. The company re- cently installed a new, complex electronics system. To prepare its maintenance workers, the company pro- vided classroom training. The trainer displayed elec- trical drawings of system components and posed prob- lems about the system. The trainer would point to a component in a drawing and ask, "What would hap- pen if this component were faulty?" Trainees would study the diagrams, describe the likely symptoms, and discuss how to repair the problem. If you were respon- sible for this company's training, how would you eval- uate the success of this training program?
8. In question 7, suppose the maintenance supervisor has complained that trainees are having difficulty trou- bleshooting problems with the new electronics sys- tem. They are spending a great deal of time on prob- lems with the system and coming to the supervisor with frequent questions that show a lack of under- standing. The supervisor is convinced that the em- ployees are motivated to learn the system, and they are well qualified. What do you think might be the problems with the current training program? What recommendations can you make for improving the program?
9. Who should be involved in orientation of new em- ployees? Why would it not be appropriate to provide employee orientation purely online?
10. Why do organizations provide diversity training? What kinds of goals are most suitable for such train- ing?

What's Your HR IQ?

The Student CD-ROM offers two more ways to check what you've learned so far. Use the Self-Assessment exer- cise to test your knowledge of training programs. Go on- line with the Web Exercise to see how well your knowl- edge works in cyberspace.

BusinessWeek Look Who's Building Online Classrooms

Corporations have quickly embraced e-learning, spawning a multimillion-dollar industry. The trend isn't limited to tech courses. Online programs also teach "soft" skills, such as leadership, coaching, and global teamwork.

Learning online has the potential to make education a high priority on the job. After all, analysts write volumes on the value of having an educated, skilled, and speedy workforce. When a lesson can be transmitted quickly to managers and sales teams worldwide through an e-learning program, it begins to show on the bottom line. Says James Moore, Sun Microsystems' director of workforce, "If you look at product development at Sun, by the time I got everyone trained [the traditional way, the product] would be obsolete."

"Our customers want learning strategies to integrate all the learning that goes on in their organization with the corporate strategy," says John W. Humphrey, chairman of Forum Corporation, a 30-year-old provider of leadership training. FT Knowledge, an e-learning company spun off from British publishing giant Pearson, announced earlier in July that it will acquire Forum for $90 million. The move points to a race among old-economy training groups to use the Web to meet company needs. The idea is to mix e-learning with some classroom sessions, using content from varied sources—executives, university professors, or private training companies.

Online learning companies are struggling to stay on top of demand. General manager Robert Brodo of 15-year-old SMG Net, the online business unit of SMG Strategic Management Group in Philadelphia, says each of the company's 40 top clients—Boeing is its largest—has had a conversation about bringing courses online. Eighty percent are implementing courses such as SMG's "simulated company." In the two-day simulation, execs can play out five to six years of business experience. "We can't keep up with the demand, and it's scary when you have to tell a customer that you can't start a project for them until October and November."

Cushing Anderson, program manager for learning-services research at International Data Corporation, is in the process of researching how companies are using e-learning for everyone from managers to sales teams and programmers. In 1999, 6 percent of all corporate training was done online, he says. Anderson's preliminary findings show that doubling in 2001, then doubling again in 2001. "Large companies tend to be more adventurous and have larger budgets to put courses online," he says, though most buy programs from outside vendors.

That isn't the case at IBM. Nancy J. Lewis, IBM's director of management development worldwide, says Big Blue will move its training programs online for 5,000 new managers, saving the company $16 million in 2000. She adds that producing five times the content at a third of the cost has helped convince all of IBM's training units to adopt the model. Her unit alone has reduced its staff from about 500 trainers worldwide to 70 this year.

IBM is so confident about its training that the company has packaged its programs to sell to customers—a side business that is already bringing in "small amounts of revenue" says Lewis's second in command, Robert MacGregor. If IBM's model for e-corporate universities works, it could become a profitable new business.

Heads of training and development have grander plans than simply offering a course online. They expect to change adults' learning habits. Pippa Wicks, CEO of FT Knowledge, says in January 2001 the company will launch a new learning program called Insight Forum. "You do your job through the training program," she says. For instance, a customer service manager would use the program to perform her daily tasks and then receive feedback about her decisions. Employees could take the training individually, or entire departments can share information in open sessions.

Los Altos, California–based Pensare, a four-year-old e-learning company, has a different vision. The company uses a model that lets employees, not trainers, decide what they need to learn, and when. "Tell [employees] what they need to do to help [execute] company strategy, then say, 'What do you think you need to know to help us?'" says Pensare cofounder Dean Hovey.

Online learning, delivered quickly and in a setting where the information can be commonly shared, will make the training process more engaging and less of a chore, experts say. And it'll give companies an advantage over competitors. 3Com, for one, places a high value on e-learning. "I've got senior people saying that they want more [online training]," says Geoff Roberts, 3Com's director of education. 3Com's agility with technology makes it imperative to train not only internal employees but also its customers. "We're selling into a market where 80 percent of the people don't understand the industry," he says.

As companies convert lessons to be delivered over intranets, one massive obstacle remains: Unless it's mandatory, most employees drop out of training. "Getting 2 percent to 3 percent [of a workforce to sign on] can't happen," says Forum's Humphrey. "There have to be more breakthroughs to make learning less intrusive to the worker." His suggestion to clients: Make lessons relevant.

The good news is that Generation Y workers—recent college grads—are more comfortable using the Web. In 2003, analysts expect 95 percent of college students to use the Internet; only 41.7 percent did in 1996. This means college grads entering the workforce in 2003, and beyond, may be more receptive to e-learning. In fact, they may expect it.

SOURCE: M. Schneider, "Look Who's Building Online Classrooms," *BusinessWeek*, July 25, 2000.

Questions

1. What features are necessary for e-learning to be effective? Explain.
2. At many organizations, online learning blurs the boundaries between training and work, because the organizations expect trainees to complete e-learning during breaks or outside of work hours. Is this expectation realistic? Why or why not?
3. What measures can an organization take to improve employees' motivation to participate in e-learning?

Case: Training Helps the Rubber Hit the Road at Tires Plus

Customers visiting an old-fashioned tire shop often encounter dirty service areas and personnel who know plenty about installing tires on cars but little about providing courteous service. Car owners used to such experiences are pleasantly surprised when they visit one of Tires Plus's 150 stores, located in the Midwestern United States. Showrooms are clean and organized, each including a customer lounge with television sets, tables, and play areas for children. Salespeople wear white shirts and ties, and they immediately greet customers as they enter. Fast, friendly service is the norm. Customers are encouraged to walk into the shop to watch the mechanics at work. No wonder, then, that Tires Plus has recently been experiencing growth of more than 20 percent a year. With sales at $200 million a year, Tires Plus has become the sixth-largest independent tire retailer and has ambitious plans for expansion nationwide.

Cofounder Tom Gegax insists that growth will not come at the expense of employees or customers. One of the company's most important goals is to ensure that Tires Plus's business strategy promotes employee growth and loyalty, as well as fairness in economic and social terms. Rapid expansion will require Tires Plus to recruit, hire, and develop a fast-growing workforce in spite of the nation's tight labor market.

To help reach its goals, the company is investing in training. As one of Tires Plus's trainers notes, "The more information and education we can give people, the better equipped they'll be to advance within the company. And if they're moving up, hopefully they'll see opportunities to expand with us." In other words, the company's intensive training and policy of internal promotion motivate employees who want to advance in their careers. This supports Tires Plus's efforts to reduce employee turnover and improve customer relations.

About 1,700 Tires Plus employees spend about 60,000 hours a year in formal training programs offered by Tires Plus University at a cost of $3 million. The company's training facility includes a 250-seat auditorium, replicas of store showrooms and service shops, a computer lab, a media center, and four full-time trainers. New hires receive a week of product, sales, or mechanical training, depending on their positions. Employees spend hours in classrooms and in the simulated tire shops, learning how to create a service environment that encourages customers to return and recommend the company to their friends.

The Tires Plus training program also supports its policy of promoting from within. Tires Plus career tracks help employees develop into mechanics and store managers. This effort has helped the company recruit new employees, retain current employees, and fill leadership positions. Tires Plus also devotes time and money to giving employees opportunities to advance, which helps recruitment and retention. For example, a tire technician who wants to become a mechanic can take an 11-week course at Tires Plus University, learning the basics of the mechanic's job. After completing this formal training, the technician works with an on-the-job mentor until ready to work alone as a mechanic. The course is free, and the prospective mechanic gets paid a full salary while participating in training. Similarly, employees who show potential to be managers receive 80 hours of leadership training.

The company's investment in training shows up in its business performance. Store surveys show a 96 percent customer satisfaction rate. Employee turnover is 8 percent—high for businesses in general, but much lower than the 20 percent average for companies in the automotive service industry. And the company's impressive growth suggests that investing in training is a winning strategy.

SOURCE: K. Dobbs, "Tires Plus Takes the Training High Road," *Training*, April 2000, pp. 57–63.

Questions

1. How does training support Tires Plus's business objectives?
2. How might the company measure the effectiveness of its training?
3. How might Tires Plus apply e-learning to its training program and training objectives?

Notes

1. E. Barker, "High-Test Education," *Inc.*, July 2001, pp. 81–82.
2. I. L. Goldstein, E. P. Braverman, and H. Goldstein, "Needs Assessment," in *Developing Human Resources*, ed. K. N. Wexley (Washington, DC: Bureau of National Affairs, 1991), pp. 5-35–5-75.
3. D. Stamps, "Deep Blue Sea," *Training*, July 1999, pp. 39–43.
4. J. Z. Rouillier and I. L. Goldstein, "Determinants of the Climate for Transfer of Training" (presented at Society of Industrial/Organizational Psychology meetings, St. Louis, MO, 1991); J. S. Russell, J. R. Terborg, and M. L. Powers, "Organizational Performance and Organizational Level Training and Support," *Personnel Psychology* 38 (1985), pp. 849–63; H. Baumgartel, G. J. Sullivan, and L. E. Dunn, "How Organizational Climate and Personality Affect the Payoff from Advanced Management Training Sessions," *Kansas Business Review* 5 (1978), pp. 1–10.
5. R. A. Noe, "Trainees' Attributes and Attitudes: Neglected Influences on Training Effectiveness," *Academy of Management Review* 11 (1986), pp. 736–49; T. T. Baldwin, R. T. Magjuka, and B. T. Loher, "The Perils of Participation: Effects of Choice on Trainee Motivation and Learning," *Personnel Psychology* 44 (1991), pp. 51–66; S. I. Tannenbaum, J. E. Mathieu, E. Salas, and J. A. Cannon-Bowers, "Meeting Trainees' Expectations: The Influence of Training Fulfillment on the Development of Commitment, Self-Efficacy, and Motivation," *Journal of Applied Psychology* 76 (1991), pp. 759–69.
6. L. H. Peters, E. J. O'Connor, and J. R. Eulberg, "Situational Constraints: Sources, Consequences, and Future Considerations," in *Research in Personnel and Human Resource Management*, ed. K. M. Rowland and G. R. Ferris (Greenwich, CT: JAI Press, 1985), vol. 3, pp. 79–114; E. J. O'Connor, L. H. Peters, A. Pooyan, J. Weekley, B. Frank, and B. Erenkranz, "Situational Constraints' Effects on Performance, Affective Reactions, and Turnover: A Field Replication and Extension," *Journal of Applied Psychology* 69 (1984), pp. 663–72; D. J. Cohen, "What Motivates Trainees?" *Training and Development Journal*, November 1990, pp. 91–93; Russell, Terborg, and Powers, "Organizational Performance."
7. J. B. Tracey, S. I. Trannenbaum, and M. J. Kavanaugh, "Applying Trade Skills on the Job: The Importance of the Work Environment," *Journal of Applied Psychology* 80 (1995), pp. 239–52; P. E. Tesluk, J. L. Farr, J. E. Mathieu, and R. J. Vance, "Generalization of Employee Involvement Training to the Job Setting: Individuals and Situational Effects," *Personnel Psychology* 48 (1995), pp. 607–32; J. K. Ford, M. A. Quinones, D. J. Sego, and J. S. Sorra, "Factors Affecting the Opportunity to Perform Trained Tasks on the Job," *Personnel Psychology* 45 (1992), pp. 511–27.
8. B. Mager, *Preparing Instructional Objectives*, 2nd ed. (Belmont, CA: Lake Publishing, 1984); B. J. Smith and B. L. Delahaye, *How to Be an Effective Trainer*, 2nd ed. (New York: Wiley, 1987).
9. J. Bailey, "Community Colleges Can Help Small Firms with Job Training," *The Wall Street Journal Online*, http://online.wsj.com, February 19, 2002.
10. R. Zemke and J. Armstrong, "How Long Does It Take? (The Sequel)," *Training*, May 1997, pp. 69–79.
11. C. Lee, "Who Gets Trained in What?" *Training*, October 1991, pp. 47–59; W. Hannum, *The Application of Emerging Training Technology* (San Diego, CA: University Associates, 1990); B. Filipczak, "Make Room for Training," *Training*, October 1991, pp. 76–82; A. P. Carnevale, L. J. Gainer, and A. S. Meltzer, *Workplace Basics Training Manual* (San Francisco: Jossey-Bass, 1990).
12. J. M. Rosow and R. Zager, *Training: The Competitive Edge* (San Francisco: Jossey-Bass, 1988).
13. T. Skylar, "When Training Collides with a 35-Ton Truck," *Training*, March 1996, pp. 32–38.
14. G. Yohe, "The Best of Both?" *Human Resource Executive*, March 6, 2002, pp. 35, 38–39.
15. D. Filipowski, "How Federal Express Makes Your Package Its Most Important," *Personnel Journal*, February 1992, pp. 40–46.
16. G. Stevens and E. Stevens, "The Truth about EPSS," *Training and Development* 50 (1996), pp. 59–61.
17. "In Your Face EPSSs," *Training*, April 1996, pp. 101–2.
18. R. W. Glover, *Apprenticeship Lessons from Abroad* (Columbus, OH: National Center for Research in Vocational Education, 1986).
19. Commerce Clearing House, *Orientation–Training* (Chicago: Personnel Practices Communications, Commerce Clearing House, 1981), pp. 501–905.
20. M. McCain, "Apprenticeship Lessons from Europe," *Training and Development*, November 1994, pp. 38–41.
21. Bailey, "Community College Can Help Small Firms with Job Training."
22. W. J. Rothwell and H. C. Kanzanas, "Planned OJT Is Productive OJT," *Training and Development Journal*, October 1990, pp. 53–56.
23. B. Filipczak, "Who Owns Your OJT?" *Training*, December 1996, pp. 44–49.
24. A. F. Cheng, "Hands-on Learning at Motorola,"

Training and Development Journal, October 1990, pp. 34–35.

25. N. Adams, "Lessons from the Virtual World," *Training*, June 1995, pp. 45–48.

26. Ibid.

27. A. Richter, "Board Games for Managers," *Training and Development Journal*, July 1990, pp. 95–97.

28. G. P. Latham and L. M. Saari, "Application of Social Learning Theory to Training Supervisors through Behavior Modeling," *Journal of Applied Psychology* 64 (1979), pp. 239–46.

29. C. Steinfeld, "Challenge Courses Can Build Strong Teams," *Training and Development*, April 1997, pp. 12–13.

30. P. F. Buller, J. R. Cragun, and G. M. McEvoy, "Getting the Most out of Outdoor Training," *Training and Development Journal*, March 1991, pp. 58–61.

31. C. Clements, R. J. Wagner, C. C. Roland, "The Ins and Outs of Experiential Training," *Training and Development*, February 1995, pp. 52–56.

32. P. Froiland, "Action Learning," *Training*, January 1994, pp. 27–34.

33. Ibid.

34. C. E. Schneier, "Training and Development Programs: What Learning Theory and Research Have to Offer," *Personnel Journal*, April 1974, pp. 288–93; M. Knowles, "Adult Learning," in *Training and Development Handbook*, 3rd ed., ed. R. L. Craig (New York: McGraw-Hill, 1987), pp. 168–79; R. Zemke and S. Zemke, "30 Things We Know for Sure about Adult Learning," *Training*, June 1981, pp. 45–52; B. J. Smith and B. L. Delahaye, *How to Be an Effective Trainer*, 2nd ed. (New York: Wiley, 1987).

35. K. A. Smith-Jentsch, F. G. Jentsch, S. C. Payne, and E. Salas, "Can Pretraining Experiences Explain Individual Differences in Learning?" *Journal of Applied Psychology* 81 (1996), pp. 110–16.

36. W. McGehee and P. W. Thayer, *Training in Business and Industry* (New York: Wiley, 1961).

37. R. M. Gagne and K. L. Medsker, *The Condition of Learning* (Fort Worth, TX: Harcourt-Brace, 1996).

38. J. C. Naylor and G. D. Briggs, "The Effects of Task Complexity and Task Organization on the Relative Efficiency of Part and Whole Training Methods," *Journal of Experimental Psychology* 65 (1963), pp. 217–24.

39. K. Mantyla, *Blended E-Learning* (Alexandria, VA: ASTD, 2001).

40. B. Gerber, "Does Your Training Make a Difference? Prove It!" *Training*, March 1995, pp. 27–34.

41. M. R. Louis, "Surprise and Sense Making: What Newcomers Experience in Entering Unfamiliar Organizational Settings," *Administrative Science Quarterly* 25 (1980), pp. 226–51.

42. Pillsbury engineering orientation program.

43. C. Joinson, "Hit the Floor Running, Start the Cart . . . and Other Neat Ways to Train New Employees," *HR Magazine* 6, no. 1 (Winter 2001), downloaded from the Society for Human Resource Management website, www.shrm.org.

44. S. M. Paskoff, "Ending the Workplace Diversity Wars," *Training*, August 1996, pp. 43-47; H. B. Karp and N. Sutton, "Where Diversity Training Goes Wrong," *Training*, July 1993, pp. 30–34.

45. Paskoff, "Ending the Workplace Diversity Wars."

46. A. Brown, "Cultural Immersion Part of Diversity Exercise," *Columbus Dispatch*, January 17, 2000, "Business Today" section, p. 3.

47. S. Rynes and B. Rosen, "A Field Study of Factors Affecting the Adoption and Perceived Success of Diversity Training," *Personnel Psychology* 48 (1995), pp. 247–70.

48. S. Rynes and B. Rosen, "What Makes Diversity Programs Work?" *HR Magazine*, October 1994, pp. 67–73; Rynes and Rosen, "A Field Survey of Factors Affecting the Adoption and Perceived Success of Diversity Training"; J. Gordon, "Different from What? Diversity as a Performance Issue," *Training*, May 1995, pp. 25–33.

VIDEO CASE

Developing a Diverse Workforce

Most jobs start with an interview, whether it's conducted in person, by phone, or even online. Interpersonal dynamics can affect those interviews, so a human resource manager who is looking to develop a diverse workforce to meet company needs must be able to ask the right questions of a candidate and listen to the answers in an objective, controlled manner. The ultimate goal is to evaluate the candidate fairly and accurately so that he or she fits well with job requirements. As you'll see in the video, two managers for the Beck 'n' Call company are interviewing two job applicants, and the way they conduct the interviews and evaluate the applicants will affect both the organization and the individuals—in the composition of the company's workforce and the way those employees later develop in their positions. Both racial and gender issues enter into play in this scenario.

The U.S. workforce is becoming increasingly diverse. Experts estimate that by the year 2006, the American workforce will be 72 percent Caucasian, 11 percent African American, 12 percent Hispanic, and 5 percent Asian and other ethnic or cultural groups. Companies that want to grow and remain competitive need to utilize the talents, experiences, and knowledge of workers from different backgrounds and cultures. If they do not, they may miss a golden opportunity to reach a larger customer base. The customer base for Beck 'n' Call is growing more and more diverse, with African American and Hispanic communities increasing in population in the area where Beck 'n' Call is located. So, it makes sense to recruit, develop, and retain employees who can relate to this broadening customer base and meet their needs in specific ways.

Managers at all companies, whether product or service oriented, can reap the rewards of diversity for their organizations if they practice ethnorelativism—the idea that groups and subcultures are inherently equal. The first step toward this practice may be consciously recognizing their own tendencies toward ethnocentrism—the idea that their own cultures are superior. Once a person recognizes and acknowledges his or her own ethnocentric attitudes and stereotypical beliefs, he or she can open up to new ideas and begin to change. For instance, conducting a structured employment interview with questions that are standardized and focused on accomplishing defined goals will help promote ethnorelativism as opposed to ethnocentrism. In addition, the interview should contain questions that allow the job applicant to respond and demonstrate his or her competencies in ways that are job related, not personal. Hunches and gut feelings should play but a tiny part in such an interview, because once a job applicant becomes an employee, it's the concrete evidence of performance that counts, not whether the interviewer and employee went to the same college or like the same sports teams.

Once employees are hired, it is important to give them opportunities to develop their skills and to advance. This practice not only enhances the employee–employer relationship but also boosts overall productivity of the company. Managers must be aware of the possibility of a glass ceiling in their organization, an invisible barrier that separates female employees or those of different cultural or ethnic backgrounds from top levels of the organization. One way to guard against such barriers to advancement is to examine workforce composition and statistics. Do certain groups of employees top out at middle management positions? Is there a cluster of women and minorities near the bottom of the employment ladder? Is upper management made up entirely of Caucasian males? If so, why? Do all employees receive equal training and opportunities for advancement, or do some receive preferential treatment, even if it isn't obvious? Some studies indicate that companies may also have "glass walls," which are invisible barriers to important lateral moves within the company. These barriers are just as important as the glass ceilings, because a glass wall can prevent an employee from receiving training or experience in certain areas that would enable him or her to move up eventually. Studies confirm the existence of glass ceilings and glass walls; one showed recently that 97 percent of the top U.S. managers are Caucasian and 95 percent of them are male. Limiting career advancement for certain groups undermines morale at a company and reduces productivity and competitiveness. If employees believe that no matter how well they perform they will never advance, they will not try their hardest for the organization. Since a company's most important asset is its employees, it makes sense to be sure they have the opportunities to perform at the highest level of creativity and productivity possible.

A firm like Beck 'n' Call can do plenty to develop its workforce to its fullest potential: If the company hires one of the candidates in the videotaped interview, it can assign a mentor to the new hire to help her learn the ropes and identify ways to further her career within the organization. It can also offer specific training and opportunities for general education. It can make sure that its approach to assessment is fair and accurate, and it can introduce benchmarking to help the employee mark her own progress. Down the road, it could consider ways to enlarge her job. Of course,

the company must review its organizational culture to be sure no glass ceiling or glass walls exist.

Thus, an interview is much more important than a casual conversation about a job. It is the first step toward shaping an organization's future workforce. If it is conducted well, both parties win.

SOURCES: Bureau of Labor Statistics, "BLS Releases New 1996–2006 Employment Projections," **www.bls.gov/new.release/ ecopro.nws.htm**; Sharon Nelton, "Nurturing Diversity," *Nation's Business*, June 1995, pp. 25–27.

Questions

1. Evaluate the interviewers in terms of their interviewing techniques and follow-up. Did either of the managers conduct their interviews with unfair or discriminating practices? Did they evaluate the best person for the job fairly and accurately? What could/should they have done differently?

2. Imagine that you were interviewing either of these candidates. How would you conduct your interview? Write four or five questions that you think should be asked to find the best applicant. Which candidate do you think you would hire, and why? (Be sure to think about long-term implications for both the employee and the organization.)

3. Think of your own experience in job interviews. Based on what you now know about interviewing, in what ways might you be able to improve your own techniques for participating in an interview as a job applicant?

Part 3

Assessing Performance and Developing Employees

Chapter 8
Managing Employees' Performance

Chapter 9
Developing Employees for Future Success

Chapter 10
Separating and Retaining Employees

237

Chapter **8**

Managing Employees' Performance

What Do I Need to Know? After reading this chapter, you should be able to:

1. Identify the activities involved in performance management.

2. Discuss the purposes of performance management systems.

3. Define five criteria for measuring the effectiveness of a performance management system.

4. Compare the major methods for measuring performance.

5. Describe major sources of performance information in terms of their advantages and disadvantages.

6. Define types of rating errors and explain how to minimize them.

7. Explain how to provide performance feedback effectively.

8. Summarize ways to produce improvement in unsatisfactory performance.

9. Discuss legal and ethical issues that affect performance management.

Introduction

When Synergy, a Philadelphia-based software company, was a start-up, its seven employees would regularly meet to discuss performance issues. Sitting around a table, they would informally discuss what changes to make in order to help the company meet its goals. Now that the company has more than 250 employees, that approach to improving performance is no longer practical. Synergy has developed a formal process for giving each employee feedback about his or her performance. That process includes a rating system used by an employee's manager, colleagues, and employees, as well as employees in other departments, to score the employee's performance four times a year. Employees also rate their own performance. This system lets employees compare their impressions of their work with other people's impressions. The regular feedback helps employees improve by focusing on what is important for the success of their careers and for Synergy as a whole.[1]

Rating employees' performance, as Synergy does, is a central part of performance management. **Performance management** is the process through which managers ensure that employees' activities and outputs contribute to the organization's goals. This process requires knowing what activities and outputs are desired, observing whether they occur, and providing feedback to help employees meet expectations. In the course of providing feedback, managers and employees may identify performance problems and establish ways to resolve those problems.

In this chapter we examine a variety of approaches to performance management. We begin by describing the activities involved in managing performance, then discuss the purpose of carrying out this process. Next, we discuss specific approaches to performance management, including the strengths and weaknesses of each approach. We also look at various sources of performance information. The next section explores the kinds of errors that commonly occur during the assessment of performance, as well as ways to reduce those errors. Then we describe ways of giving performance feedback effectively and intervening when performance must improve. Finally, we summarize legal and ethical issues affecting performance management.

performance management
The process through which managers ensure that employees' activities and outputs contribute to the organization's goals.

The Process of Performance Management

Traditional approaches to management have viewed **performance appraisal,** or the measurement of specified areas of an employee's performance, as the primary means of performance management. In the traditional approaches, the human resource department is responsible for setting up and managing a performance appraisal system. Managers conduct performance appraisals as one of their administrative duties. They tend to view the appraisals as a yearly ritual in which they quickly fill out forms and present the information to their employees, one by one. Appraisals include negative information (areas needing improvement), so the meetings for discussing performance appraisals tend to be uncomfortable for managers and employees alike. Often, managers feel they do not know how to evaluate performance effectively, and employees feel they are excluded from the process and that their contributions are not recognized.[2] The left side of Table 8.1 lists some of the criticisms that have been leveled against this style of performance management.

As indicated on the right side of Table 8.1, these problems can be solved through a more effective approach to performance management. Appraising performance need not cause the problems listed in the table. If done correctly, the process can provide valuable benefits to employees and the organization alike. For example, a performance management system can tell top performers that they are valued, encourage communication between managers and their employees, establish uniform standards for evaluating employees, and help the organization identify its strongest and weakest performers. According to the Hay Group, companies on its Global Most Admired list, which it prepares for *Fortune* magazine, have chief executive officers who understand that performance measurement helps the organization motivate people and link performance to rewards.[3] Many of these executives report that performance measurement

performance appraisal
The measurement of specified areas of an employee's performance.

TABLE 8.1

Performance Appraisal Problems and Performance Management Solutions

PROBLEM	SOLUTION
Discourages teamwork	Make collaboration a criterion on which employees will be evaluated.
Evaluators are inconsistent or use different criterion and standards	Provide training for managers; have the HR department look for patterns on appraisals that suggest bias or over- or underevaluation.
Only valuable for very good or very poor employees	Evaluate specific behaviors or results to show specifically what employees need to improve.
Encourages employees to achieve short-term goals	Include both long-term and short-term goals in the appraisal process.
Manager has complete power over the employee	Managers should be appraised for how they appraise their employees.
Too subjective	Evaluate specific behavior or results.
Produces emotional anguish	Focus on behavior; do not criticize employees; conduct appraisal on time.

SOURCE: Based on J. A. Siegel, "86 Your Appraisal Process?" *HR Magazine,* October 2000, pp. 199–202.

encourages employees to cooperate and helps the company focus on smooth operations, customer loyalty, and employee development.

LO1

To meet these objectives, performance management extends beyond mere appraisals to include several activities. As shown in Figure 8.1, these are defining performance, measuring performance, and feeding back performance information. First, the organization specifies which aspects of performance are relevant to the organization. These decisions are based on the job analysis, described in Chapter 4. Next, the organization measures the relevant aspects of performance by conducting performance appraisals. Finally, through performance feedback sessions, managers give employees information about their performance so they can adjust their behavior to meet the organization's goals. When there are performance problems, the feedback session should include efforts to identify and resolve the underlying problems. In ad-

FIGURE 8.1

Stages of the Performance Management Process

Managing Performance to Build Unity across Cultures and Jobs

General Semiconductor, which makes power magnet components for automobiles, cell phones, dishwashers, and other products, has a truly global workforce. Employees are spread from North America to Asia, and they speak many languages. Although the company is headquartered on Long Island, New York, only 200 of its 5,600 employees work in the United States. General Semiconductor facilities are located in Ireland, Continental Europe, Taiwan, and China.

General Semiconductor's management decided that for successful growth, the company needed to identify a core set of company values and to make sure that employees at all facilities worked according to those values. The company has eight values, which it calls "culture points." They are integrity; passion for customer satisfaction; respect for, responsiveness to, and empowerment of employees; technology and innovation;

continual improvement; teamwork; job satisfaction; and a winning, competitive spirit. The company's HRM staff developed a leadership and problem-solving program, which General Semiconductor used to spread the eight values throughout the company.

Consistent with these values, General Semiconductor developed a program it calls People Plus. This performance management program uses a performance appraisal conducted from several viewpoints. Each employee appraises his or her own performance and chooses managers, peers, and subordinates to contribute their assessments of the employee's performance. The various assessments are compiled, and a psychologist meets with the employee to discuss the evaluations and recommend how to improve the weaknesses identified.

People Plus focuses on identifying the unique talents and contributions of every

employee. It also helps employees understand how others on the work team view them. Employees believe that People Plus brings the company together, even though employees work at far-flung locations.

The positive results of the program are measurable. Two years after People Plus began, a survey of the senior management group showed that of 39 development areas, 36 showed improvement. The program has also contributed to a very stable workforce with a low turnover rate across all locations. General Semiconductor gives top scores to the program—and to its employees, which the company claims are the most knowledgeable and well trained in its industry.

SOURCE: C. Cole, "Eight Values Bring Unity to a Worldwide Company," *Workforce*, March 2001, pp. 44–45; General Semiconductor website, www.generalsemiconductor.com, September 2, 2001.

dition, performance feedback can come through the organization's rewards, as described in Chapter 12.

Using this performance management process in place of the traditional performance appraisal routine helps managers and employees focus on the organization's goals. The "Best Practices" box describes how General Semiconductor uses performance management to give a common focus to employees around the globe.

Computer software is available to help managers at various stages of performance management.[4] Software can help managers customize performance measurement forms. The manager uses the software to establish a set of performance standards for each job. The manager rates each employee according to the predetermined standards, and the software provides a report that compares the employee's performance to the standards and identifies the employee's strengths and weaknesses. Other software offers help with diagnosing performance problems. This type of software asks questions—for example, Does the employee work under time pressure? The answers suggest reasons for performance problems and ways the manager can help the employee improve.

Purposes of Performance Management

Organizations establish performance management systems to meet three broad purposes: strategic, administrative, and developmental. *Strategic purpose* means effective performance management helps the organization achieve its business objectives. It does this by helping to link employees' behavior with the organization's goals. Performance management starts with defining what the organization expects from each employee. It measures each employee's performance to identify where those expectations are and are not being met. This enables the organization to take corrective action, such as training, incentives, or discipline. Performance management can achieve its strategic purpose only when measurements are truly linked to the organization's goals and when the goals and feedback about performance are communicated to employees.

The *administrative purpose* of a performance management system refers to the ways in which organizations use the system to provide information for day-to-day decisions about salary, benefits, and recognition programs. Performance management can also support decision making related to employee retention, termination for poor behavior, and hiring or layoffs. Because performance management supports these administrative decisions, the information in a performance appraisal can have a great impact on the future of individual employees. Managers recognize this, which is the reason they may feel uncomfortable conducting performance appraisals when the appraisal information is negative and, therefore, likely to lead to a layoff, disappointing pay increase, or other negative outcome.

Finally, performance management has a *developmental purpose*, meaning that it serves as a basis for developing employees' knowledge and skills. Even employees who are meeting expectations can become more valuable when they hear and discuss performance feedback. Effective performance feedback makes employees aware of their strengths and of the areas in which they can improve. Discussing areas in which employees fall short can help the employees and their manager uncover the source of problems and identify steps for improvement. Although discussing weaknesses may feel uncomfortable, it is necessary when performance management has a developmental purpose.

Criteria for Effective Performance Management

In Chapter 6, we saw that there are many ways to predict performance of a job candidate. Similarly, there are many ways to measure the performance of an employee. For performance management to achieve its goals, its methods for measuring performance must be good. Selecting these measures is a critical part of planning a performance

FIGURE 8.2

Criteria for Effective
Performance Measures

management system. Criteria that determine the effectiveness of performance measures include each measure's fit with the organization's strategy, its validity, its reliability, the degree to which it is acceptable to the organization, and the extent to which it gives employees specific feedback. These criteria are summarized in Figure 8.2.

A performance management system should aim at achieving employee behavior and attitudes that support the organization's strategy, goals, and culture. If a company emphasizes customer service, then its performance management system should define the kinds of behavior that contribute to good customer service. Performance appraisals should measure whether employees are engaging in those behaviors. Feedback should help employees improve in those areas. When an organization's strategy changes, human resource personnel should help managers assess how the performance management system should change to serve the new strategy.

As we discussed in Chapter 6, *validity* is the extent to which a measurement tool actually measures what it is intended to measure. In the case of performance appraisal, validity refers to whether the appraisal measures all the relevant aspects of performance and omits irrelevant aspects of performance. Figure 8.3 shows two sets of information. The circle on the left represents all the information in a performance appraisal; the circle on the right represents all relevant measures of job performance. The overlap of the circles contains the valid information. Information that is gathered but irrelevant is "contamination." Comparing salespeople based on how many calls they make to customers could be a contaminated measure. Making a lot of calls

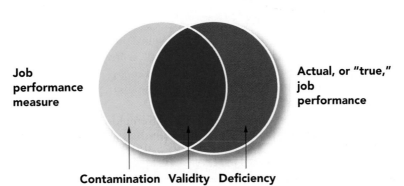

Job performance measure

Actual, or "true," job performance

Contamination   Validity   Deficiency

FIGURE 8.3

Contamination and
Deficiency of a Job
Performance Measure

does not necessarily improve sales or customer satisfaction, unless every salesperson makes only well-planned calls. Information that is not gathered but is relevant represents a deficiency of the performance measure. For example, suppose a company measures whether employees have good attendance records but not whether they work efficiently. This limited performance appraisal is unlikely to provide a full picture of employees' contribution to the company. Performance measures should minimize both contamination and deficiency.

With regard to a performance measure, reliability describes the consistency of the results that the performance measure will deliver. *Interrater reliability* is consistency of results when more than one person measures performance. Simply asking a supervisor to rate an employee's performance on a scale of 1 to 5 would likely have low interrater reliability; the rating will differ depending on who is scoring the employees. *Test-retest reliability* refers to consistency of results over time. If a performance measure lacks test-retest reliability, determining whether an employee's performance has truly changed over time will be impossible.

Whether or not a measure is valid and reliable, it must meet the practical standard of being acceptable to the people who use it. For example, the people who use a performance measure must believe that it is not too time-consuming. Likewise, if employees believe the measure is unfair, they will not use the feedback as a basis for improving their performance.

Finally, a performance measure should specifically tell employees what is expected of them and how they can meet those expectations. Being specific helps performance management meet the goals of supporting strategy and developing employees. If a measure does not specify what an employee must do to help the organization achieve its goals, it does not support the strategy. If the measure fails to point out employees' performance problems, they will not know how to improve.

Methods for Measuring Performance

LO4

Organizations have developed a wide variety of methods for measuring performance. Some methods rank each employee to compare employees' performance. Other methods break down the evaluation into ratings of individual attributes, behaviors, or results. Many organizations use a measurement system that includes a variety of the preceding measures, as in the case of applying total quality management to performance management. Table 8.2 compares these methods in terms of our criteria for effective performance management.

Making Comparisons

simple ranking
Method of performance measurement that requires managers to rank employees in their group from the highest performer to the poorest performer.

The performance appraisal method may require the rater to compare one individual's performance with that of others. This method involves some form of ranking, in which some employees are best, some are average, and others are worst. The usual techniques for making comparisons are simple ranking, forced distribution, and paired comparison.

Simple ranking requires managers to rank employees in their group from the highest performer to the poorest performer. In a variation of this approach, *alternation ranking*, the manager works from a list of employees. First, the manager decides which employee is best and crosses that person's name off the list. From the remaining

TABLE 8.2

Basic Approaches to Performance Measurement

APPROACH	CRITERIA				
	FIT WITH STRATEGY	VALIDITY	RELIABILITY	ACCEPTABILITY	SPECIFICITY
Comparative	Poor, unless manager takes time to make link	Can be high if ratings are done carefully	Depends on rater, but usually no measure of agreement used	Moderate; easy to develop and use but resistant to normative standard	Very low
Attribute	Usually low; requires manager to make link	Usually low; can be fine if developed carefully	Usually low; can be improved by specific definitions of attributes	High; easy to develop and use	Very low
Behavioral	Can be quite high	Usually high; minimizes contamination and deficiency	Usually high	Moderate; difficult to develop, but accepted well for use	Very high
Results	Very high	Usually high; can be both contaminated and deficient	High; main problem can be test–retest— depends on timing of measure	High; usually developed with input from those to be evaluated	High regarding results, but low regarding behaviors necessary to achieve them
Quality	Very high	High, but can be both contaminated and deficient	High	High; usually developed with input from those to be evaluated	High regarding results, but low regarding behaviors necessary to achieve them

names, the manager selects the worst employee and crosses off that name. The process continues with the manager selecting the second best, second worst, third best, and so on until all the employees have been ranked. The major downside of ranking involves validity. To state a performance measure as broadly as "best" or "worst" doesn't define what exactly is good or bad about the person's contribution to the organization. Ranking therefore raises questions about fairness.

Another way to compare employees' performance is with the **forced-distribution method.** This type of performance measurement assigns a certain percentage of employees to each category in a set of categories. For example, the organization might establish the following percentages and categories:

- Exceptional—5 percent
- Exceeds standards—25 percent
- Meets standards—55 percent
- Room for improvement—10 percent
- Not acceptable—5 percent

forced-distribution method
Method of performance measurement that assigns a certain percentage of employees to each category in a set of categories.

The manager completing the performance appraisal would rate 5 percent of his or her employees as exceptional, 25 percent as exceeding standards, and so on. A forced-distribution approach works best if the members of a group really do vary this much in terms of their performance. It overcomes the temptation to rate everyone high in order to avoid conflict. However, a manager who does very well at selecting, motivating, and training employees will have a group of high performers. This manager would have difficulty assigning employees to the bottom categories. In that situation, saying that some employees require improvement or are "not acceptable" not only will be inaccurate, but will hurt morale.

paired-comparison method
Method of performance measurement that compares each employee with each other employee to establish rankings.

Another variation on rankings is the **paired-comparison method.** This approach involves comparing each employee with each other employee to establish rankings. Suppose a manager has five employees, Allen, Barbara, Caitlin, David, and Edgar. The manager compares Allen's performance to Barbara's and assigns one point to whichever employer is the higher performer. Then the manager compares Allen's performance to Caitlin's, then to David's, and finally to Edgar's. The manager repeats this process with Barbara, comparing her performance to Caitlin's, David's, and Edgar's. When the manager has compared every pair of employees, the manager counts the number of points for each employee. The employee with the most points is considered the top-ranked employee. Clearly, this method is time-consuming if a group has more than a handful of employees. For a group of 15, the manager must make 105 comparisons.

In spite of the drawbacks, ranking employees offers some benefits. It counteracts the tendency to avoid controversy by rating everyone favorably or near the center of the scale. Also, if some managers tend to evaluate behavior more strictly (or more leniently) than others, a ranking system can erase that tendency from performance scores. Therefore, ranking systems can be useful for supporting decisions about how to distribute pay raises or layoffs. Some ranking systems are easy to use, which makes them acceptable to the managers who use them. A major drawback of rankings is that

Ford had to reassess its forced ranking system. Facing potential legal problems, the company was challenged to adopt a new performance ranking system. What type of performance management system might be more effective?

they often are not linked to the organization's goals. Also, a simple ranking system leaves the basis for the ranking open to interpretation. In that case, the rankings are not helpful for employee development and may hurt morale or result in legal challenges.

Rating Individuals

Instead of focusing on arranging a group of employees from best to worst, performance measurement can look at each employee's performance relative to a uniform set of standards. The measurement may evaluate employees in terms of *attributes* (characteristics or traits) believed desirable. Or the measurements may identify whether employees have *behaved* in desirable ways, such as closing sales or completing assignments. For both approaches, the performance management system must identify the desired attributes or behaviors, then provide a form on which the manager can rate the employee in terms of those attributes or behaviors. Typically, the form includes a rating scale, such as a scale from 1 to 5, where 1 is the worst performance and 5 is the best.

Rating Attributes

The most widely used method for rating attributes is the **graphic rating scale.** This method lists traits and provides a rating scale for each trait. The employer uses the scale to indicate the extent to which the employee being rated displays the traits. The rating scale may provide points to circle (as on a scale going from 1 for poor to 5 for excellent), or it may provide a line representing a range of scores, with the manager marking a place along the line. Figure 8.4 shows an example of a graphic rating scale that uses a set of ratings from 1 to 5. A drawback of this approach is that it leaves to the particular manager the decisions about what is "excellent knowledge" or

graphic rating scale
Method of performance measurement that lists traits and provides a rating scale for each trait; the employer uses the scale to indicate the extent to which an employee displays each trait.

FIGURE 8.4

Example of a Graphic Rating Scale

The following areas of performance are significant to most positions. Indicate your assessment of performance on each dimension by circling the appropriate rating.					
PERFORMANCE DIMENSION	**RATING**				
	DISTINGUISHED	**EXCELLENT**	**COMMENDABLE**	**ADEQUATE**	**POOR**
Knowledge	5	4	3	2	1
Communication	5	4	3	2	1
Judgment	5	4	3	2	1
Managerial skill	5	4	3	2	1
Quality performance	5	4	3	2	1
Teamwork	5	4	3	2	1
Interpersonal skills	5	4	3	2	1
Initiative	5	4	3	2	1
Creativity	5	4	3	2	1
Problem solving	5	4	3	2	1

"commendable judgment" or "poor interpersonal skills." The result is low reliability, because managers are likely to arrive at different judgments.

mixed-standard scales
Method of performance measurement that uses several statements describing each trait to produce a final score for that trait.

To get around this problem, some organizations use **mixed-standard scales,** which use several statements describing each trait to produce a final score for that trait. The manager scores the employee in terms of how the employee compares to each statement. Consider the sample mixed-standard scale in Figure 8.5. To create this scale, the organization determined that the relevant traits are initiative, intelligence, and relations with others. For each trait, sentences were written to describe a person having a high level of that trait, a medium level, and a low level. The sentences for the traits were rearranged so that the nine statements about the three traits are mixed together. The manager who uses this scale reads each sentence, then indicates whether the employee performs above (+), at (0), or below (−) the level described. The key in the middle section of Figure 8.5 tells how to use the pluses, zeros, and minuses to score performance. Someone who excels at every level of performance (pluses for high, medium, and low performance) receives a score of 7 for that trait. Someone who fails to live up to every description of performance (minuses for high, medium, and low) receives a score of 1 for that trait. The bottom of Figure 8.5 calculates the scores for the ratings used in this example.

Rating attributes is the most popular way to measure performance in organizations. In general, attribute-based performance methods are easy to develop and can be applied to a wide variety of jobs and organizations. If the organization is careful to identify which attributes are associated with high performance, and to define them carefully on the appraisal form, these methods can be reliable and valid. However, appraisal forms often fail to meet this standard. In addition, measurement of attributes is rarely linked to the organization's strategy. Furthermore, employees tend perhaps rightly to be defensive about receiving a mere numerical rating on some attribute. How would you feel if you were told you scored 2 on a 5-point scale of initiative or communication skill? The number might seem arbitrary, and it doesn't tell you how to improve.

Rating Behaviors

One way to overcome the drawbacks of rating attributes is to measure employees' behavior. To rate behaviors, the organization begins by defining which behaviors are associated with success on the job. Which kinds of employee behavior help the organization achieve its goals? The appraisal form asks the manager to rate an employee in terms of each of the identified behaviors.

critical-incident method
Method of performance measurement based on managers' records of specific examples of the employee acting in ways that are either effective or ineffective.

One way to rate behaviors is with the **critical-incident method.** This approach requires managers to keep a record of specific examples of the employee acting in ways that are either effective or ineffective. Here's an example of a critical incident in the performance evaluation of an appliance repairperson:

> A customer called in about a refrigerator that was not cooling and was making a clicking noise every few minutes. The technician prediagnosed the cause of the problem and checked his truck for the necessary parts. When he found he did not have them, he checked the parts out from inventory so that the customer's refrigerator would be repaired on his first visit and the customer would be satisfied promptly.

This incident provides evidence of the employee's knowledge of refrigerator repair and concern for efficiency and customer satisfaction. Evaluating performance in this specific way gives employees feedback about what they do well and what they do poorly. The manager can also relate the incidents to how the employee is helping the company achieve its goals. Keeping a daily or weekly log of critical incidents requires

FIGURE 8.5

Example of a Mixed-Standard Scale

Three traits being assessed:	Levels of performance in statements:
Initiative (INTV)	High (H)
Intelligence (INTG)	Medium (M)
Relations with others (RWO)	Low (L)

Instructions: Please indicate next to each statement whether the employee's performance is above (+), equal to (0), or below (–) the statement.

INTV	H	1.	This employee is a real self-starter. The employee always takes the initiative and his/her superior never has to prod this individual.	+
INTG	M	2.	While perhaps this employee is not a genius, s/he is a lot more intelligent than many people I know.	+
RWO	L	3.	This employee has a tendency to get into unnecessary conflicts with other people.	0
INTV	M	4.	While generally this employee shows initiative, occasionally his/her superior must prod him/her to complete work.	+
INTG	L	5.	Although this employee is slower than some in understanding things, and may take a bit longer in learning new things, s/he is of average intelligence.	+
RWO	H	6.	This employee is on good terms with everyone. S/he can get along with people even when s/he does not agree with them.	–
INTV	L	7.	This employee has a bit of a tendency to sit around and wait for directions.	+
INTG	H	8.	This employee is extremely intelligent, and s/he learns very rapidly.	–
RWO	M	9.	This employee gets along with most people. Only very occasionally does s/he have conflicts with others on the job, and these are likely to be minor.	–

Scoring Key:

STATEMENTS			SCORE
HIGH	MEDIUM	LOW	
+	+	+	7
0	+	+	6
–	+	+	5
–	0	+	4
–	–	+	3
–	–	0	2
–	–	–	1

Example score from preceding ratings:

	STATEMENTS			SCORE
	HIGH	MEDIUM	LOW	
Initiative	+	+	+	7
Intelligence	0	+	+	6
Relations with others	–	–	0	2

behaviorally anchored rating scale (BARS)
Method of performance measurement that rates behavior in terms of a scale showing specific statements of behavior that describe different levels of performance.

behavioral observation scale (BOS)
A variation of a BARS which uses all behaviors necessary for effective performance to rate performance at a task.

organizational behavior modification (OBM)
A plan for managing the behavior of employees through a formal system of feedback and reinforcement.

significant effort, however, and managers may resist this requirement. Also, critical incidents may be unique, so they may not support comparisons among employees.

A **behaviorally anchored rating scale (BARS)** builds on the critical-incidents approach. The BARS method is intended to define performance dimensions specifically, using statements of behavior that describe different levels of performance.[5] (The statements are "anchors" of the performance levels.) The scale in Figure 8.6 shows various performance levels for the behavior of "preparing for duty." The statement at the top (rating 7) describes the highest level of preparing for duty. The statement at the bottom describes behavior associated with poor performance. These statements are based on data about past performance. The organization gathers many critical incidents representing effective and ineffective performance, then classifies them from most to least effective. When experts about the job agree the statements clearly represent levels of performance, they are used as anchors to guide the rater. Although BARS can improve interrater reliability, this method can bias the manager's memory. The statements used as anchors can help managers remember similar behaviors, at the expense of other critical incidents.[6]

A **behavioral observation scale (BOS)** is a variation of a BARS. Like a BARS, a BOS is developed from critical incidents.[7] However, while a BARS discards many examples in creating the rating scale, a BOS uses many of them to define all behaviors necessary for effective performance (or behaviors that signal ineffective performance). As a result, a BOS may use 15 behaviors to define levels of performance. Also, a BOS asks the manager to rate the frequency with which the employee has exhibited the behavior during the rating period. These ratings are averaged to compute an overall performance rating. Figure 8.7 provides a simplified example of a BOS for measuring the behavior "overcoming resistance to change."

A major drawback of this method is the amount of information required. A BOS can have 80 or more behaviors, and the manager must remember how often the employee exhibited each behavior in a 6- to 12-month rating period. This is taxing enough for one employee, but managers often must rate 10 or more employees. Even so, compared to BARS and graphic rating scales, managers and employees have said they prefer BOS for ease of use, providing feedback, maintaining objectivity, and suggesting training needs.[8]

Another approach to assessment builds directly on a branch of psychology called *behaviorism*, which holds that individuals' future behavior is determined by their past experiences—specifically, the ways in which past behaviors have been reinforced. People tend to repeat behaviors that have been rewarded in the past. Providing feedback and reinforcement can therefore modify individuals' future behavior. Applied to behavior in organizations, **organizational behavior modification (OBM)** is a plan for managing the behavior of employees through a formal system of feedback and reinforcement. Specific OBM techniques vary, but most have four components:[9]

1. Define a set of key behaviors necessary for job performance.
2. Use a measurement system to assess whether the employee exhibits the key behaviors.
3. Inform employees of the key behaviors, perhaps in terms of goals for how often to exhibit the behaviors.
4. Provide feedback and reinforcement based on employees' behavior.

OBM techniques have been used in a variety of settings. For example, a community mental health agency used OBM to increase the rates and timeliness of critical job behaviors by showing employees the connection between job behaviors and the

FIGURE 8.6

Task-BARS Rating
Dimension: Patrol Officer

Preparing for Duty

7 — Always early for work, gathers all necessary equipment to go to work, fully dressed, uses time before roll call to review previous shift's activities and any new bulletins, takes notes of previous shift's activity mentioned during roll call.

Always early for work, gathers all necessary equipment to go to work, fully dressed, checks activity from previous shifts before going to roll call. — 6

5 — Early for work, has all necessary equipment to go to work, fully dressed.

On time, has all necessary equipment to go to work, fully dressed. — 4

3 — Not fully dressed for roll call, does not have all necessary equipment.

Late for roll call, does not check equipment or vehicle for damage or needed repairs, unable to go to work from roll call, has to go to locker, vehicle, or home to get necessary equipment. — 2

1 — Late for roll call majority of period, does not check equipment or vehicle, does not have necessary equipment to go to work.

SOURCE: Adapted from R. Harvey, "Job Analysis," in *Handbook of Industrial & Organizational Psychology,* 2nd ed., ed. M. Dunnette and L. Hough (Palo Alto, CA: Consulting Psychologists Press, 1991), p. 138.

FIGURE 8.7

Example of a Behavioral Observation Scale

Overcoming Resistance to Change

Directions: Rate the frequency of each behavior from 1 (Almost Never) to 5 (Almost Always).

1. Describes the details of the change to employees.
   Almost Never 1   2   3   4   5   Almost Always

2. Explains why the change is necessary.
   Almost Never 1   2   3   4   5   Almost Always

3. Discusses how the change will affect the employee.
   Almost Never 1   2   3   4   5   Almost Always

4. Listens to the employee's concerns.
   Almost Never 1   2   3   4   5   Almost Always

5. Asks the employee for help in making the change work.
   Almost Never 1   2   3   4   5   Almost Always

6. If necessary, specifies the date for a follow-up meeting
   to respond to the employee's concerns.
   Almost Never 1   2   3   4   5   Almost Always

Score: Total number of points = _____

Performance

Points	Performance Rating
6–10	Below adequate
11–15	Adequate
16–20	Full
21–25	Excellent
26–30	Superior

Scores are set by management.

agency's accomplishments.[10] This process identified job behaviors related to administration, record keeping, and service provided to clients. Feedback and reinforcement improved staff performance. OBM also increased the frequency of safety behaviors in a processing plant.[11]

Behavioral approaches such as organizational behavior modification and rating scales can be very effective. These methods can link the company's goals to the specific behavior required to achieve those goals. Behavioral methods also can generate specific feedback, along with guidance in areas requiring improvements. As a result, these methods tend to be valid. The people to be measured often help in developing the measures, so acceptance tends to be high as well. When raters are well trained, reliability also tends to be high. However, behavioral methods do not work as well for complex jobs in which it is difficult to see a link between behavior and results or there is more than one good way to achieve success.[12]

Measuring Results

Performance measurement can focus on managing the objective, measurable results of a job or work group. Results might include sales, costs, or productivity (output per worker or per dollar spent on production), among many possible measures. Two of the most popular methods for measuring results are measurement of productivity and management by objectives.

Productivity is an important measure of success, because getting more done with a smaller amount of resources (money or people) increases the company's profits. Productivity usually refers to the output of production workers, but it can be used more generally as a performance measure. To do this, the organization identifies the products—set of activities or objectives—it expects a group or individual to accomplish. At a repair shop, for instance, a product might be something like "quality of repair." The next step is to define how to measure production of these products. For quality of repair, the repair shop could track the percentage of items returned because they still do not work after a repair and the percentage of quality-control inspections passed. For each measure, the organization decides what level of performance is desired. Finally, the organization sets up a system for tracking these measures and giving employees feedback about their performance in terms of these measures. This type of performance measurement can be time-consuming to set up, but research suggests it can improve productivity.[13]

Management by objectives (MBO) is a system in which people at each level of the organization set goals in a process that flows from top to bottom, so employees at all levels are contributing to the organization's overall goals. These goals become the standards for evaluating each employee's performance. An MBO system has three components:[14]

1. Goals are specific, difficult, and objective. The goals listed in the second column of Table 8.3 provide two examples for a bank.
2. Managers and their employees work together to set the goals.
3. The manager gives objective feedback through the rating period to monitor progress toward the goals. The two right-hand columns in Table 8.3 are examples of feedback given after one year.

MBO can have a very positive effect on an organization's performance. In 70 studies of MBO's performance, 68 showed that productivity improved.[15] The productivity gains tended to be greatest when top management was highly committed to MBO. Also,

management by objectives (MBO)
A system in which people at each level of the organization set goals in a process that flows from top to bottom, so employees at all levels are contributing to the organization's overall goals; these goals become the standards for evaluating each employee's performance.

TABLE 8.3
Management by Objectives: Two Objectives for a Bank

KEY RESULT AREA	OBJECTIVE	% COMPLETE	ACTUAL PERFORMANCE
Loan portfolio management	Increase portfolio value by 10% over the next 12 months	90	Increased portfolio value by 9% over the past 12 months
Sales	Generate fee income of $30,000 over the next 12 months	150	Generated fee income of $45,000 over the past 12 months

A coach/trainer provides feedback to team members or students, just as managers give feedback to their employees. Feedback provides information about what you're doing well and how you can change to improve. Feedback can contribute to a feeling of achievement.

because staff members are involved in setting goals, it is likely that MBO systems effectively link individual employees' performance with the organization's overall goals.

In general, evaluation of results can be less subjective than other kinds of performance measurement. This makes measuring results highly acceptable to employees and managers alike. Results-oriented performance measurement is also relatively easy to link to the organization's goals. However, measuring results has problems with validity, because results may be affected by circumstances beyond each employee's performance. Also, if the organization measures only final results, it may fail to measure significant aspects of performance that are not directly related to those results. If individuals focus only on aspects of performance that are measured, they may neglect significant skills or behaviors. For example, if the organization measures only productivity, employees may not be concerned enough with customer service. The outcome may be high efficiency (costs are low) but low effectiveness (sales are low, too).[16] Finally, focusing strictly on results does not provide guidance on how to improve. If baseball players are in a hitting slump, simply telling them that their batting average is .190 may not improve their hitting. The coach would help more by providing feedback about how or what to change (for instance, taking one's eye off the ball or dropping one's shoulder).[17]

Total Quality Management

The principles of *total quality management*, introduced in Chapter 2, provide methods for performance measurement and management. Total quality management (TQM) differs from traditional performance measurement in that it assesses both individual performance and the system within which the individual works. This assessment is a process through which employees and their customers work together to set standards and measure performance, with the overall goal being to improve customer satisfaction. In this sense, an employee's customers may be inside or outside the organization; a "customer" is whoever uses the goods or services produced by the employee. The feedback aims at helping employees continuously improve the satisfaction of their customers. The focus on continuously improving customer satisfaction is intended to avoid the pitfall of rating individuals on outcomes, such as sales or profits, over which they do not have complete control.

With TQM, performance measurement essentially combines measurements of attributes and results. The feedback in TQM is of two kinds: (1) subjective feedback from managers, peers, and customers about the employee's personal qualities such as cooperation and initiative; and (2) objective feedback based on the work process.

The second kind of feedback comes from a variety of methods called *statistical quality control*. These methods use charts to detail causes of problems, measures of performance, or relationships between work-related variables. Employees are responsible for tracking these measures to identify areas where they can avoid or correct problems. Because of the focus on systems, this feedback may result in changes to a work process, rather than assuming that a performance problem is the fault of an employee. The TQM system's focus has practical benefits, but it does not serve as well to support decisions about work assignments, training, or compensation.

Sources of Performance Information

LO5

All the methods of performance measurement require decisions about who will collect and analyze the performance information. To qualify for this task, a person should have an understanding of the job requirements and the opportunity to see the employee doing the job. The traditional approach is for managers to gather information about their employees' performance and arrive at performance ratings. However, many sources are possible. As illustrated in Figure 8.8, possibilities of information sources include managers, peers, subordinates, self, and customers.

Using just one person as a source of information poses certain problems. People tend to like some people more than others, and those feelings can bias how an employee's efforts are perceived. Also, one person is likely to see an employee in a limited number of situations. A supervisor, for example, cannot see how an employee behaves when the supervisor is not watching—for example, when a service technician is at the customer's facility. To get as complete an assessment as possible, some organizations combine information from most or all of the possible sources, in what is called a **360-degree performance appraisal.** The "e-HRM" box describes how computerized 360-degree appraisals have improved performance management at Otis Elevator Company.

360-degree performance appraisal
Performance measurement that combines information from the employee's managers, peers, subordinates, self, and customers.

Managers

The most-used source of performance information is the employee's manager. It is usually safe for organizations to assume that supervisors have extensive knowledge of the job requirements and that they have enough opportunity to observe their employees. In other words, managers possess the basic qualifications for this responsibility. Another advantage of using managers to evaluate performance is that they have

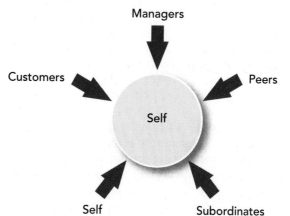

FIGURE 8.8

Sources of Performance Information

E-HRM

Otis Elevator's Appraisals Move Up, Down, and Sideways

Top executives at Otis Elevator Company decided its performance management system was stuck between floors. Otis, the world's largest builder, installer, and servicer of elevators, escalators, and moving walkways, found that its traditional approach required too much paper and time and produced feedback that employees did not consider helpful. Also, the company had just started using project teams extensively and wanted evaluations of managers to assess how well they were managing teams. Otis needed a new performance evaluation system that would accurately assess team leadership and project management skills and that would hold managers accountable for business results. Engineering managers were unused to being evaluated on leadership skills, so the new performance management system should also help them develop those skills.

To address all these issues, Otis Elevator decided to build an evaluation system that employees could access via the Internet and the company's intranet. Engineering managers' direct reports, peers, manager, and customers all log on to the system to participate in performance evaluations. At the website, they use a personal identification number to go to a screen that explains the appraisal form. The form asks them to rate the manager on a series of 75 behaviors related to team leadership in the categories of communications, leading change, customer relationships, people development, team building, process/task knowledge, and innovation and creativity. Employees can practice their evaluations, reviewing and changing ratings until they are ready to submit the completed evaluation. Evaluating a manager takes about 20 minutes, and the evaluations are anonymous.

Once the company has received all the ratings for an engineering manager, the results are compiled. Within about three days, the engineering manager receives an individual profile summarizing the results. This profile compares the manager's ratings with those of an "ideal" leader. The profile also summarizes how the manager was rated by peers, subordinates, managers, and, customers. This format gives the engineering managers specific information about their leadership strengths and weaknesses. Also, the system reduces the time needed to complete evaluations and give feedback, so the engineering managers have more time to work on their weaknesses before their next evaluation.

SOURCE: G. D. Huet-Cox, T. M. Nielsen, and E. Sundstrom, "Get the Most from 360-Degree Feedback: Put It on the Internet," *HR Magazine*, May 1999, pp. 92–103.

an incentive to provide accurate and helpful feedback, because their own success depends so much on their employees' performance.[18] Finally, when managers try to observe employee behavior or discuss performance issues in the feedback session, their feedback can improve performance, and employees tend to perceive the appraisal as accurate.[19]

Still, in some situations, problems can occur with using supervisors as the source of performance information. For employees in some jobs, the supervisor does not have enough opportunity to observe the employee performing job duties. A sales manager with many outside salespeople cannot be with the salespeople on many visits to customers. Even if the sales manager does make a point of traveling with salespeople for a few days, they are likely to be on their best behavior while the manager is there. The manager cannot observe how they perform at other times.

Peers

Another source of performance information is the employee's peers or coworkers. Peers are an excellent source of information about performance in a job where the supervisor does not often observe the employee. Examples include law enforcement and sales. For these and other jobs, peers may have the most opportunity to observe the employee in day-to-day activities. Peers have expert knowledge of job requirements. They also bring a different perspective to the evaluation and can provide extremely valid assessments of performance.[20]

Peer evaluations obviously have some potential disadvantages. Friendships (or rivalries) have the potential to bias ratings. Research, however, has provided little evidence that this is a problem.[21] Another disadvantage is that when the evaluations are done to support administrative decisions, peers are uncomfortable with rating employees for decisions that may affect themselves. Generally, peers are more favorable toward participating in reviews to be used for employee development.[22]

Subordinates

For evaluating the performance of managers, subordinates are an especially valuable source of information. Subordinates—the people reporting to the manager—often have the best chance to see how well a manager treats employees.

Subordinate evaluations have some potential problems because of the power relationships involved. Subordinates are reluctant to say negative things about the person to whom they report; they prefer to provide feedback anonymously. Managers, however, have a more positive reaction to this type of feedback when the subordinates are identified. When feedback forms require that the subordinates identify themselves, they tend to give the manager higher ratings.[23] Another problem is that when managers receive ratings from their subordinates, the employees have more power, so managers tend to emphasize employee satisfaction, even at the expense of productivity. This issue arises primarily when the evaluations are used for administrative decisions. Therefore, as with peer evaluations, subordinate evaluations are most appropriate for developmental purposes. To protect employees, the process should be anonymous and use at least three employees to rate each manager.

Self

No one has a greater chance to observe the employee's behavior on the job than does the employee himself or herself. Self-ratings are rarely used alone, but they can contribute valuable information. A common approach is to have employees evaluate their own performance before the feedback session. This activity gets employees thinking about their performance. Areas of disagreement between the self-appraisal and other evaluations can be fruitful topics for the feedback session.

The obvious problem with self-ratings is that individuals have a tendency to inflate assessments of their performance. Especially if the ratings will be used for administrative decisions, exaggerating one's contributions has practical benefits. Also, social psychologists have found that, in general, people tend to blame outside circumstances for their failures while taking a large part of the credit for their successes.

Supervisors can soften this tendency by providing frequent feedback, but because people tend to perceive situations this way, self-appraisals are not appropriate as the basis for administrative decisions.[24]

Customers

According to the Bureau of Labor Statistics, service industries will account for almost all job growth between 1996 and 2006.[25] Services are often produced and consumed on the spot—so, the customer is often the only person who directly observes the service performance, and therefore, the customer may be the best source of performance information.

Many companies in service industries have introduced customer evaluations of employee performance. Marriott Corporation provides a customer satisfaction card in every room and mails surveys to a random sample of its hotel customers. Whirlpool's Consumer Services Division conducts both mail and telephone surveys of customers after factory technicians have serviced their appliances. These surveys allow the company to evaluate an individual technician's customer-service behaviors while in the customer's home.

Using customer evaluations of employee performance is appropriate in two situations.[26] The first is when an employee's job requires direct service to the customer or linking the customer to other services within the organization. Second, customer evaluations are appropriate when the organization is interested in gathering information to determine what products and services the customer wants. That is, customer evaluations contribute to the organization's goals by enabling HRM to support the organization's marketing activities. In this regard, customer evaluations are useful both for evaluating an employee's performance and for helping to determine whether the organization can improve customer service by making changes in HRM activities such as training or compensation.

The weakness of customer surveys for performance measurement is their expense. The expenses of a traditional survey, such as printing, postage, telephone, and labor, can add up to hundreds of dollars to evaluate one individual. Many organizations therefore limit the information gathering to short periods once a year.

LO6

Errors in Performance Measurement

As we noted in the previous section, one reason for gathering information from several sources is that performance measurements are not completely objective, and errors can occur. People observe behavior, and they have no practical way of knowing all the circumstances, intentions, and outcomes related to that behavior, so they interpret what they see. In doing so, observers make a number of judgment calls, and in some situations may even distort information on purpose. Therefore, fairness in rating performance and interpreting performance appraisals requires that managers understand the kinds of distortions that commonly occur.

Types of Rating Errors

Several kinds of errors and biases commonly influence performance measurements. Usually people make these errors unintentionally, especially when the criteria for measuring performance are not very specific.

Similar to Me

A common human tendency is to give a higher evaluation to people we consider similar to ourselves. Most of us tend to think of ourselves as effective. If others seem to be like us in some way—physical characteristics, family or economic background, attitudes, or beliefs—we expect them to be effective as well. Research has demonstrated that this effect, called the **similar-to-me error,** is strong. One unfortunate result (besides inaccuracy) is that when similarity is based on characteristics such as race or sex, the decisions may be discriminatory.[27]

Errors in Distribution

Raters often tend to use only one part of a rating scale—the low scores, the high scores, or the middle of the range. Sometimes a group of employees really do perform equally well (or poorly). In many cases, however, similar ratings for all members of a group are not an accurate description of performance, but an error in distribution. When a rater inaccurately assigns high ratings to all employees, this error is called **leniency.** When a rater incorrectly gives low ratings to all employees, holding them to unreasonably high standards, the resulting error is called **strictness.** Rating all employees as somehow "average" or in the middle of the scale is called the **central tendency.**

These errors pose two problems. First, they make it difficult to distinguish among employees rated by the same person. Decisions about promotions, job assignments, and so on are more difficult if employees all seem to be performing at the same level. Second, these errors create problems in comparing the performance of individuals rated by different raters. If one rater is lenient and the other is strict, employees of the strict rater will receive significantly fewer rewards than employees of the lenient rater. The rewards are not tied to actual performance but are to some degree erroneous.

Halo and Horns

Another common problem is that raters often fail to distinguish among different aspects of performance. Consider a research lab that hires chemists. A chemist who expresses herself very well may appear to have greater knowledge of chemistry than a chemist with poor communication skills. In this example, a rater could easily fail to distinguish between communication skills and scientific skills.

This type of error can make a person look better, or worse, overall. When the rater reacts to one positive performance aspect by rating the employee positively in all areas of performance, the bias is called the **halo error.** As in the example of the chemist who communicates well, giving the impression of overall intelligence. In contrast, when the rater responds to one negative aspect by rating an employee low in other aspects, the bias is called the **horns error.** Suppose an employee is sometimes tardy. The rater takes this as a sign of lack of motivation, lack of ambition, and inability to follow through with responsibility—an example of the horns error.

When raters make halo and horns errors, the performance measurements cannot provide the specific information needed for useful feedback. Halo error signals that no aspects of an employee's performance need improvement, possibly missing opportunities for employee development. Horns error tells the employee that the rater has a low opinion of the employee. The employee is likely to feel defensive and frustrated, rather than motivated to improve.

similar-to-me error Rating error of giving a higher evaluation to people who seem similar to oneself.

leniency error Rating error of assigning inaccurately high ratings to all employees.

strictness error Rating error of giving low ratings to all employees, holding them to unreasonably high standards.

central tendency Incorrectly rating all employees at or near the middle of a rating scale.

halo error Rating error that occurs when the rater reacts to one positive performance aspect by rating the employee positively in all areas of performance.

horns error Rating error that occurs when the rater responds to one negative aspect by rating an employee low in other aspects.

Ways to Reduce Errors

Training can reduce rating errors.[28] Raters can be trained how to avoid rating errors.[29] Prospective raters watch videotapes whose scripts or story-lines are designed to lead them to make specific rating errors. After rating the fictional employees in the videotapes, raters discuss their rating decisions and how such errors affected their rating decisions. Training programs offer tips for avoiding the errors in the future.

Another training method for raters focuses not on errors in rating, but on the complex nature of employee performance.[30] Raters learn to look at many aspects of performance that deserve their attention. Actual examples of performance are studied to bring out various performance dimensions and the standards for those dimensions. The objective of this training is to help raters evaluate employees' performance more thoroughly and accurately.

Political Behavior in Performance Appraisals

Unintentional errors are not the only cause of inaccurate performance measurement. Sometimes the people rating performance distort an evaluation on purpose, to advance their personal goals. This kind of appraisal politics is unhealthy especially because the resulting feedback does not focus on helping employees contribute to the organization's goals. High-performing employees who are rated unfairly will become frustrated, and low-performing employees who are overrated will be rewarded rather than encouraged to improve. Therefore, organizations try to identify and discourage appraisal politics.

Several characteristics of appraisal systems and company culture tend to encourage appraisal politics. Appraisal politics are most likely to occur when raters are accountable to the employee being rated, the goals of rating are not compatible with one another, performance appraisal is directly linked to highly desirable rewards, top executives tolerate or ignore distorted ratings, and senior employees tell newcomers company "folklore" that includes stories about distorted ratings.

Political behavior occurs in every organization. Organizations can minimize appraisal politics by establishing an appraisal system that is fair. Some ways to promote fairness are to involve managers and employees in developing the system, use consistent standards for evaluating different employees, require that feedback be timely and complete, allow employees to challenge their evaluation, and communicate expectations about performance standards, evaluations, and rewards.[31] The organization can also help managers give accurate and fair appraisals by training them to use the appraisal process, encouraging them to recognize accomplishments that the employees themselves have not identified, and fostering a climate of openness in which employees feel they can be honest about their weaknesses.[32]

LO7

Giving Performance Feedback

Once the manager and others have measured an employee's performance, this information must be given to the employee. Only after the employee has received feedback can he or she begin to plan how to correct any shortcomings. Although the feedback stage of performance management is essential, it is uncomfortable to managers and employees. Delivering feedback feels to the manager as if he or she is standing in judgment of others—a role few people enjoy. Receiving criticism feels even worse. Fortunately, managers can do much to smooth the feedback process and make it effective.

Scheduling Performance Feedback

Performance feedback should be a regular, expected management activity. The custom or policy at many organizations is to give formal performance feedback once a year. But annual feedback is not enough. One reason is that managers are responsible for correcting performance deficiencies as soon as they occur. If the manager notices a problem with an employee's behavior in June, but the annual appraisal is scheduled for November, the employee will miss months of opportunities for improvement.

Another reason for frequent performance feedback is that feedback is most effective when the information does not surprise the employee. If an employee has to wait for up to a year to learn what the manager thinks of his work, the employee will wonder whether he is meeting expectations. Employees should instead receive feedback so often that they know what the manager will say during their annual performance review.

Preparing for a Feedback Session

Managers should be well prepared for each formal feedback session. The manager should create the right context for the meeting. The location should be neutral. If the manager's office is the site of unpleasant conversations, a conference room may be more appropriate. In announcing the meeting to an employee, the manager should

When giving performance feedback, do it in an appropriate meeting place. Meet in a setting that is neutral and free of distractions. What other factors are important for a feedback session?

Delivering Performance Feedback

Effective performance feedback communicates information that encourages continued good performance and improves poor performance. Here are some guidelines for communicating feedback to achieve those purposes:

Make feedback a common practice. Feedback should be timely so the employees understand what behaviors and performance outcomes it relates to. This means feedback should not be limited to formal appraisals. To be effective, feedback should be daily and weekly.

Praise effective performance. People often think of performance feedback as criticism and problem solving. But the purpose of the session is to give accurate feedback. Accuracy requires recognizing good performance as well as poor performance. By praising good performance, the manager encourages the employee to continue that behavior. Talking about the good as well as the bad also makes the feedback more believable.

Focus on problem solving, not punishing. When there are performance problems, the feedback should be designed to launch a problem-solving discussion, not to make the employee feel bad. Using feedback as a punishment just causes employees to become defensive and ignores the cause of the problem. The manager should therefore work with the employee to identify the cause of the problem and reach an agreement on how to solve it.

Talk about behavior and results, not about personalities. Especially when feedback is about negative performance, it is essential for the manager's words to distinguish between the person and his or her behaviors. Saying "You're not motivated" or "You're lazy" tends to make the employee defensive and angry. These assumptions about the employee's attitudes and feelings may or may not be true. Better: "You did not meet the deadline that you agreed to because you spent too much time on another project."

Keep criticism to a minimum. In the case of an individual who performs below standard, some of the feedback will have to be critical. Even then, managers should resist the temptation to reel off a list of offenses. Most employees, upon hearing a problem described, will agree that a change is needed. But if the manager keeps piling on the complaints, the employee may become less inclined to cooperate.

Agree to specific goals and a follow-up meeting. Goal setting is essential. It is one of the most effective ways to motivate employees. Focus on behaviors, knowledge, and skills that are under the employee's control. Discussions about needed improvements should end with an agreement on what the employee will do differently and by what date. Then the manager and employee should agree on a date to review the employee's progress toward this goal. Setting a date gives the employee added incentive to work on achieving the goal.

SOURCE: M. London, *Job Feedback: Giving, Seeking, and Using Feedback for Performance Improvement* (Mahwah, NJ: Lawrence Erlbaum Associates, 1997).

describe it as a chance to discuss the role of the employee, the role of the manager, and relationship between them. Managers should also say (and believe) that they would like the meeting to be an open dialogue.

Managers should also enable the employee to be well prepared. The manager should ask the employee to complete a self-assessment ahead of time. The self-assessment requires employees to think about their performance over the past rating period and to be aware of their strengths and weaknesses, so they can participate more fully in the discussion. Even though employees may tend to overstate their accomplishments, the self-assessment can help the manager and employee identify areas for discussion. When the purpose of the assessment is to define areas for development, employees may actually understate their performance. Also, differences between the manager's and the employee's rating may be fruitful areas for discussion.

Conducting the Feedback Session

During the feedback session, managers can take any of three approaches. In the "tell-and-sell" approach, managers tell the employees their ratings and then justify those ratings. In the "tell-and-listen" approach, managers tell employees their ratings and then let the employees explain their side of the story. In the "problem-solving" approach, managers and employees work together to solve performance problems in an atmosphere of respect and encouragement. Not surprisingly, research demonstrates that the problem-solving approach is superior. Perhaps surprisingly, most managers rely on the tell-and-sell approach.[33] Managers can improve employee satisfaction with the feedback process by letting employees voice their opinions and discuss performance goals.[34] The "HR How To" box provides some additional suggestions for conducting an effective feedback session.

Finding Solutions to Performance Problems   LO8

When performance evaluation indicates that an employee's performance is below standard, the feedback process should launch an effort to correct the problem. Even when the employee is meeting current standards, the feedback session may identify areas in which the employee can improve in order to contribute more to the organization in a current or future job. In sum, the final, feedback stage of performance management involves identifying areas for improvement and ways to improve performance in those areas.

As shown in Figure 8.9, the most effective way to improve performance varies according to the employee's ability and motivation. In general, when employees have high levels of ability and motivation, they perform at or above standards. But when they lack ability, motivation, or both, corrective action is needed. The type of action called for depends on what the employee lacks.

To determine an employee's ability level, the manager should consider whether the employee has the knowledge, skills, and abilities needed to perform the job effectively. Sometimes lack of ability is an issue when an employee is new or the job has changed. When a motivated employee lacks knowledge, skills, or abilities in some area, there are a number of ways to help the employee improve. The manager may offer coaching, training, and more detailed feedback. Sometimes it is appropriate to restructure the job so that its demands no longer exceed the employee's abilities.

To determine an employee's level of motivation, managers need to consider whether the employee is holding a job he or she wants. A belief that pay and other rewards are too small can also hurt motivation. Sometimes personal problems are such a distraction that they interfere with motivation. Managers with an unmotivated employee can explore ways to demonstrate that the employee is being treated fairly and rewarded adequately. The solution may be as simple as delivering more positive

FIGURE 8.9

Improving Performance

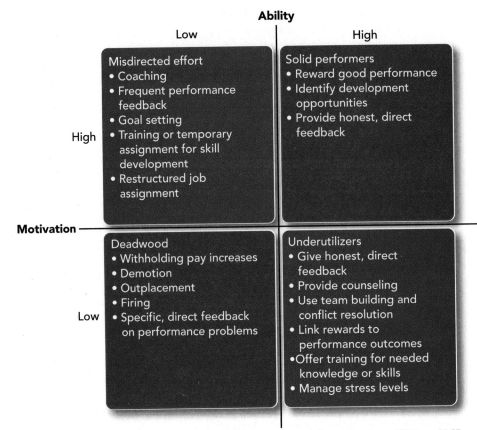

SOURCE: Based on M. London, Job Feedback (Mahwah, N.J.: Lawrence Erlbaum Associates, 1997), pp. 96-97. Used by permission.

feedback (praise). Employees may also benefit from a referral for counseling or help with stress management.

Employees whose performance is poor because they have neither the motivation nor the ability to perform the job may not be a good fit for the position. Performance may improve if the manager directs their attention to the significance of the problem by withholding rewards or by providing specific feedback. If employees do not respond by improving their performance, the organization may have to demote or terminate these underperformers.

As a rule, employees who combine high ability with high motivation are solid performers. As Figure 8.9 indicates, managers should by no means ignore these employees on the grounds of leaving well enough alone. Rather, such employees are likely to appreciate opportunities for further development. Rewards and direct feedback help to maintain these employees' high motivation levels.

LO9

Legal and Ethical Issues in Performance Management

In developing and using performance management systems, human resource professionals need to ensure that these systems meet legal requirements, such as the avoidance of discrimination. In addition, performance management systems should meet ethical standards, such as protection of employees' privacy.

Legal Requirements for Performance Management

Because performance measures play a central role in decisions about pay, promotions, and discipline, employment-related lawsuits often challenge an organization's performance management system. Lawsuits related to performance management usually involve charges of discrimination or unjust dismissal.

Discrimination claims often allege that the performance management system discriminated against employees on the basis of their race of sex. Many performance measures are subjective, and measurement errors, such as those described earlier in the chapter, can easily occur. The Supreme Court has held that the selection guidelines in the federal government's *Uniform Guidelines on Employee Selection Procedures* also apply to performance measurement.[35] (These guidelines were discussed in Chapters 3 and 6.) In general, these guidelines require that organizations avoid using criteria such as race and age as a basis for employment decisions. This requires overcoming widespread rating errors. A substantial body of evidence has shown that white and black raters tend to give higher ratings to members of their own racial group, even after rater training.[36] In addition, evidence suggests that this tendency is strongest when one group is only a small percentage of the total work group. When the vast majority of the group is male, females receive lower ratings; when the minority is male, males receive lower ratings.[37]

With regard to lawsuits filed on the grounds of unjust dismissal, the usual claim is that the person was dismissed for reasons besides the ones that the employer states. Suppose an employee who works for a defense contractor discloses that the company defrauded the government. If the company fires the employee, the employee might argue that the firing was a way to punish the employee for blowing the whistle. In this type of situation, courts generally focus on the employer's performance management system, looking to see whether the firing could have been based on poor performance. To defend itself, the employer would need a performance management system that provides evidence to support its employment decisions.

To protect against both kinds of lawsuits, it is important to have a legally defensible performance management system.[38] Such a system would be based on valid job

Getting ratings from a diverse group of employees and thus getting a variety of viewpoints could be a check on one person's rating errors. Other ways to avoid bias in performance management are to have a legally defensible rating system, to train raters in how to use the system, and to provide a way for employees to appeal an evaluation they think is inaccurate.

analyses, as described in Chapter 4, with the requirements for job success clearly communicated to employees. Performance measurement should evaluate behaviors or results, rather than traits. The organization should use multiple raters (including self-appraisals) and train raters in how to use the system. The organization should provide for a review of all performance ratings by upper-level managers and set up a system for employees to appeal when they believe they were evaluated unfairly. Along with feedback, the system should include a process for coaching or training employees to help them improve, rather than simply dismissing poor performers.

Electronic Monitoring and Employee Privacy

Computer technology now supports many performance management systems. Organizations often store records of employees' performance ratings, disciplinary actions, and work-rule violations in electronic databases. Many companies use personal computers to monitor productivity and other performance measures electronically.[39] For example, at a General Electric customer service center, agents answer over 14,000 telephone inquiries per day. The agents' calls are recorded and reviewed to help the agents improve customer service. American Airlines monitors calls to its reservation centers. Managers can hear what the agents tell customers and see what agents enter on their computers.

Congress has considered laws to regulate computer monitoring. In the meantime, organizations need to consider how employees react to this type of performance measurement. Electronic monitoring provides detailed, accurate information, but employees may find it demoralizing, degrading, and stressful. They are more likely to accept electronic monitoring if the organization explains its purpose and links it to help in improving performance. It also is essential that organizations protect the privacy of performance measurements, as they must do with other employee records.

Summary

1. Identify the activities involved in performance management.
   Performance management is the process through which managers ensure that employees' activities and outputs contribute to the organization's goals. The organization begins by specifying which aspects of performance are relevant to the organization. Next, the organization measures the relevant aspects of performance through performance appraisal. Finally, in performance feedback sessions, managers provide employees with information about their performance so they can adjust their behavior to meet the organization's goals. Feedback includes efforts to identify and solve problems.

2. Discuss the purposes of performance management systems.
   Organizations establish performance management systems to meet three broad purposes. Effective performance management helps the organization with strategic purposes, that is, meeting business objectives. It does this by helping to link employees' behavior with the organization's goals. The administrative purpose of performance management is to provide information for day-to-day decisions about salary, benefits, recognition, and retention or termination. The developmental purpose of performance management is using the system as a basis for developing employees' knowledge and skills.

3. Define five criteria for measuring the effectiveness of a performance management system.
   Performance measures should fit with the organization's strategy by supporting its goals and culture. Performance measures should be valid, so they measure all the relevant aspects of performance and do not measure irrelevant aspects of performance. These measures should also provide interrater and test-retest reliability, so that appraisals are consistent among raters and over time. Performance measurement systems should be acceptable to the people who use them or receive feedback from them. Finally, a performance measure should specifically tell employees what is expected of them and how they can meet those expectations.

4. Compare the major methods for measuring performance.

Performance measurement may use ranking systems such as simple ranking, forced distribution, or paired comparisons to compare one individual's performance with that of other employees. These methods may be time-consuming, and they will be seen as unfair if actual performance is not distributed in the same way as the ranking system requires. However, ranking counteracts some forms of rater bias and helps distinguish employees for administrative decisions. Other approaches involve rating employees' attributes, behaviors, or outcomes. Rating attributes is relatively simple but not always valid, unless attributes are specifically defined. Rating behaviors requires a great deal of information, but these methods can be very effective. They can link behaviors to goals, and ratings by trained raters may be highly reliable. Rating results, such as productivity or achievement of objectives, tends to be less subjective than other kinds of rating, making this approach highly acceptable. Validity may be a problem because of factors outside the employee's control. This method also tends not to provide much basis for determining how to improve. Focusing on quality can provide practical benefits but is not as useful for administrative and developmental decisions.

5. Describe major sources of performance information in terms of their advantages and disadvantages.

Performance information may come from an employee's self-appraisal and from appraisals by the employee's supervisor, employees, peers, and customers. Using only one source makes the appraisal more subjective. Organizations may combine many sources into a 360-degree performance appraisal. Gathering information from each employee's manager may produce accurate information, unless the supervisor has little opportunity to observe the employee. Peers are an excellent source of information about performance in a job where the supervisor does not often observe the employee. Disadvantages are that friendships (or rivalries) may bias ratings and peers may be uncomfortable with the role of rating a friend. Subordinates often have the best chance to see how a manager treats employees. Employees may be reluctant to contribute honest opinions about a supervisor unless they can provide information anonymously. Self-appraisals may be biased, but they do come from the person with the most knowledge of the employee's behavior on the job, and they provide a basis for discussion in feedback sessions, opening up fruitful comparisons and areas of disagreement between the self-appraisal and other appraisals. Customers may be an excellent source of performance information, although obtaining customer feedback tends to be expensive.

6. Define types of rating errors and explain how to minimize them.

People observe behavior often without a practical way of knowing all the relevant circumstances and outcomes, so they necessarily interpret what they see. A common tendency is to give higher evaluations to people we consider similar to ourselves. Other errors involve using only part of the rating scale: Giving all employees ratings at the high end of the scale is called leniency error. Rating everyone at the low end of the scale is called strictness error. Rating all employees at or near the middle is called central tendency. The halo error refers to rating employees positively in all areas because of strong performance observed in one area. The horns error is rating employees negatively in all areas because of weak performance observed in one area. Ways to reduce rater error are training raters to be aware of their tendencies to make rating errors and training them to be sensitive to the complex nature of employee performance so they will consider many aspects of performance in greater depth. Politics also may influence ratings. Organizations can minimize appraisal politics by establishing a fair appraisal system, involving managers and employees in developing the system, allowing employees to challenge evaluations, communicating expectations, and fostering a climate of open discussion.

7. Explain how to provide performance feedback effectively.

Performance feedback should be a regular, scheduled management activity, so that employees can correct problems as soon as they occur. Managers should prepare by establishing a neutral location, emphasizing that the feedback session will be a chance for discussion and asking the employee to prepare a self-assessment. During the feedback session, managers should strive for a problem-solving approach and encourage employees to voice their opinions and discuss performance goals. The manager should look for opportunities to praise and should limit criticism. The discussion should focus on behavior and results rather than on personalities.

8. Summarize ways to produce improvement in unsatisfactory performance.

For an employee who is motivated but lacks ability, the manager should provide coaching and training, give detailed feedback about performance, and consider restructuring the job. For an employee who has ability but lacks motivation, the manager should investigate whether outside problems are a distraction and if so, refer the employee for help. If the problem has to do with the employee's not feeling appreciated or rewarded, the manager should try to deliver more praise and evaluate whether additional pay and other rewards are appropriate. For an employee lacking both ability and motivation, the manager should consider whether the employee is a good fit for the position. Specific feedback or withholding rewards may spur improvement, or the employee may have to be demoted or terminated. Solid employees who are high in ability and motivation will continue so and may be able to contribute even more if the manager provides appropriate direct feedback, rewards, and opportunities for development.

9. Discuss legal and ethical issues that affect performance management.
Lawsuits related to performance management usually involve charges of discrimination or unjust dismissal. Managers must make sure that performance management systems and decisions treat employees equally, without regard to their race, sex, or other protected sta-

tus. Organizations can do this by establishing and using valid performance measures and by training raters to evaluate performance accurately. A system is more likely to be legally defensible if it is based on behaviors and results, rather than on traits, and if multiple raters evaluate each person's performance. The system should include a process for coaching or training employees to help them improve, rather than simply dismissing poor performers. An ethical issue of performance management is the use of electronic monitoring. This type of performance measurement provides detailed, accurate information, but employees may find it demoralizing, degrading, and stressful. They are more likely to accept it if the organization explains its purpose, links it to help in improving performance, and keeps the performance data private.

Review and Discussion Questions

1. How does a complete performance management system differ from the use of annual performance appraisals?
2. Give two examples of an administrative decision that would be based on performance management information. Give two examples of developmental decisions based on this type of information.
3. How can involving employees in the creation of performance standards improve the effectiveness of a performance management system? (Consider the criteria for effectiveness shown in Figure 8.2.)
4. Consider how you might rate the performance of three instructors from whom you are currently taking a course. (If you are currently taking only one or two courses, consider this course and two you recently completed.)
   a. Would it be harder to *rate* the instructors' performance or to *rank* their performance? Why?
   b. Write three items to use in rating the instructors—one each to rate them in terms of an attribute, a behavior, and an outcome.
   c. Which measure in (b) do you think is most valid? Most reliable? Why?
   d. Many colleges use questionnaires to gather data from students about their instructors' performance. Would it be appropriate to use the data for administrative decisions? Developmental decisions? Other decisions? Why or why not?
5. Imagine that a pet supply store is establishing a new performance management system to help employees provide better customer service. Management needs to decide who should participate in measuring the

performance of each of the store's salespeople. From what sources should the store gather information? Why?
6. Would the same sources be appropriate if the store in question 5 will use the performance appraisals to support decisions about which employees to promote? Explain.
7. Suppose you were recently promoted to a supervisory job in a company where you have worked for two years. You genuinely like almost all your coworkers, who now report to you. The only exception is one employee, who dresses more formally than the others and frequently tells jokes that embarrass you and the other workers. Given your preexisting feelings for the employees, how can you measure their performance fairly and effectively?
8. Continuing the example in question 7, imagine that you are preparing for your first performance feedback session. You want the feedback to be effective—that is, you want the feedback to result in improved performance. List five or six steps you can take to achieve your goal.
9. Besides giving employees feedback, what steps can a manager take to improve employees' performance?
10. Suppose you are a human resource professional helping to improve the performance management system of a company that sells and services office equipment. The company operates a call center that takes calls from customers who are having problems with their equipment. Call center employees are supposed to verify that the problem is not one the customer can easily handle (for example, equipment that will not

operate because it has come unplugged). Then, if the problem is not resolved over the phone, the employees arrange for service technicians to visit the customer. The company can charge the customer only if a service technician visits, so performance management of the call center employees focuses on productivity—how quickly they can complete a call and move on to the next caller. To measure this performance efficiently and accurately, the company uses electronic monitoring.

a. How would you expect the employees to react to the electronic monitoring? How might the organization address the employees' concerns?
b. Besides productivity in terms of number of calls, what other performance measures should the performance management system include?
c. How should the organization gather information about the other performance measures?

What's Your HR IQ?

The Student CD-ROM offers two more ways to check what you've learned so far. Use the Self-Assessment exercise to test your knowledge of performance management.

Go online with the Web Exercise to see how well your knowledge works in cyberspace.

BusinessWeek Case

BusinessWeek Focusing on the Softer Side of Managing

In the construction business, interpersonal skills are valued about as highly as rain on wet cement. It's a culture of muscle, not mouth.

Granite Construction, a $1.3 billion company in Watsonville, California, was no exception. For most of its 80 years, a call from the boss's office meant bad news. "Employees were only contacted when something went wrong," says division manager Bruce McGowan, a 20-year veteran who oversees a staff of 700. Because it was corrective, feedback "tended to be negative."

No longer. Spurred by a tight labor market, Granite is starting to deliver feedback of the positive kind. And to make sure the idea takes, starting next year 20 percent of every manager's bonus—which sometimes exceeds 500 percent of base salary—will depend on the person's "people skills." Explains Mike Thomas, director of human resources, "In a market where everyone is struggling to keep people, we want to foster a culture that employees choose to be part of."

Tying compensation to nonfinancial objectives isn't new—General Electric and Hewlett-Packard have done it for years. But more companies are embracing the idea. In a recent survey of 721 North American companies by management consultants Towers Perrin, 66 percent of respondents said they focused exclusively on financial results when assessing employee performance back in 1998. Today only 43 percent do. And that group will shrink to 16 percent by 2004, projects Towers Perrin, as greater attention is paid to softer skills, such as listening to subordinates and giving them opportunities to grow.

Granite, which already uses an anonymous rating system to let its 400 managers see how their coworkers, peers, and superiors perceive them, plans to use 20 touchy-feely metrics—chosen by employees themselves—when calculating bonuses next year. Two weeks ago, the company's 4,300 employees received an e-mail survey asking which skills best serve the company. According to Thomas, 81 percent mentioned integrity and ethics. An additional 79 percent cited teamwork, and 76 percent said knowledge-sharing abilities. The company is still deciding which criteria it will use next year.

Granite is modeling its approach on companies that have gone before. Wells Fargo has made worker satisfaction a top goal since its 1998 acquisition by Norwest, which took the Wells Fargo name. Accomplishing "people goals" at Wells Fargo is linked to 16–25 percent of every manager's annual bonus, which ranges from 10 to 30 percent of base salary.

Wells Fargo requires its 117,000 employees to take an automated phone survey every 18 months to answer such questions as "Do you get enough communication from management?" and "How was your training?" Now subordinates and managers talk more. Says Patricia Callahan, the company's human resource director, "Everyone is much clearer about what constitutes success." Julie Shriver, a recruitment director who has spent nine years at Wells Fargo, says, "It's nice that if you have people skills, you can be rewarded."

Still, how much business sense manager evaluations make is disputed. In a Watson Wyatt Worldwide study last year of 400 U.S. and Canadian companies, employee participation in a manager's review seemed to hurt shareholder return. Explains Brian Anderson, a senior consultant at the firm, "It's largely about implementation. If the appraisal isn't communicated properly, it can create disruption or tension that really takes you in the wrong direction."

That isn't the case at Wells Fargo, insists Callahan, a 25-year veteran. During her review last year, she heard from her nine direct reports that new employees weren't being trained well enough. "I'm not saying I didn't walk away feeling disappointed or wishing I'd done something differently," she says. But she adds, "Feedback is still a precious thing, even if it's not what you expect. Otherwise, you just don't know."

That explains why a manager's people skills may be key to a company's future performance. "Financial outcomes are results. They don't really get you ready for the future, or help you manage the process," says Jeffrey Pfeffer, a professor of organizational behavior at Stanford University's business school. Relying on them exclusively, he adds, is a little like "purchasing the present at the price of the future. If you get results in a way that's destructive of your people and culture, that performance won't last."

Granite's McGowan agrees. "Employees today are

much more concerned about life satisfaction than they used to be, and that isn't something you ignore," he says. "Besides," he adds, "if you can't figure out how to help your people improve, and accelerate the rate at which they do, you're probably not going to meet the goals you've set for your overall business."

SOURCE: C. Loizos, "Focusing on the Softer Side of Managing," *BusinessWeek*, April 10, 2001.

Questions

1. What "people skills" do you think would be important at a construction firm, such as Granite? At a bank, such as Wells Fargo?
2. According to the quality approach to management, performance measurement should take into account systems factors (conditions outside the control of the person being evaluated). What systems factors might affect the use of the skills you identified in question 1?
3. Comment on the quotation from Stanford professor Jeffrey Pfeffer: "Financial outcomes are results. They don't really get you ready for the future, or help you manage the process." What do these words tell us about the significance of measuring "soft skills" like leadership, teamwork, or communication? Does Pfeffer mean financial outcomes are unimportant? Explain.

Case: The Trials and Tribulations of Performance Management at Ford

Many U.S. companies, including Ford Motor Company, General Electric, Microsoft, and Hewlett-Packard, use a method of performance measurement called a forced-ranking system. With this method, employees are ranked as above, at, or below average, and the system requires that a certain percentage of employees fall into each category. For example, at General Electric, managers must place 20 percent of employees in the top category, 70 percent in the middle, and 10 percent in the bottom category. Typically, the bottom 10 percent receive no bonuses and may be terminated. At some companies using forced ranking, morale is poor, and some employees have filed lawsuits.

In spite of these drawbacks, Ford began using a forced-ranking system in the belief that it would help the company build a younger, more ethnically diverse management team able to succeed with new technology and rapid change. Forced rankings would serve as a way to change corporate culture by removing poor performers. (This was not Ford's first effort to remove poor performers. In the late 1990s, Ford offered a package of benefits to salaried employees who resigned or retired early. Managers were directed to tell candidates for this program that management believed they should resign or retire.)

Ford called its forced-ranking system the Performance Management Process. The process involved grading Ford's 1,800 middle managers with an A, B, or C, with 10 percent of managers receiving a C. Managers who received a C for one year received no bonus. Two years at the C level meant possible demotion and termination.

After Ford began using its Performance Management Process, a number of employees filed lawsuits, pressuring the company to change. In two separate lawsuits, 57 employees charged that the performance management system discriminated against older employees. A relatively large proportion of Ford's older workers received Cs.

Ford responded by abandoning the major elements of the Performance Management Process, including the practice of assigning a C to 10 percent of managers. The company modified the system because it had harmed teamwork and morale. Under the modified system, only 5 percent of managers are to receive the lowest grade. In addition, the names of the rankings have changed. In place of A, B, and C grades, the rankings are now called Top Achiever, Achiever, and Improvement Required. Employees ranked as requiring improvement receive counseling to help them improve their performance.

In the time since Ford acknowledged the problems and

modified the system, the company's CEO Jacques Nasser resigned, as did the head of human resources. The new CEO, William Clay Ford Jr., inherited the job of settling the lawsuits.

SOURCE: M. Boyle, "Performance Reviews: Perilous Curves Ahead," *Fortune,* May 28, 2001, pp. 187–88; N. Shirouzu, "Ford Stops Using Letter Rankings to Rate Workers," *The Wall Street Journal,* July 11, 2001, pp. B1, B4; N. Shirouzu, "Nine Ford Workers File Bias Suit Saying Ratings Curb Older Staff," *The Wall Street Journal,* February 15, 2001, p. B14; N. Shirouzu and J. B. White, "Ford Assesses Job Ratings Amid Bias Suit," *The Wall Street Journal,* July 9, 2001, pp. A3, A14; T. D. Schellhardt and S. K. Goo, "At Ford, Buyout Plan Has a Twist," *The Wall Street Journal,* July 22, 1998, pp. B1,

B6; N. Shirouzu, "Ford Is in Talks on Settling Bias Lawsuits," *The Wall Street Journal,* November 2, 2001, p. A4.

Questions

1. Why did Ford use a forced-distribution system for measuring performance? What problems did the system cause?
2. Ford modified its forced-distribution system but did not abandon it. What might be some advantages and disadvantages of its decision?
3. What changes or practices do you recommend to improve performance management at Ford?

Notes

1. P. Kiger, "Frequent Employee Feedback Is Worth the Cost and Time," *Workforce,* March 2001, pp. 62–65.
2. C. Lee, "Performance Appraisal: Can We Manage Away the Curse?" *Training,* May 1996, pp. 44–49.
3. "Measuring People Power," *Fortune,* October 2, 2000.
4. G. Bylinsky, "How Companies Spy on Employees," *Fortune,* November 4, 1991, pp. 131–40; T. L. Griffith, "Teaching Big Brother to Be a Team Player: Computer Monitoring and Quality," *Academy of Management Executive* (1993), pp. 73–80.
5. P. Smith and L. Kendall, "Retranslation of Expectations: An Approach to the Construction of Unambiguous Anchors for Rating Scales," *Journal of Applied Psychology* 47 (1963), pp. 149–55.
6. K. Murphy and J. Constans, "Behavioral Anchors as a Source of Bias in Rating," *Journal of Applied Psychology* 72 (1987), pp. 573–77; M. Piotrowski, J. Barnes-Farrel, and F. Estig, "Behaviorally Anchored Bias: A Replication and Extension of Murphy and Constans," *Journal of Applied Psychology* 74 (1989), pp. 823–26.
7. G. Latham and K. Wexley, *Increasing Productivity through Performance Appraisal* (Boston: Addison-Wesley, 1981).
8. U. Wiersma and G. Latham, "The Practicality of Behavioral Observation Scales, Behavioral Expectation Scales, and Trait Scales," *Personnel Psychology* 39 (1986), pp. 619–28.
9. D. C. Anderson, C. Crowell, J. Sucec, K. Gilligan, and M. Wikoff, "Behavior Management of Client Contacts in a Real Estate Brokerage: Getting Agents to Sell More," *Journal of Organizational Behavior Management* 4 (2001), pp. 580–90; F. Luthans and R. Kreitner, *Organizational Behavior Modification and Beyond* (Glenview, IL: Scott-Foresman, 1975).
10. K. L. Langeland, C. M. Jones, and T. C. Mawhinney, "Improving Staff Performance in a Community Mental Health Setting: Job Analysis, Training, Goal Set-

ting, Feedback, and Years of Data," *Journal of Organizational Behavior Management* 18 (1998), pp. 21–43.
11. J. Komaki, R. Collins, and P. Penn, "The Role of Performance Antecedents and Consequences in Work Motivation," *Journal of Applied Psychology* 67 (1982), pp. 334–40.
12. S. Snell, "Control Theory in Strategic Human Resource Management: The Mediating Effect of Administrative Information," *Academy of Management Journal* 35 (1992), pp. 292–327.
13. R. Pritchard, S. Jones, P. Roth, K. Stuebing, and S. Ekeberg, "The Evaluation of an Integrated Approach to Measuring Organizational Productivity," *Personnel Psychology* 42 (1989), pp. 69–115.
14. G. Odiorne, *MOBII: A System of Managerial Leadership for the 80's* (Belmont, CA: Pitman Publishers, 1986).
15. R. Rodgers and J. Hunter, "Impact of Management by Objectives on Organizational Productivity," *Journal of Applied Psychology* 76 (1991), pp. 322–26.
16. P. Wright, J. George, S. Farnsworth, and G. McMahan, "Productivity and Extra-role Behavior: The Effects of Goals and Incentives on Spontaneous Helping," *Journal of Applied Psychology* 78, no. 3 (1993), pp. 374–81.
17. Latham and Wexley, *Increasing Productivity through Performance Appraisal.*
18. R. Heneman, K. Wexley, and M. Moore, "Performance Rating Accuracy: A Critical Review," *Journal of Business Research* 15 (1987), pp. 431–48.
19. T. Becker and R. Klimoski, "A Field Study of the Relationship between the Organizational Feedback Environment and Performance," *Personnel Psychology* 42 (1989), pp. 343–58; H. M. Findley, W. F. Giles, K. W. Mossholder, "Performance Appraisal and Systems Facets: Relationships with Contextual Performance," *Journal of Applied Psychology* 85 (2000), pp. 634–40.
20. K. Wexley and R. Klimoski, "Performance Appraisal:

An Update," in *Research in Personnel and Human Resource Management*, vol. 2, ed. K. Rowland and G. Ferris (Greenwich, CT: JAI Press, 1984).

21. F. Landy and J. Farr, *The Measurement of Work Performance: Methods, Theory, and Applications* (New York: Academic Press, 1983).

22. G. McEvoy and P. Buller, "User Acceptance of Peer Appraisals in an Industrial Setting," *Personnel Psychology* 40 (1987), pp. 785–97.

23. D. Antonioni, "The Effects of Feedback Accountability on Upward Appraisal Ratings," *Personnel Psychology* 47 (1994), pp. 349–56.

24. R. Steel and N. Ovalle, "Self-Appraisal Based on Supervisor Feedback," *Personnel Psychology* 37 (1984), pp. 667–85; L. E. Atwater, "The Advantages and Pitfalls of Self-Assessment in Organizations," in *Performance Appraisal: State of the Art in Practice*, ed. J. W. Smither (San Francisco: Jossey-Bass, 1998), pp. 331–65.

25. Bureau of Labor Statistics, *Employment and Earnings* (Washington, DC: U.S. Department of Labor, 1997).

26. J. Bernardin, C. Hagan, J. Kane, and P. Villanova, "Effective Performance Management: A Focus on Precision, Customers, and Situational Constraints," in *Performance Appraisal: State of the Art in Practice*, pp. 3–48.

27. K. Wexley and W. Nemeroff, "Effects of Racial Prejudice, Race of Applicant, and Biographical Similarity on Interviewer Evaluations of Job Applicants," *Journal of Social and Behavioral Sciences* 20 (1974), pp. 66–78.

28. D. Smith, "Training Programs for Performance Appraisal: A Review," *Academy of Management Review* 11 (1986), pp. 22–40.

29. G. Latham, K. Wexley, and E. Pursell, "Training Managers to Minimize Rating Errors in the Observation of Behavior," *Journal of Applied Psychology* 60 (1975), pp. 550–55.

30. E. Pulakos, "A Comparison of Rater Training Programs: Error Training and Accuracy Training," *Journal of Applied Psychology* 69 (1984), pp. 581–88.

31. S. W. Gilliland and J. C. Langdon, "Creating Performance Management Systems That Promote Perceptions of Fairness," in *Performance Appraisal: State of the Art in Practice*, pp. 209–43.

32. S. W. J. Kozlowski, G. T. Chao, and R. F. Morrison, "Games Raters Play: Politics, Strategies, and Impression Management in Performance Appraisal," in *Performance Appraisal: State of the Art in Practice*, pp. 163–205.

33. K. Wexley, V. Singh, and G. Yukl, "Subordinate Participation in Three Types of Appraisal Interviews," *Journal of Applied Psychology* 58 (1973), pp. 54–57; K. Wexley, "Appraisal Interview," in *Performance Assessment*, ed. R. A. Berk (Baltimore: Johns Hopkins University Press, 1986), pp. 167–85.

34. D. Cederblom, "The Performance Appraisal Interview: A Review, Implications, and Suggestions," *Academy of Management Review* 7 (1982), pp. 219–27; B. D. Cawley, L. M. Keeping, and P. E. Levy, "Participation in the Performance Appraisal Process and Employee Reactions: A Meta-analytic Review of Field Investigations," *Journal of Applied Psychology* 83, no. 3 (1998), pp. 615–63; W. Giles and K. Mossholder, "Employee Reactions to Contextual and Session Components of Performance Appraisal," *Journal of Applied Psychology* 75 (1990), pp. 371–77.

35. *Brito v. Zia Co.*, 478 F.2d 1200 (10th Cir. 1973).

36. K. Kraiger and J. Ford, "A Meta-Analysis of Ratee Race Effects in Performance Rating," *Journal of Applied Psychology* 70 (1985), pp. 56–65.

37. P. Sackett, C. DuBois, and A. Noe, "Tokenism in Performance Evaluation: The Effects of Work Group Representation on Male-Female and White-Black Differences in Performance Ratings," *Journal of Applied Psychology* 76 (1991), pp. 263–67.

38. G. Barrett and M. Kernan, "Performance Appraisal and Terminations: A Review of Court Decisions since *Brito v. Zia* with Implications for Personnel Practices," *Personnel Psychology* 40 (1987), pp. 489–503; H. Feild and W. Holley, "The Relationship of Performance Appraisal System Characteristics to Verdicts in Selected Employment Discrimination Cases," *Academy of Management Journal* 25 (1982), pp. 392–406; J. M. Werner and M. C. Bolino, "Explaining U.S. Courts of Appeals Decisions Involving Performance Appraisal: Accuracy, Fairness, and Validation," *Personnel Psychology* 50 (1997), pp. 1–24; J. A. Segal, "86 Your Performance Appraisal Process," *HR Magazine*, October 2000, pp. 199–202.

39. S. E. Forrer and Z. B. Leibowitz, *Using Computers in Human Resources* (San Francisco: Jossey-Bass, 1991).

9

Developing Employees for Future Success

What Do I Need to Know? After reading this chapter, you should be able to:

1. Discuss how development is related to training and careers.

2. Identify the methods organizations use for employee development.

3. Describe how organizations use assessment of personality type, work behaviors, and job performance to plan employee development.

4. Explain how job experiences can be used for developing skills.

5. Summarize principles for setting up successful mentoring programs.

6. Tell how managers and peers develop employees through coaching.

7. Identify the steps in the process of career management.

8. Discuss how organizations are meeting the challenges of the "glass ceiling," succession planning, and dysfunctional managers.

Introduction

As we noted in Chapter 1, employees' commitment to their organization depends on how their managers treat them. To "win the war for talent" managers must be able to identify high-potential employees, make sure the organization uses the talents of these people, and reassure them of their value, so that they do not become dissatisfied and leave the organization. Managers also must be able to listen. Although new

employee development
The combination of formal education, job experiences, relationships, and assessment of personality and abilities to help employees prepare for the future of their careers.

employees need strong direction, they expect to be able to think independently and be treated with respect. In all these ways, managers provide for **employee development**—the combination of formal education, job experiences, relationships, and assessment of personality and abilities to help employees prepare for the future of their careers. Human resource management establishes a process for employee development that prepares employees to help the organization meet its goals.

This chapter explores the purpose and activities of employee development. We begin by discussing the relationships among development, training, and career management. Next, we look at development approaches, including formal education, assessment, job experiences, and interpersonal relationships. The chapter emphasizes the types of skills, knowledge, and behaviors that are strengthened by each development method, so employees and their managers can choose appropriate methods when planning for development. The third section of the chapter describes the steps of the career management process, emphasizing the responsibilities of employee and employer at each step of the process. The chapter concludes with a discussion of special challenges related to employee development—succession planning, the so-called glass ceiling, and dysfunctional managers.

LO1

Training, Development, and Career Management

Organizations and their employees must constantly expand their knowledge, skills, and behavior to meet customer needs and compete in today's demanding and rapidly changing business environment. More and more companies operate internationally, requiring that employees understand different cultures and customs. More companies organize work in terms of projects or customers, rather than specialized functions, so employees need to acquire a broad range of technical and interpersonal skills. Many companies expect employees at all levels to perform roles once reserved for management. Modern organizations are expected to provide development opportunities to employees without regard to their sex, race, ethnic background, or age, so that they have equal opportunity for advancement. In this climate, organizations are placing greater emphasis on training and development. To do this, organizations must understand development's relationship to training and career management.

Development and Training

The definition of development indicates that it is future oriented. Development implies learning that is not necessarily related to the employee's current job.[1] Instead, it prepares employees for other positions in the organization and increases their ability to move into jobs that may not yet exist.[2] Development also may help employees prepare for changes in their current jobs, such as changes resulting from new technology, work designs, or customers. So development is about preparing for change in the form of new jobs, new responsibilities, or new requirements.

In contrast, training traditionally focuses on helping employees improve performance of their current jobs. Many organizations have focused on linking training programs to business goals. In these organizations, the distinction between training and development is more blurred. Table 9.1 summarizes the traditional differences.

	TRAINING	DEVELOPMENT
Focus	Current	Future
Use of work experiences	Low	High
Goal	Preparation for current job	Preparation for changes
Participation	Required	Voluntary

TABLE 9.1

Training versus Development

Development for Careers

The concept of a career has changed in recent years. In the traditional view, a career consists of a sequence of positions within an occupation or organization.[3] For example, an academic career might begin with a position as a university's adjunct professor. It continues with appointment to faculty positions as assistant professor, then associate professor, and finally full professor. An engineer might start as a staff engineer, then with greater experience earn promotions to the positions of advisory engineer, senior engineer, and vice president of engineering. In these examples, the career resembles a set of stairs from the bottom of a profession or organization to the top.

Changes such as downsizing, restructuring, bankruptcy, and growth have become the norm in the modern business environment. As this has happened, the concept of career has become more fluid. The new concept of a career is often referred to as a **protean career**—that is, a career that frequently changes based on changes in the person's interests, abilities, and values and in the work environment. For example, an engineer might decide to take a sabbatical from her position to work in management at the United Way for a year. The purpose of this change could be to develop her managerial skills and evaluate whether she likes managerial work more than engineering. As in this example, the concept of a protean career assumes that employees will take major responsibility for managing their careers. This concept is consistent with the modern *psychological contract* we described in Chapter 2. In place of the traditional expectation of job security and advancement within a company, today's employees need to take control over their careers and personal responsibility for managing their careers. They look for organizations that will support them by providing development opportunities and flexible work arrangements so they can pursue their goals.

protean career
A career that frequently changes based on changes in the person's interests, abilities, and values and in the work environment.

In this environment, employees need to develop new skills, rather than rely on an unchanging base of knowledge. This need results from employers' efforts to respond to customer demands. The types of knowledge that an employee needs have changed.[4] The traditional career requires "knowing how," or having the appropriate skills and knowledge to provide a particular service or product. Such knowledge and skills remain important, but a protean career also requires that employees "know why" and "know whom." Knowing why means understanding the employer's business and culture in order to apply knowledge and skills in a way that contributes to the business. Knowing whom means developing relationships that contribute to the employer's success—for example, connections with vendors, suppliers, community members, customers, or industry experts. Learning these categories of knowledge requires more than formal courses and training programs. Rather, the employee must build relationships and obtain useful job experiences.

These relationships and experiences often take an employee along a career path that is far different from the traditional steps upward through an organization or profession. Although such careers will not disappear, more employees will follow a spiral career path in which they cross the boundaries between specialties and organizations. As organizations provide for employee development (and as employees take control of their own careers), they will need a pair of opportunities. First, employees need to determine their interests, skills, and weaknesses. Second, based on that information, employees seek development experiences that will likely involve jobs and relationships as well as formal courses. As discussed later in the chapter, organizations can meet these needs through a system for *career management* or *development planning*. Career management helps employees select development activities that prepare them to meet their career goals. It helps employers select development activities in line with its human resource needs.

LO2

Approaches to Employee Development

The New York City–based Metropolitan Transportation Authority (MTA) found that it needed a system for developing employees for first-level management positions.[5] To meet that need, it created its Future Managers Program. The goal of the program is to develop first-level managers who understand the transportation business and operations. It uses assessment, courses, job experiences, and relationships, combining classroom instruction that provides a learning foundation with job rotation that exposes participants to a wide variety of experiences. Class time is devoted to case studies, team building, and practice in problem solving, delegation, leadership, and communications. Working in groups, employees complete projects that involve real issues such as creating a customer service brochure in Chinese. Job rotation assignments have included working with the system road foreman, in the operations control center, and at Grand Central Terminal. Because job rotation makes employees familiar with different aspects of operations, they are prepared to move into new areas when positions become available. During the process, mentors answer questions and help participants understand the MTA's culture. Supervisors and peers provide continued performance feedback. After completing the program, a majority of graduates have received jobs they desired.

As at the MTA, employee development often focuses on managers, but development is useful for all levels of employees. For example, a grocery store manager could give clerks feedback as part of their performance appraisals. At the same time, the manager could ask the clerks to think of ways to change their weaknesses and invite them to state goals, such as positions they desire to hold in the future. In this way, the performance management process can support employee development.

The many approaches to employee development fall into four broad categories: formal education, assessment, job experiences, and interpersonal relationships.[6] Fig-

Employee development includes building relationships with key vendors, suppliers, or community members that contribute to career success.

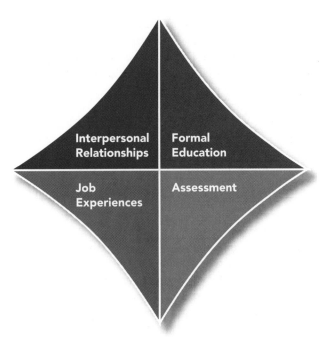

FIGURE 9.1

The Four Approaches to
Employee Development

ure 9.1 summarizes these four methods. Many organizations combine these approaches, as in the previous example of the MTA.

Formal Education

Organizations may support employee development through a variety of formal educational programs, either at the workplace or off-site. These may include workshops designed specifically for the organization's employees, short courses offered by consultants or universities, university programs offered to employees who live on campus during the program, and executive MBA programs (which enroll managers to meet on weekends or evenings to earn a master's degree in business administration). These programs may involve lectures by business experts, business games and simulations, experiential programs, and meetings with customers. Chapter 7 described most of these training methods, including their pros and cons.

Many companies, including Motorola, IBM, General Electric, and Metropolitan Financial, operate training and development centers that offer one- or two-day seminars and week-long programs. For example, GE's Management Development Institute in Crotonville, New York, teaches courses in manufacturing and sales, marketing, and advanced management training.[7] New employees may take the professional development program, with courses emphasizing preparation for a specific career path. Courses in the executive development program emphasize strategic thinking, leadership, integration of the functional specialties, global competition, and customer satisfaction. Tuition is paid by the employee's business unit.

Independent institutions offering executive education include Harvard, the Wharton School of Business, the University of Michigan, and the Center for Creative Leadership. A growing number of companies and universities are using distance learning (discussed in Chapter 7) to reach executive audiences. For example, Duke University's Fuqua School of Business offers an electronic executive MBA program. Students use personal computers to view lectures on CD-ROM, download study aids,

E-Learning Helps Build Management Talent at IBM

To compete successfully, companies need to identify employees with managerial talent and help managers become more effective. To attract and retain talented employees, companies must offer training and development opportunities. This can be challenging for a company such as IBM whose employees are geographically dispersed and dealing with many demands. IBM's solution is to apply its e-commerce expertise to its development programs.

IBM's "Basic Blue for Managers" program uses e-learning and face-to-face classroom experiences. The program helps managers understand their responsibilities in managing performance, employee relations, diversity, and multicultural issues. It moves the learning of all basic management skills to the Web, using classroom experiences for more complex management issues. It also gives managers and their bosses greater responsibility for development, while the company provides support in the form of unlimited access to development activities and support networks.

The learning model has four levels:

1. *Management quick views*— These provide practical information on over 40 common management topics related to how to conduct business, leadership and management competencies, productivity, and HRM issues.
2. *Interactive learning modules and simulations*—Interactive simulations emphasize people and task management. Employees learn by viewing videos; interacting with models of problem employees; deciding how to deal with a problem, issue, or request; and getting feedback on their decisions. Case studies also are available for review.
3. *Collaborative learning*—The learner can connect on IBM's intranet with tutors, team members, customers, or other learners to discuss problems, issues, and approaches to share learning.
4. *Learning labs*—Five-day class workshops build on the learning acquired during previous phases of e-learning. The workshops emphasize peer learning and the development of a learning community. Through challenging activities and assignments, managers gain increased awareness of themselves, their work teams, and IBM.

The program recognizes the roles of the manager's supervisor as coach, supporter, and role model. This person provides coaching and feedback, on-the-job learning experiences, assessment of the manager's development needs and progress, and help in completing individual development plans.

IBM believes that e-learning combined with the classroom environment lets managers participate in self-directed learning, try out skills in a low-risk environment, and gain access to communities of learning and just-in-time learning. Combining the advantages of e-learning with classroom experiences and support from the manager's supervisor creates a superior development program.

SOURCE: N. Lewis and P. Orton, "The Five Attributes of Innovative E-Learning," *Training and Development*, June 2000, pp. 47–51.

discuss lectures, and work on team projects using computer bulletin boards, e-mail, and live chat. They also use the Internet to research topics and companies. The nearby "e-HRM" box details how IBM is using the Web for its management development program.

Another trend in executive education is for employers and the education provider to create short courses with content designed specifically for the audience. An example of this type of customized learning is the Global Leadership Program run by Columbia University's business school. There, executives work on real problems they face in their jobs. One participant, a manager for window maker Pella Corporation, left the program with a plan for international sales.[8]

Executive education also may supplement formal courses with other types of development activities. Avon Products offers its Passport Program to employees thought to have potential to be general managers.[9] To learn Avon's global strategy, they meet for each session in a different country. The program brings a team of employees together for six-week periods spread over 18 months. University faculty and consultants give participants general background of a functional area. The team then works with Avon senior executives on a country project, such as how to enter a new market. The teams present their projects to Avon's top managers.

Assessment

Another way to provide for employee development is **assessment**—collecting information and providing feedback to employees about their behavior, communication style, or skills.[10] Information for assessment may come from the employees, their peers, managers, and customers. The most frequent uses of assessment are to identify employees with managerial potential to measure current managers' strengths and weaknesses. Organizations also use assessment to identify managers with potential to move into higher-level executive positions. Organizations that assign work to teams may use assessment to identify the strengths and weaknesses of individual team members and the effects of the team members' decision-making and communication styles on the team's productivity.

For assessment to support development, the information must be shared with the employee being assessed. Along with that assessment information, the employee needs suggestions for correcting skill weaknesses and for using skills already learned. The suggestions might be to participate in training courses or develop skills through new job experiences. Based on the assessment information and available development opportunities, employees should develop action plans to guide their efforts at self-improvement.

Organizations vary in the methods and sources of information they use in developmental assessment. Many organizations appraise performance. Organizations with sophisticated development systems use psychological tests to measure employees' skills, personality types, and communication styles. They may collect self, peer, and manager ratings of employees' behavior and style of working with others. The tools used for these assessment methods include the Myers-Briggs Type Indicator, assessment centers, the Benchmarks assessment, performance appraisal, and 360-degree feedback.

Myers-Briggs Type Indicator®

The most popular psychological test for employee development is the **Myers-Briggs Type Indicator (MBTI).** This test, taken by millions of people each year, identifies individuals' preferences for source of energy, means of information gathering, way of decision making, and lifestyle. The results of the test provide information for team building and leadership development. The test consists of more than 100 questions

LO3

assessment
Collecting information and providing feedback to employees about their behavior, communication style, or skills.

Myers-Briggs Type Indicator (MBTI)
Psychological test that identifies individuals' preferences for source of energy, means of information gathering, way of decision making, and lifestyle, providing information for team building and leadership development.

TABLE 9.2

Personality Types Used in the Myers-Briggs Type Indicator Assessment

	SENSING TYPES (S)		INTUITIVE TYPES (N)	
	THINKING (T)	FEELING (F)	FEELING (F)	THINKING (T)
Introverts (I) Judging (J)	**ISTJ** Quiet, serious, earn success by thoroughness and dependability. Practical, matter-of-fact, realistic, and responsible. Decide logically what should be done and work toward it steadily, regardless of distractions. Take pleasure in making everything orderly and organized—their work, their home, their life. Value traditions and loyalty.	**ISFJ** Quiet, friendly, responsible, and conscientious. Committed and steady in meeting their obligations. Thorough, painstaking, and accurate. Loyal, considerate, notice and remember specifics about people who are important to them, concerned with how others feel. Strive to create an orderly and harmonious environment at work and at home.	**INFJ** Seek meaning and connection in ideas, relationships, and material possessions. Want to understand what motivates people and are insightful about others. Conscientious and committed to their firm values. Develop a clear vision about how best to serve the common good. Organized and decisive in implementing their vision.	**INTJ** Have original minds and great drive for implementing their ideas and achieving their goals. Quickly see patterns in external events and develop long-range explanatory perspectives. When committed, organize a job and carry it through. Skeptical and independent, have high standards of competence and performance—for themselves and others.
Perceiving (P)	**ISTP** Tolerant and flexible, quiet observers until a problem appears, then act quickly to find workable solutions. Analyze what makes things work and readily get through large amounts of data to isolate the core of practical problems. Interested in cause and effect, organize facts using logical principles, value efficiency.	**ISFP** Quiet, friendly, sensitive, and kind. Enjoy the present moment, what's going on around them. Like to have their own space and to work within their own time frame. Loyal and committed to their values and to people who are important to them. Dislike disagreements and conflicts, do not force their opinions or values on others.	**INFP** Idealistic, loyal to their values and to people who are important to them. Want an external life that is congruent with their values. Curious, quick to see possibilities, can be catalysts for implementing ideas. Seek to understand people and to help them fulfill their potential. Adaptable, flexible, and accepting unless a value is threatened.	**INTP** Seek to develop logical explanations for everything that interests them. Theoretical and abstract, interested more in ideas than in social interaction. Quiet, contained, flexible, and adaptable. Have unusual ability to focus in depth to solve problems in their area of interest. Skeptical, sometimes critical, always analytical.

about how the person feels or prefers to behave in different situations (such as "Are you usually a good 'mixer' or rather quiet and reserved?" and so forth). The MBTI is based on the work of Carl Jung, noted psychologist who believed that differences in individuals' behavior result from their degree of extroversion–introversion and from their psychological makeup across several other dimensions. The test described these differences and individuals' preferences in the four areas:

1. The *energy* dimension indicates where individuals gain interpersonal strength and vitality, measured as their degree of introversion or extroversion. Extroverts (E) gain energy through interpersonal relationships. Introverts (I) gain energy by focusing on inner thoughts and feelings.

2. The *information-gathering* preference relates to the preparations individuals make before taking decisions. Individuals with a Sensing (S) preference tend to gather the facts and details to prepare for a decision. Intuitives (N) tend to focus less on the facts and more on possibilities and relationships among them.

3. In *decision making*, individuals differ in the amount of consideration they give to their own and others' values and feelings, as opposed to the hard facts of a situation. Individuals with a Thinking (T) preference try always to be objective in making decisions. Individuals with a Feeling (F) preference tend to evaluate the

SENSING TYPES (S)		INTUITIVE TYPES (N)	
THINKING (T)	FEELING (F)	FEELING (F)	THINKING (T)

Extroverts (E)
Perceiving (P)

ESTP	ESFP	ENFP	ENTP
Flexible and tolerant, they take a pragmatic approach focused on immediate results. Theories and conceptual explanations bore them—they want to act energetically to solve the problem. Focus on the here-and-now, spontaneous, enjoy each moment that they can be active with others. Enjoy material comforts and style. Learn best through doing.	Outgoing, friendly, and accepting. Exuberant lovers of life, people, and material comforts. Enjoy working with others to make things happen. Bring common sense and a realistic approach to their work, and make work fun. Flexible and spontaneous, adapt readily to new people and environments. Learn best by trying a new skill with other people.	Warmly enthusiastic and imaginative. See life as full of possibilities. Make connections between events and information very quickly, and confidently proceed based on the patterns they see. Want a lot of affirmation from others, and readily give appreciation and support. Spontaneous and flexible, often rely on their ability to improvise and their verbal fluency.	Quick, ingenious, stimulating, alert, and outspoken. Resourceful in solving new and challenging problems. Adept at generating conceptual possibilities and then analyzing them strategically. Good at reading other people. Bored by routine, will seldom do the same thing the same way, apt to turn to one new interest after another.

Judging (J)

ESTJ	ESFJ	ENFJ	ENTJ
Practical, realistic, matter-of-fact. Decisive, quickly move to implement decisions. Organize projects and people to get things done, focus on getting results in the most efficient way possible. Take care of routine details. Have a clear set of logical standards, systematically follow them and want others to also. Forceful in implementing their plans.	Warmhearted, conscientious, and cooperative. Want harmony in their environment, work with determination to establish it. Like to work with others to complete tasks accurately and on time. Loyal, follow through even in small matters. Notice what others need in their day-by-day lives and try to provide it. Want to be appreciated for who they are and for what they contribute.	Warm, empathetic, responsive, and responsible. Highly attuned to the emotions, needs, and motivations of others. Find potential in everyone, want to help others fulfill their potential. May act as catalysts for individual and group growth. Loyal, responsive to praise and criticism. Sociable, facilitate others in a group, and provide inspiring leadership.	Frank, decisive, assume leadership readily. Quickly see illogical and inefficient procedures and policies, develop and implement comprehensive systems to solve organizational problems. Enjoy long-term planning and goal setting. Usually well informed, well read, enjoy expanding their knowledge and passing it on to others. Forceful in presenting their ideas.

impact of the alternatives on others, as well as their own feelings; they are more subjective.

4. The *lifestyle* preference describes an individual's tendency to be either flexible or structured. Individuals with a Judging (J) preference focus on goals, establish deadlines, and prefer to be conclusive. Individuals with a Perceiving (P) preference enjoy surprises, are comfortable with changing a decision, and dislike deadlines.

The alternatives for each of the four dimensions result in 16 possible combinations, the personality types summarized in Table 9.2. Of course people are likely to be mixtures of these types; but the point of the test is that certain types predominate in individuals.

As a result of their psychological types, people develop strengths and weaknesses. For example, individuals who are Introverted, Sensing, Thinking, and Judging (known as ISTJs) tend to be serious, quiet, practical, orderly, and logical. They can organize tasks, be decisive, and follow through on plans and goals. As a consequence, however—that is, by not having the opposite preferences (Extroversion, Intuition, Feeling, and Perceiving)—ISTJs have several weaknesses. They may have difficulty responding to unexpected opportunities, appear to their colleagues to be too task-oriented or impersonal, and make decisions too fast.

Applying this kind of information about employees' preferences or tendencies helps organizations understand the communication, motivation, teamwork, work styles, and leadership of the people in their groups. For example, salespeople or executives who want to communicate better can apply what they learn about their own personality styles and the way other people perceive them. For team development, the MBTI can help teams match team members with assignments based on their preferences and thus improve problem solving.[11] The team could assign brainstorming (idea-generating) tasks to employees with an Intuitive preference and evaluation of the ideas to employees with a Sensing preference.

Research on the validity, reliability, and effectiveness of the MBTI is inconclusive.[12] People who take the MBTI find it a positive experience and say it helps them change their behavior. MBTI scores appear to be related to one's occupation; that is, people in the same occupation tend to have the same or similar personality types. Analysis of managers' scores in the United States, England, Latin America, and Japan found that a large majority of managers are ISTJ, INTJ, ESTJ, or ENTJ. However, MBTI scores are not necessarily stable over time. Studies in which the MBTI was administered at two different times found that as few as one-fourth of those who took the test were classified as exactly the same type the second time. Still, the MBTI is a valuable tool for understanding communication styles and the ways people prefer to interact with others. It is not appropriate for measuring job performance, however, or as the only means of evaluating promotion potential.

Assessment Centers

assessment center
An assessment process in which multiple raters or evaluators (assessors) evaluate employees' performance on a number of exercises, usually as they work in a group at an off-site location.

At an **assessment center,** multiple raters or evaluators (assessors) evaluate employees' performance on a number of exercises.[13] An assessment center is usually an off-site location such as a conference center. Usually 6 to 12 employees participate at one time. The primary use of assessment centers is to identify whether employees have the personality characteristics, administrative skills, and interpersonal skills needed for managerial jobs. Organizations also use them to determine whether employees have the skills needed for working in teams.

leaderless group discussion
An assessment center exercise in which a team of five to seven employees is assigned a problem and must work together to solve it within a certain time period.

The types of exercises used in assessment centers include leaderless group discussions, interviews, in-baskets, and role plays.[14] In a **leaderless group discussion,** a team of five to seven employees is assigned a problem and must work together to solve it within a certain time period. The problem may involve buying and selling supplies, nominating a subordinate for an award, or assembling a product. Interview questions typically cover each employee's work and personal experiences, skill strengths and weaknesses, and career plans. In-basket exercises, discussed as a selection method in Chapter 6, simulate the administrative tasks of a manager's job, using a pile of documents for the employee to handle. In-role plays, the participant takes the part of a manager or employee in a situation involving the skills to be assessed. For example, a participant might be given the role of a manager who must discuss performance problems with an employee, played by someone who works for the assessment center. Other exercises in assessment centers might include interest and aptitude tests to evaluate an employee's vocabulary, general mental ability, and reasoning skills. Personality tests may be used to determine employees' ability get along with others, tolerance for uncertainty, and other traits related to success as a manager or team member.

The assessors are usually managers who have been trained to look for employee behaviors that are related to the skills being assessed. Typically, each assessor observes and records one or two employees' behaviors in each exercise. The assessors review their notes and rate each employee's level of skills (for example, 5 = high level of leadership skills, 1 = low level of leadership skills). After all the employees have completed the exercises, the assessors discuss their observations of each employee. They compare their ratings and try to agree on each employee's rating for each of the skills.

As we mentioned in Chapter 6, research suggests that assessment center ratings are valid for predicting performance, salary level, and career advancement.[15] Assessment centers may also be useful for development because of the feedback that participants receive about their attitudes, skill strengths, and weaknesses.[16] Some organizations, including Eastman Kodak, offer employees training courses and development activities related to the skills evaluated in the assessment center.

Benchmarks

A development method that focuses on measuring management skills is an instrument called **Benchmarks.** This measurement tool gathers ratings of a manager's use of skills associated with success in managing. The items measured by Benchmarks are based on research into the lessons that executives learn in critical events of their careers.[17] Items measure the 16 skills and perspectives listed in Table 9.3, including how well managers deal with subordinates, acquire resources, and create a productive work climate.

Benchmarks
A measurement tool that gathers ratings of a manager's use of skills associated with success in managing.

TABLE 9.3
Skills Related to Success as a Manager

Resourcefulness	Can think strategically, engage in flexible problem solving, and work effectively with higher management.
Doing whatever it takes	Has perseverance and focus in the face of obstacles.
Being a quick study	Quickly masters new technical and business knowledge.
Building and mending relationships	Knows how to build and maintain working relationships with coworkers and external parties.
Leading subordinates	Delegates to subordinates effectively, broadens their opportunities, and acts with fairness toward them.
Compassion and sensitivity	Shows genuine interest in others and sensitivity to subordinates' needs.
Straightforwardness and composure	Is honorable and steadfast.
Setting a developmental climate	Provides a challenging climate to encourage subordinates' development.
Confronting problem subordinates	Acts decisively and fairly when dealing with problem subordinates.
Team orientation	Accomplishes tasks through managing others.
Balance between personal life and work	Balances work priorities with personal life so that neither is neglected.
Decisiveness	Prefers quick and approximate actions to slow and precise ones in many management situations.
Self-awareness	Has an accurate picture of strengths and weaknesses and is willing to improve.
Hiring talented staff	Hires talented people for the team.
Putting people at ease	Displays warmth and a good sense of humor.
Acting with flexibility	Can behave in ways that are often seen as opposites.

SOURCE: Adapted with permission from C. D. McCauley, M. M. Lombardo, and C. J. Usher, "Diagnosing Management Development Needs: An Instrument Based on How Managers Develop," *Journal of Management* 15 (1989), pp. 389–403.

Research has found that managers who have these skills are more likely to receive positive performance evaluations, be considered promotable, and be promoted.[18]

To provide a complete picture of managers' skills, the managers' supervisors, their peers, and the managers themselves all complete the instrument. The results include a summary report, which the organization provides to the manager so he or she can see the self-ratings in comparison to the ratings by others. Also available with this method is a development guide containing examples of experiences that enhance each skill and ways successful managers use the skill.

Performance Appraisals and 360-Degree Feedback

As we stated in Chapter 8, *performance appraisal* is the process of measuring employees' performance. This information can be useful for employee development under certain conditions.[19] The appraisal system must tell employees specifically about their performance problems and ways to improve their performance. Employees must gain a clear understanding of the differences between current performance and expected performance. The appraisal process must identify causes of the performance discrepancy and develop plans for improving performance. Managers must be trained to deliver frequent performance feedback and must monitor employees' progress in carrying out their action plans.

A recent trend in performance appraisals, also discussed in Chapter 8, is *360-degree feedback*—performance measurement by the employee's supervisor, peers, employees, and customers. Often the feedback involves rating the individual in terms of work-related behaviors. For development purposes, the rater would identify an area of behavior as a strength of that employee or an area requiring further development. The results presented to the employee show how he or she was rated on each item and how self-evaluations differ from other raters' evaluations. The individual reviews the results, seeks clarification from the raters, and sets specific development goals based on the strengths and weaknesses identified.[20]

Consider how US West used development planning with 360-degree feedback.[21] The 360-degree feedback results showed that one manager tended to avoid confrontation. Knowing this helped her focus her training and development activity on role-plays and discussions that would help her become more comfortable with confrontation. She left the program with an individualized list of training and development activities linked directly to the skill she needed to improve.

There are several benefits of 360-degree feedback. Organizations collect multiple perspectives of managers' performance, allowing employees to compare their own personal evaluations with the views of others. This method also establishes formal communications about behaviors and skill ratings between employees and their internal and external customers. For example, in response to feedback from the employees in his group, an AT&T executive learned to air his opinions more freely in meetings of the company's executive committee.[22] This method is most likely to be effective if the rating instrument enables reliable or consistent ratings, assesses behaviors or skills that are job related, and is easy to use. Also, the system should ensure raters' confidentiality, and managers should receive and act on the feedback.[23]

There are potential limitations of 360-degree feedback. This method demands a significant amount of time for raters to complete the evaluations. If raters, especially subordinates or peers, provide negative feedback, some managers might try to identify and punish them. A facilitator is needed to help interpret results. Finally, simply delivering ratings to a manager does not provide ways for the manager to act on the feedback (for example, development planning, meeting with raters, or taking courses). As noted earlier, any form of assessment should be accompanied by suggestions for improvement and development of an action plan.

Job Experiences

LO4

Most employee development occurs through **job experiences**[24]—the combination of relationships, problems, demands, tasks, and other features of an employee's jobs. Using job experiences for employee development assumes that development is most likely to occur when the employee's skills and experiences do not entirely match the skills required for the employee's current job. To succeed, employees must stretch their skills. In other words, they must learn new skills, apply their skills and knowledge in new ways, and master new experiences.[25] For example, companies that want to prepare employees to expand overseas markets are assigning them to a variety of international jobs.

job experiences
The combination of relationships, problems, demands, tasks, and other features of an employee's jobs.

Most of what we know about development through job experiences comes from a series of studies conducted by the Center for Creative Leadership.[26] These studies asked executives to identify key career events that made a difference in their managerial styles and the lessons they learned from these experiences. The key events included job assignments (such as fixing a failed operation), interpersonal relationships (getting along with supervisors), and types of transitions (situations in which the manager at first lacked the necessary background). Through job experiences like these, managers learn how to handle common challenges, prove themselves, lead change, handle pressure, and influence others.

The usefulness of job experiences for employee development varies depending on whether the employee views the experiences as positive or negative sources of stress. When employees view job experiences as positive stressors, the experiences challenge

Working outside one's home country is the most important job experience that can develop an employee for a career in the global economy.

FIGURE 9.2

How Job Experiences Are
Used for Employee
Development

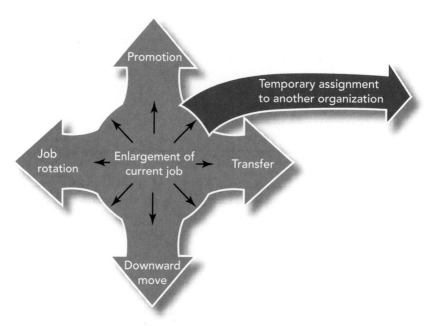

them and stimulate learning. When they view job experiences as negative stressors, employees may suffer from high levels of harmful stress. Of the job demands studied, managers were most likely to experience negative stress from creating change and overcoming obstacles (adverse business conditions, lack of management support, lack of personal support, or a difficult boss). Research suggests that all of the job demands except obstacles are related to learning.[27] Organizations should offer job experiences that are most likely to increase learning, and they should consider the consequences of situations that involve negative stress.

Although the research on development through job experiences has focused on managers, line employees also can learn through job experiences. Organizations may, for example, use job experiences to develop skills needed for teamwork, including conflict resolution, data analysis, and customer service. These experiences may occur when forming a team and when employees switch roles within a team.

Various job assignments can provide for employee development. The organization may enlarge the employee's current job or move the employee to different jobs. Lateral moves include job rotation, transfer, or temporary assignment to another organization. The organization may also use downward moves or promotions as a source of job experience. Figure 9.2 summarizes these alternatives.

Job Enlargement

As Chapter 4 stated in the context of job design, *job enlargement* involves adding challenges or new responsibilities to employees' current jobs. Examples include completing a special project, switching roles within a work team, or researching new ways to serve customers. An engineering employee might join a task force developing new career paths for technical employees. The work on the project could give the engineer a leadership role through which the engineer learns about the company's career development system while also practicing leadership skills to help the task force reach its goals. In this way, job enlargement not only makes a job more interesting, but also creates an opportunity for employees to develop new skills.

Job Rotation

Another job design technique that can be applied to employee development is *job rotation*, moving employees through a series of job assignments in one or more functional areas. At United Technologies Corporation, the job rotation program in finance moves employees into different jobs so that they understand all aspects of budgeting. Greyhound Financial Corporation has high-potential managers participate in its job rotation program, known as "muscle-building."[28] Greyhound puts managers in departments where they have to perform tasks different from those they performed in the past. The managers maintain their titles and compensation levels while moving through the assignments, which have varying status.

Job rotation helps employees gain an appreciation for the company's goals, increases their understanding of different company functions, develops a network of contacts, and improves problem-solving and decision-making skills.[29] Job rotation also helps employees increase their salary and earn promotions faster. However, job rotation poses some problems for employees and the organization. Knowing they will be rotated to another job may give the employees a short-term perspective on problems and their solutions. Employees may feel less satisfied and motivated because they have difficulty developing specialized skills and leave the position too soon to fulfill any challenging assignments. The rotation of employees through a department may hurt productivity and increase the workload of those who remain after employees are rotated out. Job rotation is most likely to succeed when it meets certain conditions:[30]

- Job rotation is used for developing skills as well as gaining experience for management careers.
- Employees understand specifically what skills rotation is to develop.
- The organization uses job rotation for all levels and types of employees.
- Job rotation is linked with the career management process so employees know what development needs each assignment addresses.
- The organization manages the timing of rotations to maximize their benefits and minimize their costs.
- All employees have equal opportunities for job rotation, regardless of their demographic group.

Transfers, Promotions, and Downward Moves

Most companies use upward, downward, and lateral moves as an option for employee development. In a **transfer,** the organization assigns an employee to a position in a different area of the company. Transfers do not necessarily increase job responsibilities or compensation. They are usually lateral moves, that is, moves to a job with a similar level of responsibility. They may involve relocation to another part of the country or even to another country.

Relocation can be stressful because of the demands of moving, especially when family members are affected. People have to find new housing, shopping, health care, and leisure facilities, and they often lack the support of nearby friends and family. These stresses come at the same time the employee must learn the expectations and responsibilities associated with the new position. Because transfers can provoke anxiety, many companies have difficulty getting employees to accept them. Employees most willing to accept transfers tend to be those with high career ambitions, a belief that the organization offers a promising future, and a belief that accepting the transfer will help the company succeed.[31]

transfer
Assignment of an employee to a position in a different area of the company, usually in a lateral move.

downward move
Assignment of an employee to a position with less responsibility and authority.

A **downward move** occurs when an employee is given less responsibility and authority. The organization may demote an employee because of poor performance or move the employee to a lower-level position in another function so that the employee can develop different skills. The temporary cross-functional move is the most common way to use downward moves for employee development. For example, engineers who want to move into management often take lower-level positions, such as shift supervisor, to develop their management skills.

Many employees have difficulty associating transfers and downward moves with development; these changes may feel more like forms of punishment. Employees often decide to leave an organization rather than accept such a change, and then the organization must bear the costs of replacing those employees. Employees will be more likely to accept transfers and downward moves as development opportunities if the organization provides information about the change and its possible benefits and involves the employee in planning the change. Employees are also more likely to be positive about such a recommendation if the organization provides clear performance objectives and frequent feedback. Employers can encourage an employee to relocate by providing financial assistance with the move, information about the new location and job, and help for family members, such as identifying schools, child-care and elder-care options, and job search assistance for the employee's spouse.[32]

promotion
Assignment of an employee to a position with greater challenges, more responsibility, and more authority than in the previous job, usually accompanied by a pay increase.

A **promotion** involves moving an employee into a position with greater challenges, more responsibility, and more authority than in the previous job. Usually promotions include pay increases. Because promotions improve the person's pay, status, and feelings of accomplishment, employees are more willing to accept promotions than lateral or downward moves. Even so, employers can increase the likelihood that employees will accept promotions by providing the same kind of information and assistance that are used to support transfers and downward moves. Organizations can more easily offer promotions if they are profitable and growing. In other conditions, opportunities for promoting employees may be limited.

Temporary Assignments with Other Organizations

In some cases, an employer may benefit from the skills an employee can learn at another organization. The employer may encourage the employee to participate in an **externship**—a full-time temporary position at another organization. Mercer Management, a consulting firm, uses externships to develop employees who want experience in a specific industry.[33] Mercer Management promises to employ the externs after their assignments end. One employee with several years' experience as a Mercer consultant became vice president of Internet services for Binney and Smith, the maker of Crayola crayons. He had been consulting on an Internet project for Binney and Smith and wanted to implement his recommendations, rather than just give them to the client and move on to another project. He started working at Binney and Smith while remaining employed by Mercer Management, though his pay comes from Binney and Smith. Mercer believes that employees who participate in its externship program will remain committed to the consulting firm because they have a chance to learn and grow professionally without the demands of a job search.

externship
Employee development through a full-time temporary position at another organization.

sabbatical
A leave of absence from an organization to renew or develop skills.

Temporary assignments can include a **sabbatical**—a leave of absence from an organization to renew or develop skills. Employees on sabbatical often receive full pay and benefits. Sabbaticals let employees get away from the day-to-day stresses of their jobs and acquire new skills and perspectives. Sabbaticals also allow employees more time for personal pursuits such as writing a book or spending more time with family members. Morningstar, which tracks and reports the performance of mutual funds, provides a six-week paid sabbatical every four years for all employees.[34] A Morningstar manager who had recently been promoted to the role of exhibit/conference manager waited an extra year before taking his sabbatical. He spent half his sabbatical on the beach in California and another three weeks pursuing his passion for modern dance. How employees spend their sabbaticals varies from company to company. Some employees may work for a nonprofit service agency; others may study at a college or university or travel and work on special projects in non-U.S. subsidiaries of the company.

Interpersonal Relationships

Employees can also develop skills and increase their knowledge about the organization and its customers by interacting with a more experienced organization member. Two types of relationships used for employee development are mentoring and coaching.

Mentors

A **mentor** is an experienced, productive senior employee who helps develop a less experienced employee, called the *protégé*. Most mentoring relationships develop informally as a result of interests or values shared by the mentor and protégé. According to research, the employees most likely to seek and attract a mentor have certain personality characteristics: emotional stability, ability to adapt their behavior to the situation, and high needs for power and achievement.[35] Mentoring relationships also can develop as part of the organization's planned effort to bring together successful senior employees with less experienced employees.

One major advantage of formal mentoring programs is that they ensure access to mentors for all employees, regardless of gender or race. Another advantage is that participants in a company-sponsored mentoring program know what is expected of them.[36] However, in an artificially created relationship, mentors may have difficulty providing counseling and coaching.[37] Mentoring programs tend to be most successful when they are voluntary and participants understand the details of the program. Rewarding managers for employee development also is important, because it signals that mentoring and other development activities are worthwhile. In addition, the organization should carefully select mentors based on their interpersonal and technical skills, train them for the role, and evaluate whether the program has met its objectives. The "HR How To" box offers tips for setting up an effective mentoring program.

New York Hospital–Cornell Medical Center developed a well-planned mentoring program for its housekeeping employees. Each mentor has between 5 and 10 protégés to meet with once each quarter. To qualify as mentors, employees must receive outstanding performance evaluations, demonstrate strong interpersonal skills, and be able to perform basic cleaning tasks and essential duties of all housekeeping positions, including safety procedures. The mentors undergo a two-day training program that emphasizes communication skills. They also learn how to convey information about the job and give directions effectively without criticizing employees. The program helps new employees learn their duties more quickly, and it gives the mentors a chance to quickly identify and correct problems.[38]

Mentors and protégés can both benefit from a mentoring relationship. Protégés receive career support, including coaching, protection, sponsorship, challenging assignments, and visibility among the organization's managers. They also receive benefits of

LO5

mentor
An experienced, productive senior employee who helps develop a less experienced employee (a protégé).

Setting Up a Mentoring Program

Mentoring is most effective if these relationships are part of a well-planned program. Here are some tips for setting up a mentoring program that supports the organization's goals:

- Make participation voluntary, for mentors and protégés alike. Establish a policy that either person may end the relationship at any time without fear of punishment.
- The process of matching mentors and protégés should not prevent relationships from developing informally. For example, the organization can establish a pool of mentors, then allow protégés to choose from a variety of qualified mentors.
- Choose mentors based on their past record of developing employees, willingness to serve in this

role, and evidence of skill in coaching, communication, and listening.
- Clearly communicate the purpose of the program and verify that all participants understand the purpose. Specify the projects and activities that the mentor and protégé are expected to complete.
- Specify the length of the program. Although a formal program has an end date, the organization should encourage the mentor and protégé to pursue the relationship beyond that date if they wish.
- Specify the minimum level of contact expected between the mentor and protégé.
- Encourage protégés to contact one another to discuss problems and share successes.
- Evaluate the mentoring program. Get immediate

feedback from interviews with mentors and protégés, and explore any areas of dissatisfaction. Use surveys to gather more detailed information regarding the benefits the participants have received from the program.
- Reward managers for employee development. The rewards signal that the effort they spend on mentoring and other development activities is worthwhile.

SOURCE: B. R. Ragins, J. Cotton, and J. S. Miller, "Marginal Mentoring: The Effects of Type of Mentor, Quality of Relationship, and Program Design on Work and Career Attitudes," *Academy of Management Journal* 43, no. 6 (2000), pp. 1177–94; S. Siebert, "The Effectiveness of Facilitated Mentoring: A Longitudinal Quasi-Experiment," *Journal of Vocational Behavior* 54 (1999), pp. 483–502; J. A. Wilson and N. S. Elman, "Organizational Benefits of Mentoring," *Academy of Management Executive* 4 (1990), pp. 88–93.

a positive relationship—a friend and role model who accepts them, has a positive opinion toward them, and gives them a chance to talk about their worries. Employees with mentors are also more likely to be promoted, earn higher salaries, and have more influence within their organization.[39] Acting as a mentor gives managers a chance to develop their interpersonal skills and increase their feelings that they are contributing something important to the organization. Working with the protégé on technical matters such as new research in the field may also increase the mentor's technical knowledge. When General Electric became involved in e-commerce, it used younger employees with Web expertise to mentor older managers. As the veterans became more familiar with the Internet, their young mentors became more comfortable working with senior managers and developed their business expertise.[40]

So that more employees can benefit from mentoring, some organizations use *group mentoring programs*, which assign four to six protégés to a successful senior employee.

Phil Jackson has a top reputation as a coach who has helped teams and individuals become champions. Career coaches motivate employees, help them develop their skills, and provide feedback for improvement.

A potential advantage of group mentoring is that protégés can learn from each other as well as from the mentor. The leader helps protégés understand the organization, guides them in analyzing their experiences, and helps them clarify career directions. Each member of the group may complete specific assignments, or the group may work together on a problem or issue.

Coaching

A **coach** is a peer or manager who works with an employee to motivate the employee, help him or her develop skills, and provide reinforcement and feedback. Coaches may play one or more of three roles:[41]

1. Working one-on-one with an employee, as when giving feedback.
2. Helping employees learn for themselves—for example, helping them find experts and teaching them to obtain feedback from others.
3. Providing resources such as mentors, courses, or job experiences.

Best Buy, a consumer-electronics retailer, has invested nearly $10 million on coaches for all top managers.[42] Once a month, top executives spend a few hours with an industrial psychologist who helps them work through leadership issues. One manager discussed with his coach how to balance the needs of some of the managers who worked for him with the company's business needs. His managers were more comfortable focusing on traditional store retailing at a time when the company needed a focus on competition on the Internet. The manager being coached needed to learn how to lead his team and push new ideas without squelching team members.

LO6

coach
A peer or manager who works with an employee to motivate the employee, help him or her develop skills, and provide reinforcement and feedback.

Systems for Career Management

LO7

Employee development is most likely to meet the organization's needs if it is part of a human resource system of career management. In practice, organizations' career management systems vary. Some rely heavily on informal relationships, while others are sophisticated programs. As shown in Figure 9.3, a basic career management system involves four steps: self-assessment, reality check, goal setting, and action planning. At each step, both the employee and the organization have responsibilities. The system is most likely to be beneficial if it is linked to the organization's objectives and needs, has support from top management, and is created with employee participation.[43] Human resource professionals can also contribute to the system's success by ensuring that

FIGURE 9.3

Steps and Responsibilities in the Career Management Process

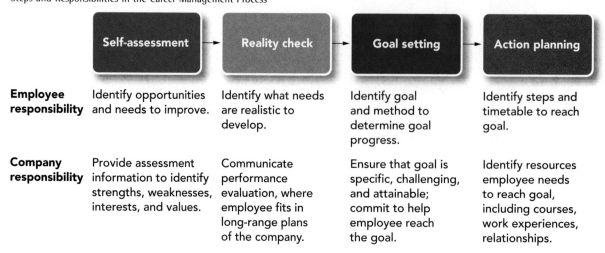

	Self-assessment	**Reality check**	**Goal setting**	**Action planning**
Employee responsibility	Identify opportunities and needs to improve.	Identify what needs are realistic to develop.	Identify goal and method to determine goal progress.	Identify steps and timetable to reach goal.
Company responsibility	Provide assessment information to identify strengths, weaknesses, interests, and values.	Communicate performance evaluation, where employee fits in long-range plans of the company.	Ensure that goal is specific, challenging, and attainable; commit to help employee reach the goal.	Identify resources employee needs to reach goal, including courses, work experiences, relationships.

it is linked to other HR practices such as performance management, training, and recruiting.

Self-Assessment

self-assessment
The use of information by employees to determine their career interests, values, aptitudes, and behavioral tendencies.

In discussing the methods of employee development, we highlighted several assessment tools. Such tools may be applied to the first stage of career development, **self-assessment.** This is the use of information by employees to determine their career interests, values, aptitudes, and behavioral tendencies. The employee's responsibility is to identify opportunities and personal areas needing improvement. The organization's responsibility is to provide assessment information for identifying strengths, weaknesses, interests, and values.

Self-assessment tools often include psychological tests such as the Myers-Briggs Type Inventory (described earlier in the chapter), the Strong-Campbell Interest Inventory, and the Self-Directed Search. The Strong-Campbell inventory helps employees identify their occupational and job interests. The Self-Directed Search identifies employees' preferences for working in different kinds of environments—sales, counseling, and so on. Tests may also help employees identify the relative values they place on work and leisure activities. Self-assessment tools can include exercises such as the one in Figure 9.4. This type of exercise helps an employee consider his or her current career status, future plans, and the fit between the career and the employee's current situation and resources. Some organizations provide counselors to help employees in the self-assessment process and to interpret the results of psychological tests.

Completing the self-assessment can help employees identify a development need. This need can result from gaps between current skills or interests and the type of work or position the employee has or wants. Ford Motor Company has a career management system that provides this type of information.[44] Ford's system, which it calls the Personal Development Roadmap (PDR), is a Web-based resource that lets marketing, sales, and service employees plan their own personal and professional development. Employees visit PDR on Ford's intranet, where they complete a profile each year.

FIGURE 9.4

Sample Self-Assessment Exercise

Step 1: Where am I?
Examine current position of life and career.
Think about your life from past and present to the future. Draw a time line to represent important events.

Step 2: Who am I?
Examine different roles.
Using 3 × 5 cards, write down one answer per card to the question "Who am I?"

Step 3: Where would I like to be, and what would I like to happen?
Begin setting goals.
Consider your life from present to future. Write an autobiography answering these questions:
• What do you want to have accomplished?
• What milestones do you want to achieve?
• What do you want to be remembered for?

Step 4: An ideal year in the future
Identify resources needed.
Consider a one-year period in the future. Answer these questions:
• If you had unlimited resources, what would you do?
• What would the ideal environment look like?
• Does the ideal environment match Step 3?

Step 5: An ideal job
Create current goal.
In the present, think about an ideal job for you with your available resources. Describe your role, resources, and type of training or education needed.

Step 6: Career by objective inventory
Summarize current situation.
• What gets you excited each day?
• What do you do well? What are you known for?
• What do you need to achieve your goals?
• What could interfere with reaching your goals?
• What should you do now to move toward reaching your goals?
• What is your long-term career objective?

SOURCE: Based on J. E. McMahon and S. K. Merman, "Career Development," in *The ASTD Training and Development Handbook,* 4th ed., ed. R. L. Craig (New York: McGraw-Hill, 1996), pp. 679–97. Reproduced with permission.

Reality Check

In the next step of career management, the **reality check,** employees receive information about their skills and knowledge and where these assets fit into the organization's plans. The employee's responsibility is to identify what skills she or he could realistically develop in light of the opportunities available. The organization's responsibility is to communicate the performance evaluation and the opportunities available to the employee, given the organization's long-range plans. Opportunities might include promotions and transfers.

reality check
Information employers give employees about their skills and knowledge and where these assets fit into the organization's plans.

Usually the employer conducts the reality check as part of a performance appraisal or as the feedback stage of performance management. In well-developed career management systems, the manager may hold separate discussions for performance feedback and career development. At Ford, the Personal Development Roadmap helps employees identify areas for development by comparing their annual profiles with the expected skill levels for their job group.

Goal Setting

Based on the information from the self-assessment and reality check, the employee sets short- and long-term career objectives. These goals usually involve one or more of the following categories:

- Desired positions, such as becoming sales manager within three years.
- Level of skill to apply—for example, to use one's budgeting skills to improve the unit's cash flow problems.
- Work setting—for example, to move to corporate marketing within two years.
- Skill acquisition, such as learning how to use the company's human resource information system.

As in these examples, the goals should be specific, and they should include a date by which the goal is to be achieved. It is the employee's responsibility to identify the goal and the method of determining her or his progress toward that goal.

Usually the employee discusses the goals with his or her manager. The organization's responsibilities are to ensure that the goal is specific, challenging, and attainable and to help the employee reach the goal. At Ford, the PDR system does this by helping employees identify areas on which to focus development and recommending development opportunities offered by the company. The PDR has also identified specific leadership behaviors associated with Ford's business success—for example, innovation and desire to serve—and helps employees focus on developing these behaviors.

Action Planning

During the final step, employees prepare an action plan for how they will achieve their short- and long-term career goals. The employee is responsible for identifying the steps and timetable to reach the goals. The employer should identify resources needed, including courses, work experiences, and relationships.

Action plans may involve any one or a combination of the development methods discussed earlier in the chapter—training, assessment, job experiences, or the help of a mentor or coach. The approach used depends on the particular developmental needs and career objectives. For example, suppose the program manager in an information systems department uses feedback from performance appraisals to determine that he needs greater knowledge of project management software. The manager plans to increase that knowledge by reading articles (formal education), meeting with software vendors, and contacting the vendors' customers to ask them about the software they have used (job experiences). The manager and his supervisor agree that six months will be the target date for achieving the higher level of knowledge through these activities.

The outcome of action planning often takes the form of a career development plan. Figure 9.5 is an example of a development plan for a product manager. Development plans usually include descriptions of strengths and weaknesses, career goals,

FIGURE 9.5

Career Development Plan

Name: **Title:** Project Manager   **Immediate Manager:**

Competencies
Please identify your three greatest strengths and areas for improvement.
Strengths
• Strategic thinking and execution (confidence, command skills, action orientation)
• Results orientation (competence, motivating others, perseverance)
• Spirit for winning (building team spirit, customer focus, respect colleagues)

Areas for Improvement
• Patience (tolerance of people or processes and sensitivity to pacing)
• Written communications (ability to write clearly and succinctly)
• Overly ambitious (too much focus on successful completion of projects rather than developing relationships with individuals involved in the projects)

Career Goals
Please describe your overall career goals.
• **Long-term:** Accept positions of increased responsibility to a level of general manager (or beyond). The areas of specific interest include but are not limited to product and brand management, technology and development, strategic planning, and marketing.
• **Short-term:** Continue to improve my skills in marketing and brand management while utilizing my skills in product management, strategic planning, and global relations.

Next Assignments
Identify potential next assignments (including timing) that would help you develop toward your career goals.
• Manager or director level in planning, development, product, or brand management. Timing estimated to be Spring 2004.

Training and Development Needs
List both training and development activities that will either help you develop in your current assignment or provide overall career development.
• Master's degree classes will allow me to practice and improve my written communications skills. The dynamics of my current position, teamwork, and reliance on other individuals allow me to practice patience and to focus on individual team members' needs along with the success of the project.

Employee _____ **Date** _____
Immediate Manager _____ **Date** _____
Mentor _____ **Date** _____

---

and development activities for reaching each goal. Ford's PDR helps employees create an annual development plan. It recommends education (Ford classes and seminars), exploration (activities outside the company), and/or experiences (job assignments and other on-the-job opportunities) geared toward meeting each employee's particular development needs. Employees also can enroll in suggested courses on Ford's intranet.

LO8

Development-Related Challenges

A well-designed system for employee development can help organizations face three widespread challenges: the glass ceiling, succession planning, and dysfunctional behavior by managers.

The Glass Ceiling

glass ceiling
Circumstances resembling an invisible barrier that keep most women and minorities from attaining the top jobs in organizations.

As we mentioned in Chapter 1, women and minorities are rare in the top level of U.S. corporations. Observers of this situation have noted that it looks as if an invisible barrier is keeping women and minorities from reaching the top jobs, a barrier that has come to be known as the **glass ceiling.** The glass ceiling is likely caused by a lack of access to training programs, appropriate developmental job experiences, and developmental relationships such as mentoring.[45] According to research, women and men have equal access to job experiences involving transitions or creating change.[46] But male managers receive significantly more assignments involving great responsibility (high stakes, managing business diversity, handling external pressure) than female managers of similar ability and managerial level. Also, female managers report experiencing more challenge due to lack of personal support (which, as we saw earlier in the chapter, is related to harmful stress). With regard to developmental relationships, women and minorities often have trouble finding mentors. They may not participate in the organization's, profession's, or community's "old boys' network." Also, managers in the organization may prefer to interact with people who have similar status or may avoid interacting with certain people because of discomfort or negative stereotypes.[47]

Organizations can use development systems to help break through the glass ceiling. Managers making developmental assignments need to carefully consider whether stereotypes are influencing the types of assignments men and women receive. A formal process for regularly identifying development needs and creating action plans can make these decisions more objective. The "Best Practices" box describes the steps that Procter & Gamble is taking to break the glass ceiling.

Another organization that is actively working to eliminate the glass ceiling is Deloitte & Touche, an accounting, tax, and consulting firm with offices throughout the United States.[48] Deloitte & Touche had been experiencing high turnover of talented women, so it set up a task force chaired by the company's chief executive officer to analyze the problem and develop recommendations. The task force gathered data by having every management professional in the company attend a workshop designed to explore how attitudes about gender affected the work environment. The workshops included discussions, videos, and case studies, such as one case in which two promising candidates, one male and one female, with identical skills were evaluated. The workshops also focused on how work assignments were allocated. The workshops found differences in the ways men and women were evaluated and in the kinds of assignments they were given, based on managers' assumptions about men and women. As a result, Deloitte & Touche began to rethink how assignments were given, to make sure women had opportunities for highly visible assignments. The company started a formal process for career planning for women and men and began offering networking events at which women could meet successful female partners and high-level managers. Deloitte & Touche began measuring turnover and promotion rates and linking rewards to meeting career development objectives. Through these changes, the company improved its retention of women, and reducing turnover has saved $250 million in hiring and training costs.

BEST PRACTICES

Procter & Gamble Selling Women on Careers

Procter & Gamble is famous for its ability to sell products like Tide detergent and Pampers diapers to women. Until recently, it was much less successful in bringing women into its management ranks. No women sat on P&G's executive committee, and few executives were female. A study of employee turnover found that two of every three high-performing employees who left the company were women. P&G has a policy of promoting from within, so retaining and promoting high performers is important for filling the company's top ranks.

To uncover the reasons women were leaving rather than moving up, P&G conducted interviews and surveys. The results showed that women felt they had a consensus-building management style that was not valued; rather, P&G executives favored quick, aggressive decision making. Career planning was not openly discussed, so women reported they didn't know where they stood with the company, and women (more than male employees) were uncomfortable with the feeling that they were not valued. Women also expressed an interest in flexible schedules so that they could put in the long hours required for success and still meet other demands on their time.

To apply these results, P&G created a task force to study the career path of the brand manager, the major route to executive-level jobs. The team set goals to lower the turnover rate among women and to achieve 40 percent women at each level of brand management by 2005.

The task force also developed a mentoring program, which it named Mentor Up. As the name suggests, the Mentor Up program directs the mentoring relationship in an unusual direction: The mentors are mid-level or junior female managers with at least a year's experience as good performers in the job. The protégés are senior-level male executives. Mentoring is intended to raise the executives' awareness of women's work-related issues. The female managers are matched with senior managers, based on their responses to a questionnaire. These protégés and mentors attend an orientation session that includes a panel discussion by past participants in the program and a series of exercises probing women's workplace issues and reasons for success at P&G. Mentors are required to meet with their protégés at least once every two months.

Mentors and protégés receive discussion guides designed to help them conduct a beneficial dialogue when they meet. For example, one discussion guide asked the mentoring pairs to explore the keys to success and failure for women and men in company leadership positions. The discussion guides also include questions designed to uncover feelings about occasions when women feel valued. The mentors and protégés answer the questions independently, then discuss their responses. By noticing similarities and differences in their answers, they can identify ways people like to be recognized.

The Mentor Up program has frequently raised two issues: the barriers that women face in balancing work and personal demands; and differences that mentoring pairs notice in the ways men and women manage people and make decisions. One of the program's biggest benefits has been that mentors and protégés have shared advice and perspectives and feel comfortable using each other to test new ideas. The junior managers also appreciate their exposure to top executives. The program has reduced the turnover rate of female managers by 25 percent, making it similar to turnover among male managers.

SOURCE: Based on T. Parker-Pope, "Inside P&G, a Pitch to Keep Women Employees," *The Wall Street Journal*, September 9, 1998, pp. B1, B6; D. Zielinski, "Mentoring Up," *Training*, October 2000, pp. 136–40.

Succession Planning

Organizations have always had to prepare for the retirement of their leaders, but the need is more intense than ever. The aging of the workforce means that a greater share of employees are reaching retirement age. Many organizations are fueling the trend by downsizing through early-retirement programs. As positions at the top of organizations become vacant, many organizations have determined that their middle managers are fewer and often unprepared for top-level responsibility. This situation has raised awareness of the need for **succession planning**—the process of identifying and tracking high-potential employees who will be able to fill top management positions when they become vacant.

Succession planning offers several benefits.[49] It forces senior management to regularly and thoughtfully review the company's leadership talent. It assures that top-level management talent is available. It provides a set of development experiences that managers must complete to be considered for top management positions, so the organization does not promote managers before they are ready. Succession planning systems also help attract and retain ambitious managerial employees by providing development opportunities.

Succession planning focuses on *high-potential employees*, that is, employees the organization believes can succeed in higher-level business positions such as general manager of a business unit, director of a function (such as marketing or finance), or chief executive officer.[50] A typical approach to development of high-potential employees is to have them complete an individual development program including education, executive mentoring and coaching, and rotation through job assignments. Job assignments are based on the successful career paths of the managers whom the high-potential employees are preparing to replace. High-potential employees may also receive special assignments, such as making presentations and serving on committees and task forces. Research shows that an effective program for developing high-potential employees has three stages:[51]

1. *Selection of high-potential employees*—Organizations may select outstanding performers and employees who have completed elite academic programs, such as earning a master's degree in business administration from a prestigious university. They may also use the results of psychological tests such as assessment centers.
2. *Developmental experiences*—As employees participate in developmental experiences, the organization identifies those who succeed in the experiences. The organization looks for employees who continue to show qualities associated with success in top jobs, such as communication skills, leadership talent, and willingness to make sacrifices for the organization. Employees who display these qualities continue to be considered high-potential employees.

GE knew that Jack Welch would be retiring, so the company planned for the succession. Welch is shown here with Jeffrey Immelt, the new CEO. What are the benefits of succession planning?

succession planning
The process of identifying and tracking high-potential employees who will be able to fill top management positions when they become vacant.

3. *Active involvement with the CEO*—High-potential employees seen by top management as fitting into the organization's culture and having personality characteristics necessary for representing the company become actively involved with the chief executive officer. The CEO exposes these employees to the organization's key people and gives them a greater understanding of the organization's culture. The development of high-potential employees is a slow process. Reaching stage 3 may take 15 to 20 years.

When American Express Financial Services wanted to develop leaders for expansion of the business, the company established a process for succession planning.[52] The process forecasts how many and what kinds of leaders the company will need over the next two years, assesses the talents of current employees, and develops employees identified as having management talent. Vice presidents recommend talented employees to participate in assessment programs that measure leadership and basic managerial skills. Employees receive personalized development plans for improving their weaknesses in knowledge, skill, or experiences. Top managers monitor their progress and provide coaching as needed.

At some organizations, succession planning systems identify a few potential managers for each position. This limited approach allows the organization to target development activities to the most talented managers, but it may not prepare enough managers to fill vacant positions. High-potential employees who are not on the short list for managerial jobs may leave. American Express's approach avoids this problem by identifying many qualified leaders, which builds commitment to the company.

Dysfunctional Managers

A manager who is otherwise competent may engage in some behaviors that make him or her ineffective or even "toxic"—someone who stifles good ideas and drives away employees. These dysfunctional behaviors include insensitivity to others, inability to be a team player, arrogance, poor conflict management skills, inability to meet business objectives, and inability to adapt to change.[53] For example, suppose a manager has great depth of technical knowledge and has excellent ability in keeping two steps ahead of competitors. But the manager is abrasive and aggressive with employees and peers and has a leadership style that discourages employees from contributing their ideas. This manager is likely to have difficulty motivating employees and may alienate people inside and outside the organization. Some of these dysfunctional manager behaviors are illustrated humorously in the popular "Dilbert" comic strip, shown in Figure 9.6.

When a manager is an otherwise valuable employee and is willing to improve, the organization may try to help him or her change the dysfunctional behavior. The usual ways to provide type of development include assessment, training, and counseling. The organization may enroll the manager in a program designed specifically to help managers with dysfunctional behavior, such as the Individual Coaching for Effectiveness (ICE) program. The ICE program includes diagnosis, coaching, and support activities, which are tailored to each manager's needs.[54] Psychologists conduct the diagnosis, coach and counsel the manager, and develop action plans for implementing new skills on the job.

During diagnosis, the psychologist collects information about the manager's personality, skills, and interests. The information comes from psychological tests and interviews with the manager, his or her supervisor, and colleagues. The psychological

FIGURE 9.6
Dysfunctional Managers

tests help the psychologist determine whether the manager will be able to change the dysfunctional behavior. For example, change will be difficult if the manager is extremely defensive. If the diagnosis indicates the manager can benefit from the program, the manager and supervisor work with the psychologist to set specific developmental objectives.

During the coaching phase of the program, the manager receives information about the target skills or behavior. This may include principles of effective communication or teamwork, tolerance of individual differences in the workplace, or conducting effective meetings. Next, the manager participates in behavior modeling training, described in Chapter 7. The manager also receives psychological counseling to overcome beliefs that may interfere with learning the desired behavior.

The support phase of the ICE program creates conditions to ensure that the manager can use the new behaviors and skills on the job. The manager's supervisor gives the manager and psychologist feedback about the manager's progress in using the new skills and behaviors. The psychologist and manager identify situations in which the manager may tend to rely on dysfunctional behavior. The coach and manager also develop action plans that outline how the manager should try to use new behaviors in daily work activities.

The effectiveness of this kind of program has not yet been thoroughly studied. Still, research suggests that managers who participate in programs like ICE improve their skills and are less likely to be terminated.[55] This suggests that organizations can benefit from offering development opportunities to valuable employees with performance problems, not just to star performers.

Summary

1. Discuss how development is related to training and careers.

   Employee development is the combination of formal education, job experiences, relationships, and assessment of personality and abilities to help employees prepare for the future of their careers. Training is more focused on improving performance in the current job, but training programs may support employee development. In modern organizations, the concept of a career is fluid—a protean career that changes along with changes in a person's interests, abilities, and values and changes in the work environment. To plan and prepare for a protean career requires active career management, which includes planning for employee development.

2. Identify the methods organizations use for employee development.

   Organizations may use formal educational programs at the workplace or off-site, such as workshops, university courses and degree programs, company-sponsored training, or programs offered by independent institutions. Organizations may use the assessment process to help employees identify strengths and areas requiring further development. Assessment can help the organization identify employees with managerial potential or identify areas in which teams need to develop. Job experiences help employees develop by stretching their skills as they meet new challenges. Interpersonal relationships with a more experienced member of the organization—often in the role of mentor or coach—can help employees develop their understanding of the organization and its customers.

3. Describe how organizations use assessment of personality type, work behaviors, and job performance to plan employee development.

   Organizations collect information and provide feedback to employees about their behavior, communication style, and skills. The information may come from the employees, their peers, managers, and customers. Many organizations use performance appraisals as a source of assessment information. Appraisals may take the form of 360-degree feedback. Some organizations use psychological tests designed for this purpose, including the Myers-Briggs Type Indicator and the Benchmarks assessment. Assessment centers combine a variety of methods to provide assessment information. Managers must share the assessments, along with suggestions for improvement.

4. Explain how job experiences can be used for developing skills.

   Job experiences contribute to development through a combination of relationships, problems, demands, tasks, and other features of an employee's jobs. The assumption is that development is most likely to occur when the employee's skills and experiences do not entirely match the skills required for the employee's current job, so employees must stretch to meet the demands of the new assignment. The impact varies according to whether the employee views the experience as a positive or negative source of stress. Job experiences that support employee development may include job enlargement, job rotations, transfers, promotions, downward moves, and temporary assignments with other organizations.

5. Summarize principles of successful mentoring programs.

   A mentor is an experienced, productive senior employee who helps develop a less experienced employee. Although most mentoring relationships develop informally, organizations can link mentoring to development goals by establishing a formal mentoring program. A formal program also provides a basis for ensuring that all eligible employees are included. Mentoring programs tend to be most successful when they are voluntary and participants understand the details of the program. The organization should reward managers for employee development, carefully select mentors based on interpersonal and technical skills, train them for the role, and evaluate whether the program has met its objectives.

6. Tell how managers and peers develop employees through coaching.

   A coach is a peer or manager who works with an employee to motivate the employee, help him or her develop skills, and provide reinforcement and feedback. Coaches should be prepared to take on one or more of three roles: working one-on-one with an employee, helping employees learn for themselves, and providing resources, such as mentors, courses, or job experiences.

7. Identify the steps in the process of career management.

   First, during self-assessment, employees use information to determine their career interests, values, aptitudes, and behavioral tendencies, looking for opportunities and areas needing improvement. Self-assessment tools often include psychological tests or exercises that ask about career status and plans. The second step is the reality check, during which the organization communicates information about the employee's skills and knowledge and how these fit into the organization's plan. The employee then sets goals and discusses them with his or her manager, who ensures that the goals are specific, challenging, and attainable. Finally, the employee works with his or her manager to create an action plan for development activities that will help the employee achieve the goals.

8. Discuss how organizations are meeting the challenges of the "glass ceiling," succession planning, and dysfunctional managers.

   The glass ceiling is a barrier that has been observed preventing women and minorities from achieving top jobs in an organization. Development programs can ensure that these employees receive access to development resources such as coaches, mentors, and developmental job assignments. Succession planning ensures that the organization prepares qualified employees to fill management jobs as managers retire. It focuses on applying employee development to high-potential employees. Effective succession planning includes methods for selecting these employees, providing them with developmental experiences, and getting the CEO actively involved with employees who display qualities associated with success as they participate in the developmental activities. For dysfunctional managers who have the potential to contribute to the organization, the organization may offer development targeted at correcting the areas of dysfunction. Typically, the process includes collecting information about the manager's personality, skills, and interests; providing feedback, training, and counseling; and ensuring that the manager can apply new, functional behaviors on the job.

Review and Discussion Questions

1. How does development differ from training? How does development support career management in modern organizations?

2. What are the four broad categories of development methods? Why might it be beneficial to combine all of these methods into a formal development program?

3. Recommend a development method for each of the following situations, and explain why you chose that method.

   a. An employee recently promoted to the job of plant supervisor is having difficulty motivating employees to meet quality standards.

   b. A sales manager annoys salespeople by dictating every detail of their work.

c. An employee has excellent leadership skills but lacks knowledge of the financial side of business.

d. An organization is planning to organize its production workers into teams for the first time.

4. A company that markets sophisticated business management software systems uses sales teams to help customers define needs and to create systems that meet those needs. The teams include programmers, salespeople who specialize in client industries, and software designers. Occasionally sales are lost as a result of conflict or communication problems among team members. The company wants to improve the effectiveness of these teams, and it wants to begin with assessment. How can the teams use 360-degree feedback and psychological tests to develop?

5. In an organization that wants to use work experiences as a method of employee development, what basic options are available? Which of these options would be most attractive to you as an employee? Why?

6. Many employees are unwilling to relocate because they like their current community and family members prefer not to move. Yet preparation for management requires that employees develop new skills, strengthen areas of weakness, and be exposed to new aspects of the organization's business. How can an organization change an employee's current job to develop management skills?

7. Many people feel that mentoring relationships should occur naturally, in situations where senior managers feel inclined to play that role. What are some advantages of setting up a formal mentoring program, rather than letting senior managers decide how and whom to help?

8. What are the three roles of a coach? How is a coach different from a mentor? What are some advantages of using someone outside the organization as a coach? Some disadvantages?

9. Why should organizations be interested in helping employees plan their careers? What benefits can companies gain? What are the risks?

10. What are the manager's roles in a career management system? Which role do you think is most difficult for the typical manager? Which is the easiest role? List reasons why managers might resist becoming involved in career management.

11. What is the glass ceiling? What are the possible consequences to an organization that has a glass ceiling? How can employee development break the glass ceiling? Can succession planning help with this problem? Explain.

12. Why might an organization benefit from giving employee development opportunities to a dysfunctional manager, rather than simply dismissing the manager? Do these reasons apply to nonmanagement employees as well?

What's Your HR IQ?

The Student CD-ROM offers two more ways to check what you've learned so far. Use the Self-Assessment exercise to test your knowledge of employee development. Go online with the Web Exercise to see how well your knowledge works in cyberspace.

BusinessWeek Case

BusinessWeek Basic Training for CEOs

Gary C. Wendt, prepare to be scared straight. On June 21, the Conseco Inc. chief and 19 other recently crowned CEOs will subject themselves to a one-day immersion course administered by a parade of corporate critics and long-time chief executives. Those instructors are convinced they might be the only thing standing between the newbie leaders and career disaster. Open only to CEOs who have held the post for less than three years, the course will be taught by professors from elite business schools, top professionals, and such executive suite veterans as Merck's Raymond V. Gilmartin, Tyco International's former CEO Dennis Kozlowski, and Larry Bossidy,

former head of AlliedSignal. "It's a boot camp for recently appointed CEOs," quips Rajiv L. Gupta, CEO of Rohm & Haas since 1999, who leapt at the chance to enlist.

To be sure, the CEO Academy is more than just a novel experiment in executive education—it may be the poshest, most expensive boot camp ever. The brainchild of an innovative CEO roundtable, the academy was conceived as a way for recently anointed CEOs to learn the perils of life in the corner office and for old-timers to discuss the trials and tribulations of CEO life before a receptive audience. It will be held in the august Harold Pratt mansion on New York city's Upper East Side. Tuition for the one-day course is a cool $10,000. But the lessons—dealing with the land mines that can bring an early end to a CEO's career—will be just as biting as the bark of any drill sergeant.

Newly minted CEOs expecting a lovefest are in for a rude awakening. The session on shareholder relations will be led in part by Nell Minow, a corporate governance agitator who has helped build bonfires under boards reluctant to deal with poor-performing CEOs. "My goal is to teach them what they need to do to avoid hearing from people like me in real life," says Minow, who will urge the CEOs to adopt performance-based pay plans, preferred by shareholders. Says Minow, "If they are responsive [to shareholders] in good times, they will have a better chance of keeping them on their side in a downturn."

If Minow's lecture reminds the new CEOs of one set of bosses, the presentation by superlawyer Ira M. Millstein, the dean of corporate governance, will urge them to pay heed to another: their board members. Millstein believes most new CEOs "would be just as happy not to have a board at all," and give it a low priority. To snap them out of that delusion, he'll warn: "There is nothing more important than getting to know the people who can fire you."

But the highlight of the CEO Academy will no doubt occur when veteran CEOs are asked to share their experiences. G. Richard Thoman, who was fired as Xerox Corporation CEO last May, will talk about the lessons he learned at both Xerox and IBM. Gilmartin, an outsider who reinvigorated Merck & Company, will discuss the special challenges facing CEOs who are brought in from the outside.

Most of the "students" can't wait to get started. "We're most able to learn when we're new in a job," says Amgen CEO Kevin W. Sharer, who got the top job a year ago and expects to benefit from people like Bossidy who have years of experience heading complex organizations.

And that, say the group's founders, is the whole point. The CEO Academy is the creation of the M&A Group Inc., a CEO club formed in 1999 as a forum to discuss and facilitate mergers and acquisitions among members. They quickly realized new CEOs needed help getting their bearings.

The reason? Although these industry titans get paid a king's ransom whether they succeed or fail, job security is a thing of the past. "This is a high-risk job," says Kozlowski, the M&A Group's chairman. "Our ranks [turn over] about 20 percent every year." And with the honeymoon period growing ever shorter, new CEOs have little time to get up to speed. Moreover, "many new CEOs have had limited experience in running a board, or in dealing with Wall Street, the business press, and shareholders," says Dennis C. Carey, a partner at headhunter Spencer-Stuart. That's why he recruited CEOs as instructors. "I wish I'd had [the chance to attend] a forum like this when I became CEO," says Kozlowski.

Of course, the ultimate test of any boot camp is whether it reduces the casualty rate among participants. It will take years to measure the effectiveness of the academy, which the M&A Group hopes to host annually. But with more CEOs crashing and burning, it sounds like a step in the right direction.

SOURCE: W. C. Symonds, "Basic Training for CEOs," *BusinessWeek*, June 11, 2001.

Questions

1. This chapter focused on employee development as a way to prepare for jobs with greater responsibility. Why would someone who has already gained an organization's top job (chief executive officer) want to participate in employee development activities such as the CEO Academy?
2. What development methods does the CEO Academy use? Can you suggest any other methods that would help a CEO become more effective?
3. A chief executive would not be able to turn to higher-level managers at the organization to serve as the CEO's mentor or coach. Who might coach or mentor a CEO or other high-level manager?

Case: Developing Employees Reduces Risk for First USA Bank

First USA Bank is the largest issuer of Visa credit cards. The company offers cards for consumers and businesses under its own name, that of its parent company (Bank One), the First Card name, and on behalf of several thousand marketing partners. These partners include leading U.S. corporations, universities, sports franchises, and financial institutions. First USA is based in Wilmington, Delaware, and has 11,000 employees.

First USA offers its employees a way to help identify their career dreams and plan what to do to achieve them. The company's Opportunity Knocks program was designed in 1998 in response to the results of an employee attitude survey showing that employees were dissatisfied with their jobs and pessimistic about their future job and career prospects within First USA. The goals of the Opportunity Knocks program are to improve job satisfaction, reduce turnover, and increase the number of employees promoted. First USA also wants its employees to take charge of their own careers and to realize that promotions are not the only desirable career path. For example, lateral moves within the company let employees work in different jobs at the same level, which can help the employees develop a greater range of experience and perspective.

The core philosophy of Opportunity Knocks is what First

USA calls "five *P*s": person, perspective, place, possibility, and plan. The *person*, or individual employee, needs to understand his or her skills, values, and interests and to communicate them so career development is possible. Employees conduct self-assessments and seek feedback on them by talking to peers and managers. These self-assessments and discussions give the employees *perspective*. Employees must gain a sense of *place*, meaning they need to understand not only First USA and their jobs, but also developments in the industry, profession, and workplace requiring changes in employees' skills. Employees need to consider different *possibilities* within First USA: moving laterally or vertically or enriching the current job. Finally, employees need *plans* for developing new skills and knowledge that will help them reach their career goals.

First USA's development program includes workshops that teach career management skills. In addition, the company set up career resource centers at each worksite. These centers offer business publications, career management literature, and computers for preparing résumés. First USA also hired employment development advisers to counsel employees about their career plans.

The program has had many benefits. Internal promotions at First USA have increased by 50 percent. Attitudes have improved as well. When First USA repeated the employee attitude survey, the company found that employee satisfaction with career development opportunities had increased more than 25 percent. Furthermore, employees who participated in the Opportunity Knocks program were far more likely to stay with the company than those who did not participate.

SOURCE: Based on P. Kiger, "At First USA Bank, Promotions and Job Satisfaction Are Up," *Workforce*, March 2001, pp. 54–56.

Questions

1. What benefits does the Opportunity Knocks program offer to employees? To First USA?
2. Suggest some ways that First USA could enhance this program with other employee development activities.
3. What if the Opportunity Knocks program leads some employees to decide they should leave the company to pursue their career objectives elsewhere? Does that make the program unwise? How might First USA address this risk?

Notes

1. M. London, *Managing the Training Enterprise* (San Francisco: Jossey-Bass, 1989).
2. R. W. Pace, P. C. Smith, and G. E. Mills, *Human Resource Development* (Englewood Cliffs, NJ: Prentice Hall, 1991); W. Fitzgerald, "Training versus Development," *Training and Development Journal*, May 1992, pp. 81–84; R. A. Noe, S. L. Wilk, E. J. Mullen, and J. E. Wanek, "Employee Development: Issues in Construct Definition and Investigation of Antecedents," in *Improving Training Effectiveness in Work Organizations*, ed. J. K. Ford (Mahwah, NJ: Lawrence Erlbaum, 1997), pp. 153–89.
3. J. H. Greenhaus and G. A. Callanan, *Career Management*, 2nd ed. (Fort Worth, TX: Dryden Press, 1994).
4. M. B. Arthur, P. H. Claman, and R. J. DeFillippi, "Intelligent Enterprise, Intelligent Careers," *Academy of Management Executive* 9 (1995), pp. 7–20.
5. K. Walter, "The MTA Travels Far with Its Future Managers Program," *Personnel Journal*, August 1995, pp. 68–72.
6. R. J. Campbell, "HR Development Strategies," in *Developing Human Resources*, ed. K. N. Wexley (Washington, DC: BNA Books, 1991), pp. 5-1–5-34; M. A. Sheppeck and C. A. Rhodes, "Management Development: Revised Thinking in Light of New Events of Strategic Importance," *Human Resource Planning* 11 (1988), pp. 159–72; B. Keys and J. Wolf, "Management Education: Current Issues and Emerging Trends," *Journal of Management* 14 (1988), pp. 205–29; L. M. Saari, T. R. Johnson, S. D. McLaughlin, and D. Zimmerle, "A Survey of Management Training and Education Practices in U.S. Companies," *Personnel Psychology* 41 (1988), pp. 731–44.
7. T. A. Stewart, "GE Keeps Those Ideas Coming," *Fortune*, August 12, 1991, pp. 41–49; N. M. Tichy, "GE's Crotonville: A Staging Ground for a Corporate Revolution," *The Executive* 3 (1989), pp. 99–106; General Electric website, www.ge.com.
8. J. Reingold, "Corporate America Goes to School," *BusinessWeek*, October 20, 1997, pp. 66–72.
9. Ibid.
10. A. Howard and D. W. Bray, *Managerial Lives in Transition: Advancing Age and Changing Times* (New York: Guilford, 1988); J. Bolt, *Executive Development* (New York: Harper Business, 1989); J. R. Hinrichs and G. P. Hollenbeck, "Leadership Development," in *Developing Human Resources*, pp. 5-221–5-237.
11. A. Thorne and H. Gough, *Portraits of Type* (Palo Alto, CA: Consulting Psychologists Press, 1993).
12. D. Druckman and R. A. Bjork, eds., *In the Mind's Eye: Enhancing Human Performance* (Washington, DC: National Academy Press, 1991); M. H. McCaulley, "The Myers-Briggs Type Indicator and Leadership," in *Measures of Leadership*, ed. K. E. Clark and M. B. Clark (West Orange, NJ: Leadership Library of America, 1990), pp. 381–418.

13. G. C. Thornton III and W. C. Byham, *Assessment Centers and Managerial Performance* (New York: Academic Press, 1982); L. F. Schoenfeldt and J. A. Steger, "Identification and Development of Management Talent," in *Research in Personnel and Human Resource Management*, vol. 7, ed. K. N. Rowland and G. Ferris (Greenwich, CT: JAI Press, 1989), pp. 151–81.

14. Thornton and Byham, *Assessment Centers and Managerial Performance*.

15. P. G. W. Jansen and B. A. M. Stoop, "The Dynamics of Assessment Center Validity: Results of a Seven-Year Study," *Journal of Applied Psychology* 86 (2001), pp. 741–53; D. Chan, "Criterion and Construct Validation of an Assessment Centre," *Journal of Occupational and Organizational Psychology* 69 (1996), pp. 167–81.

16. R. G. Jones and M. D. Whitmore, "Evaluating Developmental Assessment Centers as Interventions," *Personnel Psychology* 48 (1995), pp. 377–88.

17. C. D. McCauley and M. M. Lombardo, "Benchmarks: An Instrument for Diagnosing Managerial Strengths and Weaknesses," in *Measures of Leadership*, pp. 535–45.

18. C. D. McCauley, M. M. Lombardo, and C. J. Usher, "Diagnosing Management Development Needs: An Instrument Based on How Managers Develop," *Journal of Management* 15 (1989), pp. 389–403.

19. S. B. Silverman, "Individual Development through Performance Appraisal," in *Developing Human Resources*, pp. 5-120–5-151.

20. B. Pfau and I. Kay, "Does 360-Degree Feedback Negatively Affect Company Performance?" *HR Magazine* 47 (2002), pp. 54–59; J. F. Brett and L. E. Atwater, "360-Degree Feedback: Accuracy, Reactions, and Perceptions of Usefulness," *Journal of Applied Psychology* 86 (2001), pp. 930–42.

21. S. Caudron, "Building Better Bosses," *Workforce*, May 2000, pp. 33–39.

22. L. Atwater, P. Roush, and A. Fischthal, "The Influence of Upward Feedback on Self- and Follower Ratings of Leadership," *Personnel Psychology* 48 (1995), pp. 35–59; J. F. Hazucha, S. A. Hezlett, and R. J. Schneider, "The Impact of 360-Degree Feedback on Management Skill Development," *Human Resource Management* 32 (1993), pp. 325–51; J. W. Smither, M. London, N. Vasilopoulos, R. R. Reilly, R. E. Millsap, and N. Salvemini, "An Examination of the Effects of an Upward Feedback Program over Time," *Personnel Psychology* 48 (1995), pp. 1–34.

23. D. Bracken, "Straight Talk about Multirater Feedback," *Training and Development*, September 1994, pp. 44–51.

24. M. W. McCall Jr., *High Flyers* (Boston: Harvard Business School Press, 1998).

25. R. S. Snell, "Congenial Ways of Learning: So Near yet So Far," *Journal of Management Development* 9 (1990), pp. 17–23.

26. M. McCall, M. Lombardo, and A. Morrison, *Lessons of Experience* (Lexington, MA: Lexington Books, 1988); M. W. McCall, "Developing Executives through Work Experiences," *Human Resource Planning* 11 (1988), pp. 1–11; M. N. Ruderman, P. J. Ohlott, and C. D. McCauley, "Assessing Opportunities for Leadership Development," in *Measures of Leadership*, pp. 547–62; C. D. McCauley, L. J. Estman, and P. J. Ohlott, "Linking Management Selection and Development through Stretch Assignments," *Human Resource Management* 34 (1995), pp. 93–115.

27. C. D. McCauley, M. N. Ruderman, P. J. Ohlott, and J. E. Morrow, "Assessing the Developmental Components of Managerial Jobs," *Journal of Applied Psychology* 79 (1994), pp. 544–60.

28. M. Frase-Blunt, "Ready, Set, Rotate," *HR Magazine*, October 2001, pp. 46–53; G. B. Northcraft, T. L. Griffith, and C. E. Shalley, "Building Top Management Muscle in a Slow Growth Environment: How Different Is Better at Greyhound Financial Corporation," *The Executive* 6 (1992), pp. 32–41.

29. M. London, *Developing Managers* (San Francisco: Jossey-Bass, 1985); M. A. Camion, L. Cheraskin, and M. J. Stevens, "Career-Related Antecedents and Outcomes of Job Rotation," *Academy of Management Journal* 37 (1994), pp. 1518–42; London, *Managing the Training Enterprise*.

30. L. Cheraskin and M. Campion, "Study Clarifies Job Rotation Benefits," *Personnel Journal*, November 1996, pp. 31–38.

31. R. A. Noe, B. D. Steffy, and A. E. Barber, "An Investigation of the Factors Influencing Employees' Willingness to Accept Mobility Opportunities," *Personnel Psychology* 41 (1988), pp. 559–80; S. Gould and L. E. Penley, "A Study of the Correlates of Willingness to Relocate," *Academy of Management Journal* 28 (1984), pp. 472–78; J. Landau and T. H. Hammer, "Clerical Employees' Perceptions of Intraorganizational Career Opportunities," *Academy of Management Journal* 29 (1986), pp. 385–405; J. M. Brett and A. H. Reilly, "On the Road Again: Predicting the Job Transfer Decision," *Journal of Applied Psychology* 73 (1988), pp. 614–20.

32. J. M. Brett, "Job Transfer and Well-Being," *Journal of Applied Psychology* 67 (1992), pp. 450–63; F. J. Minor, L. A. Slade, and R. A. Myers, "Career Transitions in Changing Times," in *Contemporary Career Development Issues*, ed. R. F. Morrison and J. Adams (Hillsdale, NJ: Lawrence Erlbaum, 1991), pp. 109–20; C. C. Pinder and K. G. Schroeder, "Time to Proficiency Following Job Transfers," *Academy of Management Journal* 30 (1987), pp. 336–53; G. Flynn, "Heck No—We Won't Go!" *Personnel Journal*, March 1996, pp. 37–43.

33. R. E. Silverman, "Mercer Tries to Keep Employees through Its 'Externship' Program," *The Wall Street Journal*, November 7, 2000, p. B18.

34. B. Bounds, "Give Me a Break," *The Wall Street Journal*, May 5, 2000, pp. W1, W4.

35. D. B. Turban and T. W. Dougherty, "Role of Protégé Personality in Receipt of Mentoring and Career Success," *Academy of Management Journal* 37 (1994), pp. 688–702; E. A. Fagenson, "Mentoring: Who Needs It? A Comparison of Protégés' and Nonprotégés' Needs for Power, Achievement, Affiliation, and Autonomy," *Journal of Vocational Behavior* 41 (1992), pp. 48–60.

36. A. H. Geiger, "Measures for Mentors," *Training and Development Journal*, February 1992, pp. 65–67.

37. K. E. Kram, *Mentoring at Work: Developmental Relationships in Organizational Life* (Glenview, IL: Scott-Foresman, 1985); L. L. Phillips-Jones, "Establishing a Formalized Mentoring Program," *Training and Development Journal* 2 (1983), pp. 38–42; K. Kram, "Phases of the Mentoring Relationship," *Academy of Management Journal* 26 (1983), pp. 608–25; G. T. Chao, P. M. Walz, and P. D. Gardner, "Formal and Informal Mentorships: A Comparison of Mentoring Functions and Contrasts with Nonmentored Counterparts," *Personnel Psychology* 45 (1992), pp. 619–36.

38. C. M. Solomon, "Hotel Breathes Life into Hospital's Customer Service," *Personnel Journal*, October 1995, p. 120.

39. R. A. Noe, D. Greenberger, and S. Wang, "Mentoring: What We Know and Where We Might Go," in G. R. Ferris and J. J. Martocchio, eds., *Research in Personnel and Human Resources Management*, vol. 21 (Oxford: Elsevier Science, forthcoming).

40. M. Murray, "GE Mentoring Program Turns Underlings into Teachers of the Web," *The Wall Street Journal*, February 15, 2000, pp. B1, B16.

41. D. B. Peterson and M. D. Hicks, *Leader as Coach* (Minneapolis: Personnel Decisions, 1996).

42. J. S. Lublin, "Building a Better CEO," *The Wall Street Journal*, April 14, 2000, pp. B1, B4.

43. B. Baumann, J. Duncan, S. E. Former, and Z. Leibowitz, "Amoco Primes the Talent Pump," *Personnel Journal*, February 1996, pp. 79–84.

44. Ford Motor Company, "Personal Development Roadmap," *Ford* brochure, Detroit, 1998.

45. P. J. Ohlott, M. N. Ruderman, and C. D. McCauley, "Gender Differences in Managers' Developmental Job Experiences," *Academy of Management Journal* 37 (1994), pp. 46–67.

46. L. A. Mainiero, "Getting Anointed for Advancement: The Case of Executive Women," *Academy of Management Executive* 8 (1994), pp. 53–67; J. S. Lublin, "Women at Top Still Are Distant from CEO Jobs," *The Wall Street Journal*, February 28, 1995, pp. B1, B5; P. Tharenov, S. Latimer, and D. Conroy, "How Do You Make It to the Top? An Examination of Influences on Women's and Men's Managerial Advancements," *Academy of Management Journal* 37 (1994), pp. 899–931.

47. U.S. Department of Labor, *A Report on the Glass Ceiling Initiative* (Washington, DC: Labor Department, 1991); R. A. Noe, "Women and Mentoring: A Review and Research Agenda," *Academy of Management Review* 13 (1988), pp. 65–78; B. R. Ragins and J. L. Cotton, "Easier Said than Done: Gender Differences in Perceived Barriers to Gaining a Mentor," *Academy of Management Journal* 34 (1991), pp. 939–51.

48. D. McCracken, "Winning the Talent War for Women," *Harvard Business Review*, November–December 2000, pp. 159–67.

49. W. J. Rothwell, *Effective Succession Planning*, 2nd ed. (New York: AMACOM, 2001).

50. B. E. Dowell, "Succession Planning," in *Implementing Organizational Interventions*, ed. J. Hedge and E. D. Pulakos (San Francisco: Jossey-Bass, 2002), pp. 78–109.

51. C. B. Derr, C. Jones, and E. L. Toomey, "Managing High-Potential Employees: Current Practices in Thirty-Three U.S. Corporations," *Human Resource Management* 27 (1988), pp. 273–90; K. M. Nowack, "The Secrets of Succession," *Training and Development* 48 (1994), pp. 49–54; J. S. Lublin, "An Overseas Stint Can Be a Ticket to the Top," *The Wall Street Journal*, January 29, 1996, pp. B1, B2.

52. B. Gerber, "Who Will Replace Those Vanishing Execs?" *Training*, July 2000, pp. 49–53.

53. M. W. McCall Jr. and M. M. Lombardo, "Off the Track: Why and How Successful Executives Get Derailed," *Technical Report*, no. 21 (Greensboro, NC: Center for Creative Leadership, 1983); E. V. Veslo and J. B. Leslie, "Why Executives Derail: Perspectives across Time and Cultures," *Academy of Management Executive* 9 (1995), pp. 62–72.

54. L. W. Hellervik, J. F. Hazucha, and R. J. Schneider, "Behavior Change: Models, Methods, and a Review of Evidence," in *Handbook of Industrial and Organizational Psychology*, vol. 3, 2nd ed., ed. M. D. Dunnette and L. M. Hough (Palo Alto, CA: Consulting Psychologists Press, 1992), pp. 823–99.

55. D. B. Peterson, "Measuring and Evaluating Change in Executive and Managerial Development," paper presented at the annual conference of the Society for Industrial and Organizational Psychology, Miami, 1990.

Separating and Retaining Employees

1. Distinguish between involuntary and voluntary turnover, and describe their effects on an organization.

2. Discuss how employees determine whether the organization treats them fairly.

3. Identify legal requirements for employee discipline.

4. Summarize ways in which organizations can fairly discipline employees.

5. Explain how job dissatisfaction affects employee behavior.

6. Describe how organizations contribute to employees' job satisfaction and retain key employees.

Introduction

Manitowoc, Wisconsin, was once a center of boat-building activity, and Burger Boat developed a reputation for building high-quality yachts there. So it was a sad occurrence in 1990 when Burger became the last of the shipbuilders to leave or close down. What Burger's absentee corporate ownership did not fully appreciate, however, was the commitment of Burger's people, many of whom were their families' third generation with the company. Some even sneaked into the closed shipyard to get their tools and finish a boat they had been working on. With the help of Chicago entrepreneur David Ross, who moved to Manitowoc, a group of employees were able to revive the company. Today, orders and revenues are flowing in, and Burger is again profitable.

About his decision to invest in Burger, Ross says, "I determined that this company was zero without the people who made it famous."[1]

Every organization recognizes that it needs satisfied, loyal customers and satisfied, loyal investors. Customers and investors provide the financial resources that let an organization survive and grow. In addition, as David Ross appreciates, success requires satisfied, loyal employees. Research provides evidence that retaining employees helps retain customers and investors.[2] Organizations with low turnover and satisfied employees tend to perform better.[3] On the other side of the coin, organizations have to act when an employee's performance consistently falls short. Sometimes terminating a poor performer is the only way to show fairness, ensure quality, and maintain customer satisfaction.

This chapter explores the dual challenge of separating and retaining employees. We begin by distinguishing involuntary and voluntary turnover, describing how each affects the organization. Next we explore the separation process, including ways to manage this process fairly. Finally, we discuss measures the organization can take to encourage employees to stay. These topics provide a transition between Parts 3 and 4. The previous chapters in Part 3 considered how to assess and improve performance, and this chapter describes measures to take depending on whether performance is high or low. Part 4 discusses pay and benefits, both of which play an important role in employee retention.

Managing Voluntary and Involuntary Turnover

LO1

Organizations must try to ensure that good performers want to stay with the organization and that employees whose performance is chronically low are encouraged—or forced—to leave. Both of these challenges involve *employee turnover*, that is, employees leaving the organization. When the organization initiates the turnover (often with employees who would prefer to stay), the result is **involuntary turnover.** Examples include terminating an employee for drug use or laying off employees during a downturn. Most organizations use the word *termination* to refer only to a discharge related to a discipline problem, but some organizations call any involuntary turnover a termination. When the employees initiate the turnover (often when the organization would prefer to keep them), it is **voluntary turnover.** Employees may leave to retire or to take a job with a different organization.

In general, organizations try to avoid the need for involuntary turnover and to minimize voluntary turnover, especially among top performers. Both kinds of turnover are costly, as summarized in Table 10.1. Replacing workers is expensive, and new employees need time to learn their jobs. In addition, people today are more ready

involuntary turnover
Turnover initiated by an employer (often with employees who would prefer to stay).

voluntary turnover
Turnover initiated by employees (often when the organization would prefer to keep them).

TABLE 10.1

Costs Associated with Turnover

INVOLUNTARY TURNOVER	VOLUNTARY TURNOVER
Recruiting, selecting, and training replacements	Recruiting, selecting, and training replacements
Lost productivity	Lost productivity
Lawsuits	Loss of talented employees
Workplace violence	

to sue a former employer if they feel they were unfairly discharged. The prospect of workplace violence also raises the risk associated with discharging employees. Effective human resource management can help the organization minimize both kinds of turnover, as well as carry it out effectively when necessary. Despite a company's best efforts at personnel selection, training, and compensation, some employees will fail to meet performance requirements or will violate company policies. When this happens, organizations need to apply a discipline program that could ultimately lead to discharging the individual.

For a number of reasons, discharging employees can be very difficult. First, the decision has legal aspects that can affect the organization. Historically, if the organization and employee do not have a specific employment contract, the employer or employee may end the employment relationship at any time. This is the *employment-at-will doctrine*, described in Chapter 5. This doctrine has eroded significantly, however. Employees who have been terminated sometimes sue their employers for wrongful discharge. Some judges have considered that there could be an implied employment contract if employees meet certain criteria such as length of employment, promotions, raises, or favorable performance appraisals—even when the organization has a handbook that says there is an employment-at-will relationship.[4] In a typical lawsuit for wrongful discharge, the former employee tries to establish that the discharge violated either an implied agreement or public policy (for example, firing an employee for refusing to do something illegal). In cases of wrongful discharge, employees often win settlements of hundreds of thousands of dollars.

Along with the financial risks of dismissing an employee, there are issues related to personal safety. Distressing as it is that some former employees go to the courts, even more problematic are the employees who react to a termination decision with violence. Violence in the workplace has become a major organizational problem. Workplace homicide is the fastest-growing form of murder in the United States.[5] Although any number of organizational actions or decisions may incite violence among employees, the "nothing else to lose" aspect of an employee's dismissal makes the situation dangerous.

Retaining top performers is not always easy either, and recent trends have made this more difficult than ever. The rash of layoffs and downsizings of the early and mid-1990s reduced employees' loyalty to their organizations. This mistrust coupled with the tight labor markets of the 1990s created a workforce that is both willing and able to leave on a moment's notice.

Employee Separation

Because of the critical financial and personal risks associated with employee dismissal, it is easy to see why organizations must develop a standardized, systematic approach to discipline and discharge. These decisions should not be left solely to the discretion of individual managers or supervisors. Policies that can lead to employee separation should be based on principles of justice and law, and they should allow for various ways to intervene.

LO2

Principles of Justice

The sensitivity of a system for disciplining and possibly terminating employees is obvious, and it is critical that the system be seen as fair. Employees form conclusions about the system's fairness based on the system's outcomes and procedures and the

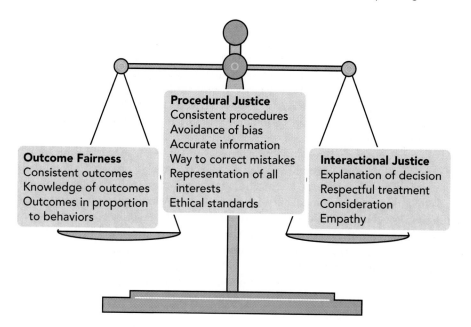

FIGURE 10.1

Principles of Justice

Outcome Fairness
Consistent outcomes
Knowledge of outcomes
Outcomes in proportion
   to behaviors

Procedural Justice
Consistent procedures
Avoidance of bias
Accurate information
Way to correct mistakes
Representation of all
   interests
Ethical standards

Interactional Justice
Explanation of decision
Respectful treatment
Consideration
Empathy

way managers treat employees when carrying out those procedures. Figure 10.1 summarizes these principles as outcome fairness, procedural justice, and interactional justice. Outcome fairness involves the ends of a discipline process, while procedural and interactional justice focus on the means to those ends.

People's perception of **outcome fairness** depends on their judgment that the consequences of a decision to employees are just. As shown in Figure 10.1, one employee's consequences should be consistent with other employees' consequences. Suppose several employees went out to lunch, returned drunk, and were reprimanded. A few weeks later, another employee was fired for being drunk at work. Employees might well conclude that outcomes are not fair because they are inconsistent. Another basis for outcome fairness is that everyone should know what to expect. Organizations promote outcome fairness when they clearly communicate policies regarding the consequences of inappropriate behavior. Finally, the outcome should be proportionate to the behavior. Terminating an employee for being late to work, especially if this is the first time the employee is late, would seem out of proportion to the offense in most situations. Employees' sense of outcome fairness usually would reserve loss of a job for the most serious offenses.

People's perception of **procedural justice** is their judgment that fair methods were used to determine the consequences an employee receives. Figure 10.1 shows six principles that determine whether people perceive procedures as fair. The procedures should be consistent from one person to another, and the manager using them should suppress any personal biases. The procedures should be based on accurate information, not rumors or falsehoods. The procedures should also be correctable, meaning the system includes safeguards, such as channels for appealing a decision or correcting errors. The procedures should take into account the concerns of all the groups affected—for example, by gathering information from employees, customers, and managers. Finally, the procedures should be consistent with prevailing ethical standards, such as concerns for privacy and honesty.

A perception of **interactional justice** is a judgment that the organization carried out its actions in a way that took the employee's feelings into account. It is a judgment

outcome fairness
A judgment that the consequences given to employees are just.

procedural justice
A judgment that fair methods were used to determine the consequences an employee receives.

interactional justice
A judgment that the organization carried out its actions in a way that took the employee's feelings into account.

about the ways that managers interact with their employees. A disciplinary action meets the standards of interactional justice if the manager explains to the employee how the action is procedurally just. The manager should listen to the employee. The manager should also treat the employee with dignity and respect and should empathize with the employee's feelings. Even when a manager discharges an employee for doing something wrong, the manager can speak politely and state the reasons for the action.

Meeting these standards can be difficult, because managers are as uncomfortable as anyone else when they have to deliver bad news. As a result, organizations sometimes handle separation and other negative actions in ways that employees find infuriating. For example, Inacom handled the layoff of 5,000 employees by directing them to call an 800 number. At that number, a recording told the employees they were off work, effective immediately. Chrysler workers didn't even make it inside the building to get the news. Workers figured out they were laid off when their ID badges no longer operated the security gates at the factory entrance. And in January 2000, Amazon.com announced job cuts by sending e-mails to employees at their homes, telling them they were no longer needed. None of these methods leaves room for such measures of interactional justice as listening to the employee. A better approach is for a direct supervisor to deliver the news, perhaps with the assistance of an HR specialist, who can answer questions about company policy.[6]

Justice issues also come into play in the use of *noncompete agreements*—contracts in which employees agree that in the future they will not take a job with a competitor of the employer.[7] Some noncompete agreements limit this restriction by preventing future employment with competitors only in a certain geographic area or within a certain time period after leaving the employer. Outside that area or after that time period, the former employee may work for a competitor without violating the agreement. During the 1990s, the use of noncompete agreements increased, as organizations looked for ways to protect their ability to compete through employees' expert knowledge. Employers see the agreements as fair because the employers have invested in training employees and providing them with the skills, information, personal contacts, and experiences that make them valuable in the workplace. From the employer's point of view, it would be unfair for an employee to obtain these advantages, then take them to a competitor in exchange for higher pay. From many employees' point of view, the agreements are unfair because they make it impractical to find another job if employees are dissatisfied—or even if they are laid off.

Consider the case of Debra Pilkerton, an optician. After working at the Annapolis office of the TLC Laser Eye Center for several months, Pilkerton had a major argument with her supervisor. She left TLC and, with 23 years of experience, found a new job at the Baltimore Laser Eye Center. Lawyers from TLC wrote to Pilkerton's employer to notify them that Pilkerton was in violation of a noncompete agreement she had signed at TLC. Rather than defend a lawsuit, Baltimore Laser Eye Center terminated Pilkerton from her new job. Two of the justice issues involved in this situation are whether the outcome was in proportion to the significance of an optician's role at a laser eye center and whether TLC handled Pilkerton's situation with procedures that were just.

Legal Requirements

LO3

The law gives employers wide latitude in hiring and firing, but employers must meet certain requirements. They must avoid wrongful discharge and illegal discrimination. They also must meet standards related to employees' privacy and adequate notice of layoffs.

Wrongful Discharge

As we noted earlier in the chapter, discipline practices must avoid the charge of wrongful discharge. First, this means the discharge may not violate an implied agreement. For instance, terminating an employee may violate an implied agreement if the employer had promised the employee job security or if the action is inconsistent with company policies. Suppose an organization has stated that an employee with an unexcused absence will receive a warning for the first violation, but an angry supervisor fires an employee for being absent on the day of an important meeting. That employee may be able to claim violation of an implied agreement. Similarly, if an organization's employee handbook or intranet Web page includes statements of employment rights, such as "permanent" employment after 90 days' probation, a court might find those statements to be an implied employment agreement.[8]

Another reason a discharge may be considered wrongful is that it violates public policy. Violations of public policy include terminating the employee for refusing to do something illegal, unethical, or unsafe. Suppose an employee refuses to dump chemicals into the sewer system; firing that employee could be a violation of public policy. It is also a violation of public policy to terminate an employee for doing what the law requires—for example, cooperating with a government investigation, reporting illegal behavior by the employer, or reporting for jury duty.

HR professionals can help organizations avoid (and defend against) charges of wrongful discharge by establishing and communicating policies for handling misbehavior. They should define unacceptable behaviors and identify how the organization will respond to them. Managers should follow these procedures consistently and document precisely the reasons for disciplinary action. In addition, the organization should train managers to avoid making promises that imply job security (for example, "As long as you keep up that level of performance, you'll have a job with us"). Finally, in writing and reviewing employee handbooks, HR professionals should avoid any statements that could be interpreted as employment contracts. When there is any doubt about a statement, the organization should seek legal advice.

Discrimination

Another benefit of a formal discipline policy is that it helps the organization comply with equal employment opportunity requirements. As in other employment matters, employers must make decisions without regard to individuals' age, sex, race, or other protected status. If two employees steal from the employer but one is disciplined more harshly than the other, the employee who receives the harsher punishment could look for the cause in his or her being of a particular race, country of origin, or some other group. Evenhanded, carefully documented discipline can avoid such claims.

Employees' Privacy

The courts also have long protected individuals' privacy in many situations.[9] At the same time, employers have legitimate reasons for learning about some personal matters, especially when behavior outside the workplace can affect productivity, workplace safety, and employee morale. Employers therefore need to ensure that the information they gather and use is relevant to these matters. For example, safety and security make it legitimate to require drug testing of all employees holding jobs such as police officer, firefighter, and airline flight crew.[10] (Governments at the federal, state, and local levels have many laws affecting drug-testing programs, so it is wise to get legal advice before planning such tests.) Likewise, an employee who has committed a violent crime outside the workplace may be prone to violent actions against coworkers or customers. Complicating this situation, an arrest does not prove a person's guilt; only a conviction does. Therefore, the organization might place an arrested employee on a leave of absence and then terminate the employee only if the arrest leads to a conviction.

The issue of off-the-job behavior took on heightened importance in the United States following the terrorist attacks of September 2001.[11] Employers became more concerned about workplace safety and security, and some prominent firms conducted background checks on current employees and contract workers. The emphasis on caution has led to some extreme responses. A pipe insulator who worked at an Eli Lilly factory in Indianapolis was banned from the facility because she had unintentionally bounced a check two years earlier while divorcing and moving to a new home. Lilly had paid for thousands of background checks of credit reports, criminal records, and motor vehicle records. According to union officials, the company banned at least 100 contract workers as a result. The company had informed the workers before the background checks, but they knew they would not be allowed to return if they refused their consent. A Lilly spokeswoman said the actions were a part of "doing what we must do to protect our company, our people, our assets, and our products," which include many widely prescribed drugs. Unions have begun challenging some of these dismissals at Lilly and other companies, including major airlines.

Privacy issues also surface when employers wish to search or monitor employees on the job. An employer that suspects theft by employees or drug use on the job may wish to search employees for evidence. In general, random searches of areas such as desks, lockers, and toolboxes are permissible, so long as the employer can justify that there is probable cause for the search and the organization has work rules that pro-

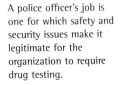

A police officer's job is one for which safety and security issues make it legitimate for the organization to require drug testing.

help the parties arrive at a settlement. To set up a panel to hear disputes as they arise, the organization may assign managers to positions on the panel and have employees elect nonmanagement panel members.

3. **Mediation**—If the peer review does not lead to a settlement, a neutral party from outside the organization hears the case and tries to help the people in conflict arrive at a settlement. The process is not binding, meaning the mediator cannot force a solution.

4. **Arbitration**—If mediation fails, a professional arbitrator from outside the organization hears the case and resolves it by making a decision. Most arbitrators are experienced employment lawyers or retired judges. The employee and employer both have to accept this person's decision. Recently, an arbitrator required Dow Chemical Company to rehire a dozen workers it had fired.[18] Dow had discovered that over 250 workers were using the company's e-mail system to send sexually explicit and violent material, but it fired only 12 of them. The rest were reprimanded. Because the discipline was not consistent, it did not stand up in arbitration.

Each stage reflects a somewhat broader involvement of people outside the dispute. The hope is that the conflict will be resolved at earlier stages, where the costs, time, and embarrassing publicity are lowest. However, even the arbitration stage tends to be much faster, simpler, and more private than a lawsuit.[19]

Experience shows that ADR can effectively save time and money. Over a four-year period of using ADR, Houston-based Brown and Root experienced a 90 percent drop in its legal fees. Of 2,000 disputes, only 30 ever reached the stage of binding arbitration. Some companies save so much money with ADR that they will even pay for lawyers to help their employees use the system. For example, Philip Morris will spend several thousand dollars to help an employee prepare a case against the company. Employees therefore feel their rights are respected and they get a fair hearing.[20]

Employee Assistance Programs

While ADR is effective in dealing with problems related to performance and disputes between people at work, many of the problems that lead an organization to want to terminate an employee involve drug or alcohol abuse. In these cases, the organization's discipline program should also incorporate an **employee assistance program (EAP).** An EAP is a referral service that employees can use to seek professional treatment for emotional problems or substance abuse. EAPs began in the 1950s with a focus on treating alcoholism, and in the 1980s they expanded into drug treatment. They continue to evolve, and many are now fully integrated into employers' overall health benefits plans, where they act as gatekeepers for use of mental health services.[21]

EAPs vary widely, but most share some basic elements. First, the programs are usually identified in official documents published by the employer, such as employee handbooks. Supervisors (and union representatives when workers belong to a union) are trained to use the referral service for employees whom they suspect of having health-related problems. The organization also trains employees to use the system to refer themselves when necessary. The organization regularly evaluates the costs and benefits of the program, usually once a year.

The variations among EAPs make evaluating these programs especially important. For example, the treatment for alcoholism varies widely, including hospitalization and participation in Alcoholics Anonymous (AA). Employers and employees tend to prefer treatment outside the hospital, which is more convenient and less expensive.

mediation
Nonbinding process in which a neutral party from outside the organization hears the case and tries to help the people in conflict arrive at a settlement.

arbitration
Binding process in which a professional arbitrator from outside the organization (usually a lawyer or judge) hears the case and resolves it by making a decision.

employee assistance program (EAP)
A referral service that employees can use to seek professional treatment for emotional problems or substance abuse.

However, when General Electric performed an experiment to compare the outcomes of these treatments, it found that employees who were hospitalized tended to fare the best in a two-year follow-up.[22] Results of a study on the treatment of drug dependency were similar.[23] The short-term savings seem to be overwhelmed by the cost of relapse. If this is true, an organization would be best served by the EAP referring employees to medical providers, rather than only to a group like AA.

Outplacement Counseling

outplacement counseling
A service in which professionals try to help dismissed employees manage the transition from one job to another.

An employee who has been discharged is likely to feel angry and confused about what to do next. If the person feels there is nothing to lose and nowhere else to turn, the potential for violence or a lawsuit is greater than most organizations are willing to tolerate. This concern is one reason many organizations provide **outplacement counseling,** which tries to help dismissed employees manage the transition from one job to another. Organizations also may address ongoing poor performance with discussion about whether the employee is a good fit for the current job. Rather than simply firing the poor performer, the supervisor may encourage this person to think about leaving. In this situation, the availability of outplacement counseling may help the employee decide to look for another job. This approach may protect the dignity of the employee who leaves and promote a sense of fairness.

Some organizations have their own staff for conducting outplacement counseling. Other organizations have contracts with outside providers to help with individual cases. Either way, the goals for outplacement programs are to help the former employee address the psychological issues associated with losing a job—grief, depression, and fear—while at the same time helping the person find a new job.

Outplacement counseling tries to help people realize that losing a job is not the end of the world and that other opportunities exist. For many people, losing a job actually has benefits. The job loss can be a learning experience that plants the seed for future success. For example, when John Morgridge was fired from his job with Honeywell, he realized that he was so assertive and loved independence so much that he would never be comfortable in a large, bureaucratic organization. Instead of trying to land a job in another company like Honeywell, he applied his skills to building computer network maker Cisco Systems, which became an industry leader.[24]

Although this was a success story for Morgridge, letting this talented manager go certainly spelled a lost opportunity for Honeywell. Retaining people who can contribute knowledge and talent is essential to business success. Therefore, the remainder of this chapter explores issues related to retaining employees.

Job Withdrawal

job withdrawal
A set of behaviors with which employees try to avoid the work situation physically, mentally, or emotionally.

Organizations need employees who are fully engaged and committed to their work. Therefore, retaining employees goes beyond preventing them from quitting. The organization needs to prevent a broader negative condition, called **job withdrawal**—or a set of behaviors with which employees try to avoid the work situation physically, mentally, or emotionally. Job withdrawal results when circumstances such as the nature of the job, supervisors and coworkers, pay levels, or the employee's own disposition cause the employee to become dissatisfied with the job. As shown in Figure 10.5, this job dissatisfaction produces job withdrawal. Job withdrawal may take the form of behavior change, physical job withdrawal, or psychological withdrawal. Some researchers believe employees engage in the three forms of withdrawal behavior in that

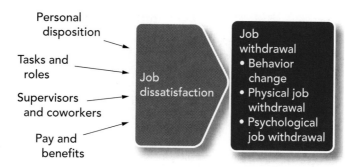

FIGURE 10.5

Job Withdrawal Process

order, while others think they select from these behaviors to address the particular sources of job dissatisfaction they experience.[25]

Job Dissatisfaction

LO5

Many aspects of people and organizations can cause job dissatisfaction, and managers and HR professionals need to be aware of them because correcting them can increase job satisfaction and prevent job withdrawal. The causes of job dissatisfaction identified in Figure 10.5 fall into four categories: personal dispositions, tasks and roles, supervisors and coworkers, and pay and benefits.

Personal Dispositions

Job dissatisfaction is a feeling experienced by individuals, so it is not surprising that many researchers have studied individual personality differences to see if some kinds of people are more disposed to be dissatisfied with their jobs. Several personal qualities have been found to be associated with job dissatisfaction, including negative affectivity and negative self-evaluations.

Negative affectivity means pervasive low levels of satisfaction with all aspects of life, compared with other people's feelings. People with negative affectivity experience feelings such as anger, contempt, disgust, guilt, fear, and nervousness more than other people do, at work and away.[26] They tend to focus on the negative aspects of themselves and others.[27] Not surprisingly, people with negative affectivity tend to be dissatisfied with their jobs, even after changing employers or occupations.[28]

Core self-evaluations are bottom-line opinions individuals have of themselves and may be positive or negative. People with a positive core self-evaluation have high self-esteem, believe in their ability to accomplish their goals, and are emotionally stable. They also tend to experience job satisfaction.[29] Part of the reason for their satisfaction is that they tend to seek out and obtain jobs with desirable characteristics, and when they are in a situation they dislike, they are more likely to seek change in socially acceptable ways.[30] In contrast, people with negative core self-evaluations tend to blame other people for their problems, including their dissatisfying jobs. They are less likely to work toward change; they either do nothing or act aggressively toward the people they blame.[31]

Tasks and Roles

As a predictor of job dissatisfaction, nothing surpasses the nature of the task itself.[32] Many aspects of a task have been linked to dissatisfaction. Of particular significance are the complexity of the task, the degree of physical strain and exertion required, and the value the employee places on the task.[33] In general, employees (especially

Military reservists who are sent overseas often experience role conflict among *three* roles: soldier, family member, and civilian employee. Overseas assignments often intensify role conflicts.

women) are bored and dissatisfied with simple, repetitive jobs.[34] People also are more dissatisfied with jobs requiring a great deal of physical strain and exertion. Because automation has removed much of the physical strain associated with jobs, employers often overlook this consideration. Still, many jobs remain physically demanding. Finally, employees feel dissatisfied if their work is not related to something they value.

Employees not only perform specific tasks, but also have roles within the organization.[35] A person's **role** consists of the set of behaviors that people expect of a person in that job. These expected behaviors include the formally defined duties of the job but also much more. Sometimes things get complicated or confusing. Coworkers, supervisors, and customers have expectations for how the employee should behave often going far beyond a formal job description and having a large impact on the employee's work satisfaction. Several role-related sources of dissatisfaction are the following:

role
The set of behaviors that people expect of a person in a particular job.

- **Role ambiguity** is uncertainty about what the organization and others expect from the employee in terms of what to do or how to do it. Employees suffer when they are unclear about work methods, scheduling, and performance criteria, perhaps because others hold different ideas about these. Employees particularly want to know how the organization will evaluate their performance. When they aren't sure, they become dissatisfied.[36]

role ambiguity
Uncertainty about what the organization expects from the employee in terms of what to do or how to do it.

- **Role conflict** is an employee's recognition that demands of the job are incompatible or contradictory; a person cannot meet all the demands. For example, a company might bring together employees from different functions to work on a team to develop a new product. Team members feel role conflict when they realize that their team leader and functional manager have conflicting expectations of them. Also, many employees may feel conflict between work roles and family roles. A role conflict may be triggered by an organization's request that an employee take an assignment overseas. Foreign assignments can be highly disruptive to family members, and the resulting role conflict is the top reason that people quit overseas assignments.[37]

role conflict
An employee's recognition that demands of the job are incompatible or contradictory.

- **Role overload** results when too many expectations or demands are placed on a person. (The opposite situation is *role underload*.) After an organization downsizes, it may expect so much of the remaining employees that they experience role overload.

role overload
A state in which too many expectations or demands are placed on a person.

Supervisors and Coworkers

Negative behavior by managers and peers in the workplace can produce tremendous dissatisfaction. Research by the Corporate Leadership Council found that employees who said they planned to leave their jobs most often said it was because managers acted as if they did not value the employees.[38] For instance, they said managers did not listen to the employees' opinions. Likewise, in their book *First Break All the Rules*, Marcus

Buckingham and Curt Coffman say people don't leave organizations, they leave managers.[39] In other cases, conflicts between employees left unaddressed by management may cause job dissatisfaction severe enough to lead to withdrawal or departure.

Pay and Benefits

For all the concern with positive relationships and interesting work, it is important to keep in mind that employees definitely care about their earnings. A job is the primary source of income and financial security for most people. Pay also is an indicator of status within the organization and in society at large, so it contributes to some people's self-worth. For all these reasons, satisfaction with pay is significant for retaining employees. Decisions about pay and benefits are so important and complex that the chapters of the next part of this book are devoted to this topic.

With regard to job satisfaction, the pay level—that is, the amount of income associated with each job—is especially important. Employers seeking to lure away another organization's employees often do so by offering higher pay. Benefits, such as insurance and vacation time, are also important, but employees often have difficulty measuring their worth. Therefore, although benefits influence job satisfaction, employees may not always consider them as much as pay itself.

Behavior Change

A reasonable expectation is that an employee's first response to dissatisfaction would be to try to change the conditions that generate the dissatisfaction. As the employee tries to bring about changes in policy or personnel, the efforts may involve confrontation and conflict with the employee's supervisor. In an organization where employees are represented by a union, as we will discuss in Chapter 14, more grievances may be filed.

From the manager's point of view, the complaints, confrontations, and grievances may feel threatening. On closer inspection, however, this is an opportunity for the manager to learn about and solve a potentially important problem. Don McAdams, a manager at Johnsonville Foods, recalls an incident in which one particular employee had been very critical of the company's incentive system. McAdams listened to the employee's concerns and asked him to head a committee charged with developing a better incentive system. The employee was at first taken aback but eventually accepted the challenge. He became so enthusiastic about the project that he was the one who presented the system to the employees. His history of criticizing the old system gave him great credibility with the other employees. In this way, the employee became a force for constructive change.[40]

In this example, the result was positive because the organization responded to legitimate concerns. When employees cannot work with management to make changes, they may look for help from outside the organization. Some employees may engage in *whistle-blowing*, taking their charges to the media in the hope that if the public learns about the situation, the organization will be forced to change. From the organization's point of view, whistle-blowing is harmful because of the negative publicity.

Another way employees may go outside the organization for help is to file a lawsuit. This way to force change is available if the employee is disputing policies on the grounds that they violate state and federal laws, such as those forbidding employment discrimination or requiring safe working conditions. Defending a lawsuit is costly, both financially and in terms of the employer's image, whether the organization wins or loses. Most employers would prefer to avoid lawsuits and whistle-blowing. Keeping employees satisfied is one way to do this.

Physical Job Withdrawal

If behavior change has failed or seems impossible, a dissatisfied worker may physically withdraw from the job. Options for physically leaving a job range from arriving late to calling in sick, requesting a transfer, or leaving the organization altogether. All these options are costly to the employer.

Finding a new job is rarely easy and can take months, so employees often are cautious about quitting. Employees who would like to quit may be late for work. Tardiness is costly because late employees are not contributing for part of the day. Especially when work is done by teams, the tardiness creates difficulties that spill over and affect the entire team's ability to work. Absenteeism is even more of a problem, costing employers hundreds of dollars a day.[41]

An employee who is dissatisfied because of circumstances related to the specific job—for example, an unpleasant workplace or unfair supervisor—may be able to resolve that problem with a job transfer. If the source of the dissatisfaction is organizational policies or practices, such as low pay scales, the employee may leave the organization altogether. These forms of physical job withdrawal contribute to high turnover rates for the department or organization. As a result, the organization faces the costs of replacing the employees, as well as lost productivity until replacement employees learn the jobs.

Organizations need to be concerned with their overall turnover rates as well as the nature of the turnover in terms of who is staying and who is leaving. For example, turnover rates among minorities at the managerial level are often two or three times the turnover among white males. One reason these managers give for leaving is that they see little opportunity for promotions. Chapter 9 discussed how organizations are addressing this problem through career management and efforts to break the glass ceiling.

Psychological Withdrawal

Employees need not leave the company in order to withdraw from their jobs. Especially if they have been unable to find another job, they may psychologically remove themselves. They are physically at work, but their minds are elsewhere.

Psychological withdrawal can take several forms. If an employee is primarily dissatisfied with the job itself, the employee may display a very low level of job involvement. **Job involvement** is the degree to which people identify themselves with their jobs. People with a high level of job involvement consider their work an important part of their life. Doing well at work contributes to their sense of who they are (their *self-concept*). For a dissatisfied employee with low job involvement, performing well or poorly does not affect the person's self-concept. The person is therefore harder to motivate.[42]

When an employee is dissatisfied with the organization as a whole, the person's organizational commitment may be low. **Organizational commitment** is the degree to which an employee identifies with the organization and is willing to put forth effort on its behalf.[43] Employees with high organizational commitment will stretch themselves to help the organization through difficult times. Employees with low organizational commitment are likely to leave at the first opportunity for a better job. They have a strong intention to leave, so like employees with low job involvement, they are hard to motivate.

job involvement
The degree to which people identify themselves with their jobs.

organizational commitment
The degree to which an employee identifies with the organization and is willing to put forth effort on its behalf.

As the *BusinessWeek* case at the end of the chapter notes, Marriott has employees who identify with the organization and will go the extra mile for it. What would give you motivation to stay with and succeed with your employer?

Job Satisfaction

LO6

Clearly, organizations want to prevent the withdrawal behaviors discussed above. As we saw in Figure 10.5, the driving force behind job withdrawal is dissatisfaction. To prevent job withdrawal, organizations therefore need to promote **job satisfaction,** a pleasant feeling resulting from the perception that one's job fulfills or allows for the fulfillment of one's important job values.[44] Several aspects of job satisfaction are:

- Job satisfaction is related to a person's values, defined as "what a person consciously or unconsciously desires to obtain."
- Different employees have different views of which values are important, so the same circumstances can produce different levels of job satisfaction.
- Job satisfaction is based on perception, not always on an objective and complete measurement of the situation. Each person compares the job situation to his or her values, and people are likely to differ in what they perceive.

In sum, values, perceptions, and ideas of what is important are the three components of job satisfaction. People will be satisfied with their jobs as long as they perceive that their jobs meet their important values. As shown in Figure 10.6, organizations can contribute to job satisfaction by addressing the four sources of job dissatisfaction we identified earlier: personal dispositions, job tasks and roles, supervisors and coworkers, and pay and benefits. These efforts are timely. Surveys have shown that job satisfaction in the United States has declined during the years from 1995 to 2000.[45]

job satisfaction
A pleasant feeling resulting from the perception that one's job fulfills or allows for the fulfillment of one's important job values.

Personal Dispositions

In our discussion of job withdrawal above, we noted that sometimes personal qualities of the employee, such as negative affectivity and negative core self-evaluation, are associated with job dissatisfaction. This linkage suggests employee selection in the first instance plays a role in raising overall levels of employee satisfaction. People making the selection decisions should look for evidence of whether employees are predisposed to being satisfied. Interviews should explore employees' satisfaction with past jobs. If an applicant says he was dissatisfied with his past six jobs, what makes the employer think the person won't be dissatisfied with the organization's vacant position?

Employers also should recognize that dissatisfaction with other facets of life can spill over into the workplace. A worker who is having problems with a family member may attribute some of the negative feelings to the job or organization. Of course, managers should not try to become clinical psychologists for their employees and applicants. Still, when employees express negativity and dissatisfaction in many

FIGURE 10.6

Increasing Job Satisfaction

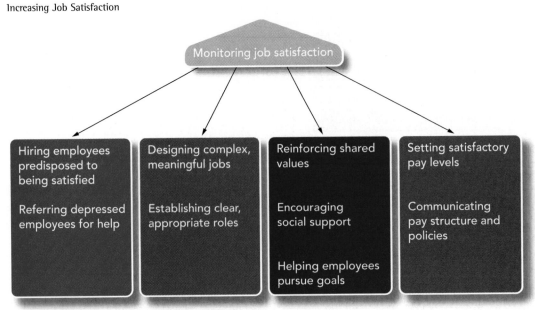

areas, managers should consider that the employee may be clinically depressed.[46] The manager should suggest that the employee contact the organization's employee assistance program or his or her physician. Depression is a common condition, but most cases can be managed with proper care. As a reasonable accommodation under the Americans with Disabilities Act, the employer may need to grant the employee time off or a flexible schedule to accommodate treatment.

Tasks and Roles

Organizations can improve job satisfaction by making jobs more complex and meaningful, as we discussed in Chapter 4. Some of the methods available for this approach to job design are job enrichment and job rotation. Organizations also can increase satisfaction by developing clear and appropriate job roles.

Job Complexity

Not only can job design add to enriching complexity, but employees themselves sometimes take measures to make their work more interesting. Some employees bring personal stereo headsets to work, so they can listen to music or radio shows while they are working. Many supervisors disapprove, worrying that the headsets will interfere with the employees' ability to provide good customer service. However, in simple jobs with minimal customer contact (like processing paperwork or entering data into computers), research suggests that personal stereo headsets can improve performance. One study examined the use of stereo headsets by workers in 32 jobs at a large retailing company. The stereo-using group outperformed the no-stereo group on simple jobs (like invoice processor) but performed worse than the stereo-free group on complex jobs (such as accountant).[47]

Attracting Workers with Technology

As use of prescription drugs skyrockets, the number of community pharmacists is not keeping pace. This has created a contest for talent among the major drugstore chains. The organization with the best recruitment and retention plan wins.

So far, one of the winners seems to be Walgreens, which recently has enjoyed record profits. Unlike its major competitor, CVS pharmacy, Walgreens has been expanding rapidly, opening hundreds of stores a year. Word-of-mouth recruiting by its employees has ensured a steady inflow of talented workers. And Walgreens' retention rate for pharmacists is the highest in the industry.

How is Walgreens attracting and keeping employees? Part of its success can be attributed to its policy of paying competitive salaries and benefits. In addition, Walgreens uses technology to make the pharmacist's job more meaningful. Walgreens Intercom Plus is a company-owned software program that streamlines the prescription process, eliminating much of the paperwork that pharmacists dread. The system processes millions of transactions a day from over 3,000 satellite-connected stores. This frees up time for customer service, so pharmacists can chat with customers and educate them about the products. Allowing pharmacists and pharmacy technicians to focus on providing personal service rather than processing paperwork increases their job satisfaction. It also fosters long-term customer relationships.

Walgreens promotes Intercom Plus in its recruitment brochures and on its website, where interested candidates are invited to apply for jobs online. Not surprisingly, many of these applicants come from competing firms. In several cases, Walgreens has accepted online applications from computers that apparently reside within CVS pharmacies. When there is no shortage of customers but a shortage of employees, using technology to make work more meaningful can give an organization a devastating edge over its competitors.

SOURCE: T. Raphael, "HR and an Rx for the Bottom Line," *Workforce*, October 2001, p. 104; J. Wolf, "Walgreen Earnings Shine," money.cnn.com, November 2001, p. 1; P. Withers, "Retention Strategies That Respond to Worker Values," *Workforce*, July 2001, pp. 37–41.

Meaningful Work

Through work design and communications with employees, organizations can make work more meaningful. After all, over a million volunteer workers in the United States perform their jobs almost exclusively because of the meaning they attach to the work. Some of these jobs are even low in complexity and high in physical exertion. The volunteers see themselves as performing a worthwhile service, and this overrides the other two factors and makes the job satisfying. Similarly, several low-paying occupations (such as social services and religious orders) explicitly try to make up for low pay by appealing to workers' nonfinancial values. The Peace Corps, for example, tries to recruit applicants by describing the work as "the toughest job you will ever love." As the "Best Practices" box above describes, employers can sometimes use technology to focus people on the aspects of work that have the most meaning for them.

Clear and Appropriate Roles

Organizations can do much to avoid role-related sources of dissatisfaction. They can define roles, clearly spelling out work methods, schedules, and performance measures. They can be realistic about the number of hours required to complete job requirements. When jobs require overtime hours, the employer must be prepared to comply with laws requiring overtime pay, as well as to help employees manage the conflict between work and family roles.

To help employees manage role conflict, employers have turned to a number of family-friendly policies. These policies may include provisions for child care, elder care, flexible work schedules, job sharing, telecommuting, and extended parental leaves.[48] Although these programs create some headaches for managers in terms of scheduling work and reporting requirements, they increase employees' commitment to the organization.[49] Organizations with family-friendly policies also have enjoyed improvements in performance, especially those that employ a large percentage of women.[50] Chapter 13 discusses such benefits in greater detail.

Organizations should also pay attention to the fit between job titles and roles, especially as more and more Americans feel overworked. A 2001 survey of U.S. workers indicated that almost half felt they were working too many hours, and roughly one-fourth worked six days and over 50 hours a week.[51] One consequence of this perception is an increase in the number of lawsuits filed by people who are suing for overtime pay. The Fair Labor Standards Act exempts managers and professionals from its requirement that the company pay overtime to employees who work more than a 40-hour week. Increasingly, employees are complaining that they have been misclassified as managers and should be treated as nonexempt workers. Their job titles sound like managerial jobs, but their day-to-day activities involve no supervision. Companies that have defended against such lawsuits include U-Haul, Taco Bell, Pepsico, Auto Zone, and Wal-Mart.[52]

role analysis technique
A process of formally identifying expectations associated with a role.

Because role problems rank just behind job problems in creating job dissatisfaction, some interventions aim directly at role elements. One of these is the **role analysis technique,** a process of formally identifying expectations associated with a role. The technique follows the steps shown in Figure 10.7. The *role occupant* (the person who fills a role) and each member of the person's *role set* (people who directly interact with this employee) each write down their expectations for the role. They meet to discuss their expectations and develop a preliminary list of the role's duties and behaviors, trying to resolve any conflicts among expectations. Next, the role occupant lists what he or she expects of others in the set, and the group meets again to reach a consensus on these expectations. Finally, the group modifies its preliminary list and reaches a consensus on the occupant's role. This process may uncover instances of overload and underload, and the group tries to trade off requirements to develop more balanced roles.

Supervisors and Coworkers

The two primary sets of people in an organization who affect job satisfaction are coworkers and supervisors. A person may be satisfied with these people for one of three reasons:

1. The people share the same values, attitudes, and philosophies. Most individuals find this very important, and many organizations try to foster a culture of shared values. Even when this does not occur across the whole organization, values shared between workers and their supervisor can increase satisfaction.[53]
2. The coworkers and supervisor may provide social support, meaning they are sympathetic and caring. Social support greatly increases job satisfaction, whether the

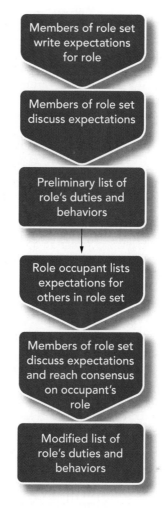

FIGURE 10.7

Steps in the Role Analysis Technique

support comes from supervisors or coworkers.[54] Turnover is also lower among employees who experience support from other members of the organization.[55]

3. The coworkers or supervisor may help the person attain some valued outcome. For example, they can help a new employee figure out what goals to pursue and how to achieve them.[56]

Because a supportive environment reduces dissatisfaction, many organizations foster team building both on and off the job (such as with softball or bowling leagues). The idea is that playing together as a team will strengthen ties among group members and develop relationships in which individuals feel supported by one another. Of course, management cannot ensure that each employee will develop friendships, but the team-building activities can make it easier for employees to interact, which is a necessary first step toward building a relationship.

Pay and Benefits

Organizations recognize the importance of pay in their negotiations with job candidates. HR professionals can support their organizations in this area by repeatedly monitoring pay levels in their industry and for the professions or trades they employ.

Coworker relationships can contribute to job satisfaction, and organizations therefore try to provide opportunities to build positive relationships. Would a strong sense of teamwork and friendship help you enjoy your work more?

As we noted in Chapter 5 and will discuss further in Chapter 11, organizations make decisions about whether to match or exceed the industry averages. Also, HR professionals can increase job satisfaction by communicating to employees the value of their benefits.

Two other aspects of pay satisfaction influence job satisfaction. One is satisfaction with pay structure—the way the organization assigns different pay levels to different levels and job categories. A manager of a sales force, for example, might be satisfied with her pay level until she discovers that some of the sales representatives she supervises are earning more than she is. The other important aspect of pay satisfaction is pay raises. People generally expect that their pay will increase over time. They will be satisfied if their expectations are met or dissatisfied if raises fall short of expectations. HR professionals can contribute to these sources of job satisfaction by helping to communicate the reasoning behind the organization's pay structure and pay raises. For example, sometimes economic conditions force an organization to limit pay raises. If employees understand the circumstances (and recognize that the same conditions are likely to be affecting other employers), they may feel less dissatisfied.

Monitoring Job Satisfaction

Employers can better retain employees if they are aware of satisfaction levels, so they can make changes if employees are dissatisfied. The usual way to measure job satisfaction is with some kind of survey. A systematic, ongoing program of employee surveys should be part of the organization's human resource strategy. This program allows the organization to monitor trends and prevent voluntary turnover. For example, if satisfaction with promotion opportunities has been falling over several years, the trend may signal a need for better career management (a topic of Chapter 9). An organizational change, such as a merger, also might have important consequences for job satisfaction. In addition, ongoing surveys give the organization a way to measure whether policies adopted to improve job satisfaction and employee retention are working. Organizations can also compare results from different departments to identify groups with successful practices that may apply elsewhere in the organization. Another benefit is that some scales provide data that organizations can use to compare themselves to others in the same industry. This information will be valuable for creating and reviewing human resource policies that enable organizations to attract and retain employees in a competitive job market. Finally, conducting surveys gives employees a chance to be heard, so the practice itself can contribute to employee satisfaction. The nearby "HR How To" box offers ideas for measuring employee satisfaction.

Measuring Employee Satisfaction

When an organization invests heavily in recruiting, training, and compensating human resources, it only makes sense to hang on to that talent. To keep valuable employees, the organization needs to know whether they are satisfied. Here are some suggestions for effectively measuring employee satisfaction:

- Make annual employee surveys part of a two-way communications program that includes messages from management, surveys, exit interviews, and other opportunities for managers and employees to hear one another's points of view.

- When preparing the survey, also prepare a way for management to apply the information. Who will review and act on the results?
- Publish survey results as soon as possible after the survey is completed.
- Along with survey results, publish information about how the organization will respond, and then follow through.
- Set up a system to gather ongoing feedback from employees, such as a toll-free phone number or e-mail address where employees can send suggestions. The system

should quickly deliver the suggestions to managers who have the ability to act on them.
- Solicit feedback through brief monthly polls at a phone number or website.
- Prepare reports highlighting trends in the ongoing employee feedback, along with recommended responses.
- Permit employees to respond to surveys and offer suggestions anonymously.

SOURCE: S. M. Lilienthal, "Screen and Glean," *Workforce*, October 2000, downloaded from FindArticles.com.

To obtain a survey instrument, an excellent place to begin is with one of the many established scales. The validity and reliability of many satisfaction scales have been tested, so it is possible to compare the survey instruments. The main reason for the organization to create its own scale would be that it wants to measure satisfaction with aspects of work that are specific to the organization (such as satisfaction with a particular health plan).

A widely used measure of job satisfaction is the Job Descriptive Index (JDI). The JDI emphasizes specific aspects of satisfaction—pay, the work itself, supervision, coworkers, and promotions. Figure 10.8 shows several items from the JDI scale. Other scales measure general satisfaction, using broad questions such as "All in all, how satisfied are you with your job?"[57] Some scales avoid language altogether, relying on pictures. The faces scale in Figure 10.9 is an example of this type of measure. Other scales exist for measuring more specific aspects of satisfaction. For example, the Pay Satisfaction Questionnaire (PSQ) measures satisfaction with specific aspects of pay, such as pay levels, structure, and raises.[58]

Conducting opinion surveys is not something an organization should take lightly. Especially when the program is new, surveys often raise employees' expectations. The organization should therefore be ready to act on the results. At Doctor's Hospital in Manteca, California, a survey of employees' opinions revealed dissatisfaction in several areas. When the hospital presented the results to the employees, each problem area was accompanied by a corresponding action plan showing how the organization

FIGURE 10.8

Example of Job Descriptive Index (JDI)

Instructions: Think of your present work. What is it like most of time? In the blank beside each word given below, write

___Y___ for "Yes" if it describes your work
___N___ for "No" if it does NOT describe your work
___?___ if you cannot decide

Work Itself
_____ Routine
_____ Satisfying
_____ Good

Pay
_____ Less than I deserve
_____ Highly paid
_____ Insecure

Promotion opportunities
_____ Dead-end job
_____ Unfair policies
_____ Based on ability

Supervision
_____ Impolite
_____ Praises good work
_____ Doesn't supervise enough

Coworkers
_____ Intelligent
_____ Responsible
_____ Boring

SOURCE: W. K. Balzar, D. C. Smith, D. E. Kravitz, S. E. Lovell, K. B. Paul, B. A. Reilly, and C. E. Reilly, *User's Manual for the Job Descriptive Index (JDI)* (Bowling Green, OH: Bowling Green State University, 1990).

intended to address the problem. For example, in the area of career development, the survey indicated that although the hospital reimbursed employees for their full tuition costs, it did so at the end of the semester. The timing of the reimbursement made it impossible for many employees to pay tuition, so they could not use this benefit. Based on the results, the hospital began paying tuition up front, along with loans to help with nontuition costs (like child care expenses) associated with taking a class. What was once a source of dissatisfaction for employees has become a source of satisfaction.[59]

In spite of surveys and other efforts to retain employees, some employees inevitably will leave the organization. This presents another opportunity to gather information for retaining employees: the **exit interview**—a meeting of the departing employee with the employee's supervisor and/or a human resource specialist to discuss the employee's reasons for leaving. A well-conducted exit interview can uncover reasons why employees leave and perhaps set the stage for some of them to return.[60] HR professionals can help make exit interviews more successful by arranging for the employee to talk to someone from the HR department (rather than the departing employee's supervisor) in a neutral location.[61] Questions should start out open-ended and general, to give the employee a chance to name the source of the dissatisfaction.

A recruiter armed with information about what caused a specific person to leave may be able to negotiate a return when the situation changes. And when several exiting employees give similar reasons for leaving, management should consider

exit interview
A meeting of a departing employee with the employee's supervisor and/or a human resource specialist to discuss the employee's reasons for leaving.

FIGURE 10.9

Example of a Simplified, Nonverbal Measure of Job Satisfaction

Job Satisfaction from the Faces Scale
Consider all aspects of your job. Circle the face that best describes your feelings about your job in general.

7   6   5   4   3   2   1

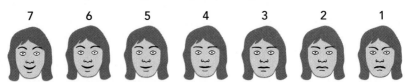

SOURCE: The faces were adapted from R. B. Dunham and J. B. Herman and published in the *Journal of Applied Psychology* 60 (1975), pp. 629–31. Copyright 1975 by the American Psychological Association. Adapted with permission.

whether this indicates a need for change. In the war for talent, the best way to manage retention is to engage in a battle for every valued employee, even when it looks as if the battle has been lost.

Summary

1. Distinguish between involuntary and voluntary turnover, and describe their effects on an organization.
   Involuntary turnover occurs when the organization requires employees to leave, often when they would prefer to stay. Voluntary turnover occurs when employees initiate the turnover, often when the organization would prefer to keep them. Both are costly because of the need to recruit, hire, and train replacements. Involuntary turnover can also result in lawsuits and even violence.

2. Discuss how employees determine whether the organization treats them fairly.
   Employees draw conclusions based on the outcomes of decisions regarding them, the procedures applied, and the way managers treat employees when carrying out those procedures. Outcome fairness is a judgment that the consequences are just. The consequences should be consistent, expected, and in proportion to the significance of the behavior. Procedural justice is a judgment that fair methods were used to determine the consequences. The procedures should be consistent, unbiased, based on accurate information, and correctable. They should take into account the viewpoints of everyone involved, and they should be consistent with prevailing ethical standards. Interactional justice is a judgment that the organization carried out its actions in a way that took the employee's feelings into account—for example, by listening to the employee and treating the employee with dignity.

3. Identify legal requirements for employee discipline.
   Employee discipline should not result in wrongful discharge, such as a termination that violates an implied contract or public policy. Discipline should be administered evenhandedly, without discrimination. Discipline should respect individual employees' privacy. Searches and surveillance should be for a legitimate business purpose, and employees should know about and consent to them. Reasons behind disciplinary actions should be shared only with those who need to know them. When termination is part of a plant closing, employees should receive the legally required notice, if applicable.

4. Summarize ways in which organizations can fairly discipline employees.
   Discipline should follow the principles of the hot-stove rule, meaning discipline should give warning and have consequences that are consistent, objective, and immediate. A system that can meet these requirements is progressive discipline, in which rules are established and communicated, and increasingly severe consequences follow each violation of the rules. Usually, consequences range from a spoken warning through written warnings, suspension, and termination. These actions should be documented in writing. Organizations also may resolve problems through alternative dispute resolution, including an open-door policy, peer review, mediation, and arbitration. When performance problems seem to result from substance abuse or mental illness, the manager may refer the employee to an employee assistance program. When a manager terminates an employee or encourages an employee to leave, outplacement counseling may smooth the process.

5. Explain how job dissatisfaction affects employee behavior.
   Circumstances involving the nature of a job, supervisors and coworkers, pay levels, or the employee's own disposition may produce job dissatisfaction. When employees become dissatisfied, they may engage in job withdrawal. This may include behavior change, as employees try to bring about changes in policy and personnel through inside action or through whistleblowing or lawsuits. Physical job withdrawal may range from tardiness and absenteeism to job transfer or leaving the organization altogether. Especially when employees cannot find another job, they may psychologically withdraw by displaying low levels of job involvement and organizational commitment.

6. Describe how organizations contribute to employees' job satisfaction and retain key employees.
   Organizations can try to identify and select employees who have personal dispositions associated with job satisfaction. They can make jobs more complex and meaningful—for example, through job enrichment and job rotation. They can use methods such as the role analysis technique to make roles clear and appropriate. They can reinforce shared values and encourage social support among employees. They can try to establish satisfactory pay levels and communicate with employees about pay structure and pay raises. Monitoring job satisfaction helps organizations identify which of these actions are likely to be most beneficial.

Review and Discussion Questions

1. Give an example of voluntary turnover and an example of involuntary turnover. Why should organizations try to reduce both kinds of turnover?

2. A member of a restaurant's serving staff is chronically late to work. From the organization's point of view, what fairness issues are involved in deciding how to handle this situation? In what ways might the employee's and other servers' ideas of fairness be different?

3. For the situation in question 2, how would a formal discipline policy help the organization address issues of fairness?

4. The progressive discipline process described in this chapter is meant to be fair and understandable, but it tends to be slow. Try to think of two or three offenses that should result in immediate discharge, rather than follow all the steps of progressive discipline. Explain why you selected these offenses. If the dismissed employee sued, do you think the organization would be able to defend its action in court?

5. A risk of disciplining employees is that some employees retaliate. To avoid that risk, what organizational policies might encourage low-performing employees to leave while encouraging high-performing employees to stay? (Consider the sources of employee satisfaction and dissatisfaction discussed in this chapter.)

6. List forms of behavior that can signal job withdrawal. Choose one of the behaviors you listed, and describe how you would respond if an otherwise valuable employee whom you supervised engaged in this kind of behavior.

7. What are the four factors that influence an employee's job dissatisfaction (or satisfaction)? Which of these do you think an employer can most easily change? Which would be the most expensive to change?

8. The section on principles of justice used noncompete agreements as an example. How would you expect the use of noncompete agreements to affect voluntary turnover? How might the use of these agreements affect job withdrawal and job satisfaction? Besides requiring noncompete agreements, how could an organization reduce the likelihood of employees leaving to work for competitors? Would these other methods have a better effect on employee satisfaction?

9. Consider your current job or a job you recently held. Overall, were you satisfied or dissatisfied with that job? How did your level of satisfaction or dissatisfaction affect your behavior on the job? Is your own experience consistent with this chapter's models of job withdrawal and job satisfaction?

10. Suppose you are an HR professional who convinced your company's management to conduct a survey of employee satisfaction. Your budget was limited, and you could not afford a test that went into great detail. Rather, you investigated overall job satisfaction and learned that it is low, especially among employees in three departments. You know that management is concerned about spending a lot for HR programs because sales are in a slump, but you want to address the issue of low job satisfaction. Suggest some ways you might begin to make a difference, even with a small budget. How will you convince management to try your ideas?

11. Why are exit interviews important? Should an organization care about the opinions of people who are leaving? How are those opinions relevant to employee separation and retention?

What's Your HR IQ?

The Student CD-ROM offers two more ways to check what you've learned so far. Use the Self-Assessment exercise to test your knowledge of employee retention. Go online with the Web Exercise to see how well your knowledge of employee separation works in cyberspace.

BusinessWeek Case

BusinessWeek Low-Wage Lessons

At 5:30 A.M. the first workers arrive for the morning shift at the Marriott Hotel in downtown Chicago. They come from the farthest reaches of the metropolitan area and from all corners of the world. Bosnian refugees and born-in-America welfare moms, Chinese immigrants, and black teenagers don their uniforms for the day. A few yards and a world removed from the crystal chandeliers and fresh flowers their guests see, a remarkable staff of hundreds whirs into motion.

Their pay: about $7 an hour. That's typical for Marriott International's 134,417 U.S. housekeepers, laundry workers, dishwashers, and other hourly staffers. It is, Marriott says, the wage that the labor market dictates. "If we pay wages in excess of the productive contribution of our people, we will become noncompetitive ourselves," says J. W. Marriott Jr., the company's chairman.

The needs of low-wage employees once were easy to ignore. If a dishwasher quit, there always was someone else happy to take the work. Not today, though. While the economy demands more and more highly educated workers, the need persists for more maids, meatpackers, and sewing machine operators. Nearly 30 percent of all U.S. employees make $7.28 an hour or less, up from 23.5 percent in 1973, according to the Economic Policy Institute.

Marriott International is coming to terms with this challenging, increasingly important group. Paying its U.S. workers a median rate of $7.40 an hour, including overtime, the hotelier resists offering the higher wages that would attract more qualified workers. It has waged often bitter battles, moreover, against attempts at unionization. Instead, it has embraced a host of informal and formal solutions—including employee stock options, a social-services referral network, day care, and welfare-to-work training classes—designed to keep workers on the job and keep guests satisfied.

Amid ever more intense competition, Marriott will thrive only if it can wring out bigger productivity gains and provide world-class service. Its human resources strategies win such results. Even without big pay hikes, Marriott employees often exhibit loyalty and even enthusiasm for their employer, and many feel they have a chance for advancement within the company. Analysts say its employee turnover rate is well below most rivals'.

There is a cost. Historically, Marriott's hotel managers and supervisors have helped solve workers' problems—playing social worker, in effect. They counsel employees confronting family problems, juggle shifts to accommodate erratic child care, or lend them money to pay pressing bills.

Yet Marriott has forged unquestionably strong bonds with many employees. "Every day I put on this uniform, just like an NBA player," proudly proclaims Thong Lee, a bartender who has worked 16 years at the Seattle Marriott. Lee has never forgotten that his boss, Sandy Olson, shut down the hotel laundry where he used to work for a day so the entire staff could attend his mother's funeral. The gesture earned Lee's loyalty for life—though the stock options the company offers all employees haven't hurt, either. Lee, who learned all the English he knows from Mar-

riott, now owns several rental properties funded by his Marriott stock and pay.

Now Marriott is launching a range of corporate programs to alleviate the demands on local hotel managers. Pathways to Independence, for example, is a company-developed class on basic work skills for former welfare recipients, offered at hotels in 15 cities. Associate Resource Line is a national toll-free referral service that hooks up its workers with local social services. And with two other hotel groups, Marriott will inaugurate Atlanta's Inn for Children, a 24-hour subsidized child-care center.

Marriott began studying its hourly-wage workforce in 1993, after realizing that child-care benefits launched three years earlier had left many problems of this population unresolved. It immediately found that a quarter have some literacy problems—mostly difficulties speaking English. Overall, Marriott workers speak and read 65 different languages.

Language barriers in this massive Babel can disrupt hotel operations—and worse. William D. Fleet, human resource director at the Seattle Marriott, where employees speak 17 languages, once fired a Vietnamese kitchen worker for wrongly accusing a chef of assault. Only after another employee was attacked by a kitchen worker did Fleet figure out that the Vietnamese employee had used the word *chef* to refer to all kitchen workers with white uniforms. The misunderstanding had led to the firing of a good staff member and delayed the arrest of a dangerous one.

Now more than half of the Marriotts in the United States offer workers ESL (English as a second language) classes—a relatively cheap and easy productivity device.

Can human resource systems sent down from headquarters reproduce the dedication that results from managers' involvement with employees? In some ways, such standardized programs could prove more effective. Marriott's Associate Resource Line is offered in more than 100 languages—more than any one manager could handle. So far, about 7,000 staffers have called and been assigned a social worker, who finds them local help. Marriott anticipates savings of five times its $2 million investment from reduced turnover, absenteeism, and tardiness.

SOURCE: "Low-Wage Lessons," *BusinessWeek*, November 11, 1996.

Questions

1. To retain low-skilled workers, what sources of job satisfaction does Marriott address?
2. What sources of job satisfaction does Marriott *not* address in the examples given?
3. What are the risks and benefits of retention policies that emphasize training and benefits, rather than higher pay?

Case: Feeling Insecure about Airline Security

Becoming an expert in any field takes some degree of training and on-the-job experience. Working as part of a team also requires time to learn about team members' strengths and weaknesses, so that the team can operate like a well-oiled machine. Therefore, when even one employee leaves the team or the organization, performance suffers. Imagine the case where an entire work unit changes every four months!

It may seem hard to believe, but this was the turnover rate at the security checkpoints at Logan International Airport in September 2001, the month two planes that departed from Logan were hijacked and used in attacks on the World Trade Center. Yet Logan was not even the worst airport in terms of employee turnover. The annual turnover rates at the airports in St. Louis and Atlanta were greater than 400 percent, meaning the entire crew was replaced every three months.

When workers have so little experience in their jobs and in working together, they cannot perform well. Regarding security at Logan, Max Cleland, chairman of the Senate Armed Services Subcommittee on Personnel, noted, "This was our front line, and what we found is we didn't have security, we had a sieve."

A number of factors contributed to the high turnover rates among airport security personnel. First, pay for these jobs is low. Most airport security personnel earn less than $6 an hour. Even workers in the airports' fast-food restaurants earn more than that. Furthermore, security jobs are dead-end jobs. There is no career path giving these employees promotions as a reward for working hard and committing to the organization. Adding to these limitations, the work itself is boring and monotonous. Interacting with travelers can be unpleasant, because travelers are in a hurry, and security screening slows them down. Airlines have pressured security personnel to keep customers moving during peak travel times, and this pressure conflicts with concern for quality in screening. Also, many travelers show little respect toward people in the airport security

jobs. Finally, these positions offer poor job security. A person can be fired for a single mistake.

The airlines, which until recently were responsible for security, blame this situation on the economics of the industry. In their struggle to be profitable, the airlines kept the costs of airport screening as low as they could. Given the nation's heightened concern for security, the government seems no longer willing to let this work go to the lowest bidder. In 2002 the federal government took over airline security duties in the United States.

What remains to be seen is how elevating security's importance and placing it under government control will affect the job satisfaction and retention of airport security workers. A variety of measures have been considered, some of them based on practices in Europe and Israel. There airline security screening is treated as a police function. Pay, training, and benefits are much better than workers have received in the United States. Many of these countries' airlines are nationalized, contributing to a closer feeling between airlines and security personnel, whose work seems more like a patriotic duty. In the United States, the revolving door of security jobs never generated anything like loyalty or emotional attachment.

SOURCE: M. Fish, "Airport Security: A System Driven by the Minimum Wage," *CNN.com*, October 31, 2001, pp. 1–5; M. Fish, "Many Warnings over Security Preceded Terrorist Attacks," *CNN.com*, November 1, 2001, pp. 1–3; S. Candiotti, "FBI Arrests Man Who Tried to Board Flight Armed with Knives," *CNN.com*, November 5, 2001, pp. 1–2; M. Fish, "Outside the U.S., a Different Approach to Air Security," *CNN.com*, November 1, 2001, pp. 1–2.

Questions

1. What were some of the characteristics of the airport security job that led to poor worker attitudes and high turnover?
2. If you were charged with fixing this system, what steps would you take to improve satisfaction and reduce turnover?
3. Which of your recommendations would you expect to be costly? Which would not increase costs very much?

Notes

1. D. Fenn, "Rescuing Tradition," *Inc.*, August 2001, pp. 48–49.
2. M. L. Schmit and S. P. Allscheid, "Employee Attitudes and Customer Satisfaction: Making Theoretical and Empirical Connections," *Personnel Psychology* 48 (1995), pp. 521–36; F. Reichheld, *The Loyalty Effect* (Cambridge, MA: Harvard Business School Press, 1996).
3. D. J. Koys, "The Effects of Employee Satisfaction, Organizational Citizenship Behavior, and Turnover on Organizational Effectiveness: A Unit-Level Longitudinal Study," *Personnel Psychology* 54 (2001), pp. 101–14.
4. M. Heller, "A Return to At-Will Employment," *Workforce*, May 2001, pp. 42–46.
5. A. Q. Nomani, "Women Likelier to Face Violence in

the Workplace," *The Wall Street Journal*, October 31, 1995, p. A16.

6. D. Spencer, "Soothing the Sting," *Human Resource Executive*, June 1, 2001, pp. 30–34; M. Conlin, "Revenge of the Downsized Nerds," *BusinessWeek*, July 30, 2001, p. 40; M. Boyle, "The Not-So-Fine Art of the Layoff," *Fortune*, March 19, 2001, pp. 209–10.

7. K. Bredemeier, "In a Bind over Non-compete Clauses," *Washington Post*, March 18, 2000, p. E1; D. M. Katz, "Non-competes: The Dark Side of the Labor Force," *CFO.com*, February 8, 2001, pp. 1–3; C. Hymowitz, "Firms That Cut Layoff Packages May Erode Employees' Loyalty," *The Wall Street Journal*, October 30, 2001, p. 1; K. Maher, "Non-compete Agreements Meet Rebels," *The Wall Street Journal*, October 23, 2001, pp. 1–2.

8. J. J. Myers, D. V. Radack, and P. M. Yenerall, "Making the Most of Employment Contracts," *HR Magazine* 43, no. 9 (August 1998), pp. 106–9; *Toussaint v. Blue Cross and Blue Shield of Michigan*, 408 Mich. 579, 292 N.W.2d 880 (1980).

9. S. Warren and L. Brandeis, "The Right to Privacy," *Harvard Law Review* 193, 205 (1890); S. C. Bennett and S. D. Locke, "Privacy in the Workplace," *Labor Law Journal* 49, no. 1 (January 1998), pp. 781–87; M. Mineham, "Debate on Workplace Privacy Likely to Intensify," *HR Magazine* 44, no. 1 (January 1999), p. 142.

10. *Harmon v. Thornburgh*, CA, DC No. 88-5265 (July 30, 1989); *Treasury Employees Union v. Von Raab*, U.S. Sup. Ct. No. 86-18796 (March 21, 1989); *City of Annapolis v. United Food & Commercial Workers Local 400*, Md. Ct. App. No. 38 (November 6, 1989); *Skinner v. Railway Labor Executives Association*, U.S. Sup. Ct. No. 87-1555 (March 21, 1989); *Bluestein v. Skinner*, 908 F.2d 451, 9th Cir. (1990).

11. A. Davis, "Firms Dig Deep into Workers' Pasts amid Post–Sept. 11 Security Anxiety," *The Wall Street Journal* Online, March 12, 2002, http://online.wsj.com; A. Davis, "Background Checks Draw Increased Scrutiny," *The Wall Street Journal Online* (2002), *Career Journal* section, www.careerjournal.com.

12. D. J. Hoekstra, "Workplace Searches: A Legal Overview," *Labor Law Journal* 47, no. 2 (February 1996), pp. 127–38.

13. G. Henshaw and K. Youmans, "Employee Privacy in the Workplace and an Employer's Right to Conduct Workplace Searches and Surveillance," *SHRM Legal Report*, Spring 1990, pp. 1–5; B. K. Repa, *Your Rights in the Workplace* (Berkeley, CA: Nolo Press, 1997).

14. G. Webster, "Respecting Employee Privacy," *Association Management*, January 1994, pp. 142–43, 146.

15. M. Denis and J. Andes, "Defamation—Do You Tell Employees Why a Coworker Was Discharged?" *Employee Relations Law Journal* 16, no. 4 (Spring 1991),

pp. 469–79; R. S. Soderstrom and J. R. Murray, "Defamation in Employment: Suits by At-Will Employees," *FICC Quarterly*, Summer 1992, pp. 395–426; R. J. Posch Jr., "Your Personal Exposure for Interoffice Communications," *Direct Marketing* 61 (August 1998).

16. N. Orkin and M. Heise, "*Weingarten* through the Looking Glass," *Labor Law Journal* 48, no. 3 (March 1997), pp. 157–63.

17. K. Karl and C. Sutton, "A Review of Expert Advice on Employment Termination Practices: The Experts Don't Always Agree," in *Dysfunctional Behavior in Organizations*, ed. R. Griffin, A. O'Leary-Kelly, and J. Collins (Stanford, CT: JAI Press, 1998).

18. "Dow Employees Fired over E-mail Misuse Win Their Jobs Back," *Miami.com*, April 3, 2002.

19. "Arbitration's Popularity Still Growing," *HRNext*, March 18, 2002, www.hrnext.com; J. Howard-Martin, "Arbitration Can Speed Resolution of Grievances," *USA Today*, March 26, 2002, http://careers.usatoday.com.

20. S. Caudron, "Blowing the Whistle on Employee Disputes," *Workforce*, May 1997, pp. 50–57.

21. J. Smith, "EAPs Evolve to Health Plan Gatekeeper," *Employee Benefit Plan Review* 46 (1992), pp. 18–19.

22. S. Johnson, "Results, Relapse Rates Add to Cost of Non-Hospital Treatment," *Employee Benefit Plan Review* 46 (1992), pp. 15–16.

23. C. Mulcany, "Experts Eye Perils of Mental Health Cuts," *National Underwriter* 96 (1992), pp. 17–18.

24. J. Jones, "How to Bounce Back if You're Bounced Out," *BusinessWeek*, January 27, 1998, pp. 22–23.

25. D. W. Baruch, "Why They Terminate," *Journal of Consulting Psychology* 8 (1944), pp. 35–46; J. G. Rosse, "Relations among Lateness, Absence and Turnover: Is There a Progression of Withdrawal?" *Human Relations* 41 (1988), pp. 517–31; C. Hulin, "Adaptation, Persistence and Commitment in Organizations," in *Handbook of Industrial & Organizational Psychology*, 2nd ed., ed. M. D. Dunnette and L. M. Hough (Palo Alto, CA: Consulting Psychologists Press, 1991), pp. 443–50; C. Hulin, M. Roznowski, and D. Hachiya, "Alternative Opportunities and Withdrawal Decisions," *Psychological Bulletin* 97 (1985), pp. 233–50.

26. D. Watson, L. A. Clark, and A. Tellegen, "Development and Validation of Brief Measures of Positive and Negative Affect: The PANAS Scales," *Journal of Personality and Social Psychology* 54 (1988), pp. 1063–70.

27. T. A. Judge, E. A. Locke, C. C. Durham, and A. N. Kluger, "Dispositional Effects on Job and Life Satisfaction: The Role of Core Evaluations," *Journal of Applied Psychology* 83 (1998), pp. 17–34.

28. B. M. Staw, N. E. Bell, and J. A. Clausen, "The

Dispositional Approach to Job Attitudes: A Lifetime Longitudinal Test," *Administrative Science Quarterly* 31 (1986), pp. 56–78; B. M. Staw and J. Ross, "Stability in the Midst of Change: A Dispositional Approach to Job Attitudes," *Journal of Applied Psychology* 70 (1985), pp. 469–80; R. P. Steel and J. R. Rentsch, "The Dispositional Model of Job Attitudes Revisited: Findings of a 10-Year Study," *Journal of Applied Psychology* 82 (1997), pp. 873–79.

29. T. A. Judge and J. E. Bono, "Relationship of Core Self-Evaluation Traits—Self-Esteem, Generalized Self-Efficacy, Locus of Control, and Emotional Stability—with Job Satisfaction and Job Performance: A Meta-Analysis," *Journal of Applied Psychology* 86 (2001), pp. 80–92.

30. T. A. Judge, J. E. Bono, and E. A. Locke, "Personality and Job Satisfaction: The Mediating Role of Job Characteristics," *Journal of Applied Psychology* 85 (2000), pp. 237–49.

31. S. C. Douglas and M. J. Martinko, "Exploring the Role of Individual Differences in the Prediction of Workplace Aggression," *Journal of Applied Psychology* 86 (2001), pp. 547–59.

32. B. A. Gerhart, "How Important Are Dispositional Factors as Determinants of Job Satisfaction? Implications for Job Design and Other Personnel Programs," *Journal of Applied Psychology* 72 (1987), pp. 493–502.

33. E. F. Stone and H. G. Gueutal, "An Empirical Derivation of the Dimensions along Which Characteristics of Jobs Are Perceived," *Academy of Managmeent Journal* 28 (1985), pp. 376–96.

34. L. W. Porter and R. M. Steers, "Organizational Work and Personal Factors in Employee Absenteeism and Turnover," *Psychological Bulletin* 80 (1973), pp. 151–76; S. Melamed, I. Ben-Avi, J. Luz, and M. S. Green, "Objective and Subjective Work Monotony: Effects on Job Satisfaction, Psychological Distress, and Absenteeism in Blue Collar Workers," *Journal of Applied Psychology* 80 (1995), pp. 29–42.

35. D. R. Ilgen and J. R. Hollenbeck, "The Structure of Work: Job Design and Roles," in *Handbook of Industrial & Organizational Psychology*, 2nd ed.

36. J. A. Breaugh and J. P. Colihan, "Measuring Facets of Job Ambiguity: Construct Validity Evidence," *Journal of Applied Psychology* 79 (1994), pp. 191–201.

37. M. A. Shaffer and D. A. Harrison, "Expatriates' Psychological Withdrawal from Interpersonal Assignments: Work, Non-work, and Family Influences," *Personnel Psychology* 51 (1998), pp. 87–118.

38. S. M. Lilienthal, "Screen and Glean," *Workforce*, October 2000, downloaded from FindArticles.com.

39. Ibid., citing M. Buckingham and C. Coffman, *First Break All the Rules* (New York: Simon & Schuster, 1999).

40. J. Cook, "Positively Negative," *Human Resource Executive*, June 15, 2001, pp. 101–4.

41. J. Jones, "Absenteeism on Rise, at $505 an Employee," *Chicago Tribune*, August 29, 1995, p. 3.

42. R. Kanungo, *Work Alienation* (New York: Praeger, 1982).

43. R. T. Mowday, R. M. Steers, and L. W. Porter, "The Measurement of Organizational Commitment," *Journal of Vocational Behavior* 14 (1979), pp. 224–47.

44. E. A. Locke, "The Nature and Causes of Job Dissatisfaction," in *The Handbook of Industrial & Organizational Psychology*, ed. M. D. Dunnette (Chicago: Rand McNally, 1976), pp. 901–69.

45. S. Caudron, "The Myth of Job Happiness," *Workforce*, April 2000, pp. 32–36.

46. E. Tanouye, "Depression Takes Annual Toll of $70 Billion on Employers," *The Wall Street Journal*, June 13, 2001, p. 1; E. Tanouye, "Mental Illness in the Workplace Afflicts Bosses, Can Affect Business," *The Wall Street Journal*, June 13, 2001, pp. 1–2; J. Vennochi, "When Depression Comes to Work," *Working Woman*, August 1995, pp. 43–51.

47. G. R. Oldham, A. Cummings, L. J. Mischel, J. M. Schmidtke, and J. Zhou, "Listen While You Work? Quasi-experimental Relations between Personal-Stereo Headset Use and Employee Work Responses," *Journal of Applied Psychology* 80 (1995), pp. 547–64.

48. B. Kaye, "Wake Up and Smell the Coffee: People Flock to Family Friendly," *BusinessWeek Online*, January 28, 2001, pp. 1–2.

49. G. Flynn, "The Legalities of Flextime," *Workforce*, October 2001, pp. 62–66.

50. J. E. Perry-Smith, "Work Family Human Resource Bundles and Perceived Organizational Performance," *Academy of Management Journal* 43 (2000), pp. 801–15.

51. B. Sorrell, "Many U.S. Employees Feel Overworked, Stressed, Study Says," *CNN.com*, May 16, 2001, pp. 1–2.

52. M. Conlin, "Revenge of the Managers," *BusinessWeek*, March 12, 2001, pp. 60–61.

53. B. M. Meglino, E. C. Ravlin, and C. L. Adkins, "A Work Values Approach to Corporate Culture: A Field Test of the Value Congruence Process and Its Relationship to Individual Outcomes," *Journal of Applied Psychology* 74 (1989), pp. 424–33.

54. G. C. Ganster, M. R. Fusilier, and B. T. Mayes, "Role of Social Support in the Experience of Stress at Work," *Journal of Applied Psychology* 71 (1986), pp. 102–11.

55. L. Rhoades, R. Eisenberger, and S. Armeli, "Affective Commitment to the Organization: The Contribution of Perceived Organizational Support," *Journal of Applied Psychology* 86 (2001), pp. 825–36.

56. R. T. Keller, "A Test of the Path-Goal Theory of Leadership with Need for Clarity as a Moderator in Research and Development Organizations," *Journal of Applied Psychology* 74 (1989), pp. 208–12.

57. R. P. Quinn and G. L. Staines, *The 1977 Quality of Employment Survey* (Ann Arbor, MI: Survey Research Center, Institute for Social Research, University of Michigan, 1979).

58. T. Judge and T. Welbourne, "A Confirmatory Investigation of the Dimensionality of the Pay Satisfaction Questionnaire," *Journal of Applied Psychology* 79 (1994), pp. 461–66.

59. T. Gray, "A Hospital Takes Action on Employee Survey," *Personnel Journal*, March 1995, pp. 74–77.

60. J. Applegaste, "Plan an Exit Interview," *CNN-Money.com*, November 13, 2000, pp. 1–2.

61. H. E. Allerton, "Can Teach Old Dogs New Tricks," *Training & Development*, November 2000, downloaded from FindArticles.com.

VIDEO CASE

Creative Staffing Solutions Pairs Workers with Employers

One of the greatest challenges for any company is to find the right workers to fill its needs, whether it's someone who can operate heavy machinery or someone who can give great haircuts. In the recent labor market, even with an economic downturn, high-tech firms have had difficulty finding enough employees who are skilled in information technology to fill the positions they have open. In addition, high-tech companies have needs that are different from firms in other industries. First, they are often looking for people who are willing to work part-time or on a temporary basis to develop and complete a particular project. Second, that temporary basis differs from "traditional" temporary assignments, which often last a week or two while a permanent employee is ill or on vacation. Instead, high-tech companies are looking for people who can stay on the job for six months or a year. Third, these firms are looking for workers with particular skills and aptitudes in information technology. "Scarcity of qualified candidates, competition from high-profile employers, and the potential for IT professionals to earn more as professional contractors were cited as top barriers for recruiting IT workers," cites a recent study conducted by the American Electronics Association (AEA). In a tight labor market, where can high-tech firms find these perfect employees?

Creative Staffing Solutions (CSS), a temporary and alternative staffing firm, provides such workers to companies. "Temping," as it used to be called, is now a $40 billion industry as more and more companies turn to staffing agencies for help. Companies are willing to pay for these employees. "For high-tech workers, this is an employees' market," notes Marc Brailov of the American Electronics Association. "It is very important for Internet companies to create and offer incentives to attract and retain employees." That's where Creative Staffing Solutions comes in.

Founded by Mel Rhone in 1996, CSS, a minority-owned firm based in Philadelphia, now has clients ranging from small companies to large organizations such as AT&T, Hershey's, and Lockheed Martin. CSS specializes in finding IT professionals, engineers, computer programmers, and other high-tech workers for its clients. On one side of the process, a CSS manager meets with and interviews the HR manager at the client firm to determine the firm's needs. On the other side, CSS managers screen, interview, and test prospective job candidates to determine their suitability for positions. CSS checks a candidate's work history and tests him or her in grammar and spelling, math, computer skills, and so forth. Recently, CSS made it possible for job hunters to post their résumés on the CSS website, where staffing managers can review them. In addition, CSS's staffing managers peruse Internet job sites in search of potential matches.

According to CSS managers, the alternative staffing solution meets both the needs of the company and the needs of the worker. Firms get screened, highly skilled, and motivated workers for a designated time period. Currently, many high-tech firms prefer to hire temporary workers because the IT economy is very volatile. And they like to hire people to complete a special project, such as development of a new computer system. Workers also benefit. "You get to make your own schedule," remarks CSS staffing manager Joy Thomas. Because CSS tests and trains candidates, people who want to improve their job skills can find plenty of opportunity through the company. Some workers are looking to change careers but are afraid to make a total commitment without knowing whether they will like the new field. Filling a temporary position can give them a good taste of what the field will be like. Occasionally, CSS sends a worker to fill one temporary position at a company, and the person moves on to a completely different job at the firm. The arrangement provides both parties with convenience and flexibility.

Creative Staffing Solutions continues to find ways to grow its own business. Now with an in-house staff of eleven people, Mel Rhone wants to expand. Recently, the company received a loan of $100,000 from the eSpeed Loans program, which is funded by ePhiladelphia, a group that represents technology companies headquartered in Philadelphia. CSS plans to use the funding to purchase hardware and software, as well as hire more staffers to train workers for all levels of technology-related jobs. Rhone, like others, foresees a future in which temporary and alternative staffing will be routine in American industry, and he wants his company to be ready to grab every opportunity that comes its way. A study by the National Association of Temporary and Staffing Services found that 90 percent of companies surveyed employ temporary help. "Companies are incorporating temp workers in long-term plans, whereas 15 years ago they used temps just to fill occasional holes," remarks Richard Wahlquist, executive vice president of the Association. The same holds true for today's workers. "The way Americans seek work has fundamentally shifted—so many young adults look to temp agencies first, to get a taste of different fields, that we are a central part of the job search process," says Wahlquist. Creative Staffing Solutions intends to remain part of the process, as well.

SOURCES: Creative Staffing Solutions website, www.cssrecruiting.com, accessed November 28, 2001; Jay Lyman, "Uncle Sam May Help Train IT Geeks," *E-Commerce Times*, April 30, 2001, www.ecommercetimes.com; Courtney Macavinta, "Study: High-Tech Worker Shortage Persists," *CNet News.com*, April 26, 2001, http://news.cnet.com; Joshua Kuriantzick, "A Temporary Boom in the Job Market," *U.S. News & World Report*, March 19, 2001, www.usnews.com; Peter Key, "Author/Innovator Gives Penn Large Gift," *Philadelphia Business Journal*, January 19, 2001, http://philadelphia.bcentral.com; Ryan Naraine, "Tech Worker Shortage Remains Despite Layoffs," *Internet.com News*, January 10, 2001, www.atnewyork.com.

Questions

1. In addition to job websites and its own site, where else might Creative Staffing Solutions look for potential job candidates?
2. How can Creative Staffing Solutions create a learning environment for job candidates before they accept a position or while they are between positions?
3. As you consider your career, would you try working through a temporary agency such as CSS? Why or why not?
4. What difficulties might Creative Staffing Solutions have to deal with in using electronic job and résumé postings?

Part 4

Compensating Human Resources

Chapter 11

Establishing a Pay Structure

Chapter 12

Recognizing Employee Contributions with Pay

Chapter 13

Providing Employee Benefits

Chapter 11

Establishing a Pay Structure

What Do I Need to Know? After reading this chapter, you should be able to:

1. Identify the kinds of decisions involved in establishing a pay structure.

2. Summarize legal requirements for pay policies.

3. Discuss how economic forces influence decisions about pay.

4. Describe how employees evaluate the fairness of a pay structure.

5. Explain how organizations design pay structures related to jobs.

6. Describe alternatives to job-based pay.

7. Summarize how to ensure that pay is actually in line with the job structure.

8. Discuss issues related to paying employees serving in the military and paying executives.

Introduction

When Internet stocks tumbled, high-tech companies' major challenge in paying employees shifted from paying them enough so they would stay on board to figuring out how to pay employees while keeping the company afloat financially. Companies that were used to crafting generous pay plans had to become more budget conscious. At Dallas-based Coollogic, the three top executives had set their pay at levels matching the pay of similar firms' executives.[1] When investment money dried up, the executives decided they couldn't afford to make such comparisons, and they slashed their pay by almost half. However, they did not force their employees to take the same bitter medicine. They feared that companywide pay cuts would demoralize the employees and inspire many to leave. Instead, they explained the software company's difficult circumstances and announced layoffs. Says Coollogic's chief executive officer and cofounder Jim Reiss Jr., "I'd rather cut bodies and add workload to the remaining crew than shear everyone and demoralize the whole crowd."

From the employer's point of view, pay is a powerful tool for meeting the organization's goals. Pay has a large impact on employee attitudes and behaviors. It influences which kinds of employees are attracted to (and remain with) the organization. By rewarding certain behaviors, it can align employees' interests with the organization's goals. Employees care about policies affecting earnings because the policies affect the employees' income and standard of living. Besides the level of pay, employees care about its fairness compared with what others earn. Also, employees consider pay a sign of status and success. They attach great importance to pay decisions when they evaluate their relationship with their employer. For these reasons, organizations must carefully manage and communicate decisions about pay.

At the same time, pay is a major cost. Its share of total costs varies widely, but across all industries, pay averages almost one-fourth of a company's revenues.[2] Some companies spend 40 percent or more of their revenues on paying employees. Managers have to keep this cost reasonable.

This chapter describes how managers weigh the importance and costs of pay to arrive at a structure for compensation and levels of pay for different jobs. We first define the basic decisions in terms of pay structure and pay level. Next, we look at several considerations that influence these decisions: legal requirements related to pay, economic forces, the nature of the organization's jobs, and employees' judgments about the fairness of pay levels. We describe methods for evaluating jobs and market data to arrive at a pay structure. We then summarize alternatives to the usual focus on jobs. The chapter closes with a look at two issues of current importance—pay for employees on leave to serve in the military and pay for executives.

Decisions about Pay

LO1

Because pay is important both in its effect on employees and on account of its cost, organizations need to plan what they will pay employees in each job. An unplanned approach, in which each employee's pay is independently negotiated, will likely result in unfairness, dissatisfaction, and rates that are either overly expensive or so low that positions are hard to fill. Organizations therefore make decisions about two aspects of pay structure: job structure and pay level. **Job structure** consists of the relative pay for different jobs within the organization. It establishes relative pay among different functions and different levels of responsibility. For example, job structure defines the difference in pay between an entry-level accountant and an entry-level assembler, as well as the difference between an entry-level accountant, the accounting department manager, and the organization's comptroller. **Pay level** is the average amount (including wages, salaries, and bonuses) the organization pays for a particular job. Together, job structure and pay levels establish a **pay structure** that helps the organization achieve goals related to employee motivation, cost control, and the ability to attract and retain talented human resources.

The organization's job structure and pay levels are policies of the organization, rather than the amount a particular employee earns. For example, an organization's pay structure could include the range of pay that a person may earn in the job of

job structure
The relative pay for different jobs within the organization.

pay level
The average amount (including wages, salaries, and bonuses) the organization pays for a particular job.

pay structure
The pay policy resulting from job structure and pay-level decisions.

FIGURE 11.1

Issues in Developing a
Pay Structure

entry-level accountant. An individual accountant could be earning an amount anywhere within that range. Typically, the amount a person earns depends on the individual's qualifications, accomplishments, and experience. The individual's pay may also depend partly on how well the organization performs. This chapter focuses on the organization's decisions about pay structure, and the next chapter will explore decisions that affect the amount of pay an individual earns.

Especially in an organization with hundreds or thousands of employees, it would be impractical for managers and the human resource department to make an entirely unique decision about each employee's pay. The decision would have to weigh so many factors that this approach would be expensive, difficult, and often unsatisfactory. Establishing a pay structure simplifies the process of making decisions about individual employees' pay by grouping together employees with similar jobs. As shown in Figure 11.1, human resource professionals develop this pay structure based on legal requirements, market forces, and the organization's goals, such as attracting a high-quality workforce and meeting principles of fairness.

Legal Requirements for Pay

LO2

Government regulation affects pay structure in the areas of equal employment opportunity, minimum wages, pay for overtime, and prevailing wages for federal contractors. All of an organization's decisions about pay should comply with the applicable laws.

Equal Employment Opportunity

Under the laws governing Equal Employment Opportunity, described in Chapter 3, employers may not base differences in pay on an employee's age, sex, race, or other protected status. Any differences in pay must instead be tied to such business-related considerations as job responsibilities or performance. The goal is for employers to provide *equal pay for equal work*. For example, being female or over 40 may not be the ba-

Two employees who do the same job cannot be paid different wages because of gender, race, or age. It would be illegal to pay these two employees differently because one is male and the other is female. Only if there are differences in their experience, skills, seniority, or job performance are there legal reasons why their pay might be different.

sis for different pay for two equally experienced lawyers or two equally experienced janitors handling equally difficult workloads equally well. Job descriptions, job structures, and pay structures can help organizations demonstrate that they are upholding these laws.

These laws do not guarantee equal pay for men and women, whites and minorities, or any other groups, because so many legitimate factors, from education to choice of occupation, affect a person's earnings. In fact, numbers show that women and racial minorities in the United States tend to earn less than white men. Among full-time workers in 2000, women on average earned 76 cents for every dollar earned by men, while black workers on average earned 79 cents for every dollar earned by white workers.[3] Even when these figures are adjusted to take into account education, experience, and occupation, the earnings gap does not completely close.[4]

One explanation for historical lower pay for women has been that employers have undervalued work performed by women—in particular, placing a lower value on occupations traditionally dominated by women. Some policy makers have proposed a remedy for this called equal pay for *comparable worth*. This policy uses job evaluation (described later in the chapter) to establish the worth of an organization's jobs in terms of such criteria as their difficulty and their importance to the organization. The employer then compares the evaluation points awarded to each job with the pay for each job. If jobs have the same number of evaluation points, they should be paid equally. If they are not, pay of the lower-paid job is raised to meet the goal of comparable worth.

Comparable-worth policies are controversial. From an economic standpoint, the obvious drawback of such a policy is that raising pay for some jobs places the employer at an economic disadvantage relative to employers that pay the market rate. In addition, a free-market economy assumes people will take differences in pay into account when they choose a career. The courts allow organizations to defend themselves against claims of discrimination by showing that they pay the going market rate.[5] Businesses are reluctant to place themselves at an economic disadvantage, but many state governments adjust pay to achieve equal pay for comparable worth. Also, at both private and government organizations, policies designed to shatter the "glass ceiling" (discussed in Chapter 9) can help to address the problem of unequal pay.

Minimum Wage

In the United States, employers must pay at least the **minimum wage** established by law. (A *wage* is the rate of pay per hour.) At the federal level, the 1938 **Fair Labor Standards Act (FLSA)** establishes a minimum wage that now stands at $5.15 per hour. In a 1990 amendment to the FLSA, Congress established a lower "training

minimum wage
The lowest amount that employers may pay under federal or state law, stated as an amount of pay per hour.

Fair Labor Standards Act (FLSA)
Federal law that establishes a minimum wage and requirements for overtime pay and child labor.

wage," which employers may pay to workers under the age of 20 for a period of up to 90 days. This subminimum wage is approximately 85 percent of the minimum wage. Some states have laws specifying minimum wages; in these states, employers must pay whichever rate is higher.

From the standpoint of social policy, an issue related to the minimum wage is that it tends to be lower than the earnings required for a full-time worker to rise above the poverty level. A number of cities have therefore passed laws requiring a so-called *living wage*, essentially a minimum wage based on the cost of living in a particular region. These local laws usually cover businesses with government contracts, but some cities have recently been considering laws to extend the living-wage requirements to the private sector.[6] Because labor costs influence the cost of providing a product or service, these laws may contribute to higher local taxes and raise the cost of doing business in an area with living-wage laws.

Overtime Pay

Another requirement of the FLSA is that employers must pay higher wages for overtime, defined as hours worked beyond 40 hours per week. The overtime rate under the FLSA is one and a half times the employee's usual hourly rate, including any bonuses and piece-rate payments (amounts paid per item produced). The overtime rate applies to the hours worked beyond 40 in one week. Time worked includes not only hours spent on production or sales but also time on such activities as attending required classes, cleaning up the work site, or traveling between work sites. Figure 11.2 shows how this applies to an employee who works 50 hours to earn a base rate of $10 per hour plus a weekly bonus of $30. The overtime pay is based on the base pay ($400) plus the bonus ($30), for a rate of $10.75 per hour. For each of the 10 hours of overtime, the employee would earn $16.13, so the overtime pay is $161.30 ($16.13 times 10). When employees are paid per unit produced or when they receive a monthly or quarterly bonus, those payments must be converted into wages per hour, so that the employer can include these amounts when figuring the correct overtime rate.

The FLSA requires overtime pay for hours worked beyond 40, whether or not the employer specifically asked or expected the employee to work those extra hours.[7] In

FIGURE 11.2

Computing Overtime Pay

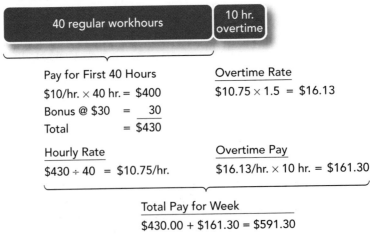

Employee's Base Pay: $10/hr. + $30/wk. (bonus)
Employee's Hours: 50 (40 regular, 10 overtime)

40 regular workhours   10 hr. overtime

Pay for First 40 Hours
$10/hr. × 40 hr. = $400
Bonus @ $30   =   30
Total   = $430

Overtime Rate
$10.75 × 1.5 = $16.13

Hourly Rate
$430 ÷ 40 = $10.75/hr.

Overtime Pay
$16.13/hr. × 10 hr. = $161.30

Total Pay for Week
$430.00 + $161.30 = $591.30

other words, if the employer knows the employee is working overtime but does not pay time and a half, the employer may be violating the FLSA. This happened to a department store when employees said the store encouraged them to perform activities like writing thank-you notes to customers after their scheduled work hours. The company denied requiring the extra work, but the employees had done the work and the company had not paid them for the time. So the store settled with the employees, providing them with back pay and legal fees totaling millions of dollars.[8]

Not everyone is eligible for overtime pay. Under the FLSA, executive, professional, administrative, and outside sales employees are considered **exempt employees,** meaning employers need not pay them one and a half times their regular pay for working more than 40 hours per week. Exempt status depends on the employee's job responsibilities and salary, and the standards can be fairly complicated. For example, the definition of an executive includes seven criteria, including whether the employee supervises two or more employees and has authority to hire and fire. For more details about the standards for exempt employees, contact the Wage and Hour Division of the Labor Department's Employment Standards Administration or refer to its website at **www.dol.gov/esa**. Any employee who is not in one of the exempt categories is called a **nonexempt employee.** Most workers paid on an hourly basis are nonexempt and therefore subject to the laws governing overtime pay. On the other hand, as the end-of-the-chapter *BusinessWeek* case shows, paying a salary does not necessarily mean a job is exempt.

exempt employees
Managers, outside salespeople, and any other employees not covered by the FLSA requirement for overtime pay.

nonexempt employees
Employees covered by the FLSA requirements for overtime pay.

Child Labor

In the early years of the Industrial Revolution, employers could pay low wages by hiring children. The FLSA now sharply restricts the use of child labor, with the aim of protecting children's health, safety, and educational opportunities.[9] The restrictions apply to children younger than 18. Under the FLSA, children aged 16 and 17 may not be employed in hazardous occupations defined by the Department of Labor, such as mining, meatpacking, and certain kinds of manufacturing using heavy machinery. Children aged 14 and 15 may work only outside school hours, in jobs defined as nonhazardous, and for limited time periods. A child under age 14 may not be employed in any work associated with interstate commerce, except work performed in a nonhazardous job for a business entirely owned by the child's parent or guardian. A few additional exemptions from this ban include acting, baby-sitting, and delivering newspapers to consumers.

Besides the FLSA, state laws also restrict the use of child labor. Many states have laws requiring working papers or work permits for minors, and many states restrict the number of hours or times of day that minors aged 16 and older may work. Before hiring any workers under the age of 18, employers must ensure they are complying with the child labor laws of their state, as well as the FLSA requirements for their industry.

Prevailing Wages

Two additional federal laws, the Davis-Bacon Act of 1931 and the Walsh-Healy Public Contracts Act of 1936, govern pay policies of federal contractors. Under these laws, federal contractors must pay their employees at rates at least equal to the prevailing wages in the area. The calculation of prevailing rates must be based on 30 percent of the local labor force. Typically, the rates are based on relevant union contracts. Pay earned by union members tends to be higher than the pay of nonunion workers in similar jobs, so the effect of these laws is to raise the lower limit of pay an employer can offer.

These laws do not cover all companies. Davis-Bacon covers construction contractors that receive more than $2,000 in federal money. Walsh-Healy covers all government contractors receiving $10,000 or more in federal funds.

Economic Influences on Pay

An organization cannot make spending decisions independent of the economy. Organizations must keep costs low enough that they can sell their products profitably, yet they must be able to attract workers in a competitive labor market. Decisions about how to respond to the economic forces of product markets and labor markets limit an organization's choices about pay structure.

Product Markets

The organization's *product market* includes organizations that offer competing goods and services. In other words, the organizations in a product market are competing to serve the same customers. To succeed in their product markets, organizations must be able to sell their goods and services at a quantity and price that will bring them a sufficient profit. They may try to win customers by being superior in a number of areas, including quality, customer service, and price. An important influence on price is the cost to produce the goods and services for sale. As we mentioned earlier, the cost of labor is a significant part of an organization's costs.

If an organization's labor costs are higher than those of its competitors, it will be under pressure to charge more than competitors charge for similar products. One study found that in the early 1990s, the amount spent on wages and benefits to produce a small car was about $1,700 at Ford, $1,800 at Chrysler, and $2,400 at General Motors.[10] Its higher spending placed General Motors at a disadvantage. The company had to offset these costs elsewhere (such as buying lower-cost components), settle for earning a lower profit, or convince car buyers to pay more for a GM car.

In this way, product markets place an upper limit on the pay an organization will offer. This upper limit is most important when labor costs are a large part of an organization's total costs and when the organization's customers place great importance on price. Organizations that want to lure top-quality employees by offering generous salaries therefore have to find ways to automate routine activities (so that labor is a smaller part of total costs) or to persuade customers that high quality is worth a premium price. Organizations under pressure to cut labor costs may respond by reducing staff levels, freezing pay levels, postponing hiring decisions, or requiring employees to bear more of the cost of benefits such as insurance premiums.

Labor Markets

Besides competing to sell their products, organizations must compete to obtain human resources in *labor markets*. In general, workers prefer higher-paying jobs and avoid employers that offer less money for the same type of job. In this way, competition for labor establishes the minimum an organization must pay to hire an employee for a particular job. If an organization pays less than the minimum, employees will look for jobs with other organizations.

An organization's competitors in labor markets typically include companies with similar products and companies in other industries that hire similar employees. For example, a truck transportation firm would want to know the pay earned by truck drivers at competing firms as well as truck drivers for manufacturers that do their own shipping, drivers for moving and storage companies, and drivers for stores that provide delivery services. In setting pay levels for its bookkeepers and secretaries, the company would probably define its labor market differently, because bookkeepers and secretaries work for most kinds of businesses. The company would likely look for data on the earnings of bookkeepers and secretaries in the region. For all these jobs, the company wants to know what others are paying so that it will pay enough to attract and keep qualified employees.

Another influence on labor markets is the *cost of living*—the cost of a household's typical expenses, such as house payments, groceries, medical care, and gasoline. In some parts of the country, the cost of living is higher than in others, so the local labor markets there will likely demand higher pay. Also, over time, the cost of living tends to rise. When the cost of living is rising rapidly, labor markets demand pay increases. The federal government tracks trends in the nation's cost of living with a measure called the Consumer Price Index (CPI). Following and studying changes in the CPI can help employers prepare for changes in the demands of the labor market.

Pay Level: Deciding What to Pay

Although labor and product markets limit organizations' choices about pay levels, there is a range within which organizations can make decisions.[11] The size of this range depends on the details of the organization's competitive environment. If many workers are competing for a few jobs, employers will have more choice. Similarly, employers can be more flexible about pay policies if they use technology and work design to get better results from employees than their competitors do.

When organizations have a broad range in which to make decisions about pay, they can choose to pay at, above, or below the rate set by market forces. Economic theory holds that the most profitable level, all things being equal, would be at the market rate. Often, however, all things are *not* equal from one employer to another. For instance, an organization may gain an advantage by paying above the market rate if it uses the higher pay as one means to attract top talent and then uses these excellent employees' knowledge to be more innovative, produce higher quality, or work more efficiently.

This approach is based on the view of employees as resources. Higher pay may be an investment in superior human resources. Having higher labor costs than your competitors is not necessarily bad if you also have the best and most effective workforce, which produces more products of better quality. Pay policies are one of the most important human resource tools for encouraging desired employee behaviors and discouraging undesired behaviors. Therefore, organizations must evaluate pay as more than a cost, but also as an investment that can generate returns in attracting, retaining, and motivating a high-quality workforce. For this reason, paying above the going rate may be advantageous for an organization that empowers employees or that cannot closely watch employees (as with repair technicians who travel to customers). Those employers might use high pay to attract and retain top candidates and to motivate them to do their best because they want to keep their high-paying jobs.[12]

Of course, employers do not always have this much flexibility. Some companies are under intense pressure to charge low prices for their products, and some companies

When a segment of the labor market is laid off, it adds to the number of people available to work and places less pressure on employers to offer high pay.

are trying to draw workers from a pool that is too small to satisfy all employers' needs. Some companies—including the small U.S. businesses that supply big manufacturers—are in the unfortunate position of trying to do both.[13] Small U.S. manufacturers often face product market competition from companies in countries where labor costs are lower. At the same time, they are struggling to find workers in a tight labor market. For example, North East Precision, a machine shop in Vermont, has had to turn down orders because it cannot find enough employees to work at a rate that lets the company charge a competitive price.[14] For unskilled labor, North East tries to match the pay of local supermarket and fast-food employees, but work at North East is more physically difficult, so many workers would rather stick with McDonald's. Organizations being squeezed between labor and product markets need to couple pay policies with creative HR, production, and marketing management to develop new recruiting sources, desirable benefits besides pay, technology and training to make workers' contributions more valuable, and more profitable product lines.

Gathering Information about Market Pay

benchmarking
A procedure in which an organization compares its own practices against those of successful competitors.

To compete for talent, organizations use **benchmarking,** a procedure in which an organization compares its own practices against those of successful competitors. In terms of compensation, benchmarking involves the use of pay surveys. These provide information about the going rates of pay at competitors in the organization's product and labor markets. An organization can conduct its own surveys, but the federal government and other organizations make a great deal of data available already.

Pay surveys are available for many kinds of industries (product markets) and jobs (labor markets). The primary collector of this kind of data in the United States is the Bureau of Labor Statistics, which conducts an ongoing National Compensation Survey measuring wages, salaries, and benefits paid to the nation's employees. The "HR How To" box provides guidelines for using the BLS website as a source of wage data.

Gathering Wage Data at the BLS Website

A convenient source of data on hourly wages is the wage query system of the Bureau of Labor Statistics (BLS). This federal agency makes data available at its website on an interactive basis. The data come from the BLS's National Compensation Survey. The user specifies the category of data desired, and the BLS provides tables of data almost instantly. Here's how to use the BLS system.

Visit the BLS website (www.bls.gov) and click on the link to "detailed statistics." You will have many options, including background information and news about the National Compensation Survey. To obtain wage data, choose the option to create customized tables. Decide whether you want to start your search by specifying geographic area, occupation, or industry.

You can start by using the map or drop-down menu to select an area. The National Compensation Survey gathers data from selected areas of the United States, designed to be representative of the entire country. Wage data cover about 90 areas, including most metropolitan areas. You can select one of these areas, or one of nine broad geographic regions, or the entire United States. When you select an area, the system allows you to select from the occupations for which the BLS has published data in that area.

The survey data cover 480 occupations, grouped into more general categories. For example, at the most specific level, you could look at civil engineers. More broadly, you could look at all engineers, or at the larger grouping of engineers, architects, and surveyors. Still more broadly, you could request data for all professional specialty occupations, which is part of the yet-broader group called professional specialty and technical occupations. This category is part of white-collar occupations, which is part of the "all workers" group. You should select the most specific grouping that covers the occupation you want to investigate. If you select occupation first, you can then select geographic areas for which the database includes data on that occupation.

After selecting an occupation, you may select a work level. This describes the level of such work features as knowledge required and the scope, complexity, and demands of the job. For instance, you could look only at data for entry-level or senior accountants, rather than all accountants. Some occupations, including artists, athletes, and announcers, are not classified by work level.

Click on the link to submit the request to the BLS. The system immediately processes the request and presents the table (or tables) in a pop-up window on your computer screen.

The Bureau of Labor Statistics is planning to make the system still more useful by offering additional categories of data. For example, the BLS is working on tools for comparing government and private-sector wages, as well as wages for full-time and part-time employees. As these options become available, users should tailor their requests as much as possible to the characteristics of their jobs and organizations.

SOURCE: Bureau of Labor Statistics website, www.bls.gov, July 2, 2002; M. Gittleman and W. J. Wiatrowski, "The BLS Wage Query System: A New Tool to Access Wage Data," *Monthly Labor Review*, October 2001, pp. 22–27.

The Society for Human Resource Management, the American Management Association, and many industry, trade, and professional groups also collect wage and salary data. Employers should check with the relevant groups to see what surveys are available. Consulting firms also will provide data, including the results of international surveys, and can tailor data to the organization's particular needs.

Human resource professionals need to determine whether to gather data focusing on particular industries or on job categories. Industry-specific data are especially relevant for jobs with skills that are specific to the type of product. For jobs with skills that can be transferred to companies in other industries, surveys of job classifications will be more relevant.

LO4

Employee Judgments about Pay Fairness

In developing a pay structure, it is important to keep in mind employees' opinions about fairness. After all, one of the purposes of pay is to motivate employees, and they will not be motivated by pay if they think it is unfair.

Judging Fairness

Employees evaluate their pay relative to the pay of other employees. Social scientists have studied this kind of comparison and developed *equity theory* to describe how people make judgments about fairness.[15] According to equity theory, people measure outcomes such as pay in terms of their inputs. For example, an employee might think of her pay in terms of her master's degree, her 12 years of experience, and her 60-hour workweeks. To decide whether a level of pay is equitable, the person compares her ratio of outcomes and inputs with other people's outcome/input ratios, as shown in Figure 11.3. The person in the previous example might notice that an employee with less education or experience is earning more than she is (unfair) or that an employee who works 80 hours a week is earning more (fair). In general, employees compare their pay and contributions against several yardsticks:

- What they think employees in other organizations earn for doing the same job.
- What they think other employees holding different jobs within the organization earn for doing work at the same or different levels.
- What they think other employees in the organization earn for doing the same job as theirs.

Employees' conclusions about equity depend on what they choose as a standard of comparison. The results can be surprising. For example, some organizations have set up two-tier wage systems as a way to cut labor costs without cutting employees' existing salaries. Typically, employers announce these programs as a way to avoid moving

FIGURE 11.3

Opinions about Fairness: Pay Equity

Equity: Pay Seems Fair

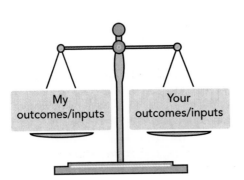

Inequity: Pay Seems Unfair

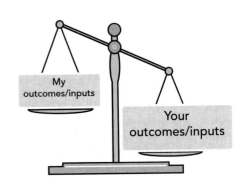

No More Secrets at Two Financial Companies

In the past, American Express, like many organizations, discouraged workplace discussions of pay. However, that policy has changed. The financial giant still doesn't actively *encourage* pay discussions, but it is attempting to be more open about its compensation practices. Employees may ask their managers for information about pay ranges. They can look up internal job postings with salary information. Explains Molly Faust, an American Express spokeswoman, "It's a way to have an open dialogue within the company."

Ohio-based North Side Bank & Trust Company also has recently dropped a ban against pay discussions. The company eliminated the prohibition from its employee handbook. The bank's human resource manager circulated a memo describing how the company's wages and salaries are determined, based on factors such as education, work experience, and seniority.

It's human nature for people to compare notes. Many experts think that it makes sense for companies to provide accurate information rather than letting rumors rule discussions. "People want to know if they're getting the best deal, so they're constantly looking to see what they're worth," says Garth Andrus, a partner with Accenture, a large management consulting firm. Evidently, American Express and North Side Bank & Trust would agree with him.

SOURCE: American Express website, www.americanexpress.com, accessed November 1, 2001; K. J. Dunham, "Employers Ease Bans on Workers Asking, 'What Do They Pay You?'" *The Wall Street Journal*, May 1, 2001, pp. B10+.

jobs out of the country or closing down altogether. In a two-tier wage system, existing employees continue on at their current (upper-tier) pay rate while new employees sign on for less pay (the lower tier). One might expect reaction among employees in the lower tier that the pay structure is unfair. But a study of these employees found that they were *more* satisfied than the top-tier employees.[16] The lower-tier employees were not comparing their pay with that of the upper-tier employees but with the other alternatives they saw for themselves: lower-paying jobs or unemployment.

The ways employees respond to their impressions about equity can have a great impact on the organization. Typically, if employees see their pay as equitable, their attitudes and behavior continue unchanged. If employees see themselves as receiving an advantage, they usually rethink the situation to see it as merely equitable. But if employees conclude that they are underrewarded, they are likely to make up the difference in one of three ways. They might put forth less effort (reducing their inputs), find a way to increase their outcomes (for example, stealing), or withdraw by leaving the organization or refusing to cooperate. Employees' beliefs about fairness also influence their willingness to accept transfers or promotions. For example, if a job change involves more work, employees will expect higher pay.

Communicating Fairness

Equity theory tells organizations that employees care about their pay relative to what others are earning and that these feelings are based on what the employees *perceive* (what they notice and form judgments about). An organization can do much to contribute to what employees know and, as a result, what they perceive. If the organization researches salary levels and concludes that it is paying its employees generously, it should communicate this. If the employees do not know what the organization learned from its research, they may reach an entirely different conclusion about their pay.

Knowing this, most organizations communicate their pay structures openly, right? Actually, until recently, few of them did. In a poll by HRNext, one-third of the 345 companies that responded said they forbid workplace discussions about pay.[17] Still, that number is smaller than five years earlier, when more than half banned such discussions, perhaps out of fear that employees would perceive inequities in their pay. Besides wanting to be more open with employees when the labor market is tight, these companies may have been responding to a ruling by the National Labor Relations Board that employees must be free to talk about pay in the workplace. These organizations also may realize that many employees prefer to work for a company with a policy of openness. The nearby "Best Practices" box describes two financial organizations with a policy of being open with employees.

Employers must also recognize that employees know much more about what other employers pay now than they did before the Internet became popular. In the past, when gathering wage and salary data was expensive and difficult, employers had more leeway in negotiating with individual employees. Today's employees can go to websites like jobstar.org or salary.com to find hundreds of links to wage and salary data. For a fee, executive search firms provide data, such as the information at www.futurestep.com, operated by Korn/Ferry. Resources like these give employees information about what other workers are earning, along with the expectation that information will be shared. This means employers will face increased pressure to clearly explain their pay policies.

Managers play the most significant role in communication because they interact with their employees each day. The HR department should prepare them to explain why the organization's pay structure is designed as it is and to judge whether employee concerns about the structure indicate a need for change. A common issue is whether to reclassify a job because its content has changed. If an employee takes on more responsibility, the employee will often ask the manager for help in seeking more pay for the job.

Organizations can also contribute to a sense of fairness by including employees in decision making about pay structures. Employee participation can take many forms. Employees may serve on task forces charged with recommending and designing a pay structure. The organization may ask them to help communicate the structure and explain its rationale. As with open communications about pay, however, employee participation in decisions about pay is fairly rare.

Job Structure: Relative Value of Jobs

LO5

Along with market forces and principles of fairness, organizations consider the relative contribution each job should make to the organization's overall performance. In general, an organization's top executives have a great impact on the organization's performance, so they tend to be paid much more than entry-level workers. Executives at the same level of the organization—for example, the vice president of marketing and the vice president of information systems—tend to be paid similar amounts. Creation of a pay structure requires that the organization develop an internal structure showing the relative contribution of its various jobs.

JOB TITLE	COMPENSABLE FACTORS			
	EXPERIENCE	EDUCATION	COMPLEXITY	TOTAL
Computer operator	40	30	40	110
Computer programmer	40	50	65	155
Systems analyst	65	60	85	210

TABLE 11.1

Job Evaluation of Three Jobs with Three Factors

One typical way of doing this is with a **job evaluation,** an administrative procedure for measuring the relative worth of the organization's jobs. Usually, the organization does this by assembling and training a job evaluation committee, consisting of people familiar with the jobs to be evaluated. The committee often includes a human re-source specialist and, if its budget permits, may hire an outside consultant.

To conduct a job evaluation, the committee identifies each job's *compensable factors*, meaning the characteristics of a job that the organization values and chooses to pay for. As shown in Table 11.1, an organization might value the experience and ed-ucation of people performing computer-related jobs, as well as the complexity of those jobs. Other compensable factors might include working conditions and responsibility. Based on the job attributes defined by job analysis (discussed in Chapter 4), the jobs are rated for each factor. The rater assigns each factor a certain number of points, giv-ing more points to factors when they are considered more important and when the job requires a high level of that factor. Often the number of points comes from one of the *point manuals* published by trade groups and management consultants. If neces-sary, the organization can adapt the scores in the point manual to the organization's situation or even develop its own point manual. As in the example in Table 11.1, the scores for each factor are totaled to arrive at an overall evaluation for each job.

The organization may evaluate its managerial and professional jobs separately, us-ing a method designed for this purpose. One of the most popular methods is the **Hay Guide-Chart Profile method,** often referred to as the Hay plan. Named for the Hay Group, the consulting firm that developed it, the Hay plan creates a profile for each position based on three variables:[18]

1. *Know-how*—the required skills, area of knowledge, and abilities.
2. *Problem solving*—the required degree of analysis, creativity, and reasoning.
3. *Accountability*—the level of responsibility and the job's impact on the organiza-tion.

A trained analyst interviews supervisors and reviews job descriptions to evaluate the organization's jobs, scoring them on one of Hay's Guide Charts developed for this purpose. The result is a score for each managerial or professional job, stated as a per-centage factor for each of the three variables. These percentages can be used to rank the jobs and arrange them into a job structure.

Job evaluations provide the basis for decisions about relative internal worth. Ac-cording to the sample assessments in Table 11.1, the job of systems analyst is worth almost twice as much to this organization as the job of computer operator. Therefore, the organization would be willing to pay almost twice as much for the work of a sys-tems analyst as it would for the work of a computer operator.

The organization may limit its pay survey to jobs evaluated as *key jobs*. These are jobs that have relatively stable content and are common among many organizations, so it is possible to obtain survey data about what people earn in these jobs. Organiza-tions can make the process of creating a pay structure more practical by defining key

job evaluation
An administrative procedure for measuring the relative internal worth of the organization's jobs.

Hay Guide-Chart Profile method
Method of job evaluation that creates a profile for each position based on its required know-how, degree of problem solving, and accountability.

jobs. Research for creating the pay structure is limited to the key jobs that play a significant role in the organization. Pay for the key jobs can be based on survey data, and pay for the organization's other jobs can be based on the organization's job structure. A job with a higher evaluation score than a particular key job would receive higher pay than that key job.

Pay Structure: Putting It All Together

hourly wage
Rate of pay for each hour worked.

piecework rate
Rate of pay for each unit produced.

salary
Rate of pay for each week, month or year worked.

As we described in the first section of this chapter, the pay structure reflects decisions about how much to pay (pay level) and the relative value of each job (job structure). The organization's pay structure should reflect what the organization knows about market forces, as well as its own unique goals and the relative contribution of each job to achieving the goals. By balancing this external and internal information, the organization's goal is to set levels of pay that employees will consider equitable and motivating. Organizations typically apply the information by establishing some combination of pay rates, pay grades, and pay ranges. Within this structure, they may state the pay in terms of a rate per hour, commonly called an **hourly wage;** a rate of pay for each unit produced, known as a **piecework rate;** or a rate of pay per month or year, called a **salary.**

Pay Rates

If the organization's main concern is to match what people are earning in comparable jobs, the organization can base pay directly on market research into as many of its key jobs as possible. To do this, the organization looks for survey data for each job title. If it finds data from more than one survey, it must weight the results based on their quality and relevance. The final number represents what the competition pays. In light of that knowledge, the organization decides what it will pay for the job.

The next step is to determine salaries for the nonkey jobs, for which the organization has no survey data. Instead, the person developing the pay structure creates a graph like the one in Figure 11.4. The vertical axis shows a range of possible pay rates,

FIGURE 11.4

Pay Policy Lines

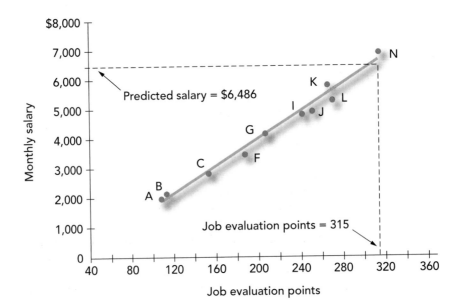

and the horizontal axis measures the points from the job evaluation. The analyst plots points according to the job evaluation and pay rate for each key job. Finally, the analyst fits a line, called a **pay policy line,** to the points plotted. (This can be done statistically on a computer, using a procedure called regression analysis.) Mathematically, this line shows the relationship between job evaluation and rate of pay. Using this line, the analyst can estimate the market pay level for a given job evaluation. Looking at the graph gives approximate numbers, or the regression analysis will provide an equation for calculating the rate of pay.

The pay policy line reflects the pay structure in the market, which does not always match rates in the organization (see key job F in Figure 11.4). Survey data may show that people in certain jobs are actually earning significantly more or less than the amount shown on the pay policy line. For example, some kinds of expertise are in short supply. People with that expertise can command higher salaries, because they can easily leave one employer to get higher pay somewhere else. Suppose, in contrast, that local businesses have laid off many warehouse employees. Because so many of these workers are looking for jobs, organizations may be able to pay them less than the rate that job evaluation points would suggest.

When job structure and market data conflict in these ways, organizations have to decide on a way to resolve the two. One approach is to stick to the job evaluations and pay according to the employees' worth to the organization. Organizations that do so will be paying more or less than they have to, so they will likely have more difficulty competing for customers or employees. A way to moderate this approach is to consider the importance of each position to the organization's goals.[19] If a position is critical for meeting the organization's goals, paying more than competitors pay may be worthwhile.

At the other extreme, the organization could base pay entirely on market forces. However, this approach also has some practical drawbacks. One is that employees may conclude that pay rates are unfair. Two vice presidents or two supervisors will expect to receive similar pay because their responsibilities are similar. If the differences between their pay are large, because of different market rates, the lower-paid employee will likely be dissatisfied. Also, if the organization's development plans include rotating managers through different assignments, the managers will be reluctant to participate if managers in some departments receive lower pay. Organizations therefore must weigh all the objectives of their pay structure to arrive at suitable rates.

Pay Grades

A large organization could have hundreds or even thousands of different jobs. Setting a pay rate for each job would be extremely complex. Therefore, many organizations group jobs into **pay grades**—sets of jobs having similar worth or content, grouped together to establish rates of pay. For example, the organization could establish five pay grades, with the same pay available to employees holding any job within the same grade.

A drawback of pay grades is that grouping jobs will result in rates of pay for individual jobs that do not precisely match the levels specified by the market and the organization's job structure. Suppose, for example, that the organization groups together its senior accountants (with a job evaluation of 255 points) and its senior systems analysts (with a job evaluation of 270 points). Surveys might show that the market rate of pay for systems analysts is higher than that for accountants. In addition, the job evaluations give more points to systems analysts. Even so, for simplicity's sake, the organization pays the same rate for the two jobs because they are in the same pay grade.

pay policy line
A graphed line showing the mathematical relationship between job evaluation points and pay rate.

pay grades
Sets of jobs having similar worth or content, grouped together to establish rates of pay.

The organization would have to pay more than the market requires for accountants or pay less than the market rate for systems analysts (so it would probably have difficulty recruiting and retaining them).

Pay Ranges

Usually, organizations want some flexibility in setting pay for individual jobs. They want to be able to pay the most valuable employees the highest amounts and to give rewards for performance, as described in the next chapter. Flexibility also helps the organization balance conflicting information from market surveys and job evaluations. Therefore, pay structure usually includes a **pay range** for each job or pay grade. In other words, the organization establishes a minimum, maximum, and midpoint of pay for employees holding a particular job or a job within a particular pay grade. Employees holding the same job may receive somewhat different pay, depending on where their pay falls within the range.

A typical approach is to use the market rate or the pay policy line as the midpoint of a range for the job or pay grade. The minimum and maximum values for the range may also be based on market surveys of those amounts. Pay ranges are most common for white-collar jobs and for jobs that are not covered by union contracts. Figure 11.5 shows an example of pay ranges based on the pay policy line in Figure 11.4. Notice that the jobs are grouped into five pay grades, each with its own pay range. In this example, the range is widest for employees who are at higher levels in terms of their job evaluation points. That is because the performance of these higher-level employees will likely have more effect on the organization's performance, so the organization needs more latitude to reward them. For instance, as discussed earlier, the organization may want to select a higher point in the range to attract an employee who is more critical to achieving the organization's goals.

pay ranges
A set of possible pay rates defined by a minimum, maximum, and midpoint of pay for employees holding a particular job or a job within a particular pay grade.

FIGURE 11.5

Sample Pay Grade Structure

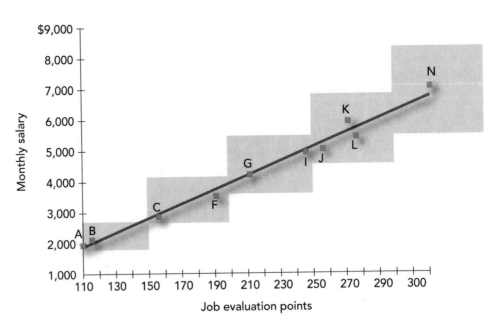

■ Current pay for job
▬ Pay policy line

Usually pay ranges overlap somewhat, so that the highest pay in one grade is somewhat higher than the lowest pay in the next grade. Overlapping ranges gives the organization more flexibility in transferring employees among jobs, because transfers need not always involve a change in pay. On the other hand, the less overlap, the more important it is to earn promotions in order to keep getting raises. Assuming the organization wants to motivate employees through promotions (and assuming enough opportunities for promotion are available), the organization will want to limit the overlap from one level to the next.

When the organization develops a pay structure, it may find that a few employees are being paid at rates that are above or below the range for their jobs. For example, an employee with exceptionally high seniority might earn above his range. Rates above the range are often called **red-circle rates.** In some cases, employees earning red-circle rates would receive no pay increases until they receive a promotion or until cost-of-living adjustments raise the pay range to include their pay rate. At the other extreme are **green-circle rates,** that is, rates below the pay range for a job. These employees usually would receive raises when the pay structure is put into practice; otherwise, their current pay rate signals that they are being paid less than their worth to the organization.

red-circle rate
Pay at a rate that falls above the pay range for the job.

green-circle rate
Pay at a rate that falls below the pay range for the job.

Pay Differentials

In some situations organizations adjust pay to reflect differences in working conditions or labor markets. For example, an organization may pay extra to employees who work the night shift, because night hours are less desirable for most workers. Similarly, organizations may pay extra to employees in locations where living expenses are higher. These adjustments are called **pay differentials.**

A survey of businesses in the United States found that over half have a formal or informal policy of providing pay differentials based on geographic location.[20] These differentials are intended as a way to treat employees fairly, without regard to where they work. The most common approach is to move an employee higher in the pay structure to compensate for higher living costs. For instance, the American Chamber of Commerce Research Association estimates that the cost of living in New York City is more than twice that of the average metropolitan area. An organization with employees in New York City and in an average U.S. city might pay its New York office manager substantially more than its office manager in the average city. This pay policy can become expensive for organizations that must operate in high-cost locations. Also, organizations need to handle the delicate issue of how to pay employees transferred to lower-cost areas.

pay differential
Adjustment to a pay rate to reflect differences in working conditions or labor markets.

Night hours are less desirable for most workers. Therefore, some companies pay a differential for night work to compensate them.

LO6

Alternatives to Job-Based Pay

The traditional and most widely used approach to developing a pay structure focuses on setting pay for jobs or groups of jobs.[21] This emphasis on jobs has some limitations. The precise definition of a job's responsibilities can contribute to an attitude that some activities "are not in my job description," at the expense of flexibility, innovation, quality, and customer service. Also, the job structure's focus on higher pay for higher status can work against an effort at empowerment. Organizations may avoid change because it requires repeating the time-consuming process of creating job descriptions and related paperwork. Another change-related problem is that when the organization needs a new set of knowledge, skills, and abilities, the existing pay structure may be rewarding the wrong behaviors. Finally, a pay structure that rewards employees for winning promotions may discourage them from gaining valuable experience through lateral career moves.

delayering
Reducing the number of levels in the organization's job structure.

Organizations have responded to these problems with a number of alternatives to job-based pay structures. Some organizations have found greater flexibility through **delayering,** or reducing the number of levels in the organization's job structure. By combining more assignments into a single layer, organizations give managers more flexibility in making assignments and awarding pay increases. These broader groupings often are called *broad bands*. IBM recently changed from a pay structure with 5,000 job titles and 24 salary grades to one with 1,200 jobs and 10 bands. When IBM began using broad bands, it replaced its point-factor job evaluation system with an approach based on matching jobs to descriptions. Figure 11.6 provides an example of how this works. Broad bands reduce the opportunities for promoting employees, so organizations that eliminate layers in their job descriptions must find other ways to reward employees.

skill-based pay systems
Pay structures that set pay according to the employees' levels of skill or knowledge and what they are capable of doing.

Another way organizations have responded to the limitations of job-based pay has been to move away from the link to jobs and toward pay structures that reward employees based on their knowledge and skills.[22] **Skill-based pay systems** are pay structures that set pay according to the employees' level of skill or knowledge and what they are capable of doing. Paying for skills makes sense at organizations where changing technology requires employees to continually widen and deepen their knowledge. For example, modern machinery often requires that operators know how to program and monitor computers to perform a variety of tasks. Skill-based pay also supports efforts to empower employees and enrich jobs because it encourages employees to add to their knowledge so they can make decisions in many areas. In this way, skill-based pay helps organizations become more flexible and innovative. More generally, skill-based pay can encourage a climate of learning and adaptability and give employees a broader view of how the organization functions. These changes should help employees use their knowledge and ideas more productively. A field study of a manufacturing plant found that changing to a skill-based pay structure led to better quality and lower labor costs.[23]

Of course, skill-based pay has its own disadvantages.[24] It rewards employees for acquiring skills but does not provide a way to ensure that employees can use their new skills. The result may be that the organization is paying employees more for learning skills that the employer is not benefiting from. The challenge for HRM is to design work so that the work design and pay structure support one another. Also, if employees learn skills very quickly, they may reach the maximum pay level so quickly that it will become difficult to reward them appropriately. Skill-based pay does not necessarily provide an alternative to the bureaucracy and paperwork of traditional pay structures, because it requires records related to skills, training, and knowledge acquired.

FIGURE 11.6

IBM's New Job Evaluation Approach

Below is an abbreviated schematic illustration of the new—and simple—IBM job evaluation approach:

POSITION REFERENCE GUIDE

Band	Skills required	Leadership/Contribution	Scope/Impact
1			
2			
3			
4			
5			
6			
7			
8			
9			
10			

Factors: Leadership/Contribution

Band 06: Understand the mission of the professional group and vision in own area of competence.

Band 07: Understand the departmental mission and vision.

Band 08: Understand departmental/functional mission and vision.

Band 09: Has vision of functional or unit mission.

Band 10: Has vision of overall strategies.

Both the bands and the approach are global. In the U.S., bands 1–5 are nonexempt; bands 6–10 are exempt. Each cell in the table contains descriptive language about key job characteristics. Position descriptions are compared to the chart and assigned to bands on a "best fit" basis. There are no points or scoring mechanisms. Managers assign employees to bands by selecting a position description that most closely resembles the work being done by an employee using an online position description library.

That's it!

SOURCE: A. S. Richter, "Paying the People in Black at Big Blue," *Compensation and Benefits Review*, May–June 1998, pp. 51–59. Reprinted with permission of Sage Publications, Inc.

Finally, gathering market data about skill-based pay is difficult, because most wage and salary surveys are job-based.

Pay Structure and Actual Pay

LO7

Usually, the human resource department is responsible for establishing the organization's pay structure. But building a structure is not the end of the organization's decisions about pay structure. The structure represents the organization's policy, but what the organization actually does may be different. As part of its management responsibility, the HR department therefore should compare actual pay to the pay structure, making sure that policies and practices match.

A common way to do this is to measure a *compa-ratio*, the ratio of average pay to the midpoint of the pay range. Figure 11.7 shows an example. Assuming the organization has pay grades, the organization would find a compa-ratio for each pay grade:

FIGURE 11.7

Finding a Compa-Ratio

Pay Grade: 1
Midpoint of Range: $2,175 per month

Salaries of Employees in Pay Grade

Employee 1	$2,306
Employee 2	$2,066
Employee 3	$2,523
Employee 4	$2,414

Average Salary of Employees
$2,306 + $2,066 + $2,523 + $2,414 = $9,309
$9,309 ÷ 4 = $2,327.25

Compa-Ratio

$$\frac{\text{Average}}{\text{Midpoint}} = \frac{\$2,327.25}{\$2,175.00} = 1.07$$

the average paid to all employees in the pay grade divided by the midpoint for the pay grade. If the average equals the midpoint, the compa-ratio is 1. More often, the compa-ratio is somewhat above 1 (meaning the average pay is above the midpoint for the pay grade) or below 1 (meaning the average pay is below the midpoint).

Assuming that the pay structure is well planned to support the organization's goals, the compa-ratios should be close to 1. A compa-ratio greater than 1 suggests that the organization is paying more than planned for human resources and may have difficulty keeping costs under control. A compa-ratio less than 1 suggests that the organization is underpaying for human resources relative to its target and may have difficulty attracting and keeping qualified employees. When compa-ratios are more or less than 1, the numbers signal a need for the HR department to work with managers to identify whether to adjust the pay structure or the organization's pay practices. The compa-ratios may indicate that the pay structure no longer reflects market rates of pay. Or maybe performance appraisals need to be more accurate, as discussed in Chapter 8.

LO8

Current Issues Involving Pay Structure

An organization's policies regarding pay structure greatly influence employees' and even the general public's opinions about the organization. Issues affecting pay structure therefore can hurt or help the organization's reputation and ability to recruit, mo-

Walt Disney Company offers to make up the difference between employees' military pay and Disney's pay for up to six months while employees perform their military service. Some companies offer this for up to five years. What advantages and disadvantages do you see for companies who offer this?

tivate, and keep employees. Recent issues related to pay structure include decisions about paying employees on active military duty and decisions about how much to pay the organization's top executives.

Pay during Military Duty

As we noted in Chapter 3, the Uniformed Services Employment and Reemployment Rights Act (USERRA) requires employers to make jobs available to their workers when they return after fulfilling military duties for up to five years. During the time these employees are performing their military service, the employer faces decisions related to paying these people. The armed services pay service members during their time of duty, but military pay often falls short of what they would earn in their civilian jobs. Some employers have chosen to support their employees by paying the difference between their military and civilian earnings for extended periods.[25] Walt Disney Company recently broadened this policy from 30 days of service to 180 days. Northrop Grumman will make up the difference in pay for one year. A notable holdout is the federal government, which also employs more National Guard members and reservists than any company.[26] The government has maintained its policy of paying a reservist's salary for only 22 days.

Policies to make up the difference between military and civilian pay are costly. The employer is paying employees while they are not working for the organization. United Parcel Service, for example, pays reservists on active duty the difference in their salary plus their health benefits for up to a year. Between October 2001 and April 2002, 650 UPS employees were called up, at a cost to UPS of $800,000 per month in salary and benefits for those absent employees.[27] In addition, the organization must pay people to fill in while the service members are on active duty for periods that can last as long as four years. This challenge has posed a significant hardship on some employers since the fall of 2001, when the U.S. government's actions against terrorism included the call-up of thousands of reservists and National Guard members. Even so, as the nation copes with this challenge, hundreds of employers have decided that maintaining positive relations with employees—and the goodwill of the American public—makes the expense worthwhile.

Pay for Executives

The media have drawn public attention to the issue of executive pay. The issue attracts notice because of the very high pay that the top executives of major U.S. companies have received in recent years. A significant form of executive compensation comes in the form of company stock (a type of compensation discussed in the next chapter). Because the stock market soared during the 1990s, so did executive pay. Figure 11.8 shows the salary, bonus, and total compensation paid to CEOs of large U.S. companies between 1996 and 2000. Notice that the majority of the growth in total compensation came from compensation other than salary and bonus—primarily from increases in the value of the company's stock given to the CEO. Also keep in mind that the numbers do not represent many managers; *BusinessWeek* surveyed "365 of the country's largest companies" to arrive at the data in Figure 11.9. A more representative 2000 survey found that at companies with at least $500 million in sales, total CEO pay averaged $1.4 million.[28]

Although these high amounts apply to only a small proportion of the total workforce, the issue of executive pay is relevant to pay structure in terms of equity theory.

FIGURE 11.8

CEO Compensation at 365 of the Largest U.S. Companies

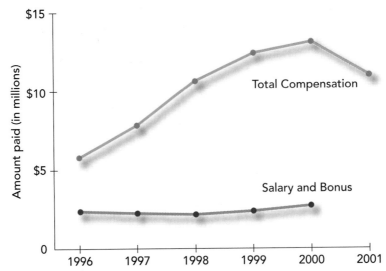

SOURCE: "Executive Pay," *BusinessWeek,* April 21, 1997; April 20, 1998; April 19, 1999; April 17, 2000; April 16, 2001; April 5, 2002).

As we discussed earlier in the chapter, employees draw conclusions about the fairness of pay by making comparisons among employees' inputs and outcomes. By many comparisons, U.S. CEOs' pay is high. Figure 11.9 compares CEO pay in several industrialized countries: the United States, France, Germany, and Japan. Measured in U.S. dollars, the pay of a CEO in the United States is much higher. According to equity theory, employees would see this as fair if the U.S. CEOs also do more for their organizations than CEOs in other countries do. The situation becomes more complex

FIGURE 11.9

Pay for Chief Executive Officers in Four Industrialized Countries

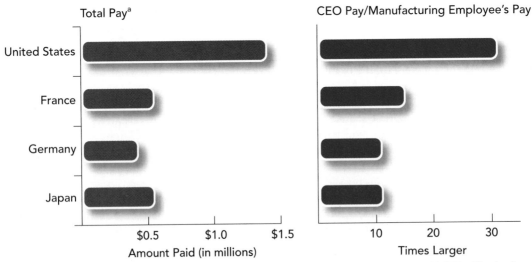

[a]Includes salary, bonus, company contributions, perquisites, and long-term incentives. Data based on a company with $500 million in sales.

SOURCE: Towers Perrin, "2000 Worldwide Total Remuneration," New York: Towers Perrin, 2000.

Chapter 12

Recognizing Employee Contributions with Pay

What Do I Need to Know? After reading this chapter, you should be able to:

1. Discuss the connection between incentive pay and employee performance.

2. Describe how organizations recognize individual performance.

3. Identify ways to recognize group performance.

4. Explain how organizations link pay to their overall performance.

5. Describe how organizations combine incentive plans in a "balanced scorecard."

6. Summarize processes that can contribute to the success of incentive programs.

7. Discuss issues related to performance-based pay for executives.

Introduction

In 2001 Baxter International's chief executive officer, Harry M. Jansen Kraemer Jr., decided he deserved a pay cut. The company had met its financial objectives, so Kraemer was eligible for a bonus of up to one and a half times his base pay. But not everything had gone well for the maker of drugs and medical equipment. Dozens of kidney dialysis patients had died because of defects in a blood filter sold by Baxter. Closing two factories and settling with the families cost $156 million. Kraemer believed it simply would be wrong for the company to reward him for the year's performance. Following Kraemer's request, Baxter's board of directors cut his bonus to 60 percent of base pay and cut the bonuses of the other company executives to 80 percent.

Accountability is far from a new idea for Kraemer. He links employees' rewards to company performance by granting stock options (the right to buy stock in the company) to all Baxter's employees. Regarding executive pay, Kraemer had these remarks for a *BusinessWeek* reporter:[1]

> I'm in favor of a very, very significant portion of pay being based on the stock price. My view of compensation would be to pay [the executive] a reasonable salary. I don't know precisely what it is, but it certainly wouldn't be more than $1 million under any scenario. The fact that people can make millions and millions of dollars and the shareholder not get anything—I'm sort of amazed that shareholders let people get away with that. It strikes me as beyond absurd.

The preceding chapter discussed setting pay for jobs. In this chapter we focus on using pay to recognize and reward employees' contributions to the organization's success. Employees' pay does not depend solely on the jobs they hold. Instead, organizations vary the amount paid according to differences in performance of the individual, group, or whole organization, as well as differences in employee qualities such as seniority and skills.[2]

incentive pay
Forms of pay linked to an employee's performance as an individual, group member, or organization member.

In contrast to decisions about pay structure, organizations have wide discretion in setting performance-related pay, called **incentive pay.** Organizations can tie incentive pay to individual performance, profits, or many other measures of success. They select incentives based on their costs, expected influence on performance, and fit with the organization's broader HR and company policies and goals. These decisions are significant. A study of 150 organizations found that the way organizations paid employees was strongly associated with their level of profitability.[3]

This chapter explores the choices available to organizations with regard to incentive pay. First, the chapter describes the link between pay and employee performance. Next, we discuss ways organizations provide a variety of pay incentives to individuals. The following two sections describe pay related to group and organizational performance. We then explore the organization's processes that can support the use of incentive pay. Finally, we discuss incentive pay for the organization's executives.

LO1

Incentive Pay

Along with wages and salaries, many organizations offer *incentive pay*—that is, pay specifically designed to energize, direct, or control employees' behavior. Incentive pay is influential because the amount paid is linked to certain predefined behaviors or outcomes. For example, as we will see in this chapter, an organization can pay a salesperson a *commission* for closing a sale, or the members of a production department can earn a *bonus* for meeting a monthly production goal. Usually, these payments are in addition to wages and salaries. Knowing they can earn extra money for closing sales or meeting departmental goals, the employees often try harder or get more creative than they might without the incentive pay. In addition, the policy of offering higher pay for higher performance may make an organization attractive to high performers when it is trying to recruit and retain these valuable employees.[4]

For incentive pay to motivate employees to contribute to the organization's success, the pay plans must be well designed. In designing incentive pay plans, organizations should consider whether the pay encourages the kinds of behavior that are most needed, whether employees believe they have the ability and resources to meet the performance standards, and whether they value the rewards and think the pay plan is fair. These principles are summarized in Figure 12.1.

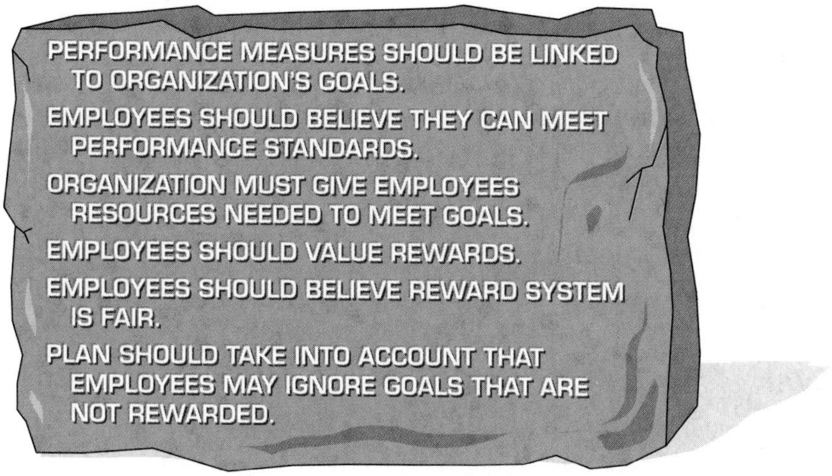

FIGURE 12.1

Principles of Effective
Incentive Pay Plans

PERFORMANCE MEASURES SHOULD BE LINKED
TO ORGANIZATION'S GOALS.

EMPLOYEES SHOULD BELIEVE THEY CAN MEET
PERFORMANCE STANDARDS.

ORGANIZATION MUST GIVE EMPLOYEES
RESOURCES NEEDED TO MEET GOALS.

EMPLOYEES SHOULD VALUE REWARDS.

EMPLOYEES SHOULD BELIEVE REWARD SYSTEM
IS FAIR.

PLAN SHOULD TAKE INTO ACCOUNT THAT
EMPLOYEES MAY IGNORE GOALS THAT ARE
NOT REWARDED.

Since incentive pay is linked to particular outcomes or behaviors, the organization is encouraging them to demonstrate those chosen outcomes and behaviors. As obvious as that may sound, the implications are more complicated. If incentive pay is extremely rewarding, employees may focus on only the performance measures rewarded under the plan and ignore measures that are not rewarded. Suppose an organization pays managers a bonus when employees are satisfied; this policy may interfere with other management goals. A manager who doesn't quite know how to inspire employees to do their best might be tempted to fall back on overly positive performance appraisals, letting work slide in order to keep everyone happy. Similarly, many call centers pay employees based on how many calls they handle, as an incentive to work quickly and efficiently. However, speedy call handling does not necessarily foster good customer relationships. Gallup Organization depends on good relationships to keep the people in its research samples from hanging up on its telephone pollsters, so its incentive pay is based on customer evaluations, rather than number of calls.[5] As we will see in this chapter, organizations may combine a number of incentives so employees do not focus on one measure to the exclusion of others.

Employees must also believe they have the ability and resources to meet the performance standards. For rewards to be motivating, employees have to believe they can earn them. As we will discuss in the section on rewards for organizational performance, this is a challenge in the case of incentives based on an organization's profits or stock price. Employees at lower levels of the organization may doubt that they have much influence over these performance measures. Therefore, these incentives likely will not have much effect on these employees' behavior, at least in large companies. For the same reason, if organizations want to reward employees for meeting goals, they must give the employees access to the resources needed for meeting those goals. If rewards are tied to customer satisfaction, for example, employees must be empowered to satisfy customers.

Other attitudes that influence the success of incentive pay include whether employees value the rewards and think the pay plan is fair. Most, if not all, employees value pay, but it is important to remember that earning money is not the only reason people try to do a good job. As we have discussed in other chapters (see Chapters 4, 8, and 13), people also want interesting work, appreciation for their efforts, flexibility, and a sense of belonging to the work group—not to mention the inner satisfaction of work well done. Therefore, a complete plan for motivating and compensating employees has many components, from pay to work design to developing managers so they can exercise positive leadership.

With regard to the fairness of incentive pay, the preceding chapter described equity theory, which explains how employees form judgments about the fairness of a pay structure. The same process applies to judgments about incentive pay. In general, employees compare their efforts and rewards with other employees', considering a plan to be fair when the rewards are distributed according to what the employees contribute.

The remainder of this chapter identifies elements of incentive pay systems. We consider each option's strengths and limitations with regard to these principles. The many kinds of incentive pay fall into three broad categories: incentives linked to individual, group, or organizational performance. Choices from these categories should consider not only their strengths and weaknesses, but also their fit with the organization's goals. The choice of incentive pay may affect not only the level of motivation, but also the kinds of employees who are attracted to and stay with the organization. For example, there is some evidence that organizations with team-based rewards will tend to attract employees who are more team-oriented, while rewards tied to individual performance make an organization more attractive to those who think and act independently, as individuals.[6]

LO2

Pay for Individual Performance

Organizations may reward individual performance with incentives such as piecework rates, standard hour plans, merit pay, individual bonuses, and sales commissions. These alternatives are summarized in Figure 12.2.

Piecework Rates

piecework rate
A wage based on the amount workers produce.

As an incentive to work efficiently, some organizations pay production workers a **piecework rate,** a wage based on the amount they produce. This rate is often paid in addition to employees' base pay. The amount paid per unit is set at a level that rewards employees for above-average production volume. For example, suppose that on

FIGURE 12.2

Types of Pay for Individual Performance

| Piecework Rates (Straight or Differential) | Standard Hours Plan | Merit Pay | Performance Bonus | Sales Commissions |

FIGURE 12.3

How Incentives Sometimes "Work"

SOURCE: DILBERT reprinted by permission of United Features Syndicate, Inc.

average, assemblers can finish 10 components in an hour. If the organization wants to pay its average assemblers $8 per hour, it can pay a piecework rate of $8/hour divided by 10 components/hour, or $.80 per component. An assembler who produces the average of 10 components per hour earns an amount equal to $8 per hour. An assembler who produces 12 components in an hour would earn $.80 × 12, or $9.60 each hour. This is an example of a **straight piecework plan,** because the employer pays the same rate per piece, no matter how much the worker produces.

A variation on straight piecework is **differential piece rates** (also called *rising* and *falling differentials*), in which the piece rate depends on the amount produced. If the worker produces more than the standard output, the piece rate is higher. If the worker produces at or below the standard, the amount paid per piece is lower. In the preceding example, the differential piece rate could be $1 per component for components exceeding 12 per hour and $.80 per component for up to 12 components per hour.

In one study, the use of piece rates increased production output by 30 percent—more than any other motivational device evaluated.[7] An obvious advantage of piece rates is the direct link between how much work the employee does and the amount the employee earns. This type of pay is easy to understand and seems fair to many people, if they think the production standard is reasonable. In spite of their advantages, piece rates are relatively rare for several reasons.[8] Most jobs, including those of managers, have no physical output, so it is hard to develop an appropriate performance measure. This type of incentive is most suited for very routine, standardized jobs with output that is easy to measure. For complex jobs or jobs with hard-to-measure outputs, piecework plans do not apply very well. Also, unless a plan is well designed to include performance standards, it may not reward employees for focusing on quality or customer satisfaction if it interferes with the day's output. In Figure 12.3, the employees quickly realize they can earn huge bonuses by writing software "bugs" and then fixing them, while writing bug-free software affords no chance to earn bonuses. More seriously, a bonus based on number of faucets produced gives production workers no incentive to stop a manufacturing line to correct a quality-control problem. Production-oriented goals may do nothing to encourage employees to learn new skills or cooperate with others. Therefore, individual incentives such as these may be a poor incentive in an organization that wants to encourage teamwork. They may not be helpful in an organization with complex jobs, employee empowerment, and team-based problem solving.

straight piecework plan
Incentive pay in which the employer pays the same rate per piece, no matter how much the worker produces.

differential piece rates
Incentive pay in which the piece rate is higher when a greater amount is produced.

Standard Hour Plans

standard hour plan
An incentive plan that pays workers extra for work done in less than a preset "standard time."

Another quantity-oriented incentive for production workers is the **standard hour plan,** an incentive plan that pays workers extra for work done in less than a preset "standard time." The organization determines a standard time to complete a task, such as tuning up a car engine. If the mechanic completes the work in less than the standard time, the mechanic receives an amount of pay equal to the wage for the full standard time. Suppose the standard time for tuning up an engine is 2 hours. If the mechanic finishes a tune-up in 1½ hours, the mechanic earns 2 hours' worth of pay in 1½ hours. Working that fast over the course of a week could add significantly to the mechanic's pay.

In terms of their pros and cons, standard hour plans are much like piecework plans. They encourage employees to work as fast as they can, but not necessarily to care about quality or customer service. Also, they only succeed if employees want the extra money more than they want to work at a pace that feels comfortable.

Merit Pay

merit pay
A system of linking pay increases to ratings on performance appraisals.

Almost all organizations have established some program of **merit pay**—a system of linking pay increases to ratings on performance appraisals. (Chapter 8 described the content and use of performance appraisals.) Merit pay is most common for white-collar employees. To make the merit increases consistent, so they will be seen as fair, many merit pay programs use a *merit increase grid,* such as the sample for Merck, the giant drug company, in Table 12.1. As the table shows, the decisions about merit pay are based on two factors: the individual's performance rating and the individual's compa-ratio (pay relative to average pay, as defined in Chapter 11). This system gives the biggest pay increases to the best performers and to those whose pay is relatively low for their job. At the highest extreme, an exceptional employee earning 80 percent of the average pay for his job could receive a 15 percent merit raise. An employee rated as having "room for improvement" would receive a raise only if that employee was earning relatively low pay for the job (compa-ratio of .95 or less).

TABLE 12.1

Sample Merit Increase Grid

	SUGGESTED MERIT INCREASE PERCENTAGE			
PERFORMANCE RATING	COMPA-RATIO 80.00–95.00	COMPA-RATIO 95.01–110.00	COMPA-RATIO 110.01–120.00	COMPA-RATIO 120.01–125.00
EX (Exceptional within Merck)	13–15%	12–14%	9–11%	To maximum of range
WD (Merck Standard with Distinction)	9–11	8–10	7–9	—
HS (High Merck Standard)	7–9	6–8	—	—
RI (Merck Standard Room for Improvement)	5–7	—	—	—
NA (Not Adequate for Merck)	—	—	—	—

SOURCE: K. J. Murphy, "Merck & Co., Inc. (B)," Boston: Harvard Business School, Case 491-006. Copyright © 1990 by the President & Fellows of Harvard College. Reprinted with permission.

By today's standards, all of these raises are large, because they were created at a time when inflation was strong and economic forces demanded big pay increases to keep up with the cost of living. The range of percentages for a policy used today would be lower. Organizations establish and revise merit increase grids in light of changing economic conditions. When organizations revise pay ranges, employees have new compa-ratios. A higher pay range would result in lower compa-ratios, causing employees to become eligible for bigger merit increases. An advantage of merit pay is therefore that it makes the reward more valuable by relating it to economic conditions. A drawback is that conditions can shrink the available range of increases. During recent years, budgets for merit pay increases were about 3 to 5 percent of pay, so average performers could receive a 4 percent raise, and top performers perhaps as much as 6 percent. The 2-percentage-point difference, after taxes and other deductions, would amount to only a few dollars a week on a salary of $40,000 per year. Over an entire career, the bigger increases for top performers can grow into a major change, but viewed on a year-by-year basis, they are not much of an incentive to excel.[9]

Another advantage of merit pay is that it provides a method for rewarding performance in all of the dimensions measured in the organization's performance management system. If that system is appropriately designed to measure all the important job behaviors, then the merit pay is linked to the behaviors the organization desires. This link seems logical, although so far there is little research showing the effectiveness of merit pay.[10]

A drawback of merit pay, from the employer's standpoint, is that it can quickly become expensive. Managers at a majority of organizations rate most employees' performance in the top two categories (out of four or five).[11] Therefore, the majority of employees are eligible for the biggest merit increases, and their pay rises rapidly. This cost is one reason that some organizations have established guidelines about the percentage of employees that may receive the top rating, as discussed in Chapter 8.

Another drawback of merit pay is that it makes assumptions that may be misleading. Rewarding employees for superior performance ratings assumes that those ratings depend on employees' ability and motivation. But performance may actually depend on forces outside the employee's control, such as managers' rating biases, the level of cooperation from coworkers, or the degree to which the organization gives employees the authority, training, and resources they need. Under these conditions, employees will likely conclude that the merit pay system is unfair.

Quality guru W. Edwards Deming also criticizes merit pay for discouraging teamwork. In Deming's words, "Everyone propels himself forward, or tries to, for his own good, on his own life preserver. The organization is the loser."[12] For example, if employees in the purchasing department are evaluated based on the number or cost of contracts they negotiate, they may have little interest in the quality of the materials they buy, even when the manufacturing department is having quality problems. In reaction to such problems, Deming advocated the use of group incentives. Another alternative is for merit pay to include ratings of teamwork and cooperation. Some employers ask coworkers to provide such ratings.

Performance Bonuses

Like merit pay, performance bonuses reward individual performance, but bonuses are not rolled into base pay. The employee must re-earn them during each performance period. In some cases, the bonus is a one-time reward. Bonuses may also be linked to objective performance measures, rather than subjective ratings.

Bonuses for individual performance can be extremely effective and give the organization great flexibility in deciding what kinds of behavior to reward. For example, as we saw in Chapter 2, Continental Airlines pays employees a quarterly bonus for ranking in the top three airlines for on-time arrivals, a measure of service quality. In many cases, employees receive bonuses for meeting such routine targets as sales or production numbers. Such bonuses encourage hard work. But an organization that focuses on growth and innovation may get better results from rewarding employees for learning new skills than from linking bonuses to mastery of existing jobs.

Adding to this flexibility, organizations also may motivate employees with one-time bonuses. For example, when one organization acquires another, it usually wants to retain certain valuable employees in the organization it is buying. Therefore, it is common for organizations involved in an acquisition to pay *retention bonuses*—one-time incentives paid in exchange for remaining with the company—to top managers, engineers, top-performing salespeople, and information technology specialists. When AMR Corporation, the parent company of American Airlines, acquired Trans World Airlines, it paid key TWA managers bonuses if they stayed on after the acquisition.[13] Each manager who stayed received a bonus equaling 15 to 30 percent of his or her salary.

Many car salespeople earn a straight commission, meaning that 100% of their pay comes from commission instead of a salary. What type of individual might enjoy a job like this?

HR
HOW TO

Using Incentives to Motivate Salespeople

During the recent economic boom, employers scrambled to keep good salespeople by putting together the most generous package of pay and benefits. A thornier problem is how to keep the sales reps motivated when demand slows down and profits tumble. Here are some ideas from several companies.

Set performance goals that are clear and achievable. If salespeople have to fill a quota before they earn a commission or bonus, make sure the quota is realistic for the current economic climate. Or pay an incentive for meeting a fraction of the goal. Provide training to help salespeople meet their quotas.

Establish adjustable goals related to market conditions. *The New York Times* has a "push goal" for its advertising sales force. Teams that meet the goal earn a preset bonus. The size of the goal depends on business conditions. At times, business has been so good that teams have met the push goal before year-end. When that happens, the *Times* creates additional push goals, so there is an incentive to keep selling.

Along with commissions, offer daily and weekly rewards tied to activities. Typical examples are number of customers visited and prospects phoned. These incentives, known as *activity-based pay*, can encourage salespeople to build customer relationships, preparing for a time when they are ready to start spending again. Rewards can be as inexpensive as $20 or lunch at a local restaurant.

Supplement pay incentives with nonpay motivation. Tom Salonek, founder of an e-commerce consulting firm called Go-e-biz.com, uses a personal touch. He revived an earlier practice of visiting key customers along with his sales reps, and he starts each day with what he calls a "15-minute huddle." Every morning at 7:25, Salonek and the salespeople dial the company's conference call center and share their experiences of the day before, and Salonek uses the time for a pep talk.

Offer a choice. Business consulting firm Artis & Associates offers bigger potential rewards to salespeople willing to shoulder more of the risk. Salespeople have two alternatives. They can accept a straight commission at a higher rate or a small salary plus commission at a lower rate. The rates are set so that the salespeople on straight commission have the potential to earn more than their colleagues earning a salary.

SOURCE: S. Greco, "Sales: What Works Now," *Inc.*, February 2002, pp. 52–59.

Sales Commissions

A variation on piece rates and bonuses is the payment of **commissions,** or pay calculated as a percentage of sales. For instance, a furniture salesperson might earn commissions equaling 6 percent times the price of the furniture the person sells during the period. Selling a $2,000 couch would add $120 to the salesperson's commissions for the period. At most organizations today, commissions range from 5 percent to 20 percent of sales.[14] In a growth-oriented organization, sales commissions need not be limited to salespeople. Many of the technical experts at Scientific & Engineering Solutions are eligible for commissions and bonuses tied to the profitability of the sales they help to close. One member of the Maryland company's technical staff, Steve Newcomb, helped to develop a small contract into a $700,000 sale. He earned the commission on the sale, along with an additional prize—tickets to the Super Bowl.[15]

commissions
Incentive pay calculated as a percentage of sales.

Some salespeople earn a commission in addition to a base salary; others earn only commissions—a pay arrangement called a *straight commission plan*. Straight commissions are common among insurance and real estate agents and car salespeople. Other salespeople earn no commissions at all, but a straight salary. Paying most or all of a salesperson's compensation in the form of salary frees the salesperson to focus on developing customer goodwill. Paying most or all of a salesperson's compensation in the form of commissions encourages the salesperson to focus on closing sales. In this way, differences in salespeople's compensation directly influence how they spend their time, how they treat customers, and how much the organization sells.

The nature of salespeople's compensation also affects the kinds of people who will want to take and keep sales jobs with the organization. Hard-driving, ambitious, risk-taking salespeople might enjoy the potential rewards of a straight commission plan. An organization that wants salespeople to concentrate on listening to customers and building relationships might want to attract a different kind of salesperson by offering more of the pay in the form of a salary. Basing part or all of a salesperson's pay on commissions assumes that the organization wants to attract people with some willingness to take risks—probably a reasonable assumption about people whose job includes talking to strangers and encouraging them to spend money. An example of such a person is Beth Bruck, who sells legal publications for CCH, earning $70,000 to $110,000 each year, with more than half coming from commissions. Bruck says new CCH sales reps have to work as long as a year before they begin to earn "decent commissions."[16]

The "HR How To" box on page 381 provides additional suggestions for incentive pay to motivate salespeople.

LO3

Pay for Group Performance

Employers may address the drawbacks of individual incentives by including group incentives in the organization's compensation plan. To win group incentives, employees must cooperate and share knowledge so that the entire group can meet its performance targets. As shown in Figure 12.4, common group incentives include gainsharing, bonuses, and team awards.

Gainsharing

gainsharing
Group incentive program that measures improvements in productivity and effectiveness and distributes a portion of each gain to employees.

Organizations that want employees to focus on efficiency may adopt a **gainsharing** program, which measures increases in productivity and effectiveness and distributes a portion of each gain to employees. For example, if a factory enjoys a productivity gain worth $30,000, half the gain might be the company's share. The other $15,000 would be distributed among the employees in the factory. Knowing that they can enjoy a financial benefit from helping the company be more productive, employees supposedly will look for ways to work more efficiently and improve the way the factory operates.

Gainsharing addresses the challenge of identifying appropriate performance measures for complex jobs. For example, how would a hospital measure the production of its nurses—in terms of satisfying patients, keeping costs down, or completing a number of tasks? Each of these measures oversimplifies the complex responsibilities involved in nursing care. Even for simpler jobs, setting acceptable standards and measuring performance can be complicated. Gainsharing frees employees to determine how to improve their own and their group's performance. It also broadens employees' focus beyond their individual interests. But in contrast to profit sharing, discussed

FIGURE 12.4

Types of Pay for Group Performance

Gainsharing
• Scanlon plans
• Rucker plans
• Improshare programs

Bonuses

Team Awards

later, it keeps the performance measures within a range of activity that most employees believe they can influence. Organizations can enhance the likelihood of a gain by providing a means for employees to share knowledge and make suggestions, as we will discuss in the last section of this chapter.

Gainsharing is most likely to succeed when organizations provide the right conditions. Among the conditions identified, the following are among the most common:[17]

• Management commitment.
• Need for change or strong commitment to continuous improvement.
• Management acceptance and encouragement of employee input.
• High levels of cooperation and interaction.
• Employment security.
• Information sharing on productivity and costs.
• Goal setting.
• Commitment of all involved parties to the process of change and improvement.
• Performance standard and calculation that employees understand and consider fair and that is closely related to managerial objectives.
• Employees who value working in groups.

Gainsharing plans have many variations. Among the most widely used gainsharing plans are Scanlon plans, Rucker plans, and Improshare programs.

Scanlon Plans

A popular form of gainsharing is the **Scanlon plan,** developed in the 1930s by Joseph N. Scanlon, president of a union local at Empire Steel and Tin Plant in Mansfield, Ohio. The Scanlon plan gives employees a bonus if the ratio of labor costs to the sales value of production is below a set standard. To keep this ratio low enough to earn the

Scanlon plan
A gainsharing program in which employees receive a bonus if the ratio of labor costs to the sales value of production is below a set standard.

FIGURE 12.5

Finding the Gain in a
Scanlon Plan

Target Ratio: $\dfrac{\text{Labor Costs}}{\text{Sales Value of Production}} = \dfrac{20}{100}$

Sales Value of Production: $1,200,000

Goal: $\dfrac{20}{100} \times \$1,200,000 = \$240,000$

Actual: $210,000

Gain: $240,000 − $210,000 = $30,000

SOURCE: Example adapted from B. Graham-Moore and
Timothy L. Ross, *Gainsharing: Plans for Improving
Performance* (Washington, DC: Bureau of National Affairs,
1990), p. 57.

bonus, workers have to keep labor costs to a minimum and produce as much as possible with that amount of labor. Figure 12.5 provides an example. In this example, the standard is a ratio of 20/100, or 20 percent, and the workers produced parts worth $1.2 million. To meet the standard, the labor costs should be less than 20 percent of $1.2 million, or $240,000. Since the actual labor costs were $210,000, the workers will get a gainsharing bonus based on the $30,000 difference between the $240,000 target and the actual cost.

Typically, an organization does not pay workers all of the gain immediately. First, the organization keeps a share of the gain to improve its own bottom line. A portion of the remainder goes into a reserve account. This account offsets losses in any months when the gain is negative (that is, when costs rise or production falls). At the end of the year, the organization closes out the account and distributes any remaining surplus. If there were a loss at the end of the year, the organization would absorb it.

Rucker plan
A gainsharing program in which the ratio measuring the gain compares labor costs to the value added in production (output minus the cost of materials, supplies, and services).

Rucker Plans
A **Rucker plan** is similar to a Scanlon plan but takes a broader view of production expenses. The ratio used as a basis for measuring the gain takes into account the use of materials, supplies, and services. These production costs are subtracted from production output to find the *value added* in production. The Rucker plan formula measures the ratio of labor costs to value added; the organization then shares gains in this ratio with employees. Since workers can improve the ratio by reducing any production costs (not just the cost of labor), as well as by increasing output, this plan offers an incentive to reduce production-related costs such as wasteful use of supplies. As with the Scanlon plan, the organization keeps a share of the gain, places a portion in a reserve account, and distributes the rest to the employees in the group.

Improshare
A gainsharing program in which the gain is the decrease in the labor hours needed to produce one unit of product, with the gains split equally between the organization and its employees.

Improshare
Industrial engineer Mitchell Fein devised a form of gainsharing he called **Improshare,** a shortened form of "improved productivity through sharing." An Improshare program is similar to a standard hour plan. The organization measures the labor hours needed to produce one unit of product. Gains in this measure—that is, the hours saved in production—are the basis for computing a bonus to be split equally between the organization and its employees.

Group members that meet a sales goal or a product development team that meets a deadline or successfully launches a product may be rewarded with a bonus for group performance. What are some advantages and disadvantages of group bonuses?

To implement an Improshare program, the organization would use engineering procedures to determine how long it takes to produce a unit of product. Applying this rate to the amount produced, the organization establishes a baseline number of hours. If the group produces more than this baseline amount, the difference is the gain to be shared between organization and employees. Like the individual incentive of a piecework rate, Improshare focuses strictly on quantity. In contrast to piecework, Improshare counts not only production workers' time, but also the indirect hours of management and support staff. This gives employees an incentive to cooperate to get the job done.

Group Bonuses and Team Awards

In contrast to gainsharing plans, which typically reward the performance of all employees at a facility, bonuses for group performance tend to be for smaller work groups.[18] These bonuses reward the members of a group for attaining a specific goal, usually measured in terms of physical output. Team awards are similar to group bonuses, but they are more likely to use a broad range of performance measures, such as cost savings, successful completion of a project, or even meeting deadlines.

Both types of incentives have the advantage that they encourage group or team members to cooperate so that they can achieve their goal. However, depending on the reward system, competition among individuals may be replaced by competition among groups. Competition may be healthy in some situations, as when groups try to outdo one another in satisfying customers. On the downside, competition may also prevent necessary cooperation among groups. To avoid this, the organization should carefully set the performance goals for these incentives so that concern for costs or sales does not obscure other objectives, such as quality, customer service, and ethical behavior.

Pay for Organizational Performance   LO4

Two important ways organizations measure their performance are in terms of their profits and their stock price. In a competitive marketplace, profits result when an organization is efficiently providing products that customers want at a price they are willing to pay. Stock is the owners' investment in a corporation; when the stock price is rising, the value of that investment is growing. Rather than trying to figure out what performance measures will motivate employees to do the things that generate high profits and a rising stock price, many organizations offer incentive pay tied to those organizational performance measures. The expectation is that employees will focus on what is best for the organization.

These organization-level incentives can motivate employees to align their activities with the organization's goals. For example, when Harry Kraemer, the CEO described at the beginning of this chapter, joined Baxter International as chief financial officer, he observed that the executives in charge of the company's divisions operated so independently that Baxter lacked focus. To align the executives' efforts, Kraemer directed the company to change its incentive pay policy. Instead of relying on bonuses linked to divisional results, Baxter encouraged managers to purchase the company's stock and later began granting stock options to all employees.[19]

Linking incentives to the organization's profits or stock price exposes to employees to a high degree of risk. Profits and stock price can soar very high very fast, but they can also fall. The result is a great deal of uncertainty about the amount of incentive pay each employee will receive in each period. Therefore, these kinds of incentive pay are likely to be most effective in organizations that emphasize growth and innovation, which tend to need employees who thrive in a risk-taking environment.[20]

Profit Sharing

profit sharing
Incentive pay in which payments are a percentage of the organization's profits and do not become part of the employees' base salary.

Under **profit sharing,** payments are a percentage of the organization's profits and do not become part of the employees' base salary. For example, General Motors provides for profit sharing in its contract with its workers' union, the United Auto Workers. Depending on how large GM's profits are in relation to its total sales for the year, at least 6 percent of the company's profits are divided among the workers according to how many hours they worked during the year.[21] The formula for computing and dividing the profit-sharing bonus is included in the union contract.

Organizations use profit sharing for a number of reasons. It may encourage employees to think more like owners, taking a broad view of what they need to do in order to make the organization more effective. They are more likely to cooperate and less likely to focus on narrow self-interests. Also, profit sharing has the practical advantage of costing less when the organization is experiencing financial difficulties. If the organization has little or no profit, this incentive pay is small or nonexistent, so employers may not need to rely as much on layoffs to reduce costs.[22]

Does profit sharing help organizations perform better? The evidence is not yet clear. Although research supports a link between profit-sharing payments and profits, researchers have questioned which of these causes the other.[23] For example, Ford, Chrysler, and GM have similar profit-sharing plans in their contracts with the United Auto Workers, but the payouts are not always similar. In one year, the average worker received $4,000 from Ford, $550 from GM, and $8,000 from Chrysler. Since the plans are similar, something other than the profit sharing must have made Ford and Chrysler more profitable than GM.

Differences in payouts, as in the preceding example, raise questions not only about the effectiveness of the plans, but about equity. Assuming workers at Ford, Chrysler, and GM have similar jobs, they would expect to receive similar profit-sharing checks. In the year of this example, GM workers might have seen their incentive pay as highly inequitable unless GM could show how Chrysler workers did more to earn their big checks. Employees also may feel that small profit-sharing checks are unfair because they have little control over profits. If profit sharing is offered to all employees but most employees think only management decisions about products, price, and marketing have much impact on profits, they will conclude that their is little con-

Incentives for Tough Times

Companies began tying more pay to stock price and profits when both were soaring, so workers were delighted to receive these incentives. More recently, stocks and profit sharing have been a lot less valuable. How to avoid punishing employees for the poor performance of the economy? Some employers have found creative solutions to this dilemma.

Some employers are considering what their workers want besides money. According to Watson Wyatt Worldwide, a benefits consulting firm, many people care about flexible schedules. Employees also want opportunities for advancement and skill development.

Consulting giant Accenture addressed its need to cut costs by appealing to the desire for flexibility. Instead of reducing salary expenses primarily through layoffs, the company established a program called FlexLeave, which offers employees 6 to 12 months of leave at 20 percent of pay and full benefits. Employees can use the leave to do anything except work for a rival firm or a client of Accenture. For example, Michael Chapman, a media and entertainment strategy consultant, left Accenture's New York office to spend six months as a producer and engineer in the recording industry. He says he thought, "How many times would you have the opportunity to do what you want to do, receive some of your pay, full benefits, and a job when you return?" Along with Chapman, more than 2,000 other Accenture employees enrolled in the program.

James O'Shaughnessy, vice president and chief intellectual-property counsel for Rockwell Automation Corporation, focuses on the engineers he has identified as being especially innovative thinkers. Besides offering raises and bonuses, O'Shaughnessy dishes out the kinds of nonpay incentives that appeal to this kind of employee: opportunities to be creative and recognition for work well done. Calling himself MOM, for "Mentor of Mavericks," O'Shaughnessy makes a point of praising these "mavericks" in management meetings. Even when staffing budgets require that these engineers handle routine work, he pulls them away about once a month to meet in groups focusing on innovative projects.

When sales are down, some companies look for incentives to bring them back up. Since commissions are supposed to be an incentive to sell, David Weekley Homes, a Houston home builder, increased commission rates when sales plunged in the fall of 2001. The move was financially possible because the company's sales consultants work on straight commission. Cyrus Varsh responded to the incentive as intended, and he produced above-average sales for the fourth quarter of 2001. Explains Varsh, "I worked hard, obviously. But there is a lot of emotion involved in a home purchase—my emotion, too. And when I have confidence in my situation, that translates to the home buyer, too."

SOURCE: S. Jones, "When the Perks Fade," *The Wall Street Journal Online*, April 11, 2002, http://online.wsj.com.

nection between their actions and their rewards. In that case, profit-sharing plans will have little impact on employee behavior. This problem is even greater when employees have to wait months before profits are distributed. The time lag between high-performance behavior and financial rewards is simply too long to be motivating.

An organization setting up a profit-sharing plan should consider what to do if profits fall. If the economy slows and profit-sharing payments disappear along with profits, employees may become discouraged or angry. Consider the case of the

Du Pont Fibers Division, which linked a portion of employees' pay to the division's profits.[24] Under the plan, employees' base salary was about 4 percent lower than salaries for similar employees in other Du Pont divisions unless the Fibers Division reached 100 percent of its profit goal. If the division reached its profit goal, its employees' earnings would match that of employees in other divisions; if the division exceeded its profit goal, its employees would earn substantially more. In the first year, the division exceeded its goal, and employees earned slightly more than their counterparts in other divisions. In the next year, profits fell significantly, and employees' pay fell below that of other divisions. The Fibers Division eliminated the profit-sharing plan and returned to the original fixed salaries. One way to avoid this kind of problem is to design profit-sharing plans to reward employees for high profits but not penalize them when profits fall. This solution may be more satisfactory to employees but does not offer the advantage of reducing labor costs without layoffs during economic downturns. The "Best Practices" box on page 387 describes how some companies are meeting the challenge of rewarding performance during a slow economy.

Given the limitations of profit-sharing plans, one strategy is to use them as a component of a pay system that includes other kinds of pay more directly linked to individual behavior. This increases employees' commitment to organizational goals while addressing concerns about fairness.

Stock Ownership

While profit-sharing plans are intended to encourage employees to "think like owners," a stock ownership plan actually makes employees part owners of the organization. Like profit sharing, employee ownership is intended as a way to encourage employees to focus on the success of the organization as a whole. The drawbacks of stock ownership as a form of incentive pay are similar to those of profit sharing. Specifically, it may not have a strong effect on individuals' motivation. Employees may not see a strong link between their actions and the company's stock price, especially in larger organizations. The link between pay and performance is even harder to appreciate because the financial benefits mostly come when the stock is sold—typically when the employee leaves the organization.

Ownership programs usually take the form of *stock options* or *employee stock ownership plans*. These are illustrated in Figure 12.6.

Stock Options

stock options
Rights to buy a certain number of shares of stock at a specified price.

One way to distribute stock to employees is to grant them **stock options**—the right to buy a certain number of shares of stock at a specified price. (Purchasing the stock is called *exercising* the option.) Suppose that in 2000 a company's employees received

FIGURE 12.6

Types of Pay for Organizational Performance

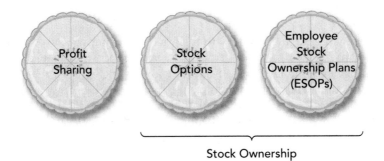

Stock Ownership

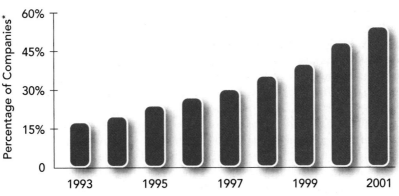

FIGURE 12.7

Share of Large
Corporations Granting
Stock Options to at Least
Half Their Employees

*Based on a survey of 350 large, public companies.

SOURCE: G. Hitt and J. M. Schlesinger, "Perk Police: Stock Options Come under Fire in Wake of Enron's Collapse," *The Wall Street Journal Online,* March 26, 2002, http://online.wsj.com.

options to purchase the company's stock at $10 per share. The employees will benefit if the stock price rises above $10 per share, because they can pay $10 for something (a share of stock) that is worth more than $10. If in 2005 the stock is worth $30, they can exercise their options and buy stock for $10 a share. If they want to, they can sell their stock for the market price of $30, receiving a gain of $20 for each share of stock. Of course, stock prices can also fall. If the 2005 stock price is only $8, the employees would not bother to exercise the options.

Traditionally, organizations have granted stock options to their executives. During the 1990s, many organizations pushed eligibility for options further down in the organization's structure. As Figure 12.7 shows, the share of companies granting stock options to at least half of their employees has grown from less than one-quarter to more than half. Wal-Mart and PepsiCo are among the large companies that have granted stock options to employees at all levels. Stock options were a popular way to lure employees to Internet start-ups during the last decade. Stock values were rising so fast during the 1990s that options were extremely rewarding for a time. But when stock prices tumbled in the current decade, options lost their attractiveness as a way to reward employees at all levels.

Some studies suggest that organizations perform better when a large percentage of top and middle managers are eligible for long-term incentives such as stock options. This evidence is consistent with the idea of encouraging employees to think like owners.[25] It is not clear whether these findings would hold up for lower-level employees. They may see much less opportunity to influence the company's performance in the stock market.

Recent scandals have drawn attention to another challenge of using stock options as incentive pay. As with other performance measures, employees may focus so much on stock price that they lose sight of other goals, including ethical behavior. Ideally, managers would bring about an increase in stock price by adding value in terms of efficiency, innovation, and customer satisfaction. But there are other, unethical ways to increase stock price by tricking investors into thinking the organization is more valuable and more profitable than it actually is. Hiding losses and inflating the recorded value of revenues are just two of the ways some companies have boosted stock prices, enriching managers until these misdeeds come to light. The 2002 bankruptcy of WorldCom demonstrated on a massive scale that the short-term benefits of an inflated stock price may not be in a company's long-term best interests.

Employee Stock Ownership Plans

employee stock ownership plan (ESOP)
An arrangement in which the organization distributes shares of stock to all its employees by placing it in a trust.

While stock options are most often used with top management, a broader arrangement is the **employee stock ownership plan (ESOP).** In an ESOP, the organization distributes shares of stock to its employees by placing the stock into a trust managed on the employees' behalf. Employees receive regular reports on the value of their stock, and when they leave the organization, they may sell the stock to the organization or (if it is a publicly traded company) on the open market.

ESOPs are the most common form of employee ownership, with the number of employees in such plans increasing from 4 million in 1980 to over 10 million in 1999 in the United States.[26] In Japan, 91 percent of companies listed on Japanese stock markets have an ESOP, and these companies appear to have higher average productivity than non-ESOP companies.[27] One reason for ESOPs' popularity in the United States is that earnings of the trust holdings are exempt from income taxes.

ESOPs raise a number of issues. On the negative side, they carry a significant risk for employees. By law, an ESOP must invest at least 51 percent of its assets in the company's own stock (in contrast to other kinds of stock funds that hold a wide diversity of companies). Problems with the company's performance therefore can take away significant value from the ESOP. Many companies set up ESOPs to hold retirement funds, so these risks directly affect employees' retirement income. Adding to the risk, funds in an ESOP are not guaranteed by the Pension Benefit Guarantee Corporation (described in Chapter 13). Sometimes employees use an ESOP to buy their company when it is experiencing financial problems; this is a highly risky investment.

Still, ESOPs can be attractive to employers. Along with tax and financing advantages, ESOPs give employers a way to build pride in and commitment to the organization. Employees have a right to participate in votes by shareholders (if the stock is registered on a national exchange, such as the New York Stock Exchange).[28] This means employees participate somewhat in corporate-level decision making. Still, the overall level of participation in decisions appears to vary significantly among organi-

Many companies now have an employee stock ownership plan (ESOP). What are some of the benefits and drawbacks of ESOPs?

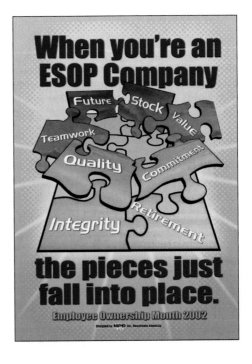

zations with ESOPs. Some research suggests that the benefits of ESOPs are greatest when employee participation is greatest.[29]

Balanced Scorecard

As the preceding descriptions indicate, any form of incentive pay has advantages and disadvantages. For example, relying exclusively on merit pay or other individual incentives may produce a workforce that cares greatly about meeting those objectives but competes to achieve them at the expense of cooperating to achieve organizational goals. Relying heavily on profit sharing or stock ownership may increase cooperation but do little to motivate day-to-day effort or to attract and retain top individual performers. Because of this, many organizations design a mix of pay programs. The aim is to balance the disadvantages of one type of incentive pay with the advantages of another type.

LO5

One way of accomplishing this goal is to design a **balanced scorecard**—a combination of performance measures directed toward the company's long- and short-term goals and used as the basis for awarding incentive pay. A corporation would have financial goals to satisfy its stockholders (owners), quality- and price-related goals to satisfy its customers, efficiency goals to ensure better operations, and goals related to acquiring skills and knowledge for the future to fully tap into employees' potential. Different jobs would contribute to those goals in different ways. For example, an engineer could develop products that better meet customer needs and can be produced more efficiently. The engineer could also develop knowledge of new technologies, in order to contribute more to the organization in the future. A salesperson's goals would include measures related to sales volume, customer service, and learning about product markets and customer needs. Organizations customize their balanced scorecards according to their markets, products, and objectives. The scorecards of a company that is emphasizing low costs and prices would be different from the scorecards of a company emphasizing innovative use of new technology.

balanced scorecard
A combination of performance measures directed toward the company's long- and short-term goals and used as the basis for awarding incentive pay.

Table 12.2 shows the kinds of information that go into a balanced scorecard. This scorecard for a manager in a manufacturing company includes four performance measures. The financial performance measure is return on capital employed (that is, profits divided by capital used during the period). A higher percentage means the capital (money and equipment) generated more profits. The measure of customer satisfaction is product returns. If customers return 1 product out of 1,000, they are better satisfied than if they return 1 product out of 800. The measure of internal operations is the percentage by which the manager's group reduces *cycle time*, the amount of time required to complete the group's process, such as fulfilling an order or getting a new product into production. Finally, the manager's objective for learning and growth in the group is to reduce voluntary turnover among employees. This goal assumes that the manager can develop a more experienced, valuable group of employees by reducing turnover.

For each of these goals, the balanced scorecard assigns a target incentive payment for the manager to earn and four levels of performance. If the manager achieves the top level of performance, the manager will earn 150 percent of the target incentive. The payout would fall to 100 percent of the incentive for achieving the second level of performance, 50 percent of the incentive for achieving the third level, and nothing for achieving the bottom level. In this example, the manager's target incentive is $2,000 per time period (e.g., per month), but the manager could earn $3,000 per period for exceeding all of the performance objectives—or nothing for failing to achieve all of the objectives.

TABLE 12.2

Sample Balanced Scorecard for a Production Manager

PERFORMANCE MEASURE	INCENTIVE SCHEDULE		
	TARGET INCENTIVE PER MONTH	PERFORMANCE LEVEL	% TARGET EARNED
Financial	$1000	20%+	150%
• Return on capital employed		16–20%	100%
		12–16%	50%
		Below 12%	0%
Customer	$ 400	1 in:	1
• Product returns		1,000 +	150%
		900–999	100%
		800–899	50%
		Below 800	0%
Internal	$ 300	9%+	150%
• Cycle time reduction (%)		6–9%	100%
		3–6%	50%
		0–3%	0%
Learning and growth	$ 300	Below 5%	150%
• Voluntary employee turnover		5–8%	100%
		8–12%	50%
Total	$2000		

SOURCE: Adapted from F. C. McKenzie and M. P. Shilling, "Avoiding Performance Traps: Ensuring Effective Incentive Design and Implementation," *Compensation and Benefits Review*, July–August 1998, pp. 57–65. Reprinted with permission.

Not only does the balanced scorecard combine the advantages of different incentive-pay plans, it helps employees understand the organization's goals. By communicating the balanced scorecard to employees, the organization shows employees information about what its goals are and what it expects employees to accomplish. In Table 12.2, for example, the organization not only indicates that the manager should meet the four performance objectives, but also that it is especially concerned with the financial target, because half the incentive is based on this one target.

Tellabs, which provides communication service products around the world, uses a balanced scorecard. The company tracks performance measures such as revenue growth, customer satisfaction, time to market for new products, and employee satisfaction.[30] Each department has objectives that support the goals on the scorecard. Every employee has a bonus plan; bonuses are tied to performance as measured by the objectives. The company conducts quarterly meetings at which employees learn how their performance will be evaluated according to the scorecard. The company also makes this information available on its intranet.

LO6

Processes That Make Incentives Work

As we explained in Chapter 11, communication and employee participation can contribute to a belief that the organization's pay structure is fair. In the same way, the process by which the organization creates and administers incentive pay can help it use incentives to achieve the goal of motivating employees. The monetary rewards of gainsharing, for example, can substantially improve productivity,[31] but the organization can set up the process to be even more effective. In a study of an automotive parts plant, productivity rose when the gainsharing plan added employee participation in the form of monthly meetings with managers to discuss the gainsharing plan and ways to increase productivity. A related study asked employees what motivated them to participate actively in the plan (for example, by making suggestions for improvement). According to employees, other factors besides the pay itself were important—especially the ability to influence and control the way their work was done.[32]

Participation in Decisions

Employee participation in pay-related decisions can be part of a general move toward employee empowerment. If employees are involved in decisions about incentive pay plans and employees' eligibility for incentives, the process of creating and administering these plans can be more complex.[33] There is also a risk that employees will make decisions that are in their interests, at the expense of the organization's interests. However, employees have hands-on knowledge about the kinds of behavior that can help the organization perform well, and they can see whether individuals are displaying that behavior.[34] Therefore, in spite of the potential risks, employee participation can contribute to the success of an incentive plan. This is especially true when monetary incentives encourage the monitoring of performance and when the organization fosters a spirit of trust and cooperation.

Communication

Along with empowerment, communicating with employees is important. It demonstrates to employees that the pay plan is fair. Also, when employees understand the requirements of the incentive pay plan, the plan is more likely to influence their behavior as desired.

It is particularly important to communicate with employees when changing the plan. Employees tend to feel concerned about changes. Pay is a frequent topic of rumors and assumptions based on incomplete information, partly because of pay's importance to employees. When making any changes, the human resource department should determine the best ways to communicate the reasons for the change. Some organizations rely heavily on videotaped messages from the chief executive officer. Other means of communication include brochures that show examples of how employees will be affected. The human resource department may also conduct small-group interviews to learn about employees' concerns, then address those concerns in the communications effort.

Incentive Pay for Executives   LO7

Because executives have a much stronger influence over the organization's performance than other employees do, incentive pay for executives warrants special attention. Assuming that incentives influence performance, decisions about incentives for executives should have a great impact on how well the executives and the organization perform. Along with overall pay levels for executives (discussed in Chapter 11), organizations need to create incentive plans for this small but important group of employees.

BusinessWeek publishes a list of top executives who give their shareholders the most for the pay that they earn. There is no easy answer to the question of what is fair compensation for executives. Are there factors that could justify executives' receiving up to 400 times the average worker's pay?

PAY FOR PERFORMANCE: BOTH ENDS OF THE SCALE

To see how pay measures up to performance, *BusinessWeek* compares what the boss made over a three-year period with how he did for shareholders

EXECUTIVES WHO GAVE SHAREHOLDERS THE MOST FOR THEIR PAY...

	TOTAL PAY* MILLIONS OF DOLLARS	SHAREHOLDER RETURN**	RELATIVE INDEX
1 B.WAYNE HUGHES Public Storage	$0.3	47%	579
2 MARK LEVIN Millennium Pharmaceuticals	1.7	279	225
3 GEORGE PERLEGOS Atmel	1.3	92	150
4 DANE MILLER Biomet	1.2	75	143
5 IRWIN JACOBS Qualcomm	5.8	680	133

...AND THOSE WHO GAVE SHAREHOLDERS THE LEAST

1 LAWRENCE ELLISON Oracle	795.1	92	0.24
2 JOHN CHAMBERS Cisco Systems	279.3	-22	0.28
3 PETER KARMANOS JR. Compuware	93.9	-70	0.32
4 LOUIS GERSTNER IBM	303.2	33	0.44
5 L. DENNIS KOZLOWSKI Tyco Intl.	331.9	57	0.47

*Salary, bonus, and long-term compensation, including exercised stock options, for the 1999, 2000, and 2001 fiscal years
**Stock price on Dec. 31, 2001, plus dividends reinvested for three years, divided by stock price on Dec. 31, 1998

Data: Standard & Poor's EXECUCOMP

To encourage executives to develop a commitment to the organization's long-term success, executive compensation often combines short-term and long-term incentives. *Short-term incentives* include bonuses based on the year's profits, return on investment, or other measures related to the organization's goals. Sometimes, to gain tax advantages, the actual payment of the bonus is deferred (for example, by making it part of a retirement plan). *Long-term incentives* include stock options and stock purchase plans. The rationale for these long-term incentives is that executives will want to do what is best for the organization because that will cause the value of their stock to grow.

Each year *BusinessWeek* publishes a list of top executives who did the most for their pay (that is, their organizations performed best) and those who did the least. The performance of the latter group has prompted much of the negative attention that executive pay has received. The problem seems to be that in some organizations, the chief executive's pay is high every year, regardless of the organization's profitability or performance in the stock market. In terms of people's judgments about equity, it seems fairer if high-paid executives must show results to justify their pay levels.

A corporation's shareholders—its owners—want the corporation to encourage managers to act in the owners' best interests. They want managers to care about the company's profits and stock price, and incentive pay can encourage this interest. One way to achieve these goals is to tie a large share of executives' pay to performance. In the *BusinessWeek* survey we discussed in Chapter 11, almost 80 percent of chief executives' pay comes in the form of stock options and other incentive pay based on long-term performance objectives. Another study has found that relying on such long-term incentives is associated with greater profitability.[35]

Performance Measures for Executives

The balanced-scorecard approach is useful in designing executive pay. Whirlpool, for example, has used a balanced scorecard that combines measures of whether the organization is delivering value to shareholders, customers, and employees. These measures are listed in Table 12.3. Similarly, at Eastman Kodak, the CEO's bonus has been based on the satisfaction of shareholders, customers, and employees. In one year, for example, only shareholder satisfaction received a "strong" rating relative to the year

TYPE OF VALUE CREATION	MEASURES
Shareholder value	Economic value added
	Earnings per share
	Cash flow
	Total cost productivity
Customer value	Quality
	Market share
	Customer satisfaction
Employee value	High-performance culture index
	High-performance culture deployment
	Training and development diversity

TABLE 12.3

Balanced Scorecard for Whirlpool Executives

SOURCE: E. L. Gubman, *The Talent Solution* (New York: McGraw-Hill, 1998).

before, so chief executive George Fisher's annual bonus was reduced by $290,000. However, Fisher's total compensation was mostly based on stock options, so it remained high, at $5.5 million. The next year Fisher agreed to a new contract that tied even more of his bonus to the three criteria.[36]

Since a decade ago, regulators and shareholders have pressured companies to do a better job of linking executive pay and performance. The Securities and Exchange Commission (SEC) has required companies to more clearly report executive compensation levels and the company's performance relative to that of competitors over a five-year period. These reporting requirements shine a light on situations where executives of poorly performing companies receive high pay, so companies feel more pressure to link pay to performance. Some forms of incentive pay also have tax advantages. Under the Omnibus Budget Reconciliation Act of 1993, companies may not deduct executive pay that exceeds $1 million, but performance-related pay (including stock options) is exempt, so it is deductible even over $1 million.

Ethical Issues

Incentive pay for executives lays the groundwork for significant ethical issues. When an organization links pay to its stock performance, executives need the ethical backbone to be honest about their company's performance even when dishonesty or clever shading of the truth offers the tempting potential for large earnings. As recent scandals involving WorldCom, Enron, Global Crossing, and other companies have shown, the results can be disastrous when unethical behavior comes to light.

Among these issues is one we have already touched on in this chapter: the difficulty of setting performance measures that encourage precisely the behavior desired. In the case of incentives tied to stock performance, executives may be tempted to inflate the stock price in order to enjoy bonuses and valuable stock options. The intent is for the executive to boost stock value through efficient operations, technological innovation, effective leadership, and so on. Unfortunately, individuals at some companies have determined that they can obtain faster results through accounting practices that stretch the norms in order to present the company's performance in the best light. When (and if) these practices are discovered to be misleading, stock prices plunge and the company's reputation is damaged, sometimes beyond repair.

A related issue when executive pay includes stock or stock options is insider trading. When executives are stockholders, they have a dual role as owners and managers. This places them at an advantage over others who want to invest in the company. An individual, a pension fund, or other investors have less information about the company than its managers do—for example, whether product development is proceeding on schedule, whether a financing deal is in the works, and so on. An executive who knows about these activities could therefore reap a windfall in the stock market by buying or selling stock based on knowledge about the company's future. The SEC places strict limits on this "insider trading," but some executives have violated these limits. In the worst cases executives have sold stock, secretly knowing their company was failing, before the stock price collapsed. The losers are the employees, retirees, and other investors who hold the now-worthless stock.

As recent news stories have reminded us, linking pay to stock price can reward unethical behavior, at least in the short term and at least in the minds of a handful of executives. Yet, given the motivational power of incentive pay, organizations cannot afford to abandon incentives for their executives. These temptations are among the reasons that executive positions demand individuals who maintain high ethical standards.

Summary

1. Discuss the connection between incentive pay and employee performance.
   Incentive pay is pay tied to individual performance, profits, or other measures of success. Organizations select forms of incentive pay to energize, direct, or control employees' behavior. It is influential because the amount paid is linked to predefined behaviors or outcomes. To be effective, incentive pay should encourage the kinds of behavior that are most needed, and employees must believe they have the ability to meet the performance standards. Employees must value the rewards, have the resources they need to meet the standards, and believe the pay plan is fair.

2. Describe how organizations recognize individual performance.
   Organizations may recognize individual performance through such incentives as piecework rates, standard hour plans, merit pay, sales commissions, and bonuses for meeting individual performance objectives. Piecework rates pay employees according to the amount they produce. Standard hour plans pay workers extra for work done in less than a preset "standard time." Merit pay links increases in wages or salaries to ratings on performance appraisals. Bonuses are similar to merit pay, because they are paid for meeting individual goals, but they are not rolled into base pay, and they usually are based on achieving a specific output, rather than subjective performance ratings. A sales commission is incentive pay calculated as a percentage of sales closed by a salesperson.

3. Identify ways to recognize group performance.
   Common group incentives include gainsharing, bonuses, and team awards. A gainsharing program measures increases in productivity and distributes a portion of each gain to employees. Types of gainsharing programs include Scanlon plans, Rucker plans, and Improshare programs. Group bonuses reward the members of a group for attaining a specific goal, usually measured in terms of physical output. Team awards are more likely to use a broad range of performance measures, such as cost savings, successful completion of a project, or meeting a deadline.

4. Explain how organizations link pay to their overall performance.
   Incentives for meeting organizational objectives include profit sharing and stock ownership. Profit-sharing plans pay workers a percentage of the organization's profits; these payments do not become part of the employees' base salary. Stock ownership incentives may take the form of stock options or employee stock ownership plans. A stock option is the right to buy a certain number of shares at a specified price. The employee benefits by exercising the option at a price lower than the market price, so the employee benefits when the company's stock price rises. An employee stock ownership plan (ESOP) is an arrangement in which the organization distributes shares of its stock to employees by placing the stock in a trust managed on the employees' behalf. When employees leave the organization, they may sell their shares of the stock.

5. Describe how organizations combine incentive plans in a "balanced scorecard."

   A balanced scorecard is a combination of performance measures directed toward the company's long- and short-term goals and used as the basis for awarding incentive pay. Typically, it includes financial goals to satisfy stockholders, quality- and price-related goals for customer satisfaction, efficiency goals for improved operations, and goals related to acquiring skills and knowledge for the future. The mix of pay programs is intended to balance the disadvantages of one type of incentive with the advantages of another type. The balanced scorecard also helps employees to understand and care about the organization's goals.

6. Summarize processes that can contribute to the success of incentive programs.

   Communication and participation in decisions can contribute to employees' feeling that the organization's incentive pay plans are fair. Employee participation in pay-related decisions can be part of a general move toward employee empowerment. Employees may put their own interests first in developing the plan, but they also have firsthand insight into the kinds of behavior that can contribute to organizational goals. Communicating with employees is important because it demonstrates that the pay plan is fair and helps them understand what is expected of them. Communication is especially important when the organization is changing its pay plan.

7. Discuss issues related to performance-based pay for executives.

   Because executives have such a strong influence over the organization's performance, incentive pay for them receives special attention. Executive pay usually combines long-term and short-term incentives. By motivating executives, these incentives can significantly affect the organization's performance. The size of incentives should be motivating but also meet standards for equity. Performance measures should encourage behavior that is in the organization's best interests, including ethical behavior. Executives need ethical standards that keep them from insider trading or deceptive practices designed to manipulate the organization's stock price.

Review and Discussion Questions

1. With some organizations and jobs, pay is primarily wages or salaries, and with others, incentive pay is more important. For each of the following jobs, state whether you think the pay should emphasize base pay (wages and salaries) or incentive pay (bonuses, profit sharing, and so on). Give a reason for each.
   a. An accountant at a manufacturing company.
   b. A salesperson for a software company.
   c. A chief executive officer.
   d. A physician in a health clinic.

2. Consider your current job or a job that you have recently held. Would you be most motivated in response to incentives based on your individual performance, your group's performance, or the organization's overall performance (profits or stock price)? Why?

3. What are the pros and cons of linking incentive pay to individual performance? How can organizations address the negatives?

4. Suppose you are a human resource professional at a company that is setting up work teams for production and sales. What group incentives would you recommend to support this new work arrangement?

5. Why do some organizations link incentive pay to the organization's overall performance? Is it appropriate to use stock performance as an incentive for employees at all levels? Why or why not?

6. Stock options have been called the pay program that "built Silicon Valley," because of their key role as incentive pay for employees in high-tech companies. They were popular during the 1990s, when the stock market was rising rapidly. Since then, stock prices have fallen.
   a. How would you expect this change to affect employees' attitudes toward stock options as incentive pay?
   b. How would you expect this change to affect the effectiveness of stock options as an incentive?

7. Based on the balanced scorecard in Table 12.2, what would be the total incentive paid to a manager if the group's return on capital employed was 12 percent, customers returned 1 product out of every 1,200 products delivered, cycle time was reduced by 5 percent, and employee turnover was 4 percent? (For each measure, find the performance level, then multiply the corresponding percentage by the target incentive to find the incentive earned.)

8. Why might a balanced scorecard like the one in question 7 be more effective than simply using merit pay for a manager?

9. How can the way an organization creates and carries out its incentive plan improve the effectiveness of that plan?

10. In a typical large corporation, the majority of the chief executive's pay is tied to the company's stock price. What are some benefits of this pay strategy? Some risks? How can organizations address the risks?

What's Your HR IQ?

The Student CD-ROM offers two more ways to check what you've learned so far. Use the Self-Assessment exercise to test your knowledge of incentive pay. Go online with the Web Exercise to see how well your knowledge works in cyberspace.

BusinessWeek Case

BusinessWeek A Little Less in the Envelope This Week

A decade ago, the deal didn't get any better than at IBM. Big Blue's generous compensation packages offered medical coverage that was virtually free, cushy pensions, and salaries that rose dependably each year. Today, those guarantees are gone.

The convulsive change—in which IBM ripped out the ramparts of its entitlement culture and replaced them with more pay-for-performance and leaner benefits—began in the early 1990s and took on an added urgency during the late 90s' war for talent. Cast as the crusty stalwart in the battle against all those cash-gorged start-ups coughing up options, IBM realized its compensation structure was about as appealing as its old Selectric typewriters. A workaholic up-and-comer could exceed every goal and still wind up with the same raise as the incompetent in the next office. Worse, fewer than 1,000 employees had stock options. In a climate that was all about risk and reward, IBM was more about security and one-size-fits-all pay.

So the company instituted rigorous performance reviews, spread stock options to 70,000 workers, and made an average of 10 percent of employee pay variable—meaning it would swell and shrink depending on the worker's performance and that of the company. Benefits were also overhauled. For example, health coverage has ended up costing as much as $157 a month.

Now, employees across Corporate America are realizing just how much their deals have changed. In the first months of 2002, many workers at companies as diverse as Ford Motor Company and Texas Instruments won't see a penny in bonuses—something that during the boom was a guaranteed slam-dunk, swelling pay by 10 percent to 70 percent.

Even in a recession, there is still one big plus for workers in the new payroll fluidity: It gives companies other ways besides layoffs to deal with the turbulence of the global market.

Still, it's hard to believe how fast—and drastically—things have changed. A decade ago, Corporate America prided itself on offering employees an impressive array of benefits and a steady, if slow, climb in pay. But handing out supersized raises to compete with start-ups during the boom would have wrecked profits and locked in higher fixed costs. So companies started doling out stock options and implementing variable-pay schemes. The gamble paid off as everyone from secretaries to CEOs saw five years of dizzying, double-digit gains in stock portfolios, lavish bonuses, and a sizzling job market that made it seem like personal fortunes could only go in one direction—up.

This year, employees are seeing the dark side of the deal: vanishing variable pay, tougher performance reviews, and shrinking benefits. A year ago, Silicon Valley sales and marketing executives like Madeleine Xavier were making more than six figures. Today, Xavier, a 36-year-old University of California, Berkeley, grad, works at online registration outfit Acteva.com—for a salary of nothing. Like many, she has taken a commission-only sales job to tide herself over during the bust. "Now a company's attitude is that you have to take a percent of the risk with them," Xavier says.

Today, more than 75 percent of salaried and hourly workers have variable pay, up from fewer than half that number 10 years ago. The number of companies with pay-for-performance programs also doubled in the 1990s. Moreover, more than 40 percent of companies now offer stock options to employees, up from just 8 percent in 1991.

The boom-time bounty pushed nearly everyone up the ladder and made it easy for companies to get employees to buy in. Now, though, there is more uncertainty. Goldman, Sachs & Company senior economist John Youngdahl estimates that the evaporation of variable pay alone, not including disappearing stock-option income, could subtract as much as $440 billion in compensation in the first and second quarters—more than last summer's tax rebates combined.

Still, it's not as if all employees deserve to moan. During the 1990s, in survey after survey, workers said they wanted more skin in the game, thereby opting for more measurements of their performance. "We take risks, and we can't whine when the economy goes south," says Intel Corporation's director of consumer Internet strategy, David Nash, who has seen his bonus shrivel to nothing this year. But many employees say they didn't realize that while they could be whipsawed by the ups and downs of variable pay, many executives would be insulated. At the same time that companies were cutting retirement benefits for employees, for example, some were also creating special supplemental plans for their highest-paid executives that guaranteed lush retirements.

The crunched pay and benefits create more inequality. Employers are using variable pay to lavish financial resources on their most prized employees, creating a kind of corporate star system.

No doubt, dismantling the old entitlement culture is bound to create a whole new set of questions. "How do you communicate to a workforce that it isn't created equally?" asks Jay Schuster of Los Angeles–based compensation consultants Schuster-Zingheim & Associates. "How do you treat a workforce in which everyone has a different deal?"

SOURCE: M. Conlin, "A Little Less in the Envelope This Week," *BusinessWeek*, February 18, 2002, pp. 64+.

Questions

1. The case says many organizations shifted to greater use of variable pay during the 1990s, a time of rapid economic growth. What forms of variable pay are mentioned? What were some advantages of switching to variable pay during a growth period?
2. Variable pay helped IBM compete in the labor market during the 1990s. Since then, economic conditions have changed. How does variable pay affect IBM's competitiveness now?
3. At the end of this case, consultant Jay Schuster asks, "How do you communicate to a workforce that it isn't created equally?" and "How do you treat a workforce in which everyone has a different deal?" Considering that the way an organization implements its pay plan will affect that plan's success, how would you answer Schuster's questions?

Case: Paying for Good Employee Relations

Organizations understand that their ability to reach financial goals depends largely on how well they manage relationships with customers and employees. Therefore, many organizations link incentive pay to customer satisfaction and employee satisfaction. Eastman Kodak, for example, has since 1995 used employee opinion results as one measure of executive performance upon which bonuses are based. Similarly, United Airlines, which is employee owned, has been moving toward a system in which executive bonuses will depend partly on the results of employee satisfaction surveys.

Although the idea of rewarding managers for good employee relations has some intuitive appeal, this practice may have some unintended consequences. Gordon Bethune, chief executive officer of Continental Airlines, has described such an idea as "absolutely stupid." Bethune argues, "Being an effective leader and having a company where people enjoy coming to work is not a popularity contest. When you run popularity contests, you tend to do things that may get you more points. That may not be good for shareholders and may not be good for the company."

These words do not mean that Bethune and Continental place little importance on employee relations. In fact, *Air Transport World* named Continental the 2001 airline of the year, and *Fortune* ranked Continental number 18 on its list of best companies to work for in America. The issue that concerns Bethune and managers at other companies is the kind of behavior that will result from linking bonuses to employee surveys. Will an incentive plan that directly rewards employee satisfaction produce only the intended positive consequences? Or might this practice also produce unintended and less desirable consequences?

Eastman Kodak and United are two examples of companies that have decided some direct incentive makes sense, even if the incentive is small compared with the rewards for satisfying other measures such as financial performance. Other companies have shied away from these incentives out of concern for unintended consequences. In this way, we can see that the organizations' pay strategies are related to their business goals.

SOURCE: "Bottom-up Pay: Companies Regularly Survey How Employees Feel about Their Bosses, but They Rarely Use Ratings to Set Compensation," *The Wall Street Journal*, April 6, 2000, pp. R5+.

Questions

1. What might be some positive results of rewarding managers for employee satisfaction? In other words, how might that incentive encourage managers to behave in ways that benefit the organization?
2. What might be some negative results of rewarding managers for employee satisfaction? Do you agree with Gordon Bethune's statement that such an incentive is "absolutely stupid"? Why or why not?
3. Besides employees, who else must managers satisfy? Think of as many groups as you can. For each of these groups, suggest a performance measure that would be appropriate for an incentive plan.

Notes

1. D. Harbrecht, "Baxter's Harry Kraemer: 'I Don't Golf,'" *BusinessWeek Online*, March 28, 2002, www.businessweek.com (interview with Harry Kraemer Jr.).

2. This chapter draws freely on several literature reviews: B. Gerhart and G. T. Milkovich, "Employee Compensation: Research and Practice," in *Handbook of Industrial and Organizational Psychology*, vol. 3, 2nd ed., ed. M. D. Dunnette and L. M. Hough (Palo Alto, CA: Consulting Psychologists Press, 1992); B. Gerhart, G. T. Milkovich, and B. Murray, "Pay, Performance, and Participation," in *Research Frontiers in Industrial Relations and Human Resources*, ed. D. Lewin, O. S. Mitchell, and P. D. Sherer (Madison, WI: Industrial Relations Research Association, 1992); B. Gerhart and R. D. Bretz, "Employee Compensation," in *Organization and Management of Advanced Manufacturing*, ed. W. Karwowski and G. Salvendy (New York: John Wiley & Sons, 1994).

3. B. Gerhart and G. T. Milkovich, "Organizational Differences in Managerial Compensation and Financial Performance," *Academy of Management Journal* 33 (1990), pp. 663–91.

4. G. T. Milkovich and A. K. Wigdor, *Pay for Performance* (Washington, DC: National Academy Press, 1991); Gerhart and Milkovich, "Employee Compensation"; C. Trevor, B. Gerhart, and J. W. Boudreau, "Voluntary Turnover and Job Performance: Curvilinearity and the Moderating Influences of Salary Growth and Promotions," *Journal of Applied Psychology* 82 (1997), pp. 44–61.

5. "Who's Answering the Phone? Your Company's Fortunes Hang on It," *Gallup Management Journal*, Fall 2001.

6. R. D. Bretz, R. A. Ash, and G. F. Dreher, "Do People Make the Place? An Examination of the Attraction-Selection-Attrition Hypothesis," *Personnel Psychology* 42 (1989), pp. 561–81; T. A. Judge and R. D. Bretz, "Effect of Values on Job Choice Decisions," *Journal of Applied Psychology* 77 (1992), pp. 261–71; D. M. Cable and T. A. Judge, "Pay Performance and Job Search Decisions: A Person-Organization Fit Perspective," *Personnel Psychology* 47 (1994), pp. 317–48.

7. E. A. Locke, D. B. Feren, V. M. McCaleb, K. N. Shaw, and A. T. Denny, "The Relative Effectiveness of Four Methods of Motivating Employee Performance," in *Changes in Working Life*, ed. K. D. Duncan, M. M. Gruenberg, and D. Wallis (New York: Wiley, 1980), pp. 363–88.

8. Gerhart and Milkovich, "Employee Compensation."

9. E. E. Lawler III, "Pay for Performance: A Strategic Analysis," in *Compensation and Benefits*, ed. L. R. Gomez-Mejia (Washington, DC: Bureau of National Affairs, 1989); A. M. Konrad and J. Pfeffer, "Do You Get What You Deserve? Factors Affecting the Relationship between Productivity and Pay," *Administrative Science Quarterly* 35 (1990), pp. 258–85; J. L. Medoff and K. G. Abraham, "Are Those Paid More Really More Productive? The Case of Experience," *Journal of Human Resources* 16 (1981), pp. 186–216; K. S. Teel, "Are Merit Raises Really Based on Merit?" *Personnel Journal* 65, no. 3 (1986), pp. 88–95.

10. R. D. Bretz, G. T. Milkovich, and W. Read, "The Current State of Performance Appraisal Research and Practice," *Journal of Management* 18 (1992), pp. 321–52; R. L. Heneman, "Merit Pay Research," *Research in Personnel and Human Resource Management* 8 (1990), pp. 203–63; Milkovich and Wigdor, *Pay for Performance*.

11. Bretz et al., "Current State of Performance Appraisal Research."

12. W. E. Deming, *Out of the Crisis* (Cambridge, MA: Center for Advanced Engineering Study, Massachusetts Institute of Technology, 1986), p. 110.

13. D. J. Hanford, "Stay, Please," *The Wall Street Journal Online*, April 12, 2001, http://interactive.wsj.com.

14. J. Bennett, "A Career on Commission Can Be a Hard Sell," *Chicago Tribune*, March 24, 2002, sec. 5, p. 5.

15. S. Greco, "Sales: What Works Now," *Inc.*, February 2002, pp. 52–59.

16. Bennett, "A Career on Commission."

17. T. L. Ross and R. A. Ross, "Gainsharing: Sharing Improved Performance," in *The Compensation Handbook*, 3rd ed., ed. M. L. Rock and L. A. Berger (New York: McGraw-Hill, 1991).

18. T. M. Welbourne and L. R. Gomez-Mejia, "Team Incentives in the Workplace," in *The Compensation Handbook*, 3rd ed.

19. Harbrecht, "Baxter's Harry Kraemer."

20. L. R. Gomez-Mejia and D. B. Balkin, *Compensation, Organizational Strategy, and Firm Performance* (Cincinnati: South-Western, 1992).

21. J. A. Fossum, *Labor Relations* (New York: McGraw-Hill, 2002).

22. This idea has been referred to as the "share economy." See M. L. Weitzman, "The Simple Macroecnomics of Profit Sharing," *American Economic Review* 75 (1985), pp. 937–53. For supportive research, see the following studies: J. Chelius and R. S. Smith, "Profit Sharing and Employment Stability," *Industrial and Labor Relations Review* 43 (1990), pp. 256S–73S; B. Gerhart and L. O. Trevor, "Employment Stability under Different Managerial Compensation Systems," work-

ing paper (Cornell University Center for Advanced Human Resource Studies, 1995); D. L. Kruse, "Profit Sharing and Employment Variability: Microeconomic Evidence on the Weitzman Theory," *Industrial and Labor Relations Review* 44 (1991), pp. 437–53.

23. Gerhart and Milkovich, "Employee Compensation"; M. L. Weitzman and D. L. Kruse, "Profit Sharing and Productivity," in *Paying for Productivity*, ed. A. S. Blinder (Washington, DC: Brookings Institution, 1990); D. L. Kruse, *Profit Sharing: Does It Make a Difference?* (Kalamazoo, MI: Upjohn Institute, 1993).

24. American Management Association, *CompFlash*, April 1991, p. 3.

25. Gerhart and Milkovich, "Organizational Differences in Managerial Compensation."

26. *EBRI Databook on Employee Benefits* (Washington, DC: Employee Benefit Research Institute, 1995); National Center for Employee Ownership website, www.nceo.org.

27. D. Jones and T. Kato, "The Productivity Effects of Employee Stock Ownership Plans and Bonuses: Evidence from Japanese Panel Data," *American Economic Review* 185, no. 3 (June 1995), pp. 391–414.

28. M. A. Conte and J. Svejnar, "The Performance Effects of Employee Ownership Plans," in *Paying for Productivity*, pp. 245–94.

29. Ibid.; T. H. Hammer, "New Developments in Profit Sharing, Gainsharing, and Employee Ownership," in *Productivity in Organizations*, ed. J. P. Campbell, R. J. Campbell, et al. (San Francisco: Jossey-Bass, 1988);

K. J. Klein, "Employee Stock Ownership and Employee Attitudes: A Test of Three Models," *Journal of Applied Psychology* 72 (1987), pp. 319–32.

30. E. Raimy, "A Plan for All Seasons," *Human Resource Executive*, April 2001, pp. 34–38.

31. R. T. Kaufman, "The Effects of Improshare on Productivity," *Industrial and Labor Relations Review* 45 (1992), pp. 311–22; M. H. Schuster, "The Scanlon Plan: A Longitudinal Analysis," *Journal of Applied Behavioral Science* 20 (1984), pp. 23–28; J. A. Wagner III, P. Rubin, and T. J. Callahan, "Incentive Payment and Nonmanagerial Productivity: An Interrupted Time Series Analysis of Magnitude and Trend," *Organizational Behavior and Human Decision Processes* 42 (1988), pp. 47–74.

32. C. R. Gowen III and S. A. Jennings, "The Effects of Changes in Participation and Group Size on Gainsharing Success: A Case Study," *Journal of Organizational Behavior Management* 11 (1991), pp. 147–69.

33. D. I. Levine and L. D. Tyson, "Participation, Productivity, and the Firm's Environment," in *Paying for Productivity.*

34. T. Welbourne, D. Balkin, and L. Gomez-Mejia, "Gainsharing and Mutual Monitoring: A Combined Agency–Organizational Justice Interpretation," *Academy of Management Journal* 38 (1995), pp. 881–99.

35. Gerhart and Milkovich, "Organizational Differences in Managerial Compensation."

36. Eastman Kodak 1996 proxy statement.

Chapter 13

Providing Employee Benefits

1. Discuss the importance of benefits as a part of employee compensation.

2. Summarize the types of employee benefits required by law.

3. Describe the most common forms of paid leave.

4. Identify the kinds of insurance benefits offered by employers.

5. Define the types of retirement plans offered by employers.

6. Describe how organizations use other benefits to match employees' wants and needs.

7. Explain how to choose the contents of an employee benefits package.

8. Summarize the regulations affecting how employers design and administer benefits programs.

9. Discuss the importance of effectively communicating the nature and value of benefits to employees.

Introduction

Hewitt Associates signals to its employees that it cares about them, body, mind, and spirit. Employees participate in plans that help them pay for medical, dental, and vision care expenses, stop-smoking programs, and care expenses for sick children. Employees who travel on business can receive reimbursement for overnight dependent care and overnight care for their pets. Employees enjoy paid time off for vacations and holidays, plus additional "Splash" time off in their fifth year of service and every five years after that. Through the LifeWorks referral service, Hewitt employees can find help with family, education, legal, and financial issues. A tuition reimbursement program pays 85 percent of employees' tuition for approved courses. The company also encourages employees to participate in charitable activities. Employees who wish to volunteer time in their communities can recive up to two days of paid time off. These and other benefits attract qualified employees and keep them loyal to Hewitt.[1]

Like Hewitt's employees, employees at almost every organization receive more than dollars and cents in exchange for their efforts. They also receive a package of **employee benefits**—compensation in forms other than cash. Besides the use of corporate fitness centers, examples include paid vacation time, employer-paid health insurance, and pension plans, among a wide range of possibilities.

employee benefits
Compensation in forms other than cash.

This chapter describes the contents of an employee benefits package and the way organizations administer employee benefits. We begin by discussing the important role of benefits as a part of employee compensation. The following sections define major types of employee benefits: benefits required by law, paid leave, insurance policies, retirement plans, and other benefits. We then discuss how to choose which of these alternatives to include in an employee benefits package so that it contributes to meeting the organization's goals. The next section summarizes the regulations affecting how employers design and administer benefits programs. Finally, we explain why and how organizations should effectively communicate with employees about their benefits.

The Role of Employee Benefits

LO1

As a part of the total compensation paid to employees, benefits serve functions similar to pay. Benefits contribute to attracting, retaining, and motivating employees. The variety of possible benefits also helps employers tailor their compensation to the kinds of employees they need. Different employees look for different types of benefits. Employers need to examine their benefits package regularly to see whether they meet the needs of today. At the same time, benefits packages are more complex than pay structures, so benefits are harder for employees to understand and appreciate. Even if employers spend large sums on benefits, if employees do not understand how to use them or why they are valuable, the cost of the benefits will be largely wasted.[2] Employers need to communicate effectively so that the benefits succeed in motivating employees.

Employees have come to expect that benefits will help them maintain economic security. Social Security contributions, pensions, and retirement savings plans help employees prepare for their retirement. Insurance plans help to protect employees from unexpected costs such as hospital bills. This important role of benefits is one reason that benefits are subject to government regulation. Some benefits, such as Social Security, are required by law. Other regulations establish requirements that benefits must meet to obtain the most favorable tax treatment. Later in the chapter, we will describe some of the most significant regulations affecting benefits.

Even though many kinds of benefits are not required by law, they have become so common that today's employees expect them. Many employers find that attracting qualified workers requires them to provide medical and retirement benefits of some sort. A large employer without such benefits would be highly unusual and would have difficulty competing in the labor market. Still, the nature of the benefits package changes over time, as we will discuss at various points throughout the chapter.

FIGURE 13.1

Benefits as a Percentage
of Total Compensation

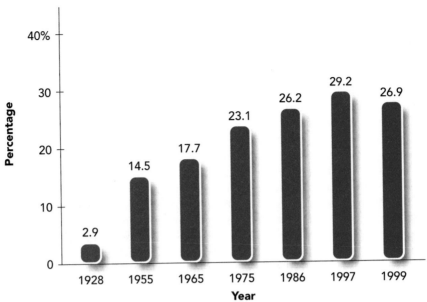

SOURCE: U.S. Chamber of Commerce Research Center, *Employee Benefits 1990, Employee Benefits 1997, Employee Benefits 2000* (Washington, DC: U.S. Chamber of Commerce, 1991, 1997, and 2000.

Like other forms of compensation, benefits impose significant costs. On average, out of every dollar spent on compensation, about 27 cents go to benefits. As Figure 13.1 shows, this share has grown over the past decades. These numbers indicate that an organization managing its labor costs must pay careful attention to the cost of its employee benefits.

Why do organizations pay a growing share of compensation in the form of benefits? It would be simpler to pay all compensation in cash and let employees buy their own insurance and contribute to their own savings plans. That arrangement would also give employees greater control over what their compensation buys. However, several forces have made benefits a significant part of compensation packages. One is that laws require employers to provide certain benefits, such as contributions to Social Security and unemployment insurance. Also, tax laws can make benefits favorable. For example, employees do not pay income taxes on most benefits they receive, but they pay income taxes on cash compensation. Therefore, an employee who receives a $1,000 raise "takes home" less than the full $1,000, but an employee who receives an additional $1,000 worth of benefits receives the full benefits. Another cost advantage of paying benefits is that employers, especially large ones, often can get a better deal on insurance or other programs than employees can obtain on their own. Finally, some employers assemble creative benefits packages that set them apart in the competition for talent. Examples include Hewitt Associates, described in the Introduction, and SAS Institute, described in the *BusinessWeek* case at the end of this chapter.

Benefits Required by Law

The federal and state governments require various forms of social insurance to protect workers from the financial hardships of being out of work. In general, Social Security provides support for retired workers, unemployment insurance assists laid-off workers, and workers' compensation insurance provides benefits and services to workers in-

TABLE 13.1

Benefits Required by Law

BENEFIT	EMPLOYER REQUIREMENT
Social Security	Flat payroll tax on employees and employers
Unemployment insurance	Payroll tax on employers that depends on state requirements and experience rating
Workers' compensation insurance	Provide coverage according to state requirements. Premiums depend on experience rating
Family and medical leave	Up to 12 weeks of unpaid leave for childbirth, adoption, or serious illness

jured on the job. Employers must also provide unpaid leave for certain family and medical needs. Because these benefits are required by law, employers cannot gain an advantage in the labor market by offering them, nor can they design the nature of these benefits. Rather, the emphasis must be on complying with the details of the law. Table 13.1 summarizes legally required benefits.

Social Security

In 1935 the federal Social Security Act established old-age insurance and unemployment insurance. Congress later amended the act to add survivor's insurance (1939), disability insurance (1956), hospital insurance (Medicare Part A, 1965), and supplementary medical insurance (Medicare Part B, 1965) for the elderly. Together, the law and its amendments created what is now the Old Age, Survivors, Disability, and Health Insurance (OASDHI) program, informally known as **Social Security.** This program covers over 90 percent of U.S. employees. The main exceptions are railroad and federal, state, and local government employees, who often have their own plans.

Workers who meet eligibility requirements receive the retirement benefits according to their age and earnings history. If they elect to begin receiving benefits at age 65, they can receive full benefits, or if they elect to begin receiving benefits at age 62, they receive benefits at a permanently reduced level. The amount rises with the person's past earnings, but the level goes up very little after a certain level, and in 2002, the maximum monthly benefit was $1,660. The government increases the payments each year according to the growth in the consumer price index. Also, spouses of covered earners receive benefits, even if they have no covered earnings. They receive either the benefit associated with their own earnings or one-half of the amount received by the covered earner, whichever is greater.

Benefits may be reduced if the worker is still earning wages above a maximum, called the *exempt amount.* In 2002, the exempt amount was $11,280 for beneficiaries aged 62 to 64. A beneficiary in that age range who earns more than the exempt amount sees a reduction in his or her benefit. The amount of the reduction is $1 for every $2 the person earns above the exempt amount. For example a 63-year-old who earned $13,280 in 2002 would have earned $2,000 above the exempt amount, so the person's Social Security benefits would have been reduced by $1,000. During the year a worker reaches 65, the maximum untaxed earnings are $30,000 (in 2002), and benefits are reduced $1 for every $3 in earnings. As of January 2000, workers aged 65 or older face no penalty. For workers under the age of 65, the penalty increases the incentive to retire or at least reduce the number of hours worked. Adding to this incentive, Social Security benefits are free from federal income taxes and free from state taxes in about half the states.

Social Security
The federal Old Age, Survivors, Disability, and Health Insurance (OASDHI) program, which combines old age (retirement) insurance, survivor's insurance, disability insurance, hospital insurance (Medicare Part A), and supplementary medical insurance (Medicare Part B) for the elderly.

Employers and employees share the cost of Social Security through a payroll tax. The percentage is set by law and has changed from time to time. In 2002, employers and employees each paid a tax of 7.65 percent on the first $84,900 of the employee's earnings, with 6.2 percent of earnings going to OASDHI and 1.45 percent going to Medicare (Part A). For earnings above $84,900, only the 1.45 percent for Medicare is assessed.

Unemployment Insurance

unemployment insurance
A federally mandated program to minimize the hardships of unemployment through payments to unemployed workers, help in finding new jobs, and incentives to stabilize employment.

Along with OASDHI, the Social Security Act of 1935 established a program of **unemployment insurance.** This program has four objectives related to minimizing the hardships of unemployment. It provides payments to offset lost income during involuntary unemployment, and it helps unemployed workers find new jobs. The payment of unemployment insurance taxes gives employers an incentive to stabilize employment. And providing workers with income during short-term layoffs preserves investments in worker skills because workers can afford to wait to return to their employer, rather than start over with another organization. Technically, the federal government left it to each state's discretion to establish an unemployment insurance program. At the same time, the Social Security Act created a tax incentive structure that quickly led every state to establish the program.

Most of the funding for unemployment insurance comes from federal and state taxes on employers. The federal tax rate is currently 0.8 percent of the first $7,000 of each employee's wages. The state tax rate varies. The minimum is 5.4 percent on the first $7,000 of wages, but many states have a higher rate or tax more than $7,000 of each employee's wages.

experience rating
The number of employees a company has laid off in the past and the cost of providing them with unemployment benefits.

No state imposes the same tax rate on every employer in the state. The size of the unemployment insurance tax imposed on each employer depends on the employer's **experience rating**—the number of employees the company laid off in the past and the cost of providing them with unemployment benefits. Employers with a history of laying off a large share of their workforces pay higher taxes than those with few layoffs. In some states, an employer with very few layoffs may pay no state tax. In contrast, an employer with a poor experience rating could pay a tax as high as 5 to 10 percent, depending on the state.[3] The use of experience ratings gives employers some control over the cost of unemployment insurance. Careful human resource planning can minimize layoffs and keep their experience rating favorable.

To receive benefits, workers must meet four conditions:

1. They meet requirements demonstrating they had been employed (often 52 weeks or four quarters of work at a minimum level of pay).
2. They are available for work.
3. They are actively seeking work. This requirement includes registering at the local unemployment office.
4. They were not discharged for cause (such as willful misconduct), did not quit voluntarily, and are not out of work because of a labor dispute (such as a union member on strike).

Workers who meet these conditions receive benefits at the level set by the state—typically about half the person's previous earnings—for a period of 26 weeks. States with a sustained unemployment rate above a particular threshold or significantly above recent levels also offer extended benefits for up to 13 weeks. Sometimes Congress funds emergency extended benefits, as it did with passage of the Job Creation and Worker Assistance Act of 2002. All states have minimum and maximum weekly benefit levels.

Workers' compensation laws are intended to protect the incomes of workers injured on the job, without the workers having to sue or the employers having to admit responsibility.

Workers' Compensation

Decades ago, workers who suffered work-related injury or illness had to bear the cost unless they won a lawsuit against their employer. Those who sued often lost the case because of the defenses available to employers. Today, the states have passed **workers' compensation** laws, which help workers with the expenses resulting from job-related accidents and illnesses.[4] These laws operate under a principle of *no-fault liability*, meaning that an employee does not need to show that the employer was grossly negligent in order to receive compensation, and the employer is protected from lawsuits. The employer loses this protection if it intentionally contributes to a dangerous workplace. Employees are not eligible if their injuries are self-inflicted or if they result from intoxication or "willful disregard of safety rules."[5]

About 9 out of 10 U.S. workers are covered by state workers' compensation laws, with the level of coverage varying from state to state. The benefits fall into four major categories:

1. Disability income
2. Medical care
3. Death benefits
4. Rehabilitative services

The amount of income varies from state to state but is typically two-thirds of the worker's earnings before the disability. The benefits are tax free.

The states differ in terms of how they fund workers' compensation insurance. Some states have a single state fund. Most states allow employers to purchase coverage from private insurance companies. Most also permit self-funding by employers. The cost of the workers' compensation insurance depends on the kinds of occupations involved, the state where the company is located, and the employer's experience rating. Premiums for low-risk occupations may be less than 1 percent of payroll. For some of the most hazardous occupations, the cost may be as high as 100 percent of payroll. Costs also vary from state to state, so that one state's program requires higher premiums than another state's program. As with unemployment insurance, unfavorable experience ratings lead to higher premiums. Organizations can minimize the cost of this benefit by keeping workplaces safe and making employees and their managers conscious of safety issues, as discussed in Chapter 3.

Unpaid Family and Medical Leave

In the United States, unpaid leave is required by law for certain family needs. Specifically, the **Family and Medical Leave Act (FMLA)** of 1993 requires organizations with 50 or more employees within a 75-mile radius to provide as much as 12 weeks of

workers' compensation
State programs that provide benefits to workers who suffer work-related injuries or illnesses, or to their survivors.

Family and Medical Leave Act (FMLA)
Federal law requiring organizations with 50 or more employees to provide up to 12 weeks of unpaid leave after childbirth or adoption; to care for a seriously ill family member; or for an employee's own serious illness.

unpaid leave after childbirth or adoption; to care for a seriously ill child, spouse, or parent; or for an employee's own serious illness.[6] Employers must also guarantee these employees the same or a comparable job when they return to work. The law does not cover employees who have less than one year of service, work fewer than 25 hours per week, or are among the organization's 10 percent highest paid. The 12 weeks of unpaid leave amount to a smaller benefit than is typical of Japan and most countries in Western Europe. Japan and West European nations typically require paid family leave.

Experience with the Family and Medical Leave Act suggests that a majority of those opting for this benefit fail to take the full 12 weeks. According to Department of Labor statistics, the median amount of time taken is 10 days.[7] This is especially the case among female executives. Many are eager to return to their careers, and others fear that staying away for three months would damage their career opportunities.[8] Of course, another reason for not taking the full 12 weeks is that not everyone can afford three months without pay, especially when responsible for the expenses that accompany childbirth, adoption, or serious illness.

When employees experience pregnancy and childbirth, employers must also comply with the Pregnancy Discrimination Act, described in Chapter 3. If an employee is temporarily unable to perform her job due to pregnancy, the employer must treat her in the same way as any other temporarily disabled employee. For example, the employer may provide modified tasks, alternative assignments, disability leave, or leave without pay.

Optional Benefits Programs

Other types of benefits are optional. These include various kinds of insurance, retirement plans, and paid leave. Figure 13.2 shows the percentage of full-time workers receiving the most common employee benefits. (Part-time workers often receive fewer benefits.) The most widely offered benefits are paid leave for vacations and holidays, life and medical insurance, and retirement plans. In general, benefits packages at smaller companies tend to be more limited than at larger companies.

Benefits such as health insurance often extend to employees' dependents. Traditionally, these benefits have covered employees, their spouses, and dependent children. Today, many employers also cover *domestic partners*, defined either by local law or by the companies themselves. Typically, a domestic partner is an adult nonrelative who lives with the employee in a relationship defined as permanent and financially interdependent. Some local governments provide for registration of domestic partners. Organizations offering coverage to domestic partners generally require that the partners sign a document stating they meet the requirements for a domestic partnership. Benefits provided to domestic partners do not have the same tax advantages as benefits provided to spouses. The partner's benefits are taxed as wages of the employee receiving the benefits.

LO3

Paid Leave

The major categories of paid leave are vacations, holidays, and sick leave. Employers also should establish policies for other situations that may require time off. Organizations often provide for paid leave for jury duty, funerals of family members, and military duty. Some organizations provide for other paid leave, such as time off to vote or

FIGURE 13.2

Percentage of Full-Time Workers Who Participate in Selected Benefit Programs

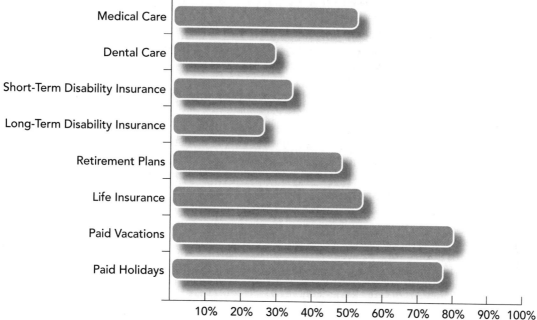

SOURCE: Bureau of Labor Statistics, http://stats.bls.gov.

to donate blood. Establishing policies communicates the organization's values, clarifies what employees can expect, and prevents situations in which unequal treatment leads to claims of unfairness.

At first blush, paid vacation, holidays, sick leave, and other paid leave may not seem to make economic sense. The employer pays the employee for time spent not working, so the employer receives nothing in return for the pay. Some employers may see little direct advantage. This may be the reason that Western European countries require a minimum number of paid vacation days, with new employees receiving 30 days off in many countries. The United States, in contrast, has no such legal requirement. It is up to U.S. employers to decide whether paid leave has a payoff in recruiting and retaining employees. At large U.S. companies, paid vacation is typically 10 days a year for the first few years. To receive as much vacation as European employees, U.S. workers must typically stay with an employer for 20 to 25 years.[9]

Paid time off is a way for employees to enjoy time with their families and to refresh their bodies and spirits. Is paid time off an important criteria for you when accepting a position?

Paid holidays are time off on specified days in addition to vacation time. In Western Europe and the United States, employees typically have about 10 paid holidays each year, regardless of length of service. The most common paid holidays in the United States are New Year's Day, Memorial Day, Independence Day, Labor Day, Thanksgiving Day, and Christmas Day.

Sick leave programs pay employees for days not worked because of illness. The amount of sick leave is often based on length of service, so that it accumulates over time—for example, one day added to sick leave for each month of service. Employers must decide how many sick days to grant and whether to let them continue accumulating year after year. If sick days accumulate without limit, employees can "save" them in case of disability. If an employee becomes disabled, the employee can use up the accumulated sick days, receiving full pay rather than smaller payments from disability insurance, discussed later. Some employers let sick days accumulate for only a year, and unused sick days "disappear" at year-end. This may provide an unintended incentive to use up sick days. Some healthy employees may call in sick near the end of the year so that they can obtain the benefit of the paid leave before it disappears. Employers may counter this tendency by paying employees for some or all of their unused sick days at year-end or when the employees retire or resign.

An organization's policies for time off may include other forms of paid and unpaid leave. For a workforce that values flexibility, the organization may offer paid *personal days*, days off that employees may schedule according to their personal needs, with the supervisor's approval. Typically, organizations offer a few personal days in addition to sick leave. *Floating holidays* are paid holidays that vary from year to year. The organization may schedule floating holidays so that they extend a Tuesday or Thursday holiday into a long weekend. Organizations may also give employees discretion over the scheduling of floating holidays. Employers should establish policies for leaves without pay—for example, leaves of absence to pursue nonwork goals or to meet family needs. Unpaid leave is an employee benefit because the employee usually retains seniority and benefits during the leave.

Group Insurance

LO4

As we noted earlier, rates for group insurance are typically lower than for individual policies. Also, insurance benefits are not subject to income tax, as wages and salaries are. When employees receive insurance as a benefit, rather than higher pay so they can buy their own insurance, employees can get more for their money. Because of this, most employees value group insurance. The most common types of insurance offered as employee benefits are medical, life, and disability insurance.

Medical Insurance

For the average person, the most important benefit by far is medical insurance.[10] As Figure 13.2 shows, a slight majority of full-time employees receive medical benefits. The policies typically cover three basic types of medical expenses: hospital expenses, surgical expenses, and visits to physicians. Some employers offer additional coverage, such as dental care, vision care, birthing centers, and prescription drug programs. Currently under debate is whether insurance plans should cover mental illnesses in the same way as other illnesses. Many plans limit coverage for mental illnesses, while some people expect that workplace stress and greater openness about mental illness will lead to a rise in the demand for mental health benefits.[11] Over the last few years,

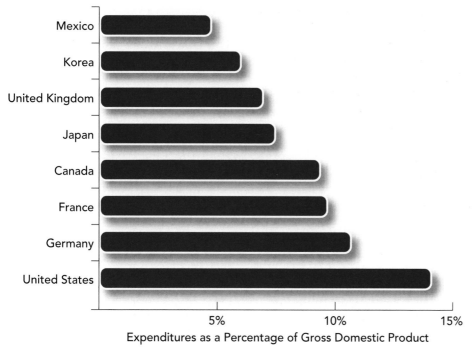

FIGURE 13.3

Health Care Costs in Various Countries

Expenditures as a Percentage of Gross Domestic Product

SOURCE: Organization for Economic Cooperation and Development, *OECD Health Data 99* (Paris: OECD, 1999); U.S. Census Bureau, International Database, www.census.gov.

mental health claims have held steady at about 6.5 percent of short-term claims and 9 to 10 percent of long-term disability claims.

Employers that offer medical insurance must meet the requirements of the **Consolidated Omnibus Budget Reconciliation Act (COBRA)** of 1985. This federal law requires employers to permit employees to extend their health insurance coverage at group rates for up to 36 months following a "qualifying event." Qualifying events include termination (except for gross misconduct), a reduction in hours that leads to loss of health insurance, and the employee's death (in which case the surviving spouse or dependent child would extend the coverage). To extend the coverage, the employee or the surviving spouse or dependent must pay for the insurance, but the payments are at the group rate. These employees and their families must have access to the same services as those who did not lose their health insurance.

As we will discuss later in the chapter, health insurance is a significant and fast-growing share of benefits costs at U.S. organizations. Figure 13.3 shows that the United States spends much more of its total wealth on health care than other countries do. Most Western European countries have nationalized health systems, but the majority of Americans with coverage for health care expenses get it through their own or a family member's employer.[12]

Managed Care. As the cost of health care coverage has risen, employers have looked for ways to control the cost while keeping this valuable benefit. To address employer concerns about cost, most insurers have offered forms of *managed care*, in which the insurer plays a role in decisions about health care, aimed at avoiding unnecessary procedures. The "Best Practices" box describes some organizations that have found creative applications of managed care. Managed care may include claims review, in

Consolidated Omnibus Budget Reconciliation Act (COBRA)
Federal law that requires employers to permit employees or their dependents to extend their health insurance coverage at group rates for up to 36 months following a qualifying event, such as a layoff, reduction in hours, or the employee's death.

Giving Employees the Health Care Benefits They Want

With health care costs rising, the workforce aging, and companies feeling a profit squeeze, finding the right health insurance can be a nightmare for employers. One solution at some companies is to use a consumer-oriented benefit plan. With this kind of plan, patients (employees and their family members) are more involved in treatment decisions. Helping employees make good choices not only can save money but can empower the employees. In the words of Jonathan Lord, chief clinical strategy and innovation officer for Humana, "When people are more engaged in their care, they end up using fewer resources because they have a sense of comfort and control." Humana, a managed-care company, plans to use the Internet to communicate directly with its patients.

WellPoint, another managed-care company, learned from surveys and other research that when premiums for health insurance went up, healthy customers (especially individuals and members of small groups) simply dropped their coverage. Health insurers can't afford to lose their healthy subscribers, who pay premiums without using a lot of services. So WellPoint decided to find out what customers really want from their health plans. The objective was to find out how much employees are willing to pay out of their own pockets and create a package of health benefits that this amount would buy. (This reverses the traditional approach of defining coverage first, then setting the price to cover the cost.)

Applying its research, WellPoint came up with two plans: PlanScape for individual insurance purchasers and FlexScape for groups of 2 to 50. With PlanScape, customers can choose the size of their monthly premium. The higher the premium, the richer the benefits will be, and the lower the out-of-pocket expenses. PlanScape can also be part of an employee benefits package. Instead of buying a group insurance policy, the employer can let employees shop for the PlanScape plan that best meets each employee's needs. FlexScape lets each employee choose from a series of benefit packages offered by the employer.

Other employers are trying to manage health care costs by helping employees stay healthier. Some are insisting on health care plans that include disease management programs. Textron, General Motors, Coca-Cola, and Georgia Power are among the large companies doing this. Their disease management programs include calls from nurses to employees at home, checking on such measures as blood pressure and weight gain. Why is this significant? "Sixty percent of my costs over the next decade will be basically in a dozen to 18 chronic diseases," remarks Allen Feezor, head of health benefits for the California Public Employees' Retirement System. Preventing even a few of those diseases can mean tremendous savings for the system, which employs 1.2 million insured workers.

SOURCE: M. D. Dalzell, "Where Will Health Plans Find the Next Generation of Savings?" *Managed Care,* September 2001, www.managedcaremag.com; M. Freudenheim, "A Changing World Is Forcing Changes on Managed Care," *New York Times,* July 2, 2001, www.nytimes.com.

which the insurer studies claims to determine whether procedures are effective for the type of illness or injury. Patients may be required to obtain approval before hospital admissions, and the insurer may require alternatives to hospital stays—for example, outpatient surgery or home health care. Managed care often involves two variations on the design of health insurance: health maintenance organizations and preferred provider organizations.

A **health maintenance organization (HMO)** is a health care plan that requires patients to receive their medical care from the HMO's health care professionals, who are often paid a flat salary, and provides all services on a prepaid basis. In other words, the premiums paid for the HMO cover all the patient's visits and procedures, without an additional payment from the patient. By paying physicians a salary, rather than a fee for each service, the HMO hopes to remove any incentive to provide more services than the patients really need. HMO coverage tends to cost less than traditional health insurance. The downside is that employees sometimes complain cost-control incentives work so well that they are denied access to services they actually need.

A **preferred provider organization (PPO)** is a health care plan that contracts with health care professionals to provide services at a reduced fee. Often, the PPO does not require employees to use providers in the network, but it pays a larger share of the cost of services from PPO providers. For example, the employee might pay 10 percent of the cost of a test by an in-network provider and 20 percent if the employee goes out of the PPO network. In general, PPOs seem to be less expensive than traditional insurance but more expensive than HMOs.[13]

Flexible Spending Accounts. Another alternative to traditional employer-provided insurance is a **flexible spending account,** in which employees may set aside a portion of pretax earnings to pay for uncovered health care expenses (for example, payment of premiums). To avoid taxation, the money in the account must meet IRS requirements. Contributions to this account may not exceed $5,000 per year and must be designated in advance. The money in the flexible spending account may be spent on health care expenses of the employee and employee's dependents during the plan year. At the end of the year, any remaining funds in the account revert to the employer.[14]

The major advantage of flexible spending accounts is that the money in the account is not taxed, so employees will have more take-home pay. For example, if they were in a 30 percent tax bracket and saved $5,000, they could keep the $1,500 (.30 × $5,000) they otherwise would have paid in income taxes. Because of the tax savings, employees will benefit if they use a flexible spending account and actually need all the money in the account for health care expenses. But if they do not use all the money in the flexible spending account, they lose the amount they do not spend. Therefore, employees are most likely to benefit from a flexible spending account if they have predictable health care expenses, such as insurance premiums.

Wellness Programs. Another way to lower the cost of health insurance is to reduce employees' need for health care services. Employers may try to do this by offering an **employee wellness program (EWP),** a set of communications, activities, and facilities designed to change health-related behaviors in ways that reduce health risks. Typically, an EWP aims at specific health risks, such as high blood pressure, high cholesterol levels, smoking, and obesity, by encouraging preventive measures such as exercise and good nutrition.

EWPs are either passive or active. Passive programs provide information and services, but no formal support or motivation to use the program. Examples include health education (such as lunchtime courses) and fitness facilities. These programs are passive because they rely on employees to identify the services they need and act on their own to obtain the services, such as participating in classes. Active wellness programs assume that behavior change requires support and reinforcement along with awareness and opportunity. These programs provide for outreach and follow-up. For

health maintenance organization (HMO)
A health care plan that requires patients to receive their medical care from the HMO's health care professionals, who are often paid a flat salary, and provides all services on a prepaid basis.

preferred provider organization (PPO)
A health care plan that contracts with health care professionals to provide services at a reduced fee and gives patients financial incentives to use network providers.

flexible spending account
A portion of pretax earnings set aside to pay for an employee's uncovered health care expenses during the same year.

employee wellness program (EWP)
A set of communications, activities, and facilities designed to change health-related behaviors in ways that reduce health risks.

Kellogg's employees can use the company's "Feeling Gr-r-reat" Fitness Center to make sure the Frosted Flakes they eat don't expand their waistlines. Can you think of firms that offer other unique fringe benefits?

example, the program may include counselors who tailor programs to individual employees' needs, take baseline measurements (for example, blood pressure and weight), and take follow-up measures for comparison to the baseline. Active programs often set goals and provide symbolic rewards as individuals make progress toward meeting their goals. In general, passive health education programs cost less than fitness facilities and active wellness programs.[15] All these variations have had success in reducing risk factors associated with cardiovascular disease (obesity, high blood pressure, smoking, lack of exercise), but the follow-up method is most successful.

Life Insurance

Employers may provide life insurance to employees or offer the opportunity to buy coverage at low group rates. With a *term life insurance* policy, if the employee dies during the term of the policy, the employee's beneficiaries receive a payment called the death benefit. In policies purchased as an employee benefit, the usual death benefit is twice the employee's yearly pay. The policies may provide additional benefits for accidental death and dismemberment (loss of a body part such as a hand or foot). Along with a basic policy, the employer may give employees the option of purchasing additional coverage, usually at a nominal cost.

Disability Insurance

Employees risk losing their incomes if a disability makes them unable to work. Disability insurance provides protection against this loss of income. Typically, **short-term disability insurance** provides benefits for six months or less. **Long-term disability insurance** provides benefits after that initial period, potentially for the rest of the disabled employee's life. Disability payments are a percentage of the employee's salary— typically 50 to 70 percent. Payments under short-term plans may be higher. Often the policy sets a maximum amount that may be paid each month. Because its limits make it more affordable, short-term disability coverage is offered by more employers. Fewer than half of employers offer long-term plans.

In planning an employee benefits package, the organization should keep in mind that Social Security includes some long-term disability benefits. To manage benefits costs, the employer should ensure that the disability insurance is coordinated with Social Security and any other programs that help workers who become disabled.

short-term disability insurance
Insurance that pays a percentage of a disabled employee's salary as benefits to the employee for six months or less.

long-term disability insurance
Insurance that pays a percentage of a disabled employee's salary after an initial period and potentially for the rest of the employee's life.

Long-Term Care Insurance

The cost of long-term care, such as care in a nursing home, can be devastating. Today, with more people living to an advanced age, many people are concerned about affording long-term care. Some employers address this concern by offering long-term care insurance. These policies provide benefits toward the cost of long-term care and related medical expenses.

Retirement Plans

LO5

Despite the image of retired people living on their Social Security checks, Figure 13.4 shows that those checks amount to less than half of a retired person's income. Among persons over age 65, pensions provided a significant share of income in 2000. Employers have no obligation to offer retirement plans beyond the protection of Social Security, but most offer some form of pension or retirement savings plan. About half of employees working for private businesses (that is, nongovernment jobs) have employer-sponsored retirement plans. These plans are most common for higher-earning employees. Among employees earning the top one-fifth of incomes, almost three-quarters have a pension plan, and about one out of six employees in the bottom fifth have pensions.[16]

FIGURE 13.4

Sources of Income for Persons 65 and Older

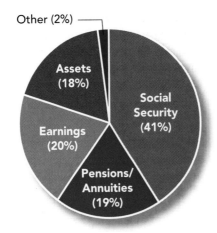

SOURCE: Employee Benefit Research Institute, *Income of the Elderly, 2000* (Washington, DC: EBRI).

contributory plan
Retirement plan funded by contributions from the employer and employee.

noncontributory plan
Retirement plan funded entirely by contributions from the employer.

defined benefit plan
Pension plan that guarantees a specified level of retirement income.

Employee Retirement Income Security Act (ERISA)
Federal law that increased the responsibility of pension plan trustees to protect retirees, established certain rights related to vesting and portability, and created the Pension Benefit Guarantee Corporation.

Pension Benefit Guarantee Corporation (PBGC)
Federal agency that insures retirement benefits and guarantees retirees a basic benefit if the employer experiences financial difficulties.

Retirement plans may be **contributory plans,** meaning they are funded by contributions from the employer and employee, or **noncontributory plans,** meaning all the contributions come from the employer.

Defined Benefit Plans

Employers have a choice of using retirement plans that define the amount to be paid out after retirement or plans that define the amount the employer will invest each year. A **defined benefit plan** guarantees a specified level of retirement income. Usually the amount of this defined benefit is calculated for each employee based on the employee's years of service, age, and earnings level (for example, the average of the employee's five highest-earnings years). These calculations typically result in pension payments that range from 20 percent of final salary for an employee who is relatively young and has few years of service to 35 percent of the final salary of an older employee who has spent many years with the organization. Using years of service as part of the basis for calculating benefits gives employees an incentive to stay with the organization as long as they can, so it can help to reduce voluntary turnover.

Defined benefit plans must meet the funding requirements of the **Employee Retirement Income Security Act (ERISA)** of 1974. This law increased the responsibility of pension plan trustees to protect retirees, established certain rights related to *vesting* (earning a right to receive the pension) and *portability* (being able to move retirement savings when changing employers), and created the **Pension Benefit Guarantee Corporation (PBGC).** The PBGC is the federal agency that insures retirement benefits and guarantees retirees a basic benefit if the employer experiences financial difficulties. To fund the PBGC, employers must make annual contributions of $19 per fund participant. Plans that are *underfunded*—meaning the employer does not contribute enough to the plan each year to meet future obligations—must pay an additional premium as high as $72 per participant.[17] The PBGC's protection applies to the pensions of 44 million workers.

With a defined benefit plan, the employer sets up a pension fund to invest the contributions. As required by ERISA, the employer must contribute enough for the plan to cover all the benefits to be paid out to retirees. Defined benefit plans protect employees from the risk that the pension fund will not earn as much as expected. If the pension fund earns less than expected, the employer makes up the difference from other sources. If the employer experiences financial difficulties so that it must end or reduce employee pension benefits, the PBGC provides a basic benefit, which does not necessarily cover the full amount promised by the employer's pension plan. The PBGC establishes a maximum; in 2002, it was $42,954.60 per year.

Defined Contribution Plans

An alternative to defined benefits is a **defined contribution plan,** which sets up an individual account for each employee and specifies the size of the investment into that account, rather than the amount to be paid out upon retirement. The amount the retiree receives will depend on the account's performance. Many kinds of defined contribution plans are available, including the following:

- *Money purchase plan*—The employer specifies a level of annual contributions (for example, 10 percent of salary). The contributions are invested, and when the employee retires, he or she is entitled to receive the amount of the contributions plus the investment earnings. ("Money purchase" refers to the fact that when employees retire, they often buy an annuity with the money, rather than taking it as a lump sum.)
- *Profit-sharing and employee stock ownership plans*—As we saw in Chapter 12, incentive pay may take the form of profit sharing and employee stock ownership plans (ESOPs). These payments may be set up so that the money goes into retirement plans. By defining its contributions in terms of stock or a share of profits, the organization has more flexibility to contribute less dollar value in lean years and more in good years.
- *Section 401(k) plans*—Employees contribute a percentage of their earnings, and employers may make matching contributions. The amount employees contribute is not taxed as part of their income until they receive it from the plan. The federal government limits the amount that may be contributed each year. In 2002 the limit was $11,000; it increases by $1,000 a year through 2005 and by $500 a year from 2006 through 2010.[18]

These plans free employers from the risks that investments will not perform as well as expected. They put the responsibility for wise investing squarely on the shoulders of each employee. A defined contribution plan is also easier to administer. The employer need not calculate payments based on age and service, and payments to the PBGC are not required. Considering the advantages to employers, it is not surprising that a growing share of retirement plans are defined contribution plans, especially at relatively small organizations. For instance, 401(k) plans provided about 15 percent of retirement income in 1992 and are expected to provide as much as 50 percent by 2012.[19] In terms of contributions, a majority of dollars went into defined benefit plans in 1980, but 85 percent went to defined contribution plans in 1999.[20] Still, many organizations offer both kinds of retirement plans.

When retirement plans make individual employees responsible for investment decisions, the employees need information about retirement planning. Retirement savings plans often give employees much control over decisions about when and how much to invest. Many employees do not appreciate the importance of beginning to save early in their careers. As Figure 13.5 shows, an employee who invests $3,000 a year ($250 a month) between the ages of 21 and 29 will have far more at age 65 than

defined contribution plan
Retirement plan in which the employer sets up an individual account for each employee and specifies the size of the investment into that account.

FIGURE 13.5

Value of Retirement
Savings Invested at
Different Ages

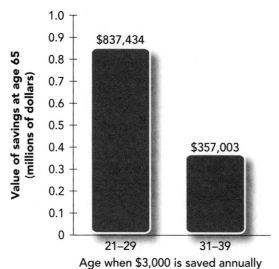

Note: Investment portfolio consists of 60 percent stocks, 30 percent
bonds, and 10 percent cash (e.g., money-market funds, bank savings
accounts), assuming average rates of return based on historical rates
from 1946 to 1990.

an employee who invests the same amount between ages 31 and 39. Another important lesson is to diversify investments. Based on investment performance between
1946 and 1990, stocks earned an average of 11.4 percent per year, bonds earned 5.1
percent, and bank savings accounts earned 5.3 percent. But in any given year, one of
these types of investments might outperform the other. And within the categories of
stocks and bonds, it is important to invest in a wide variety of companies. If one company performs poorly, the investments in other companies might perform better. To
help employees handle the risks, some organizations provide financial planning services as another employee benefit. Some employers require that a certain percentage
of retirement funds be invested in the company's own stock. This requirement increases the risk borne by the employees. One company with such a requirement was
Enron Corporation. When Enron declared bankruptcy, the retirement savings of
many employees were wiped out.

Defined contribution plans also offer an advantage to employees in today's highly
mobile workforce. They do not penalize employees for changing jobs. With these
plans, retirement earnings are less related to the number of years an employee stays
with a company.

cash balance plan
Retirement plan in
which the employer
sets up an individual
account for each
employee and
contributes a
percentage of the
employee's salary;
the account earns
interest at a
predefined rate.

Cash Balance Plans

An increasingly popular way to combine the advantages of defined benefit plans and
defined contribution plans is to use a **cash balance plan.** This type of retirement plan
consists of individual accounts, as in a 401(k) plan. But in contrast to a 401(k), all
the contributions come from the employer. Usually, the employer contributes a percentage of the employee's salary, say, 4 or 5 percent. The money in the cash balance
plan earns interest according to a predetermined rate, such as the rate paid on U.S.
Treasury bills. Employers guarantee this rate as in a defined benefit plan. This
arrangement helps employers plan their contributions and helps employees predict
their retirement benefits. If employees change jobs, they generally can roll over the
balance into an individual retirement account.

Many organizations have switched from traditional defined benefit plans to cash balance plans. The change, like any major change, requires employers to consider the effects on employees as well as on the organization's bottom line. Defined benefit plans are most generous to older employees with many years of service, and cash balance plans are most generous to young employees who will have many years ahead in which to earn interest. For an organization with many experienced employees, switching from a defined benefit plan can produce great savings in pension benefits. In that case, the older workers are the greatest losers, unless the organization adjusts the program to retain their benefits.

Government Requirements for Vesting and Communication

Along with requirements for funding defined benefit plans, ERISA specifies a number of requirements related to eligibility for benefits and communication with employees. ERISA guarantees employees that when they become participants in a pension plan and work a specified number of years, they earn a right to a pension upon retirement. These rights are called **vesting rights.**[21] Employees whose contributions are *vested* have met the requirements (enrolling and length of service) to receive a pension at retirement age, regardless of whether they remained with the employer until that time. Employees' own contributions to their pension plans are always completely vested. In most cases, the vesting of employer-funded pension benefits must take place under one of two schedules selected by the employer:

1. The employer may vest employees after five years and may provide zero vesting until that time.
2. The employer may vest employees over a three- to seven-year period, with at least 20 percent vesting in the third year and at least an additional 20 percent in each year after the third year.

vesting rights Guarantee that when employees become participants in a pension plan and work a specified number of years, they will receive a pension at retirement age, regardless of whether they remained with the employer.

These two schedules represent minimum requirements. Employers may vest employees more quickly if they wish. Two less-common situations have different vesting requirements. One is a "top-heavy" pension plan, meaning pension benefits for *key employees* (such as highly paid top managers) exceed a government-specified share of total pension benefits. A top-heavy plan requires faster vesting for nonkey employees. Another exception from the usual schedule involves multiemployer pension plans. These plans need not provide vesting until after 10 years of employment.

The intent of vesting requirements is to protect employees by preventing employers from terminating them before they meet retirement age in order to avoid paying pension benefits. In addition, it is illegal for employers to transfer or lay off employees as a way to avoid pension obligations, even if these changes are motivated partly by business need.[22] One way employers may legally try to minimize pension costs is in choosing a vesting schedule. For example, if many employees leave after three or four years of employment, the five-year vesting schedule would minimize pension costs.

ERISA's reporting and disclosure requirements involve the Internal Revenue Service, the Department of Labor, and employees.[23] Within 90 days after employees enter a plan, they must receive a **summary plan description (SPD),** a report that describes the plan's funding, eligibility requirements, risks, and other details. If the employee requests one, the employer must also make available an individual benefit statement, which describes the employee's vested and unvested benefits. Many employers provide such information regularly, without waiting for employee requests. This type of communication helps employees understand and value their retirement benefits.

summary plan description Report that describes a pension plan's funding, eligibility requirements, risks, and other details.

LO6

"Family-Friendly" Benefits

As employers have recognized the significance of employees' need to manage conflicts between their work and family roles, many have added "family-friendly" benefits to their employee benefits. These benefits include family leave policies and child care. The programs discussed here apply directly to the subset of employees with family responsibilities. However, family-friendly benefits often have spillover effects in the form of loyalty because employees see the benefits as evidence that the organization cares about its people.[24]

Family Leave

Family-friendly benefits often include some form of family or parental leave granting employees time off to care for children and other dependents. As discussed earlier in the chapter, federal law requires 12 weeks of unpaid leave. Companies may choose to offer more generous leave policies. Paid family leave remains rare in the United States, however, despite some state laws. By contrast, more than 120 countries provide paid family leave by law. The norm in Western Europe is three to four months at 80 to 100 percent of pay.[25]

Child Care

Many companies provide some form of child-care benefits. These benefits may take several forms, requiring different levels of organizational involvement.[26] As shown in Figure 13.6, the lowest level of involvement, offered by 36 percent of companies, is for the organization to supply and help employees collect information about the cost and quality of available child care. At the next level, organizations provide vouchers

Offices at Excite.com have a red tube slide that employees can use to get from the second to the first floor at its headquarters. Excite and other Internet-related companies often have such playground activities to help employees relax during their long workdays. What types of on-site benefits do you think would help to alleviate stress at your workplace?

FIGURE 13.6

Percentage of Employers Offering Various Levels of Child-Care Benefits

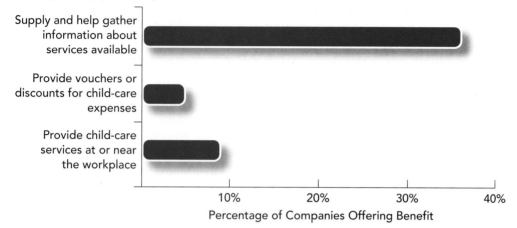

Note: Data based on a nationally representative survey of employers with 100 or more employees.

SOURCE: Families and Work Institute, "The Families and Work Institute's 1998 Business Work-Life Study," www.familiesandwork.org.

or discounts for employees to use at existing child-care facilities. At the highest level of involvement, the employer provides child care at or near the work site. Cisco Systems, a software company in San Jose, California, operates a day-care center at company headquarters.[27] In spite of the costs of this benefit and the recent economic slowdown, Cisco continued operating the day-care center because it believes the center helps employees work more productively, and productivity is especially important during difficult economic times.

An organization should not take lightly the decision to staff its own child-care facility. Such an operation is costly and involves important liability concerns. At the same time, the results of this type of benefit, in terms of reducing absenteeism and enhancing productivity, have been mixed. Some organizations have simply offered day care to follow a trend in employee benefits, rather than to address the needs of specific employees.[28] One large U.S. corporation found that less than 2 percent of its workforce used a flexible spending account the company offered as its main child-care benefit. Organizations can avoid such wasted benefits by conducting a thorough needs analysis before selecting programs to offer.[29] For example, Memphis-based First Tennessee Bank was losing 1,500 worker-days a year because of child-care problems, so the bank surveyed its employees about their needs. The results indicated that most child-care problems involved the inability to use existing child care because either the child or the provider was sick. The bank addressed this need by setting up a sick-child care center, which was smaller and less expensive than a full-time center. Absenteeism dropped so much that the program paid for itself in its first nine months.[30]

College Savings

As workers' children grow up, their needs shift from maternity leave and child care to college tuition. Some organizations have supported this concern by sponsoring tax-favored *529 savings plans*. These plans, named after the section of the Internal Revenue Code that regulates them, let parents and other family members defer taxes on the earnings of their deposits into the 529 account. Some states also provide a (limited) tax deduction for these contributions. As an employee benefit, organizations can arrange with a broker to offer direct deposit of a portion of employees' paychecks into their accounts. Besides offering the convenience of direct deposit, employers can negotiate lower management fees. For example, Merrill Lynch charges half its usual management fee on 529 accounts set up through employers.[31]

Elder Care

As the population of the nation's elderly grows, so do the demands on adult children to care for elderly parents, aunts, and uncles. When these people become ill or disabled, they rely on family or professional caregivers. Responsibilities such as providing assistance, paying for professional caregivers, and locating services can be expensive, time-consuming, and exhausting, often distracting employees from their work roles. In response, many employers have added elder-care benefits. These benefits typically emphasize information and support, rather than direct financial assistance. For example, organizations may provide access to counseling, flexible schedules, and printed resources. Even companies that cannot afford to offer counseling or referral services can use intranets to provide links to helpful websites such as the National Alliance for Caregiving (**www.caregiving.org**), the National Council on Aging (www.benefitscheckup.org), and the federal government's benefits information site (**govbenefits.gov**).[32]

Other Benefits

The scope of possible employee benefits is limited only by the imagination of the organization's decision makers. Organizations have developed a wide variety of benefits to meet the needs of employees and to attract and keep the kinds of workers who will be of value to the organization. Traditional extras include subsidized cafeterias, on-site health care for minor injuries or illnesses, and moving expenses for newly hired or relocating employees. Stores and manufacturers may offer employee discounts on their products.

To encourage learning and attract the kinds of employees who wish to develop their knowledge and skills, many organizations offer *tuition reimbursement* programs. A typical program covers tuition and related expenses for courses that are relevant to the employee's current job or future career at the organization. Employees are reimbursed for these expenses after they demonstrate they have completed an approved course.

Especially for demanding, high-stress jobs, organizations may look for benefits that help employees put in the necessary long hours and alleviate stress. Recreational activities such as on-site basketball courts or company-sponsored softball teams provide for social interaction as well as physical activity. Employers may reward hardworking groups or individuals with a trip for a weekend, a meal, or any activity employees are likely to enjoy. At one accounting firm, a manager made a practice of occasionally taking her team of women to a manicure salon for a break to relax and converse.[33]

LO7

Selecting Employee Benefits

Although the government requires certain benefits, employers have wide latitude in creating the total benefits package they offer employees.[34] Decisions about which benefits to include should take into account the organization's goals, its budget, and the expectations of the organization's current employees and those it wishes to recruit in the future. Employees have come to expect certain things from employers. An organization that does not offer the expected benefits will have more difficulty attracting and keeping talented workers. Also, if employees believe their employer feels no commitment to their welfare, they are less likely to feel committed to their employer.

Organization's Objectives

A logical place to begin selecting employee benefits is to establish objectives for the benefits package. This helps an organization select the most effective benefits and monitor whether the benefits are doing what they should. Table 13.2 is an example of one organization's benefits objectives. Unfortunately, research suggests that most organizations do not have written benefits objectives.

Metzger Associates, a technology public relations company, set the objective of reducing voluntary turnover and improving recruitment results by making its benefits more attractive than what competitors were offering.[35] The Boulder, Colorado, company started by looking at what other PR firms offered, concluding that many of the "extras" were designed to keep employees at work as many hours as possible. Special services like a concierge or free pizza in the evening made it easier to stay at the office. Metzger decided it would distinguish itself by helping employees rest and refresh themselves away from work. The company assigned its more than 30 employees to design a package it calls its Live Long and Prosper benefit. The benefit includes reimbursement in four categories: $600 for physical fitness (for example, a personal

TABLE 13.2

An Organization's Benefits Objectives

- To establish and maintain an employee benefit program that is based primarily on the employees' needs for leisure time and on protection against the risks of old age, loss of health, and loss of life.
- To establish and maintain an employee benefit program that complements the efforts of employees on their own behalf.
- To evaluate the employee benefit plan annually for its effect on employee morale and productivity, giving consideration to turnover, unfilled positions, attendance, employees' complaints, and employees' opinions.
- To compare the employee benefit plan annually with that of other leading companies in the same field and to maintain a benefit plan with an overall level of benefits based on cost per employee that falls within the second quintile of these companies.
- To maintain a level of benefits for nonunion employees that represents the same level of expenditures per employee as for union employees.
- To determine annually the costs of new, changed, and existing programs as percentages of salaries and wages and to maintain these percentages as much as possible.
- To self-fund benefits to the extent that a long-run cost savings can be expected for the firm and catastrophic losses can be avoided.
- To coordinate all benefits with social insurance programs to which the company makes payments.
- To provide benefits on a noncontributory basis except for dependent coverage, for which employees should pay a portion of the cost.
- To maintain continual communications with all employees concerning benefit programs.

trainer or a membership at a health club), $500 for outdoor living (such as lift tickets for skiing), $600 for relaxation (music lessons, trips, and so on), and $1,000 for education. The new benefit produced results in its first year and a half, as turnover fell to 2 percent from 15 percent.

Employees' Expectations and Values

To meet employee expectations about benefits, it can be helpful to see what other organizations offer. Employers can purchase survey information about benefits packages from private consultants. In addition, the Bureau of Labor Statistics gathers benefits data. The BLS website (**www.bls.gov**) is therefore a good place to check for free information about employee benefits in the United States.

Employers should also consider that the value employees place on various benefits is likely to differ from one employee to another. At a broad level, basic demographic factors such as age and sex can influence the kinds of benefits employees want. An older workforce is more likely to be concerned about (and use) medical coverage, life insurance, and pensions. A workforce with a high percentage of women of childbearing age may care more about disability or family leave. Young, unmarried men and women often place more value on pay than on benefits. However, these are only general observations; organizations should check which considerations apply to their own employees and identify more specific needs and differences. One approach is to use surveys to ask employees about the kinds of benefits they value. The survey should be carefully worded not to raise employees' expectations by seeming to promise all the benefits asked about at no cost to the employee.

The choice of benefits may influence current employees' satisfaction and may also affect the organization's recruiting, in terms of both the ease of recruiting and the kinds of employees attracted to the organization. For example, a benefits package that has strong medical benefits and pensions may be particularly attractive to older people or to those with many dependents. Such benefits may attract people with extensive experience and those who wish to make a long-term commitment to the organization. This strategy may be especially beneficial when turnover costs are very high. On the other hand, offering generous health care benefits may attract and retain people with high health care costs. Thus, organizations need to consider the signals sent by their benefits package as they set goals for benefits and select benefits to offer.

Cafeteria-Style Benefits

cafeteria-style plan
A benefits plan that offers employees a set of alternatives from which they can choose the types and amounts of benefits they want.

Organizations can address differences in employees' needs and empower their employees by offering flexible benefits plans in place of a single benefits package for all employees. These plans, often called **cafeteria-style plans,** offer employees a set of alternatives from which they can choose the types and amounts of benefits they want. The plans vary. Some impose minimum levels for certain benefits, such as health care coverage; some allow employees to receive money in exchange for choosing a "light" package; and some let employees pay extra for the privilege of receiving more benefits. For example, some plans let employees give up vacation days for more pay or to purchase extra vacation days in exchange for a reduction in pay.

Cafeteria-style plans have a number of advantages.[36] The selection process can make employees more aware of the value of the benefits, particularly when the plan assigns each employee a sum of money to allocate to benefits. Also, the individual choice in a cafeteria plan enables each employee to match his or her needs to the company's benefits, increasing the plan's actual value to the employee. And because employees would not select benefits they don't want, the company avoids the cost of providing employees with benefits they don't value. Another way to control costs is to give employees incentives to choose lower-cost options. For example, the employee's deductible on a higher-cost health plan could be larger than on a relatively low-cost HMO.

A drawback of cafeteria-style plans is that they have a higher administrative cost, especially in the design and start-up stages. Organizations can avoid some of the higher cost, however, by using software packages and standardized plans that have been developed for employers wishing to offer cafeteria-style benefits. Another possible drawback is that employee selection of benefits will increase rather than decrease costs because employees will select the kinds of benefits they expect to need the most. For example, an employee expecting to need a lot of dental work is more likely to sign up for a dental plan. The heavy use of the dental coverage would then drive up the employer's premiums for that coverage. Costs can also be difficult to estimate when employees select their benefits.

Customized Benefits

Some organizations go so far as to consider the needs and interests of each individual employee. A portion of the company's spending on benefits and incentives is available for this "one-to-one management."[37] At Technology Professionals Group, the vice president of corporate culture, Linda Connor, routinely takes notes about the interests and concerns of the company's employees and uses the information to devise customized rewards. Ideas have included a weekend getaway with several rounds of golf for a TPG consultant who loves the game and housekeeping and lawn-mowing services for an employee who is affected by work-related stress that carries over at home. This customized approach to benefits is one way that a small company, where employees are better able to know one another, can compete in the labor market.

Benefits' Costs

Employers also need to consider benefits costs. One place to start is with general information about the average costs of various benefits types. A widely used source of cost data is the U.S. Chamber of Commerce's annual survey about employee benefits. As shown in Table 13.3, this survey indicates the cost of various benefits, stated as a percentage of total payroll costs as well as in dollar terms.

TYPE OF BENEFIT	PERCENTAGE OF PAYROLL	COST IN DOLLARS
Legally required	9.1%	$ 3,458
Retirement and savings plans	6.8	2,584
Medical and other insurance	9.7	3,686
Payments for time not worked	10.7	4,066
Miscellaneous[a]	0.7	266
Total Benefits	36.8	14,060

TABLE 13.3

Costs of Employee Benefits

[a] Includes employee services and extra cash payment categories.

SOURCE: Adapted from the U.S. Chamber of Commerce Research Center, *2000 Employee Benefits Study* (Washington, DC: U.S. Chamber of Commerce, April 2001).

Controlling the Cost of Benefits

Even though organizations are still competing for high-quality, talented workers, the lure of a "chill out" room or an on-site foosball table may not be worth the cost to install and maintain it. In fact, in leaner times, organizations are looking for ways to cut back on certain perks without losing their employees' trust or loyalty. Their actions provide ideas for other employers seeking control over benefits costs.

Dave Stum, president of Aon Consulting's Loyalty Institute, suggests, "Organizations need to take a good, hard look at the basics before launching new and trendy benefits or other human resources packages. Start by ensuring that you offer a safe, secure work environment and equitable compensation and benefits packages." According to Stum, these basics form the foundation of the employer's compensation system. Any additional benefits should be laid on a firm foundation.

Jean Wilson, membership director of the Employee

Services Management Association in Oak Brook, Illinois, advises comparing benefits costs to the potential cost of higher employee turnover. According to Wilson, the cost of a benefit is often much less than that of replacing an employee coaxed away by a more generous employer.

Even so, organizations must sometimes cut back on some of their employee services. When this happens, says Cathy Ohmes, organizations should clearly communicate the decision to employees before the change occurs. The communication prepares employees to understand and absorb the information before the services are eliminated.

Another tip from Ohmes is for employers to establish a "perks philosophy." This philosophy puts into words the mission of employee benefits. It explains how employee services fit into the organization's overall compensation and benefits package. A perks philosophy avoids confusion about what types of services the

organization offers and why.

Instead of cutting services altogether, organizations can look for new, cheaper ways to offer comparable services. At Intel, HR managers were frustrated that the company was offering lunchtime seminars on health topics but no one was attending them. Concerned that many workers were already skipping meals, exercise, and sleep, Intel didn't want to give up its health program. So the company linked its intranet to the Mayo Clinic HealthQuest service, which creates personalized Web pages detailing how individuals can improve their health habits. Information covers exercise programs, healthful recipes, and more. The site is cheaper to manage than the lunchtime lectures, and employees are more apt to use it.

SOURCE: "Benefits for Your Workers," *Business Owner's Toolkit*, October 30, 2001, www.toolkit.cch.com; L. Lawrence, "Companies Still Offering Perks, but HR's Taking Another Look," *HR News*, June 2001, p. 4; B. Brady, "The Cost of Health," *Business 2.0*, January 2000, www.business2.com.

Employers can use data about costs to help them select the kinds of benefits to offer. But in balancing these decisions against organizational goals and employee benefits, the organization may decide to offer certain high-cost benefits while also looking for ways to control the cost of those benefits. The highest-cost items tend to offer the most room for savings, but only if the items permit choice or negotiation. Also, as we noted earlier, organizations can control certain costs such as workers' compensation by improving their experience ratings. Cost control is especially important—and difficult—when economic growth slows or declines. The "HR How To" box provides some guidelines for coping with this challenge.

In recent years, benefits related to health care have attracted particular attention because these costs have risen very rapidly and because employers have a number of options. Concern over costs has prompted many employers to shift from traditional health insurance to HMOs and PPOs. Some employers shift more of the cost to employees. They may lower the employer's payments by increasing the amounts employees pay for deductibles and coinsurance (the employee's share of the payment for services). Or they may require employees to pay some or all of the difference in cost between traditional insurance and an HMO or PPO plan. Excluding or limiting coverage for certain types of claims also can slow the increase in health insurance costs. Employee wellness programs, especially when they are targeted to employees with risk factors and include follow-up and encouragement, can reduce risk factors for disease.[38] A study published by the President's Council on Physical Fitness and Sports found that fitness programs provided by employers saved between $1.15 and $5.52 for every dollar spent.[39] As a result, employee wellness programs should contribute to lower health insurance costs.

Since the 1990s, efforts to control the growth in health care costs have borne fruit only temporarily. From 1980 through 1993, the growth rate in health care costs was in the double digits, but employer expenses for health care fell by almost 20 percent from 1993 to 1996. The trend again reversed from 1996 to 2000, with a cost increase of 24 percent. The Health Care Financing Administration projects that health care spending in the United States will continue to grow. Already 85 percent of working Americans with health care coverage participate in some form of managed care, so employers cannot repeat the savings of switching to managed care. Also, the profit margins of many managed-care providers are already slim, so they are limited in how to find new savings.

Legal Requirements for Employee Benefits   LO8

As we discussed earlier in this chapter, some benefits are required by law. This requirement adds to the cost of compensating employees. Organizations looking for ways to control staffing costs may look for ways to structure the workforce so as to minimize the expense of benefits. They may require overtime rather than adding new employees, hire part-time rather than full-time workers (because part-time employees generally receive much smaller benefits packages), and use independent contractors rather than hire employees. Some of these choices are limited by legal requirements, however. For example, the Fair Labor Standards Act requires overtime pay for nonexempt workers, as discussed in Chapter 11. Also, the Internal Revenue Service strictly limits the definition of "independent contractors," so that employees cannot avoid legal obligations by classifying workers as self-employed when the organization receives the benefits of a permanent employee. Other legal requirements involve tax treatment of benefits, antidiscrimination laws, and accounting for benefits.

Tax Treatment of Benefits

The IRS provides more favorable tax treatment of benefits classified as *qualified plans*. The details vary from one type of benefit to another. In the case of retirement plans, the advantages include the ability for employees to immediately take a tax deduction for the funds they contribute to the plans, no immediate tax on employees for the amount the employer contributes, and tax-free earnings on the money in the retirement fund.[40]

To obtain status as a qualified plan, a benefit plan must meet certain requirements.[41] In the case of pensions, these involve vesting and nondiscrimination rules. The nondiscrimination rules provide tax benefits to plans that do not discriminate in favor of the organization's "highly compensated employees." To receive the benefits, the organization cannot set up a retirement plan that provides benefits exclusively to the organization's owners and top managers. The requirements encourage employers to provide important benefits such as pensions to a broad spectrum of employees. Before offering pension plans and other benefits, organizations should have them reviewed by an expert who can advise on whether the benefits are qualified plans.

Antidiscrimination Laws

As we discussed in Chapter 3, a number of laws are intended to provide equal employment opportunity without regard to race, sex, age, disability, and several other protected categories. Some of these laws apply to the organization's benefits policies.

Legal treatment of men and women includes equal access to benefits, so the organization may not use the employee's gender as the basis for providing more limited benefits. That is the rationale for the Pregnancy Discrimination Act, which requires that employers treat pregnancy as it treats any disability. If an employee needs time off for conditions related to pregnancy or childbirth, the employee would receive whatever disability benefits the organization offers to employees who take disability leave for other reasons. Another area of concern in the treatment of male and female employees is pension benefits. On average, women live longer than men, so on average, pension benefits for female employees are more expensive (because the organization pays the pension longer), other things being equal. Some organizations have used this difference as a basis for requiring that female employees contribute more than male employees to defined benefit plans. The Supreme Court in 1978 determined that such a requirement is illegal.[42] According to the Supreme Court, the law is intended to protect individuals, and when women are considered on an individual basis (not as averages), not every woman outlives every man.

Age discrimination is also relevant to benefits policies. Two major issues have received attention under the Age Discrimination in Employment Act (ADEA) and amendments. First, employers must take care not to discriminate against workers over age 40 in providing pay or benefits. For example, employers may not set an age at which retirement benefits stop growing as a way to pressure older workers to retire.[43] Also, early-retirement incentive programs need to meet certain standards. The programs may not coerce employees to retire, they must provide accurate information about the options available, and they must give employees enough time to make a decision. In effect, employees must really have a choice about whether they retire.

When employers offer early retirement, they often ask employees to sign waivers saying they will not pursue claims under the ADEA. The Older Workers Benefit Protection Act of 1990 set guidelines for using these waivers.[44] The waivers must be voluntary and understandable to the employee and employer, and they must spell out the employee's rights under the ADEA. Also, in exchange for signing the waiver, the employee must receive "compensation," that is, greater benefits than he or she would otherwise receive upon retirement. The employer must inform employees that they may consult a lawyer before signing, and employees must have time to make a decision about signing—21 days before signing plus 7 days afterward in which they can revoke the agreement.

Tapping into Benefits Online

Information about benefits is a key part of most company intranets. Employees often have questions about their health insurance, retirement savings, vacation time, and the like. They can get answers conveniently and inexpensively when the employer posts the facts online. An intranet provides information securely, respecting employees' privacy, while giving the organization control over how the message is presented.

It is expensive to have employees use a paper form to add a new baby to a health plan or call a service representative to learn whether a doctor is in the PPO. This kind of information is easy to make available online. Many companies post links to enrollment forms, which employees can fill out and submit online. Links to health plans can provide lists of doctors in the PPO or HMO network, as well as information about coverage for different medications.

Creative sites extend beyond basic enrollment and coverage information to support employees' efforts to maintain good health. Links can lead employees to information on healthy life habits or management of chronic conditions. Some intranets let employees report absences online. According to Veronica Hellwig, a senior health and productivity consultant at the consulting firm Watson Wyatt, "Some employers are providing hyperlinks from their benefit intranets to other websites, such as job accommodation or online interactive health and lifestyle connections." According to Hellwig, the information helps employees provide better care for themselves, promoting their health so they can return to work sooner after an illness or injury.

Benefits affect employees' well-being in large and small ways, and there are just as many ways to connect employees to benefits online.

The intranet home page might feature links to information on vacation days remaining, the employees' medical deductibles, or even menus for the company cafeteria. At PeopleSoft, employees have to go online if they want to see their paycheck statements. The virtual pay stubs are available only on the software company's intranet. Not only does eliminating the paper check stubs save money on printing and mailing, the practice also meets the company's goal of encouraging intranet use. In the words of Robert Geib, a business development specialist at PeopleSoft, "People care about their paychecks. And if they want to see what they're getting paid, they need to come to our intranet."

SOURCE: G. Anders, "Inside Job," *Fast Company,* September 2001, p. 176; "More Pressure to Control Absences," *HR Daily News Page,* March 15, 2002, BenefitsNext website, www.benefitsnext.com.

The Americans with Disabilities Act imposes requirements related to health insurance. Under the ADA, employees with disabilities must have "equal access to whatever health insurance coverage the employer provides other employees." Even so, the terms and conditions of health insurance may be based on risk factors—as long as the employer does not use this basis as a way to escape offering health insurance to someone with a disability. From the standpoint of avoiding legal challenges, an employer who has risk-based insurance and then hires an employee with a disability is in a stronger position than an employee who switches to a risk-based policy after hiring a disabled employee.[45]

Accounting Requirements

Companies' financial statements must meet the many requirements of the Financial Accounting Standards Board (FASB). These accounting requirements are intended to ensure that financial statements are a true picture of the company's financial status and that outsiders, including potential lenders and investors, can understand and compare financial statements. Under FASB standards, employers must set aside the funds they expect to need for benefits to be paid after retirement, rather than funding those benefits on a pay-as-you-go basis. On financial statements, those funds must appear as future cost obligations.[46] For companies with substantial retirement benefits, reporting those benefits as future cost obligations greatly lowers income each year. Along with rising benefits costs, this reporting requirement has encouraged many companies to scale back benefits to retirees.

LO9

Communicating Benefits to Employees

Organizations must communicate benefits information to employees so that they will appreciate the value of their benefits. This is essential so that benefits can achieve their objective of attracting, motivating, and retaining employees. Employees are interested in their benefits, and they need a great deal of detailed information to take advantage of benefits such as health insurance and 401(k) plans. It follows that electronic technology such as the Internet and supporting databases can play a significant role in modern benefit systems. The "e-HRM" box discusses how some companies are putting benefits information on their intranets.

In actuality, employees and job applicants often have a poor idea of what benefits they have and what the market value of their benefits is. Research asking employees about their benefits has shown that employees significantly underestimate the cost and value of their benefits.[47] Probably a major reason for their lack of knowledge is a lack of communications from employers. Although employers spend about $14,000 per worker per year on benefits, by one account, they spend less than $10 per worker per year on communicating information about those benefits.[48]

Employers have many options for communicating information about benefits. To increase the likelihood that employees will receive and understand the messages, em-

FIGURE 13.7

Techniques for Communicating Employee Benefits

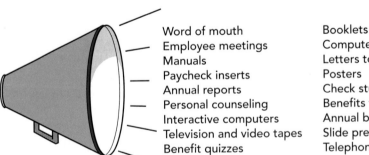

Word of mouth
Employee meetings
Manuals
Paycheck inserts
Annual reports
Personal counseling
Interactive computers
Television and video tapes
Benefit quizzes

Booklets
Computerized statements
Letters to employees
Posters
Check stubs
Benefits fairs
Annual benefits review
Slide presentations
Telephone hot lines

SOURCE: "An Evaluation of Benefit Communication Strategy," by Michael C. Giallourakis and G. Stephen Taylor, which appeared in the 4th Quarter 1991 issue, was reprinted with permission from the *Employee Benefits Journal*, published by the International Foundation of Employee Benefit Plans, Brookfield, WI. Statements or opinions expressed in this article are those of the author and do not necessarily represent the views or positions of the International Foundation, its officers, directors, or staff.

ployers can combine several media, such as brochures, question-and-answer meetings, intranet pages, memos, and e-mail. Figure 13.7 identifies a variety of options for communicating messages to employees about their benefits. An investment of creativity in employee communication can reap great returns in the form of committed, satisfied employees.

Summary

1. Discuss the importance of benefits as a part of employee compensation.
Like pay, benefits help employers attract, retain, and motivate employees. The variety of possible benefits also helps employers tailor their compensation packages to attract the right kinds of employees. Employees expect at least a minimum level of benefits, and providing more than the minimum helps an organization compete in the labor market. Benefits are also a significant expense, but employers provide benefits because employees value them and many benefits are required by law.

2. Summarize the types of employee benefits required by law.
Employers must contribute to the Old Age, Survivors, Disability, and Health Insurance program known as Social Security through a payroll tax shared by employers and employees. Employers must also pay federal and state taxes for unemployment insurance, based on each employer's experience rating, or percentage of employees a company has laid off in the past. State laws require that employers purchase workers' compensation insurance. Under the Family and Medical Leave Act, employees who need to care for a baby following birth or adoption or for an ill family member must be granted unpaid leave of up to 12 weeks.

3. Describe the most common forms of paid leave.
The major categories of paid leave are vacations, holidays, and sick leave. Paid time off may seem uneconomical, which may be the reason U.S. employers tend to offer much less vacation time than is common in Western Europe. At large U.S. companies, paid vacation is typically 10 days. The typical number of paid holidays is 10 in both Western Europe and the United States. Sick leave programs often provide full salary replacement for a limited period of time, with the amount of sick leave usually based on length of service. Policies are needed to determine how the organization will handle unused sick days at the end of each year. Some organizations let employees roll over some or all of the unused sick days into the next year, and others let unused days expire at the end of the year. Other forms of paid leave include personal days and floating holidays.

4. Identify the kinds of insurance benefits offered by employers.
Medical insurance is one of the most valued employee benefits. Such policies typically cover hospital expenses, surgical expenses, and visits to physicians. Some employers offer additional coverage, such as dental care, vision care, birthing centers, and prescription drug programs. Under the Consolidated Omnibus Budget Reconciliation Act of 1985, employees must be permitted to extend their health insurance coverage at group rates for up to 36 months after they leave the organization. To manage the costs of health insurance, many organizations offer coverage through a health maintenance organization or preferred provider organization, or they may offer flexible spending accounts. Some encourage healthy behaviors through an employee wellness program. Life insurance usually takes the form of group term life insurance, with the usual benefit being two times the employee's yearly pay. Employers may also offer short-term and/or long-term disability insurance, with disability payments being a percentage of the employee's salary. Some employers provide long-term care insurance to pay the costs asssociated with long-term care such as nursing home care.

5. Define the types of retirement plans offered by employers.
Retirement plans may be contributory, meaning funded by contributions from employer and employee, or noncontributory, meaning funded only by the employer. These plans may be defined benefit plans, which guarantee a specified level of retirement income, usually based on the employee's years of service, age, and earnings level. Benefits under these plans are protected by the Pension Benefit Guarantee Corporation. An alternative is to set up a defined contribution plan, such as a 401(k) plan. The employer sets up an individual account for each employee and guarantees the size of the investment into that account, rather than the amount to be paid out on retirement. Because employees have control over investment decisions, the organization may also offer financial planning services as an employee benefit. A cash balance plan combines some advantages of defined benefit plans and defined contribution plans. The employer sets up individual

accounts and contributes a percentage of each employee's salary. The account earns interest at a predetermined rate, so the contributions and benefits are easier to predict.

6. Describe how organizations use other benefits to match employees' wants and needs.
   Employers have responded to work-family role conflicts by offering family-friendly benefits, including paid family leave, child-care services or referrals, college savings plans, and elder-care information and support. Other employee benefits have traditionally included subsidized cafeterias, on-site health clinics, and reimbursement of moving expenses. Stores and manufacturers may offer discounts on their products. Tuition reimbursement encourages employees to continue learning. Recreational services and employee outings provide social interaction as well as stress relief.

7. Explain how to choose the contents of an employee benefits package.
   A logical place to begin is to establish organizational objectives and select benefits that support those objectives. Organizations should also consider employees' expectations and values. At a minimum, organizations offer the benefits employees have come to view as basic; some organizations go so far as to match extra benefits to individual employees' needs and interests. Cafeteria-style plans are an intermediate step that gives employees control over the benefits they receive. Employers must also weigh the costs of benefits, which are significant.

8. Summarize the regulations affecting how employers design and administer benefits programs.
   Employers must provide the benefits that are required by law, and they may not improperly classify employees as "independent contractors" to avoid paying benefits. Tax treatment of qualified plans is favorable, so organizations need to learn the requirements for setting up benefits as qualified plans—for example, ensuring that pension plans do not discriminate in favor of the organization's highly compensated employees. Employers may not use employees' gender as the basis for discriminating against anyone, as in pension benefits on the basis that women as a group may live longer. Nor may employers discriminate against workers over age 40 in providing pay or benefits, such as pressuring older workers to retire by limiting retirement benefits. When employers offer early retirement, they must meet the requirements of the Older Workers Benefit Protection Act of 1990. Under the Americans with Disabilities Act, employers must give disabled employees equal access to health insurance. To meet the requirements of the Financial Accounting Standards Board, employers must set aside the funds they expect to need for retirement benefits ahead of time, rather than funding the benefits on a pay-as-you-go basis.

9. Discuss the importance of effectively communicating the nature and value of benefits to employees.
   Communicating information about benefits is important so that employees will appreciate the value of their benefits. Communicating their value is the main way benefits attract, motivate, and retain employees. Employers have many options for communicating information about benefits, brochures, meetings, intranets, memos, e-mail. Using a combination of such methods increases employees' understanding.

Review and Discussion Questions

1. Why do employers provide employee benefits, rather than providing all compensation in the form of pay and letting employees buy the services they want?
2. Of the benefits discussed in this chapter, list the ones you consider essential—that is, the benefits you would require in any job offer. Why are these benefits important to you?
3. Define the types of benefits required by law. How can organizations minimize the cost of these benefits while complying with the relevant laws?
4. What are some advantages of offering a generous package of insurance benefits? What are some drawbacks of generous insurance benefits?
5. Imagine that you are the human resource manager of a small architectural firm. You learn that the monthly premiums for the company's existing health insurance policy will rise by 15 percent next year. What can you suggest to help your company manage this rising cost?
6. In principle, health insurance would be most attractive to employees with large medical expenses, and retirement benefits would be most attractive to older employees. What else might a company include in its benefits package to appeal to young, healthy employees? How might the company structure its benefits so these employees can take advantage of the benefits they care about most?
7. What issues should an organization consider in selecting a package of employee benefits? How should an employer manage the trade-offs among these considerations?
8. How do tax laws and accounting regulations affect benefits packages?

9. What legal requirements might apply to a family leave policy? Suggest how this type of policy should be set up to meet those requirements.

10. Why is it important to communicate information about employee benefits? Suppose you work in the HR department of a company that has decided to add new benefits—dental and vision insurance plus an additional two days of paid time off for "personal days." How would you recommend communicating this change? What information should your messages include?

What's Your HR IQ?

The Student CD-ROM offers two more ways to check what you've learned so far. Use the Self-Assessment Exercise to determine if you're likely to find a job that provides the benefits you want. Go online with the Web Exercise to see how your knowledge of employee benefits works in cyberspace.

BusinessWeek Case

BusinessWeek **Dr. Goodnight's Company Town**

The war for talent has businesses transforming their corporate campuses into country clubs—offering everything from five-star lunches to concierges willing to arrange employees' lawn mowing and haircuts. But long before the words "labor crunch" put employee perks in vogue, SAS Institute Inc. founder James Goodnight was lavishing money on programmers instead of headhunters. It worked: SAS turnover is 4 percent in an industry for which 20 percent is typical. The Cary, North Carolina–based company may compete against PeopleSoft Inc. and Oracle Corporation, but SAS employees aren't asked to mimic their Silicon Valley brethren's sleep-starved lifestyle. Goodnight, a shy billionaire who until recently drove a Buick Roadmaster wagon, believes in leaving the office at 5 P.M. sharp. Dinner, he says, should be spent with your family, not at your desk.

Goodnight remembers working as a programmer for NASA—a place so cheap it wouldn't even spring for workers' sodas. Insulted, he vowed to do things differently. Today he's become a Willy Wonka to his workers, creating a corporate perk factory where even the plain and peanut-filled M&Ms, replenished like clockwork every Wednesday, are free. Goodnight believes that if you treat people as if they make a difference, they will. The turnover savings he reaps from his largesse are huge: an estimated $75 million a year. This means Goodnight can afford all those banana trees and cracker-and-cheese-stocked snack rooms. It may be too Stepford-like for cynics, but the T-shirt and Teva-sporting SAS employees say they wouldn't have it any other way.

On-site benefits at the Institute include day care, Montessori school, the Atrium, and lunchtime entertainment. For $25 a month, the day care center will take babies after SAS's six-week paid maternity leave. Sixty percent of the employees use the on-site day care; parents can visit or pick up their kids for lunch. Employees also get private offices and open spaces for impromptu meetings and breaks.

The perks aren't limited to the on-site stuff. Goodnight offers discounts on everything from land in his ritzy subdivision to memberships at his country club. Employees make only industry-average salaries, but they get a generous year-end bonus, profit sharing, and an extra week of paid vacation at Christmas. Employees can also enjoy Shiatsu, Swedish, and deep tissue massages—all available between meetings—right down the hall. A free clinic is available so employees can get care at work, even if it's a child that's ill.

This is just the beginning. SAS also has a 55,000-square-foot athletic facility worthy of Olympic games—plus tennis courts, walking trails, picnic shelters, and a lake, canoes provided. In summer the place looks more like a raucous college campus than a headquarters for wireheads. After your workout, the company takes your gym clothes and returns them to you freshly laundered the next day. Hungry? Head over to the subsidized cafeteria, where it's hard to spend more than $3 for a feast.

When Goodnight decided he didn't like Cary's local high school, he built a new private college prep called Cary Academy right next to SAS. (His own son though didn't want to switch schools to attend.) Employees receive a 10 percent discount off the $9,000-per-year tuition. If that's too steep, they can still enjoy a smorgasbord of free services like the car wash and detailing, farmer's market, and advice on financial planning for college and retirement. But the all-time favorite SAS perk is the seven-hour workday, which leaves time for family or personal obligations. While the Silicon Valley set grinds away, SAS's gates close shut. For Goodnight, seven hours of work a day are plenty.

Goodnight believes that workers' environments can inspire or depress them. To that end, he has hired a full-time ergonomics specialist and built an on-site greenhouse that provides fresh flowers. His 7,000 employees also enjoyed the $16 million in bonuses and $30 million in profit sharing shelled out last year, when the company's revenues hit $1.02 billion. The payoff: similar software companies lose and replace 1,000 people a year, while SAS loses 130. Says one SAS employee, "We're spoiled rotten."

SOURCE: *BusinessWeek Online*, www.businessweek.com, June 19, 2000.

Questions

1. Would you like to work at SAS? Why or why not? Would you prefer to work at SAS or Microsoft?
2. What are the advantages and disadvantages of SAS's benefits strategy?
3. SAS is sometimes criticized for being too paternalistic. What is your opinion?

Case: Is Retirement a Luxury?

A generation ago, a worker's pension was too sacred to be touched. Employees could secure a safe retirement by staying with their employer for years, even decades. Today, retirement security is going the way of employment security—replaced by flexibility and workers' individual responsibility.

Many companies have replaced defined benefit pension plans with defined contribution plans, such as 401(k) plans. The worth of those plans at retirement depends on the employee's investment decisions and the performance of stocks, bonds, and other investments in general. Often, a sizable share of 401(k) investments are in the stock of the employer. Lucent Technologies, for example, has a 401(k) plan for hourly employees. For every dollar contributed by an employee, Lucent contributes 66 cents of Lucent stock, which the employee must hold for a certain number of years. When the company was riding high, so were the retirement plans. But in 2000, Lucent stock dropped 80 percent. Younger employees' investments have years to recover, but for employees nearing retirement age, retirement may become unaffordable overnight.

The usual advice to investors is to diversify, but defined contribution plans like Lucent's conflict with that goal. Similarly, Owens Corning has a plan that includes 44 percent company stock, and Dell Computer's plan requires 88 percent in company assets. Fidelity Investments studied 7,000 defined contribution programs and learned that the average plan has more than 30 percent of its total assets invested in the employer's stock. As the downside of this strategy has become apparent in the recent stock slide, some companies have begun capping the percentage of company stock employees may have in their retirement plans.

Along with retirement income, elderly workers and retirees are concerned about retirement expenses, especially the cost of health care and prescription drugs. The government-run Medicare program provides assistance with medical care, and many retirees supplement Medicare coverage by purchasing health insurance or receiving insurance as a benefit from former employers. But the share of employers providing retiree health coverage has been declining as employers struggle to control the cost of this benefit. A decade ago, 45 percent of retirees too young for Medicare (that is, younger than 65) had supplementary coverage from their employers, and 40 percent of Medicare-eligible retirees had such coverage. By 2001, the share of employees with this benefit had fallen to below 30 percent for retirees under 65 and below 25 percent for Medicare-eligible retirees.

Coverage for prescriptions is also becoming a thing of the past, even as drug costs are skyrocketing. Some companies and unions are turning to organizations like Solutions for Progress, a consulting firm in Philadelphia that tries to help retirees pay for their medicine after prescription-drug coverage ends. Solutions for Progress uses a database with information about retirees and the requirements of government and manufacturer discount plans to find matches between each retiree's situation and the plan requirements. As you might expect, some retirees easily qualify for assistance, while others are difficult to help.

The struggle to afford retirement is likely to intensify as the workforce ages and a growing share of the population is retired. The steel industry provides an early example. The companies in this industry face about $10 billion in "legacy costs"—fulfilling the promises made to provide health insurance, life insurance, and pensions for retirees. Because of cutbacks, greater efficiency, and an aging workforce, retired steelworkers now outnumber active employees. Steel companies are paying benefits to people who are no longer contributing through employment at a time when many of the companies are unprofitable. Over 30 have declared bankruptcy, ending benefits payments to retirees. These companies are unattractive to buy and salvage through a reorganization, because the legacy costs are so high. Some companies have taken desperate measures. LTV, operating at a loss and unable to find a buyer, closed its doors and auctioned off its assets. Bethlehem Steel Corporation is arranging to have other companies operate its steel plants, leaving Bethlehem merely to hold its assets and let retirees compete with its creditors during bankruptcy proceedings.

These changes are making government benefits essential to many retirees. Take Donna Louise Wilson, whose husband worked for LTV. After her husband died and LTV went out of business, the Pension Benefit Guaranty Corporation began paying about 85 percent of the pension that had been paid to Wilson as a survivor's benefit. However, Wilson is responsible for the $125 she pays for prescription drugs each month, an expense that had been covered as a retiree benefit.

How did the steel workers get into such a position? The situation is complex, but many of the decisions involved trade-offs in union negotiations. In the short-term, the companies benefited from granting generous retirement benefits rather than large wage increases. Now in an even more competitive market, the companies must pay the costs of those decisions, and they are facing trade-offs between the demands of current employees and retirees, as well as customers and creditors. In the meantime, many retirees are facing trade-offs between the cost of medicine and the cost of housing.

SOURCES: B. Healy, "Taking Stock of Options," *Boston Globe*, August 6, 2001, http://digitalmass.boston.com; L. Graham, "Company Stock Could Sink Your Ship," *BusinessWeek*, July 30, 2001, p. 86; C. Tejada, "EEOC May Allow Companies to Reduce Retirees' Benefits," *The Wall Street Journal Online*, June 26, 2002, http://online.wsj.com; C. Tejada, "How Much Longer Can Employees Expect Workplace Health Benefits?" *The Wall Street Journal Online*, July 24, 2002, http://online.wsj.com; R. G. Matthews, "Legacy Costs Drive Big Changes in Steel, and Retirees Lose Out," *The Wall Street Journal Online*, April 25, 2002, http://online.wsj.com.

Questions

1. During the 1990s, many employees expected their stock investments to pay for a comfortable retirement, and in the years before that, many employees expected employer-funded pension plans to do the same. Other employees expect to rely on government Social Security payments. In your opinion, what should employees rely on—personal savings and investments, employers, the government, their families, or some other source? How does your opinion affect your own decisions about saving and employment?

2. With the share of the population above retirement age expected to rise, the growth in retirement income could come from required benefits such as Social Security or from voluntary benefits such as pensions. For an employer, what would be some advantages of offering generous retirement plans? What would be some disadvantages?

3. Does cutting benefits to retirees affect a company's ability to compete in the labor market? Explain.

Notes

1. "Benefits—United States," Hewitt Associates website, http://was.hewitt.com, downloaded August 27, 2002.
2. B. Gerhart and G. T. Milkovich, "Employee Compensation: Research and Practice," in *Handbook of Industrial and Organizational Psychology*, vol. 3, 2nd ed., ed. M. D. Dunnette and L. M. Hough (Palo Alto, CA: Consulting Psychologists Press, 1992).
3. J. A. Penczak, "Unemployment Benefit Plans," in *Employee Benefits Handbook*, 3rd ed., ed. J. D. Mamorsky (Boston: Warren, Gorham & Lamont, 1992).
4. J. V. Nackley, *Primer on Workers' Compensation* (Washington, DC: Bureau of National Affairs, 1989); T. Thomason, T. P. Schmidle, and J. F. Burton, *Workers' Compensation* (Kalamazoo, MI: Upjohn Institute, 2001).
5. B. T. Beam Jr. and J. J. McFadden, *Employee Benefits*, 6th ed. (Chicago: Real Estate Education Co., 2001).
6. U.S. Department of Labor website, www.dol.gov.
7. U.S. Department of Labor, "Balancing the Needs of Families and Employers," Labor Department website, www.dol.gov, 2000.
8. P. Hardin, "Women Execs Should Feel at Ease about Taking Full Maternity Leave," *Personnel Journal*, September 1995, p. 19; U.S. Department of Labor website, www.dol.gov, 2000.
9. "Summer Vacation Highlights Global Differences in Paid Time Off," Hewitt Associates, June 6, 2001.
10. Employee Benefit Research Institute, "Health-Care Reform: Trade-Offs and Implications," *EBRI Issue Brief*, no. 125 (Washington, DC, April 1992), summarizing data collected by Gallup.
11. C. Tejada, "Mental-Health Claims Grow Slowly amid White House Push for Benefits," *The Wall Street Journal Online*, May 8, 2002, http://online.wsj.com.
12. Employee Benefit Research Institute, "Health-Care Reform."
13. Beam and McFadden, *Employee Benefits*.
14. P. Biggins, "Flexible/Cafeteria Plans," in *Employee Benefits Handbook*.
15. J. C. Erfurt, A. Foote, and M. A. Heirich, "The Cost-Effectiveness of Worksite Wellness Programs for Hypertension Control, Weight Loss, Smoking Cessation and Exercise," *Personnel Psychology* 45 (1992), pp. 5–27.
16. D. Wessel, "Enron and a Bigger Ill: Americans Don't Save," *The Wall Street Journal Online*, March 7, 2002, http://online.wsj.com.
17. M. Slate, "The Retirement Protection Act," *Labor Law Journal*, April 1995, pp. 245–50.

18. Internal Revenue Service website, www.irs.gov.

19. R. A. Ippolito, "Toward Explaining the Growth of Defined Contribution Plans," *Industrial Relations* 34 (1995), pp. 1–20.

20. Wessel, "Enron and a Bigger Ill."

21. Pension Benefit Guarantee Corporation website, www.pbgc.gov.

22. "Supreme Court Lets Stand Third Circuit Ruling That Pension Avoidance Scheme Is ERISA Violation," *Daily Labor Report*, no. 234 (December 8, 1987), p. A-14, summarizing *Continental Can Company v. Gavalik*.

23. Beam and McFadden, *Employee Benefits*.

24. S. L. Grover and K. J. Crooker, "Who Appreciates Family Responsive Human Resource Policies: The Impact of Family-Friendly Policies on the Organizational Attachment of Parents and Non-parents," *Personnel Psychology* 48 (1995), pp. 271–88.

25. International Labor Office, "More than 120 Nations Provide Paid Maternity Leave," ILO website, www.ilo.org, 1998.

26. Families and Work Institute (FWI), "The Families and Work Institute's 1998 Business Work-Life Study," FWI website, www.familiesandwork.org.

27. "Benefits and the Bottom Line," *(Raleigh, N.C.) News and Observer*, October 14, 2001.

28. E. E. Kossek, "Diversity in Child Care Assistance Needs: Employee Problems, Preferences, and Work-Related Outcomes," *Personnel Psychology* 43 (1990), pp. 769–91.

29. E. E. Kossek, *The Acceptance of Human Resource Innovation: Lessons from Management* (Westport, CT: Quorum, 1989).

30. G. Flynn, "Some of Your Best Ideas May Be Working against You," *Personnel Journal*, October 1995, pp. 77–83.

31. T. Cullen, "Workplace 529 Plans May Have Lower Fees, but Also Drawbacks," *The Wall Street Journal Online*, May 9, 2002, http://online.wsj.com.

32. S. Shellenbarger, "Web Sites Can Help to Ease Burden of Caring for Elders," *The Wall Street Journal Online*, February 27, 2002, http://online.wsj.com.

33. S. Shellenbarger, "From Catnaps to Lunchtime Jobs: Tales about 'Undertime' at Work," *The Wall Street Journal Online*, May 16, 2002, http://online.wsj.com.

34. R. Broderick and B. Gerhart, "Nonwage Compensation," in *The Human Resource Management Handbook*, ed. D. Lewin, D. J. B. Mitchell, and M. A. Zadi (San Francisco: JAI Press, 1996).

35. L. Buchanan, "Managing One-to-One," *Inc.*, October 16, 2001, pp. 83–89.

36. Beam and McFadden, *Employee Benefits*.

37. Buchanan, "Managing One-to-One."

38. D. A. Harrison and L. Z. Liska, "Promoting Regular Exercise in Organizational Fitness Programs: Health-Related Differences in Motivational Building Blocks," *Personnel Psychology* 47 (1994), pp. 47–71; Erfurt et al., "The Cost-Effectiveness of Worksite Wellness Programs."

39. Beck, "Your Company Needs Its Own Best Practices"; Chase, "Healthy Assets."

40. Beam and McFadden, *Employee Benefits*, p. 359.

41. For a description of these rules, see M. M. Sarli, "Nondiscrimination Rules for Qualified Plans: The General Test," *Compensation and Benefits Review* 23, no. 5 (September–October 1991), pp. 56–67.

42. *Los Angeles Department of Water & Power v. Manhart*, 435 U.S. S. Ct. 702 (1978), 16 E.P.D. 8250.

43. S. K. Hoffman, "Discrimination Litigation Relating to Employee Benefits," *Labor Law Journal*, June 1992, pp. 362–81.

44. P. J. Kennedy, "Take the Money and Sue," *HRMagazine* 43, no. 5 (April 1998), pp. 105–8.

45. Hoffman, "Discrimination Litigation," p. 375.

46. Ibid.

47. M. Wilson, G. B. Northcraft, and M. A. Neale, "The Perceived Value of Fringe Benefits," *Personnel Psychology* 38 (1985), pp. 309–20; H. W. Hennessey, P. L. Perrewe, and W. A. Hochwarter, "Impact of Benefit Awareness on Employee and Organizational Outcomes: A Longitudinal Field Experiment," *Benefits Quarterly* 8, no. 2 (1992), pp. 90–96.

48. M. C. Giallourakis and G. S. Taylor, "An Evaluation of Benefit Communication Strategy," *Employee Benefits Journal* 15, no. 4 (1991), pp. 14–18.

Compensating Workers through Pay and Benefits

Today's human resource managers face a wide range of challenges in helping their organizations determine what types of compensation and benefits best suit their employees' needs. Because of the diversity of today's workers in mid-sized to large organizations, the choices can be mind boggling, but HR managers must work to get the right mix to attract and retain talented employees. Older employees are more concerned about how their retirement accounts are shaping up; working parents are desperate for child care; younger workers want opportunities to move up the ladder fast. Thus, HR managers and other executives must come up with creative ways to motivate and empower employees through compensation and benefits plans.

The following companies have combined some innovative perks with traditional ones.

- The S. C. Johnson Company in Racine, Wisconsin, has a company-owned, employee-directed 146-acre park with an outdoor recreation center, child-care center, softball fields, tennis courts, golf driving range, miniature golf course, and other attractions. It also offers a paid sabbatical program and an expanded maternity/paternity/adoption policy, with time off for the adoption process.
- CIGNA Insurance Company employs 33,000 people worldwide and also combines a variety of traditional and alternative benefits for its employees, from medical and dental insurance plans to a company chef who will make

meals to order for employees to take home to their families at the end of the day. CIGNA also offers flexible work arrangements, health and wellness programs, and a tuition reimbursement program for workers who want to continue their education.
- Employees at Wilton Connor Packaging, Inc., in Charlotte, North Carolina, can actually bring their dirty laundry to work and have it cleaned for $1 per load. The company also offers child-care services, on-site tutoring for children, and English classes for employees. In addition, Wilton Connor conducts a six-week summer school program for children of full-time employees. Workers at Wilton Connor seem to be satisfied; only two leave the company on average every year.
- Financial services firm Salomon Smith Barney provides time off for special needs, such as caring for an ailing relative; child care discounts and referral services; adoption assistance; a Volunteer Incentive Program that encourages employees to volunteer for nonprofit organizations; a LifeWorks Program that is designed to help workers balance work and personal responsibilities; on-site medical attention and prescription fulfillment; and investment opportunities.
- Accenture (formerly Andersen Consulting) actually employs a concierge to run errands such as grocery shopping or dry-cleaning pickup for employees who have to stay late or can't take time out at lunch for these errands. The company also focuses on professional

development of its new hires and offers Student Leadership Conferences to final-year college students in the United States, Europe, and Asia.
- Both Coca-Cola and Home Depot provide wellness and fitness programs designed to reduce stress and enhance employee health. Coca-Cola has found that employees who use these programs are not only healthier but more productive on the job. Home Depot has taken its program a step further by offering on-site classes in smoking cessation, nutrition, proper exercise, and balancing work and home life. The Center for Disease Control in Atlanta strongly recommends these types of classes for the well-being of workers.

On another front, Home Depot has recently launched a new type of class for employees: an in-house course in personal finance. The company states that the financial health of its 250,000 employees is a priority. "We want to be an employer of choice, and we see helping associates [employees] manage their finances as one more way to do that," explains Layne Thome, director of associate services for the company. "We want to win the war for talent. We see this as another tool for improving recruitment and retention." Managers were spurred to develop the course after realizing that many of the company's employees were having financial trouble. "We . . . found that associates were cashing out of their retirement accounts early and they were making early withdrawals on their stock purchase plans, which also concerned us," says Thome. "We saw we had a population in trouble." So the company has done something about it. Partnering with the Fannie Mae Foundation and the Consumer Credit Counseling Service, Home Depot has custom-developed classes for its employees.

Developing the right compensation packages for employees can help ensure low turnover and higher productivity—just what every company wants.

SOURCES: S. C. Johnson website, www.scjohnsonwax.com, accessed November 29, 2001; Cigna website, www.cigna.com, accessed November 29, 2001; Salomon Smith Barney website, http://careers.ssmb.com, accessed November 29, 2001; Accenture website, http://careers.accenture.com, accessed November 29, 2001; Home Depot website, www.homedepot.com, accessed November 29, 2001; J. Lee Howard, "Expansion at Westlake to Add 400 Jobs," *The Business Journal of Charlotte*, June 2, 2000, http://charlotte.bcentral.com.

QUESTIONS

1. You've seen a range of advantages of the creative benefits programs just described. But what might be some disadvantages?
2. What special challenges might companies such as Coca-Cola face in developing and implementing compensation packages for employees in other countries?
3. As an employee, which is more important to you: your pay or other benefits? Why? Do you think this ratio might change as you grow older and progress in your career?
4. Do you think these types of benefits have the greatest influence on: attracting new employees? Motivating current employees? Keeping current employees? Explain your answer.

Part

5

Meeting Other HR Goals

Chapter 14
Collective Bargaining and Labor Relations

Chapter 15
Managing Human Resources Globally

Chapter 16
Creating and Maintaining High-Performance Organizations

Chapter 14

Collective Bargaining and Labor Relations

What Do I Need to Know? After reading this chapter, you should be able to:

1. Define unions and labor relations and their role in organizations.

2. Identify the labor relations goals of management, labor unions, and society.

3. Summarize laws and regulations that affect labor relations.

4. Describe the union organizing process.

5. Explain how management and unions negotiate contracts.

6. Summarize the practice of contract administration.

7. Describe more cooperative approaches to labor-management relations.

Introduction

The pay for Southwest Airlines pilots is set out in the company's 10-year contract with the Southwest Airlines Pilots Association, negotiated in 1994. But on more than one occasion, the union and Southwest have negotiated revisions to that contract. The pilots originally agreed to a five-year pay freeze in exchange for stock options—a mutually beneficial trade-off, considering the company's excellent performance. In 1998 the pilots negotiated pay increases of 3 percent a year from 1999 through 2003. Still, even with those raises, Southwest pilots earn less than pilots in the rest of the airline industry. The pilots' goal, in the words of the union's president, is "to be industry average in pay but industry leading in pay and [stock] options combined." Responding to the union's request for more money, Southwest offered to raise pay at least 20 percent in 2003 and 2004. The company will also extend the contract with more pay raises in the two following years. Southwest spokeswoman Linda Rutherford said this offer "helps us predict our future labor costs and provide pay increases for the best pilot group in the airline industry."[1]

In contrast to the discussion of compensation in Part 4, the pay decisions made by Southwest come in response to demands by the pilots as a group (that is, by their union). The presence of unions at Southwest changes this aspect of human resource management by directing more attention to the interests of employees as a group. To some degree, employers and employees share the same interests. They both benefit when the organization is strong and growing, providing employees with jobs and employers with profits. And the pilots have stock options, so the pilots and company alike benefit from a higher stock price. But although the interests of employers and employees overlap, they obviously are not identical. In the case of pay, workers benefit from higher pay, but high pay cuts into the organization's profits, unless pay increases are associated with higher productivity or better customer service. Workers may negotiate these differences with their employers individually, or they may form unions to negotiate on their behalf. In the example of Southwest, the pilots union and the company agreed that pilots' compensation should be partly tied to company performance (by giving stock options).

This chapter explores human resource activities in organizations where employees belong to unions or where employees are seeking to organize unions. We begin by formally defining unions and labor relations, then describe the scope and impact of union activity. We next summarize government laws and regulations affecting unions and labor relations. The following three sections detail types of activities involving unions: union organizing, contract negotiation, and contract administration. Finally, we identify ways in which unions and management are working together in arrangements that are more cooperative than the traditional labor-management relationship.

Role of Unions and Labor Relations

LO1

In the United States today, most workers act as individuals to select jobs that are acceptable to them and to negotiate pay, benefits, flexible hours, and other work conditions. Especially when there is stiff competition for labor and employees have hard-to-replace skills, this arrangement produces satisfactory results for most employees. At times, however, workers have believed their needs and interests do not receive enough consideration from management. One response by workers is to act collectively by forming and joining labor **unions,** organizations formed for the purpose of representing their members' interests and resolving conflicts with employers.

Unions have a role because some degree of conflict is inevitable between workers and management.[2] As we commented earlier, for example, managers can increase profits by lowering workers' pay, but workers benefit in the short-term if lower profits result because their pay is higher. Still, this type of conflict is more complex than a simple trade-off, such as wages versus profits. Rising profits can help employees by driving up profit sharing or other benefits, and falling profits can result in layoffs and a lack of investment. Although employers can use programs like profit sharing to help align employee interests with their own, some remaining divergence of interests is inevitable. Labor unions represent worker interests and the collective bargaining process provides a way to manage the conflict. In other words, through systems for hearing complaints and negotiating labor contracts, unions and managers resolve conflicts between employers and employees.

unions
Organizations formed for the purpose of representing their members' interests in dealing with employers.

labor relations
Field that emphasizes skills managers and union leaders can use to minimize costly forms of conflict (such as strikes) and seek win-win solutions to disagreements.

As unionization of workers became more common, universities developed training in how to manage union-management interactions.[3] This specialty, called **labor relations,** emphasizes skills that managers and union leaders can use to foster effective labor-management cooperation, minimize costly forms of conflict (such as strikes), and seek win-win solutions to disagreements. Labor relations involves three levels of decisions:[4]

1. *Labor relations strategy*—For management, the decision involves whether the organization will work with unions or develop (or maintain) nonunion operations. This decision is influenced by outside forces such as public opinion and competition. For unions, the decision involves whether to fight changes in how unions relate to the organization or accept new kinds of labor-management relationships.
2. *Negotiating contracts*—As we will describe later in the chapter, contract negotiations in a union setting involve decisions about pay structure, job security, work rules, workplace safety, and many other issues. These decisions affect workers' and the employer's situation for the term of the contract.
3. *Administering contracts*—These decisions involve day-to-day activities in which union members and the organization's managers may have disagreements. Issues include complaints of work rules being violated or workers being treated unfairly in particular situations. A formal grievance procedure is typically used to resolve these issues.

Later sections in this chapter describe how managers and unions carry out the activities connected with these levels of decisions, as well as the goals and legal constraints affecting these activities.

National and International Unions

Most union members belong to a national or international union. Figure 14.1 shows the membership of the 10 largest national unions in the United States. Half of these have memberships of over a million workers.

craft union
Labor union whose members all have a particular skill or occupation.

These unions may be either craft of industrial unions. The members of a **craft union** all have a particular skill or occupation. Examples include the International Brotherhood of Electrical Workers for electricians and the United Brotherhood of Carpenters and Joiners of America for carpenters. Craft unions are often responsible for training their members through apprenticeships and for supplying craft workers to employers. For example, an employer would send requests for carpenters to the union hiring hall, which would decide which carpenters to send out. In this way, craft workers may work for many employers over time but have a constant link to the union. A craft union's bargaining power depends greatly on its control over the supply of its workers.

John Sweeney (left), president of the AFL-CIO, works with his organization to improve the lives of working families and to bring economic justice to the workplace. Most national unions are affiliated with the AFL-CIO.

FIGURE 14.1

10 Largest Unions in the United States

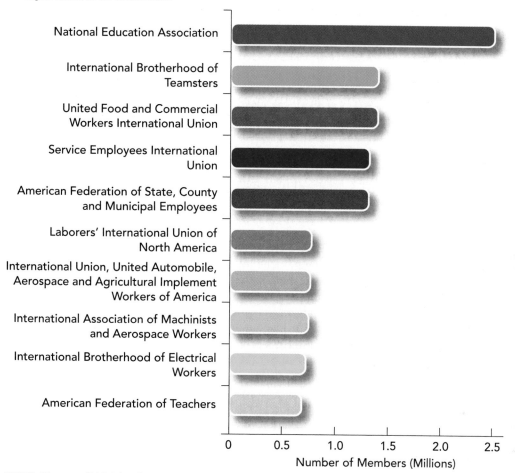

SOURCE: *Directory of U.S. Labor Organizations*, 2000 ed. Copyright © 2000 by the Bureau of National Affairs, Inc., Washington, DC, 20037.

In contrast, **industrial unions** consist of members who are linked by their work in a particular industry. Examples include the United Steelworkers of America and the Communication Workers of America. Typically, an industrial union represents many different occupations. Membership in the union is the result of working for a particular employer in the industry. Changing employers is less common than it is among craft workers, and employees who change employers remain members of the same union only if they happen to move to other employers covered by that union. Another difference is that whereas a craft union may restrict the number of skilled craftsmen—say, carpenters—to maintain higher wages, industrial unions try to organize as many employees in as wide a range of skills as possible.

Most national unions are affiliated with the **American Federation of Labor and Congress of Industrial Organizations (AFL-CIO).** The AFL-CIO is not a labor union but an association that seeks to advance the shared interests of its member unions at the national level, much as the Chamber of Commerce and the National Association of Manufacturers do for their member employers. Approximately 72 national and international unions are affiliated with the AFL-CIO. An important responsibility of the AFL-CIO is to represent labor's interests in public policy issues

industrial union
Labor union whose members are linked by their work in a particular industry.

American Federation of Labor and Congress of Industrial Organizations (AFL-CIO)
An association that seeks to advance the shared interests of its member unions at the national level.

such as labor law, economic policy, and occupational safety and health. The organization also provides information and analysis that member unions can use in their activities.

Local Unions

Most national unions consist of multiple local units. Even when a national union plays the most critical role in negotiating the terms of a collective bargaining contract, negotiation occurs at the local level for work rules and other issues that are locally determined. In addition, administration of the contract largely takes place at the local union level. As a result, most day-to-day interaction between labor and management involves the local union.

Membership in the local union depends on the type of union. For an industrial union, the local may correspond to a single large facility or to a number of small facilities. In a craft union, the local may cover a city or a region.

Typically, the local union elects officers, such as president, vice president, and treasurer. The officers may be responsible for contract negotiation, or the local may form a bargaining committee for that purpose. When the union is engaged in bargaining, the national union provides help, including background data about other settlements, technical advice, and the leadership of a representative from the national office.

Individual members participate in local unions in various ways. At meetings of the local union, they elect officials and vote on resolutions to strike. Most of workers' contact is with the **union steward,** an employee elected by union members to represent them in ensuring that the terms of the contract are enforced. The union steward helps to investigate complaints and represents employees to supervisors and other managers when employees file grievances alleging contract violations.[5] When the union deals with several employers, as in the case of a craft union, a *business representative* performs some of the same functions as a union steward. Because of union stewards' and business representatives' close involvement with employees, it is to management's advantage to cultivate positive working relationships with them.

union steward
An employee elected by union members to represent them in ensuring that the terms of the labor contract are enforced.

Trends in Union Membership

Union membership in the United States peaked in the 1950s, reaching over one-third of employees. Since then, the share of employees who belong to unions has fallen. It now stands at 14 percent overall and 9 percent of private-sector employment.[6] As Figure 14.2 indicates, union membership fell steadily during the 1980s and 1990s. Union membership among government workers has held steady, with the decline occurring in the private sector.

The decline in union membership has been attributed to several factors.[7] The factor that seems to be cited most often is change in the structure of the economy. Much recent job growth has occurred among women and youth in the service sector of the economy, while union strength has traditionally been among urban blue-collar workers, especially middle-aged workers. Women are less likely than men to belong to unions, and services industries such as finance, insurance, and real estate have lower union representation than manufacturing. Also, much business growth has been in the South, where workers are less likely to join unions.[8]

Another force working against union membership is management efforts against union organizing. In a survey, almost half of large employers said their most important labor goal was to be union-free. Efforts to control costs have contributed to employer

FIGURE 14.2

Union Membership Density among U.S. Wage and Salary Workers, 1973–2000

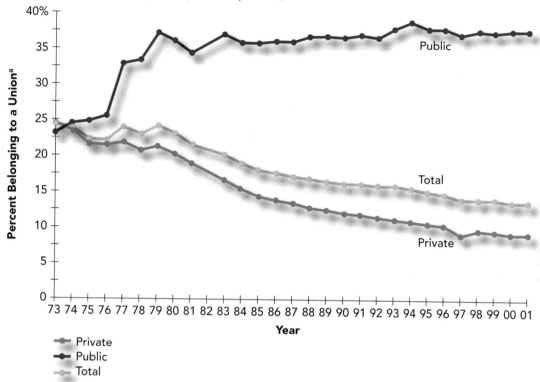

[a]Percentage of total, private-sector, and public-sector wage and salary workers who are union members. Beginning in 1977, workers belonging to "an employee association similar to a union" are included as members.

SOURCE: 1973–81—May Current Population Surveys (CPS); 1983–2001—CPS Outgoing Rotation Group (ORG) Earning Files. Values for 1982 are linearly interpolated from 1981 and 1983 values. From B. T. Hirsch and D. A. MacPherson, *Union Membership and Earnings Data Book 2001* (Washington, DC: Bureau of National Affairs, 2002). Reprinted with permission.

resistance to unions.[9] On average, unionized workers receive higher pay than their nonunionized counterparts, and the pressure is greater because of international competition. In the past, union membership across an industry such as automobiles or steel resulted in similar wages and work requirements for all competitors. Today, U.S. producers must compete with companies that have entirely different pay scales and work rules, often placing the U.S. companies at a disadvantage. Another way in which management may contribute to the decline in union membership is by adopting human resource practices that increase employees' commitment to their job and employer. Competition for scarce human resources can lead employers to offer much of what employees traditionally sought through union membership. Government regulations, too, can make unions seem less important. Stricter regulation in such areas as workplace safety and equal employment opportunity leaves fewer areas in which unions can show an advantage over what employers must already offer.

Trends such as these have raised questions about the role of unions in the Internet Age. As described in the "e-HRM" box on page 446, unions have experienced setbacks in efforts to organize e-commerce workers. Still, the role of unions in the new economy is not yet decided.

Will Unions Play a Role in High-Tech Industries?

Unions used to be the domain of auto workers, truck drivers, electricians, teachers, movie actors, and other employees in traditional jobs. But with the changing economy, union membership has had to change as well. Will unions survive in the new economy? If so, what will their role be?

Although unions have turned to the information technology industry for potential growth, they have been snubbed on many occasions. Perhaps this is because traditional union values seem outdated. For instance, the mostly young IT workforce lacks older workers' level of concern for job security. "The philosophy is, 'Til death do us part—until I get a better offer," says Harris Miller, president of the Information Technology Association of America, an industry trade group. "That's a very different attitude from saying, 'I'll work for this steel mill for the rest of my life,' and it makes it very hard for high-tech workers to see the appeal of joining a union."

The Communication Workers of America's efforts to organize workers at Amazon.com have failed thus far, along with a similar drive at CNBC, the cable counterpart of NBC. The failure of the CNBC drive is a mystery to many because cable TV workers are generally paid much less than their network counterparts. But local CWA vice president Bill Freeh says, "It was a very hard sell. These were workers who weren't looking for the security a union can provide. They just didn't want to jeopardize their jobs." During the organization drive, CNBC hosted pizza parties and bowling nights for employees, many of whom were recent college graduates.

In spite of setbacks like these, organized labor has not lost hope of a significant part in the new economy. Marcus Courtney, cofounder and president of WashTech, an advocacy and advice group based in Washington, admits that it is difficult to convince high-tech workers to join a union. Even so, Courtney says, "Some things don't change, and one of them is that individuals have no power unless they're organized." The challenge may be to figure out what high-tech workers want a union to achieve with its power. To interest tech workers, unions may have to focus more on issues of quality of life, seeking benefits such as child care or time off to take care of aging parents.

This kind of adaptability can help unions meet workers' needs while meeting the unions' own need for growth. According to Katie Quan, labor policy specialist at the Center for Labor Research and Education at the University of California at Berkeley, the e-commerce sector is a "sunrise industry." Says Quan, "It's quite important for the labor movement to get a foothold and grow with it."

SOURCES: L. M. Prencipe, "E-Mail and the Internet Age Changing the Labor/Management Power Play," *InfoWorld*, March 12, 2001, www.infoworld.com; T. Wolverton, "Labor Pains," *CNet News.com*, January 16, 2001, http://news.cnet.com; Y. J. Dreezen, "Old Labor Tries to Establish Role in New Economy," *The Wall Street Journal*, August 15, 2001, pp. B1, B10.

As Figure 14.3 indicates, the percentage of U.S. workers who belong to unions is lower than in many countries. More dramatic is the difference in "coverage"—the percentage of employees whose terms and conditions of employment are governed by a union contract, whether or not the employees are technically union members. In Western Europe, it is common to have coverage rates of 80 to 90 percent, so the influence of labor unions far outstrips what membership levels would imply.[10] Also, em-

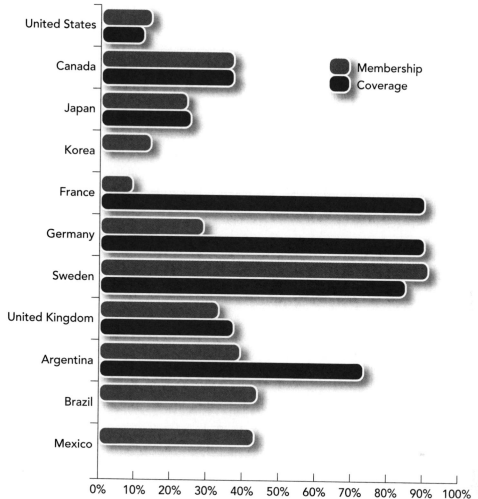

SOURCE: International Labour Office, *World Labour Report, 1997–98* (Geneva, Switzerland).

FIGURE 14.3

Union Membership Rates and Coverage in Selected Countries

ployees in Western Europe tend to have a larger formal role in decision making than in the United States. This role, including worker representatives on boards of directors, is often mandated by the government. But as markets become more and more global, pressure to cut labor costs and increase productivity is likely to be stronger in every country. Unless unions can help companies improve productivity or organize new production facilities opened in lower-wage countries, union influence may decline in countries where it is now strong.

Although union members are a smaller share of the U.S. workforce, they are a significant part of many industries' labor markets. Along with strength in numbers, large unions have strength in dollars. Union retirement funds, taken together, are huge. Unions try to use their investment decisions in ways that influence businesses. For example, in a recent year, union retirement funds held $1.4 trillion worth of corporate stock, or about 14 percent of outstanding shares. Unions share control of these assets with company-appointed trustees, but they hope to use their power to influence the policies of the companies whose stock they hold.[11]

Unions in Government

Unlike union membership for workers in businesses, union membership among government workers has remained strong. Union membership in the public sector grew during the 1960s and 1970s and has remained steady ever since. Over one-third of government employees are union members, and a larger share are covered by collective bargaining agreements. One reason for this strength is that government regulations and laws support the right of government workers to organize. In 1962 Executive Order 10988 established collective bargaining rights for federal employees. By the end of the 1960s, most states had passed similar laws.

An interesting aspect of union growth among government workers is that much of it has occurred in the service industry and among white-collar employees—groups that have been viewed as difficult to organize. The American Federation of State, County and Municipal Employees (AFSCME) has 1.3 million members. These include 325,000 members in health care, 325,000 in clerical jobs, and more than 400,000 in all white-collar occupations.[12]

Labor relations with government workers is different in some respects, such as regarding the right to strike. Strikes are illegal for federal workers and for state workers in most states. At the local level, all states prohibit strikes by police (Hawaii being a partial exception) and firefighters (Idaho being the exception). Teachers and state employees are somewhat more likely to have the right to strike, depending on the state. Legal or not, strikes by government workers do occur. Of the 39 strikes involving 1,000 or more workers in 2000, eight involved workers in state and local government.

Impact of Unions on Company Performance

Organizations are concerned about whether union organizing and bargaining will hurt their performance, in particular, unions' impact on productivity, profits, and stock performance. Researchers have studied the general relationship between unionization and these performance measures. Through skillful labor relations, organizations can positively influence outcomes.

There has been much debate regarding the effects of unions on productivity.[13] The view that unions decrease productivity is based on work rules and limits on workloads set by union contracts and production lost to such union actions as strikes and work slowdowns. At the same time, unions can have positive effects on productivity.[14] They can reduce turnover by giving employees a route for resolving problems.[15] Unions emphasize pay systems based on seniority, which remove incentives for employees to compete rather than cooperate. The introduction of a union also may force an employer to improve its management practices and pay greater attention to employee ideas.

Although there is evidence that unions have both positive and negative effects on productivity, most studies have found that union workers are more productive than nonunion workers. Are highly productive workers more likely to form unions, or does a union make workers more productive? The answer is unclear. In theory, if unions caused greater productivity, we would expect union membership to be rising, not falling as it has been.[16]

Even if unions do raise productivity, a company's profits and stock performance may still suffer if unions raise wage and benefits costs by more than the productivity gain. On average, union members receive higher wages and more generous benefits

Harley-Davidson and the International Association of Machinists and Aerospace Workers have cooperated to produce good results. In general, though, companies wishing to become more competitive need to continually monitor their labor relations strategies.

than nonunion workers, and evidence shows that unions have a large negative effect on profits. Also, union coverage tends to decline faster in companies with a lower return to shareholders.[17] In summary, companies wishing to become more competitive must continually monitor their labor relations strategy.

These studies look at the average effects of unions, not at individual companies or innovative labor relations. Some organizations can report success stories in labor relations. Harley-Davidson, for example, has developed a cooperative relationship with the International Association of Machinists and Aerospace Workers (IAM).[18] The two parties negotiated a contract that provides for employment security and joint labor-management decision making in many areas. The company shares technical and financial information and expects a high level of participation in improving productivity and satisfying customers. The IAM's Lou Kiefer explains, "We know that if we increase productivity and lower costs, we're not working ourselves out of a job." Under this arrangement, Harley-Davidson earned record profits in 2001, while the overall U.S. economy was experiencing a recession.

Goals of Each Group   LO2

Resolving conflicts in a positive way is usually easiest when the parties involved understand each other's goals. Although individual cases vary, we can draw some general conclusions about the goals of labor unions and management. Society, too, has goals for labor and business, given form in the laws regulating labor relations.

Goals of Management

Management goals are to increase the organization's profits. Managers tend to prefer options that lower costs and raise output. When deciding whether to discourage employees from forming a union, a concern is that a union will create higher costs for wages and benefits, as well as raise the risk of work stoppages. Managers may also fear that a union will make managers and workers into adversaries or limit management's discretion in making business and employment decisions.

When an employer has recognized a union, management's goals continue to emphasize restraining costs and improving output. Managers continue to prefer to keep the organization's operations flexible, so they can adjust activities to meet competitive challenges and customer demands. Therefore, in their labor relations managers prefer to limit increases in wages and benefits and to retain as much control as they can over work rules and schedules.

Goals of Labor Unions

checkoff provision
Contract provision under which the employer, on behalf of the union, automatically deducts union dues from employees' paychecks.

closed shop
Union security arrangement under which a person must be a union member before being hired; illegal for those covered by the National Labor Relations Act.

union shop
Union security arrangement that requires employees to join the union within a certain amount of time (30 days) after beginning employment.

agency shop
Union security arrangement that requires the payment of union dues but not union membership.

maintenance of membership
Union security rules not requiring union membership but requiring that employees who join the union remain members for a certain period of time.

In general, labor unions have the goals of obtaining pay and working conditions that satisfy their members and of giving members a voice in decisions that affect them. Traditionally, they obtain these goals by gaining power in numbers. The more workers who belong to a union, the greater the union's power. More members translates into greater ability to halt or disrupt production. Larger unions also have greater financial resources for continuing a strike; the union can help to make up for the wages the workers lose during a strike. The threat of a long strike—stated or implied—can make an employer more willing to meet the union's demands.

As we noted earlier, union membership is indeed linked to better compensation. In 2000, private-sector unionized workers received, on average, wages 19 percent higher than nonunion workers in similar jobs.[19] Union membership has an even greater effect on benefits packages. Total compensation (pay plus benefits) was 36 percent higher for union members in 2000. Taking into account other influences, such as the greater ease with which unions are able to organize relatively highly paid, productive workers, researchers estimate that the total "union effect" on wages is about 10 percent.[20] In other words, for every $1 paid to a nonunion worker, a union worker in the same job would earn about $1.10.

Unions typically want to influence the *way* pay and promotions are determined. Unlike management, which tries to consider employees as individuals so that pay and promotion decisions relate to performance differences, unions try to build group solidarity and avoid possible arbitrary treatment of employees. To do so, unions focus on equal pay for equal work. They try to have any pay differences based on seniority, on the grounds that this measure is more objective than performance evaluations. As a result, where workers are represented by a union, it is common for all employees in a particular job classification to be paid at the same rate.

The survival and security of a union depend on its ability to ensure a regular flow of new members and member dues to support the services it provides. Therefore, unions typically place high priority on negotiating two types of contract provisions with an employer that are critical to a union's security and viability: checkoff provisions and provisions relating to union membership or contribution.

Under a **checkoff provision,** the employer, on behalf of the union, automatically deducts union dues from employees' paychecks. Security provisions related to union membership are *closed shop, union shop, agency shop,* and *maintenance of membership.*

The strongest union security arrangement is a **closed shop,** under which a person must be a union member before being hired. Under the National Labor Relations Act, discussed later in this chapter, closed shops are illegal. A legal membership arrangement that supports the goals of labor unions is the **union shop,** an arrangement that requires an employee to join the union within a certain time (30 days) after beginning employment. A similar alternative is the **agency shop,** which requires the payment of union dues but not union membership. **Maintenance of membership** rules do not require union membership but do require that employees who join the union remain members for a certain period of time, such as the length of the contract. As we will discuss later in the chapter, some states forbid union shops, agency shops, and maintenance of membership.

All these provisions are ways to address unions' concern about "free riders"—employees who benefit from union activities without belonging to a union. By law, all members of a bargaining unit, whether union members or not, must be represented by the union. If the union must offer services to all bargaining unit members but some of them are not dues-paying union members, the union may not have enough financial resources to operate successfully.

Goals of Society

The activities of unions and management take place within the context of society, with society's values driving the laws and regulations that affect labor relations. As long ago as the late 1800s and early 1900s, industrial relations scholars saw unions as a way to make up for individual employees' limited bargaining power.[21] At that time, clashes between workers and management could be violent, and many people hoped that unions would replace the violence with negotiation. Since then, observers have expressed concern that unions in certain industries have become too strong, achieving their goals at the expense of employers' ability to compete or meet other objectives. But even Senator Orrin Hatch, described by *BusinessWeek* as "labor's archrival on Capitol Hill," has spoken of a need for unions:

> There are always going to be people who take advantage of workers. Unions even that out, to their credit. We need them to level the field between labor and management. If you didn't have unions, it would be very difficult for even enlightened employers not to take advantage of workers on wages and working conditions, because of [competition from less-enlightened] rivals. I'm among the first to say I believe in unions.[22]

Senator Hatch's statement implies that society's goal for unions is to ensure that workers have a voice in how they are treated by their employers. As we will see in the next section, this view has produced a set of laws and regulations intended to give workers the right to join unions if they so wish.

Laws and Regulations Affecting Labor Relations

LO3

The laws and regulations pertaining to labor relations affect unions' size and bargaining power, so they significantly affect the degree to which unions, management, and society achieve their varied goals. These laws and regulations set limits on union structure and administration and the ways in which unions and management interact.

National Labor Relations Act (NLRA)

Perhaps the most dramatic example of labor laws' influence is the 1935 passage of the Wagner Act (also known as the **National Labor Relations Act,** or **NLRA),** which actively supported collective bargaining. After Congress passed the NLRA, union membership in the United States nearly tripled, from 3 million in 1933 to 8.8 million (19.2 percent of employment) in 1939.[23]

Before the 1930s, the U.S. legal system was generally hostile to unions. The courts tended to view unions as coercive organizations that hindered free trade. Unions' focus on collective voice and collective action (such as strikes and boycotts) did not fit well with the U.S. emphasis on capitalism, individualism, freedom of contract, and property rights.[24] Then the Great Depression of the 1930s shifted public attitudes toward business and the free-enterprise system. Unemployment rates as high as 25 percent and a steep fall in production between 1929 and 1933 focused attention on

National Labor Relations Act (NLRA)
Federal law that supports collective bargaining and sets out the rights of employees to form unions.

TABLE 14.1

Workers Excluded from the NLRA's Coverage

Workers employed under the following conditions are not covered by the NLRA:
- Employed as a supervisor.
- Employed by a parent or spouse.
- Employed as an independent contractor.
- Employed in the domestic service of any person or family in a home.
- Employed as agricultural laborers.
- Employed by an employer subject to the Railway Labor Act.
- Employed by a federal, state, or local government.
- Employed by any other person who is not an employer as defined in the NLRA.

SOURCE: National Labor Relations Board website, www.nlrb.gov.

employee rights and the shortcomings of the economic system of the time. The nation was in crisis, and President Franklin Roosevelt responded dramatically with the New Deal. On the labor front, the 1935 NLRA ushered in an era of public policy for labor unions, enshrining collective bargaining as the preferred way to settle labor-management disputes.

Section 7 of the NLRA sets out the rights of employees, including the "right to self-organization, to form, join, or assist labor organizations, to bargain collectively through representatives of their own choosing, and to engage in other concerted activities for the purpose of collective bargaining."[25] Employees also have the right to refrain from these activities, unless union membership is a condition of employment. The following activities are among those protected under the NLRA:

- Union organizing.
- Joining a union, whether recognized by the employer or not.
- Going out on strike to secure better working conditions.
- Refraining from activity on behalf of the union.

Most employees in the private sector are covered by the NLRA. As shown in Table 14.1, however, certain workers are excluded, including supervisors, independent contractors, agricultural workers, and government employees. State or local laws may provide additional coverage. For example, California's 1975 Agricultural Labor Relations Act covers agricultural workers in that state.

In Section 8(a), the NLRA prohibits certain activities by employers as unfair labor practices. In general, employers may not interfere with, restrain, or coerce employees in exercising their rights to join or assist a labor organization or to refrain from such activities. Employers may not dominate or interfere with the formation or activities of a labor union. They may not discriminate in any aspect of employment that attempts to encourage or discourage union activity, nor may they discriminate against employees for providing testimony related to enforcement of the NLRA. Finally, employers may not refuse to bargain collectively with a labor organization that has standing under the act. For more guidance in complying with the NLRA, see the examples in the "HR How To" box.

When employers or unions violate the NLRA, remedies typically include ordering that unfair labor practices stop. Employers may be required to rehire workers, with or without back pay. The NLRA is not a criminal law, and violators may not be assigned punitive damages (fines to punish, rather than merely make up for the harm done).

HR HOW TO

Avoiding Unfair Labor Practices

The National Labor Relations Act prohibits employers and unions from engaging in unfair labor practices. For employers, this means they must not interfere with employees' decisions about whether to join a union and engage in union-related activities. Employers may not discriminate against employees for being involved in union activities or testifying in court about actions under the NLRA. Here are some specific examples of unfair labor practices that *employers must avoid:*

- Threatening employees with loss of their jobs or benefits if they join or vote for a union.
- Threatening to close down a plant if it is organized by a union.
- Questioning employees about their union membership or activities in a way that restrains or coerces them.

- Spying or pretending to spy on union meetings.
- Granting wage increases timed to discourage employees from forming or joining a union.
- Taking an active part in organizing a union or committee to represent employees.
- Providing preferential treatment or aid to one of several unions trying to organize employees.
- Discharging employees for urging other employees to join a union.
- Refusing to hire applicants because they are union members.
- Refusing to reinstate workers when job openings occur, on the grounds that the workers participated in a lawful strike.
- Ending operations at one facility and opening the same operations at another facility with new employees because employees at the first joined a union.

- Demoting or firing employees for filing an unfair labor practice complaint or testifying at an NLRB meeting.
- Refusing to meet with employees' representatives because the employees are on strike.
- Refusing to supply the employees' representative with cost and other data concerning a group insurance plan covering employees.
- Announcing a wage increase without consulting the employees' representative.
- Failing to bargain about the effects of a decision to close one of the employer's facilities.

SOURCE: National Labor Relations Board, *A Guide to Basic Law and Procedures under the National Labor Relations Act* (Washington, DC: U.S. Government Printing Office, 1991); National Labor Relations Board website, www.nlrb.gov.

Laws Amending the NLRA

Originally, the NLRA did not list any unfair labor practices by unions. In later amendments to the NLRA—the Taft-Hartley Act of 1947 and the Landrum-Griffin Act of 1959—Congress established some restrictions on union practices deemed unfair to employers and union members.

Under the Taft-Hartley Act, unions may not restrain employers through actions such as the following:[26]

- Mass picketing in such numbers that nonstriking employees physically cannot enter the workplace.
- Engaging in violent acts in connection with a strike.

453

FIGURE 14.4

States with Right-to-Work Laws

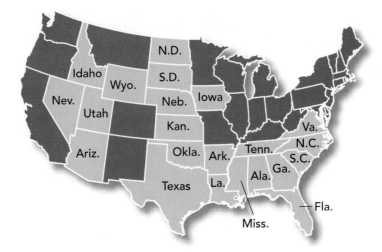

SOURCE: National Right to Work Legal Defense Foundation, cited in K. Chen, "Wooing Companies: Do 'Right-to-Work' Laws Make a Difference?" *The Wall Street Journal Online*, July 10, 2002, http://online.wsj.com.

- Threatening employees with physical injury or job loss if they do not support union activities.
- During contract negotiations, insisting on illegal provisions, provisions that the employer may hire only workers who are union members or "satisfactory" to the union, or working conditions to be determined by a group to which the employer does not belong.
- Terminating an existing contract and striking for a new one without notifying the employer, the Federal Mediation and Conciliation Service, and the state mediation service (where one exists).

right-to-work laws
State laws that make union shops, maintenance of membership, and agency shops illegal.

The Taft-Hartley Act also allows the states to pass so-called **right-to-work laws,** which make union shops, maintenance of membership, and agency shops illegal. The idea behind such laws is that requiring union membership or the payment of union dues restricts the employees' right to freedom of association. In other words, employees should be free to choose whether they join a union or other group. Of course, unions have a different point of view. The union perspective is that unions provide services to all members of a bargaining unit (such as all of a company's workers), and all members who receive the benefits of a union should pay union dues. Figure 14.4 indicates which states currently have right-to-work laws.

The Landrum-Griffin Act regulates unions' actions with regard to their members, including financial disclosure and the conduct of elections. This law establishes and protects rights of union members. These include the right to nominate candidates for union office, participate in union meetings and secret-ballot elections, and examine unions' financial records.

National Labor Relations Board (NLRB)
Federal government agency that enforces the NLRA by conducting and certifying representation elections and investigating unfair labor practices.

National Labor Relations Board (NLRB)

Enforcement of the NLRA rests with the **National Labor Relations Board (NLRB).** This federal government agency consists of a five-member board, the general counsel, and 33 regional offices. Because the NLRB is a federal agency, its enforcement actions are limited to companies that have an impact on interstate commerce, but as a practical matter, this extends to all but purely local businesses. For federal government workers under the Civil Service Reform Act of 1978, Title VII, the Federal Labor

Ballots are counted at the Seattle International Association of Machinists as aerospace machinists voted on the latest Boeing contract offer (Sept. 13, 2002). The members rejected Boeing's contract offer but failed to approve a strike, thus putting the contract into effect.

Relations Authority has a role similar to that of the NLRB. Many states have similar agencies to administer their laws governing state and local government workers.

The NLRB has two major functions: to conduct and certify representation elections and to prevent unfair labor practices. It does not initiate either of these actions but responds to requests for action.

Representation Elections

The NLRB is responsible for ensuring that the organizing process follows certain steps, described in the next section. Depending on the response to organizing efforts, the NLRB conducts elections. When a majority of workers vote in favor of a union, the NLRB certifies it as the exclusive representative of a group of employees. The NLRB also conducts elections to decertify unions, following the same process as for representation elections.

The NLRB is also responsible for determining the appropriate bargaining unit and the employees who are eligible to participate in organizing activities. As we stated earlier, bargaining units may not include certain types of employees, such as agricultural laborers, independent contractors, supervisors, and managers. Beyond this, the NLRB attempts to group together employees who have a community of interest in their wages, hours, and working conditions. A unit may cover employees in one facility or multiple facilities within a single employer, or the unit may cover multiple employers. In general, employees on the payroll just before the ordering of an election are eligible to vote, although this rule is modified in some cases, for example, when employment in the industry is irregular. Most employees who are on strike and who have been replaced by other employees are eligible to vote in an election (such as a decertification election) that occurs within 12 months of the onset of the strike.

Prevention of Unfair Labor Practices

The handling of complaints regarding unfair labor practices begins when someone files a charge. The deadline for filing a charge is six months after the alleged unfair practice. All parties must be served with a copy of the charge. (Registered mail is recommended.) The charge is investigated by a regional office. If, after investigating, the NLRB finds the charge has merit and issues a complaint, two actions are possible. The NLRB may defer to a grievance procedure agreed on by the employer and the union; grievances are discussed later in this chapter. Or a hearing may be held before an administrative law judge. The judge makes a recommendation, which either party may appeal.

The NLRB has the authority to issue cease-and-desist orders to halt unfair labor practices. It also can order the employer to reinstate workers, with or without back pay. The NLRB can set aside the results of an election if it believes either the union or the employer has created "an atmosphere or confusion or fear of reprisals."[27] If an employer or union refuses to comply with an NLRB order, the board has the authority to petition the U.S. Court of Appeals. The court may enforce the order, recommend it to the NLRB for modification, change the order itself, or set it aside altogether.

LO4

Union Organizing

Unions begin their involvement with an organization's employees by conducting an organizing campaign. To meet its objectives, a union needs to convince a majority of workers that they should receive better pay or other employment conditions and that the union will help them do so. The employer's objectives will depend on its strategy—whether it seeks to work with a union or convince employees that they are better off without union representation.

The Process of Organizing

The organizing process begins with authorization cards, such as the example shown in Figure 14.5. Union representatives make contact with employees, present their message about the union, and invite them to sign an authorization card. For the organization process to continue, at least 30 percent of the employees must sign an authorization card.

If over half the employees sign an authorization card, the union may request that the employer voluntarily recognize the union. If the employer agrees, the NLRB certifies the union as the exclusive representative of employees. If the employer refuses, or if only 30 to 50 percent of employees signed cards, the NLRB conducts a secret-ballot election. The arrangements are made in one of two ways:

1. For a *consent election*, the employer and the union seeking representation arrive at an agreement stating the time and place of the election, the choices included on the ballot, and a way to determine who is eligible to vote.
2. For a *stipulation election*, the parties cannot agree on all of these terms, so the NLRB dictates the time and place, ballot choices, and method of determining eligibility.

On the ballot, workers vote for or against union representation, and they may also have a choice from among more than one union. If the union (or one of the unions on the ballot) wins a majority of votes, the NLRB certifies the union. If the ballot in-

YES, I WANT THE IAM

FIGURE 14.5

Authorization Card

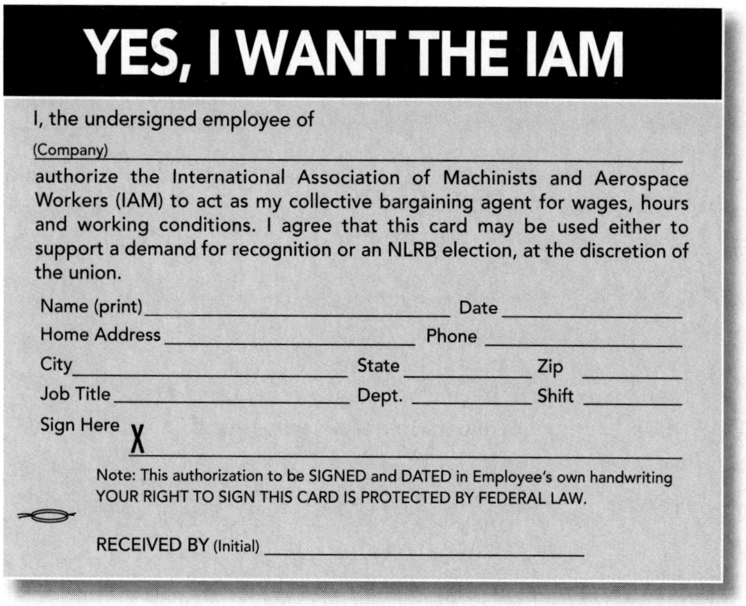

I, the undersigned employee of

(Company) _____

authorize the International Association of Machinists and Aerospace Workers (IAM) to act as my collective bargaining agent for wages, hours and working conditions. I agree that this card may be used either to support a demand for recognition or an NLRB election, at the discretion of the union.

Name (print)_____ Date _____

Home Address _____ Phone _____

City_____ State _____ Zip _____

Job Title _____ Dept. _____ Shift _____

Sign Here X

_____

Note: This authorization to be SIGNED and DATED in Employee's own handwriting
YOUR RIGHT TO SIGN THIS CARD IS PROTECTED BY FEDERAL LAW.

RECEIVED BY (Initial) _____

SOURCE: From J. A. Fossum, *Labor Relations: Development, Structure and Process, 2002.* Copyright © 2002 The McGraw-Hill Companies, Inc. Reprinted with permission.

cludes more than one union and neither gains a simple majority, the NLRB holds a runoff election.

As noted earlier, if the NLRB finds the election was not conducted fairly, it may set aside the results and call for a new election. Conduct that may lead to an election result's being set aside include the following examples:[28]

- Threats of loss of jobs or benefits by an employer or union to influence votes or organizing activities.
- A grant of benefits or a promise of benefits as a means of influencing votes or organizing activities.
- Campaign speeches by management or union representatives to assembled groups of employees on company time less than 24 hours before an election.
- The actual use of threat of physical force or violence to influence votes or organizing activities.

After certification, there are limits on future elections. Once the NLRB has certified a union as the exclusive representative of a group of employees, it will not permit additional elections for one year. Also, after the union and employer have finished negotiating a contract, an election cannot be held for the time of the contract period or for three years, whichever comes first. The parties to the contract may agree not to hold an election for longer than three years, but an outside party (another union) cannot be barred for more than three years.

Management Strategies

Sometimes an employer will recognize a union after a majority of employees have signed authorization cards. More often, there is a hotly contested election campaign. During the campaign, unions try to persuade employees that their wages, benefits, treatment by employers, and chances to influence workplace decisions are too poor or

TABLE 14.2

What Supervisors Should and Should Not Do to Discourage Unions

WHAT TO DO:
Report any direct or indirect signs of union activity to a core management group.
Deal with employees by carefully stating the company's response to pro-union arguments. These responses should be coordinated by the company to maintain consistency and to avoid threats or promises. Take away union issues by following effective management practices all the time:
Deliver recognition and appreciation.
Solve employee problems.
Protect employees from harassment or humiliation.
Provide business-related information.
Be consistent in treatment of different employees.
Accommodate special circumstances where appropriate.
Ensure due process in performance management.
Treat all employees with dignity and respect.
WHAT TO AVOID:
Threatening employees with harsher terms and conditions of employment or employment loss if they engage in union activity.
Interrogating employees about pro-union or anti-union sentiments that they or others may have or reviewing union authorization cards or pro-union petitions.
Promising employees that they will receive favorable terms or conditions of employment if they forgo union activity.
Spying on employees known to be, or suspected of being, engaged in pro-union activities.

SOURCE: J. A. Segal, "Unshackle Your Supervisors to Stay Union Free," *HRMagazine*, June 1998, pp. 177–84.

small and that the union will be able to obtain improvements in these areas. Management typically responds with its own messages providing an opposite point of view. Management messages say the organization has provided a valuable package of wages and benefits and has treated employees well. Management also argues that the union will not be able to keep its promises but will instead create costs for employees, such as union dues and lost income during strikes.

Employers use a variety of methods to oppose unions in organizing campaigns.[29] Their efforts range from hiring consultants to distributing leaflets and letters to presenting the company's viewpoint at meetings of employees. Some management efforts go beyond what the law permits, especially in the eyes of union organizers. This impression is supported by an increase in charges of employer unfair labor practices and awards of back pay since the late 1960s.[30] Why would employers break the law? One explanation is that the consequences, such as reinstating workers with back pay, are small compared to the benefits.[31] If coercing workers away from joining a union saves the company the higher wages, benefits, and other costs of a unionized workforce, management may feel an incentive to accept costs like back pay.

Supervisors have the most direct contact with employees. Thus, as Table 14.2 indicates, it is critical that they establish good relationships with employees even before there is any attempt at union organizing. Supervisors also must know what *not* to do if a union drive takes place. They should be trained in the legal principles discussed earlier in this chapter.

Union Strategies

The traditional union organizing strategy has been for organizers to call or visit employees at home, when possible, to talk about issues like pay and job security. For a young, educated workforce, unions have been learning new tactics. In Madison, Wisconsin, the United Food and Commercial Workers union organized the employees of the local Whole Foods Market when regional union leaders learned that many employees felt their concerns were being ignored by management. The union arranged for interested workers to develop their own website, research the relevant labor law, and invite their coworkers out for coffee or beer after work. Whole Foods unintentionally reinforced the union message that the company was pushy and insensitive by requiring that employees attend meetings to discuss the union. The union's strategy emphasized speed, personal attention, and employee empowerment, and it succeeded when employees voted 65 to 54 in favor of the union.[32]

Beyond encouraging workers to sign authorization cards and vote for the union, organizers use some creative alternatives to traditional organizing activities. They sometimes offer workers **associate union membership,** which is not linked to an employee's workplace and does not provide representation in collective bargaining. Rather, an associate member receives other services, such as discounts on health and life insurance or credit cards.[33] In return for these benefits, the union receives membership dues and a broader base of support for its activities. Associate membership may be attractive to employees who wish to join a union but cannot because their workplace is not organized by a union.

Another alternative to traditional organizing is to conduct **corporate campaigns**—bringing public, financial, or political pressure on employers during union organization and contract negotiation.[34] For example, the Building and Construction Trades Department of the AFL-CIO successfully lobbied Congress to eliminate $100 million in tax breaks for a Toyota truck plant in Kentucky until Toyota agreed to use union construction workers and pay union wages.[35] The Amalgamated Clothing and Textile Workers Union (ACTWU) corporate campaign against textile maker J. P. Stevens during the late 1970s was one of the first successful corporate campaigns and served as a model for those that followed. The ACTWU organized a boycott of J. P. Stevens products and threatened to withdraw its pension funds from financial institutions where J. P. Stevens officers acted as directors. The company eventually agreed to a contract with ACTWU.[36]

In some recent success stories unions have eschewed elections in favor of strikes and negative publicity to pressure corporations to accept a union.[37] The Hotel Employees and Restaurant Employees (HERE) organized 9,000 workers in 2001, with 80 percent of these memberships resulting from pressure on employers rather than a vote. The Union of Needletrade, Industrial and Textile Employees (UNITE), which organized 15,000 workers in 2001, has also succeeded with this approach. After losing an election by just two votes among employees of Up-to-Date Laundry, which cleans linens for Baltimore hotels and hospitals, UNITE decided to try other tactics, including a corporate campaign. It called a strike to demand that Up-to-Date recognize the union. It also persuaded several major customers of the laundry to threaten to stop using the laundry's services, shared claims of racial and sexual harassment with state agencies and the NAACP, and convinced the Baltimore city council to require testimony from Up-to-Date. Eventually, the company gave in, recognized the union, and negotiated a contract that raised the workers' $6-an-hour wages and gave them better benefits.

associate union membership
Alternative form of union membership in which members receive discounts on insurance and credit cards rather than representation in collective bargaining.

corporate campaigns
Bringing public, financial, or political pressure on employers during union organization and contract negotiation.

Another winning union organizing strategy is to negotiate employer neutrality and card-check provisions into a contract. Under a *neutrality provision*, the employer pledges not to oppose organizing attempts elsewhere in the company. A *card-check provision* is an agreement that if a certain percentage—by law, at least a majority—of employees sign an authorization card, the employer will recognize their union representation. An impartial outside agency, such as the American Arbitration Association, counts the cards. The Communication Workers of America negotiated these provisions in its dispute with Verizon (described in the case at the end of this chapter). Evidence suggests that this strategy can be very effective for unions.[38]

Decertifying a Union

The Taft-Hartley act expanded union members' right to be represented by leaders of their own choosing to include the right to vote out an existing union. This action is called *decertifying* the union. Decertification follows the same process as a representation election. An election to decertify a union may not take place when a contract is in effect.

Research indicates that when decertification elections are held, unions typically do not fare well.[39] During the mid-1990s, unions lost about 7 out of 10 decertification elections. In another blow to unions, the number of decertification elections has increased from about 5 percent of all elections in the 1950s and 1960s to about 14 percent in the mid-1990s.

collective bargaining
Negotiation between union representatives and management representatives to arrive at a contract defining conditions of employment for the term of the contract and to administer that contract.

LO5

Collective Bargaining

When the NLRB has certified a union, that union represents employees during contract negotiations. In **collective bargaining,** a union negotiates on behalf of its members with management representatives to arrive at a contract defining conditions of employment for the term of the contract and to resolve differences in the way they interpret the contract. Typical contracts include provisions for pay, benefits, work rules, and resolution of workers' grievances. Table 14.3 shows typical provisions negotiated in collective bargaining contracts.

TABLE 14.3

Typical Provisions in Collective Bargaining Contracts

Establishment and administration of the agreement	Bargaining unit and plant supplements
	Contract duration and reopening and renegotiation provisions
	Union security and the checkoff
	Special bargaining committees
	Grievance procedures
	Arbitration and mediation
	Strikes and lockouts
	Contract enforcement
Functions, rights, and responsibilities	Management rights clauses
	Plant removal
	Subcontracting
	Union activities on company time and premises
	Union–management cooperation
	Regulation of technological change
	Advance notice and consultation

TABLE 14.3

Concluded

Wage determination and administration	General provisions
	Rate structure and wage differentials
	Allowances
	Incentive systems and production bonus plans
	Production standards and time studies
	Job classification and job evaluation
	Individual wage adjustments
	General wage adjustments during the contract period
Job or income security	Hiring and transfer arrangements
	Employment and income guarantees
	Reporting and call-in pay
	Supplemental unemployment benefit plans
	Regulation of overtime, shift work, etc.
	Reduction of hours to forestall layoffs
	Layoff procedures; seniority; recall
	Worksharing in lieu of layoff
	Attrition arrangements
	Promotion practices
	Training and retraining
	Relocation allowances
	Severance pay and layoff benefit plans
	Special funds and study committees
Plant operations	Work and shop rules
	Rest periods and other in-plant time allowances
	Safety and health
	Plant committees
	Hours of work and premium pay practices
	Shift operations
	Hazardous work
	Discipline and discharge
Paid and unpaid leave	Vacations and holidays
	Sick leave
	Funeral and personal leave
	Military leave and jury duty
Employee benefit plans	Health and insurance plans
	Pension plans
	Profit-sharing, stock purchase, and thrift plans
	Bonus plans
Special groups	Apprentices and learners
	Workers with disabilities and older workers
	Women
	Veterans
	Union representatives
	Nondiscrimination clauses

SOURCE: T. A. Kochan, *Collective Bargaining and Industrial Relations* (Homewood, IL: Richard D. Irwin, 1980), p. 29. Original data from J. W. Bloch, "Union Contracts—A New Series of Studies," *Monthly Labor Review* 87 (October 1964), pp. 1184–85.

Collective bargaining differs from one situation to another in terms of *bargaining structure*—that is, the range of employees and employers covered by the contract. A contract may involve a narrow group of employees in a craft union or a broad group in an industrial union. Contracts may cover one or several facilities of the same employer, or the bargaining structure may involve several employers. Many more interests must be considered in collective bargaining for an industrial union with a bargaining structure that includes several employers than in collective bargaining for a craft union in a single facility.

The majority of contract negotiations take place between unions and employers that have been through the process before. In the typical situation, management has come to accept the union as an organization it must work with. The situation can be very different when a union has just been certified and is negotiating its first contract. In over one-fourth of negotiations for a first contract, the parties are unable to reach an agreement.[40]

Bargaining over New Contracts

Clearly, the outcome of contract negotiations can have important consequences for labor costs, productivity, and the organization's ability to compete. Therefore, unions and management need to prepare carefully for collective bargaining. Preparation includes establishing objectives for the contract, reviewing the old contract, gathering data (such as compensation paid by competitors and the company's ability to survive a strike), predicting the likely demands to be made, and establishing the cost of meeting the demands.[41] This preparation can help negotiators develop a plan for how to negotiate. Different situations and goals call for different approaches to bargaining, such as the following alternatives proposed by Richard Walton and Robert McKersie:[42]

- *Distributive bargaining* divides an economic "pie" between two sides—for example, a wage increase means giving the union a larger share of the pie.
- *Integrative bargaining* looks for win-win solutions, or outcomes in which both sides benefit. If the organization's labor costs hurt its performance, integrative bargaining might seek to avoid layoffs in exchange for work rules that improve productivity.
- *Attitudinal structuring* focuses on establishing a relationship of trust. The parties are concerned about ensuring that the other side will keep its part of any bargain.
- *Intraorganizational bargaining* addresses conflicts within union or management groups or objectives, such as between new employees and workers with high seniority or between cost control and reduction of turnover.

The collective bargaining process may involve any combination of these alternatives.

Negotiations go through various stages.[43] In the earliest stages, many more people are often present than in later stages. On the union side, this may give all the various internal interest groups a chance to participate and voice their goals. Their input helps communicate to management what will satisfy union members and may help the union achieve greater solidarity. At this stage, union negotiators often present a long list of proposals, partly to satisfy members and partly to introduce enough issues that they will have flexibility later in the process. Management may or may not present proposals of its own. Sometimes management prefers to react to the union's proposals.

During the middle stages of the process, each side must make a series of decisions, even though the outcome is uncertain. How important is each issue to the other side?

Failing to reach a contract under collective bargaining can result in a strike or boycott. Here actor Rob Schneider encourages the public to boycott Procter & Gamble products because the company used nonunion workers in its commercials in place of striking members of the Screen Actors Guild.

How likely is it that disagreement on particular issues will result in a strike? When and to what extent should one side signal its willingness to compromise?

In the final stage of negotiations, pressure for an agreement increases. Public negotiations may be only part of the process. Negotiators from each side may hold one-on-one meetings or small-group meetings where they escape some public relations pressures. A neutral third party may act as a go-between or facilitator. In some cases, bargaining breaks down as the two sides find they cannot reach a mutually acceptable agreement. The outcome depends partly on the relative bargaining power of each party. That power, in turn, depends on each party's ability to withstand a strike, which costs the workers their pay during the strike and costs the employer lost production and possibly lost customers.

When Bargaining Breaks Down

The intended outcome of collective bargaining is a contract with terms acceptable to both parties. If one or both sides determine that negotiation alone will not produce such an agreement, bargaining breaks down. To bring this impasse to an end, the union may strike, or the parties may bring in outside help to resolve their differences.

Strikes

A **strike** is a collective decision of the union members not to work until certain demands or conditions are met. The union members vote, and if the majority favors a strike, they all go on strike at that time or when union leaders believe the time is right. Strikes are typically accompanied by *picketing*—the union stations members near the worksite with signs indicating the union is on strike. During the strike, the union members do not receive pay from their employer, but the union may be able to make up for some of the lost pay. The employer loses production unless it can hire replacement workers, and even then, productivity may be reduced. Often, other unions support striking workers by refusing to cross their picket line—for example, refusing to make deliveries to a company during a strike.

strike
A collective decision by union members not to work until certain demands or conditions are met.

FIGURE 14.6

Strikes Involving 1,000
or More Workers

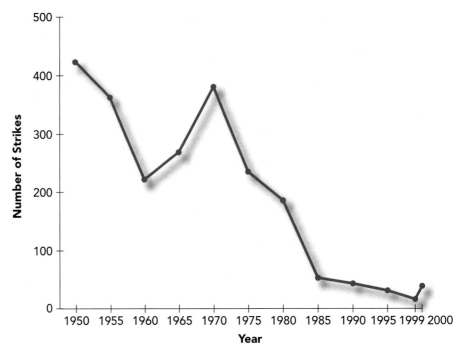

Note: Because strikes are most likely in large bargaining units, these numbers represent most lost working time in the United States.

SOURCE: Bureau of Labor Statistics website, http://stats.bls.gov.

The vast majority of labor-management negotiations do not result in a strike, and the number of strikes has plunged since the 1950s, as shown in Figure 14.6. The percentage of total working time lost to strikes in 2000 was a mere 0.06 percent—that is, less than one-tenth of 1 percent of working time. A primary reason strikes are rare is that a strike is seldom in the best interests of either party. Not only do workers lose wages and employers lose production, but the negative experience of a strike can make future interactions more difficult. When strikes do occur, the conduct of each party during the strike can do lasting harm to labor-management relations. Violence by either side or threats of job loss or actual job loss because jobs went to replacement workers can make future relations difficult. Finally, many government employees do not have a right to strike, and their percentage among unionized employees overall has risen in recent decades, as we discussed earlier.

Alternatives to Strikes

mediation
Conflict resolution procedure in which a mediator hears the views of both sides and facilitates the negotiation process but has no formal authority to dictate a resolution.

Because strikes are so costly and risky, unions and employers generally prefer other methods for resolving conflicts. Three of the most common alternatives are mediation, fact finding, and arbitration. All of these rely on a neutral third party, who usually is provided by the Federal Mediation and Conciliation Service (FMCS).

The least formal and most widely used of these procedures is **mediation.** In this procedure, a mediator hears the views of both sides and facilitates the negotiation process. The mediator has no formal authority to dictate a resolution, so a strike remains a possibility. In a survey studying negotiations between unions and large businesses, mediation was used in almost 4 out of 10 negotiation efforts.[44]

A **fact finder,** most often used for negotiations with governmental bodies, typically reports on the reasons for the dispute, the views and arguments of both sides, and (sometimes) a recommended settlement, which the parties may decline. The public nature of these recommendations may pressure the parties to reach a settlement. Even if they do not accept the fact finder's recommended settlement, the hope of this process is that the fact finder will identify or frame issues in a way that makes agreement easier. Sometimes merely devoting time to this process gives the parties a chance to reach an agreement. Again, however, there is no guarantee that a strike will be avoided.

The most formal type of outside intervention is **arbitration,** under which an arbitrator or arbitration board determines a settlement that is *binding,* meaning the parties have to accept it. In conventional arbitration, the arbitrator fashions the solution. In "final-offer arbitration," the arbitrator must choose either management's or the union's final offer for each issue or for the contract as a whole. There is wide acceptance of "rights arbitration," which focuses on enforcing or interpreting contract terms, but arbitration in the writing of contracts or setting of contract terms has traditionally been reserved for special circumstances such as negotiations between unions and government agencies, where strikes may be illegal or especially costly. Occasionally, arbitration has also been used with businesses in situations where strikes have been extremely damaging. Arbitration is uncommon in the private sector and one reason is the general opinion that union and management representatives are in the best position to resolve conflicts themselves, because they are closer to the situation than an arbitrator can be.

Contract Administration

LO6

Although the process of negotiating a labor agreement (including the occasional strike) receives the most publicity, other union-management activities occur far more often. Bargaining over a new contract typically occurs only about every three years, but administering labor contracts goes on day after day, year after year. The two activities are linked, of course. Vague or inconsistent language in the contract can make administering the contract more difficult. The difficulties can create conflict that spills over into the next round of negotiations.[45] Events during negotiations—strikes, the use of replacement workers, or violence by either side—also can lead to difficulties in working successfully under a conflict.

Contract administration includes carrying out the terms of the agreement and resolving conflicts over interpretation or violation of the agreement. Under a labor contract, the process for resolving these conflicts is called a **grievance procedure.** This procedure has a key influence on success in contract administration. A grievance procedure may be started by an employee or discharged employee who believes the employer violated the contract or by a union representative on behalf of a group of workers or union representatives.

For grievances launched by an employee, a typical grievance procedure follows the steps shown in Figure 14.7. The grievance may be settled during any of the four steps. In the first step, the employee talks to his or her supervisor about the problem. If this conversation is unsatisfactory, the employee may involve the union steward in further discussion. The union steward and employee decide whether the problem has been resolved and, if not, whether it is a contract violation. If the problem was not resolved and does seem to be a contract violation, the union moves to step 2, putting the

fact finder
Third party to collective bargaining who reports the reasons for a dispute, the views and arguments of both sides, and possibly a recommended settlement, which the parties may decline.

arbitration
Conflict resolution procedure in which an arbitrator or arbitration board determines a binding settlement.

grievance procedure
The process for resolving union-management conflicts over interpretation or violation of a collective bargaining agreement.

FIGURE 14.7

Steps in an Employee-
Initiated Grievance
Procedure

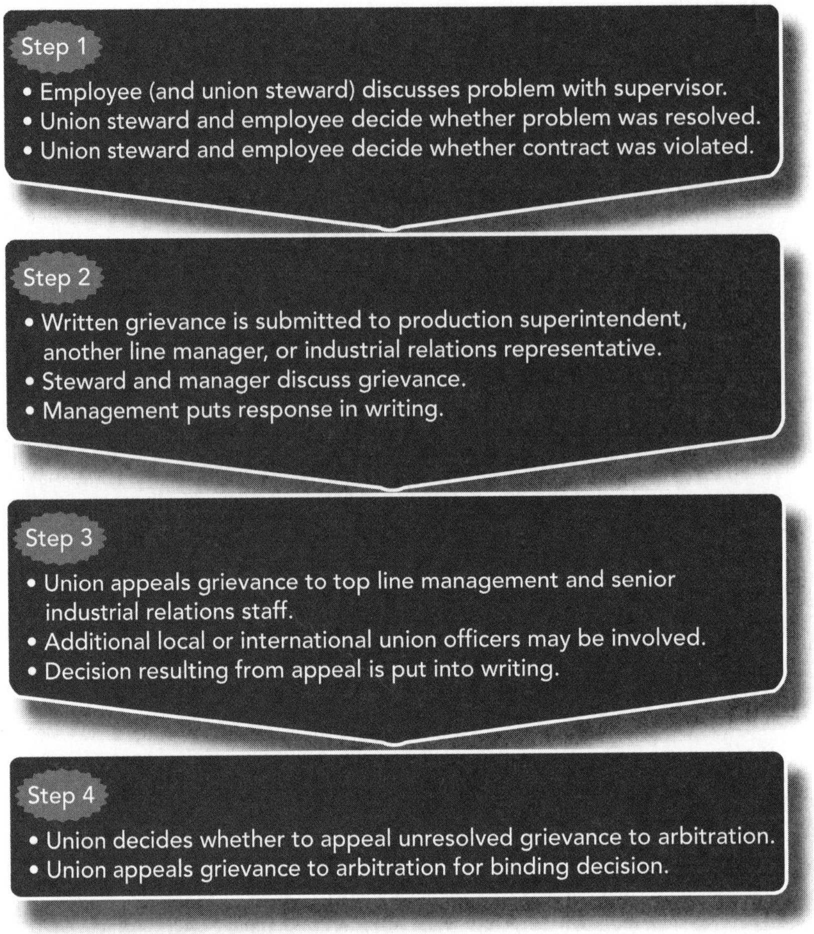

Step 1

- Employee (and union steward) discusses problem with supervisor.
- Union steward and employee decide whether problem was resolved.
- Union steward and employee decide whether contract was violated.

Step 2

- Written grievance is submitted to production superintendent, another line manager, or industrial relations representative.
- Steward and manager discuss grievance.
- Management puts response in writing.

Step 3

- Union appeals grievance to top line management and senior industrial relations staff.
- Additional local or international union officers may be involved.
- Decision resulting from appeal is put into writing.

Step 4

- Union decides whether to appeal unresolved grievance to arbitration.
- Union appeals grievance to arbitration for binding decision.

SOURCE: Adapted from T. A. Kochan, *Collective Bargaining and Industrial Relations* (Homewood, IL: Richard D. Irwin, 1980), p. 395; J. A. Fossum, *Labor Relations* (Boston: McGraw-Hill/Irwin, 2002), pp. 448–52.

grievance in writing and submitting it to a line manager. The union steward meets with a management representative to try to resolve the problem. Management consults with the industrial relations staff and puts its response in writing too at this second stage. If step 2 fails to resolve the problem, the union appeals the grievance to top line management and representatives of the industrial relations staff. The union may involve more local or international officers in discussions at this stage (see step 3 in Figure 14.7). The decision resulting from the appeal is put into writing. If the grievance is still not resolved, the union may decide (step 4) to appeal the grievance to an arbitrator. If the grievance involves a discharged employee, the process may begin at step 2 or 3, however, and the time limits between steps may be shorter. Grievances filed by the union on behalf of a group may begin at step 1 or step 2.

The majority of grievances are settled during the earlier steps of the process. This reduces delays and avoids the costs of arbitration. If a grievance does reach arbitration, the arbitrator makes the final ruling in the matter. Based on a series of Supreme Court decisions, courts generally avoid reviewing arbitrators' decisions and focus only on whether the grievance involved an issue that is subject to arbitration under the contract.[46]

From the point of view of employees, the grievance procedure is an important means of getting fair treatment in the workplace. Its success depends on whether it provides for all the kinds of problems that are likely to arise (such as how to handle a business slowdown), whether employees feel they can file a grievance without being punished for it, and whether employees believe their union representatives will follow through. Under the National Labor Relations Act, the union has a *duty of fair representation*, which means the union must give equal representation to all members of the bargaining unit, whether or not they actually belong to the union. Too many grievances may indicate a problem—for example, the union members or line supervisors do not understand how to uphold the contract or have no desire to do so. At the same time, a very small number of grievances may also signal a problem. A very low grievance rate may suggest a fear of filing a grievance, a belief that the system does not work, or a belief that employees are poorly represented by their union.

What types of issues most commonly reach arbitration? According to data from the Federal Mediation and Conciliation Service, the majority of arbitration cases involved discharge or other disciplinary actions.[47] Other issues that often reach arbitration are subcontracting; the use of seniority in decisions about promotions, layoffs, transfers, work assignments, and scheduling; and the distribution of overtime or requirement of overtime. In reaching decisions about these and other issues, arbitrators consider a number of criteria, such as employees' understanding of the rules, the employer's consistency and fairness, and the employees' chance to present a defense and appeal a decision.[48]

Labor–Management Cooperation

LO7

The traditional understanding of union-management relations is that the two parties are adversaries, meaning each side is competing to win at the expense of the other. There have always been exceptions to this approach. And since at least the 1980s, there seems to be wider acceptance of the view that greater cooperation can increase employee commitment and motivation while making the workplace more flexible.[49] Also, evidence suggests that employees who worked under traditional labor relations systems and then under the new, more cooperative systems prefer the cooperative approach.[50]

Cooperation between labor and management may feature employee involvement in decision making, self-managing employee teams, labor-management problem-solving teams, broadly defined jobs, and sharing of financial gains and business information with employees.[51] The search for a win-win solution requires that unions and their members understand the limits on what an employer can afford in a competitive marketplace. The "Best Practices" box on the next page describes how a factory in Buffalo, New York, has met this challenge.

Without the union's support, efforts at employee empowerment are less likely to survive and less likely to be effective if they do survive.[52] Unions have often resisted employee empowerment programs, precisely because the programs try to change workplace relations and the role that unions play. Union leaders have often feared that such programs will weaken unions' role as independent representatives of employee interests. Indeed, the National Labor Relations Act makes it an unfair labor practice for an employer to "dominate or interfere with the formation or administration of any labor organization or contribute financial or other support to it."

This legal requirement gave rise to concern that self-managing work teams set up by an employer could violate the NLRA. Several widely publicized rulings by the

Brass Factory Polishes Employees' Understanding—And Morale, Too

During the recent economic slowdown, some companies have been giving employees training in economics and personal finance so they will understand the tough decisions managers have to make in hard times. A good example is the Outokumpu American Brass factory in Buffalo, New York. There, treating blue-collar workers like thinking human beings has strengthened morale—and profits.

The Buffalo factory is a renovated copper and brass plant almost shut down in 1984 by the Atlantic Richfield Company because of flagging sales and labor unrest. Local investors bought the plant, which makes a variety of metal products from brass buttons to electrical connectors for cell phones, and quickly turned it around. In 1990 the investors sold the company to Outokumpu Oyj, a mining and metals company based in Finland.

Outokumpu bought the plant, one of the largest copper and brass rolling mills in the United States, to gain a greater presence in the global market. To make the investment profitable, Outokumpu determined it would have to raise productivity. Management thought one way to meet that goal would be to teach workers the economic and financial basics of the company's markets and ask for ideas on how to run the plant (as the local investors had done).

Outokumpu hired Cornell University's School of Industrial and Labor Relations in Buffalo to teach employees the basics of the brass industry.

At first employees reacted negatively. Lou Jean Fleron, the school's director, recalls that when she visited the factory to talk about the global economy, she saw a startling amount of worker hostility toward their new employer. Fleron says, "They saw [the new ownership] as us against them, a takeover by this evil foreign company." But the Cornell instructors persisted. In a session on global economic changes, Fleron explained that investments by foreign companies in American plants were increasing. She distributed

National Labor Relations Board in the mid-1990s found that worker-management committees were illegal when they were dominated by management and dealt with issues such as wages, grievances, and working conditions.[53] Table 14.4 provides some guidance on when the use of teams might be illegal.

Although employers must be careful to meet legal requirements, the NLRB has clearly supported employee involvement in decision making. For example, in a 2001 ruling, the NLRB found that employee participation committees at Crown Cork & Seal's aluminum-can factory did not violate federal labor law.[54] Those committees make and carry out decisions regarding a wide range of issues, including production, quality, training, safety, and certain types of discipline. The NLRB determined that the committees were not employer dominated. Instead of "dealing with" management, where employees make proposals for management to accept or reject, the committees exercise authority within boundaries set by management, similar to the authority of a first-line supervisor. In spite of the legal concerns, cooperative approaches to labor relations seem to contribute to an organization's success.[55]

Beyond avoiding any taint of misuse of employee empowerment, employers build cooperative relationships by the way they treat employees—with respect and fairness,

an article by Robert B. Reich, the former U.S. labor secretary, outlining the benefits, including examples of overseas capital saving American jobs. And in workshops scheduled during all three shifts throughout the next year, the instructors taught subjects ranging from the impact of technology on the workplace to the details of corporate income statements and the pricing of commodities.

Eventually employees began to see connections between the classroom discussions and their working conditions. For example, after learning about manufacturing costs in developing countries, they more clearly understood how their own wages were set. Employees also have a better grasp of who their customers are and what goes on in other departments.

The workshops now take place every three years. Management also holds quarterly meetings for all 850 employees to discuss plant operations, market conditions, and investments in new equipment. According to Warren E. Bartel, president of Outokumpu American Brass, "The questions—about pricing, competition, and customers— seem to get better every year." Outokumpu invites customers to tour the production lines and talk to workers about the factory's products, and it has begun seeking employees' views on how to increase productivity. As one instance, management turned to a respected machinist for advice on capital procurement— replacing a metal-turning lathe used to repair equipment.

Outsiders are impressed with the way the company works. The AFL-CIO gave the company a national award for its labor-management cooperation, and the U.S. Department of Commerce uses it as a case study for effective employee involvement. Representatives from companies in Ireland, Poland, Pittsburgh, and Australia have visited to learn how workers and management have come to get along so well.

SOURCE: W. Royal, "A Factory's Crash Course in Economics Pays Off," *New York Times*, April 25, 2001, p. 9.

TABLE 14.4

When Teams May Be Illegal

Primary factors to look for that could mean a team violates national labor law:	
Representation	Does the team address issues affecting nonteam employees? (Does it represent other workers?)
Subject matter	Do these issues involve matters such as wages, grievances, hours of work, and working conditions?
Management involvement	Does the team deal with any supervisors, managers, or executives on any issue?
Employer domination	Did the company create the team or decide what it would do and how it would function?

SOURCE: T. Kochan and P. Osterman, *The Mutual Gains Enterprise* (Boston: Harvard Business School Press, 1994), p. 202; originally from A. Bernstein, "Making Teamwork Work—And Appeasing Uncle Sam," *BusinessWeek*, January 25, 1993, p. 101.

in the knowledge that attracting talent and minimizing turnover are in the employer's best interests. A business owner who appreciates this approach is Kenn Ricci, founder of Flight Options, which offers clients the use of a private plane.[56] Clients buy a share in the ownership of a plane, and Flight Options provides a pilot to fly the plane. A pilot himself, Ricci built his company on values many pilots share, including flexibility and trust. When Flight Options prepared to acquire Raytheon Travel Air, Ricci inherited a union organizing effort at that company. In a climate of rumors and mistrust, a Travel Air pilot sent Ricci an e-mail message asking if he planned to lay off the Travel Air pilots if they voted in favor of the union. Ricci replied with a simple *no*—and the pilots voted down the union. When it came time to merge the two company's seniority lists (the basis for assigning pilots to aircraft and routes), Ricci called together a group of pilots representing both companies to identify alternatives. He posted the ideas on the Flight Options website, gathered reactions, and narrowed the choices to two, which pilots voted on. Ricci's active involvement with employees and the company's culture of trust have kept pilot turnover at a fraction of the industry average and made labor relations positive in an industry racked with disputes.

Summary

1. Define unions and labor relations and their role in organizations.
   A union is an organization formed for the purpose of representing its members in resolving conflicts with employers. Labor relations is the management specialty emphasizing skills that managers and union leaders can use to minimize costly forms of conflict and to seek win-win solutions to disagreements. Unions—often locals belonging to national and international organizations—engage in organizing, collective bargaining, and contract administration with businesses and government organizations. In the United States, union membership has been declining among businesses but has held steady with government employees. Unionization is associated with more generous compensation and higher productivity but lower profits. Unions may reduce a business's flexibility and economic performance.

2. Identify the labor relations goals of management, labor unions, and society.
   Management goals are to increase the organization's profits. Managers generally expect that unions will make these goals harder to achieve. Labor unions have the goal of obtaining pay and working conditions that satisfy their members. They obtain these results by gaining power in numbers. Society's values have included the hope that the existence of unions will replace conflict or violence between workers and employers with fruitful negotiation.

3. Summarize laws and regulations that affect labor relations.

The National Labor Relations Act supports the use of collective bargaining and sets out the rights of employees, including the right to organize, join a union, and go on strike. The NLRA prohibits unfair labor practices by employers, including interference with efforts to form a labor union and discrimination against employees who engage in union activities. The Taft-Hartley Act and Landrum-Griffin Act establish restrictions on union practices that restrain workers, such as their preventing employees from working during a strike or determining who an employer may hire. The Taft-Hartley Act also permits state right-to-work laws.

4. Describe the union organizing process.
   Organizing begins when union representatives contact employees and invite them to sign an authorization card. If over half the employees sign a card, the union may request that the employer voluntarily recognize the union. If the employer refuses or if 30 to 50 percent of employees signed authorization cards, the NLRB conducts a secret-ballot election. If the union wins, the NLRB certifies the union. If the union loses but the NLRB finds that the election was not conducted fairly, it may set aside the results and call a new election.

5. Explain how management and unions negotiate contracts.
   Negotiations take place between representatives of the union and the management bargaining unit. The majority of negotiations involve parties that have been through the process before. The process begins with preparation, including research into the other side's

strengths and demands. In the early stages of negotiation, many more people are present than at later stages. The union presents its demands, and management sometimes presents demands as well. Then the sides evaluate the demands and the likelihood of a strike. In the final stages, pressure for an agreement increases, and a neutral third party may be called on to help reach a resolution. If bargaining breaks down, the impasse may be broken with a strike, mediation, fact finder, or arbitration.

6. Summarize the practice of contract administration.
   Contract administration is a daily activity under the labor agreement. It includes carrying out the terms of the agreement and resolving conflicts over interpretation or violation of the contract. Conflicts are resolved through a grievance procedure. Typically, the grievance procedure begins with an employee talking to his or her supervisor about the problem and possibly involving the union steward in the discussion. If this does not resolve the conflict, the union files a written grievance with a line manager, and union and management representatives meet to discuss the problem. If this effort fails, the union appeals the grievance to top line management and the industrial relations staff. If the appeal fails, the union may appeal the grievance to an arbitrator.

7. Describe more cooperative approaches to labor-management relations.
   In contrast to the traditional view that labor and management are adversaries, some organizations and unions work more cooperatively. Cooperation may feature employee involvement in decision making, self-managing employee teams, labor-management problem-solving teams, broadly defined jobs, and sharing of financial gains and business information with employees. If such cooperation is tainted by attempts of the employer to dominate or interfere with labor organizations, however, such as by dealing with wages, grievances, or working conditions, it may be illegal under the NLRA. In spite of such legal concerns, cooperative labor relations seem to contribute to an organization's success.

Review and Discussion Questions

1. Why do employees join labor unions? Did you ever belong to a labor union? If you did, do you think union membership benefited you? If you did not, do you think a union would have benefited you? Why or why not?
2. Why do managers at most companies prefer that unions not represent their employees? Can unions provide benefits to an employer? Explain.
3. How has union membership in the United States changed over the past few decades? How does union membership in the United States compare with union membership in other countries? How might these patterns in union membership affect the HR decisions of an international company?
4. What legal responsibilities do employers have regarding unions? What are the legal requirements affecting unions?
5. Suppose you are the HR manager for a chain of clothing stores. You learn that union representatives have been encouraging the stores' employees to sign authorization cards. What events can follow in this process of organizing? Suggest some ways that you might respond in your role as HR manager.
6. If the parties negotiating a labor contract are unable to reach an agreement, what actions can resolve the situation?
7. Why are strikes uncommon? Under what conditions might management choose to accept a strike?
8. What are the usual steps in a grievance procedure? What are the advantages of resolving a grievance in the first step? What skills would a supervisor need so grievances can be resolved in the first step?
9. The "Best Practices" box in the chapter gives an example of union-management cooperation at Outokumpu American Brass. What does the company gain from this effort? What do workers gain? Do you think the cooperative effort eliminates the union's role at Outokumpu American Brass? Explain.
10. What are the legal restrictions on labor-management cooperation?

What's Your HR IQ?

The Student CD-ROM offers two more ways to check what you've learned so far. Use the Self-Assessment exercise to test your judgments about labor relations. Go online with the Web Exercise to see how well your knowledge of labor relations works in cyberspace.

BusinessWeek **Case**

BusinessWeek # A World of Sweatshops

If you tour Tong Yang Indonesia (TYI) shoe factory, an 8,500-worker complex of hot, dingy buildings outside Jakarta, company president Jung Moo Young will show you the improvements he has made in the past two years. He did so to satisfy his biggest customer, Reebok International, accused by activists of using sweatshops.

Last year Jung bought machinery to apply a water-based solvent to glue on shoe soles instead of toluene, which may be hazardous to workers. He installed a ventilation system after Reebok auditors found the old one inadequate. TYI bought new chairs with backs, so that its young seamstresses have some support while seated at their machines, and bought back braces for 500 workers who do heavy lifting. In all, TYI, which has $100 million in annual sales, spent $2 million to satisfy Reebok. But to Jung's surprise, it was a sound investment. "We should make it all back after three years," he says. "The workers are more productive, and the new machinery is more efficient."

TYI's efforts show how much progress Western consumer goods companies can make in cleaning up sweatshop conditions. In the early 1990s, many companies adopted codes of conduct requiring contractors to fix harsh or abusive conditions. Several companies—such as Reebok, Nike, and Liz Claiborne—have begun enforcing their codes in the past year or two.

More than a dozen companies have joined efforts to create an industrywide system for verifying that consumer goods sold in the United States are made under humane conditions. The most ambitious effort involves the Fair Labor Association, which grew out of a presidential task force of companies and human rights groups. It plans to send outside monitors to factories worldwide to ensure they meet minimum standards on everything from health and safety to workers' rights to join unions.

The problem is that such conscientious companies are the exceptions. Although many multinationals operate facilities in Asia and Latin America that are run as well as any in the West, most still buy from factories where practices are appalling. The claims of many companies that they adhere to labor codes are no more than window-dressing.

Then there are the tougher issues that even companies such as Reebok haven't yet grappled with. How can companies respect workers' rights to collectively bargain in China, for instance, where free unions are banned and the country's own labor laws often aren't enforced? Nor have most Western companies improved wages, which are often below what even governments like Indonesia's define as enough to support a family.

Investigators for U.S. labor and human rights groups estimate that Asia and Latin America have thousands of sweatshops, which force employees to work 16-hour days and cheat them out of already meager wages. "It would be extremely generous to say that even 10 percent of [Western companies charged with abuses] have done anything meaningful about labor conditions," says S. Prakash Sethi, a Baruch College business professor. Price hikes in U.S. retail garments have lagged inflation since 1982, and Asian factory owners complain they are under intense pressure to squeeze out costs.

Liz Claiborne's attempt to improve conditions at a factory in Guatemala shows how hard it is for companies to clean up sweatshops. In 1998 the U.S. apparel giant began working with the Commission for the Verification of Corporate Codes of Conduct (Coverco) to monitor one of its suppliers, a Korean-owned factory near Guatemala City. Coverco found a litany of problems, beginning with workers' claims that they didn't receive proper overtime payments or promised production bonuses. Workers lacked adequate protection when handling hazardous chemicals. Toilets and canteens were unsanitary. Some managers screamed at workers and pressured those who complained to resign. Many workers said they were denied time off for doctors' appointments. Coverco says the plant is slowly improving under Liz Claiborne's pressure.

The inability to form free unions means that workers often lack power to make much beyond subsistence wages. The Modas Uno Korea plant in a Guatemala City suburb stopped paying workers on time in August 2000 and fired 22 who complained to the Labor Ministry. That September, workers stormed the plant demanding back pay—and the company relented. Workers who stayed on said they were offered sewing machines instead of severance pay when the factory shut down in early October.

Workers' pay, even if it's better than average for the country, is still pitiful considering the nearly 40 percent profit margins (profit as a percent of expenses) Nike and Reebok earn before taxes. TYI pays about 22 cents an hour, just over Indonesia's minimum wage. It gets around $13 for every pair of shoes it makes for Reebok, paying only $1 for labor. Still, TYI says that after paying for materials and overhead, its margins are just 10 percent. It can't just hike its price to Reebok. "They look for suppliers who sell for the lowest price," says a TYI manager.

Given the huge oversupply of cheap labor in many developing nations, more widespread gains in the workplace are unlikely until workers can organize unions to demand changes—or unless there is a system to punish violators of international codes.

SOURCE: "A World of Sweatshops," *BusinessWeek Online*, November 6, 2000, www.businessweek.com.

Questions

1. What would you expect to happen if the workers in this case were able to join unions?

2. What might happen to a shoe company like Reebok if it began to sell union-made shoes?

3. Would you be willing to pay more for shoes made under better working conditions? Explain.

Case: Verizon Strikes Out against Unions

Although union membership in the United States has declined, organized-labor groups that are willing and able to adapt to new industries and a new economy are surviving. Granted, not every attempt to organize young workers in high-tech fields succeeds. Employees at Amazon.com and CNBC knocked down union drives at those two companies. But workers at telecommunications companies such as Verizon Communications and aerospace companies such as Lockheed Martin do have unions—and fairly strong ones. The Communication Workers of America (CWA) and the International Brotherhood of Electrical Workers (IBEW) represent over half of Verizon's 250,000 employees.

Recently both of those unions won on a major issue in a strike against Verizon. The issue had its roots in the merger of Bell Atlantic, GTE, and Vodafone into Verizon. The unions wanted a chance to sign up nonunion employees from the old GTE and Vodafone companies. Verizon management tried to sidestep the issue by offering a five-year contract with large wage increases. The unions opted instead to pursue union contracts for cable and wireless employees. They also disputed Verizon's right to transfer work from union to nonunion units, as well as workload and overtime issues. The latter issues were considered especially significant to call center workers, who were under pressure to deliver service to often-frustrated customers as quickly as possible by following marketing scripts. Work rules permitted only two-second breaks between calls.

To be more competitive, Verizon's managers hoped to use less union labor as a way to reduce costs and increase flexibility. From its point of view, the CWA saw that its future depended on being able to organize workers in nonunionized parts of Verizon. The conflict eventually resulted in a strike that lasted 18 days and idled 85,000 workers. In the end, the unions won the right to organize the company's nonunion divisions, as well as concessions on the other issues.

Perhaps one reason the CWA and IBEW fought so hard at Verizon was that the CWA had already lost ground at AT&T, where union membership has decreased to about one-quarter of the workforce following AT&T's mergers with other companies. With such a low share of union membership at AT&T, the company's management has taken a hard line against organized labor—so much so that it has ignored a previous agreement allowing the CWA to organize workers in nonunion divisions free of executive interference. AT&T has also refused to cooperate with any arbitration proceedings. Based on this experience, CWA representatives don't want to find themselves banging on closed doors at other companies.

Executives at many telecommunications companies see organized labor as a threat to their ability to compete in a marketplace that demands extreme flexibility and speed. Perhaps they view the traditional union relationship as one that saddles them with workers comfortable to meet basic job requirements in exchange for job security and guaranteed pay raises. Some observers question that point of view. In *BusinessWeek*, Robert Kuttner writes, "Most of the economy's recent productivity gains reflect technological breakthroughs, not the downgrading of labor." This point of view leaves room for cooperation between labor and management.

When the economy, especially the high-tech sector, was growing rapidly, the question facing unions and management was how to divide the gains. More recently, the economic slowdown has raised the question of how to share the burden of cutbacks.

SOURCES: T. Wolverton, "Labor Pains," *CNet News.com*, January 16, 2001, http://news.cnet.com; R. Kuttner, "Verizon's Crash Course in High-Tech Unionism," *BusinessWeek*, September 11, 2000, p. 28; Y. J. Dreazen, "Old Labor Tries to Establish Role in New Economy," *The Wall Street Journal*, August 15, 2000, pp. B1, B10.

Questions

1. The traditional image of a union member is a male blue-collar worker in a factory. From the CWA union's point of view, what might be challenges of convincing Verizon's high-tech workers that they should join a union? Would some of those challenges be different for a call center employee in contrast to a software engineer?

2. From Verizon's perspective, why do you think the company was willing to offer a contract with large wage increases in place of expanding union representation? What would be some costs and benefits of this labor relations strategy?

3. How might the Communication Workers of America and Verizon have resolved their differences without a strike? Do you think the results would have been better for the company? For the employees? Was a strike necessary?

Notes

1. M. Trottman, "Southwest Offers Pilots Union a Minimum Pay Raise of 20%," *The Wall Street Journal Online*, May 20, 2002, http://online.wsj.com.
2. J. T. Dunlop, *Industrial Relations Systems* (New York: Holt, 1958); C. Kerr, "Industrial Conflict and Its Mediation," *American Journal of Sociology* 60 (1954), pp. 230–45.
3. See A. M. Glassman and T. G. Cummings, *Industrial Relations: A Multidimensional View* (Glenview, IL: Scott, Foresman, 1985); W. H. Holley Jr. and K. M. Jennings, *The Labor Relations Process* (Chicago: Dryden Press, 1984).
4. T. A. Kochan, *Collective Bargaining and Industrial Relations* (Homewood, IL: Richard D. Irwin, 1980), p. 25; H. C. Katz and T. A. Kochan, *An Introduction to Collective Bargaining and Industrial Relations* (New York: McGraw-Hill, 1992), p. 10.
5. Whether the time the union steward spends on union business is paid for by the employer, the union, or a combination is a matter of negotiation between the employer and the union.
6. B. T. Hirsch and D. A. MacPherson, *Union Membership and Earnings Data Book 2001* (Washington, DC: Bureau of National Affairs, 2002).
7. Katz and Kochan, *An Introduction to Collective Bargaining,* building on J. Fiorito and C. L. Maranto, "The Contemporary Decline of Union Strength," *Contemporary Policy Issues* 3 (1987), pp. 12–27; G. N. Chaison and J. Rose, "The Macrodeterminants of Union Growth and Decline," in *The State of the Unions,* ed. G. Strauss et al. (Madison, WI: Industrial Relations Research Association, 1991).
8. Bureau of Labor Statistics website, www.bls.gov; AFL-CIO website, www.aflcio.org.
9. T. A. Kochan, R. B. McKersie, and J. Chalykoff, "The Effects of Corporate Strategy and Workplace Innovations in Union Representation," *Industrial and Labor Relations Review* 39 (1986), pp. 487–501; Chaison and Rose, "The Macrodeterminatnts of Union Growth and Decline"; J. Barbash, *Practice of Unionism* (New York: Harper, 1956), p. 210; W. N. Cooke and D. G. Meyer, "Structural and Market Predictors of Corporate Labor Relations Strategies," *Industrial and Labor Relations Review* 43 (1990), pp. 280–93; T. A. Kochan and P. Capelli, "The Transformation of the Industrial Relations and Personnel Function," in *Internal Labor Markets,* ed. P. Osterman (Cambridge, MA: MIT Press, 1984).
10. C. Brewster, "Levels of Analysis in Strategic HRM: Questions Raised by Comparative Research," Conference on Research and Theory in HRM, Cornell University, October 1997.
11. A. Bernstein, "Working Capital: Labor's New Weapon?" *BusinessWeek,* September 27, 1997.
12. American Federation of State, County and Municipal Employees website, www.afscme.org.
13. J. T. Addison and B. T. Hirsch, "Union Effects on Productivity, Profits, and Growth: Has the Long Run Arrived?" *Journal of Labor Economics* 7 (1989), pp. 72–105; R. B. Freeman and J. L. Medoff, "The Two Faces of Unionism," *Public Interest* 57 (Fall 1979), pp. 69–93.
14. L. Mishel and P. Voos, *Unions and Economic Competitiveness* (Armonk, NY: M. E. Sharpe, 1991); Freeman and Medoff, "Two Faces"; S. Slichter, J. Healy, and E. R. Livernash, *The Impact of Collective Bargaining on Management* (Washington, DC: Brookings Institution, 1960).
15. A. O. Hirschman, *Exit, Voice, and Loyalty* (Cambridge, MA: Harvard University Press, 1970); R. Batt, A. J. S. Colvin, and J. Keefe, "Employee Voice, Human Resource Practices, and Quit Rates: Evidence from the Telecommunications Industry," *Industrial and Labor Relations Review* 55 (1970), pp. 573–94.
16. R. B. Freeman and J. L. Medoff, *What Do Unions Do?* (New York: Basic Books, 1984); E. E. Herman, J. L. Schwatz, and A. Kuhn, *Collective Bargaining and Labor Relations* (Englewood Cliffs, NJ: Prentice Hall, 1992); Addison and Hirsch, "Union Effects on Productivity"; Katz and Kochan, *An Introduction to Collective Bargaining;* P. D. Lineman, M. L. Wachter, and W. H. Carter, "Evaluating the Evidence on Union Employment and Wages," *Industrial and Labor Relations Review* 44 (1990), pp. 34–53.
17. B. E. Becker and C. A. Olson, "Unions and Firm Profits," *Industrial Relations* 31, no. 3 (1992), pp. 395–415; B. T. Hirsch and B. A. Morgan, "Shareholder Risks and Returns in Union and Nonunion Firms," *Industrial and Labor Relations Review* 47, no. 2 (1994), pp. 302–18.
18. "Eighth Biennial National Labor-Management Conference," *Monthly Labor Review,* January 1999, pp. 29–45; "Companies Breaking Records in Hard Times," *Milwaukee Journal Sentinel* (October 13, 2001).
19. Bureau of Labor Statistics website, http://stats.bls.gov.
20. S. B. Jarrell and T. D. Stanley, "A Meta-Analysis of the Union-Nonunion Wage Gap," *Industrial and Labor Relations Review* 44 (1990), pp. 54–67.
21. S. Webb and B. Webb, *Industrial Democracy* (London: Longmans, Green, 1987); J. R. Commons, *Institutional Economics* (New York: Macmillan, 1934).
22. "Why America Needs Unions, but Not the Kind It Has Now," *BusinessWeek,* May 23, 1994, p. 70.

23. Herman et al., *Collective Bargaining.*

24. Kochan, *Collective Bargaining and Industrial Relations,* p. 61.

25. National Labor Relations Board, *Basic Guide to the National Labor Relations Act* (Washington, DC: U.S. Government Printing Office, 1997).

26. Ibid.

27. Ibid.

28. Ibid.

29. R. B. Freeman and M. M. Kleiner, "Employer Behavior in the Face of Union Organizing Drives," *Industrial and Labor Relations Review* 43, no. 4 (April 1990), pp. 351–65.

30. Freeman and Medoff, *What Do Unions Do?;* National Labor Relations Board annual reports for 1980s and 1990s.

31. J. A. Fossum, *Labor Relations,* 5th ed. (Homewood, IL: Richard D. Irwin, 1992), p. 149.

32. C. Tejada, "Young, Educated Employees Are Seen as Boon for Union," *The Wall Street Journal Online,* August 21, 2002, http://online.wsj.com.

33. Herman et al., *Collective Bargaining;* P. Jarley and J. Fiorito, "Associate Membership: Unionism or Consumerism?" *Industrial and Labor Relations Review* 43 (1990), pp. 209–24.

34. Katz and Kochan, *An Introduction to Collective Bargaining;* R. L. Rose, "Unions Hit Corporate Campaign Trail," *The Wall Street Journal,* March 8, 1993, p. B1.

35. P. Jarley and C. L. Maranto, "Union Corporate Campaigns: An Assessment," *Industrial and Labor Relations Review* 44 (1990), pp. 505–24.

36. Katz and Kochan, *An Introduction to Collective Bargaining.*

37. D. Wessel, "Aggressive Tactics by Unions Target Lower-Paid Workers," *The Wall Street Journal Online,* January 31, 2002, http://online.wsj.com.

38. A. E. Eaton and J. Kriesky, "Union Organizing under Neutrality and Card Check Agreements," *Industrial and Labor Relations Review* 55 (2001), pp. 42–59.

39. National Labor Relations Board annual reports.

40. Chaison and Rose, "The Macrodeterminants of Union Growth and Decline."

41. Fossum, *Labor Relations,* p. 262.

42. R. E. Walton and R. B. McKersie, *A Behavioral Theory of Negotiations* (New York: McGraw-Hill, 1965).

43. C. M. Steven, *Strategy and Collective Bargaining Negotiations* (New York: McGraw-Hill, 1963): Katz and Kochan, *An Introduction to Collective Bargaining.*

44. Kochan, *Collective Bargaining and Industrial Relations,* p. 272.

45. Katz and Kochan, *An Introduction to Collective Bargaining.*

46. *United Steelworkers v. American Manufacturing Company,* 363 U.S. 564 (1960); *United Steelworkers v.*

Warrior Gulf and Navigation Company, 363 U.S. 574 (1960); *United Steelworkers v. Enterprise Wheel and Car Corporation,* 363 U.S. 593 (1960).

47. U.S. Federal Mediation and Conciliation Service, *Fiftieth Annual Report, Fiscal Year 1997* (Washington, DC: U.S. Government Printing Office, 1997).

48. J. R. Redecker, *Employee Discipline: Policies and Practices* (Washington, DC: Bureau of National Affairs, 1989).

49. T. A. Kochan, H. C. Katz, and R. B. McKersie, *The Transformation of American Industrial Relations* (New York: Basic Books, 1986), chap. 6; E. Appelbaum, T. Bailey, and P. Berg, *Manufacturing Advantage: Why High-Performance Work Systems Pay Off* (Ithaca, NY: Cornell University Press, 2000).

50. L. W. Hunter, J. P. MacDuffie, and L. Doucet, "What Makes Teams Take? Employee Reactions to Work Reforms," *Industrial and Labor Relations Review* 55 (2002), pp. 448–472.

51. J. B. Arthur, "The Link between Business Strategy and Industrial Relations Systems in American Steel Minimills," *Industrial and Labor Relations Review* 45 (1992), pp. 488–506; M. Schuster, "Union Management Cooperation," in *Employee and Labor Relations,* ed. J. A. Fossum (Washington, D.C.: Bureau of National Affairs, 1990); E. Cohen-Rosenthal and C. Burton, *Mutual Gains: A Guide to Union-Management Cooperation,* 2nd ed. (Ithaca, NY: ILR Press, 1993); T. A. Kochan and P. Osterman, *The Mutual Gains Enterprise* (Boston: Harvard Business School Press, 1994); E. Applebaum and R. Batt, *The New American Workplace* (Ithaca, NY: ILR Press, 1994).

52. A. E. Eaton, "Factors Contributing to the Survival of Employee Participation Programs in Unionized Settings," *Industrial and Labor Relations Review* 47, no. 3 (1994), pp. 371–89.

53. A. Bernstein, "Putting a Damper on That Old Team Spirit," *BusinessWeek,* May 4, 1992, p. 60; Bureau of National Affairs, "Polaroid Dissolves Employee Committee in Response to Labor Department Ruling," *Daily Labor Report,* June 23, 1992, p. A-3; K. G. Salwen, "DuPont Is Told It Must Disband Nonunion Panels," *The Wall Street Journal,* June 7, 1993, p. A2.

54. "NLRB 4–0 Approves Crown Cork & Seal's Use of Seven Employee Participation Committees," *HR News,* September 3, 2001.

55. Kochan and Osterman, *The Mutual Gains Enterprise;* J. P. MacDuffie, "Human Resource Bundles and Manufacturing Performance: Organizational Logic and Flexible Production Systems in the World Auto Industry," *Industrial and Labor Relations Review* 48, no. 2 (1995), pp. 197–221; W. N. Cooke, "Employee Participation Programs, Group-Based Incentives, and Company Performance: A Union-Nonunion

Comparison," *Industrial and Labor Relations Review* 47, no. 4 (1994), pp. 594–609; C. Doucouliagos, "Worker Participation and Productivity in Labor-Managed and Participatory Capitalist Firms: A Meta-Analysis," *Industrial and Labor Relations Review* 49, no. 1 (1995), pp. 58–77.

56. P. Thomas, "Aviation Firm Learns to Deal with Strained Labor Relations," *The Wall Street Journal Online*, July 30, 2002, http://online.wsj.com.

Chapter 15

Managing Human Resources Globally

What Do I Need to Know? After reading this chapter, you should be able to:

1. Summarize how the growth in international business activity affects human resource management.

2. Identify the factors that most strongly influence HRM in international markets.

3. Discuss how differences among countries affect HR planning at organizations with international operations.

4. Describe how companies select and train human resources in a global labor market.

5. Discuss challenges related to compensating employees from other countries.

6. Explain how employers prepare managers for international assignments and for their return home.

Introduction

According to a survey of almost 3,000 line executives and HR executives from 12 countries, international competition is the number one factor affecting human resource management. The globalization of business structures and globalization of the economy ranked fourth and fifth, respectively.[1] Business decisions such as whether to enter foreign markets or set up operations in other countries are complex, and in the course of moving and executing them many human resource issues surface.

This chapter discusses the HR issues that organizations must address in a world of global competition. We begin by describing how the global nature of business is affecting human resource management in modern organizations. Next, we identify how global differences among countries affect the organization's decisions about human resources. In the following sections we explore HR planning, selection, training, and compensation practices in international settings. Finally, we examine guidelines for managing employees sent on international assignments.

LO1

HRM in a Global Environment

The environment in which organizations operate is rapidly becoming a global one. More and more companies are entering international markets by exporting their products, building facilities in other countries, and entering into alliances with foreign companies. At the same time, companies based in other countries are investing and setting up operations in the United States. Indeed, most organizations now function in the global economy.

What is behind the trend toward expansion into global markets? Foreign countries can provide a business with new markets in which there are millions or billions of new customers; developing countries often provide such markets, but developed countries do so as well. Companies set up operations overseas because they can operate with lower labor costs—for example, in Mexico near the U.S. border, thousands of manufacturing plants called *maquiladoras*, most of them owned by U.S. companies, employ Mexican laborers at an average wage of less than $3 per hour.[2]

Global activities are simplified and encouraged by trade agreements among nations; for example, most countries in Western Europe belong to the European Union and have begun to share a common currency, the euro. Canada, Mexico, and the United States have encouraged trade among themselves with the North American Free Trade Agreement (NAFTA). The World Trade Organization (WTO) resolves trade disputes among more than 100 participating nations.

As these trends and arrangements encourage international trade, they increase and change the demands on human resource management. Organizations with customers or suppliers in other countries need employees who understand those customers or suppliers. Organizations that operate facilities in foreign countries need to understand the laws and customs that apply to employees in those countries. They may have to prepare managers and other personnel to take international assignments. They have to adapt their human resource plans and policies to different settings. Even if some practices are the same worldwide, the company now has to communicate them to its international workforce. A variety of international activities require managers to understand HRM principles and practices prevalent in global markets.

Mexican workers sew pants for export to the United States in a *maquiladora*. U.S. companies set up these operations over the border in Mexico because of lower labor costs. Mexico needs the jobs. Arrangements such as these increase the demands on human resource management.

Employees in an International Workforce

When organizations operate globally, their employees are very likely to be citizens of more than one country. Employees may come from the employer's parent country, a host country, or a third country. The **parent country** is the country in which the organization's headquarters is located. For example, the United States is the parent country of General Motors, because GM's headquarters is in Michigan. A GM employee who was born in the United States and works at GM's headquarters or one of its U.S. factories is therefore a *parent-country national.*

A **host country** is a country (other than the parent country) in which an organization operates a facility. Great Britain is a host country of General Motors because GM has operations there. Any British workers hired to work at GM's British facility would be *host-country nationals,* that is, employees who are citizens of the host country.

A **third country** refers to a country that is neither the parent country nor the host country. (The organization may or may not have a facility in the third country.) In the example of GM's operations in Great Britain, the company could hire an Australian manager to work there. The Australian manager would be a *third-country national* because the manager is neither from the parent country (the United States) nor from the host country (Great Britain).

When organizations operate overseas, they must decide whether to hire parent-country nationals, host-country nationals, or third-country nationals for the overseas operations. Usually, they hire a combination of these. In general, employees assigned to work in another country are called **expatriates.** In the GM example, the U.S. and Australian managers working in Great Britain would be expatriates during those assignments.

The extent to which organizations use parent-country, host-country, or third-country nationals varies. According to one study, Japanese firms with overseas operations use Japanese (parent-country) managers for their foreign assignments relatively often.[3] European and U.S. companies are less likely to emphasize parent-country nationals. (In the same study, HRM practices emphasizing the use of managers from the parent country were associated with more HRM problems.)

parent country
The country in which an organization's headquarters is located.

host country
A country (other than the parent country) in which an organization operates a facility.

third country
A country that is neither the parent country nor the host country of an employer.

expatriates
Employees assigned to work in another country.

Employers in the Global Marketplace

Just as there are different ways for employees to participate in international business—as parent-country, host-country, or third-county nationals—so there are different ways for employers to do business globally, ranging from simply shipping products to customers in other countries to transforming the organization into a truly global one, with operations, employees, and customers in many countries. Figure 15.1 shows the major levels of global participation.

Most organizations begin by serving customers and clients within a domestic marketplace. Typically, a company's founder has an idea for serving a local, regional, or national market. The business must recruit, hire, train, and compensate employees to produce the product, and these people usually come from the business owner's local labor market. Selection and training focus on employees' technical abilities and, to some extent, on interpersonal skills. Pay levels reflect local labor conditions. If the product succeeds, the company might expand operations to other domestic locations, and HRM decisions become more complex as the organization draws from a larger labor market and needs systems for training and motivating employees in several locations. As the employer's workforce grows, it is also likely to become more diverse.

FIGURE 15.1

Levels of Global Participation

international organization

An organization that sets up one or a few facilities in one or a few foreign countries.

multinational company

An organization that builds facilities in a number of different countries in an effort to minimize production and distribution costs.

global organization

An organization that chooses to locate a facility based on the ability to effectively, efficiently, and flexibly produce a product or service, using cultural differences as an advantage.

Even in small domestic organizations, a significant share of workers may be immigrants. In this way, even domestic companies are affected by issues related to the global economy.

As organizations grow, they often begin to meet demand from customers in other countries. The usual way that a company begins to enter foreign markets is by *exporting*, or shipping domestically produced items to other countries to be sold there. Eventually, it may become economically desirable to set up operations in one or more foreign countries. An organization that does so becomes an **international organization.** The decision to participate in international activities raises a host of HR issues, including the basic question of whether a particular location provides an environment where the organization can successfully acquire and manage human resources.

While international companies build one or a few facilities in another country, **multinational companies** go overseas on a broader scale. They build facilities in a number of different countries as a way to keep production and distribution costs to a minimum. In general, when organizations become multinationals, they move production facilities from relatively high-cost locations to lower-cost locations. The lower-cost locations may have lower average wage rates, or they may reduce distribution costs by being nearer to customers. The HRM challenges faced by a multinational company are similar but larger than those of an international organization, because more countries are involved. More than ever, the organization needs to hire managers who can function in a variety of settings, give them necessary training, and provide flexible compensation systems that take into account the different pay rates, tax systems, and costs of living from one country to another.

At the highest level of involvement in the global marketplace are **global organizations.** These flexible organizations compete by offering top products tailored to segments of the market while keeping costs as low as possible. A global organization locates each facility based on the ability to effectively, efficiently, and flexibly produce a product or service, using cultural differences as an advantage. Rather than treating differences in other countries as a challenge to overcome, a global organization treats different cultures as equals. It may have multiple headquarters spread across the globe, so decisions are more decentralized. This type of organization needs HRM practices that encourage flexibility and are based on an in-depth knowledge of differences among countries. Global organizations must be able to recruit, develop, retain, and use managers who can get results across national boundaries.

A global organization needs a **transnational HRM system**[4] that features decision making from a global perspective, managers from many countries, and ideas contributed by people from a variety of cultures. Decisions that are the outcome of a transnational HRM system balance uniformity (for fairness) with flexibility (to account for cultural and legal differences). This balance and the variety of perspectives should work together to improve the quality of decision making. The participants from various countries and cultures contribute ideas from a position of equality, rather than the parent country's culture dominating.

transnational HRM system
Type of HRM system that makes decisions from a global perspective, includes managers from many countries, and is based on ideas contributed by people representing a variety of cultures.

LO2

Factors Affecting HRM in International Markets

Whatever their level of global participation, organizations that operate in more than one country must recognize that the countries are not identical and differ in terms of many factors. To simplify this discussion, we focus on four major factors: culture, education, economic systems, and political-legal systems. These influences on human resource management are shown in Figure 15.2.

Culture

By far the most important influence on international HRM is the culture of the country in which a facility is located. *Culture* is a community's set of shared assumptions about how the world works and what ideals are worth striving for.[5] Cultural influences may be expressed through customs, languages, religions, and so on.

Culture is important to HRM for two reasons. First, it often determines the other three international influences. Culture can greatly affect a country's laws, because

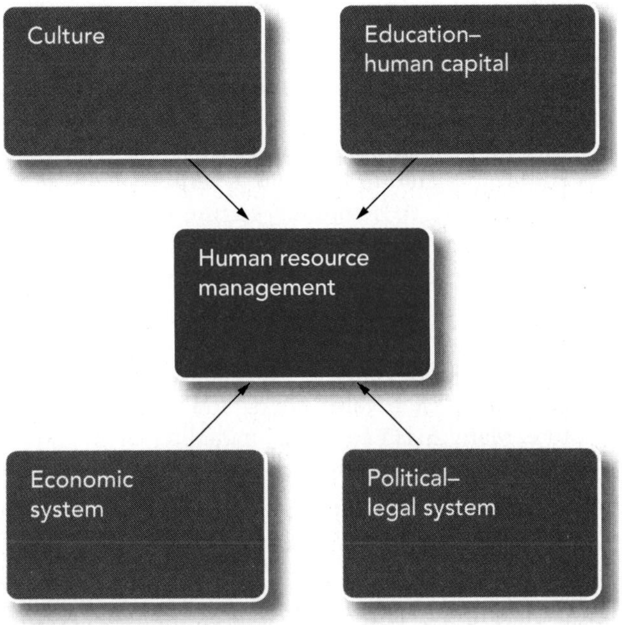

FIGURE 15.2

Factors Affecting Human Resource Management in International Markets laws often are based on the culture's definitions of right and wrong. Culture also influences what people value, so it affects people's economic systems and efforts to invest in education.

Even more important for understanding human resource management, culture often determines the effectiveness of various HRM practices. Practices that are effective in the United States, for example, may fail or even backfire in a country with different beliefs and values.[6] Consider the five dimensions of culture that Geert Hofstede identified in his classic study of culture:[7]

1. *Individualism/collectivism* describes the strength of the relation between an individual and other individuals in the society. In a culture that is high in individualism, such as the United States, Great Britain, and the Netherlands, people tend to think and act as individuals rather than as members of a group. People in these countries are expected to stand on their own two feet, rather than be protected by the group. In a culture that is high in collectivism, such as Colombia, Pakistan, and Taiwan, people think of themselves mainly as group members. They are expected to devote themselves to the interests of the community, and the community is expected to protect them when they are in trouble.

2. *Power distance* concerns the way the culture deals with unequal distribution of power and defines the amount of inequality that is normal. In countries with large power distances, including India and the Philippines, the culture defines it as normal to maintain large differences in power. In countries with small power distances, such as Denmark and Israel, people try to eliminate inequalities. One way to see differences in power distance is in the way people talk to one another. In the high-power-distance countries of Mexico and Japan, people address one another with titles (Señor Smith, Smith-san). At the other extreme, in the United States, in most situations people use one another's first names—behavior that would be disrespectful in other cultures.

3. *Uncertainty avoidance* describes how cultures handle the fact that the future is unpredictable. High uncertainty avoidance refers to a strong cultural preference for structured situations. In countries such as Greece and Portugal, people tend to rely heavily on religion, law, and technology to give them a degree of security and clear rules about how to behave. In countries with low uncertainty avoidance, including Singapore and Jamaica, people seem to take each day as it comes.

4. *Masculinity/femininity* is the emphasis a culture places on practices or qualities that have traditionally been considered masculine or feminine. A "masculine" culture is a culture that values achievement, money making, assertiveness, and competition. A "feminine" culture is one that places a high value on relationships, service, care for the weak, and preserving the environment. In this model, Germany and Japan are examples of masculine cultures, and Sweden and Norway are examples of feminine cultures.

5. *Long-term/short-term orientation* suggests whether the focus of cultural values is on the future (long term) or the past and present (short term). Cultures with a long-term orientation value saving and persistence, which tend to pay off in the future. Many Asian countries, including Japan and China, have a long-term orientation. Short-term orientations, as in the cultures of the United States, Russia, and West Africa, promote respect for past tradition, and for fulfilling social obligations in the present. Figure 15.3 summarizes these five cultural dimensions.

Such cultural characteristics as these influence the ways members of an organization behave toward one another, as well as their attitudes toward various HRM prac-

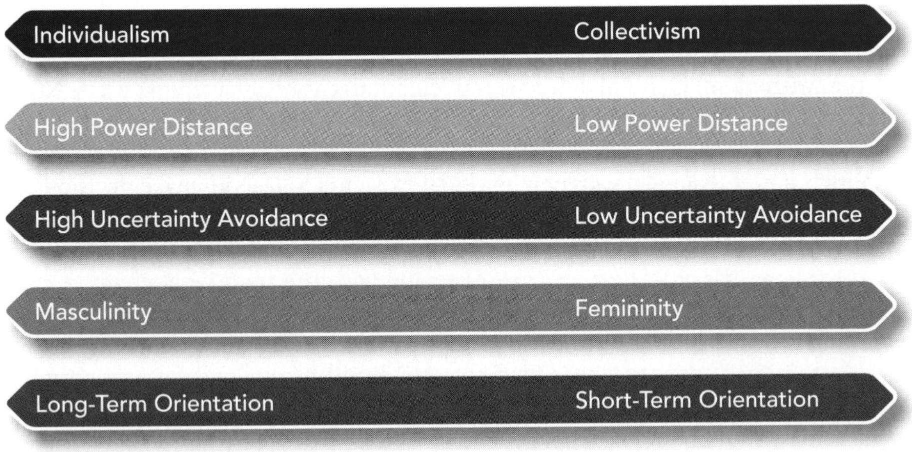

Individualism	Collectivism

High Power Distance	Low Power Distance

High Uncertainty Avoidance	Low Uncertainty Avoidance

Masculinity	Femininity

Long-Term Orientation	Short-Term Orientation

FIGURE 15.3

Five Dimensions of Culture

SOURCE: G. Hofstede, "Dimensions of National Cultures in Fifty Countries and Three Regions," in *Expectations in Cross-Cultural Psychology*, eds. J. Deregowski, S. Dziurawiec, and R. C. Annis (Lisse, Netherlands: Swets and Zeitlinger, 1983); G. Hofstede, "Cultural Constraints in Management Theories," *Academy of Management Executive* 7 (1993), pp. 81–90.

tices. For instance, cultures differ strongly in their opinions about how managers should lead, how decisions should be handled, and what motivates employees. In Germany, managers achieve their status by demonstrating technical skills, and employees look to managers to assign tasks and resolve technical problems. In the Netherlands, managers focus on seeking agreement, exchanging views, and balancing the interests of the people affected by a decision.[8] Clearly, differences like these would affect how an organization selects and trains its managers and measures their performance.

Cultures strongly influence the appropriateness of HRM practices. For example, the extent to which a culture is individualist or collectivist will affect the success of a compensation program. Compensation tied to individual performance may be seen as fairer and more motivating by members of an individualist culture; a culture favoring individualism will be more accepting of great differences in pay between the organization's highest- and lowest-paid employees. Collectivist cultures tend to have much flatter pay structures.

Job design aimed at employee empowerment can be problematic in cultures with high "power distance." In a Mexican slipper-manufacturing plant, an effort to expand the decision-making authority of production workers stumbled when the workers balked at doing what they saw as the supervisor's proper responsibility.[9] Realizing they had moved too quickly, the plant's managers narrowed the scope of the workers' decision-making authority so they could adapt to the role. On the other hand, a factor in favor of empowerment at that plant was the Mexican culture's high collectivism. The workers liked discussing team-related information and using the information to benefit the entire team. As in this example, a culture does not necessarily rule out a particular HRM practice, such as employee empowerment, but it should be a consideration in deciding how to carry out the practice.

Finally, cultural differences can affect how people communicate and how they coordinate their activities. In collectivist cultures, people tend to value group decision making, as in the previous example. When a person raised in an individualistic culture must work closely with people from a collectivist culture, communication problems and conflicts often occur. People from the collectivist culture tend to collaborate heavily and may evaluate the individualistic person as unwilling to cooperate and share information with them. Cultural differences in communication affected the way a North American agricultural company embarked on employee empowerment at its facilities in the United States and Brazil.[10] Empowerment requires information sharing, but in Brazil, high power distance leads employees to expect managers to make decisions, so they do not desire information that is appropriately held by managers. Empowering the Brazilian employees required involving managers directly in giving and sharing information to show that this practice was in keeping with the traditional chain of command. Also, because uncertainty avoidance is another aspect of Brazilian culture, managers explained that greater information sharing would reduce uncertainty about their work. At the same time, greater collectivism in Brazil made employees comfortable with the day-to-day communication of teamwork. The individualistic U.S. employees needed to be sold more on this aspect of empowerment.

Because of these challenges, organizations must prepare managers to recognize and handle cultural differences. They may recruit managers with knowledge of other cultures or provide training, as described later in the chapter. For expatriate assignments, organizations may need to conduct an extensive selection process to identify individuals who can adapt to new environments.

Education and Skill Levels

Countries also differ in the degree to which their labor markets include people with education and skills of value to employers. As discussed in Chapter 1, the United States suffers from a shortage of skilled workers in many occupations, and the problem is expected to increase. For example, the need for knowledge workers (engineers, teachers, scientists, health care workers) is expected to grow almost twice as fast as the overall rate of job growth in the United States.[11] On the other hand, the labor markets in many countries are very attractive because they offer high skills and low wages.

Educational opportunities also vary from one country to another. In general, spending on education is greater per pupil in high-income countries than in poorer countries.[12] In the Netherlands, government funding of school systems allows students to go all the way through graduate school without paying.[13] Similarly, the free education provided to citizens in the former Soviet bloc resulted in a highly educated workforce, in spite of the region's economic difficulties. Some Third World countries, such as Nicaragua and Haiti, have relatively low educational levels because those countries have not invested in education.

Companies with foreign operations locate in countries where they can find suitable employees. The education and skill levels of a country's labor force affect how and the extent to which companies want to operate there. In countries with a poorly educated population, companies will limit their activities to low-skill, low-wage jobs. In Ireland, a high rate of college education, along with a strong work ethic and high unemployment, attracted employers looking for skilled workers, high productivity, and low turnover.[14]

Economic System

A country's economic system whether capitalist or socialist, as well as the government's involvement in the economy through taxes or compensation, price controls, and other activities, influences human resource management practices in a number of ways.

As with all aspects of a region's or country's life, the economic system and culture are likely to be closely tied, providing many of the incentives or disincentives for developing the value of the labor force. Socialist economic systems provide ample opportunities for educational development because the education system is free to students. At the same time, socialism may not provide economic rewards (higher pay) for increasing one's education. In capitalist systems, students bear more of the cost of their education, but employers reward those who invest in education.

The health of an economic system affects human resource management. In developed countries with great wealth, labor costs are relatively high. Such differences show up in compensation systems and in recruiting and selection decisions.

In general, socialist systems take a higher percentage of each worker's income as the worker's income increases. Capitalist systems tend to let workers keep more of their earnings. In this way, socialism redistributes wealth from high earners to the poor, while capitalism apparently rewards individual accomplishments. In any case, since the amount of take-home pay a worker receives after taxes may thus differ from country to country, in an organization that pays two managers in two countries $100,000 each, the manager in one country might take home more than the manager

Students at the University of Warsaw in Poland are provided with a government-supported education. In general, former Soviet bloc countries tend to be generous in funding education, so they tend to have highly educated and skilled labor forces. Capitalist countries such as the United States generally leave higher education up to individual students to pay for, but the labor market rewards students who earn a college degree.

in the other country. Such differences make pay structures more complicated when they cross national boundaries, and they can affect recruiting of candidates from more than one country.

Political-Legal System

A country's political-legal system—its government, laws, and regulations—strongly impinges on human resource management. The country's laws often dictate the requirements for certain HRM practices, such as training, compensation, hiring, firing, and layoffs. As we noted in the discussion of culture, the political-legal system arises to a large degree from the culture in which it exists, so laws and regulations reflect cultural values.

For example, the United States has led the world in eliminating discrimination in the workplace. Because this value is important in U.S. culture, the nation has legal safeguards such as the equal employment opportunity laws discussed in Chapter 3, which affect hiring and other HRM decisions. As a society, the United States also has strong beliefs regarding the fairness of pay systems. Thus, the Fair Labor Standards Act (discussed in Chapter 11), among other laws and regulations, sets a minimum wage for a variety of jobs. Other laws and regulations dictate much of the process of negotiation between unions and management. All these are examples of laws and regulations that affect the practice of HRM in the United States.

Similarly, laws and regulations in other countries reflect the norms of their cultures. In Germany employees have a legal right to "codetermination" at the level of the company, facility, and individual. At the company level, an organization's employees have direct influence on the important decisions that affect them, such as large investments or new strategies. This influence comes from employee representatives on each company's supervisory council. At the level of each facility, codetermination exists through work councils. The councils have no rights in the economic management of the company, but they can influence HRM policies on issues such as working hours, payment methods, hirings, and transfers. Finally, at the individual level, employees have contractual rights, such as the right to read their personnel files and the right to be informed about how their pay is calculated.[15]

As this example suggests, an organization that expands internationally must gain expertise in the host country's legal requirements and ways of dealing with its legal system, often leading organizations to hire one or more host-country nationals to help in the process. Some countries have laws requiring that a certain percentage of the employees of any foreign-owned subsidiary be host-country nationals, and in the context of our discussion here, this legal challenge to an organization's HRM may hold an advantage if handled creatively.

LO3

Human Resource Planning in a Global Economy

As economic and technological change creates a global environment for organizations, human resource planning is involved in decisions about participating as an exporter or as an international, multinational, or global company. Even purely domestic companies may draw talent from the international labor market. As organizations consider decisions about their level of international activity, HR professionals should provide information about the relevant human resource issues, such as local market pay rates and labor laws. When organizations decide to operate internationally or globally, human resource planning involves decisions about where and how many employees are needed for each international facility.

In Chapter 5, we saw that human resource planning includes decisions to hire and lay off workers to prepare for the organization's expected needs. Compared with other countries, the United States allows employers wide latitude in reducing their workforce, giving U.S. employers the option of hiring for peak needs, then laying off employees if needs decline. Other governments place more emphasis on protecting workers' jobs. As described in the *BusinessWeek* Case at the end of this chapter, European countries, and France in particular, tend to be very strict in this regard.

Until recently, Japanese law and culture supported the concept of "lifetime employment," but this practice is changing to help companies weather a difficult recession.[16] HR planning at Japanese companies now includes more decisions to shrink or close Japanese facilities in favor of production elsewhere. At its peak in the mid-1990s, Nissan Motor Company's Murayama plant was a symbol of Japanese automaking efficiency, producing almost a half million cars a year. In 2001, Nissan closed the plant, displacing all 5,000 workers. As Nissan was closing plants in Japan, it was expanding production of its Maxima sedan in Tennessee and planning a new Mississippi factory to produce minivans and sport utility vehicles. The company's home market was weak, and demand for its product was strong in North America, so the decisions made economic sense. Producing in the United States keeps transportation costs down and protects the company from shifts in the relative value of the dollar and yen. As can be easily imagined, many HR issues come into play in consequence of and especially in planning for such shifts, in both home country and host country.

Selecting Employees in a Global Labor Market LO4

Many companies such as Microsoft have headquarters in the United States plus facilities in locations around the world. To be effective, employees in the Microsoft Mexico operations in Mexico City must understand that region's business and social culture. Organizations often meet this need by hiring host-country nationals to fill most of their foreign positions.[17] A key reason is that a host-country national can more easily understand the values and customs of the local workforce than someone from another part of the world can. Also, training for and transporting families to foreign assignments is more expensive than hiring people in the foreign country. Employees may be reluctant to take a foreign assignment because of the difficulty of moving overseas. Sometimes the move requires the employee's spouse to quit a job, and some countries will not allow the employee's spouse to seek work, even if jobs might be available.

Even so, organizations fill many key foreign positions with parent-country or third-country nationals. Sometimes a person's technical and human relations skills outweigh the advantages of hiring locally. In other situations, such as the shortage of U.S. knowledge workers, the local labor market simply does not offer enough qualified people. At organizations located where needed skills are in short supply, hiring immigrant employees may be part of an effective recruitment and selection strategy.[18] Of the two largest categories of foreign workers employed in the United States, one group consists of professionals with the particular qualifications needed to fill a job.[19] The other group comprises employees of multinational companies who are transferred to the United States from their employer's facilities in another country. The terrorist attacks of September 11, 2001, have not changed the basics of selecting these employees, but they have raised some security issues. One is that the government may move more deliberately (and thus more slowly) in approving visas for immigrants from certain countries, such as Libya and Iraq. Another issue is that foreign travelers to and from the United States, including the organization's immigrant workers, may have to contend with more delays and red tape. The primary impact on employers is that they must be more patient in completing the hiring process.[20]

Whether the organization is hiring immigrants or selecting parent-country or third-country nationals for foreign assignments, some basic principles of selection apply. Selection of employees for foreign assignments should reflect criteria that have been associated with success in working overseas:

- Competency in the employee's area of expertise.
- Ability to communicate verbally and nonverbally in the foreign country.
- Flexibility, tolerance of ambiguity, and sensitivity to cultural differences.
- Motivation to succeed and enjoyment of challenges.
- Willingness to learn about the foreign country's culture, language, and customs.
- Support from family members.[21]

In research conducted a number of years ago, the factor most strongly influencing whether an employee completed a foreign assignment was the comfort of the employee's spouse and family.[22] Personality may also be important. Research has found successful completion of overseas assignments to be most likely among employees who are extroverted (outgoing), agreeable (cooperative and tolerant), and conscientious (dependable and achievement oriented).[23]

Qualities of flexibility, motivation, agreeableness, and conscientiousness are so important because of the challenges involved in entering another culture. The emotions that accompany an overseas assignment tend to follow a cycle like that in Figure 15.4.[24] For a month or so after arriving, the foreign worker enjoys a "honeymoon" of fascination and euphoria as the employee enjoys the novelty of the new culture and compares its interesting similarities to or differences from the employee's own culture. Before long, the employee's mood declines as he or she notices more unpleasant differences and experiences feelings of isolation, criticism, stereotyping, and even hostility. As the mood reaches bottom, the employee is experiencing **culture shock,** the

culture shock
Disillusionment and discomfort that occur during the process of adjusting to a new culture.

Qualities associated with success in foreign assignments are the ability to communicate in the foreign country, flexibility, enjoying a challenging situation, and support from family members. What would persuade you to take a foreign assignment?

FIGURE 15.4

Emotional Cycle
Associated with a
Foreign Assignment

SOURCE: Adapted from C. Lachnit, "Low-Cost Tips for Successful Inpatriation,"
Workforce, August 2001, p. 44.

disillusionment and discomfort of ideas that occur during the process of adjusting
to a new culture and its norms, values, and perspectives. Eventually, if employees
persist and continue learning about their host country's culture, they develop a
greater understanding and a support network. As the employee's language skills and
comfort increase, the employee's mood should improve as well. Eventually, the employee reaches a stage of adjustment in which he or she accepts and enjoys the host
country's culture.

Even if the organization determines that the best candidate for a position is someone from another country, employers often have difficulty persuading candidates to accept foreign assignments. Not only do the employee and employee's family have to
contend with culture shock, but the employee's spouse commonly loses a job when an
employee makes a foreign move. Some organizations solve this problem with a compromise: the use of **virtual expatriates,** or employees who manage an operation abroad
without locating permanently in that country.[25] They take frequent trips to the foreign
country, and when they are home, they use modern technology such as videoconferencing and e-mail to stay in touch. An assignment as a virtual expatriate may be less
inconvenient to family members and less costly to the employer. The arrangement
does have disadvantages. Most notably, by limiting personal contact to sporadic trips,
the virtual expatriate will likely have a harder time building relationships.

virtual expatriates
Employees who
manage an
operation abroad
without permanently
locating in the
country.

Training and Developing a Global Workforce

In an organization whose employees come from more than one country, some special
challenges arise with regard to training and development: (1) Training and development programs should be effective for all participating employees, regardless of their
country of origin. (2) When organizations hire employees to work in a foreign country or transfer them to another country, the employer needs to provide the employees
with training in how to handle the challenges associated with working in the foreign
country.

Training Programs for an International Workforce

Developers of effective training programs for an international workforce must ask certain questions.[26] The first is to establish the objectives for the training and its content. Decisions about the training should support those objectives. The developers
should next ask what training techniques, strategies, and media to use. Some will be
more effective than others, depending on the learners' language and culture, as well
as the content of the training. For example, in preparation U.S. employees might expect to discuss and ask questions about the training content, whereas employees from
other cultures might consider this level of participation to be disrespectful, so for
them some additional support might be called for. Language differences will require
translations and perhaps a translator at training activities. Next, the developers

should identify any other interventions and conditions that must be in place for the training to meet its objectives. For example, training is more likely to meet its objectives if it is linked to performance management and has the full support of management. Finally, the developers of a training program should identify who in the organization should be involved in reviewing and approving the training program.

The plan for the training program must consider international differences among trainees. For example, economic and educational differences might influence employees' access to and ability to use Web-based training. Cultural differences may influence whether they will consider it appropriate to ask questions and whether they expect the trainer to spend time becoming acquainted with employees or to get down to business immediately. Table 15.1 provides examples of how cultural characteristics can affect training design. These differences may call for extra planning and creativity on the part of the training program's developer. To meet the needs of trainees in China, for instance, the training program should take into account that culture's high power distance.[27] The instructor needs to encourage audience feedback, perhaps by inviting the group's senior member to speak. If the instructor gives other trainees a chance to forward questions to this person, they can avoid embarrassing a high-status participant by asking a better question. Also, extra time is needed to prepare translations and practice delivering presentations with a translator.

An example of successful international training was a unit on avoiding sexual harassment presented to employees of four multinational companies working on the Sea Launch vessel, a rocket launch platform located in the Pacific Ocean.[28] The Sea Launch employees came from the United States, Norway, Russia, Ukraine, and the Philippines. The training was essential because one of the employers in this joint venture, the Boeing Company, is a U.S. business and therefore must comply with U.S. laws forbidding sex discrimination. However, the other three companies participating in the joint venture are based in other countries, so the law did not apply to them, and they had differing standards on what is appropriate in male-female interactions. The objective of the training was therefore to explain how employees should behave to succeed in an American work environment, emphasizing shared values of personal responsibility and respect for individuals, rather than "right" or "wrong" behavior.

TABLE 15.1

Effects of Culture on Training Design

CULTURAL DIMENSION	IMPACT ON TRAINING
Individualism	Culture high in individualism expects participation in exercises and questioning to be determined by status in the company or culture.
Uncertainty avoidance	Culture high in uncertainty avoidance expects formal instructional environments. Less tolerance for impromptu style.
Masculinity	Culture low in masculinity values relationships with fellow trainees. Female trainers less likely to be resisted in low-masculinity cultures.
Power distance	Culture high in power distance expects trainer to be expert. Trainers expected to be authoritarian and controlling of session.
Time orientation	Culture with a long-term orientation will have trainees who are likely to accept development plans and assignments.

SOURCE: Based on B. Filipczak, "Think Locally, Act Globally," *Training*, January 1997, pp. 41–48.

The trainers selected the most common and accepted training methods for their audience: a lecture followed by a question-and-answer session. To establish the training's importance and credibility, the training sessions included an introduction by top executives and presentations by experts in the subject matter. Also, upper management was involved in the design of the program, which helped to demonstrate management's commitment to the training content. Classes brought together participants from all the cultures, and a translator enabled the material to be presented in the two dominant languages, English and Russian. Employee satisfaction surveys later showed a positive contribution to the attitudes of Boeing's Sea Launch employees.

Cross-Cultural Preparation

When an organization selects an employee for a position in a foreign country, it must prepare the employee for the foreign assignment. This kind of training is called **cross-cultural preparation,** preparing employees to work across national and cultural boundaries, and it often includes family members who will accompany the employee on the assignment. The training is necessary for all three phases of an international assignment:

cross-cultural preparation
Training to prepare employees and their family members for an assignment in a foreign country.

1. Preparation for *departure*—language instruction and an orientation to the foreign country's culture.
2. The *assignment* itself—some combination of a formal program and mentoring relationship to provide ongoing further information about the foreign country's culture.
3. Preparation for the *return* home—providing information about the employee's community and home-country workplace (from company newsletters, local newspapers, and so on).

Methods for providing this training may range from lectures for employees and their families to visits to culturally diverse communities.[29] Employees and their families may also spend time visiting a local family from the country where they will be working. In the later section on managing expatriates, we provide more detail about cross-cultural preparation.

U.S.-based companies sometimes need to be reminded that foreign employees who come to the United States ("inpatriates") need cross-cultural preparation as much as U.S. employees sent on foreign assignments.[30] In spite of the many benefits of living in the United States, relocation can be challenging for inpatriates. In fact, in the Global Relocation Trends 2000 Survey Report, the United States was listed as among the most challenging foreign assignments.[31] For example, inpatriates exposed to the United States through Hollywood and TV shows often worry about safety in their new homes. In many parts of the world, a middle manager or professional's lifestyle may include servants, and the cost of rental housing is far less. As with expatriates, organizations can prepare inpatriate employees by providing information about getting the resources they need to live safely and comfortably in their new surroundings. HR personnel may be able to identify local immigrant communities where their inpatriate employees can go to shop for familiar foods and hear their native language.

Global Employee Development

At global organizations, international assignments are a part of many career paths. The organization benefits most if it applies the principles of employee development in deciding which employees should be offered jobs in other countries. Career development helps expatriate and inpatriate employees make the transitions to and from

Deloitte Develops a Global Workforce

Deloitte Touche Tohmatsu is an accounting and consulting firm whose 95,000 employees work in 700 offices located in 140 different countries around the world. An organization like that has the human resources to know the ins and outs of international business—but only if it gives employees international experience. Deloitte does just that with its Global Development Program.

The Global Development Program, based on a curriculum developed by the human resource department, identifies midcareer employees in Deloitte's worldwide locations and assigns them to work in other countries. HR coordinators work with applicants to identify countries that offer experiences likely to be relevant to future work in the applicants' own countries. Often, employees wind up working with the same multinational client but in another country where that client operates. Through the program, these employees learn the languages, business practices, and cultures of the countries where they are assigned. They also have plenty of opportunity to interact with other expatriate employees.

For example, Fabian Gomez left Mexico for a year and a half at Deloitte's New York office. When he returned to León, a city northwest of Mexico City, Gomez was well prepared to serve an international clientele as an audit partner. Explains Gomez, "A lot of our business is serving Mexican subsidiaries of international companies, and the executives usually come from other places" as far from Mexico as Japan.

Hundreds of employees and Deloitte offices in 50 countries participate in the Global Development Program. Executives give the program some of the credit for the firm's 11 percent growth in global revenue in 2001—growth that is particularly impressive because it occurred during a time of economic slowdown. The company expects further benefits down the road, as Deloitte increases its ability to serve the multinational needs of its clients.

The participants praise the program, too. Gomez says, "People are very excited about [the Global Development Program], because they know that if they have international experience, both they and the company are going to get ahead."

SOURCE: P. J. Kiger, "How Deloitte Builds Global Expertise," *Workforce*, June 2002, pp. 62–64, 66.

their assignments and helps the organization apply the knowledge the employees obtain from these assignments. An example of a company with a strong program for global employee development is Deloitte Touche Tohmatsu, described in the "Best Practices" box.

Performance Management across National Boundaries

The general principles of performance management may apply in most countries, but the specific methods that work in one country may fail in another. Therefore, organizations have to consider legal requirements, local business practices, and national cultures when they establish performance management methods in other countries.

Differences may include which behaviors are rated, how and the extent to which performance is measured, who performs the rating, and how feedback is provided.[32]

For example, National Rental Car uses a behaviorally based rating scale for customer service representatives. To measure the extent to which customer service representatives' behaviors contribute to the company's goal of improving customer service, the scale measures behaviors such as smiling, making eye contact, greeting customers, and solving customer problems. Depending on the country, different behaviors may be appropriate. In Japan, culturally defined standards for polite behavior include the angle of bowing as well as proper back alignment and eye contact. In Ghana and many other African nations, appropriate measures would include behaviors that reflect loyalty and repaying of obligations as well as behaviors related to following regulations and procedures.

The extent to which managers measure performance may also vary from one country to another. In rapidly changing regions, such as Southeast Asia, the organization may have to update its performance plans more often than once a year.

Not every culture values the independence and freedom from surveillance that American workers and managers desire. Ito-Yokado, the Japanese company that controls 7-Eleven convenience stores in that country, has installed cash registers that let headquarters monitor every time a sale is made and the frequency with which managers use the system's analytical tools to track product sales.[33] American managers, in contrast, tend to think they know how to stock shelves and make changes in product mix, taking into account the weather and special events.

Feedback is another area in which differences can occur. Employees around the world appreciate positive feedback, but U.S. employees are much more used to direct feedback than are employees in other countries. In Mexico managers are expected to provide positive feedback before focusing the discussion on behaviors the employee needs to improve.[34] At the Thai office of Singapore Airlines, managers resisted giving negative feedback to employees because they feared this would cause them to have bad karma, contributing to their reincarnation at a lower level in their next life.[35] The airlines therefore allowed the managers to adapt their feedback process to fit local cultures.

Compensating an International Workforce   LO5

The chapters in Part 4 explained that compensation includes decisions about pay structure, incentive pay, and employee benefits. All these decisions become more complex when an organization has an international workforce.

Pay Structure

As Figure 15.5 shows, market pay structures can differ substantially across countries in terms of both pay level and the relative worth of jobs. For example, compared with the labor market in Frankfurt, Germany, the markets in Budapest, Hungary, and in Bombay, India, provide much lower pay levels overall. The latter two labor markets also exhibit less of a pay difference for jobs requiring greater skill and education.

Differences such as these create a dilemma for global companies: Should pay levels and differences reflect what workers are used to in their own countries? Or should they reflect the earnings of colleagues in the country of the facility, or earnings at the company headquarters? For example, should a German engineer posted to Bombay be

FIGURE 15.5

Earnings in Selected Occupations in Seven Cities

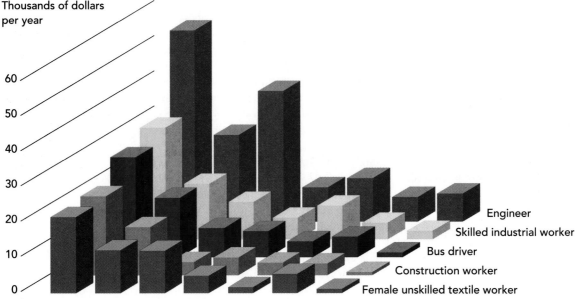

Note: Earnings are adjusted to reflect purchasing power.

SOURCE: World Bank, *World Development Report 1995* (Oxford: Oxford University Press, 1995), p. 11. Reprinted with permission of World Bank via Copyright Clearance Center.

paid according to the standard in Frankfurt or the standard in Bombay? If the standard is Frankfurt, the engineers in Bombay will likely see the German engineer's pay as unfair. If the standard is Bombay, the company will likely find it impossible to persuade a German engineer to take an assignment in Bombay. Typically, companies have resolved this dilemma by linking pay and benefits more closely to those of the employee's country. However, evidence suggests this link is slowly weakening and now depends more on the nature and length of the foreign assignment.[36]

These decisions affect a company's costs and ability to compete. The average hourly labor costs in industrialized countries such as the United States, Germany, and Japan are far higher than these costs in newly industrialized countries such as Mexico, Hong Kong, and Korea.[37] As a result, we often hear that U.S. labor costs are too high to allow U.S. companies to compete effectively unless the companies shift operations to low-cost foreign subsidiaries. That conclusion oversimplifies the situation for many companies. Merely comparing wages ignores differences in education, skills, and productivity.[38] If an organization gets more or higher-quality output from a higher-wage workforce, the higher wages may be worth the cost. Besides this, if the organization has many positions requiring highly skilled workers, it may need to operate in (or hire immigrants from) a country with a strong educational system, regardless of labor costs. Finally, labor costs may be outweighed by other factors, such as transportation costs or access to resources or customers.

At the same time, the challenge of competing with organizations in low-wage countries can be very difficult. China, for example, has invested in vocational schools,

A large number of journalists found shelter in the old building of the French nongovernmental organization in Afghanistan in the fall of 2001. Taking an overseas assignment, especially in a harsh or potentially dangerous climate, requires the challenge of adjusting to life in a new country, so many companies pay employees higher salaries to compensate for this hardship.

which provide training for skilled factory jobs. Chinese universities graduate a much larger share of engineers than U.S. universities. These schools are flooding the Chinese labor market with talent, so that even as high-tech manufacturing spreads to many Chinese cities, the need for workers is easy to fill. For Chinese workers, even experienced engineers, the result is that pay is growing but remains low compared to rates in other countries. An example is Li Guangxiang, a senior engineer and assistant manager at a Flextronics International computer parts factory, who earns just $10,000 a year.[39]

Incentive Pay

Besides setting a pay structure, the organization must make decisions with regard to incentive pay, such as bonuses and stock options. Although stock options became a common form of incentive pay in the United States during the 1990s, European businesses did not begin to embrace this type of compensation until the end of that decade. European companies with North American operations have felt the greatest pressure to join the stock option "club."[40] For instance, executives at Alcatel, a French manufacturer of telecommunications equipment, recently realized they needed to broaden the scope of their compensation when they began to acquire North American firms such as Canada's Newbridge Networks. Afraid that failure to offer stock options would result in a loss of qualified employees, Alcatel announced a plan that would award options to over one-third of its engineers and middle managers outside the United States (and three-quarters of them inside the United States).

The United States and Europe differ in the way they award stock options. European companies usually link the options to specific performance goals, such as the increase in a company's share price compared with that of its competitors. German law actually requires this, and British firms such as Barclays are beginning to enforce stricter guidelines. Belgium and Switzerland still discourage the use of stock options by imposing high taxes on this form of compensation. Italy and Norway have passed laws and tax changes that make stock options more attractive to employers and employees. As competition in European labor markets increases, experts predict that companies not offering options will have a harder time recruiting the best employees.

Employee Benefits

As in the United States, compensation packages in other countries include benefits. Decisions about benefits must take into account the laws of each country involved, as well as employees' expectations and values in those countries. Some countries require

FIGURE 15.6

Normal Annual Hours Worked in Manufacturing Relative to United States

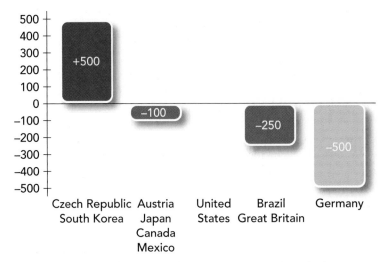

SOURCE: *Key Indicators of the Labor Market 2001–2002* (Geneva, Switzerland: International Labour Office, 2001).

paid maternity leave, and some countries have nationalized health care systems, which would affect the value of private health insurance in a compensation package. Pension plans are more widespread in parts of Western Europe than in the United States and Japan. Over 90 percent of workers in Switzerland have pension plans, as do all workers in France. Among workers with pension plans, U.S. workers are significantly less likely to have defined benefit plans than workers in Japan or Germany.

Paid vacation, discussed in Chapter 13, tends to be more generous in Western Europe than in the United States. Figure 15.6 compares the number of hours the average manufacturing employee works in various countries. Of these countries, only in the Czech Republic and South Korea do manufacturing workers put in more hours than U.S. workers—500 more hours per year. In the other countries, the norm is to work 100 to 500 hours less than a U.S. worker over the course of a year.

International Labor Relations

Companies that operate across national boundaries often need to work with unions in more than one country. Organizations establish policies and goals for labor relations, overseeing labor agreements, and monitoring labor performance (for example, output and productivity).[41] The day-to-day decisions about labor relations are usually handled by each foreign subsidiary. The reason is that labor relations on an international scale involve differences in laws, attitudes, and economic systems, as well as differences in negotiation styles.

At least in comparison with European organizations, U.S. organizations exert more centralized control over labor relations in the various countries where they operate.[42] U.S. management therefore must recognize differences in how various countries understand and regulate labor relations. For example, in the United States, collective bargaining usually involves negotiations between a union local and an organization's management, but in Sweden and Germany, collective bargaining generally involves negotiations between an employers' organization and a union representing an entire industry's employees.[43] Legal differences range from who may form a union to how much latitude an organization is allowed in laying off workers. In China, for example, efforts at economic reform have resulted in many thousands of layoffs. In the spring of 2002, as many as 20,000 workers at a time have rallied to protest layoffs by PetroChina, angry that early-retirement packages did not include expected medical insurance and social security payments. The workers resort to public protest because the country's legal and economic system allows only government-controlled unions and does not provide them with recourse when the government does not support their position.[44] In Germany, because labor representatives participate on companies' boards of directors, the way management handles labor relations can affect a broad range of decisions.[45] Management therefore has an incentive to build cooperative relationships.

International labor relations must also take into account that negotiations between labor and management take place in a different social context, not just different economic and legal contexts. Cultural differences that affect other interactions come into play in labor negotiations as well. Negotiators will approach the process differently depending on whether the culture views the process as primarily cooperative or competitive and whether it is local practice to negotiate a deal by starting with the specifics or agreeing on overall principles.[46] Working with host-country nationals can help organizations navigate such differences in negotiation style.

Managing Expatriates

At some point, most international and global organizations assign managers to foreign posts. These assignments give rise to significant human resource challenges, from selecting managers for these assignments to preparing them, compensating them, and helping them adjust to a return home. In a global marketplace, expatriate assignments are important, but evidence suggests that U.S. companies have not yet learned to select and use expatriates. Out of every hundred U.S. expatriates, between 16 and 40 return before their assignment is complete, a rate about two to three times that of foreign nationals.[47] Other research found that between one-third and one-half of U.S. expatriates perform at a level that, according to employers' evaluations, is either ineffective or marginally effective.[48]

Selecting Expatriate Managers

The challenge of managing expatriate managers begins with determining which individuals in the organization are most capable of handling an assignment in another country. Expatriate managers need technical competence in the area of operations, in part to help them earn the respect of subordinates. In the past and at many organizations even today, technical competence has been almost the only basis upon which U.S. companies have selected expatriate managers.[49] Of course, many other skills are also necessary for success in any management job, especially one that involves working overseas. Depending on the nature of the assignment and the culture where it is located, the organization should consider each candidate's skills, learning style, and approach to problem solving.[50]

A successful expatriate manager must be sensitive to the host country's cultural norms, flexible enough to adapt to those norms, and strong enough to survive the culture shock of living in another culture. In addition, if the manager has a family, the family members must be able to adapt to a new culture. Adaptation requires three kinds of skills:[51]

1. Ability to maintain a positive self-image and feeling of well-being.
2. Ability to foster relationships with the host-country nationals.
3. Ability to perceive and evaluate the host country's environment accurately.

In a study that drew on the experience of people holding international assignments, expatriates told researchers that the most important qualities for an expatriate manager are, in order of importance, family situation, flexibility and adaptability, job knowledge and motivation, relational skills, and openness to other cultures.[52] To assess candidates' ability to adapt to a new environment, interviews should address topics such as the ones listed in Table 15.2. The interviewer should be certain to give candidates a clear and complete preview of the assignment and the host-country culture. This helps the candidate evaluate the assignment and consider it in terms of his or her family situation, so the employer does not violate the employee's privacy.[53]

A final issue with regard to selecting expatriates is the use of women in international assignments. For a long time, U.S. firms believed that women would have little success as managers in countries where women have not traditionally been promoted to management positions (such as in Japan and other Asian countries). In spite of this view, some organizations have taken a chance on female managers, and evidence suggests the original assumption was wrong. Robin Abrams, working for Apple Computer in Hong Kong, found that nobody cares whether "you are wearing trousers or a skirt if you have demonstrated core competencies." Some female expatriates' experience has been that the novelty of being a woman in a group of men gives them an extra sort of credibility with host-country nationals. With such successes, organizations in the 1990s began rapidly increasing the share of women assigned to foreign countries.[54]

TABLE 15.2

Topics for Assessing Candidates for Overseas Assignments

Motivation
- Investigate reasons and degree of interest in wanting to be considered.
- Determine desire to work abroad, verified by previous concerns such as personal travel, language training, reading, and association with foreign employees or students.
- Determine whether the candidate has a realistic understanding of what working and living abroad requires.
- Determine the basic attitudes of the spouse toward an overseas assignment.

Health
- Determine whether any medical problems of the candidate or his or her family might be critical to the success of the assignment.
- Determine whether he or she is in good physical and mental health, without any foreseeable change.

Language ability
- Determine potential for learning a new language.
- Determine any previous language(s) studied or oral ability (judge against language needed on the overseas assignment).
- Determine the ability of the spouse to meet the language requirements.

Family considerations
- How many moves has the family made in the past among different cities or parts of the United States?
- What problems were encountered?
- How recent was the last move?

TABLE 15.2 Concluded

Family considerations *(continued)*
- What is the spouse's goal in this move?
- What are the number of children and the ages of each?
- Has divorce or its potential, or death of a family member, weakened family solidarity?
- Will all the children move? Why or why not?
- What are the location, health, and living arrangements of grandparents and the number of trips normally made to their home each year?
- Are there any special adjustment problems that you would expect?
- How is each member of the family reacting to this possible move?
- Do special educational problems exist within the family?

Resourcefulness and initiative
- Is the candidate independent; can he make and stand by his decisions and judgments?
- Does she have the intellectual capacity to deal with several dimensions simultaneously?
- Is he able to reach objectives and produce results with whatever personnel and facilities are available, regardless of the limitations and barriers that might arise?
- Can the candidate operate without a clear definition of responsibility and authority on a foreign assignment?
- Will the candidate be able to explain the aims and company philosophy to the local managers and workers?
- Does she possess sufficient self-discipline and self-confidence to overcome difficulties or handle complex problems?
- Can the candidate work without supervision?
- Can the candidate operate effectively in a foreign environment without normal communications and supporting services?

Adaptability
- Is the candidate sensitive to others, open to the opinions of others, cooperative, and able to compromise?
- What are his reactions to new situations, and efforts to understand and appreciate differences?
- Is she culturally sensitive, aware, and able to relate across the culture?
- Does the candidate understand his own culturally derived values?
- How does the candidate react to criticism?
- What is her understanding of the U.S. government system?
- Will he be able to make and develop contacts with peers in the foreign country?
- Does she have patience when dealing with problems?
- Is he resilient; can he bounce back after setbacks?

Career planning
- Does the candidate consider the assignment anything other than a temporary overseas trip?
- Is the move consistent with her progression and that planned by the company?
- Is his career planning realistic?
- What is the candidate's basic attitude toward the company?
- Is there any history or indication of interpersonal problems with this employee?

Financial
- Are there any current financial and/or legal considerations that might affect the assignment, such as house purchase, children and college expenses, car purchases?
- Are financial considerations negative factors? Will undue pressures be brought to bear on the employee or her family as a result of the assignment?

SOURCE: Reprinted with permission, from D. M. Noer, *Multinational People Management*, pp. 55–57. Copyright © 1989 by the Bureau of National Affairs, Inc., Washington, DC, 20037.

Of course, selection decisions are not just about finding employees who can do the job; the organization needs to select people who *want* an expatriate assignment. It is nothing new that many people are reluctant to move to a foreign country. Since the terrorist attacks of September 2001 and the subsequent war on terrorism, however, the reluctance of some employees has grown, because they fear being targets of another attack or civil unrest related to anger about U.S. policies. Organizations can and should address these concerns.[55] They should prepare evacuation plans in case of emergency and should tell the employees about those plans. They should provide strong channels of communication for expatriate workers, as well as access to employee assistance plans (EAPs). Above all, they should ensure that employees are well trained for their assignments, prepared for the culture, and knowledgeable about the transportation and geography in their host country, so that they do not unintentionally draw negative attention to themselves or expose themselves unduly. Finally, employers should take a global perspective that recognizes the present heightened anxiety felt by all—"inpatriates" (foreign workers in the United States) as well as expatriates.

Preparing Expatriates

LO6

Once the organization has selected a manager for an overseas assignment, it is necessary to prepare that person through training and development. Because expatriate success depends so much on the entire family's adjustment, the employee's spouse should be included in the preparation activities. Employees selected for expatriate assignments already have job-related skills, so preparation for expatriate assignments often focuses on cross-cultural training—that is, training in what to expect from the host country's culture. The general purpose of cross-cultural training is to create an appreciation of the host country's culture so expatriates can behave appropriately.[56] Paradoxically, this requires developing a greater awareness of one's own culture, so that the expatriate manager can recognize differences and similarities between the cultures and, perhaps, home-culture biases. Consider, for example, the statements in Figure 15.7, which are comments made by visitors to the United States. Do you think these observations accurately describe U.S. culture?

On a more specific level, cross-cultural training for foreign assignments includes the details of how to behave in business settings in another country—the ways people behave in meetings, how employees expect managers to treat them, and so on. As an example, Germans value promptness for meetings to a much greater extent than do Latin Americans—and so on. How should one behave when first meeting one's business counterparts in another culture? The "outgoing" personality style so valued in the United States may seem quite rude in other parts of the world.[57]

Employees preparing for a foreign assignment also need information about such practical matters as housing, schools, recreation, shopping, and health care facilities in the country where they will be living. This is a crucial part of the preparation.

Communication in another country often requires a determined attempt to learn a new language. Some employers try to select managers who speak the language of the host country, and a few provide language training. Most companies assume that employees in the host country will be able to speak the host country's language. Even if this is true, host country nationals are not likely to be fluent in the home country's language, so language barriers remain. The nearby "HR How To" box on page 502 provides suggestions for communicating across language barriers.

Along with cross-cultural training, preparation of the expatriate should include career development activities. Before leaving for a foreign assignment, expatriates

FIGURE 15.7

Impressions of Americans: Comments by Visitors to the United States

"Americans seem to be in a perpetual hurry. Just watch the way they walk down the street. They never allow themselves the leisure to enjoy life; there are too many things to do."
—A visitor from India

"The American is very explicit; he wants a 'yes' or 'no.' If someone tries to speak figuratively, the American is confused."
—A visitor from Ethiopia

"The tendency in the United States to think that life is only work hits you in the face. Work seems to be the one type of motivation."
—A visitor from Colombia

"The first time . . . my [American] professor told me, 'I don't know the answer, I will have to look it up,' I was shocked. I asked myself, 'Why is he teaching me?' In my country, a professor would give the wrong answer rather than admit ignorance."
—A visitor from Iran

SOURCE: J. Feig and G. Blair, *There Is a Difference*, 2nd ed. (Washington, DC: Meridian House International, 1980), cited in N. Adler, *International Dimensions of Organizational Behavior*, 2nd ed. (Boston: PWS-Kent, 1991).

should discuss with their managers how the foreign assignment fits into their career plans and what types of positions they can expect upon their return. This prepares the expatriate to develop valuable skills during the overseas assignment and eases the return home when the assignment is complete.

When the employee leaves for the assignment, the preparation process should continue.[58] Employees need a chance to discuss their experiences with other expatriates, so they can learn from their failures and successes. The organization may provide a host-country mentor or "assimilator" to help expatriates understand their experiences. Successful expatriates tend to develop a bicultural or multicultural point of view, so as they spend more time in the host country, the value of their connections to other expatriates may actually increase.

Compensating Expatriates

One of the greatest challenges of managing expatriates is determining the compensation package. Most organizations use a *balance sheet approach* to determine the total amount of the package. This approach adjusts the manager's compensation so that it

HR HOW TO

Communicating across Language Barriers

Not only do citizens of different countries, who probably speak different languages, face communication problems, but even among countries where the same language is spoken, dialects and variations—such as differences between American English, Australian English, and Nigerian English—can present language barriers. Moreover, people who speak the local language but only as a second language may have difficulty understanding at times. Here are some ideas for how to communicate effectively in spite of language barriers:

- Speak clearly and slowly. Enunciate each word. No need to shout, however!
- Use basic words. Avoid slang and idioms (expressions that mean something other than their literal meaning—for example, "don't lose your head").
- Repeat important ideas, using different words to explain the same concept.
- Use short, simple sentences with the active form of verbs—"Please do this," not "It should be done."

- Supplement spoken or written messages with pictures and graphs.
- Use gestures and facial expressions to emphasize the meaning of words.
- Pause more often than you would with someone who speaks your language well.
- When you present a long spoken message, hand out a written summary for your audience to follow while you speak. They can also refer to the handout later.
- When the other person is silent, allow time for the person to translate and think about what you have said. Don't jump in quickly just to fill the silence.
- When you notice errors in a person's speech or writing, don't assume the errors are a sign of low intelligence. They may simply mean the person is unfamiliar with the language.
- If you are unsure whether the other person understands, assume the person does not understand.
- To check the other person's understanding, ask the person to summarize what

you have said. Do not simply ask, "Do you understand?" In some cultures, politeness or pride requires a "yes," whether or not the message was understood.
- Allow for more frequent breaks. Understanding a second language is exhausting.
- Divide messages into short segments.
- Allow extra time to deliver a message, whether it is a training session, a meeting, a slide presentation, or other material.
- Ask questions of quiet participants to encourage their ideas. Give them time to think and respond.
- Do not embarrass inexperienced speakers of your language. For example, do not look impatient or draw attention to mistakes.
- Offer sincere praise and nonverbal encouragement to those who make the effort to communicate in your language.

SOURCE: Based on N. Adler, *International Dimensions of Organizational Behavior*, 2nd ed. (Boston: PWS-Kent, 1991).

gives the manager the same standard of living as in the home country plus extra pay for the inconvenience of locating overseas. As shown in Figure 15.8, the balance sheet approach begins by determining the purchasing power of compensation for the same type of job in the manager's own country—that is, how much a person can buy, after taxes, in terms of housing, goods and services, and a reserve for savings. Next, this amount is compared with the cost (in dollars, for a U.S. company) of these same expenses in the foreign country. In Figure 15.8, the greater size of the second column

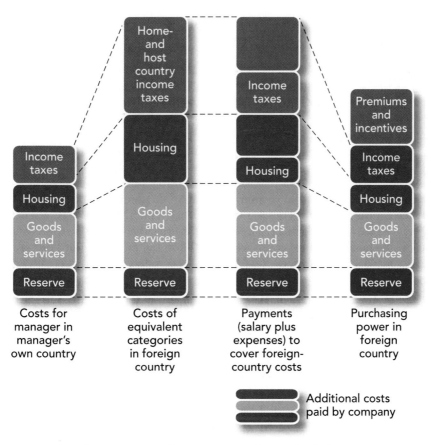

FIGURE 15.8

The Balance Sheet for Determining Expatriate Compensation

SOURCE: C. Reynolds, "Compensation of Overseas Personnel," in *Handbook of Human Resource Administration*, 2nd ed., J. J. Famularo, ed. (New York: McGraw-Hill, 1986), p. 51. Reprinted with permission.

means the costs for a similar standard of living in the foreign country are much higher in every category except the reserve amount. For the expatriate in this situation, the employer would pay the additional costs, as shown by the third column. Finally, the expatriate receives additional purchasing power from premiums and incentives. Because of these added incentives, the expatriate's purchasing power is more than what the manager could buy at home with the salary for an equivalent job. (Compare the fourth column with the first.) In practice, allowances for hardship and higher costs can more than double total compensation.[59]

After setting the total pay, the organization divides this amount into the four components of a total pay package. First, there is a base salary. Determining the base salary is complex because different countries use different currencies (dollars, yen, euros, and so on). The exchange rate—the rate at which one currency may be exchanged for another—constantly shifts in response to a host of economic forces, so the real value of a salary in terms of dollars is constantly changing. Also, as discussed earlier, the base salary may be comparable to the pay of other managers at headquarters or comparable to other managers at the foreign subsidiary. Because many organizations pay a salary premium as an incentive to accept an overseas assignment, expatriates' salaries are often higher than pay for staying at headquarters. This incentive role of pay has been especially important in recruiting expatriate managers for the Mexican *maquiladoras*. As demand for manufacturing in these facilities has increased, so has the need for qualified managers. To meet the demand, salaries for managers of *maquiladoras* have risen much faster than the average salary growth in the United States.[60]

A second component of total pay is a *tax equalization allowance*. Companies have different systems for taxing income, and in many countries, tax rates are much higher than in the United States. Usually, the employer of an expatriate withholds the amount of tax to be paid in the parent country, then pays all of the taxes due in the country where the expatriate is working.

A third component, benefits, presents additional challenges. Most of these have to do with whether an employee can use the same benefits in the foreign country. For example, if an expatriate has been contributing to a pension plan in the United States, does this person have a new pension in the foreign country? Or can the expatriate continue to contribute to the U.S. pension plan? Similarly, health benefits may involve receiving care at certain health facilities. While the person is abroad, does the same health plan cover services received in the foreign country? In one case, flying a manager back to the United States for certain procedures actually would have cost less than having the procedures done in the country where the person was working. But the company's health plans did not permit this alternative.

An employer may offer expatriates additional benefits to address the problem of uprooting the spouse when assigning an employee overseas. Pfizer, a pharmaceutical company, provides a $10,000 allowance that the spouse can use in many different ways.[61] A person in the foreign country helps the spouse with professional development and locating educational or other resources. In countries where the spouse is allowed to work, Pfizer tries to find him or her a job within the company. Pfizer also provides cross-cultural counseling and language assistance and tries to connect the family with the area's expatriate community.

The final component of pay packages is some set of allowances to make a foreign assignment more attractive. Cost-of-living allowances make up the differences in expenses for day-to-day needs. Housing allowances ensure that the expatriate can maintain the same standard of living as in the United States. Education allowances reimburse expatriates who pay tuition for their children to attend private English-speaking schools. Relocation allowances cover the expenses of making the move to the foreign country, including transportation, shipping or storage of possessions, and expenses for temporary housing until the employee can rent or purchase a home. Figure 15.9 is an example of a summary sheet for an expatriate manager's compensation package, showing a variety of allowances.

Helping Expatriates Return Home

repatriation
The process of preparing expatriates to return home from a foreign assignment.

As the expatriate's assignment nears its end, the human resource department faces a final challenge: helping the expatriate make the transition back to his or her home country. The process of preparing expatriates to return home from a foreign assignment is called **repatriation**. Reentry is not as simple as it might sound. Culture shock takes place in reverse. The experience has changed the expatriate, and the company's and expatriate's home culture have changed as well. Also, because of differences in economies and compensation levels, a returning expatriate may experience a decline in living standards. The standard of living for an expatriate in many countries includes maid service, a limousine, private schools, and clubs.

Companies are increasingly making efforts to help expatriates through this transition. Two activities help the process along: communication and validation.[62] Com-

John H. Doe		1 October 2001	
Name		**Effective date**	
Singapore		Manager, SLS./Serv. AP/ME	
Location of assignment		**Title**	
Houston, Texas	1234	202	202
Home base	**Emp. no.**	**LCA code**	**Tax code**

Reason for Change: _____ International Assignment _____

	Old	New
Monthly base salary		$5,000.00
Living cost allowance		$1,291.00
Foreign service premium		$ 750.00
Area allowance		- 0 -
Gross monthly salary		$7,041.00
Housing deduction		$ 500.00
Hypothetical tax		$ 570.00
Other		
Net monthly salary		$5,971.00

Prepared by	**Date**
Vice President, Human Resources	**Date**

FIGURE 15.9

International Assignment
Allowance Form

munication refers to the expatriate receiving information and recognizing changes while abroad. The more the organization keeps in contact with the expatriate, the more effective and satisfied the person will be upon return. The expatriate plays a role in this process as well. Expatriates should work at maintaining important contacts in the company and industry. Communication related to career development before and during the overseas assignment also should help the employee return to a position that is challenging and interesting. Validation means giving the expatriate recognition for the overseas service when this person returns home. Expatriates who receive praise and recognition from colleagues and top managers for their overseas service and future contribution have fewer troubles with reentry than those whose contributions are disregarded. Validation should also include planning for how the returning employee will contribute to the organization. What skills will this person bring back? What position will he or she fill? The new skills may be much more than knowledge of a particular culture. For example, the person may have learned how to lead or negotiate with a diverse group of people.[63]

Monsanto, a large agricultural, chemical, and pharmaceutical company, has an extensive repatriation program that begins long before the expatriate returns. Before the employee begins a foreign assignment, the employee and the sending and receiving managers develop an agreement that expresses their understanding of the assignment, including its fit with the company's business objectives and employee's career path. When the assignment is nearing its end, Monsanto gives expatriates information about the potential culture shock that can accompany the return home, as well as information about possible changes in family members, friends, and the office environment. Repatriating employees also share their experiences with American peers, superiors, and subordinates. A few months after the expatriate has returned, he or she holds "debriefing" sessions with several colleagues to help work through difficulties. According to Monsanto, this program makes the company more competitive in benefiting from international assignments. Not only does the process help employees return home, it helps their U.S. colleagues better understand different cultural issues and business environments.[64]

Summary

1. Summarize how the growth in international business activity affects human resource management.
   More and more companies are entering international markets by exporting and operating foreign facilities. Organizations therefore need employees who understand customers and suppliers in other countries. They need to understand local laws and customs and be able to adapt their plans to local situations. To do this organizations may hire a combination of parent-country, host-country, and third-country nationals. They may operate on the scale of an exporter or an international, global, or multinational organization. A global organization needs a transnational HRM system, which makes decisions from a global perspective, includes managers from many countries, and is based on ideas contributed by people representing a variety of cultures.

2. Identify the factors that most strongly influence HRM in international markets.
   By far the most important influence is the culture of each market—its set of shared assumptions about how the world works and what ideals are worth striving for. A culture has the dimensions of individualism/collectivism, high or low power distance, high or low uncertainty avoidance, masculinity/femininity, and long-

term or short-term orientation. Countries also differ in the degree to which their labor markets include people with education and skills of value to employers. Another influence on international HRM is the foreign country's political-legal system—its government, laws, and regulations. Finally, a country's economic system, capitalist or socialist, as well as the government's involvement in the country's economy, such as through taxes and price controls, is a strong factor determining HRM practices.

3. Discuss how differences among countries affect HR planning at organizations with international operations.
   As organizations consider decisions about their level of international activity, HR professionals should provide information about the relevant human resource issues. When organizations decide to operate internationally or globally, HR planning involves decisions about where and how many employees are needed for each international facility. Some countries limit employers' ability to lay off workers, so organizations would be less likely to staff for peak periods. Other countries allow employers more flexibility in meeting human resource needs. HRM professionals need to be conversant with such differences.

4. Describe how companies select and train human resources in a global labor market.

   Many organizations with foreign operations fill most positions with host-country nationals. These employees can more easily understand the values and customs of the local workforce, and hiring locally tends to be less expensive than moving employees to new locations. Organizations also fill foreign positions with parent-country and third-country nationals who have human relations skills associated with success in foreign assignments. They also may use "virtual expatriates," who do not go abroad for an extended period. When sending employees on foreign assignments, organizations prepare the employees (and often their families) through cross-cultural training. Before the assignment, the training provides instruction in the foreign country's language and culture. During the assignment, there is communication with the home country and mentoring. For the return home the employer provides further training.

5. Discuss challenges related to compensating employees from other countries.

   Pay structures can differ substantially among countries in terms of pay level and the relative worth of jobs. Organizations must decide whether to set pay levels and differences in terms of what workers are used to in their own countries or in terms of what employees' colleagues earn at headquarters. Typically, companies have resolved this dilemma by linking pay and benefits more closely to those of the employee's country, but this practice may be weakening so that it depends more on the nature and length of the foreign assignment. These decisions affect the organization's costs and ability to compete, so organizations consider local labor costs in their location decisions. Along with the basic pay structure, organizations must make decisions regarding incentive pay, such as bonuses and stock options. Laws may dictate differences in benefit packages, and the value of benefits will differ if a country requires them or makes them a government service.

6. Explain how employers prepare managers for international assignments and for their return home.

   When an organization has selected a manager for an overseas assignment, it must prepare the person for the experience. In cross-cultural training the soon to-be expatriate learns about the foreign culture he or she is heading to, and studies her or his own home-country culture as well for insight. The trainee is given a detailed briefing on how to behave in business settings in the new country. Along with cross-cultural training, preparation of the expatriate should include career development activities to help the individual acquire valuable career skills during the foreign assignment and at the end of the assignment to handle repatriation successfully. Communication of changes at home and validation of a job well done abroad help the expatriate through the repatriation process.

Review and Discussion Questions

1. Identify the parent country, host country(ies), and third country(ies) in the following example: A global soft-drink company called Cold Cola has headquarters in Atlanta, Georgia. It operates production facilities in Athens, Greece, and in Jakarta, Indonesia. The company has assigned a manager from Boston to head the Athens facility and a manager from Hong Kong to manage the Jarkarta facility.

2. What are some HRM challenges that arise when a U.S. company expands from domestic markets by exporting? When it changes from simply exporting to operating as an international company? When an international company becomes a global company?

3. In recent years, many U.S. companies have invested in Russia and sent U.S. managers there in an attempt to transplant U.S.-style management. According to Hofstede (see Figure 15.3), U.S. culture has low power distance, uncertainty avoidance, and long-term orientation and high individuality and masculinity. Russia's culture has high power distance and uncertainty avoidance, low masculinity and long-term orientation, and moderate individuality. In light of what you know about cultural differences, how well do you think U.S. managers can succeed in each of the following U.S.-style HRM practices? (Explain your reasons.)

   a. Selection decisions based on extensive assessment of individual abilities.
   b. Appraisals based on individual performance.
   c. Systems for gathering suggestions from workers.
   d. Self-managing work teams.

4. Besides cultural differences, what other factors affect human resource management in an organization with international operations?

5. Suppose you work in the HR department of a company that is expanding into a country where the law and culture make it difficult to lay off employees. How should your knowledge of that difficulty affect human resource planning for the overseas operations?

6. Why do multinational organizations hire host-country nationals to fill most of their foreign positions, rather than sending expatriates for most jobs?

7. Suppose an organization decides to improve collaboration and knowledge sharing by developing an intranet to link its global workforce. It needs to train employees in several different countries to use this system. List the possible cultural issues you can think of that the training program should take into account.

8. For an organization with operations in three different countries, what are some advantages and disadvantages of setting compensation according to the labor markets in the countries where the employees live and work? What are some advantages and disadvantages of setting compensation according to the labor market in the company's headquarters? Would the best arrangement be different for the company's top executives and its production workers? Explain.

9. What abilities make a candidate more likely to succeed in an assignment as an expatriate? Which of these abilities do you have? How might a person acquire these abilities?

10. In the past, a large share of expatriate managers from the United States have returned home before successfully completing their foreign assignments. Suggest some possible reasons for the high failure rate. What can HR departments do to increase the success of expatriates?

What's Your HR IQ?

The Student CD-ROM offers two more ways to check what you've learned so far. Use the Self-Assessment exercise to test your knowledge of global HRM. Go online with the Web Exercise to see how well your knowledge works in cyberspace.

BusinessWeek Case

BusinessWeek The High Cost of France's Aversion to Layoffs

It was a sad ending for appliance maker Moulinex, once considered an icon of French industry. On October 22, 2001, a bankruptcy court approved the sale of most Moulinex assets and brands to French rival SEB. Nearly two-thirds of Moulinex's 8,800 employees will lose their jobs as a result.

France's Socialist government reacted with predictable dismay, promising to help workers find new jobs. But government officials—not just the Socialists but their conservative predecessors—bear blame for the company's demise. As Moulinex slid deeper into the red over the past decade, authorities repeatedly blocked management's efforts to cut costs. In August the government rejected a plan to shutter a refrigerator factory and lay off 670 workers. Instead, the company was ordered to resume talks with unions. By then it was too late. Moulinex had racked up $120 million in losses the year before on sales of $1.1 billion. Bankruptcy loomed.

The Moulinex saga underscores a growing worry in corporate France. To stay competitive, companies need flexibility to trim their payrolls, especially now that Europe faces its steepest economic downturn in nearly a decade. But laying off workers in France is nightmarishly difficult. Labor laws require lengthy negotiations with unions over planned job reductions and expensive severance packages for laid-off workers. On October 23, 2001, 56 leading French chief executives sent a letter to Prime Minister Lionel Jospin's government, warning that layoff policies were hurting French competitiveness.

French executives have reason to worry. Germany, where governments traditionally have been as layoff-averse as in France, is looking a lot more open-minded these days. Companies ranging from electronics giant Siemens to chipmaker Infineon Technologies to Commerzbank have announced thousands of job cuts with only muted government response. Such flexibility could help German companies recover more quickly when the economy improves, says Antonella Mei-Pochtler, a senior vice president at Boston Consulting Group in Munich.

In France it's another story. When consulting firm Bain & Company recently polled chief executives of 125 leading French and German companies on their plans to weather the downturn, the German CEOs listed trimming payrolls as a top priority. But French bosses put layoffs well down their list, saying they would first cut back on purchasing, investment, and marketing. Apart from bankruptcy cases like Moulinex, virtually no companies have announced big layoffs in France this year. "We are still a civilized company," said a France Télécom spokesman recently, denying rumors that the phone operator was planning to eliminate jobs.

An analysis by the Organization for Economic Cooperation and Development shows that Germany's anti-layoff laws are just as tough as France's. But French executives know even modest job cuts will ignite a political firestorm. Consider what happened to Groupe Danone CEO Frank Riboud last spring when he moved to close two factories employing 570 people. Riboud offered every worker a job at another factory or an attractive severance package. No matter. Protesters marched through Paris calling for a boycott of the foodmaker, and the government introduced legislation, now pending, to fatten mandatory severance pay.

With unemployment creeping back up to 9 percent and national elections due next year, the pressure to protect jobs will only intensify. Already the government is pushing state-controlled Air France, which is reeling from a steep drop in traffic, to hire workers laid off by a bankrupt regional carrier, AOM-Air Liberté.

France Inc. may be ready to fight back. The October 23 letter was signed by top bosses like Thierry Desmarest of TotalFinaElf and Jean-Martin Folz of Peugeot. Ultimately, they warn, workers will suffer if companies cannot restructure quickly enough to save themselves. But don't take the CEOs' word on that. Just ask the ex-employees of Moulinex.

SOURCE: "The High Cost of France's Aversion to Layoffs," *BusinessWeek Online*, November 5, 2001, www.businessweek.com.

Questions

1. According to this case, how does France's political-legal system affect HRM decisions? (Consider, for example, human resource planning and decisions about separating and retaining employees.)
2. What cultural values might be at the root of France's laws limiting job cuts? What reasons do French managers give for wanting to loosen the legal requirements? Which point of view is more like your own?
3. In the United States, employers have much wider latitude in making layoff decisions than in France. Still, some U.S. companies have no-layoff policies, which help them attract and keep talented workers. Suppose two U.S. companies are opening French subsidiaries, and one of those companies has a no-layoff policy. Would the company with a no-layoff policy have an advantage in France? Explain.

Case: Human Resource Management in a World with Terrorism

As we have seen in this chapter, human resource management cannot function apart from world events. Certainly the link was made tragically clear during and after the events of September 11, 2001. Terrorists with Middle-Eastern roots (allegedly part of Osama bin Laden's al-Qaida network) hijacked four U.S. planes, then crashed two of them into the World Trade Center's twin towers and one into the Pentagon. (The fourth crashed in a field after passengers scuffled with the hijackers.) After no response to U.S. warnings that the Taliban government in Afghanistan must turn over bin Laden and his deputies, the United States and United Kingdom began military action against the Taliban and al-Qaida in Afghanistan. Bombing in that country started on October 7, 2001.

As of the writing of this chapter, we do not know what the ultimate result of the military action will be. But we do know that the terrorist attacks and the U.S. war on terrorism have intensified the challenges faced by multinational companies. The impact is especially strong for global companies that must manage employees from a variety of nationalities and religions, and do so across many countries.

First, U.S. companies doing business overseas must recognize that many parts of the world have the potential to become hostile territory. Particularly sensitive areas include Muslim-dominated countries such as the Arab states and Indonesia, where many citizens hold the opinion that the past–September 11 U.S. bombings of Afghanistan were hostile to their religion. In these parts of the world, companies must manage their workforce—especially U.S. and British citizens—in light of the greater risk to their security. Following the terrorist attacks and the U.S. response, many of these employees were afraid, and some asked to return to their home countries. Accounting giant KPMG surveyed HR executives about the impact of terrorism, and some said that at least half their expatriate workforce had asked to return to the United States. Those most likely to request a return home were employees working in high-risk countries such as Egypt and Pakistan.

Before September 11, 2001, many of these employees had lived relatively normal lives, free from security concerns. Recent threats on American interests have shattered that sense of security. Expatriate assignments are more risky in the eyes of many employees. Consider the impact on the Global Gateway pages of the Monster.com job website, which lists jobs outside the United States. In September 2001, the number of visitors to Global Gateway dropped 12 percent from the month before.

One result of these trends is that compensation for expatriates is likely to rise. Candidates for overseas jobs are more likely to look for help in paying for housing that offers security as well as the comforts of home. Many may ask for more frequent trips home to be with family as well.

Another challenge is that companies with global workforces must manage across boundaries that are more nationalistic. While many U.S. citizens have felt united in actions they justify as a valid response to an act of war, many citizens of other countries consider the U.S. military response as an act of aggression. For example, an executive at a global oil company has noted the difficulty of managing a workforce that is approximately one-quarter Arab. That executive heard from many of his Arab colleagues that "While we know that you are concerned about the events of September 11, you should know that we are equally concerned about the events of October 7."

SOURCE: E. Tahmincioglu, "Opportunities Mingle with Fear Overseas," *New York Times,* October 24, 2001, p. G1.

Questions

1. Give an example of how the experience of the September 11 attacks and the U.S. war on terrorism might affect each of the HRM functions of recruiting, training, and compensating employees for a global company.

2. Do the issues in question 1 differ depending on the countries where employees are located? (For example, would the issues and HRM practices have the same effect on employees in Germany, Colombia, and Saudi Arabia?) Explain.

3. The case points out that although people in different parts of the world condemn terrorism, they do not necessarily view events in the same context. For a global or international organization, what challenges to HRM do these different viewpoints present? In a U.S.-based organization with subsidiaries in Muslim-dominated countries, how might HR staff address these challenges?

Notes

1. Towers Perrin, *Priorities for Competitive Advantage: A Worldwide Human Resource Study* (Valhalla, NY: Towers Perrin, 1991).

2. B. P. Sunoo, "Over the Border," *Workforce,* July 2000, pp. 40–44; C. Sparks, T. Bikoi, and L. Moglia, "A Perspective on U.S. and Foreign Compensation Costs in Manufacturing," *Monthly Labor Review,* June 2002, pp. 36–50.

3. R. Kopp, "International Human Resource Policies and Practices in Japanese, European, and United States Multinationals," *Human Resource Management* 33 (1994), pp. 581–99.

4. N. Adler and S. Bartholomew, "Managing Globally Competent People," *The Executive* 6 (1992), pp. 52–65.

5. V. Sathe, *Culture and Related Corporate Realities* (Homewood, IL: Richard D. Irwin, 1985); M. Rokeach, *Beliefs, Attitudes, and Values* (San Francisco: Jossey-Bass, 1968).

6. N. Adler, *International Dimensions of Organizational Behavior,* 2nd ed. (Boston: PWS-Kent, 1991).

7. G. Hofstede, "Dimensions of National Cultures in Fifty Countries and Three Regions," in *Expectations in Cross-Cultural Psychology,* eds. J. Deregowski, S. Dziurawiec, and R. C. Annis (Lisse, Netherlands: Swets and Zeitlinger, 1983); G. Hofstede, "Cultural Constraints in Management Theories," *Academy of Management Executive* 7 (1993), pp. 81–90.

8. Hofstede, "Cultural Constraints in Management Theories."

9. W. A. Randolph and M. Sashkin, "Can Organizational Empowerment Work in Multinational Settings?" *Academy of Management Executive* 16, no. 1 (2002), pp. 102–115.

10. Ibid.

11. L. A. West Jr. and W. A. Bogumil Jr., "Foreign Knowledge Workers as a Strategic Staffing Option," *Academy of Management Executive* 14, no. 4 (2000), pp. 71–83.

12. National Center for Education Statistics (NCES), "International Comparisons of Education," *Digest of Education Statistics, 2000,* chapter 6, NCES website, http://nces.ed.gov, downloaded September 23, 2002.

13. Adler and Bartholomew, "Managing Globally Competent People."

14. B. O'Reilly, "Your New Global Workforce," *Fortune,* December 14, 1992, pp. 52–66.

15. P. Conrad and R. Peiper, "Human Resource Management in the Federal Republic of Germany," in *Human Resource Management: An International Comparison,* ed. R. Peiper (Berlin: Walter de Gruyter, 1990).

16. I. M. Kunii, "Under the Knife," *BusinessWeek,* September 10, 2001, p. 62; C. Dawson, "Saying Sayonara," *BusinessWeek,* September 24, 2001, pp. 108–9; I. M. Kunii, "Japan's Jobless Need More than a Handout," *BusinessWeek,* September 24, 2001, p. 110.

17. B. Ettore, "Let's Hear It for Local Talent," *Management Review,* October 1994, p. 9; S. Franklin, "A New World Order for Business Strategy," *Chicago Tribune,* May 15, 1994, sec. 19, pp. 7–8.

18. West and Bogumil, "Foreign Knowledge Workers as a Strategic Staffing Option."

19. G. Flynn, "Hiring Foreign Workers in a Post-9/11 World," *Workforce,* July 2002, pp. 78–79.

20. Ibid.

21. W. A. Arthur Jr. and W. Bennett Jr., "The International Assignee: The Relative Importance of Factors

Perceived to Contribute to Success," *Personnel Psychology* 48 (1995), pp. 99–114; G. M. Spreitzer, M. W. McCall Jr., and J. D. Mahoney, "Early Identification of International Executive Potential," *Journal of Applied Psychology* 82 (1997), pp. 6–29.

22. J. S. Black and J. K. Stephens, "The Influence of the Spouse on American Expatriate Adjustment and Intent to Stay in Pacific Rim Overseas Assignments," *Journal of Management* 15 (1989), pp. 529–44.

23. P. Caligiuri, "The Big Five Personality Characteristics as Predictors of Expatriates' Desire to Terminate the Assignment and Supervisor-Rated Performance," *Personnel Psychology* 53 (2000), pp. 67–88.

24. C. Lachnit, "Low-Cost Tips for Successful Inpatriation," *Workforce*, August 2001, pp. 42–44, 46–47.

25. J. Flynn, "E-mail, Cell Phones, and Frequent-Flier Miles Let 'Virtual' Expats Work Abroad but Live at Home," *The Wall Street Journal*, October 25, 1999, p. A26.

26. D. M. Gayeski, C. Sanchirico, and J. Anderson, "Designing Training for Global Environments: Knowing What Questions to Ask," *Performance Improvement Quarterly* 15, no. 2 (2002), pp. 15–31.

27. B. Filipczak, "Think Locally, Train Globally," *Training* (January 1997), pp. 41–48.

28. Ibid.

29. J. S. Black and M. Mendenhall, "A Practical but Theory-Based Framework for Selecting Cross-Cultural Training Methods," in *Readings and Cases in International Human Resource Management*, eds. M. Mendenhall and G. Oddou (Boston: PWS-Kent, 1991), pp. 177–204.

30. Lachnit, "Low-Cost Tips for Successful Inpatriation."

31. Ibid., citing research jointly sponsored by GMAC Global Relocation Services/Windham International, the National Foreign Trade Council, and SHRM Global Forum.

32. D. D. Davis, "International Performance Measurement and Management," in *Performance Appraisal: State of the Art in Practice*, ed. J. W. Smither (San Francisco: Jossey-Bass, 1998), pp. 95–131.

33. N. Shirouzu and J. Bigness, "7-Eleven Operators Resist System to Monitor Managers," *The Wall Street Journal*, June 16, 1997, pp. B1, B5.

34. M. Gowan, S. Ibarreche, and C. Lackey, "Doing the Right Things in Mexico," *Academy of Management Executive* 10 (1996), pp. 74–81.

35. L. S. Chee, "Singapore Airlines: Strategic Human Resource Initiatives," in *International Human Resource Management: Think Globally, Act Locally*, ed. D. Torrington (Upper Saddle River, NJ: Prentice Hall, 1994), pp. 143–59.

36. C. M. Solomon, "Global Compensation: Learn the ABCs," *Personnel Journal*, July 1995, p. 70; R. A. Swaak, "Expatriate Management: The Search for Best Practices," *Compensation and Benefits Review*, March–April 1995, p. 21.

37. Sparks, Bikoi, and Moglia, "A Perspective on U.S. and Foreign Compensation Costs in Manufacturing."

38. See, for example, A. E. Cobet and G. A. Wilson, "Comparing 50 Years of Labor Productivity in U.S. and Foreign Manufacturing," *Monthly Labor Review*, June 2002, pp. 51–63.

39. P. Wonacott, "China's Secret Weapon: Smart, Cheap Labor for High-Tech Goods," *The Wall Street Journal*, March 14, 2002, pp. A1, A6.

40. "Taxation of European Stock Options," *The European Commission*, June 26, 2001, http://europa.eu.int; D. Woodruff, "Europe: A Latecomer, Embraces Options Even as Market Swoons," *The Wall Street Journal*, May 15, 2001, www.wsj.com; "Eager Europeans Press Their Noses to the Glass," *BusinessWeek Online*, April 19, 1999, www.businessweek.com.

41. P. J. Dowling, D. E. Welch, and R. S. Schuler, *International Human Resource Management*, 3rd ed. (Cincinnati: South-Western, 1999), pp. 235–36.

42. Ibid.; J. La Palombara and S. Blank, *Multinational Corporations and National Elites: A Study of Tensions* (New York: Conference Board, 1976); A. B. Sim, "Decentralized Management of Subsidiaries and Their Performance: A Comparative Study of American, British and Japanese Subsidiaries in Malaysia," *Management International Review* 17, no. 2 (1977), pp. 45–51; Y. K. Shetty, "Managing the Multinational Corporation: European and American Styles," *Management International Review* 19, no. 3 (1979), pp. 39–48; J. Hamill, "Labor Relations Decision-Making within Multinational Corporations," *Industrial Relations Journal* 15, no. 2 (1984), pp. 30–34.

43. Dowling, Welch, and Schuler, *International Human Resource Management*, p. 231.

44. P. Wonacott, "PetroChina Unit, after Job Cuts, Is Besieged by Protesters," *The Wall Street Journal*, March 14, 2002, pp. A9, A12.

45. J. K. Sebenius, "The Hidden Challenge of Cross-Border Negotiations," *Harvard Business Review*, March 2002, pp. 76–85.

46. Ibid.

47. R. Tung, "Selection and Training Procedures of U.S., European, and Japanese Multinational Corporations," *California Management Review* 25, no. 1 (1982), pp. 57–71.

48. L. Copeland and L. Griggs, *Going International* (New York: Random House, 1985).

49. M. Mendenhall, E. Dunbar, and G. R. Oddou, "Expatriate Selection, Training, and Career-Pathing: A Review and Critique," *Human Resource Management Review* 25, no. 1 (1982), pp. 57–71; A. Halcrow,

"Expats: The Squandered Resource," *Workforce*, April 1999, pp. 42–44, 46, 48.

50. M. Harvey and M. M. Novicevic, "Selecting Expatriates for Increasingly Complex Global Assignments," *Career Development International* 6, no. 2 (2001), pp. 69–86.

51. M. Mendenhall and G. Oddou, "The Dimensions of Expatriate Acculturation," *Academy of Management Review* 10 (1985), pp. 39–47.

52. Arthur and Bennett, "The International Assignee."

53. J. I. Sanchez, P. E. Spector, and C. L. Cooper, "Adapting to a Boundaryless World: A Developmental Expatriate Model," *Academy of Management Executive* 14, no. 2 (2000), pp. 96–106.

54. "Work Week," *The Wall Street Journal*, September 5, 1995, p. A1.

55. A. Freedman, "Alien Nation," *Human Resource Executive*, February 2002, pp. 51–54; B. McConnell, "Terrorism Changes Managers' Thinking about Overseas Assignments," *HR News*, January 2002, p. 14.

56. P. Dowling and R. Schuler, *International Dimensions of Human Resource Management* (Boston: PWS-Kent, 1990).

57. Sanchez, Spector, and Cooper, "Adapting to a Boundaryless World."

58. Ibid.; Lachnit, "Low-Cost Tips for Successful Inpatriation."

59. P. Evans, V. Pucik, and J.-L. Barsoux, *The Global Challenge: Frameworks for International Human Resource Management* (New York: McGraw-Hill/Irwin, 2002), p. 131; F. Higgins, "Survey on Expatriate Compensation and Benefits, 1996," cited in B. Fitzgerald-Turner, "Myths of Expatriate Life," *HRMagazine* 42, no. 6 (June 1997), pp. 65–74.

60. Sunoo, "Over the Border," p. 42.

61. J. Flynn, "Multinationals Help Career Couples Deal with Strains Affecting Expatriates," *The Wall Street Journal*, August 8, 2000, p. A19; C. Solomon, "The World Stops Shrinking," *Workforce*, January 2000, pp. 48–51; C. Solomon, "Unhappy Trails," *Workforce*, August 2000, pp. 36–41.

62. Adler, *International Dimensions of Organizational Behavior*.

63. L. G. Klaff, "The Right Way to Bring Expats Home," *Workforce*, July 2002, pp. 40–44.

64. C. Solomon, "Repatriation: Up, Down, or Out?" *Personnel Journal*, 1995, pp. 28–37.

Creating and Maintaining High-Performance Organizations

What Do I Need to Know? After reading this chapter, you should be able to:

1. Define high-performance work systems and identify the elements of such a system.

2. Summarize the outcomes of a high-performance work system.

3. Describe the conditions that create a high-performance work system.

4. Explain how human resource management can contribute to high performance.

5. Discuss the role of HRM technology in high-performance work systems.

6. Summarize ways to measure the effectiveness of human resource management.

Introduction

Blackmer/Dover Resources, which makes heavy-duty pumps, experienced some resistance while trying to get performance improvements flowing.[1] To boost efficiency and cut inventory costs, the company redesigned its production process. Replacing jobs in which assemblers built most of each pump at a single workstation, Blackmer set up an assembly line. The redesign was done by consultants without input from the production workers. The results included slower production, higher costs, and lower job satisfaction. Workers who intimately knew their machines and products felt that their expertise no longer mattered.

With sales declining, the company hired a new president, Carmine Bosco. Bosco brought a desire to learn from workers. Under Bosco, workers provided ideas for correcting problems in the production system. Production workers still learn different jobs so that they can move to different parts of the factory as needed. Not everyone likes the change. Bill Fowler, whose job involves the precision cutting of metal shafts for the pumps, says, "I don't want to move around, because I love my routine—it helps me get through the day." To avoid unfamiliar assignments, Fowler—a 24-year veteran with a track record of working faster than his coworkers—keeps his extensive knowledge to himself. He figures his strategy also prevents management from using his knowledge against him by raising production standards. In spite of Fowler's reaction, Blackmer's management believes that most employees will be won over to the spirit of knowledge sharing. The company intends to convince them by building trust and setting up the right incentives so that employees know they will be rewarded, not punished, for sharing their know-how.

Blackmer's efforts at achieving high performance show that technology alone cannot do the trick. Someone in the organization has to recognize how changes will affect the organization's people. The organization must design work and performance management systems so that they bring out the best in the employees. These challenges are some of the most crucial responsibilities of human resource management.

This chapter summarizes the role of human resource management in creating an organization that achieves a high level of performance, measured in such terms as long-term profits, quality, and customer satisfaction. We begin with a definition of *high-performance work systems* and a description of these systems' elements and outcomes. Next, we identify the conditions that contribute to high performance. We explain how the various HRM functions can contribute to high performance. Finally, we introduce ways to measure the effectiveness of human resource management.

High-Performance Work Systems

LO1

high-performance work system
The right combination of people, technology, and organizational structure that makes full use of the organization's resources and opportunities in achieving its goals.

The challenge facing managers today is how to make their organizations into **high-performance work systems,** with the right combination of people, technology, and organizational structure to make full use of resources and opportunities in achieving their organizations' goals. To function as a high-performance work system, each of these elements must fit well with the others in a smoothly functioning whole. Many manufacturers use the latest in processes including flexible manufacturing technology, total quality management, and just-in-time inventory control (meaning parts and supplies are automatically restocked as needed), but of course, these processes do not work on their own; they must be run by qualified people. Organizations need to determine what kinds of people fit their needs, and then locate, train, and motivate those special people.[2] According to research, organizations that introduce integrated high-performance work practices usually experience increases in productivity and long-term financial performance.[3]

Creating a high-performance work system contrasts with traditional management practices. In the past, decisions about technology, organizational structure, and human resouces were treated as if they were unrelated. An organization might acquire a new information system, restructure jobs, or add an office in another country without considering the impact on its people.[4] More recently, managers have realized that success depends on how well all the elements work together.

Elements of a High-Performance Work System

As shown in Figure 16.1, in a high-performance work system, the elements that must work together include organizational structure, task design, people (the selection, training, and development of employees), reward systems, and information systems, and human resource management plays an important role in establishing all these.

Organizational structure is the way the organization groups its people into useful divisions, departments, and reporting relationships. The organization's top management makes most decisions about structure, for instance, how many employees report to each supervisor and whether employees are grouped according to the functions they carry out or the customers they serve. Such decisions affect how well employees coordinate their activities and respond to change. In a high-performance work system, organizational structure promotes cooperation, learning, and continuous improvement.

Task design determines how the details of the organization's necessary activities will be grouped, whether into jobs or team responsibilities. In a high-performance work system, task design makes jobs efficient while encouraging high quality. In Chapter 4, we discussed how to carry out this HRM function through job analysis and job design.

The right *people* are a key element of high-performance work systems. HRM has a significant role in providing people who are well suited and well prepared for their jobs. Human resource personnel help the organization recruit and select people with the needed qualifications. Training, development, and career management ensure that these people are able to perform their current and future jobs with the organization.

Reward systems contribute to high performance by encouraging people to strive for objectives that support the organization's overall goals. Reward systems include the performance measures by which employees are judged, the methods of measuring performance, and the incentive pay and other rewards linked to success. Human resource management plays an important role in developing and administering reward systems, as we saw in Chapters 8 through 12.

The final element of high-performance work systems is the organization's *information systems*. Managers make decisions about the types of information to gather and the sources of information. They also must decide who in the organization should have access to the information and how they will make the information available.

FIGURE 16.1

Elements of a High-Performance Work System

In a high-performance work system, all the elements—people, technology, and organizational structure—work together for success.

Modern information systems, including the Internet, have enabled organizations to share information widely. HR departments take advantage of this technology to give employees access to information about benefits, training opportunities, job openings, and more, as we will describe later in this chapter.

Outcomes of a High-Performance Work System

Consider the practices of steel minimills in the United States. Some of these mills have strategies based on keeping their costs below competitors' costs; low costs let them operate at a profit while winning customers with low prices. Other steel minimills focus on "differentiation," meaning they set themselves apart in some way other than low price—for example, by offering higher quality or unusual product lines. Research has found that the minimills with cost-related goals tend to have highly centralized structures, so managers can focus on controlling through a tight line of command. These organizations have low employee participation in decisions, relatively low wages and benefits, and pay highly contingent on performance.[5] At minimills that focus on differentiation, structures are more complex and decentralized, so authority is more spread out. These minimills encourage employee participation and have higher wages and more generous benefits. They are high-performance work systems. In general, these differentiator mills enjoy higher productivity, lower scrap rates, and lower employee turnover than the mills that focus on low costs.

Outcomes of a high-performance work system thus include higher productivity and efficiency. These outcomes contribute to higher profits. A high-performance work system may have other outcomes, including high product quality, great customer satisfaction, and low employee turnover. Some of these outcomes meet intermediate goals that lead to higher profits (see Figure 16.2). For example, high quality contributes to customer satisfaction, and customer satisfaction contributes to growth of the business. Likewise, improving productivity lets the organization do more with less, which satisfies price-conscious customers and may help the organization win over customers from its competitors. Other ways to lower cost and improve quality are to reduce absenteeism and turnover, providing the organization with a steady supply of experienced workers. In the previous example of minimills, some employers keep turnover and scrap rates low. Meeting those goals helps the minimills improve productivity, which helps them earn more profits.

In a high-performance work system, the outcomes of each employee and work group contribute to the system's overall high performance. The organization's individuals and groups work efficiently, provide high-quality goods and services, and so

LO2

FIGURE 16.2

Outcomes of a High-Performance Work System

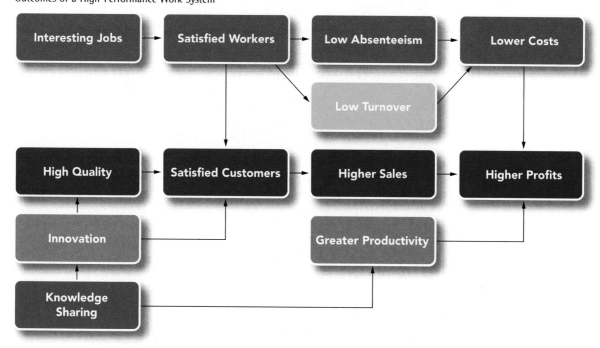

on, and in this way, they contribute to meeting the organization's goals. When the organization adds or changes goals, people are flexible and make changes as needed to meet the new goals. For example, an especially important outcome of human resource departments during the high-growth 1990s was obtaining enough talented employees. When the economy began to slow in 2000 and 2001, many organizations relied on HR departments to help them focus more on the efficiency of their workforces. Yet another issue surfaced following the September 2001 terrorist attacks on the Pentagon and World Trade Center: knowing that all the organization's employees are safe and accounted for.[6] As employers of people working at those locations struggled to locate their employees on September 11, 2001, they appreciated more than ever the importance of having accurate data about all personnel, including up-to-date emergency contact information. This tragic lesson illustrates the importance of good HR information systems as an outcome that helps an organization perform even under the worst circumstances.

Conditions that Contribute to High Performance

LO3

Certain conditions underlie the formation of a high-performance work system. Table 16.1 shows examples of such conditions—common practices in high-performing organizations. These practices, such as those involving rewards, employee empowerment, and jobs with variety, contribute to high performance by giving employees skills, incentives, knowledge, anatomy—and satisfaction, another condition associated with high performance. Finally, ethical behavior is a necessary condition of high

TABLE 16.1

Conditions for High
Performance

> - Teams perform work.
> - Employees participate in selection.
> - Employees receive formal performance feedback and are actively involved in the performance improvement process.
> - Ongoing training is emphasized and rewarded.
> - Employees' rewards and compensation relate to the company's financial performance.
> - Equipment and work processes are structured and technology is used to encourage maximum flexibility and interaction among employees.
> - Employees participate in planning changes in equipment, layout, and work methods.
> - Work design allows employees to use a variety of skills.
> - Employees understand how their jobs contribute to the finished product or service.
> - Ethical behavior is encouraged.

SOURCE: Based on J. A. Neal and C. L. Tromley, "From Incremental Change to Retrofit: Creating High-Performance Work Systems," *Academy of Management Executive* 9 (1995), pp. 42–54; M. A. Huselid, "The Impact of Human Resource Management Practices on Turnover, Productivity, and Corporate Financial Performance," *Academy of Management Journal* 38 (1995), pp. 635–72.

performance because it contributes to good long-term relationships with employees, customers, and the public.

Teamwork and Empowerment

As we discussed in Chapter 2, today's organizations empower employees. They expect employees to make more decisions about how they perform their jobs. One of the most popular ways to empower employees is to design work so that it is performed by teams. On a work team, employees bring together various skills and experiences to produce goods or provide services. The organization may charge the team with making decisions traditionally made by managers, such as hiring team members and planning work schedules. Teamwork and empowerment contribute to high performance when they improve job satisfaction and give the organization fuller use of employees' ideas and expertise.

For empowerment to succeed, managers must serve in linking and coordinating roles[7] and providing the team with the resources it needs to carry out its work. The manager should help the team and its members interact with employees from other departments or teams and should make sure communication flows in both directions—the manager keeps the team updated on important issues and ensures that the team shares information and resources with others who need it. Along with these efforts at coordination, the team's manager should help team members resolve problems as needed. To provide such help, the manager may have to refer team members to resources outside the team or organization.

Knowledge Sharing

learning organization
An organization in which people continually expand their capacity to achieve the results they desire.

For the last decade, managers have been interested in creating a **learning organization,** that is, an organization in which people continually expand their capacity to achieve the results they desire.[8] The people in a learning organization are constantly

Continuous learning

Critical, systematic thinking

Knowledge generation and sharing

Learning Organization

Encourgement of flexibility and experimentation

Valuing of employees

Learning culture

FIGURE 16.3

Key Features of a Learning Organization

SOURCE: Adapted from M. A. Gephart, V. J. Marsick, M. E. Van Buren, and M. S. Spiro, "Learning Organizations Come Alive," *Training and Development* 50 (1996), pp. 34–45.

learning. Their learning results from monitoring the business environment, taking in information, making decisions, and making changes in the organization based on what they learn. An organization's information systems, discussed later in this chapter, have an important role in making this learning activity possible. Information systems capture knowledge and make it available even after individual employees who provided the knowledge have left the organization. Ultimately, people are the essential ingredients in a learning organization. They must be committed to learning and willing to share what they have learned. A learning organization has the key features identified in Figure 16.3: continuous learning, generation and sharing of knowledge, thinking that is critical and systematic, a culture that values learning, encouragement of flexibility and experimentation, and appreciation of the value of each employee.

Continuous learning is each employee's and each group's ongoing efforts to gather information and apply the information to their decisions. In many organizations, the process of continuous learning is aimed at improving quality. To engage in continuous learning, employees must understand the entire work system they participate in, the relationships among jobs, their work units, and the organization as a whole. Employees who continuously learn about their work system are adding to their ability to improve performance.

Knowledge is most valuable to the organization when it is *shared*. Therefore, to create a learning organization, one challenge is to shift the focus of training away from merely teaching skills and toward a broader focus on generating and sharing knowledge.[9] In this view, training is an investment in the organization's human resources; it increases employees' value to the organization. Also, training content should be related to the organization's goals. Human resource departments can support the creation of a learning organization by planning training programs that meet these criteria, and they can help to create systems for creating, capturing, and sharing knowledge.

Critical, systematic thinking occurs when organizations encourage employees to see relationships among ideas and to test assumptions and observe the results of their actions. Reward systems can be set up to encourage employees and teams to think in new ways.

continuous learning
Each employee's and each group's ongoing efforts to gather information and apply the information to their decisions in a learning organization.

A *learning culture* is an organizational culture in which learning is rewarded, promoted, and supported by managers and organizational objectives. This culture may be reflected in performance management systems and pay structures that reward employees for gathering and sharing more knowledge. A learning culture creates the conditions in which managers encourage *flexibility* and *experimentation*. The organization should encourage employees to take risks and innovate, which means it cannot be quick to punish ideas that do not workout as intended.

Finally, in a learning organization, *employees are valued.* The organization recognizes that employees are the source of its knowledge. It therefore focuses on ensuring the development and well-being of each employee.

An example of a learning organization is Viant, a consulting firm that specializes in building e-businesses.[10] When employees join the company, they start in the home office in Boston, where they learn team skills, the company's consulting strategy, and the organization's culture. There they meet members of upper management. On the job, Viant employees work in settings that encourage interaction; no walls separate desks, and snack areas are located conveniently nearby. Performance reviews emphasize growth in employees' skills, and the company rewards knowledge sharing with incentives in the form of stock options. Before each project, consultants complete a brief document describing the knowledge they need, the knowledge they can use from other projects, what they need to create, and what they hope to learn that they can share with their colleagues. These documents are posted on Viant's internal website. Every six weeks, Viant's knowledge management group posts an online summary of what has been learned.

Job Satisfaction

A condition underpinning any high-performance organization is that employees experience job satisfaction—they experience their jobs as fulfilling or allowing them to fulfill important values. Research supports the idea that employees' job satisfaction and job performance are related.[11] Higher performance at the individual level should contribute to higher performance for the organization as a whole. One study looked at job satisfaction in teachers and the overall performance of their schools.[12] It found a significant link between teachers' satisfaction and their schools' performance according to a variety of measures, including students' behavior and academic achievement. More recently, a study by Watson Wyatt Worldwide found that companies with high employee commitment (which includes employees' satisfaction with their jobs and the company) enjoyed higher total returns to shareholders, a basic measure of a company's financial performance.[13]

Chapter 10 described a number of ways organizations can promote job satisfaction. They include making jobs more interesting, setting clear and challenging goals, and providing valued rewards that are linked to performance in a performance management system that employees consider fair.

Some organizations are moving beyond concern with mere job satisfaction and are trying to foster employees' *passion* for their work. Passionate people are fully engaged with something so that it becomes part of their sense of who they are. Feeling this way about one's work has been called *occupational intimacy.*[14] People experience occupational intimacy when they love their work, when they and their coworkers care about one another, and when they find their work meaningful. Human resource managers have a significant role in creating these conditions. For example, they can select people who care about their work and customers, provide methods for sharing knowledge,

Research has found that teachers' job satisfaction is associated with high performance of the schools where they teach. What are other ways in which organizations can promote and foster job satisfaction?

design work to make jobs interesting, and establish policies and programs that show concern for employees' needs. Such efforts may become increasingly important as the business world increasingly uses employee empowerment, teamwork, and knowledge sharing to build flexible organizations.[15]

These trends rely on positive employee relationships. Perhaps that is why, when the Gallup Organization studied more than 105,000 employees, it found that one of the 13 circumstances associated with high productivity was "having a best friend at work."[16] A case in point is David Liggett, who developed important friendships at work. Those friends encouraged him, provided helpful feedback, and pitched in whenever one of the friends needed help to meet a deadline. Fifteen years after meeting, the friends continue to get together.

Ethics

In the long run, a high-performance organization meets high ethical standards. Ethics, defined in Chapter 1, establishes fundamental principles for behavior, such as honesty and fairness. Organizations and their employees must meet these standards if they are to maintain positive long-term relationships with their customers and their community.

Ethical behavior is most likely to result from values held by the organization's leaders combined with systems that promote ethical behavior. Charles O. Holliday Jr., the chairman and chief executive officer of DuPont Company, is an example of an executive who cares about ethics. For Holliday, ethics is a matter of behaving in ways that promote trust: "Just saying you're ethical isn't very useful. You have to earn trust by what you do every day."[17] Holliday experienced this kind of leadership himself when he first joined DuPont. The CEO at that time, Dick Heckert, told him, "This company lives by the letter of its contracts and the intent of those contracts," speaking with such conviction that he imprinted the lesson on Holliday's mind.

A number of organizational systems can promote ethical behavior.[18] These include a written code of ethics that the organization distributes to employees and expects them to use in decision making. Publishing a list of ethical standards is not enough, however. The organization should reinforce ethical behavior. For example, performance measures should include ethical standards, and misdeeds should receive swift discipline, as described in Chapter 10. The organization should provide channels employees can use to ask questions about ethical behavior or to seek help if they are expected to do something they believe is wrong. Organizations also can provide training in ethical decision making.

As these examples suggest, ethical behavior is a human resource management concern. The systems that promote ethical behavior include such HRM functions as training, performance management, and discipline policies. In today's business climate, ethical behavior also can affect recruiting. Recent scandals such as those at Enron and Arthur Andersen have hastened the collapse of some companies and put thousands of employees out of work. (The second case at the end of this chapter describes the situation at Arthur Andersen.) Job candidates want to avoid employers whose misdeeds might cost them their jobs and their reputations. Many job candidates have asked recruiters how well their organizations promote ethical behavior.[19] At United Technologies, for example, Patrick Gnazzo says the company's formal practices to promote ethics are "a great recruiting tool." United Technologies and many other companies are finding that ethical behavior and the reputation for it help them keep the best employees as well as the best customers.

LO4

HRM'S Contribution to High Performance

Management of human resources plays a critical role in determining companies' success in meeting the challenges of a rapidly changing, highly competitive environment.[20] Compensation, staffing, training and development, performance management, and other HRM practices are investments that directly affect employees' motivation and ability to provide products and services that are valued by customers. A study by Watson Wyatt Worldwide found that significant improvements in major HR practices, including reward systems, recruitment, and employee retention, led to significant increases in the value of a company's stock.[21] Table 16.2 lists examples of HRM practices that contribute to high performance.

Research suggests that it is more effective to improve HRM practices as a whole than to focus on one or two isolated practices, such as the organization's pay structure or selection system.[22] Also, to have the intended influence on performance, the HRM practices must fit well with one another and the organization as a whole.[23] An example of an organization that has achieved this fit is FedEx, described in the nearby "Best Practices" box.

Job Design

For the organization to benefit from teamwork and employee empowerment, jobs must be designed appropriately. Often, a high-performance work system places em-

TABLE 16.2

HRM Practices That Can Help Organizations Achieve High Performance

• HRM practices match organization's goals.	• Performance management system measures customer satisfaction and quality.
• Individuals and groups share knowledge.	• Organization monitors employees' satisfaction.
• Work is performed by teams.	• Discipline system is progressive.
• Organization encourages continuous learning.	• Pay systems reward skills and accomplishments.
• Work design permits flexibility in where and when tasks are performed.	• Skills and values of a diverse workforce are valued and used.
• Selection system is job related and legal.	• Technology reduces time and costs of tasks while preserving quality.

HR Policies Deliver High Performance for FedEx

At FedEx, the well-known provider of express package delivery, human resource management uses a strategy based on the company's philosophy that "employees should be doing the kind of work they want to do." To match candidates with the right jobs, the company hosts a virtual career center on its website (www.fedex.com). The career center invites visitors to identify their ideal job by choosing location, type of work, and other variables from drop-down lists. Candidates also enter information about their skills. As new positions become available, FedEx uses this system to sort through the data and find candidates with the right interests and skills.

According to FedEx, the online recruiting produces a pool of candidates who are more intelligent than average, even for jobs requiring manual labor. Their intelligence contributes to FedEx's performance at all levels. According to Larry McMahan, the company's vice president of human resources performance and support, "Brighter people are better employees in every category, in every way. They're safer, don't take as much time

off from work, and are better performers."

The selection process at FedEx builds on its electronic recruiting. Candidates take skills tests that measure their reasoning, reading, and math skills. The company also measures physical abilities and conducts background checks. From the test results, hiring managers can select the most qualified candidates.

FedEx's award-winning training programs prepare employees for their jobs. First comes an orientation program, which lasts up to one month. Electronic instruction materials tell employees about FedEx and the employee's job in relation to the compnay. Additional training prepares employees for specific kinds of jobs. Couriers, for example, receive an additional three weeks of training. Managers receive 6 to 10 weeks of training during their first year with FedEx. Each year after that, they participate in another 40 hours of training. The training program supports the company's position tht better-informed employees will be better-performing employees.

Human resource policies also contribute to productivity by

encouraging good attendance. To correct a problem with high absenteeism, the company adopted a policy for sick leave. Employees receive five days of paid sick leave. If they are sick longer, they may use vacation days. If they use fewer than five days, the company pays them for unused sick days at the end of the year. When the company adopted this policy, unscheduled medical absences fell by almost one-third. FedEx also helps employees get back to work after an injury. The company helps disabled employees coordinate their medical benefits, encourages them to stick to their treatment plan, and provides answers to questions about the health care system. When employees can return to work but still must restrict their activities, the company tries to arrange for jobs they can handle as they finish their recovery.

Together, HR programs and policies at FedEx bring talented people onboard, then motivate them and provide them with resources they need to do their jobs.

SOURCE: C. M. Solomon, "HR's Push for Productivity," *Workforce*, August 2002, pp. 28–33.

ployees in work teams where employees collaborate to make decisions and solve problems. A good example of this approach to job design is GE Fanuc Automation North America, a joint venture between General Electric Company and FANUC Ltd. of Japan.[24] GE Fanuc Automation employs 1,500 people and maintains a strong commitment to quality. Its work design is based on the principle that employees who are closest to the work have the best ideas for improvement. To encourage these employees to contribute their ideas, the venture organized work into more than 40 work teams. The teams set their own goals and measure their success based on factors related to the venture's business goals. Each team spends at least one hour per week measuring performance relative to the goals and discussing ways to improve. Each function team within the business has a dedicated HR manager who helps the team develop its strategies, accompanies the team on sales calls, and supports the team as needed.

Recruitment and Selection

At a high-performance organization, recruitment and selection aim at obtaining the kinds of employees who can thrive in this type of setting. These employees are enthusiastic about and able to contribute to teamwork, empowerment, and knowledge sharing. Qualities such as creativity and ability to cooperate as part of a team may play a large role in selection decisions. High-performance organizations need selection methods that identify more than technical skills like ability to perform accounting and engineering tasks. Employers may use group interviews, open-ended questions, and psychological tests to find employees who innovate, share ideas, and take initiative.

Training and Development

When organizations base hiring decisions on qualities like decision-making and teamwork skills, training may be required to teach employees the specific skills they need to perform the duties of their job. Extensive training and development also are part of a learning organization, described earlier in this chapter. And when organizations delegate many decisions to work teams, the members of those teams likely will benefit from participating in team development activities that prepare them for their roles as team members. In the previous example of GE Fanuc Automation North America, training supports the effectiveness of the joint venture's work teams. All GE Fanuc employees receive more than 100 hours of training.[25]

Employee development is an important factor in IBM's top ranking in a study of the "Top 20 Companies for Leaders," jointly conducted by Hewitt Associates and *Chief Executive* magazine. According to Randall MacDonald, IBM's senior vice president of human resources, IBM had determined that leadership was one of four areas it had to focus on to achieve high performance. So the company charged all its existing leaders with developing future leaders. Once a year, IBM calls together its top managers to select candidates for leadership development, and they work with the candidates to create a development plan that meets their personal goals. By making leadership development a part of the company's routine processes, IBM removes the fear that coaching one's replacement threatens one's own career. MacDonald points out that planning for leadership is at least as important as other types of planning: "The [chief financial officer], when he gives one of our line guys $3 billion to go build a new plant, he doesn't say, 'Go build the plant and do what you want with it.' No, that CFO and that line person are going to manage that asset. . . . Whatever happened to the concept of people being our most important asset? Well if they are, we ought to manage them."[26]

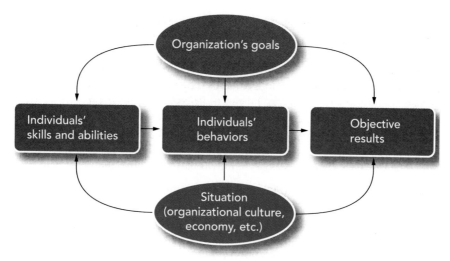

FIGURE 16.4

Employee Performance as a Process

Performance Management

In a high-performance organization, employees know the organization's goals and what they must do to help achieve those goals. HR departments can contribute to this ideal through the design of the organization's performance management system. As we discussed in Chapter 8, performance management should be related to the organization's goals. For example, teamwork is central to the success of the joint venture at GE Fanuc Automation. Therefore, managers must support their teams, and support of teamwork is one performance measure in the managers' performance evaluations.[27] At Extreme Logic, high performance comes from clear communication about what kinds of behavior are needed. On its intranet, the Atlanta-based software company publishes attributes and behaviors associated with success in each job, as well as the performance standard for each attribute and behavior. Employees can go online at any time to gauge whether they are meeting those standards.[28]

To set up a performance management system that supports the organization's goals, managers need to understand the process of employee performance. As shown in Figure 16.4, individual employees bring a set of skills and abilities to the job, and by applying a set of behaviors, they use those skills to achieve certain results. But success is more than the product of individual efforts. The organization's goals should influence each step of the process. The organization's culture and other factors influence the employees' abilities, behaviors, and results. Sometimes uncontrollable forces such as the current economic conditions enter the picture, it mustn't be forgotten—for

To create high-performance work systems, organizations should establish performance goals that are linked to meeting customers' needs. Customers can be external or internal, such as the ones pictured here attending a training/orientation session conducted by someone in the company.

example, a salesperson can probably sell more during an economic expansion than during an economic slowdown.

This model suggests some guidelines for performance management. First, each aspect of performance management should be related to the organization's goals. Business goals should influence the kinds of employees selected and their training, the requirements of each job, and the measures used for evaluating results. Generally, this means the organization identifies what each department must do to achieve the desired results, then defines how individual employees should contribute to their department's goals. More specifically, the following guidelines describe how to make the performance management system support organizational goals:[29]

- *Define and measure performance in precise terms*. Focus on outcomes that can be defined in terms of how frequently certain behaviors occur. Include criteria that describe ways employees can add value to a product or service (such as through quantity, quality, or timeliness). Include behaviors that go beyond the minimum required to perform a job (such as helping coworkers).
- *Link performance measures to meeting customer needs*. "Customers" may be the organization's external customers, or they may be internal customers (employees receiving services from a coworker). Service goals for internal customers should be related to satisfying external customers.
- *Measure and correct for the effect of situational constraints*. Monitor economic conditions, the organization's culture, and other influences on performance. Measures of employees' performance should take these influences into account.

This approach gives employees the information they need to behave in ways that contribute to high performance. In addition, organizations should help employees identify and obtain the abilities they need to meet their performance goals.

Compensation

Organizations can reinforce the impact of this kind of performance management by linking compensation in part to performance measures. Chapter 12 described a number of methods for doing this, including merit pay, gainsharing, and profit sharing. A small manufacturer called Headsets.com improved productivity by linking bonuses to sales volume; employees share a fixed percentage of the company's total sales.[30] Employees at Headsets.com can see that if the company grows by hiring more workers, rather than by using the same number of workers to produce and sell more, the bonus will be divided among more people. They can earn a bigger bonus if they get the same results by working more efficiently. Since starting this bonus plan, Headsets.com has been able to grow more profitably. Compensation systems also can help to create the conditions that contribute to high performance, including teamwork, empowerment, and job satisfaction. For example, as discussed in Chapter 12, compensation can be linked to achievement of team objectives.

Organizations can increase empowerment and job satisfaction by including employees in decisions about compensation and by communicating the basis for decisions about pay. When the organization designs a pay structure, it can set up a task force that includes employees with direct experience in various types of jobs. Some organizations share financial information with their employees and invite them to recommend pay increases for themselves, based on their contributions. Employees also may participate in setting individual or group goals for which they can receive bonuses. Research has found that employee participation in decisions about pay poli-

Using Information Systems in a Learning Organization

A learning organization uses information technology to encourage employees to share information with each other, and HR professionals can help establish these applications. Here are some ideas:

- Set up an intranet that allows employees to store and share knowledge through Web pages and e-mail.
- Publish directories listing what employees do, what kinds of knowledge they have, and how to contact them.
- Develop "informational maps," or charts that identify where specific knowledge is stored in the organization.
- Create the position of chief information officer, which includes the responsibility for cataloging information and enabling the sharing of information within the organization.
- When employees attend training programs, require that they give their coworkers presentations or post summaries on the intranet of what they have learned from the programs.
- Allow employees to take time off from work to acquire knowledge or study problems. Establish policies for sabbaticals, attendance at training programs, and other time away from the workplace for learning, and communicate these on the intranet.
- Create an online library of learning resources, such as journals, technical manuals, training opportunities, and seminars. These can be available through the organization's intranet.

cies is linked to greater satisfaction with the pay and the job.[31] And as we discussed in Chapter 11, when organizations explain their pay structures to employees, the communication can enhance employees' satisfaction and belief that the system is fair.

HRM Technology

LO5

Human resource departments can improve their own and their organization's performance by appropriately using new technology. New technology usually involves *automation*—that is, using equipment and information processing to perform activities that had been performed by people. Over the last few decades, automation has improved HRM efficiency by reducing the number of people needed to perform routine tasks. Information technology also provides ways to build and improve systems for knowledge generation and sharing, as part of a learning organization. The "HR How-To" box describes some ways of using information technology to create and share knowledge.

HRM Applications

As computers become ever more powerful, new technologies continue to be introduced. In fact, so many HRM applications are developed for use on personal computers that publications serving the profession (such as *HR Magazine* and *Personnel Journal*) devote annual issues to reviewing this software. Some of the technologies that have been widely adopted are transaction processing, decision support systems, and expert systems.[32]

transaction processing
Computations and calculations involved in reviewing and documenting HRM decisions and practices.

Transaction processing refers to computations and calculations involved in reviewing and documenting HRM decisions and practices. It includes documenting decisions and actions associated with employee relocation, training expenses, and enrollments in courses and benefit plans. Transaction processing also includes the activities required to meet government reporting requirements, such as filling out EEO-1 reports, on which employers report information about employees' race and gender by job category. Computers enable companies to perform these tasks more efficiently. Employers can fill out computerized forms and store HRM information in databases (data stored electronically in user-specified categories), so that it is easier to find, sort, and report.

decision support systems
Computer software systems designed to help managers solve problems by showing how results vary when the manager alters assumptions or data.

Decision support systems are computer software systems designed to help managers solve problems. They usually include a "what if?" feature that managers can use to enter different assumptions or data and see how the likely outcomes will change. This type of system can help managers make decisions for human resource planning. The manager can, for example, try out different assumptions about turnover rates to see how those assumptions affect the number of new employees needed. Or the manager can test a range of assumptions about the availability of a certain skill in the labor market, looking at the impact of the assumptions on the success of different recruiting plans. Possible applications for a decision support system include forecasting (discussed in Chapter 5) and succession planning (discussed in Chapter 9).

expert systems
Computer systems that support decision making by incorporating the decision rules used by people who are considered to have expertise in a certain area.

Expert systems are computer systems that incorporate the decision rules used by people who are considered to have expertise in a certain area. The systems help users make decisions by recommending actions based on the decision rules and the information provided by the users. An expert system is designed to recommend the same actions that a human expert would in a similar situation. For example, an expert system could guide an interviewer during the selection process. Some organizations use expert systems to help employees decide how to allocate their money for benefits (as in a cafeteria plan) and help managers schedule the labor needed to complete projects. Expert systems can deliver both high quality and lower costs. By using the decision processes of experts, an expert system helps many people to arrive at decisions that reflect the expert's knowledge. An expert system helps avoid the errors that can result from fatigue and decision-making biases, such as biases in appraising employee performance, described in Chapter 8. An expert system can increase efficiency by enabling fewer or less-skilled employees to do work that otherwise would require many highly skilled employees.

In modern HR departments, transaction processing, decision support systems, and expert systems often are part of a human resource information system. Also, these technologies may be linked to employees through a network such as an intranet. Information systems and networks have been evolving rapidly; the following descriptions provide a basic introduction.

Human Resource Information Systems

A standard feature of a modern HRIS is the use of *relational databases*, which store data in separate files that can be linked by common elements. These common elements are fields identifying the type of data. Commonly used fields for an HR database include name, Social Security number, job status (full- or part-time), hiring date, position, title, rate of pay, citizenship status, job history, job location, mailing address, birth date, and emergency contacts. A relational database lets a user sort the data by any of the fields. For example, depending on how the database is set up, the user might be able to look up tables listing employees by location, rates of pay for various jobs, or employees who have completed certain training courses. This system is far more sophisticated than the old-fashioned method of filing employee data by name, with one file per employee.

The ability to locate and combine many categories of data has a multitude of uses in human resource management. Databases have been developed to track employee benefit costs, training courses, and compensation. The system can meet the needs of line managers as well as the HR department. On an oil rig, for example, management might look up data listing employee names along with safety equipment issued and appropriate skill certification. HR managers at headquarters might look up data on the same employees to gather information about wage rates or training programs needed. Another popular use of an HRIS is applicant tracking, or maintaining and retrieving records of job applicants. This is much faster and easier than trying to sort through stacks of résumés. Nike, for example, had to throw away most of the 35,000 unsolicited résumés it received until it began using the *Resumix* applicant tracking program.[33] With relational databases, HR staff can retrieve information about specific applicants or obtain lists of applicants with specific skills, career goals, work history, and employment background. Such information is useful for HR planning, recruitment, succession planning, and career development. Taking the process a step further, the system could store information related to hiring and terminations. By analyzing such data, the HR department could measure the long-term success of its recruiting and selection processes.

Human Resource Management Online: E-HRM

During the last decade or so, organizations have seen the advantages of sharing information in computer networks. At the same time, the widespread adoption of the Internet has linked people around the globe. As we discussed in Chapter 2, more and more organizations are engaging in e-HRM, providing HR-related information over the Internet. Because much human resource information is confidential, organizations may do this with an intranet, which uses Internet technology but allows access only to authorized users (such as the organization's employees). For HR professionals, Internet access also offers a way to research new developments, post job openings, trade ideas with colleagues in other organizations, and obtain government documents. In this way, e-HRM combines company-specific information on a secure intranet with links to the resources on the broader Internet.

Apple's recruiting home page. Online recruiting offers potential benefits for companies. Employers can retrieve résumés at their own websites. They can also use online testing services to help make selection decisions. Potential employees benefit because they can read more about the company directly on the site and easily apply or submit their résumé.

Oracle Spells Human Resource Management "B2E"

The promise and challenge of Internet technology in organizations is that it enables them to review and restructure their processes, including those of human resource management. Oracle Corporation is among the companies that have realized great improvements in efficiency from applying this technology to HRM. Using e-business software has saved Oracle over a billion dollars, and a significant part of the savings came from the transformation of HRM.

Oracle, the world's second largest independent software company, must manage administrative activities for a huge global workforce. Not surprisingly for a technology leader, the company does so efficiently through its use of automation to create a "B2E"

(business-to-employee) relationship. Oracle has moved routine, day-to-day administrative tasks online. A variety of self-service tools let managers and employees find answers and provide information on their computers. Before the change, HR staff had been spending 6 out of every 10 hours on simple administrative tasks. By automating those tasks, HR professionals have freed up more time to focus on activities that are more directly productive—for instance, recruiting, staffing, training, and compensation.

The savings of the B2E approach go straight to Oracle's bottom line. To carry out all the HRM tasks, Oracle once needed an HR staff person for every 800 employees. Now the human

resource staff can meet the needs of more employees—1 staffer for every 3,000 employees. This efficiency has enabled Oracle to grow in other departments without increasing the budget for human resource management. At the same time, the focus of HRM has shifted from paperwork to business success. In the words of Joyce Westerdahl, Oracle's vice president of human resources, "We will continue to add more and more capabilities to empower employees and managers with the tools and knowledge they need to be as effective and as productive as possible."

SOURCE: C. Collett, "Business to Employee: Automating the HR Function," *CMA Management* 75, no. 7 (October 1, 2001), p. 20.

A benefit of e-HRM is that employees can help themselves to the information they need when they need it, instead of contacting an HR staff person. For example, employees can go online to enroll in or select benefits, submit insurance claims, or fill out employee satisfaction surveys. This can be more convenient for the employees, as well as more economical for the HR department. The "e-HRM" box describes how Oracle Corporation has obtained these benefits by moving many HRM services online. Similarly, at Cisco Systems, many HR activities are automated online.[34] When employees join the company, they log on, visit the "New Hire" page, and sign up for benefits. They also see that the website is the place to file expense reports, look up project information, and more. The site lets employees know when it is time for their performance review and lets them start the process with their supervisor. The employee reviews an evaluation form, studies the expected behaviors, fills in needed information, and sends the form to the supervisor. If the form requires information from someone else in the company, the supervisor clicks on a link to request that information. The supervisor receives any requested information, completes the appraisal form, and meets with the employee to discuss the review. So much of the process is automated that supervisors have more time to focus on the actual meeting with the employee.

Most administrative and information-gathering activities in human resource management can be part of e-HRM. For example, online recruiting has become a significant part of the total recruiting effort, as candidates submit résumés online. Employers go online to retrieve suitable résumés from job search sites or retrieve information from forms they post at their own websites. For selection decisions, the organization may have candidates use one of the online testing services available; these services conduct the tests, process the results, and submit reports to employers. Online appraisal systems can help managers make pay decisions consistent with company policies and employee performance. Many types of training can be conducted online, as we discussed in Chapter 7. Online surveys of employee satisfaction can be quick and easy to fill out. Besides providing a way to administer the survey, an intranet is an effective vehicle for communicating the results of the survey and management's planned response.

Not only does e-HRM provide efficient ways to carry out human resource functions, it also poses new challenges to employees and new issues for HR managers to address. The Internet's ability to link people anytime, anywhere has accelerated such trends as globalization, the importance of knowledge sharing within organizations, and the need for flexibility.[35] These trends, in turn, change the work environment for employees. For example, employees in the Internet age are expected to be highly committed but flexible, able to move from job to job. Employees also may be connected to the organization 24/7. In the car, on vacation, in airports, and even in the bathroom, employees with handheld computers can be interrupted by work demands. Organizations depend on their human resource departments to help prepare employees for this changing work world through such activities as training, career development, performance management, and benefits packages that meet the need for flexibility and help employees manage stress.

Effectiveness of Human Resource Management

LO6

In recent years, human resource management at some organizations has responded to the quest for total quality management by taking a customer-oriented approach. For an organization's human resource division, "customers" are the organization as a whole and its other divisions. They are customers of HRM because they depend on HRM to provide a variety of services that result in a supply of talented, motivated employees. Taking this customer-oriented approach, human resource management defines its customer groups, customer needs, and the activities required to meet those needs, as shown in Figure 16.5. These definitions give an organization a basis for defining goals and measures of success.

One company that uses this approach is Whirlpool Corporation. The company's HR managers identify their customer, define the need they can satisfy or the value they can provide, and identify the methods they must use to satisfy the customer. When Whirlpool planned to start a centralized service center, its plan called for

FIGURE 16.5

Customer-Oriented Perspective of Human Resource Management

Who Are Our Customers?
Line managers
Strategic planners
Employees

What Do Our Customers Need?
Committed employees
Competent employees

How Do We Meet Customer Needs?
Qualified staffing
Performance management
Rewards
Training and development

Human Resource Management

hiring of 100 to 150 employees as call takers to process service requests from customers owning Whirlpool appliances and to schedule service calls. Whirlpool gave an HR manager the responsibility for developing a selection system for call takers. The manager determined the customer in this instance was the operations manager in charge of phone service and the need was the delivery of qualified call takers. To meet this need, the HR manager decided to use a combination of structured interviews and paper-and-pencil tests. The company can evaluate the success of this program in terms of whether it efficiently produces enough qualified call takers.

Depending on the situation, a number of techniques are available for measuring HRM's effectiveness in meeting its customers' needs. These techniques include reviewing a set of key indicators, measuring the outcomes of specific HRM activity, and measuring the economic value of HRM programs.

Human Resource Management Audits

HRM audit
A formal review of the outcomes of HRM functions, based on identifying key HRM functions and measures of business performance.

An **HRM audit** is a formal review of the outcomes of HRM functions. To conduct the audit, the HR department identifies key functions and the key measures of business performance and customer satisfaction that would indicate each function is succeeding. Table 16.3 lists examples of these measures for a variety of HRM functions: staffing, compensation, benefits, training, appraisal and development, and overall effectiveness. The audit may also look at any other measure associated with successful management of human resources—for instance, compliance with equal employment opportunity laws, succession planning, maintaining a safe workplace, and positive labor relations. An HRM audit using customer satisfaction measures supports the customer-oriented approach to human resource management.

After identifying performance measures for the HRM audit, the staff carries out the audit by gathering information. The information for the key business indicators is usually available in the organization's documents. Sometimes the HR department has to create new documents for gathering specific types of data. The usual way to measure

TABLE 16.3

Key Measures of Success for an HRM Audit

BUSINESS INDICATORS	CUSTOMER SATISFACTION MEASURES
Staffing	
Average days taken to fill open requisitions	Anticipation of personnel needs
Ratio of acceptances to offers made	Timeliness of referring qualified workers to line supervisors
Ratio of minority/women applicants to representation in local labor market	Treatment of applicants
Per capita requirement costs	Skill in handling terminations
Average years of experience/education of hires per job family	Adaptability to changing labor market conditions
Compensation	
Per capita (average) merit increases	Fairness of existing job evaluation system in assigning grades and salaries
Ratio of recommendations for reclassification to number of employees	Competitiveness in local labor market
Percentage of overtime hours to straight time	Relationship between pay and performance
Ratio of average salary offers to average salary in community	Employee satisfaction with pay
Benefits	
Average unemployment compensation payment (UCP)	Promptness in handling claims
Average workers' compensation payment (WCP)	Fairness and consistency in the application of benefit policies
Benefit cost per payroll dollar	Communication of benefits to employees
Percentage of sick leave to total pay	Assistance provided to line managers in reducing potential for unnecessary claims
Training	
Percentage of employees participating in training programs per job family	Extent to which training programs meet the needs of employees and the company
Percentage of employees receiving tuition refunds	Communication to employees about available training opportunities
Training dollars per employee	Quality of introduction/orientation programs
Employee appraisal and development	
Distribution of performance appraisal ratings	Assistance in identifying management potential
Appropriate psychometric properties of appraisal forms	Organizational development activities provided by HRM department
Overall effectiveness	
Ratio of personnel staff to employee population	Accuracy and clarity of information provided to managers and employees
Turnover rate	
Absenteeism rate	Competence and expertise of staff
Ratio of per capita revenues to per capita cost	Working relationship between organizations and HRM department
Net income per employee	

SOURCE: Reprinted with permission excerpts from Chapter 1.5, "Evaluating Human Resource Effectiveness," pp. 187–227, by Anne S. Tsui and Luis R. Gomez-Mejia, from *Human Resource Management: Evolving Roles and Responsibilities;* edited by Lee Dyer. Copyright © 1988 by The Bureau of National Affairs, Inc., Washington DC 20037.

customer satisfaction is to conduct surveys. Employee attitude surveys, discussed in Chapter 10, provide information about the satisfaction of these internal customers. Many organizations conduct surveys of top line executives to get a better view of how HRM practices affect the organization's business success.

Analyzing the Effect of HRM Programs

Another way to measure HRM effectiveness is to analyze specific programs or activities. The analysis can measure a program's success in terms of whether it achieved its objectives and whether it delivered value in an economic sense. For example, if the organization sets up a training program, it should set up goals for that program, such as the training's effects on learning, behavior, and performance improvement (results). The analysis would then measure whether the training program achieved the preset goals.

The analysis can take an economic approach that measures the dollar value of the program's costs and benefits. Successful programs should deliver value that is greater than the programs' costs. Costs include employees' compensation as well as the costs to administer HRM programs such as training, employee development, or satisfaction surveys. Benefits could include a reduction in the costs associated with employee absenteeism and turnover, as well as improved productivity associated with better selection and training programs.

In general, HR departments should be able to improve their performance through some combination of greater efficiency and greater effectiveness. Greater efficiency means the HR department uses fewer and less-costly resources to perform its functions. Greater effectiveness means that what the HR department does—for example, selecting employees or setting up a performance management system—has a more beneficial effect on employees' and the organization's performance.

HRM's potential to affect employees' well-being and the organization's performance makes human resource management an exciting field. As we have shown throughout the book, every HRM function calls for decisions that have the potential to help individuals and organizations achieve their goals. For HR managers to fulfill that potential, they must ensure that their decisions are well grounded. As an example, we discussed telework in Chapter 4, as an option for work design that many organizations have embraced to promote greater productivity and job satisfaction. At the same time, a review of the research literature shows that these assumptions about telework's benefits are largely untested.[36] Telework is but one example of an issue that can dramatically affect employees' lives and organizations' success yet remains open for future investigation. The field of human resource management provides tremendous opportunity to future researchers and managers who want to make a difference in many people's lives.

Summary

1. Define high-performance work systems and identify the elements of such a system.
A high-performance work system is the right combination of people, technology, and organizational structure that makes full use of the organization's resources and opportunities in achieving its goals. The elements of a high-performance work system are organizational structure, task design, people, reward systems, and information systems. These elements must work together in a smoothly functioning whole.

2. Summarize the outcomes of a high-performance work system.

   A high-performance work system achieves the organization's goals, typically including growth, productivity, and high profits. On the way to achieving these overall goals, the high-performance work system meets such intermediate goals as high quality, innovation, customer satisfaction, job satisfaction, and reduced absenteeism and turnover.

3. Describe the conditions that create a high-performance work system.

   Many conditions contribute to high-performance work systems by giving employees skills, incentives, knowledge, autonomy, and employee satisfaction. Teamwork and empowerment can make work more satisfying and provide a means for employees to improve quality and productivity. Organizations can improve performance by creating a learning organization, in which people constantly learn and share knowledge so that they continually expand their capacity to achieve the results they desire. In a high-performance organization, employees experience job satisfaction or even "occupational intimacy." For long-run high performance, organizations and employees must be ethical as well.

4. Explain how human resource management can contribute to high performance.

   Jobs should be designed to foster teamwork and employee empowerment. Recruitment and selection should focus on obtaining employees who have the qualities necessary for teamwork, empowerment, and knowledge sharing. When the organization selects for teamwork and decision-making skills, it may have to provide training in specific job tasks. Training also is important because of its role in creating a learning organization. The performance management system should be related to the organization's goals, with a fo-

cus on meeting internal and external customers' needs. Compensation should include links to performance, and employees should be included in decisions about compensation. Research suggests that it is more effective to improve HRM practices as a whole than to focus on one or two isolated practices.

5. Discuss the role of HRM technology in high-performance work systems.

   Technology can improve the efficiency of the human resource management functions and support knowledge sharing. HRM applications involve transaction processing, decision support systems, and expert systems, often as part of a human resource information system using relational databases, which can improve the efficiency of routine tasks and the quality of decisions. With Internet technology, organizations can use e-HRM to let all the organization's employees help themselves to the HR information they need whenever they need it.

6. Summarize ways to measure the effectiveness of human resource management.

   Taking a customer-oriented approach, HRM can improve quality by defining the internal customers who use its services and determining whether it is meeting those customers' needs. One way to do this is with an HRM audit, a formal review of the outcomes of HRM functions. The audit may look at any measure associated with successful management of human resources. Audit information may come from the organization's documents and surveys of customer satisfaction. Another way to measure HRM effectiveness is to analyze specific programs or activities. The analysis can measure success in terms of whether a program met its objectives and whether it delivered value in an economic sense, such as by leading to productivity improvements.

Review and Discussion Questions

1. What is a high-performance work system? What are its elements? Which of these elements involve human resource management?

2. As it has become clear that HRM can help create and maintain high-performance work systems, it appears that organizations will need two kinds of human resource professionals: One kind focuses on identifying how HRM can contribute to high performance. The other kind develops expertise in particular HRM functions, such as how to administer a benefits program that complies with legal requirements. Which aspect of HRM is more interesting to you? Why?

3. How can teamwork, empowerment, knowledge sharing, and job satisfaction contribute to high performance?

4. If an organization can win customers, employees, or investors through deception, why would ethical behavior contribute to high performance?

5. How can an organization promote ethical behavior among its employees?

6. Summarize how each of the following HR functions can contribute to high performance.
   a. Job design
   b. Recruitment and selection

c. Training and development
d. Performance management
e. Compensation

7. How can HRM technology make a human resource department more productive? How can technology improve the quality of HRM decisions?

8. Why should human resource departments measure their effectiveness? What are some ways they can go about measuring effectiveness?

What's Your HR IQ?

The student CD-ROM offers two more ways to check what you've learned so far. Use the Self-Assessment exercise to test your ethical judgment. Then go online with the Web Exercise to learn more about global organizations that have high-performance work systems.

BusinessWeek Case

BusinessWeek **From Devastation to High Performance**

Hanging in the New York office of Keefe, Bruyette & Woods Inc. is a painting of the American flag. A close look reveals that the stripes are in fact names. These are the 67 people who worked at KBW's offices on the 88th and 89th floors of the World Trade Center and died on September 11, 2001. The flag is the only obvious reference to the tragedy. Indeed, to all appearances, KBW—which makes its money by researching, trading, and advising banks and financial-services firms—is prospering. It's a bittersweet success. "No matter what horrible things you've been through, life goes on," says President Andrew M. Senchak. "It's horrifying and glorious at the same time."

Going on meant rebuilding the shattered firm, which was among the hardest hit. Since that day, as they have grieved for their lost colleagues, Senchak, CEO John G. Duffy, and their staff have done more. Today, the reconstituted KBW employs more people, takes in just as much in commissions, and covers almost as many stocks as it did when the Twin Towers fell. Revenues are down 13 percent from a year ago, but that's an impressive achievement given the economic climate. The firm's resurrection is a result of Herculean efforts by surviving employees, plus dozens of outsiders, some of whom radically changed their lives to join. And, Duffy says, KBW "caught some breaks along the way."

The first two weeks were the toughest. The company had lost its co-chairman, a third of its staff, and all of its New York documents and computer files. Senchak—then KBW's vice chairman and the man who ran the company while Duffy was home mourning the death of his son, Christopher, an employee—recalls those early days as "fundamental chaos. There was no road map for what we had to do." Still, order soon emerged. KBW set up temporary digs at the offices of Wachtell, Lipton, Rosen & Katz, a midtown law firm where Senchak had been on the morning of September 11. KBW also shipped traders up to its Boston offices until securing temporary space at the Banc National de Paris.

A huge hurdle was filling the vacancies, a task made immeasurably simpler when Wall Street veterans, ex-Keefe employees, and even rivals began offering their services. One such person was Michael Corasaniti, an ex–portfolio manager for Newberger Berman LLC who had quit the rat race to teach part-time at Columbia University, work at boutique research shop Graham Fisher Company, and spend more time with his young son. As he scanned the list of missing employees on KBW's website, Corasaniti realized the firm needed his help. "It was like a phone call from God," he says.

Corasaniti's decision to accept a job as director of research marked a turning point. His presence prompted former colleagues to come aboard, too. First to sign up were two of Corasaniti's partners from Graham Fisher. "That was huge," says Duffy. "It sent the message that Keefe was in good enough shape to join." KBW's reputation for solid research helped, too. Before long, most of Morgan Stanley's San Francisco bank-analyst team had joined. Then two UBS Warburg analysts came on. "It was like a waterfall," says Corasaniti.

As KBW set about rebuilding its business, employees had to be creative. At Wachtell Lipton, where the investment bankers set up shop, there weren't enough phones to go around. So they used public ones to contact clients. "You'd see this Harvard MBA go into a booth, open his briefcase, and put the finishing touches on a deal," says Senchak. "Then he'd leave, and another banker would go into the same booth."

Whatever it took to keep deals flowing, they did. By December 2001, KBW had closed 13, including a record-setting deal with First Tennessee National Corporation

(FTN). The complicated deal with FTN required coordinating 85 small banks and creating and selling three types of bonds. "Everyone at Keefe worked around the clock," says Gary Grear, president of FTN Financial Securities Corporation, FTN's investment bank. "They were going to get that deal done."

There has been no letup this year [2002]. Corasaniti has taken up the goals laid out by his late predecessor, David S. Berry. "David projected 10 percent growth for 2002. I want his budget met," he says. That has put a strain on the new researchers. "No one has gotten a vacation since they got here," says Corasaniti. "Maybe in late September they can have a little time off."

While KBW seems back on track, its execs concede their work is far from finished. In early September, construction at the new headquarters on Seventh Avenue and 51st Street still wasn't complete. Wires hung from the ceiling. Doors were barricaded with Wet Cement signs. Duffy's office was a cramped, unadorned space filled with boxes.

There is a nagging worry they all share: What if operating in crisis mode was the easy part?

SOURCE: H. Timmons, "Keefe Bruyette: Up from Ground Zero," *BusinessWeek Online*, September 16, 2002, www.businessweek.com.

Questions

1. In terms of human resource management, what do you think were the biggest challenges facing Keefe, Bruyette & Woods in the weeks after September 11, 2001? Will the focus of HRM at the firm need to change in the future? Why or why not?

2. In the period described by this case, what elements of a high-performance work system do you see? Which of the conditions that contribute to high performance are present?

3. Why do you think the firm's people are worried that "operating in crisis mode" might be "the easy part"? What can be "easy" about a crisis? What principles of high-performance organizations might help in this situation?

Case: A Giant Falls

Arthur Andersen, once a giant of the accounting world, crumbled into bankruptcy in a scandal that made international headlines. The firm bears the name of its founder, Arthur Andersen, a principled accountant who founded it to conduct audits. Basically, auditing involves reviewing a sample of a client's paperwork to make sure transactions are being recorded properly. Andersen had a reputation for strictly adhering to auditing principles. If a client threatened to go elsewhere unless Andersen signed off on questionable reports, Andersen would say good-bye. Thanks to Andersen's good reputation, the small Chicago firm grew to one of the nation's Big Eight (and eventually, as firms merged, Big Six and Big Five).

From its early days, Andersen's firm offered more services than auditing. If an audit uncovered a problem, the firm offered to develop solutions—that is, it offered business consulting. During the 1980s, Andersen succeeded so well at developing computerized business solutions that its auditing became more automated and less profitable. In a climate where Andersen's consultants were generating far more profits than the auditors, tension developed between the two groups.

The differences between the auditors and the consultants involved more than profitability. The two groups represented wholly different cultures. For an auditor, independence and accuracy are core values. The quality of an auditor's work depends on accurate reporting of the facts as they are, not as the client wishes them to be. Consultants must care about accuracy, too, but a consultant's aim is to

improve the client's success. The consultant is more directly committed to the client's interests. Also, consultants build their practice by looking for areas in which they can help organizations improve, so Andersen's consultants were more oriented to selling than its auditors were. These differences shaped the way the auditors and consultants made decisions. In the words of Gresham Brebach, a head of consulting for Andersen during the 1960s, "When you've got a gray area, the auditors would always push you toward . . . the conservative view." Consultants, in contrast, are "there to influence change, to convince the client to do something different, not to conform or comply."

As the consultants' role grew, the firm went hunting for dramatic revenue growth. In the 1970s, the firm's Detroit office, headed by Dick Measelle, won the account of the short-lived DeLorean Motor Company, owned by the flamboyant John DeLorean. Tipped off by the motor company's own financial executives, auditors discovered that DeLorean was charging a wide range of personal expenses to the company. But when Measelle and other Andersen auditors met with DeLorean, they accepted the CEO's explanations and let the expenses stand. Later, DeLorean's company collapsed, leaving the British government empty-handed after giving tens of millions of dollars in loans and grants to bring a DeLorean plant to Belfast. The British government sued Andersen for vouching for DeLorean rather than disclosing the questionable accounting. Andersen settled the suits—and promoted Measelle. He became the head of Andersen's U.S. audit division in 1987, and two years later, he took the helm of Andersen's worldwide audit and tax practice.

Measelle and CEO Larry Weinbach charged Jim Edwards, head of the U.S. audit practice, with making that practice more profitable. They encouraged Edwards and his managers to reduce the number of auditors, often through retirement incentives for the most experienced auditors—the ones most steeped in the old auditing culture. To win more business from existing clients, the audit practice offered internal auditing, which studies a company's financial statements to answer management questions such as whether the company is operating efficiently. Traditionally, companies use their own accountants for internal audits, and outside auditors review the books to report on the fairness and accuracy of the financial statements. When Andersen began doing internal audits, it typically would put the client's accountants on its own payroll.

The pressure on the auditors continued to intensify. The consulting business eventually dwarfed auditing; it then split away from Andersen to operate as a separate company named Accenture. Growth had to come from the audit division. The company rewarded partners who brought in new business, even when audits failed to uncover scandalous problems, including the collapse of Lincoln Savings and Loan in 1992, allegations of fraud against Waste Management Inc. in 1999, and the collapse of Enron Energy Services in 2001. Settling the associated lawsuits cost the firm tens of millions of dollars.

The Enron collapse was the final straw. Andersen employees worked at Enron's Houston headquarters, and former Andersen employees were on Enron's payroll doing internal audits. The close ties between the auditor and its important client (Enron paid Andersen $58 million in 2000 alone) made it difficult for Andersen's auditors to be impartial. As Enron crafted questionable deals in an apparent effort to hide losses, Andersen's auditors felt pressured to go along. Patricia Grutzmacher, a former senior manager at Andersen who worked on the Enron account, testified that when auditors insisted on unfavorable requirements, Enron managers would call Andersen senior partners and persuade them to overrule the auditors' advice. Carl Bass, an auditor and member of Andersen's Professional Standards Group, remained steadfast, but Enron eventually persuaded Andersen to exclude him from the account.

When Enron's schemes began to unravel and its stock plunged, many people questioned Andersen's role in signing off on Enron's financial statements. The scandal worsened following publicity that Andersen employees had been shredding documents related to the Enron account. In light of Andersen's earlier questionable practices, including the audit of Waste Management, the Justice Department indicted Andersen for obstruction of justice.

The mighty accounting firm could not withstand this blow to its reputation. On June 15, 2002, a jury found Andersen guilty of obstruction of justice, and on August 31, Andersen shut down its auditing business.

SOURCE: "Civil War Splits Andersen," *Chicago Tribune*, September 2, 2002, sec. 1, pp. 1, 14–15; "Ties to Enron Blinded Andersen," *Chicago Tribune*, September 3, 2002, sec. 1, pp. 1, 8–9; "Repeat Offender Gets Stiff Justice," *Chicago Tribune*, September 4, 2002, sec. 1, pp. 1, 12–13.

Questions

1. What elements and conditions of a high-performance work system did Arthur Andersen possess? Which did it lack?
2. How would human resource management at Arthur Andersen have needed to change when the firm's goals shifted from an emphasis on independence and technical skill to an emphasis on profit growth?
3. How could human resource management have promoted ethical behavior and affected the course of events described in this case?

Notes

1. T. Aeppel, "On Factory Floors, Top Workers Hide Secrets to Success," *The Wall Street Journal*, July 1, 2002, pp. A1, A10.
2. S. Snell and J. Dean, "Integrated Manufacturing and Human Resource Management: A Human Capital Perspective," *Academy of Management Journal* 35 (1992), pp. 467–504.
3. M. A. Huselid, "The Impact of Human Resource Management Practices on Turnover, Productivity, and Corporate Financial Performance," *Academy of Management Journal* 38 (1995), pp. 635–72; U.S. Department of Labor, *High-Performance Work Practices and Firm Performance* (Washington, DC: U.S. Government Printing Office, 1993).
4. R. N. Ashkenas, "Beyond the Fads: How Leaders Drive Change with Results," *Human Resource Planning* 17 (1994), pp. 25–44.
5. J. Arthur, "The Link between Business Strategy and Industrial Relations Systems in American Steel Mini-Mills," *Industrial and Labor Relations Review* 45 (1992), pp. 488–506.
6. "9/11: A Look Back," *Human Resource Executive*, 2002, pp. 1, 26+.
7. D. McCann and C. Margerison, "Managing High-Performance Teams," *Training and Development Journal*, November 1989, pp. 52–60; S. Sheman, "Secrets of HP's 'Muddled' Team," *Fortune*, March 18, 1996, pp. 116–20.

8. T. Stewart, "Brace for Japan's Hot New Strategy," *Fortune*, September 21, 1992, pp. 62–76.

9. T. T. Baldwin, C. Danielson, and W. Wiggenhorn, "The Evolution of Learning Strategies in Organizations: From Employee Development to Business Redefinition," *Academy of Management Executive* 11 (1997), pp. 47–58; J. J. Martocchio and T. T. Baldwin, "The Evolution of Strategic Organizational Training," in *Research in Personnel and Human Resource Management* 15, ed. G. R. Ferris (Greenwich, CT: JAI Press, 1997), pp. 1–46.

10. T. Stewart, "The House That Knowledge Built," *Fortune*, October 2, 2000, pp. 278–80; Viant website, www.viant.com.

11. T. A. Judge, C. J. Thoresen, J. E. Bono, and G. K. Patton, "The Job Satisfaction–Job Performance Relationship: A Qualitative and Quantitative Review," *Psychological Bulletin* 127 (2001), pp. 376–407; R. A. Katzell, D. E. Thompson, and R. A. Guzzo, "How Job Satisfaction and Job Performance Are and Are Not Linked," *Job Satisfaction*, ed. C. J. Cranny, P. C. Smith, and E. F. Stone (New York: Lexington Books, 1992), pp. 195–217.

12. C. Ostroff, "The Relationship between Satisfaction, Attitudes, and Performance," *Journal of Applied Psychology* 77, no. 6 (1992), pp. 963–74.

13. Watson Wyatt Worldwide, *WorkUSA 2002: Weathering the Storm* (Watson Wyatt, October 2002, www.humancapitalonline.com).

14. P. E. Boverie and M. Kroth, *Transforming Work: The Five Keys to Achieving Trust, Commitment, and Passion in the Workplace* (Cambridge, MA: Perseus Publishing, 2001), pp. 71–72, 79.

15. R. P. Gephart Jr., "Introduction to the Brave New Workplace: Organizational Behavior in the Electronic Age," *Journal of Organizational Behavior* 23 (2002), pp. 327–44.

16. S. Shellenbarger, "Along with Benefits and Paychecks, Employees Value Workplace Friends," *The Wall Street Journal Online*, February 20, 2002, http://online.wsj.com.

17. C. Hymowitz, "CEOs Must Work Hard to Maintain Faith in the Corner Office," *The Wall Street Journal*, July 9, 2002, p. B1.

18. K. Maher, "Wanted: Ethical Employer," *The Wall Street Journal*, July 9, 2002, pp. B1, B8.

19. Ibid.

20. W. F. Cascio, *Costing Human Resources: The Financial Impact of Behavior in Organizations*, 3rd ed. (Boston: PWS-Kent, 1991); Watson Wyatt Worldwide, *Watson Wyatt's Human Capital Index: Human Capital as a Lead Indicator of Shareholder Value*, 2001/2002 Survey Report (Watson Wyatt, October 2002, www.humancapitalonline.com).

21. Watson Wyatt, *Watson Wyatt's Human Capital Index*.

22. B. Becker and M. A. Huselid, "High-Performance Work Systems and Firm Performance: A Synthesis of Research and Managerial Implications," in *Research in Personnel and Human Resource Management* 16, ed. G. R. Ferris (Stamford, CT: JAI Press, 1998), pp. 53–101.

23. B. Becker and B. Gerhart, "The Impact of Human Resource Management on Organizational Performance: Progress and Prospects," *Academy of Management Journal* 39 (1996), pp. 779–801.

24. G. Flynn, "HR Leaders Stay Close to the Line," *Workforce*, February 1997, p. 53; General Electric Company, "World Class Excellence," GE Fanuc Corporate Profile, GE website, www.ge.com/gemis/gefanuc.

25. Flynn, "HR Leaders Stay Close to the Line"; GE, "World Class Excellence."

26. "Leadership: Ripe for Change," *Human Resource Executive*, 2002, pp. 60, 62+ (interview with Randall MacDonald).

27. Flynn, "HR Leaders Stay Close to the Line"; GE, "World Class Excellence."

28. C. M. Solomon, "HR's Push for Productivity," *Workforce*, August 2002, pp. 28–33.

29. H. J. Bernardin, C. M. Hagan, J. S. Kane, and P. Villanova, "Effective Performance Management: A Focus on Precision, Customers, and Situational Constraints," in *Performance Appraisal: State of the Art in Practice*, ed. J. W. Smither (San Francisco: Jossey-Bass, 1998), p. 56.

30. J. Bailey, "Entrepreneurs Share Their Tips to Boost a Firm's Productivity," *The Wall Street Journal*, July 9, 2002, p. B4.

31. L. R. Gomez-Mejia and D. B. Balkin, *Compensation, Organizational Strategy, and Firm Performance* (Cincinnati: South-Western, 1992); G. D. Jenkins and E. E. Lawler III, "Impact of Employee Participation in Pay Plan Development," *Organizational Behavior and Human Performance* 28 (1981), pp. 111–28.

32. R. Broderick and J. W. Boudreau, "Human Resource Management, Information Technology, and the Competitive Edge," *Academy of Management Executive* 6 (1992), pp. 7–17.

33. J. Cohan, "Nike Uses *Resumix* to Stay Ahead in the Recruitment Game," *Personnel Journal*, November 1992, p. 9 (supplement).

34. Solomon, "HR's Push for Productivity," p. 31.

35. Gephart, "Introduction to the Brave New Workplace."

36. D. E. Bailey and N. B. Kurland, "A Review of Telework Research: Findings, New Directions, and Lessons for the Study of Modern Work," *Journal of Organizational Behavior* 23 (2002), pp. 383–400.

VIDEO CASE

Workplace Ergonomics Is Good Business

During the Industrial Revolution a century ago, workplace injuries were so commonplace that they were simply considered one of the hazards of having a job. Children and adults were often maimed or disfigured in factory accidents. Today, strict regulations cover safety in the workplace, guided by the U.S. Department of Labor's Occupational Safety and Health Administration (OSHA). But during the past couple of decades, as industry itself has changed, a different type of injury has emerged: musculoskeletal disorders (MSDs). MSDs are injuries resulting from overexertion and repetitive motion, such as constantly lifting heavy loads or grabbing and twisting a piece of machinery. People who sit at computer workstations all day are susceptiable to MSDs as well, particularly carpal tunnel syndrome, which affects the nerves of the hand, wrist, and arm. According to OSHA, about one-third of repetitive stress injuries, or 600,000, are serious enough to require time off the job, which means that businesses pay for these injuries not only in medical costs but in lost productivity. They can also contribute to high employee turnover. No one disputes that these injuries occur. But various experts, industry leaders, and politicians argue about how severe the injuries are, who should pay for them, what should be done about them, and who takes ultimate responsibility for the safety of workers.

One aspect of the whole issue of workplace injuries is ergonomics—"the applied science of equipment design, intended to reduce operator fatigue and discomfort, or as OSHA puts it, the science of fitting the job to the worker," explains news correspondent Gwen Ifill. Ergonomics involves everything from developing new equipment, including desk chairs that support the back properly and flexible splints to support the wrist while typing, to designing better ways to use the equipment, such as the proper way to hold a computer mouse. Ergonomics standards are "about helping real people suffering real problems, problems like back injuries and carpal tunnel syndrome, tendonitis—not minor aches or pains, but serious, life-altering injuries," notes Alexis Herman, former Secretary of Labor.

Several years ago, OSHA proposed new guidelines for better ergonomic standards, targeting jobs where workers perform repetitive tasks, whether they are engaged in poultry processing or delivering packages. The proposal required employers that received reports from workers who were suffering from MSDs to respond promptly with an evaluation and follow-up health care. Workers who needed time off could receive 90 percent of their pay and 100 percent of their benefits. Not surprisingly, arguments for and against the proposal broke out. OSHA spokesperson Charles Jeffers claimed that the guidelines "will save employers $9 billion every year from what they've currently been spending on these problems." Peg Seminario of the AFL-CIO noted that the guidelines did not go far enough, since they did not cover "workers in construction, agriculture, or maritime, who have very serious problems." Pat Cleary, of the National Association of Manufacturers, argued that "there's a central flaw here and that is that there is no scientific—or no consensus in the scientific or medical community about the causes of ergonomics injuries." Debates over the proposed rules' merit were further clouded by the Small Business Administration's prediction that implementing the standards would cost industries $18 billion; OSHA had forecast a mere $4.2 billion.

Just before he left office, President Bill Clinton signed the bill into law, which was overturned by incoming President George W. Bush and the new Congress. Calling the workplace safety regulations "unduly burdensome and overly broad," Bush signed the measure to roll back the new rules.

Where do these actions leave workers and businesses in regard to workplace injuries? Legally, businesses are not required to redesign work systems or continue full pay and benefits for an extended period after a work-related injury. But if the goal of a company is to find and keep the best employees, perhaps developing good ergonomic practices makes good business sense. The high cost of treatment and turnover, not to mention lowered productivity, points toward prevention as a competitive strategy. "Good ergonomics in the office should not be a big burden on a company and may be a way to retain good employees," notes Peter Budnick, president and CEO of Ergo Web Inc., an ergonomics consulting firm in Utah. Gary Allread, program director at the Institute

540

for Ergonomics at The Ohio State University, remarks, "In my opinion, there's enough research out there to show that implementing some of these types of controls can significantly reduce workers compensation costs. . . . [But] there are also a lot of companies that aren't as concerned about the health and welfare of their employees, so they're not attuned to the things that can be done" to minimize workplace repetitive stress injuries. In fact, they may not even realize that shifting an employee's computer screen from the side to direclty in front of the employee could actually prevent an injury.

So perhaps the more savvy companies can use good erogonomics as a competitive strategy—to retain the best workers, boost morale, and even enhance productivity. "Employers have every incentive to protect employees," says Tim Hammonds, president of the Food Marketing Institute. To that end many supermarkets and grocery stores have already put ergonomics programs in place to prevent workplace injuries—with or without federal regulations.

SOURCE: "Ergonomics Rules," *Workforce*, June 19, 2001, www.workforce.com; Jennifer Jones, "Bush Expected to Rescind OSHA Rules," *InfoWorld*, March 22, 2001, www.cnn.com; Mike Allen, "Bush Signs Repeal of Ergonomics Rules," *Washington Post*, March 21, 2001, www.washingtonpost.com; James Kuhnhenn, "House Joins Senate in Repeal of Workplace Ergonomics Rules," *San Jose Mercury News*, www.siliconvalley.com; Kathy Kiely, "House Votes to Repeal Ergonomics Rules," *USA Today*, March 7, 2001, www.usatoday.com; David Espo, "Senate Votes to Repeal Ergonomics Rules," *ABCNews.com*, March 6, 2001, www.abcnews.go.com; Patrick Thibodeau, "OSHA Releases Final Version of Workplace Ergonomics Rules," *Computerworld*, November 13, 2000, www.computerworld.com; "Working Better," *Online NewsHour*, video transcript, November 22, 1999, www.pbs.org.

QUESTIONS

1. Do you agree or disagree that ergonomics in the workplace should be covered by federal regulations? Explain your answer.
2. Choose a job with which you are familiar and discuss the possibilities for repetitive stress injuries that could occur on this job and ways they could be prevented.
3. Imagine that you are the human resource manager for a company that hires workers for the job described in question 2. What steps might you encourage company officials to take to identify and prevent potential MSDs?

Glossary

achievement tests   Tests that measure a person's existing knowledge and skills.

action learning   Training in which teams get an actual problem, work on solving it and commit to an action plan, and are accountable for carrying it out.

affirmative action   An organization's active effort to find opportunities to hire or promote people in a particular group.

agency shop   Union security arrangement that requires the payment of union dues but not union membership.

alternative dispute resolution (ADR)   Methods of solving a problem by bringing in an impartial outsider but not using the court system.

alternative work arrangements   Methods of staffing other than the traditional hiring of full-time employees (for example, use of independent contractors, on-call workers, temporary workers, and contract company workers).

American Federation of Labor and Congress of Industrial Organizations (AFL-CIO)   An association that seeks to advance the shared interests of its member unions at the national level.

apprenticeship   A work-study training method that teaches job skills through a combination of on-the-job training and classroom training.

aptitude tests   Tests that assess how well a person can learn or acquire skills and abilities.

arbitration   Conflict resolution procedure in which an arbitrator or arbitration board determines a binding settlement.

assessment center   A wide variety of specific selection programs that use multiple selection methods to rate applicants or job incumbents on their management potential.

assessment   Collecting information and providing feedback to employees about their behavior, communication style, or skills.

associate union membership   Alternative form of union membership in which members receive discounts on insurance and credit cards rather than representation in collective bargaining.

balanced scorecard   A combination of performance measures directed toward the company's long- and short-term goals and used as the basis for awarding incentive pay.

behavior description interview (BDI)   A structured interview in which the interviewer asks the candidate to describe how he or she handled a type of situation in the past.

behavioral observation scale (BOS)   A variation of a BARS which uses all behaviors necessary for effective performance to rate performance at a task.

behaviorally anchored rating scale (BARS)   Method of performance measurement that rates behavior in terms of a scale showing specific statements of behavior that describe different levels of performance.

benchmarking   A procedure in which an organization compares its own practices against those of successful competitors.

Benchmarks   A measurement tool that gathers ratings of a manager's use of skills associated with success in managing.

bona fide occupational qualification (BFOQ)   A necessary (not merely preferred) qualification for performing a job.

cafeteria-style plan   A benefits plan that offers employees a set of alternatives from which they can choose the types and amounts of benefits they want.

cash balance plan   Retirement plan in which the employer sets up an individual account for each employee and contributes a percentage of the employee's salary; the account earns interest at a predefined rate.

central tendency   Incorrectly rating all employees at or near the middle of a rating scale.

checkoff provision   Contract provision under which the employer, on behalf of the union, automatically deducts union dues from employees' paychecks.

closed shop   Union security arrangement under which a person must be a union member before being hired; illegal for those covered by the National Labor Relations Act.

coach   A peer or manager who works with an employee to motivate the employee, help him or her develop skills, and provide reinforcement and feedback.

cognitive ability tests   Tests designed to measure such mental abilities as verbal skills, quantitative skills, and reasoning ability.

collective bargaining   Negotiation between union representatives and management representatives to arrive at a contract defining conditions of employment for the term of the contract and to administer that contract.

commissions   Incentive pay calculated as a percentage of sales.

compensatory model   Process of arriving at a selection decision in which a very high score on one type of assessment can make up for a low score on another.

concurrent validation   Research that consists of administering a test to people who currently hold a job, then comparing their scores to existing measures of job performance.

Consolidated Omnibus Budget Reconciliation Act (COBRA)   Federal law that requires employers to permit employees or their dependents to extend their health insurance coverage at group rates for up to 36 months following a qualifying event, such as a layoff, reduction in hours, or the employee's death.

construct validity   Consistency between a high score on a test and high level of a construct such as intelligence or leadership ability, as well as between mastery of this construct and successful performance of the job.

content validity   Consistency between the test items or problems and the kinds of situations or problems that occur on the job.

continuous learning   Each employee's and each group's ongoing efforts to gather information and apply the information to their decisions in a learning organization.

contributory plan   Retirement plan funded by contributions from the employer and employee.

coordination training   Team training that teaches the team how to share information and make decisions to obtain the best team performance.

core competency   A set of knowledges and skills that make the organization superior to competitors and create value for customers.

corporate campaigns   Bringing public, financial, or political pressure on employers during union organization and contract negotiation.

craft union   Labor union whose members all have a particular skill or occupation.

criterion-related validity   A measure of validity based on showing a substantial correlation between test scores and job performance scores

critical-incident method   Method of performance measurement based on managers' records of specific examples of the employee acting in ways that are either effective or ineffective.

cross-cultural preparation   Training to prepare employees and their family members for an assignment in a foreign country.

cross-training   Team training in which team members understand and practice each other's skills so that they are prepared to step in and take another member's place.

culture shock   Disillusionment and discomfort that occur during the process of adjusting to a new culture.

decision support systems   Computer software systems designed to help managers solve problems by showing how results vary when the manager alters assumptions or data.

defined benefit plan   Pension plan that guarantees a specified level of retirement income.

defined contribution plan   Retirement plan in which the employer sets up an individual account for each employee and specifies the size of the investment into that account.

delayering   Reducing the number of levels in the organization's job structure.

development   The acquisition of knowledge, skills, and behaviors that improve an employee's ability to meet changes in job requirements and in customer demands.

Dictionary of Occupational Titles   Created by the Department of Labor in the 1930s, the DOT listed over 12,000 jobs and requirements.

differential piece rates   Incentive pay in which the piece rate is higher when a greater amount is produced.

direct applicants   People who apply for a vacancy without prompting from the organization.

disability   Under the Americans with Disabilities Act, a physical or mental impairment that substantially limits one or more major life activities, a record of having such an impairment, or being regarded as having such an impairment.

disparate impact   A condition in which employment practices are seemingly neutral yet disproportionately exclude a protected group from employment opportunities.

disparate treatment   Differing treatment of individuals, where the differences are based on the individuals' race, color, religion, sex, national origin, age, or disability status.

diversity training Training designed to change employee attitudes about diversity and/or develop skills needed to work with a diverse workforce.

downsizing The planned elimination of large numbers of personnel with the goal of enhancing the organization's competitiveness.

downward move Assignment of an employee to a position with less responsibility and authority.

due-process policies Policies that formally lay out the steps an employee may take to appeal the employer's decision to terminate that employee.

EEO-1 report The EEOC's Employer Information Report, which details the number of women and minorities employed in nine different job categories.

e-learning Receiving training via the Internet or the organization's intranet.

electronic business (e-business) Any process that a business conducts electronically, especially business involving use of the Internet.

electronic human resource management (e-HRM) The processing and transmission of digitized HR information, especially using computer networking and the Internet.

employee assistance program (EAP) A referral service that employees can use to seek professional treatment for emotional problems or substance abuse.

employee benefits Compensation in forms other than cash.

employee development The combination of formal education, job experiences, relationships, and assessment of personality and abilities to help employees prepare for the future of their careers.

employee empowerment Giving employees responsibility and authority to make decisions regarding all aspects of product development or customer service.

Employee Retirement Income Security Act (ERISA) Federal law that increased the responsibility of pension plan trustees to protect retirees, established certain rights related to vesting and portability, and created the Pension Benefit Guarantee Corporation.

employee stock ownership plan (ESOP) An arrangement in which the organization distributes shares of stock to all its employees by placing it in a trust.

employee wellness program (EWP) A set of communications, activities, and facilities designed to change health-related behaviors in ways that reduce health risks.

employment at will Employment principle that if there is no specific employment contract saying otherwise, the employer or employee may end an employment relationship at any time, regardless of cause.

equal employment opportunity (EEO) The condition in which all individuals have an equal chance for employment, regardless of their race, color, religion, sex, age, disability, or national origin.

Equal Employment Opportunity Commission (EEOC) Agency of the Department of Justice charged with enforcing Title VII of the Civil Rights Act of 1964 and other antidiscrimination laws.

ergonomics The study of the interface between individuals' physiology and the characteristics of the physical work environment.

ethics The fundamental principles of right and wrong.

exempt employees Managers, outside salespeople, and any other employees not covered by the FLSA requirement for overtime pay.

exit interview A meeting of a departing employee with the employee's supervisor and/or a human resource specialist to discuss the employee's reasons for leaving.

expatriates Employees assigned to work in another country.

experience rating The number of employees a company has laid off in the past and the cost of providing them with unemployment benefits.

experiential programs A teamwork and leadership training program based on the use of challenging, structured outdoor activities.

expert systems Computer systems that support decision making by incorporating the decision rules used by people who are considered to have expertise in a certain area.

external labor market Individuals who are actively seeking employment.

externship Employee development through a full-time temporary position at another organization.

fact finder Third party to collective bargaining who reports the reasons for a dispute, the views and arguments of both sides, and possibly a recommended settlement, which the parties may decline.

Fair Labor Standards Act (FLSA) Federal law that establishes a minimum wage and requirements for overtime pay and child labor.

Family and Medical Leave Act (FMLA) Federal law requiring organizations with 50 or more employees to provide up to 12 weeks of unpaid leave after childbirth or adoption; to care for a seriously ill family member; or for an employee's own serious illness.

Fleishman Job Analysis System   Job analysis technique that asks subject-matter experts to evaluate a job in terms of the abilities required to perform the job.

flexible spending account   A portion of pretax earnings set aside to pay for an employee's uncovered health care expenses during the same year.

flextime   A scheduling policy in which full-time employees may choose starting and ending times within guidelines specified by the organization.

forced-distribution method   Method of performance measurement that assigns a certain percentage of employees to each category in a set of categories.

forecasting   The attempts to determine the supply of and demand for various types of human resources to predict areas within the organization where there will be labor shortages or surpluses.

four-fifths rule   Rule of thumb that finds evidence of discrimination if an organization's hiring rate for a minority group is less than four-fifths the hiring rate for the majority group.

gainsharing   Group incentive program that measures improvements in productivity and effectiveness objectives and distributes a portion of each gain to employees.

generalizable   Valid in other contexts beyond the context in which the selection method was developed.

glass ceiling   Circumstances resembling an invisible barrier that keep most women and minorities from attaining the top jobs in organizations.

global organization   An organization that chooses to locate a facility based on the ability to effectively, efficiently, and flexibly produce a product or service, using cultural differences as an advantage.

graphic rating scale   Method of performance measurement that lists traits and provides a rating scale for each trait; the employer uses the scale to indicate the extent to which an employee displays each trait.

green-circle rate   Pay at a rate that falls below the pay range for the job.

grievance procedure   The process for resolving union-management conflicts over interpretation or violation of a collective bargaining agreement.

group-building methods   Training methods in which trainees share ideas and experiences, build group identity, understand interpersonal relationships, and learn the strengths and weaknesses of themselves and their coworkers.

halo error   Rating error that occurs when the rater reacts to one positive performance aspect by rating the employee positively in all areas of performance.

hands-on methods   Training methods which actively involve the trainee in trying out skills being taught.

Hay Guide-Chart Profile method   Method of job evaluation that creates a profile for each position based on its required know-how, degree of problem solving, and accountability.

health maintenance organization (HMO)   A health care plan that requires patients to receive their medical care from the HMO's health care professionals, who are often paid a flat salary, and provides all services on a prepaid basis.

high-performance work system   An organization in which technology, organizational structure, people, and processes all work together to give an organization an advantage in the competitive environment.

horns error   Rating error that occurs when the rater responds to one negative aspect by rating an employee low in other aspects.

host country   A country (other than the parent country) in which an organization operates a facility.

hot-stove rule   Principle of discipline that says discipline should be like a hot stove, giving clear warning and following up with consistent, objective, immediate consequences.

hourly wage   Rate of pay for each hour worked.

HRM audit   A formal review of the outcomes of HRM functions, based on identifying key HRM functions and measures of business performance.

human capital   An organization's employees, described in terms of their training, experience, judgment, intelligence, relationships, and insight.

human resource information system (HRIS)   A computer system used to acquire, store, manipulate, analyze, retrieve, and distribute information related to an organization's human resources.

human resource management (HRM)   The policies, practices, and systems that influence employees' behavior, attitudes, and performance.

human resource planning   Identifying the numbers and types of employees the organization will require in order to meet its objectives.

Improshare   A gainsharing program in which the gain is the decrease in the labor hours needed to produce one unit of product, with the gains split equally between the organization and its employees.

incentive pay Forms of pay linked to an employee's performance as an individual, group member, or organization member.

industrial engineering The study of jobs to find the simplest way to structure work in order to maximize efficiency.

industrial union Labor union whose members are linked by their work in a particular industry.

instructional design A process of systematically developing training to meet specified needs.

interactional justice A judgment that the organization carried out its actions in a way that took the employee's feelings into account.

internal labor force An organization's workers (its employees and the people who have contracts to work at the organization).

international organization An organization that sets up one or a few facilities in one or a few foreign countries.

internship On-the-job learning sponsored by an educational institution as a component of an academic program.

involuntary turnover Turnover initiated by an employer (often with employees who would prefer to stay).

job analysis The process of getting detailed information about jobs.

job description A list of the tasks, duties, and responsibilities (TDRs) that a particular job entails.

job design The process of defining how work will be performed and what tasks will be required in a given job.

job enlargement Broadening the types of tasks performed in a job.

job enrichment Empowering workers by adding more decision-making authority to jobs.

job evaluation An administrative procedure for measuring the relative internal worth of the organization's jobs.

job experiences The combination of relationships, problems, demands, tasks, and other features of an employee's jobs.

job extension Enlarging jobs by combining several relatively simple jobs to form a job with a wider range of tasks.

job hazard analysis technique Safety promotion technique that involves breaking down a job into basic elements, then rating each element for its potential for harm or injury.

job involvement The degree to which people identify themselves with their jobs.

job posting The process of communicating information about a job vacancy on company bulletin boards, in employee publications, on corporate intranets, and anywhere else the organization communicates with employees.

job rotation Enlarging jobs by moving employees among several different jobs.

job satisfaction A pleasant feeling resulting from the perception that one's job fulfills or allows for the fulfillment of one's important job values.

job sharing A work option in which two part-time employees carry out the tasks associated with a single job.

job specification A list of the knowledge, skills, abilities, and other characteristics (KSAOs) that an individual must have to perform a particular job.

job structure The relative pay for different jobs within the organization.

job withdrawal A set of behaviors with which employees try to avoid the work situation physically, mentally, or emotionally.

job A set of related duties.

knowledge workers Employees whose main contribution to the organization is specialized knowledge, such as knowledge of customers, a process, or a profession.

labor relations Field that emphasizes skills managers and union leaders can use to minimize costly forms of conflict (such as strikes) and seek win-win solutions to disagreements.

leaderless group discussion An assessment center exercise in which a team of five to seven employees is assigned a problem and must work together to solve it within a certain time period.

leading indicators Objective measures that accurately predict future labor demand.

learning organization An organization in which people continually expand their capacity to achieve the results they desire.

leniency error Rating error of assigning inaccurately high ratings to all employees.

long-term disability insurance Insurance that pays a percentage of a disabled employee's salary after an initial period and potentially for the rest of the employee's life.

maintenance of membership Union security rules not requiring union membership but requiring that employees who join the union remain members for a certain period of time.

management by objectives (MBO) A system in which people at each level of the organization set goals in a process that flows from top to bottom, so employees at all levels are contributing to the organization's overall goals;

these goals become the standards for evaluating each employee's performance.

material safety data sheets (MSDSs) Forms on which chemical manufacturers and importers identify the hazards of their chemicals.

mediation Conflict resolution procedure in which a mediator hears the views of both sides and facilitates the negotiation process but has no formal authority to dictate a resolution.

mentor An experienced, productive senior employee who helps develop a less experienced employee (a protégé).

merit pay A system of linking pay increases to ratings on performance appraisals.

minimum wage The lowest amount that employers may pay under federal or state law, stated as an amount of pay per hour.

mixed-standard scales Method of performance measurement that uses several statements describing each trait to produce a final score for that trait.

multinational company An organization that builds facilities in a number of different countries in an effort to minimize production and distribution costs.

multiple-hurdle model Process of arriving at a selection decision by eliminating some candidates at each stage of the selection process.

Myers-Briggs Type Indicator (MBTI) Psychological test that identifies individuals' preferences for source of energy, means of information gathering, way of decision making, and lifestyle, providing information for team building and leadership development.

National Labor Relations Act (NLRA) Federal law that supports collective bargaining and sets out the rights of employees to form unions.

National Labor Relations Board (NLRB) Federal government agency that enforces the NLRA by conducting and certifying representation elections and investigating unfair labor practices.

needs assessment The process of evaluating the organization, individual employees, and employees' tasks to determine what kinds of training, if any, are necessary.

nepotism The practice of hiring relatives.

noncontributory plan Retirement plan funded entirely by contributions from the employer.

nondirective interview A selection interview in which the interviewer has great discretion in choosing questions to ask each candidate.

nonexempt employees Employees covered by the FLSA requirements for overtime pay.

Occupational Safety and Health Act (OSH Act) U.S. law authorizing the federal government to establish and enforce occupational safety and health standards for all places of employment engaging in interstate commerce.

Occupational Safety and Health Administration (OSHA) Labor Department agency responsible for inspecting employers, applying safety and health standards, and levying fines for violation.

Office of Federal Contract Compliance Procedures (OFCCP) The agency responsible for enforcing the executive orders that cover companies doing business with the federal government.

on-the-job training (OJT) Training methods in which a person with job experience and skill guides trainees in practicing job skills at the workplace.

open-door policy An organization's policy of making managers available to hear complaints.

organization analysis A process for determining the appropriateness of training by evaluating the characteristics of the organization.

organizational behavior modification (OBM) A plan for managing the behavior of employees through a formal system of feedback and reinforcement.

organizational commitment The degree to which an employee identifies with the organization and is willing to put forth effort on its behalf.

orientation Training designed to prepare employees to perform their jobs effectively, learn about their organization, and establish work relationships.

outcome fairness A judgment that the consequences given to employees are just.

outplacement counseling A service in which professionals try to help dismissed employees manage the transition from one job to another.

outsourcing Contracting with another organization to perform a broad set of services.

outsourcing The practice of having another company (a vendor, third-party provider, or consultant) provide services.

paired-comparison method Method of performance measurement that compares each employee with each other employee to establish rankings.

panel interview Selection interview in which several members of the organization meet to interview each candidate.

parent country The country in which an organization's headquarters is located.

pay differential Adjustment to a pay rate to reflect differences in working conditions or labor markets.

pay grades Sets of jobs having similar worth or content, grouped together to establish rates of pay.

pay level The average amount (including wages, salaries, and bonuses) the organization pays for a particular job.

pay policy line A graphed line showing the mathematical relationship between job evaluation points and pay rate.

pay ranges A set of possible pay rates defined by a minimum, maximum, and midpoint of pay for employees holding a particular job or a job within a particular pay grade.

pay structure The pay policy resulting from job structure and pay level decisions.

peer review Process for resolving disputes by taking them to a panel composed of representatives from the organization at the same levels as the people in the dispute.

Pension Benefit Guarantee Corporation (PBGC) Federal agency that insures retirement benefits and guarantees retirees a basic benefit if the employer experiences financial difficulties.

performance appraisal The measurement of specified areas of an employee's performance.

performance management The process through which managers ensure that employees' activities and outputs contribute to the organization's goals.

person analysis A process for determining individuals' needs and readiness for training.

personnel selection The process through which organizations make decisions about who will or will not be allowed to join the organization.

piecework rate Rate of pay for each unit produced.

Position Analysis Questionnaire (PAQ) A standardized job analysis questionnaire containing 194 questions about work behaviors, work conditions, and job characteristics that apply to a wide variety of jobs.

position The set of duties (job) performed by a particular person.

predictive validation Research that uses the test scores of all applicants and looks for a relationship between the scores and future performance of the applicants who were hired.

preferred provider organization (PPO) A health care plan that contracts with health care professionals to provide services at a reduced fee and gives patients financial incentives to use network providers.

presentation methods Training methods in which trainees receive information provided by instructors or via computers or other media.

procedural justice A judgment that fair methods were used to determine the consequences an employee receives.

profit sharing Incentive pay in which payments are a percentage of the organization's profits and do not become part of the employees' base salary.

progressive discipline A formal discipline process in which the consequences become more serious if the employee repeats the offense.

promotion Assignment of an employee to a position with greater challenges, more responsibility, and more authority than in the previous job, usually accompanied by a pay increase.

protean career A career that frequently changes based on changes in the person's interests, abilities, and values and in the work environment.

psychological contract A description of what an employee expects to contribute in an employment relationship and what the employer will provide the employee in exchange for those contributions.

readability The difficulty level of written materials.

readiness for training A combination of employee characteristics and positive work environment that permit training.

realistic job preview Background information about a job's positive and negative qualities.

reality check Information employers give employees about their skills and knowledge and where these assets fit into the organization's plans.

reasonable accommodation An employer's obligation to do something to enable an otherwise qualified person to perform a job.

recruiting Any activity carried on by the organization with the primary purpose of identifying and attracting potential employees.

recruitment The process through which the organization seeks applicants for potential employment.

red-circle rate Pay at a rate that falls above the pay range for the job.

reengineering A complete review of the organization's critical work processes to make them more efficient and able to deliver higher quality.

referrals People who apply for a vacancy because someone in the organization prompted them to do so.

reliability The extent to which a measurement is from random error.

repatriation The process of preparing expatriates to return home from a foreign assignment.

right-to-know laws State laws that require employers to provide employees with information about the health risks associated with exposure to substances considered hazardous.

right-to-work laws State laws that make union shops, maintenance of membership, and agency shops illegal.

role ambiguity Uncertainty about what the organization expects from the employee in terms of what to do or how to do it.

role analysis technique A process of formally identifying expectations associated with a role.

role conflict An employee's recognition that demands of the job are incompatible or contradictory.

role overload A state in which too many expectations or demands are placed on a person.

role The set of behaviors that people expect of a person in a particular job.

Rucker plan A gainsharing program in which the ratio measuring the gain compares labor costs to the value added in production (output minus the cost of materials, supplies, and services).

sabbatical A leave of absence from an organization to renew or develop skills.

salary Rate of pay for each week, month, or year worked.

Scanlon plan A gainsharing program in which employees receive a bonus if the ratio of labor costs to the sales value of production is below a set standard.

selection The process by which the organization attempts to identify applicants with the necessary knowledge, skills, abilities, and other characteristics that will help the organization achieve its goals.

self-assessment The use of information by employees to determine their career interests, values, aptitudes, and behavioral tendencies.

self-service System in which employees have online access to information about HR issues and go online to enroll themselves in programs and provide feedback through surveys.

sexual harassment Unwelcome sexual advances as defined by the EEOC.

short-term disability insurance Insurance that pays a percentage of a disabled employee's salary as benefits to the employee for six months or less.

similar-to-me error Rating error of giving a higher evaluation to people who seem similar to oneself.

simple ranking Method of performance measurement that requires managers to rank employees in their group from the highest performer to the poorest performer.

simulation A training method that represents a real-life situation, with trainees making decisions resulting in outcomes that mirror what would happen on the job.

situational interviews A structured interview in which the interviewer describes a situation likely to arise on the job, then asks the candidate what he or she would do in that situation.

skill-based pay systems Pay structures that set pay according to the employees' levels of skill or knowledge and what they are capable of doing.

Social Security The federal Old Age, Survivors, Disability, and Health Insurance (OASDHI) program, which combines old age (retirement) insurance, survivor's insurance, disability insurance, hospital insurance (Medicare Part A), and supplementary medical insurance (Medicare Part B) for the elderly.

standard hour plan An incentive plan that pays workers extra for work done in less than a preset "standard time."

stock options Rights to buy a certain number of shares of stock at a specified price.

straight piecework plan Incentive pay in which the employer pays the same rate per piece, no matter how much the worker produces.

strictness error Rating error of giving low ratings to all employees, holding them to unreasonably high standards.

strike A collective decision by union members not to work until certain demands or conditions are met.

structured interview A selection interview that consists of a predetermined set of questions for the interviewer to ask.

succession planning The process of identifying and tracking high-potential employees who will be able to fill top management positions when they become vacant.

summary plan description Report that describes a pension plan's funding, eligibility requirements, risks, and other details.

task analysis inventory Job analysis method that involves listing the tasks performed in a particular job and rating each task according to a defined set of criteria.

task analysis The process of identifying and analyzing tasks to be trained for.

teamwork The assignment of work to groups of employees with various skills who interact to assemble a product or provide a service.

technic of operations review (TOR) Method of promoting safety by determining which specific element of a job led to a past accident.

third country A country that is neither the parent country nor the host country of an employer.

360-degree performance appraisal Performance measurement that combines information from the employee's managers, peers, subordinates, self, and customers.

total quality management (TQM) A companywide effort to continuously improve the ways people, machines, and systems accomplish work.

training An organization's planned efforts to help employees acquire job-related knowledge, skills, abilities, and behaviors, with the goal of applying these on the job.

transaction processing Computations and calculations involved in reviewing and documenting HRM decisions and practices.

transfer of training On-the-job use of knowledge, skills, and behaviors learned in training.

transfer Assignment of an employee to a position in a different area of the company, usually in a lateral move.

transitional matrix A chart that lists job categories held in one period and shows the proportion of employees in each of those job categories in a future period.

transnational HRM system Type of HRM system that makes decisions from a global perspective, includes managers from many countries, and is based on ideas contributed by people representing a variety of cultures.

trend analysis Constructing and applying statistical models that predict labor demand for the next year, given relatively objective statistics from the previous year.

unemployment insurance A federally mandated program to minimize the hardships of unemployment through payments to unemployed workers, help in finding new jobs, and incentives to stabilize employment.

Uniform Guidelines on Employee Selection Procedures Guidelines issued by the EEOC and other agencies to identify how an organization should develop and administer its system for selecting employees so as not to violate antidiscrimination laws.

union shop Union security arrangement that requires employees to join the union within a certain amount of time (30 days) after beginning employment.

union steward An employee elected by union members to represent them in ensuring that the terms of the labor contract are enforced.

unions Organizations formed for the purpose of representing their members' interests in dealing with employers.

utility The extent to which something provides economic value greater than its cost.

validity The extent to which performance on a measure (such as a test score) is related to what the measure is designed to assess (such as job performance).

vesting rights Guarantee that when employees become participants in a pension plan and work a specified number of years, they will receive a pension at retirement age, regardless of whether they remained with the employer.

virtual expatriates Employees who manage an operation abroad without permanently locating in the country.

virtual reality A computer-based technology that provides an interactive, three-dimensional learning experience.

voluntary turnover Turnover initiated by employees (often when the organization would prefer to keep them).

work flow design The process of analyzing the tasks necessary for the production of a product or service.

workers' compensation State programs that provide benefits to workers who suffer work-related injuries or illnesses, or to their survivors.

workforce utilization review A comparison of the proportion of employees in protected groups with the proportion that each group represents in the relevant labor market.

yield ratio A ratio that expresses the percentage of applicants who successfully move from one stage of the recruitment and selection process to the next.

Photo Credits

Page 4   Courtesy Southwest Airlines
Page 10   Ray Stubblebine/Reuters/TimePix
Page 16   AP Wide World Photos
Page 18   Richard Carson/Reuters/TimePix
Page 22   SHRM 2002 Annual Conference: Steven Purcell
Page 31   © Joe Radele/Getty Images
Page 39   © Brownie Harris/Corbis
Page 47   AP Wide World Photos
Page 51   Photo Courtesy of Integral Systems, Inc.
Page 57   © Dick Blume/The Image Works
Page 67   AP Wide World Photos
Page 81   Source: U.S. Equal Employment Opportunity
                Commission
Page 85   AP Wide World Photos
Page 91   The Occupational Safety and Health
                Administration (OSHA)
Page 104   EyeWire Collection/Getty Images
Page 110   AP Wide World Photos
Page 115   © Forestier Yves/Corbis
Page 119   © Jack Hollingsworth/Getty Images
Page 121   ©Francisco Cruz/SuperStock
Page 123   © Michael Newman/ PhotoEdit
Page 142   AP Wide World Photos
Page 145   AP Wide World Photos
Page 152   Courtesy of Johnson and Johnson
Page 153   © Jon Riley/Getty Images
Page 181   © Jack Hollingsworth /Getty Images
Page 184   © Paula Bronstein/Getty Images
Page 188   © Julie Houck/Stock Boston/Picture Quest
Page 206   Courtesy of Tires Plus
Page 219   Used by permission of General Motors Corp.
Page 223   © Bruce Ayres/Getty Images
Page 246   © Alon Reininger/Contact Press
                Images/PictureQuest
Page 254   AP Wide World Photos

Page 261   © Ryan McVay/Getty Images
Page 265   Pepsi-Cola Company
Page 276   © Michael Newman/PhotoEdit
Page 285   © Howard Grey/Getty Images
Page 291   AP Wide World Photos
Page 298   © Erik Freeland/Corbis
Page 314   AP Wide World Photos
Page 322   © David McNew/Getty Images
Page 325   © Le Segretain Pascal/Corbis
Page 329   © Steve Chenn/Corbis
Page 347   © Walter Hodges/Getty Images
Page 352   AP Wide World Photos
Page 361   © John Boykin/PhotoEdit
Page 364   © John Neubauer/PhotoEdit
Page 380   © Harry Bartlett/Getty Images
Page 385   © Kwame Zikomo/SuperStock
Page 390   All rights reserved, The ESOP Association, 2002.
Page 394   Reprinted from the April 15, 2002 of BusinesWeek
                by permission.
                Copyright 2002 by The McGraw-Hill Companies.
Page 407   AP Wide World Photos
Page 409   © Elie Bernager/Getty Images
Page 414   © Seth Resnick/Stock Boston
Page 420   © Mark Richards/PhotoEdit
Page 442   © Chris Hondros/Getty Images
Page 449   © Steven Rubin/The Image Works
Page 455   AP Wide World Photos
Page 463   AP Wide World Photos
Page 478   © Lou Dematteis/The Image Works
Page 485   © Paul Almasy/Corbis
Page 488   © Rob Brimson/Getty Images
Page 495   © Patrick Robert/Corbis Sygma
Page 516   © Peter Beck/Corbis
Page 521   © Chris Hondros/Getty Images
Page 525   © PS Productions/Getty Images

Name/Company Index

(Included in this index are names of Government Agencies, Institutions, Organizations, and Publications)

See also SUBJECT INDEX

Note: Titles of specific books or publications and names of specific acts of legislation or legal cases can be found in the SUBJECT INDEX.

ABB Asea Brown Boveri, 47
Abbott Laboratories, 195
Abrams, Robin, 498
Accenture Ltd., 25, 165–66, 355, 387, 538
Acteva.com, 398
Acxiom Corporation, 109–10
ADP, 61
Advanced Financial Solutions, 176
Air France, 509
Air Transport World, 399
Alcatel, 165, 495
Alcoholics Anonymous (AA), 319
Aligned Fiber Composites, 144
Allen, Ron, 62, 63
AlliedSignal, 303
Allread, Gary, 540–41
Alternative Technology Resources, 165
Amalgamated Clothing and Textile Workers Union (ACTWU), 459
Amazon.com, 115, 312, 446, 473
American Airlines, 146, 266
American Arbitration Association, 460
American Chamber of Commerce Research Association, 361
American Express, 299, 355
American Federation of Labor and Congress of Industrial Organizations (AFL-CIO), 442, 443–44, 459, 469, 540
American Federation of State, County, and Municipal Employees (AFSCME), 448
American Foundation for the Blind, 85
American Management Association, 353
American Society for Training and Development, 208
AmeriCorps, 25
Amgen, 304
Amoco Oil, 44
Ampro Computers, 140
AMR Corporation, 380
Andersen, Arthur, 522, 537

Anderson, Brian, 270
Anderson, Cushing, 230
Andrus, Garth, 355
Anheuser-Busch Company, 195
AOM-Air Liberté, 509
Aon Consulting, 128, 426
APCOA, 181
Apple Computer, 146, 498, 529
Arant, Rusty, 127
Army, U.S., 152–53
Artis & Associates, 381
Athleta Corporation, 3–4
Atlantic Richfield Company, 468
AT&T, 227, 284, 473
ATX Forms, 7–8
August, Kelsey, 149
AutoZone, 370
Avert Inc., 181–82
Avon Products, 156, 279

Bain & Company, 508
Bakke, Alan, 69
Baltimore Laser Eye Center, 312
Bank of America, 49
Barrios, Lisa, 153
Bartel, Warren E., 469
Bass, Carl, 538
Baxter International, 373–74, 386
Bell, Jess, 73
Bell Atlantic, 147
Berry, David S., 537
Best Buy, 291
Bethlehem Steel Corporation, 434
Bethune, Gordon, 42, 399
Binney and Smith, 288
Blackmer/Dover Resources, 513–14
Blake, Anthony J., 196
Blind Cow restaurant, 76
BMW, 157
Boeing Company, 47, 98, 218, 455, 490–91
Bonne Bell, 83
Borden Foods, 216

Bosco, Carmine, 514
Bossidy, Larry, 303
Boston Consulting Group, 508
Botello, Rhonda Mae, 61, 62
Boys and Girls Club of America, 111
Braxton, Mark, 46
Brebach, Gresham, 537
British Petroleum, 42
Brodo, Robert, 230
Brown and Root, 319
Bruck, Beth, 382
Buckingham, Marcus, 322–23
Buckman, Robert, 39–40
Buckman Laboratories, 39–40
Budnick, Peter, 540
Buker, Edwin, 157
Bureau of Labor Statistics (BLS), 32, 37, 38, 57, 93, 138, 352–53, 424
Burger Boat, 308–309
Burger King, 94
Bush, George W., 66–67, 540
Business Week, 365–67, 394, 451, 473

Cablevision, 214
California Public Employees' Retirement System, 412
Callahan, Patricia, 269, 270
Cardstore.com Inc., 61
CareerBuilder, 160
Carey, Dennis C., 304
Carier, Dan, 56
Carlton, Juliana, 73
Carrig, Ken, 42
Center for Creative Leadership, 285
Centra Software, 214
Chamber of Commerce, 425
Channell Commerical Corporation, 53, 54
Chapman, Michael, 387
Charles Schwab Corporation, 25
ChemConnect, 226
Chief Executive magazine, 524
Christian and Timbers, 196
Chrysler, 312, 350, 386

CIO.com, 160
CIO Magazine, 160
Cisco Systems, 14, 44, 55, 166, 320, 421, 530
Citicorp, 44
Citizens Financial Group, 367
Clapp, Elissa, 101
Cleary, Pat, 540
Cleland, Max, 336
Clinton, Bill, 540
CNBC, 446, 473
Coffman, Curt, 323
Columbia University, 83, 279
Commerzbank, 508
Commission for the Verification of Corporate Codes of Conduct (Coverco), 472
Communication Workers of America (CWA), 147, 443, 446, 460, 473
Compaq Computer, 16, 42
Connor, Linda, 425
Conseco Inc., 15, 303
Container Store, The, 26–27, 225
Continental Airlines, 42–43, 380, 399
Coollogic, 344–45
Cooper, Kimberley, 31–32
Corasaniti, Michael, 536, 537
Corio, 61
Cornell University, 468
Corporate Leadership Council, 322
Council for Adult & Experiential Learning, 127
Courtney, Marcus, 446
Cronin and Company, 10
Crown Cork & Seal, 468
CVS Drugstores, 327

Dataquest, 61, 62
David Weekley Homes, 387
Dell Computer, 434
Deloitte & Touche, 61, 296, 492
DeLorean, John, 537
DeLorean Motor Company, 537–38
Delta Air Lines, 62–63
Deming, W. Edwards, 379
Department of Commerce, 469
Department of Labor, 77, 88, 111, 114
Desmarest, Thierry, 509
Digital Equipment Corporation, 211
Diversified Communications Group, 172
Dobry, Diane, 83
Doctor's Hospital (California), 331–32
Dominguez, Cari M., 67
Donovan, John, 61
Dow Chemical Company, 122, 152, 319
Drinan, Helen, 143
Duffy, John G., 536
Duke University, 277–78
Dun & Bradstreet, 158
DuPont Company, 388, 521

Eastman Kodak, 211, 283, 394–95, 399
Ebay, 51
eBenefits.com, 61, 62
Economy.com Inc., 26
Edwards, Jim, 538
Elgia, 134–35
Ellis, Becky, 41
Eli Lilly, 314
Employease Inc., 61
EmployeeService.com, 61, 62
Employee Services Management, 426
Enron Corporation, 18, 151, 395, 418, 522, 538
Equal Employment Opportunity Commission (EEOC), 37, 67, 77–81, 86, 98, 114
Ergo Web Inc., 540
Ernst & Young, 58
Espresso Connection, 199–200
E*Trade Group Inc., 62
Excite.com
Express Scripts, 44
Extreme Logic, 525
Exult Inc., 49

Fair Labor Association, 472
FANUC Ltd., 523–24
Farmers Insurance Group, 370
Faust, Molly, 355
Federal Express, 212–13, 523
Federal Mediation and Conciliation Service (FMCS), 464, 467
Feezor, Allen, 412
Fein, Mitchell, 384
Feldman, David L., 140
Fidelity Investments, 434
Financial Accounting Standards Board (FASB), 430
First Tennessee Bank, 421
First Tennessee National Corporation (FTN), 536–37
First USA Bank, 304–305
Fish, Larry, 367
Fisher, George, 395
Fleet, William D., 335
Fleron, Lou Jean, 468–69
Flextronics International computer, 495
Flight Options, 470
Fols, Jean-Martin, 509
Fontan, Joseph, 105
Food Marketing Institute, 541
Ford, William Clay, Jr., 271
Ford Motor Company, 146, 246, 270–71, 292, 294, 295, 350, 386, 398
Fortune magazine, 41, 239, 399
Forum Corporation, 230
Fowler, Bill, 514
Fraser, John, 114
Freeh, Bill, 446
Fruit of the Loom, 141

FTD, 51
FT Knowledge, 230

Gallup Organization, 375, 521
Geert Hofstede, 482
Gegax, Tom, 231
Geib, Robert, 429
General Electric, 266, 269, 270, 277, 290, 298, 320, 523–24
General Motors, 45, 53, 54, 350, 386–87, 479
General Semiconductor, 241
Gerstner, Lou, 128
Giambi, Jason, 10
Gilmartin, Raymond V., 303, 304
Global Crossing, 395
GM Onstar-Europe, 46
Gnazzo, Patrick, 522
Go-e-biz.com, 381
Goldman, Sachs & Company, 398
Gomez, Fabian, 492
Goodnight, James, 433–34
Granite Construction, 269, 270
Greyhound Financial Corporation, 287
Groupe Danone, 509
Grutzmacher, Patricia, 538
Gupta, Rajiv L., 303

Hackman, Richard, 117
Hagans, Phil, 150
Hammonds, Tim, 541
Harley Davidson, 449
Hatch, Orrin, 451
Hay Group, 239
Headsets.com, 526
Health Care Financing Administration, 427
Heckert, Dick, 521
Hellwig, Veronica, 429
Herman, Alexis, 540
Herzberg, Frederick, 118
Hewitt Associates, 402–403, 524
Hewlett-Packard Computers, 16, 58, 120, 269
Holliday, Charles O., Jr., 521
Home Depot, 98–99
Honda, 157
Honeywell, 320
Horner, James, 370
Hotel Employees and Restaurant Employees (HERE), 459
HotJobs, 52, 160
Hovey, Dean, 230
Hsu, Jessica, 31
Humana, 412
Humphrey, John W., 230

IBM, 45, 121–22, 128, 166, 211, 223, 230, 278, 363, 398, 524
Ifill, Gwen, 540

IHS Help Desk, 114
Immelt, Jeffrey, 298
Inacom, 312
Independence Center (Missouri), 157
Infineon Technologies, 508
Information Technology Association of America (ITAA), 26, 166, 446
Inova Health Systems, 154–55
Insight Management, 61
Institute for the Study of Distributed Work, 122
Intel Corporation, 398
Internal Revenue Service, 427–28
International Association of Machinists and Aerospace Workers (IAM), 449
International Brotherhood of Electrical Workers (IBEW), 442, 473
International Data Corporation, 230
International Paper, 58
International Truck and Engine Corporation, 122–23
Interpath Communications, 61
Intuit Corporation, 180
Ito-Yokado, 493

J. P. Stevens Co., 459
Jackson, Phil, 291
Jeffers, Charles, 540
Johnson, Lyndon, 68, 77
Johnson Controls, 83, 146
Johnsonville Foods, 323
Jones, David P., 128
Jones, Julie, 25
Jung, Carl, 280
Jung Moo Young, 472

Kalina, Rick, 157
Kant, Immanuel, 18
Kar, Christian, 199–200
Keefe, Bruyette & Woods Inc., 536
Keim, Jessica, 52
Keller, Joanne, 226
Kellogg, 414
Key Resources, 144
Kiefer, Lou, 449
King, Martin Luther, Jr., 71
Kinzer, Allen, 157
Kirkwood Community College, 215
Kirkwood Insurance Agency, 157
Knoll Associates, 196
Knowledge Company, 182
Korn/Ferry, 356
Kozlowski, Dennis, 303, 304
KPMG Accounting, 509
Kraemer, Harry M. Jansen, Jr., 373–74, 386
Kuttner, Robert, 473

Larrave, Rene, 17
Lee, Thong, 335

Levi Strauss, 189
Lewis, Nancy J., 230
Liggett, David, 521
Li Guangxiang, 495
Lincoln Electric Company, 58
Lincoln Savings and Loan, 538
Liz Claiborne clothing, 472
Lockheed Martin Corporation, 97, 98
Logan International Airport, 336
Lone Star Direct, 149
Long, Bob, 122
Lord, Abbett and Company, 145
Lord, Jonathan, 412
LTV, 434–35
Lucent Technologies, 434

M&A Group Inc., 304
MacDonald, Randall, 524
Mackey, John, 41
MacTemps, 146
Macy's West, 14
Maiorino, Fred, 72
Maricopa Community College, 207
Marlowe, Barbara, 20
Marriott Corporation, 258, 325, 334–35
Matsushita Corporation, 138–39
Mayo Clinic HealthQuest, 426
McAdams, Don, 323
McDonald's restaurants, 150
McDonnell Douglas, 144, 145
McElroy, Kay, 101–102
McGill, Carrie, 102
McGowan, Bruce, 269, 270
MCI Worldcom, 53
McKersie, Robert, 462
McKinney, Matt, 26
McMahan, Larry, 523
MCN Corporation, 146
McNeal, Michael L., 166
Measelle, Dick, 537–38
Mercer Management, 288
Merck & Company, 303, 304, 378
Merrill Lynch, 422
Metropolitan Life Insurance, 146
Metropolitan Transportation Authority (MTA), 276
Metzger Associates, 423–24
Microsoft, 103, 166, 487
Midway Airlines, 166
Miller, Harris, 446
Millstein, Ira M., 304
Minow, Nell, 304
Mintz, Levin, Cohn, Ferris, Glovsky, and Popeo, 20
Mobil Corporation, 182
Modas Uno Korea plant, 472
Moffat, Al, 1–2
Moffat/Rosenthal Advertising Agency, 1–2
Molina Healthcare, 35

Monsanto Corporation, 14, 153, 506
Monster.com, 51, 160, 509
Monthly Labor Review, 138
Moore, James, 230
Morgridge, John, 320
Morningstar, 289
Morse-Brothers Trucking, 212
Moses, Joyce, 370
Motorola, 216
Moulinex, 508
MTW, 55–56
Mullin, Leo, 63
Multex.com, 52
Multi-Media, 195

NAACP, 459
Nash, David, 398
Natella, Tony, 172
National Academy of Sciences, 186
National Alliance for Caregiving, 422
National Association of Manufacturers, 36, 540
National Council on Aging, 422
National Guard, 365
National Institute for Occupational Safety and Health (NIOSH), 88, 90
National Labor Relations Board (NLRB), 454–56, 457, 468
National Rental Car, 493
National Safety Council, 94, 95
National Society to Prevent Blindness, 95
National Technological University, 211
Navarro, Bobbi, 181
Navin, Peter, 226
Net-Folio, 52
New Balance Athletic Shoes, 104
Newcomb, Steve, 381
New York Hospital-Cornell Medical Center, 289
New York Times, 381
New York Yankees, 10
Nike, 472, 529
Nissan Motor Company, 487
Nixon, Richard, 77
North East Precision, 352
Northeast Tool & Manufacturing Company, 127–28
Northern Telecom, 50
Northrop Grumman, 365
North Side Bank & Trust Company, 355
Northwest Airlines Corporation, 98, 166
Now Audio Video chain, 31

O'Brien, Dick, 54
Occupational Outlook Quarterly, 138
Occupational Safety and Health Administration (OHSA), 37, 88–93, 95, 123, 540
Office of Personnel Management, 77

Ohio State University, 541
Ohmes, Cathy, 426
Oldham, Greg, 117
Olson, Sandy, 335
Oracle Corporation, 530
Organization for Economic Cooperation and Development, 508–509
O'Shaughnessy, James, 387
Otis Elevator Company, 256
Outback Steakhouse, 71, 82
Outokumpu American Brass factory, 468–69
Outokumpu Oyi, 468
Owens Corning, 370–71, 434

Pan Am, 62
Paradiso, Jane, 226
Parker Hannifin, 135
Parker, Jim, 167
Peace Corps, 31, 327
Pella Corporation, 279
Pensare, 230
Pension Benefit Guarantee Corporation (PBGC), 390, 416, 435
PeopleSoft, 429
PepsiCo, 207, 389
PetroChina, 497
Peugeot, 509
Pfeffer, Jeffrey, 270
Pfizer pharmaceutical company, 504
Philip Morris, 319
Pilkerton, Debra, 312
Pillsbury Foods, 225
Pinnacle Decision Systems, 226
Pinpoint Networks, 196
Pitasky, Scott, 115
President's Council on Physical Fitness and Sports, 427
Price, Fred, 127
Procter & Gamble, 296, 297, 463
Proscio, Tony, 36

Quan, Katie, 446

Rall, Jean, 114
Raytheon Company, 19
Raytheon Travel Air, 470
Red Dot Corporation, 120
Reebok International, 472
Reich, Robert B., 469
Riboud, Frank, 509
Ricci, Kenn, 470
Roberts, Geoff, 230
Roche Holding, 142
Rockwell Automation Corporation, 387
Rohm & Haas, 303
Roosevelt, Franklin D., 452
Rosenthal, Rob, 1–2
Ross, David, 308–309

Ross, Ruth K., 25
Royal Bank of Scotland Group, 367

Salonek, Tom, 381
SAS Institute Inc., 14–15, 433–34
Scapini, Kathleen, 195
Schachtman, Richard, 31
Schering-Plough, 72–73
Schlager, Seymour, 195
Schneider, Rob, 463
Scholl, Rebecca, 61, 62
Schuster, Jay, 399
Schuster-Zingheim & Associates, 399
Schwab, Charles, 14
Scientific & Engineering Solutions, 381
SCJohnson, 58
Scott, Stacey, 134–35
Screen Actors Guild, 463
Seattle International Association of Machinists, 455
Securities and Exchange Commission (SEC), 395
Seminario, Peg, 540
Senchak, Andrew M., 536
Sethi, S. Prakash, 472
Seyfarth, Shaw, Fairweather & Geraldson, 98
Sharer, Kevin W., 304
Sherman Assembly Systems, 10
Shriver, Julie, 269
Siemens, 508
Singapore Airlines, 493
Skrzyniarz, Beth, 52
SMG Strategic Management Group, 230
Smith, Al, 156
Society for Human Resource Management (SHRM), 21, 22, 37, 49, 143, 353
Soderberg, Jeff, 170–71
Software Technology Group (STG), 170–71
Solomon, Larry, 25
Soluri, Jeff, 195
Solutions for Progress, 434
Southwest Airlines, 4, 166–67, 440–41
Southwest Airlines Pilots Association, 440–41
Spencer-Stuart, 304
Spielman, Jorge, 76
Standard & Poor's, 26
Standridge, Jeff, 109–10
Starbucks Coffee, 47
Stieber, Gus, 62
StorageTek, 214
Strydom, Hugo, 195
Stum, Dave, 426
Suburban Hospital (Maryland), 105
Sun Microsystems, 14, 230
Supreme Court, 68, 189, 265, 428, 466

Sweeney, John, 442
Sweet, Ken, 135
Synergy, 238–39
Syntex Corporation, 142

Tactica Consulting, 17
Tate, Pamela J., 127
Teach for America, 101–102
Technology Professionals Group, 425
Telecommcareers.net, 160
Texaco, 34–35, 98
Texas Instruments, 26, 398
Thoman, G. Richard, 304
Thomas, Mike, 269
3Com, 230
3M Corporation, 123, 158
Tires Plus, 206, 231
TLC Laser Eye Center, 312
Tong Yang Indonesia (TYI), 472
TotalFinaElf, 509
Towers Perrin, 269
Toyota, 459
Transocean Offshore, 202–203
Transit Ltd. (South Africa), 195
Traveller's Group Insurance, 44
Travelocity, 51
Tricon Restaurants, 7, 48
TWA Airline, 380
Tyco International, 303

U-Haul, 370
Union of Needletrade, Industrial and Textile Employees (UNITE), 459
Unisys, 214
United Airlines, 399
United Auto Workers, 45, 386
United Brotherhood of Carpenters and Joiners of America, 442
United Food and Commercial Workers Union, 459
United Parcel Service (UPS), 144, 365
U.S. Employment Service (USES), 157
United Steelworkers of America, 93, 443
United Technologies Corporation, 287, 522
Universal Studios, 141
University of California at Berkeley, 446
University of California at Davis, 69
University of Warsaw, 485
Up-to-Date Laundry, 459
US West, 284

ValueRx, 44
Van Derven, George, 165
Varsh, Cyrus, 387
Verizon, 460, 473
Verner, Colleen, 61
Viant consulting, 520

VMC Behavioral Health Care Services, 62

Wachtell, Lipton, Rosen & Katz, 536
Walgreen's Drugstores, 327, 223–24
Wall Street Journal, 18, 31
Wal-Mart, 85, 87, 389
Walton, Richard, 462
Walt Disney Company, 195, 364, 365
WashTech, 446
Waste Management Inc., 538
Watson Wyatt Worldwide, 226, 269–70, 387, 429, 520
Weinbach, Larry, 538

Welch, Jack, 298
WellPoint, 412
Wells Fargo, 260–70
Wendt, Gary C., 303
Westerdahl, Joyce, 530
Whirlpool Corporation, 219, 258, 394, 531–32
Whitlatch, Brian, 215
Whole Foods Market, 41, 42, 459
Wicks, Pippa, 230
Williams, Lynn, 93
Wilson, Donna Louise, 435
Wilson, Jean, 426
Winningham, Aly, 41

Workers Against Discrimination, 97
Workplace Learning Connection, 215
WorldCom, 389, 395
World Trade Organization (WTO), 478
Wyss, David, 26

Xavier, Madeleine, 398
Xerox Corporation, 55, 304
Xikes, Greg, 31

Youngdahl, John, 398

Zandi, Mark M., 26
ZF Micro Devices, 140

Subject Index

See also NAME/COMPANY INDEX

Note: Names of government agencies, institutions, organizations, and publications will be found in NAME/COMPANY INDEX

ability, of employee. *See also* cognitive ability
   definition of, 109
   performance management, 263, 264
absenteeism, 324
accountability, and incentive pay, 374
accounting. *See also* audits
   employee benefits, 430
   scandals, 537–39
achievement tests, 182
acquisitions, and company strategy, 44
action learning, 218–19
action planning, 294–95
action steps, 82
activity-based pay, 381
actual pay, 363–64
administration
   contracts, 465–67
   performance management, 242
   training programs, 209
administrative information, and job description, 107
advertising, and recruiting, 152–53, 156, 160
affirmative action, 73, 84–85, 148
age, and changes in labor force, 32–33
Age Discrimination in Employment Act (ADEA), 70, 72–73, 428
agency shop, 450
airline industry, 166–67
Airline Quality Rating, 63
alcoholism, and employee assistance programs, 319
alternation ranking, 244–45
alternative dispute resolution (ADR), 318–19
alternative work arrangements, 56–57
American Sign Language, 85
Americans with Disabilities Act (ADA), 12, 70, 73–75, 85, 114, 176, 429
antidiscrimination laws, and employee benefits, 428–29
application forms, and selection, 178–80

application service providers (ASPs), 61–62
apprenticeships, 215
aptitude tests, 182
Arab-Americans, and discrimination, 67
arbitration, 319, 465
Argentina, 95
assessment, and employee development, 279–84
assessment centers, 184, 282–83
associate union membership, 459
attitudes, and incentive pay, 375–76. *See also* morale; motivation; personality
attitudinal structuring, 462
attributes, and performance measurement, 247–48
audiovisual training, 212
audits, of human resource management, 532–34. *See also* accounting
automation, 527

background checks, and selection, 181–82, 196
balanced scorecard, and incentive pay, 391–92, 394
balance sheet approach, to compensation, 501–503, 504
banding, and cognitive ability, 183
bargaining structure, 462
behavior. *See also* attitudes; motivation; personality
   employee separation, 314
   job dissatisfaction, 323
   performance feedback, 262
   performance measurement, 248–53, 260
   of recruiters, 162, 163–64
   training and modeling of, 217
behaviorally anchored rating scale (BARS), 250
behavioral observation scale (BOS), 250, 252
behavior description interview (BDI), 188

behaviorism, 250
benchmarks
   employee development, 283–84
   pay structure, 352
benefits, employee
   communication of, 430–31
   definition of, 403
   education, 433–34
   global workforce, 495–96, 504
   job dissatisfaction and satisfaction, 323, 330
   legal requirements, 404–408, 427–30
   optional programs, 408–22
   responsibilities of human resource department, 10
   role of, 403–404
   selection of, 422–27
   unions, 450
Bill of Rights, 18
binding arbitration, 465
bona fide occupational qualification (BFOQ), 83
bonuses, and incentive pay, 374, 379–80, 385
Brazil, 484
broad bands, and pay levels, 362
B2E (business-to-employee relationship), 530
business representative, and union, 444
business games, and training, 216–17
buyout plan, 147

cafeteria-style benefits, 424–25
California, 452
capitalism, 485–86
card-check provision, 460
careers, planning and management of
   employee development, 275–76, 291–95
   expatriates, 500–501
   in human resource management, 20–21
   job analysis, 114
case studies, and training, 216–17

cash balance plans, and retirement, 418–19
cash registers, 124
central tendency, and rating errors, 259
CEOs. *See also* executives
    basic training for, 303–304
    pay for, 365–67
    succession planning, 299
certification, in human resource management, 21
checkoff provision, 450
chief executive officer. *See* CEO
child care, 335, 420–21
child labor, 349
China
    global workforce, 494–95, 497
    labor rights, 472
    training of employees, 490
churning, of employees, 45
citizenship, and selection process, 178
Civil Rights Acts, 68, 69, 70, 71, 75, 176, 183
Civil Service Reform Act of 1978, 454–55
classroom instruction, 210–12
closed shop, 450
coaching, and development, 291
CODAP method, for task analysis inventory, 112
codetermination, and culture, 486
cognitive ability, 175, 183. *See also* mental capabilities and limitations
collective bargaining, and unions, 460–65
collectivism, and culture, 482
colleges. *See also* universities
    employee benefits and savings plans, 421–22
    recruiting, 158
commissions, and incentive pay, 374, 380, 381–82
communication. *See also* language
    culture and global workforce, 483–84, 500, 502, 504–506
    employee benefits, 430–31
    incentive pay, 393
    layoffs, 143
    pay fairness, 355–56
    selection decisions, 192
    training programs, 209
company culture. *See also* culture; organizations
    executive pay, 367
    learning and, 520
    performance appraisals and politics, 260
company performance, 2, 3–5
comparable worth, 347
compa-ratio, 363–64
comparisons, and performance appraisal, 244–47

compensation. *See* pay structure
compensatory damages, and equal employment opportunity, 75
compensatory model, of selection, 192
compressed workweek, 121
computers and computer software. *See also* Internet; World Wide Web
    employer surveillance, 315
    high-performance work systems, 527–31
    performance management, 241–42, 266
    training programs, 211, 212–13, 230–31
concurrent validation, and selection, 174
conscience, and employee rights, 18–19
conscientiousness, and personality inventories, 184
consent, as employee right, 18, 20
consent election, 456
Consolidated Omnibus Budget Reconciliation Act (COBRA), 411
Constitution, U.S., 18, 69, 70
construct validity, and selection, 175
consultants, and scandals, 537
consumer-oriented benefit plan, 412
Consumer Price Index (CPI), 351
contact information, and job application, 178
contamination, of performance measures, 243–44
content validity, and selection, 174–75
continuous learning, 519
contract company workers, 57
contracts
    labor relations and administration of, 465–67
    unions and negotiation of, 442, 462–63
contributory plans, 416
cooperation, between labor and management, 467–70
coordination training, 218
core competency, 140–41
core self-evaluations, 321
corporate campaigns, and unions, 459
correlation coefficients, and reliability, 173
cost/benefit analysis
    effectiveness of human resource management programs, 534
    of training programs, 223
cost of living
    allowances for expatriates, 504
    labor markets, 351
costs
    benefits, 404, 425–27
    downsizing, 141
    global workforce, 494
    pay as percent of total, 345

coverage, and union membership, 446–47
coworkers, and job dissatisfaction/satisfaction, 322–23, 329–30
craft union, 442
criminal background checks, 182
criterion-related validity, 173–74
critical-incident method, and performance measurement, 248, 250
critical thinking, 519
criticism, and performance feedback, 262
cross-cultural preparation, for foreign assignments, 491, 500
cross-training, 218
cultural diversity, and changes in labor force, 34–35
culture. *See also* company culture; globalization; society
    global workforce, 488–89, 490, 491, 493
    international markets, 481–84
    safety and international management, 95
    selection for overseas assignments, 7
"culture points," and performance management, 241
culture shock, 488–89
customers, and performance evaluations, 258, 526
customer service, and performance management, 243–44
customized benefits, 425
cycle time, and incentive pay, 391

Davis-Bacon Act of 1931, 349–50
decertification, of union, 460
decision making
    incentive pay and employee participation, 393
    personality type, 280–81
    selection process, 191–92
    skills of human resource professionals, 15–16
    support systems, 528
defamation, and references, 181
deficiencies, in performance measures, 243–44
defined benefit plans, 416–17, 434
defined contribution plans, 417–18, 434
dejobbing, 115
delayering, of pay levels, 362
development, of employees
    approaches to, 276–91
    basic training for CEOs, 303–304
    career management, 275–76
    challenges in, 296–301
    definition of, 274
    global workforce, 489–92
    high-performance work system, 524

development, of employees—*Cont.*
  performance management, 242
  responsibilities of human resource
    department, 8–9
  risk reduction, 304–305
  training, 274
development planning, 276
Dictionary of Occupational Titles (DOT),
  111
differential piece rates, 377
direct applicants, 155–56
disabilities and disabled persons
  Americans with Disabilities Act, 74,
    429
  medical leave, 408
  reasonable accommodation, 85
  sick leave programs, 410
  veterans, 76–77
disability insurance, 415
disease management programs, 412
discipline. *See* progressive discipline
discrimination. *See also* equal
    employment opportunity; glass
    ceiling; reverse discrimination
  avoidance of 82–85
  disabled persons, 74–75, 85, 429
  employee benefits, 428–29
  employee separation, 313
  ethnicity, 67, 296
  gender, 98, 99, 296, 347
  pay structure, 347
  performance management, 265
  racism, 97–98, 98–99, 347
disparate impact, of discrimination,
  82–84
distance learning, 211–12
distribution, and performance
    measurement, 259
distributive bargaining, 462
diversity
  cultural, 34–35
  equal employment opportunity, 87
  training programs, 225–27
documentation, and progressive
    discipline, 317. *See also* records and
    recordkeeping
domestic partners, and employee benefits,
  408
dot-coms, 51, 52
downsizing. *See also* layoffs; separation
  company strategy and, 44–46, 128
  executive pay, 367
  planning, 141–42
  temporary workers, 145
downward move, 288
drug abuse, and employee assistance
    programs, 319–20
drug tests, and selection, 185–87
due process, and employee rights, 19, 20,
  69, 152

duty of fair representation, 467
dysfunctional managers, and
    development, 299–301

early retirement programs, 45–46, 72,
  143–44. *See also* retirement
economy
  changes in, 50–51
  globalization and systems of, 484–86
  pay structure, 350–54, 367
education. *See also* learning; teaching;
    training
  employee benefits, 433–34
  employee development, 277–79
  globalization, 484, 504
  job application, 178
  job satisfaction, 335
  skill deficiencies in workforce, 36
effectiveness, of human resource
    management, 531–34. *See also*
    evaluation; measures and
    measurement
e-HRM. *See* electronic human resource
    management
elder care, 422
e-learning, 213, 214, 230–31, 278. *See
  also* Internet
elections, and unions, 455, 456–57, 460
electronic business (e-business), 50–52
electronic human resource management
    (e-HRM), 52–55, 529–31
electronic monitoring, and performance
    management, 266
electronic performance support systems
    (EPSSs), 213
electronic recruiting, 159–60
e-mail, 124–25, 315. *See also* Internet
employability, 55
employee assistance programs (EAPs),
  319–20, 500
employee relations. *See* labor relations
Employee Retirement Income Security
    Act (ERISA), 416–17
employee rights, and ethical human
    resource management, 18–19
employees. *See* benefits; development;
    equal employment opportunity;
    empowerment; labor relations;
    morale; recruitment; safety;
    selection; separation; training;
    turnover
employee stock ownership plans
    (ESOPs), 390–91, 417
employee wellness program (EWP),
  413–15
Employer Information Report (EEO-1),
  78, 79–80
employer-sponsored safety and health
    programs, 94–95
employment agencies, 156–58

employment relationship, and current
    trends, 55–58
employment tests, 182–87
employment-at-will policies, 152, 310
empowerment, of employees. *See also*
    power
  culture and, 483, 484
  high-performance work systems, 40,
    518
  job enrichment, 118
  layoffs, 143
  unions, 467
energy, and personality type, 280
enforcement, of Occupational Safety and
    Health Act, 91–92
equal employment opportunity
  businesses' role in, 82–87
  definition of, 68–69
  constitutional amendments, 69, 70
  government's role in, 77–82
  legislation, 69–77
  pay structure, 346–47
Equal Pay Act of 1963, 70, 71
equipment, and training programs, 209
equitable relief, 75
equity theory, and pay structure, 354–56,
  365–67, 376
ergonomics, 122–23
ESL (English as second language), 335
essential duties, and job description, 107
ethics
  high-performance work systems,
    521–22
  in human resource management,
    17–20
  incentive pay, 395–96
  performance management, 264–66
ethnicity. *See also* race and racism
  changes in labor force, 34–35
  discrimination and harassment in
    workplace, 66–67, 296
Europe. *See also* France; Germany
  European Union and global recruiting,
    159
  nationalized health systems, 411
  paid family leave, 408, 420
  paid vacation, 409, 496
  stock options, 495
  unions, 446–47
evaluation. *See also* effectiveness;
    measures and measurement
  of human resource plan, 147
  of training programs, 222–23
executive orders, 68, 70, 77
executive search firm (ESF), 157–58
executives, and pay structure, 365–67,
  393–96, 398–99. *See also* CEOs
exempt amount, and Social Security, 405
exempt employees, 349
exit interview, 331

expanded hours, and labor shortages, 147
expatriates, and globalization, 48, 479, 489, 491, 497–506
expectations, and employee benefits, 424
expectations agreement, 56
experience rating, and unemployment insurance, 406
experiential programs, 217–18
expert systems, 528
export centers, 138–39
external labor force, 32
external recruiting, 150, 155–60
externship, 288
extroverted personality type, 281

faces scale, and job satisfaction, 331, 332
fact finder, 465
factory workers, and work analysis, 127–28
Fair Credit Reporting Act, 177
fair employment practices, 12. *See also* unfair labor practices
Fair Labor Standards Act, 121, 328, 347–49, 427
fairness, and pay structure, 354–56
family
    family-friendly policies, 328, 420–22
    global workforce, 491, 498
Family and Medical Leave Act (FMLA), 407–408
fast food industry, 7
Federal Register, 81
feedback
    employee development, 284–85
    job satisfaction, 331
    performance management, 240–41, 260–63
    recruiters, 163
    total quality management, 255
    training programs, 221
final-offer arbitration, 465
fitness-for-duty testing, 186
529 savings plans, 421, 422
Fleishman Job Analysis System, 112–13
flexibility
    employment relationship, 56–58
    pay structure, 370–71, 387
    work schedules, 57–58, 120–21
flexible spending accounts, 413
flextime, 120–21
floating holidays, 410
follow-up meetings, and performance feedback, 262
forced-distribution method, of performance measurement, 245–46
forecasting, of labor demand and supply, 136–39
foreign assignments, and selection, 7, 488–89. *See also* expatriates; international assignments

four-fifths rule, 83, 84
401(k) plans, 151, 417, 418, 434
Fourteenth Amendment, to Constitution, 69, 70
France. *See also* Europe
    layoffs, 508–509
    pay of CEOs, 366
freedom of speech, and employee rights, 19, 20
free riders, 450–51
friendships, and peer evaluations, 257

gainsharing, 382–85
gender, and culture, 482. *See also* discrimination; sex discrimination
General Aptitude Test Battery (GATB), 182
generalizable method, and selection, 175
Generation Y, 33
geographic location, and pay differentials, 361
Germany. *See also* Europe
    culture and, 483
    layoffs, 508
    pay of CEOs, 366
    political-legal system, 486
Ghana, 493
glass ceiling, and development, 296
globalization. *See also* culture; *specific countries*
    company strategy and expansion, 46–48
    compensation, 493–96
    environment of HRM, 478–81
    human resource planning, 486–87
    international markets, 481–86
    job specialization, 110
    labor relations, 496–97
    managing expatriates, 497–506
    outsourcing, 146
    performance management, 492–93
    recruiting, 159
    safety programs, 95
    selection, 487–89
    sweatshops, 472
    terrorism, 509–10
    training and development, 489–92
global organizations, 480–81
Global Relocation Trends 2000 Survey Report, 491
goals and goal setting. *See also* objectives
    career management, 294
    equal employment opportunity, 81
    incentive pay, 381
    performance feedback, 262
    strategic planning, 138–47
government. *See also* laws and legal system; legislation; states; *specific agencies* (in NAME/COMPANY INDEX)
    elder care, 422

government—*Cont.*
    equal employment opportunity, 67–68, 77–82
    military duty and pay structure, 365
    pension plans, 419
    regulation of human resource management, 68
    unions in, 448
    workplace safety and health, 67–68, 88–93
graphic rating scale, and performance measurement, 247–48
Great Depression, and labor relations, 451–52
green-circle rates, 361
grievance procedure, 465–67
group-building methods, of training, 210
group insurance, and employee benefits, 410
group mentoring programs, 290–91
group performance, and incentive pay, 382–85
Guatemala, 472

halo error, and performance measurement, 259
hands-on methods, of training, 210, 211
handwriting analysis, 185
harassment, and workplace discrimination, 98. *See also* sexual harassment
Hay Guide-Chart Profile method, 357
Hazard Communication Standard, 92–93
health insurance. *See* medical insurance
health maintenance organization (HMO), 413, 427, 429
high-performance work system
    conditions contributing to, 517–22
    current trends, 36–42
    definition of, 5, 514
    elements of, 515–16
    management and, 522–31
    outcomes of, 516–17
    rebuilding of business after September 11, 2001, 536–37
high-potential employees, and succession planning, 298
holidays, and benefits, 409, 410
honesty tests, 185
horns error, and performance measurement, 259
hospitals, and team-based jobs, 105
host country, 479
hot-stove rule, 315, 317
hourly wage, 358
housing, and expatriates, 504

human capital, 3
human relations, and skills of human resource professionals, 14–16. *See also* labor relations
human resource information system (HRIS), 49–50
human resource management (HRM). *See also* benefits; development; equal employment opportunity; globalization; job analysis; labor relations; pay structure; performance management; planning; selection; separation; training
    careers in, 20–21
    case study of excellence in, 26–27
    company performance, 2, 3–5
    current trends in, 30–58
    definition of, 2
    effectiveness of, 531–34
    ethics in, 17–20
    responsibilities of departments, 5–13
    responsibilities of supervisors, 16–17
    skills of professionals, 13–16
human resource planning, and job analysis, 113–14

image advertising, 152–53
Immigration Reform and Control Act of 1986, 178
impairment tests, 186
implementation
    of human resources plan, 147
    of training program, 219–21
Improshare program, 384–85
incentive pay. *See also* pay structure
    balanced scorecard, 391–92, 394
    employee motivation and attitudes, 374–76, 399
    executives, 393–96, 398–99
    global workforce, 495
    group performance, 382–85
    individual performance, 376–82
    organizational performance, 385–91
    processes of, 392–93
incentive programs, and safety, 95. *See also* early retirement programs
independent contractors, 57, 427
India
    global labor market, 15
    outsourcing, 146
Individual Coaching for Effectiveness (ICE) program, 299, 301
individualism, and culture, 482
Indonesia, 472
industrial accidents, 93
industrial engineering, 116–17
Industrial Revolution, and child labor, 349
industrial unions, 443–44

information
    high-performance work system and systems of, 515–16, 527, 528–29
    job analysis, 110–11
information-gathering, and personality type, 280
Information Revolution, and recruiting, 166
inpatriates, 491
inputs, and work flow, 104
insider trading, 396
instructional design, 200
integrative bargaining, 462
intensive-care unit (ICU), 105
interactional justice, 311–12
interactive video, 212–13
internal labor force, 32
internal recruiting, 150, 153–55
international assignments, and company strategy, 48. *See also* expatriates; foreign assignments
international markets, 481–86
international organization, 480
Internet. *See also* computers and computer software; e-learning; World Wide Web
    e-business and, 51
    E-HRM, 529–31
    employee benefits, 429
    orientation of new employees, 226
    recruiting, 159–60
    telecommuting, 122
    unions, 445–46
    wage and salary data, 356
interns and internships, 158, 215
interpersonal relationships, and employee development, 289–91
interrater reliability, 244
interviews
    employee separation and exit interview, 332
    selection process, 177, 187–91
intranet, and electronic human resource management, 52, 54
intraorganizational bargaining, 462
introverted personality type, 280, 281
involuntary turnover, 309–10
Ireland, 15

Japan
    culture, 487, 493
    downsizing, 142
    employee stock ownership plans, 390
    forecasts for labor demand and supply, 138
    overseas operations, 479
    paid family leave, 408
    pay of CEOs, 366
job, definition of, 102

job analysis
    definition of, 6
    importance of, 113–15
    process of, 105–13
    trends in, 115, 127–28
job applications, 178–82
job categories, 137
Job Characteristics Model, 117
job complexity, 326
Job Creation and Worker Assistance Act of 2002, 406
job descriptions, 106–108
job design
    culture and, 483
    definition of, 6
    high-performance work system, 522–24
    process of, 116–25
Job Descriptive Index (JDI), 331, 332
job dissatisfaction, 321–23. *See also* job satisfaction
job enlargement, 118, 286
job enrichment, 118
job evaluation, 114, 357, 363
job experiences, and development, 285–89
job extension, 118
job hazard analysis technique, 94
job information, 110–11
job involvement, 324
job offer, communication of, 192
job performance tests, 184
job posting, 153–54
job rotation, 118, 287
job satisfaction, 325–33, 334–35, 520–21. *See also* job dissatisfaction
job security, 152, 313
job sharing, 121
job specifications, 108–10
job structure, and pay structure, 356–58
job withdrawal, 320–24
justice, and employee separation, 310–12

key jobs, 357–58
knowledge
    definition of, 109
    high-performance work systems, 37–40, 518–20
knowledge, skills, abilities, and other characteristics (KSAOs), 108–10

labor. *See also* labor markets; labor relations; unions
    changes in labor force, 32–36
    forecasting demand for, 136–39
labor markets
    forecasting, 138
    globalization, 159, 487–89
    pay structure, 350–51
    shortages, 138–39, 147, 196
    surpluses, 138–39

labor relations. *See also* collective bargaining; employment relationship; human relations
  contract administration, 465–67
  globalization and, 472, 496–97
  goals of groups, 449–51
  incentive pay, 399
  labor-management cooperation, 467–70
  laws and regulations, 451–56
  responsibilities of human resource department, 11
  role of unions, 441–49
Landrum-Griffin Act of 1959, 453, 454
language. *See also* communication
  misunderstandings and employee separation, 335
  training and development of global workforce, 489, 500, 502
Latin America, and sweatshops, 472
layoffs. *See also* downsizing; separation
  France and aversion to, 508–509
  minimizing pain of, 143
  notification of, 315–18
laws and legal systems. *See also* government; legislation; states; Supreme Court (in NAME/COMPANY INDEX)
  airline industry, 166–67
  compliance as responsibility of human resource department, 11–12
  culture and definitions of rights and wrong, 482
  employee benefits, 404–408, 427–30
  employee separation, 310, 312–15
  employment-at-will policies, 152
  globalization, 486
  job analysis, 114
  job descriptions, 115
  job dissatisfaction, 323–24
  labor relations, 451–56
  pay structure, 346–50
  performance management, 264–66
  selection, 176–78
leaderless group discussion, 282
leadership skills, of human resource management professionals, 16
leading indicators, 136
lead-the-market pay strategies, 150–51
learning, principles of, 219–21. *See also* education
learning culture, 519, 520
learning organization, 518–19, 527
legislation, and equal employment opportunity, 69–77. *See also* laws and legal systems
leniency, and rating errors, 259
lie detector tests, 185
life insurance, 415
lifestyle, and personality type, 281

living wage, 348
local unions, 444
Log of Work-Related Injuries, 89, 90
long-term care insurance, 415
long-term disability insurance, 415
long-term incentives, 394
long-term orientation, and culture, 482

magazines, and job advertisements, 156. *See also* media
managed care, 411–13
management by objectives (MBO), 253–54
managers and management. *See also* executives; supervisors
  benchmarks for skills, 283, 284
  employee development and dysfunctional, 299–301
  labor relations, 449, 467–70
  pay structure, 369–70
  performance evaluations, 255–57, 261–63, 269–70
  subordinate evaluations of, 257
  support for training, 206
  union organizing, 457–58, 473
maquiladoras, 478, 503–504
market pay, 352–54
material safety data sheets (MSDs), 92–93
MBA programs, 277–78
meaningful work, 327
measures and measurement. *See also* effectiveness; evaluation
  performance management, 244–55, 269–70
  training programs, 221–24
media. *See also* newspapers
  pay for CEOs, 365
  whistle-blowing, 323
mediation
  collective bargaining, 464–65
  employee separation, 319
medical examinations, and selection, 187
medical insurance, and benefits, 410–15, 427
medical leave, 407–408
Medicare, 406, 434
membership, of unions, 444–47, 450
mental capabilities and limitations, and job design, 124–25. *See also* cognitive ability
mentors, and development, 289–91, 297, 501
mergers
  company strategy and, 44
  downsizing, 141
merit pay, 378–79
Mexico, and globalization, 478, 483, 503–504

military
  pay structure, 364, 365
  terrorism, 509, 510
minimum wage, 347–48
misrepresentation, and job application, 181
mixed-standard scales, and performance measurement, 248, 249
money purchase plan, 417
monitoring, of job satisfaction, 330–33
morale. *See also* attitudes
  after downsizing, 46
  labor relations, 468–69
motivation. *See also* attitudes
  downsizing, 142
  incentive pay, 374–75, 381
  job design, 117
  performance management, 263–64
multiemployer pension plans, 419
multinational companies, 480
multiple-hurdle model, for selection decisions, 192
multitasking, 31–32
Myers-Briggs Type Indicator (MBTI), 279–82

National Compensation Survey, 353
National Labor Relations Act (NLRA), 451–54, 467
needs assessment, and training, 201–204
negative affectivity, 321
nepotism, 156
Netherlands, 483, 484
neutrality provision, 460
New Deal, and labor relations, 452
newspapers, and job advertisements, 156, 160. *See also* media
New York City, and pay differentials, 361
"niche boards," 160
night shifts, 110, 361. *See also* schedules and scheduling
no-fault liability, and workers' compensation, 407
noncomplete agreements, 312
noncontributory plans, 416
nondirective interview, 187–88
nonexempt employees, and overtime pay, 349
North American Free Trade Agreement (NAFTA), 478
notification, of layoffs, 315

objectives. *See also* goals and goal setting
  selection of benefits and organizational, 423–24
  of training programs, 207
Occupational Information Network (O*NET), 111
occupational intimacy, 520–21

Occupational Safety and Health Act (OSH Act), 88–93
Office of Federal Contract Compliance Procedures (OFCCP), 73, 81–82
Old Age, Survivors, Disability, and Health Insurance (OASDHI) program, 405
older workers, and changes in labor force, 33. *See also* elder care
Older Workers Benefit Protection Act of 1990, 428
Omnibus Budget Reconciliation Act of 1993, 395
on-call workers, 57
on-the-job training (OJT), 214–16
open-door policy, 318
open-ended questions, and interviews, 187–88
opinion surveys, and job satisfaction, 331–32
opposition, and equal employment opportunity, 71
organizational behavior modification (OBM), 250, 252–53
organizational commitment, 324
organization analysis, 202–203
organizations. *See also* company culture
  employee benefits, 423–24
  high-performance work system and structure of, 515–16
  incentive pay, 385–91
  project-based structures, 115
  training and needs of, 200, 202–203
  work flow, 102–104
organizing, and unions, 456–60, 473
orientation, of new employees, 224–25, 226
outcome fairness, and employee separation, 311
outplacement counseling, 320
outputs, and work flow, 104
outsourcing
  company strategy, 49
  temporary workers, 146–47
overqualified job applicants, 192
overtime
  labor shortages, 147
  pay structure, 348–49
overwork, and job satisfaction, 328

paid leave, 408–10
paired-comparison method, of performance measurement, 246
panel interview, 188–89
parent country, 479, 488
participation in a proceeding, and equal employment opportunity, 71
pay differentials, 361
pay grades, 359–60
pay level, 345, 351–52

pay policy line, 358, 359
pay ranges, 360–61
pay rates, 358–59
payroll tax, and Social Security, 406
Pay Satisfaction Questionnaire (PSQ), 331
pay strategy, and lead-the-market, 150–51
pay structure. *See also* incentive pay
  actual pay, 363–64
  culture and, 483
  current issues involving, 364–67
  decisions about, 345–46
  definition of, 345
  economic influences on, 350–54
  elements of, 358–63
  employee judgments about fairness, 354–56
  flexibility in, 370–71
  global workforce, 493–96, 501–504
  high-performance work systems, 526–27
  job dissatisfaction and satisfaction, 323, 330, 334–35
  job structure, 356–58
  legal requirements, 346–50
  managers and lawsuits, 369–70
  responsibilities of human resource department, 10
  unions and, 440–41, 445, 450
peers
  employee separation and review by, 318–19
  as source of performance information, 257
  support of and training, 205–206
pensions. *See* retirement
performance appraisal. *See also* performance management
  comparisons, 244–47
  definition of, 239
  employee development, 284–85
  job analysis, 114
  political behavior in, 260
  problems in, 240
  360–degree performance appraisal, 255, 284–85
performance bonuses, 379–80
performance management. *See also* performance appraisal
  criteria for effective, 242–44
  definition of, 239
  errors in measurement, 258–60
  feedback, 260–63
  globalization, 492–93
  high-performance work system, 525–26
  incentive pay, 376–82
  legal and ethical issues in, 264–66
  measurement methods, 244–55, 269–70, 394–95
  process of, 239–42

performance management—*Cont.*
  purposes of, 242
  responsibilities of human resource department, 9
  solutions to problems in, 263–64, 270–71
  sources of information for, 255–58
  unions and, 448–49
performance standards, and training, 207
"perks philosophy," 426
Personal Development Roadmap (PDR), 292, 294, 295
personal dispositions, and job satisfaction, 321, 325–26
personality. *See also* attitudes; behavior
  Myers-Briggs Type Indicator and types of, 280–81
  overseas assignments, 7
  selection and personality inventories, 184–85
person analysis, 203
personnel selection, 171
pharmacists, and job satisfaction, 327
phased-retirement program, 144
physical ability tests, 182–83
physical job withdrawal, 324
picketing, 463
piecework rates, 358, 376–77
planning
  global economy, 486–87
  interviews, 190
  process of, 135–48
  responsibilities of human resource department, 10, 13
  training programs, 206–10
Poland, 485
police officers, 314
policies, personnel. *See also* public policy
  equal employment opportunity, 84
  planning and recruitment, 149–53
  responsibilities of human resource department, 11
political behavior, in performance appraisals, 260
political systems, and globalization, 486
polygraph, 185
position, definition of, 102
Position Analysis Questionnaire (PAQ), 111–12
power. *See also* empowerment
  culture and distance of, 482, 483
  knowledge workers, 39
  subordinate evaluations, 257
practical value, of selection methods, 175–76
praise, and performance management, 262
predictive validation, and selection, 174
preferred provider organization (PPO), 413, 427, 429

Pregnancy Discrimination Act of 1978, 70, 73, 408, 428
preparation
   of expatriates, 500–501
   for interviews, 189–91
   for performance feedback, 261–63
presentation methods, and training programs, 210
pretests, and training programs, 209
prevailing wages, 349–50
preventive health care, 412
privacy
   employee rights, 18, 20, 177
   employee separation, 313–15
   performance management systems, 266
private employment agencies, 157–58
problem solving, and performance management, 262, 263
procedural justice, 311
productivity
   incentive pay, 393
   performance measurement, 253
   unions and, 448
product markets, and pay structure, 350
profit sharing, 386–88, 417
progressive discipline, and separation, 315–18
project-based organizational structures, 115
promotion
   employee development, 288
   promote-from-within policies, 150
   unions and labor relations, 450
protean career, 275
protégé, and mentor, 289
psychological contract, and employment relationship, 55–56, 275
psychological job withdrawal, 324
psychological testing, and selection, 196
public employment agencies, 156–57
public policy. See also government; society
   employee separation and violations of, 313
   minimum wage, 348
punitive damages, and equal employment opportunity, 75
push goal, 381

qualifying events, and medical insurance, 411
quality standards, and high-performance work systems, 43–44
questionnaires, and task analysis, 204
quid pro quo harassment, 87

race and racism
   changes in labor force, 34–35
   cognitive ability tests and race norming, 183

race and racism—Cont.
   discrimination in workplace, 97–98, 98–99, 347
rating errors, and performance measurement, 258–59
rating of individuals, and performance measurement, 247–53
readability, and training programs, 221
readiness, for training, 205–206
realistic job preview, 163
reality check, and career management, 293–94
reasonable accommodation, 85–86
records and recordkeeping, and training, 209. See also documentation
recreational activities, 422
recruitment, of employees
   high-performance work system, 524
   process of, 148–49, 165–66
   recruiter traits and behaviors, 161–64
   responsibilities of human resources department, 6–8
   sources for, 153–61
   strategies for, 14
red-circle rates, 361
reengineering, and company strategy, 48–49
references, and job application, 180–81
referrals, and recruiting, 155–56
Rehabilitation Act of 1973, 70
reinforcement, of safe practices, 95
relational databases, 528–29
reliability, of selection process, 172–73
religion, and discrimination, 85
relocation
   allowances for expatriates, 504
   downsizing, 141
   employee development, 287
repatriation, of expatriates, 504–506
request for proposal (RFP), 208
results, and performance measurement, 253–54, 262
résumés, 180
Resumix applicant tracking program, 529
retention bonuses, 380
retirement. See also early retirement programs; 401K plans
   employee benefits, 415, 434–35
   succession planning, 298
return on investment, of training program, 223
reverse discrimination, 69, 84
reward systems, and high-performance work system, 515
rights arbitration, 465
right-to-know laws, 92
right-to-work laws, 454
risk, development and reduction of, 304–305
role analysis technique, 328

roles, and job satisfaction, 322, 328
Rucker plan, 384

sabbaticals, 288–89
safety, workplace
   drug testing, 187
   employer-sponsored safety and health programs, 94–95
   government regulation of, 67–68
   Occupational Safety and Health Act, 88–93
salary, and pay structure, 358
sales associates, and job description and specifications, 108, 109
salespeople, and commissions, 380, 381–82
scandals
   accounting and auditing, 537–39
   stock options, 389, 395
Scanlon plans, 383–84
schedules and scheduling. See also night shifts
   flexible, 57–58, 120–21
   performance feedback, 261
Sea Launch vessel, 490
searches, and employee privacy, 314–15
selection, of employees
   decision making, 191–92
   employment tests, 182–87
   global labor market, 487–89, 497–500
   high-performance work system, 524
   interviews, 187–91
   job analysis, 114
   job applications, 178–82
   process of, 171–78
   responsibilities of human resources department, 6–8
self-assessment, and employee development, 292, 293
Self-Directed Search, 292
self-employment, 427
self-evaluation, and performance measurement, 257–58
self-managing work teams, 119–20
self-selection, and recruiting, 155
self-service, and sharing of information, 53
seniority, and unions, 450
separation, of employees. See also downsizing; layoffs
   job withdrawal, 320–24
   legal requirements, 312–15
   principles of justice, 310–12
   progressive discipline and, 315–18
September 11, 2001 (terrorist attack on World Trade Center), 66, 167, 314, 365, 488, 500, 509, 517, 536–37. See also terrorism
service industries
   job growth, 38
   performance measurement, 258

severance pay, 143
sex discrimination, 98, 99, 296, 347
sexual harassment, 86–87
shared knowledge, 519
short-term disability insurance, 415
short-term incentives, 394
short-term orientation, and culture, 482
sick leave, and benefits, 409, 410
signature, and job application, 178
signing bonuses, 150
similar-to-me error, 259
simple ranking, and performance
    measures, 244–45
simplification, of jobs, 124
simulations, as training method, 216
situational constraints
    performance measurement, 526
    training, 205
situational interviews, 188
skill-based pay systems, 362–63
skills
    benchmarks for managerial, 283, 284
    deficiencies in workforce, 36
    definition of, 109
    globalization, 484
    of human resource professionals,
        13–16
    interviewing, 190
slavery, and Thirteenth Amendment, 69
socialism, 485–86
Social Security, 405–406, 415
Social Security Act of 1935, 156–57
society. See also culture; public policy
    labor relations and goals of, 451
    minimum wage and social policy, 348
South Africa, 195
spam (electronic junk mail), 125
staffing levels, and flexibility, 56–57
standard hour plan, 378
standards, for ethical behavior, 19–20
states. See also laws and legal systems;
        legislation
    child labor laws, 349
    college savings plans, 421–22
    labor relations, 452
    unions and strikes, 448
    workers' compensation laws, 407
statistical quality control, 255
steel industry
    high-performance work systems, 516
    pensions, 434–35
stereo headsets, 326
stipulation election, 456
stocks
    incentive pay, 386, 388–91, 395–96,
        495
    pay for executives and options, 365
    pay strategies, 150–51
    retirement plans, 418
straight commission plan, 382

straight piecework plan, 377
strategic approach, to personnel
    selection, 172
strategic planning, 139–47
strategy, and high-performance work
    system, 42–49
strictness, and rating errors, 259
strikes, and unions, 448, 450, 463–64
Strong-Campbell Interest Inventory, 292
structured interview, 187
subjectivity, and interviews, 189
subordinates, and evaluation of
        performance of managers, 257
succession planning, 298–99
summary plan description (SPD), 419
supervisors. See also managers
    human resource responsibilities of,
        16–17
    job satisfaction and dissatisfaction,
        322–23, 329–30
surveillance, and employee privacy, 315
surveys
    job satisfaction and employee, 331
    market pay, 352
    performance management and
        customer, 258
sustainable competitive advantage, 4
sweatshops, 472

Taft-Hartley Act of 1947, 453–54, 460
task analysis and task analysis inventory,
    112, 203–204
task-BARS rating dimension, 251
tasks, duties, and responsibilities (TDRs),
    106, 107
tasks
    high-performance work system and
        design of, 515
    job dissatisfaction, 321–22, 326–28
task statement questionnaire, 204
taxation, and employee benefits, 427–28,
    504
tax equalization allowance, 504
teaching, elements of job, 102. See also
        education
team training, 218
teamwork
    high-performance work systems,
        40–42, 528
    hospitals and team-based jobs, 105
    incentive pay, 385
    recruiting, 163
    self-managing work teams, 119–20
technical skills, of human resource
        management professionals, 16
technic of operations review (TOR), 94
technology
    current trends in human resource
        management, 49–55
    downsizing, 141

technology—Cont.
    high-performance work systems,
        527–31
    job satisfaction, 327
telecommuting and telework, 121–22,
    534
temporary assignments, and employee
        development, 288–89
temporary workers, 57, 144–46
term life insurance, 415
terrorism. See also September 11, 2001
    global workforce, 509–10
    pay during military duty, 365
test-retest reliability, 244
Texas, 111
theft, by employees, 315
third country, and international
        organizations, 479, 488
Thirteenth Amendment, to
        Constitution, 69, 70
360–degree performance appraisal, 255,
    284–85
title, and job description, 107
Title VII, of Civil Rights Act, 68, 70, 71,
    75
"top-heavy" pension plan, 419
total quality management (TQM)
    high quality standards and, 43–44
    performance measurement, 254–55
training, of employees. See also education
    applications of, 224–27
    cross-cultural for expatriates, 500
    definition of, 200
    employee development, 274
    global workforce, 489–92
    high-performance work system, 524
    implementation of, 219–21
    job analysis, 114
    measuring results of, 221–24
    methods of, 210–19
    needs assessment, 201–204
    online classrooms, 230–31
    organizational needs, 200
    orientation, 195
    performance measurement errors, 260
    planning of programs, 206–10
    readiness for, 205–206
    responsibilities of human resource
        department, 8–9
    safety, 94
training administration, 208–209
transaction processing, 528
transfers
    employee development, 287–88
    of training, 222
transitional matrix, 137
transnational HRM system, 481
travel industry, 51
trend analysis, 136
tuition reimbursement programs, 422

turnover, of employees, 309–10, 324
two-tier wage system, 355

uncertainty avoidance, and culture, 482
underfunding, of pension funds, 416
unemployment insurance, 406
unfair labor practices, 453, 456. *See also* fair employment practices
Uniformed Services Employment and Reemployment Rights Act of 1994, 70, 75–77, 365
Uniform Guidelines on Employee Selection Procedures, 78, 80, 173, 265
unions, labor
  collective bargaining, 460–65
  employee separation, 318
  goals of, 450–51
  labor relations and role of, 441–49, 473
  organizing, 456–60
  pay structure, 349–50, 440–41
union shop, 450
union steward, 444
universities, and recruiting, 158, 160–61. *See also* colleges; *specific institutions* (in NAME/COMPANY INDEX)
unpaid family and medical leave, 407–408, 420
utility, and selection process, 175
utilization analysis, 81

vacation, and employee benefits, 409, 496
validation, and repatriation of expatriates, 504–506
validity
  of performance management, 243–44
  of selection process, 173–75
value-added production, 384
values
  employee benefits, 424
  selection decisions, 192
variable pay, 398–99
vesting rights, and pension plans, 419
veterans, disabled, 76–77
Veterans' Employment and Training Service, 77
videotapes, and training, 212
Vietnam Era Veteran's Readjustment Act of 1974, 73
violence, in workplace and discharging of employees, 310
virtual expatriates, 489
virtual reality, 216
virtual teams, 105
Vocational Rehabilitation Act of 1973, 73
voluntary turnover, 309, 310
volunteer workers, 327

Walsh-Healy Public Contracts Act of 1936, 349–50

warnings, and progressive discipline, 315
"welfare to work" programs, 157
wellness programs, 413–15
whistle-blowing, 323
women, as percent of labor force, 34. *See also* gender; sex discrimination
work environment, and training, 205–206
worker-management committees, 468, 469
Workers Adjustment Retraining and Notification Act, 315
workers' compensation, 407
work experience, and job application, 178
work flow, 102–104
workforce utilization review, 148
work processes, 103
work redesign, and job analysis, 113
work samples, 184
World Wide Web. *See also* computers and computer software; Internet
  recruiting, 159, 166
  wage data, 353, 356
wrongful discharge, 313

yield ratios, 160
youth, and labor force, 32